THE ANCIENT MARTYRDOM ACCOUNTS OF PETER AND PAUL

Society of Biblical Literature

Writings from the Greco-Roman World

General Editors

Craig A. Gibson and Ronald Hock
David Konstan and Johan C. Thom

Editorial Board

Erich S. Gruen
Wendy Mayer
Margaret M. Mitchell
Teresa Morgan
Ilaria L. E. Ramelli
Michael Roberts
Karin Schlapbach
James C. VanderKam
L. Michael White

Number 39

Volume Editors
Andrew Cain and Ute Possekel

THE ANCIENT MARTYRDOM ACCOUNTS OF PETER AND PAUL

David L. Eastman

SBL Press
Atlanta

Copyright © 2015 by SBL Press

All rights reserved. No part of this work may be reproduced or transmitted in any form or by any means, electronic or mechanical, including photocopying and recording, or by means of any information storage or retrieval system, except as may be expressly permitted by the 1976 Copyright Act or in writing from the publisher. Requests for permission should be addressed in writing to the Rights and Permissions Office, SBL Press, 825 Houston Mill Road, Atlanta, GA 30329 USA.

Library of Congress Cataloging-in-Publication Data

Eastman, David L., author.
The ancient martyrdom accounts of Peter and Paul / by David L. Eastman.
p. cm. — (Writings from the Greco-Roman world ; number 39)
Includes bibliographical references and index.
ISBN 978-1-62837-090-4 (paper binding : alk. paper) — ISBN 978-1-62837-092-8 (electronic format) — ISBN 978-1-62837-091-1 (hardcover binding : alk. paper)
1. Peter, the Apostle, Saint—Death and burial. 2. Paul, the Apostle, Saint—Death and burial. 3. Martyrdom—Christianity. 4. Christian literature, Early—History and criticism. I. Title. II. Series: Writings from the Greco-Roman world ; no. 39.
BS2510.E27 2015
225.9'22—dc23 2015007483

Printed on acid-free, recycled paper conforming to
ANSI/NISO Z39.48-1992 (R1997) and ISO 9706:1994
standards for paper permanence.

In memory of François Bovon,
an enthusiastic supporter of this project
who was taken from us before its completion

Contents

Part 4. Patristic Literature

ACKNOWLEDGMENTS

I am very grateful to the many colleagues who provided assistance during the production of this volume. John T. Fitzgerald was the first to suggest the pursuit of this project, while series editors Johan Thom and David Konstan, succeeded by Ron Hock and Craig A. Gibson, shepherded the book from proposal to completion. I was aided greatly along the way by the insights and support of François Bovon, Larry L. Welborn, Cilliers Breytenbach, Adela Yarbro Collins, Jeremy F. Hultin, Celia E. Schultz, Michael W. Holmes, Joshua Ezra Burns, Siam Bhayro, Dylan M. Burns, Yonatan Moss, Tony Burke, Brent Landau, Aaron M. Butts, Chris Keith, Tobias Nicklas, Père Louis Soltner, Gérard Poupon, Eric Junod, and Jean-Daniel Kaestli. Billie Paulus, Sonja G. Anderson, Daniel Schriever, Makenna D. Huff, and Brice C. Jones assisted with various elements of the formatting of the manuscript, while Ute Possekel and Andrew Cain provided constructive feedback on the translations. I am also grateful to President Rock Jones of Ohio Wesleyan University, who provided a grant for research travel through the Thomas E. Wenzlau Presidential Discretionary Fund.

Abbreviations

Primary Sources

1 Apol.	Justin Martyr, *Apologia i*
Act. apost.	Arator, *De actibus apostolorum*
Acta mart. Scillit.	Acts of the Scillitan Martyrs
Acta Phil.	Acta Phileae
Acts Paul	Acts of Paul
Acts Paul Thec.	Acts of Paul and Thecla
Acts Pet.	Acts of Peter
Acts Pet. Paul	Acts of the Holy Apostles Peter and Paul (ch. 10b)
Acts Phil. Mart.	Acts of Philip, Martyrdom
Acts Pil.	Acts of Pilate
Adv. Donat.	Optatus of Milev, *Adversus Donatistas*
Adv. Marc.	Tertullian, *Adversus Marcionem*
Adv. nat.	Arnobius of Sicca, *Adversus nationes*
Agr.	Tacitus, *Agricola*
Ann.	Tacitus, *Annales*
Ant.	Josephus, *Antiquities*
Ap. John	Apocryphon of John
Apol.	*Apologia/Apologeticum* (various authors)
Apos. Con.	Constitutiones apostolicae
Aux.	Ambrose, *Sermo contra Auxentium de basilicis tradendis*
Bapt.	Tertullian, *De baptismo*
Car.	Theodoret of Cyrus, *De caritate*
Carm.	*Carmina* (various authors)
CD	Cairo Genizah copy of the Damascus Document
Chron.	Eusebius of Caesarea, *Chronicon*
Civ.	Augustine, *De civitate Dei*
Cod. Bern.	*Martyrology of Jerome*, Codex of Berne

Comm. Gen.	Origen, *Commentarii in Genesim*
Comm. Jo.	Origen, *Commentarii in evangelium Joannis*
Comm. ser. Matt.	Origen, *Commentarium series in evangelium Matthaei*
Dial. Sav.	Dialogue of the Savior
Doct. Apost.	Doctrine of the Apostles (ch. 14)
Ennarat. Ps.	Augustine, *Ennarationes in Psalmos*
Ep.	*Epistles* (various authors)
Ep. Demet.	Pelagius, *Epistle to Demetrias*
Ep. Tim.	Pseudo-Dionysius, *Epistle to Timothy on the Death of the Apostles Peter and Paul* (ch. 12)
Exc. Hier.	Pseudo-Hegesippus, *De excidio urbis Hierosolymitanae*
Fast.	Ovid, *Fasti*
Galba	*Vita Galbae* (Suetonius and Plutarch)
Glor. mart.	Gregory of Tours, *De gloria martyrum*
Gos. Thom.	Gospel of Thomas
Gyn.	Soranus of Ephesus, *Gynecology*
Haer.	*Adversus haereses* (various authors)
Hist.	*Historia* (various authors)
Hist. eccl.	*Historia ecclesiastica* (various authors)
Hist. laus.	Palladius, *Historia Lausiaca*
Hist. Paul	History of the Holy Apostle My Lord Paul (ch. 8)
Hist. Shim.	History of Shimeon Kepha the Chief of the Apostles (ch. 4)
Hom.	Pseudo-Clementine *Homilies*
Ignatius *Rom.*	Ignatius of Antioch, *Epistle to the Romans*
Inst.	Lactantius, *Divinae institutiones*
Instr	Commodian, *Instructions*
IP	Instrumenta Patristica
Itiner. Salz.	Salzburg Itinerary
J.W.	Josephus, *Jewish War*
Job	Ambrose, *De interpellatione Job et David*
Laps.	Cyprian, *On the Lapsed*
Leg. aur.	Jacobus de Voragine, *The Golden Legend*
Lib. apis	Solomon of Basra, *Book of the Bee (Liber apis)*
Lib. pontif.	Liber pontificalis
Mart. Ascen. Isa.	Martyrdom and Ascension of Isaiah
Mart. Paul	Pseudo-Linus, *Martyrdom of the Blessed Apostle Paul* (ch. 6)

Mart. Paul	Martyrdom of the Holy Apostle Paul in Rome [from Acts of Paul] (ch. 5)
Mart. Paul Head	Martyrdom of Paul the Apostle and the Discovery of His Severed Head (ch. 9)
Mart. Pet.	Pseudo-Linus, *Martyrdom of Blessed Peter the Apostle* (ch. 2)
Mart. Pet.	Martyrdom of the Holy Apostle Peter [from Acts of Peter] (ch. 1)
Mart. Pol.	Martyrium Polycarpi
Menaḥ.	Menaḥot Treatise
MT	Masoretic Text of the Hebrew Bible
Nat.	Pliny the Elder, *Naturalis historia*
Nero	Suetonius, *Vita neronis (De vita caesarum)*
Pass. Apost.	Passion of the Apostles Peter and Paul (ch. 11)
Pass. Holy	Pseudo-Marcellus, *Passion of the Holy Apostles Peter and Paul* (ch. 10a)
Pass. Paul	Pseudo-Abdias, *Passion of Saint Paul* (ch. 7)
Pass. Pet.	Pseudo-Abdias, *Passion of Saint Peter* (ch. 3)
Pass. Sebast.	Passio Sebastiani
Perist.	Prudentius, *Peristephanon (De coronis martyrum)*
Pist. soph.	Pistis Sophia
Praep. ev.	Eusebius of Caesarea, *Praepartio evangelica*
Praescr.	Tertullian, *De praesciptione haereticorum*
Prax.	Tertullian, *Adversus Praxean*
Princ.	Origen, *De principiis (Peri archōn)*
Pulchr.	Dio Chrysostom, *De pulchritudine (Or. 21)*
Recog.	Pseudo-Clementine *Recognitions*
Rom.	Plutarch, *Vita Romuli (Vitae parallelae)*
Sat.	Horace, *Satirae*
Serm.	*Sermones* (various authors)
Teach. Shim.	Teaching of Shimeon Kepha in the City of Rome (ch. 13)
Theb.	Caecilius Statius, *Thebaid*
Tract. Ps.	Jerome, *Tractatus sive homiliae in psalmos*
Unit. eccl.	Cyprian, *De unitate ecclesiae*
Var.	Cassiodorus, *Variae*
Vir. ill.	Jerome, *De viris illustribus*
Virginit.	Ambrose of Milan, *De virginitate*
Vita Ad. Ev.	Vita Adae et Evae

Secondary Sources

AASS	*Acta sanctorum*
ABD	*Anchor Bible Dictionary.* Edited by David Noel Freedman. 6 vols. New York: Doubleday, 1992.
ABRL	Anchor Bible Reference Library
AMS	*Acta martyrum et sanctorum Syriace*
AJSL	*American Journal of Semitic Languages and Literatures*
AnBoll	*Analecta Bollandiana*
ANCL	Ante-Nicene Christian Library
ANF	*The Ante-Nicene Fathers.* Edited by Alexander Roberts and James Donaldson. Revised by A. Cleveland Coxe. New York: Christian Literature Publishing, 1886.
ANRW	*Aufstieg und Niedergang der römischen Welt: Geschichte und Kultur Roms im Spiegel der neueren Forschung*
AnTard	*Antiquité tardive*
ANZJOG	Australian and New Zealand Journal of Obstetrics and Gynecology
BARIS	British Archaeological Reports International Series
BBR	*Bulletin for Biblical Research*
BegC	*The Beginnings of Christianity.* Part 1: *The Acts of the Apostles.* Edited by Frederick J. Foakes-Jackson and Kirsopp Lake. 5 vols. London: Macmillan, 1922.
BETL	Bibliotheca ephemeridum theologicarum Lovaniensium
BHG	*Bibliotheca Hagiographica Graeca*
BHL	*Bibliotheca Hagiographica Latina*
BHO	*Bibliotheca Hagiographica Orientalis*
BIFCS	*Book of Acts in Its First Century Setting.* Edited by Bruce W. Winter. Grand Rapids: Eerdmans, 1994.
BMRP	British Museum Research Publication
ca.	circa
CANT	Clavis Apocryphum Novi Testamenti
CCSA	Corpus Christianorum, Series Apocryphorum
CCSL	Corpus Christianorum, Series Latina
CFHB.SB	Corpus Fontium Historiae Byzantinae. Series Berolinensis
CP	*Classical Philology*
ClQ	*The Classical Quarterly*

CSCO	Corpus Scriptorum Christianorum Orientalium
CSEL	Corpus Scriptorum Ecclesiasticorum Latinorum
DOP	Dumbarton Oaks Papers
esp.	especially
FontC	Fontes Christiani
GCS	Die griechischen christlichen Schriftsteller der ersten Jahrhunderte
GSAT	*Giornale della Società asiatica italiana*
HTR	*Harvard Theological Review*
JAJ	*Journal of Ancient Judaism*
JECS	*Journal of Early Christian Studies*
JQR	*Jewish Quarterly Review*
JSAH	*Journal of the Society of Architectural Historians*
JSJSup	Journal for the Study of Judaism in the Persian, Hellenistic, and Roman Periods: Supplement Series
MACr	Monumenti di antichità cristiana
MATS	Miscellanea Agostiniana Testi e studi
MEFR	*Mélanges d'archéologie et d'histoire de l'école française de Rome*
MGH.AA	Monumenta Germaniae Historica. Auctores antiquissimi
MGH.SRM	Monumenta Germaniae Historica. Scriptores rerum merovingicarum
MS(S)	Manuscript(s)
NHS	Nag Hammadi Studies
NovT	*Novum Testamentum*
NTAbh	Neutestamentliche Abhandlungen
OAF	Oxford Apostolic Fathers
OTM	Oxford Theological Monographs
OTP	*Old Testament Pseudepigrapha.* Edited by James H. Charlesworth. 2 vols. New York: Doubleday, 1983.
PG	Patrologia graeca. Edited by J .P Migne. 162 vols. Paris, 1857–1886.
PL	Patrologia latina. Edited by J. P. Migne. 217 vols. Paris, 1844–1864.
PPSD	Pauline and Patristic Scholars in Debate
PTS	Patristische Texte und Studien
REAug	*Revue des études augustiniennes*
RGRW	Religions in the Graeco-Roman World

RHE	*Revue d'histoire ecclésiastique*
ROC	*Revue de l'Orient chrétien*
SBLDS	Society of Biblical Literature Dissertation Series
SC	Sources chrétiennes
SECA	Studies on Early Christian Apocrypha
SPM	Stromata Patristica et Mediaevalia
TAPA	*Transactions of the American Philological Association*
TT	Textes et Traditions
TUGAL	Texte und Untersuchungen zur Geschichte der altchristlichen Literatur
UALG	Untersuchungen zur antiken Literatur und Geschichte
VC	*Vigiliae Christianae*
VetChr	*Vetera Christianorum*
VOHDSupp	Verzeichnis der orientalischen Handschriften in Deutschland Supplementband
WGRW	Writings from the Greco-Roman World
WGRWSup	Writings from the Greco-Roman World Supplement Series
WUNT	Wissenschaftliche Untersuchungen zum Neuen Testament
ZAC	*Zeitschrift für Antikes Christentum/Journal of Ancient Christanity*
ZDMG	*Zeitschrift der deutschen morgenländischen Gesellschaft*
ZNW	*Zeitschrift für die Neutestamentliche Wissenschaft und die Kunde der älteren Kirche*

Introduction

According to Gal 2:9, an important deal was struck in Antioch that was to determine the shape of early Christian missionary activity. Peter would focus his efforts on evangelizing "the circumcised," while Paul would go and preach to the gentiles. As a result, Peter is remembered as the *apostle to the Jews*,[1] while Paul is remembered as the *apostle to everyone else*. This vision of the apostles as the two pillars of the church is witnessed as early as the Acts of the Apostles, in which act 1 (Acts 1–12) features Peter in Jerusalem and its vicinity, and act 2 (Acts 13–28) recounts Paul's missionary journeys all the way to Rome, the capital of the gentile world. And yet, Luke's rendition of these early stages of the spread of the gospel omits many important details. His narrative leaves Peter rather abruptly and does not go on to tell what happens subsequently. Is Peter successful in his further evangelistic endeavors? And if so, where does he go? Or does he meet with resistance and even violence?[2] And what about Paul? The author of Acts specifies that Paul spends two years in custody in Rome. If he knows how long Paul's incarceration lasted, then presumably he knows what happened after it ended. Why does he not provide these details? And what eventually happened to both Peter and Paul? Where and when did they die?

---

1. A lively scholarly debate has been going on for some time concerning the translation of *Ioudaios* as "Jew" or "Judean" when speaking about the ancient world. I have been strongly influenced by recent work by Jewish scholars favoring the translation "Jew" and will follow that convention throughout this volume. See Daniel R. Schwartz, "'Judaean' or 'Jew'? How Should We Translate Ioudaios in Josephus?" in *Jewish Identity in the Greco-Roman World/Jüdische Identität in Der Griechisch-Römischen Welt*, ed. Jörg Frey, Daniel R. Schwartz, and Stephanie Gripentrog (Leiden: Brill, 2007), 3–27; Seth Schwartz, "How Many Judaisms Were There? A Critique of Neusner and Smith on Definition and Mason and Boyarin on Categorization," *JAJ* 2 (2011): 208–38; Adele Reinhartz, "The Vanishing Jews of Antiquity," *Marginalia*, http://marginalia.lareviewofbooks.org/vanishing-jews-antiquity-adele-reinhartz/.

2. The author of 1 Clement, writing at the very end of the first century or in the early years of the second century, suggests this latter experience. See ch. 15, Text 1 in this volume.

Scholars have spilled considerable amounts of ink speculating on what happened "after Acts," but this is not a new phenomenon. As early as the second century, authors began filling in the gaps in the apostolic stories. They recounted the sometimes extraordinary adventures of not just Paul and Peter, but also the apostles John, Thomas, and Andrew. In later centuries the subjects and scope of these stories grew exponentially, and almost any figure associated with the apostles, even if mentioned only in passing in the canonical writings, could become the subject of such an account.

The Role of "Apocryphal" Literature

These writings are known collectively as the apocryphal acts of the apostles, yet this is a misnomer. The word *apocryphos* in Greek means "hidden" or "secret," and these texts were anything but hidden. The fact that they were not eventually included in the canon did not mean they were unknown or even suppressed. Rather, they served important functions in early Christian identity formation, liturgical and cultic development, and competing claims to ecclesiastical authority. If we consider even just the texts included in this volume, we find evidence of all three of these dynamics.

(1) *Identity formation*. What did it mean to be a Christian, a *true* Christian, among the early followers of Jesus? The evidence suggests that a key element in this definition was *suffering*. A true Christian followed the example of Jesus to suffering and even death, and Peter and Paul were models for this. The Acts of Peter and Acts of Paul recount the many trials and persecutions that the apostles endured during their later careers. Often challenged and threatened, they eventually suffered martyrdom for bearing witness to the faith. The base meaning of the Greek word *martyros* is "witness," so dying for the faith was their final and ultimate act of evangelism. As a result of these actions, Paul and Peter became idealized models for later Christians. We see this, for example, in the Acts of the Scillitan Martyrs, which dates from 180 CE and purports to be the trial transcript for a group of Christians in North Africa. They are from a village called Scillium but are brought to Carthage for trial, likely some of the last victims of the sporadic persecutions that occurred during the reign of Marcus Aurelius (161–180 CE). Most of the text consists of verbal sparring between the proconsul Saturninus and the Christians, led by a certain Speratus. Speratus proclaims that the Christians do not recognize earthly authority, but only God's authority: "I do not know the emperor of this age, but I serve instead that God whom no man sees nor is able to see with these eyes" (Acta mart.

Scillit. 18–20). This is a paraphrase of a passage in the Pauline corpus, where God is described as dwelling "in unapproachable light, whom no one has ever seen or can see" (1 Tim 6:16, NRSV). Threatened with death, Speratus appeals to Pauline language to express the Christian position. There is yet another reference to Paul at the climax of the text. The proconsul asks what the Christians have in a box they are carrying, and Speratus responds, "Books and epistles of Paul, a just man." I have demonstrated elsewhere that this reference to Paul, which seems strikingly out of place within the narrative, is actually the focal point of a chiasm.[3] That is, this entire section of the martyrdom account is constructed in order to bring attention to this reference to Paul. Immediately after this exchange about Paul's letters, the Christians are sentenced to death by the sword, just as Paul had been. Behind this narrative lies the image of Paul as a model martyr. Paul is prominent in the story even in his absence, for these Christians quote Paul, carry Paul with them in the form of his letters, and by standing firm for their faith end up dying in the same manner as the apostle. They effectively become "new Pauls." Thus, the account of Paul's death in the Acts of Paul has influenced the way in which the Scillitan martyrs are remembered and their martyrdom account is constructed.[4]

(2) *Liturgical and cultic development*. The apocryphal acts also served as foundation stories for the development of various apostolic cults, thereby contributing to the construction and adaptation of Christian time and space. The stories about Peter and Paul led to the establishment of a joint apostolic festival day (at least in the West) on June 29. Although this date is not mentioned in the earliest martyrdom accounts (i.e., the Acts of Peter and Acts of Paul) it is attested by the middle of the third century CE[5] and becomes an important detail in the liturgical calendar and in many of the later renditions of their deaths. It is also a detail picked up by other authors, such as Jerome, Ambrose, Augustine, and the Christian poet Prudentius.[6]

3. The term comes from the Greek letter Chi, which resembles a capital X. In a chiasm, the main point sits at the center of the Chi and is surrounded by parallel phrases as you move toward and then back away from that point.

4. See David L. Eastman, *Paul the Martyr: The Cult of the Apostle in the Latin West*, WGRWSup 4 (Atlanta: Society of Biblical Literature, 2011), 156–63.

5. The Burying of the Martyrs assigns the celebration of a joint apostolic festival on June 29 to 258 CE.

6. See e.g., Jerome (*Vir. ill.* 5; *Tract. Ps.* 96.10), Ambrose (*Virginit.* 19.124), Augustine (*Serm.* 295.7; 381.1), Prudentius (*Perist.* 12).

Just as the Romans prior to Christianity had ordered their year around a series of festivals, so did the Christians of Rome construct a liturgical calendar based at least in part on dates designated in apocryphal literature. Sources confirm that in the case of Paul and Peter, readings from their writings and from the writings about them, in particular their martyrdom accounts, were part and parcel of the celebration of their annual feast.

The precise locations of the apostolic deaths and burials as given in the apocryphal acts also served as justification for cultic sites in Rome. In the case of Peter, references to the Vatican hill (near the Naumachia) appear frequently in texts after the time of Constantine, who had constructed a large basilica at the Vatican in honor of the chief of the apostles. It is difficult to establish the original reason for the location of the Petrine cult site, but its inclusion in the later apocryphal accounts confirmed and reinforced cultic practice and justified in the minds of Roman Christians their particular association with the apostle. Similarly, the Pauline apocryphal stories after Constantine are typically careful to specify that the apostle died along the Ostian Road outside the walls of Rome. These narratives justify the foundation of the cult at this particular location and the basilicas built there in the fourth century.[7]

(3) *Competing claims to ecclesiastical authority*. Rome began its rise to ecclesiastical prominence at a distinct disadvantage, for its apostolic associations in the New Testament are rather meager. Yes, Paul writes to the Romans, and the author of Acts states that Paul spent two years preaching in Rome, but this does not compare with cities like Jerusalem, Antioch, and Corinth, where both Pauline and Petrine traditions are witnessed in the canonical sources. Rome was a latecomer, a city whose church was divided by internal strife and by controversies between various expressions of Christianity, especially during the second century (e.g., Justin Martyr, Marcion, and Valentinus, to name a few). If Rome was to rise to a position of authority, it needed a trump card to play, and that card came in the form of the claim that Peter (the apostle to the Jews) and Paul (the apostle to everyone else) had preached and died in Rome as martyrs. In these two apostles, then, the entire Christian world was represented and placed under Rome.

---

7. I have noted elsewhere, however, the existence of one apocryphal account (ch. 10, text 10b in this volume) that places Paul's death at a different location along the Laurentinian Road (Aquae Salvias), thus bearing witness to cultic competition between multiple sites. See Eastman, *Paul the Martyr*, 62–69.

The utilization of this claim as political capital became particularly important beginning in the fourth century. Constantine established his new capital of Constantinople in the Greek East, and the first "ecumenical" council took place in nearby Nicaea in 325 CE. Of the 314 bishops reportedly at the council, only two represented Rome and Bishop Sylvester I, and they seem to have had no impact on the proceedings. In 341 CE, a gathering of bishops at Antioch sent a letter to Bishop Julius of Rome reminding him that Peter and Paul had been in Antioch before they had gone to Rome. The implication was clear. Because Paul and Peter preached in Antioch before going to Rome, the Syrian city enjoyed preeminence. This letter marked a direct challenge to any Roman claim to primacy over the Eastern cities based on an association with the apostles. A few decades later, the First Council of Constantinople took place in 381 without the presence or influence of Damasus of Rome, and his attempts to summon the Eastern bishops to Rome the subsequent year were ignored. Damasus was facing the reality that the balance of theological and ecclesiastical influence had clearly shifted East, and he responded by reasserting the Roman claim to Peter and Paul. In a hymn reportedly placed on the Appian Road at a shared cult site for the apostles, he claimed them as Rome's "own citizens," even if no one in the East was listening to his plea.[8]

The apocryphal acts, however, presented another opportunity to restate and perpetuate the Roman claims to the two greatest apostles. On one level there was no novelty in the martyrdom accounts of the fourth, fifth, and sixth centuries, which placed the apostolic deaths in Rome. Yet at the same time, the stakes riding on this claim had grown higher. If the churches of the East were tempted to ignore or claim greater authority than Rome, then they needed to be reminded where the blood of Peter and Paul had flowed on behalf of the faith. After Christ himself, these were the two greatest martyrs of Christianity. They had died on Roman soil, and their bodies still lay in Roman soil. In the minds of Roman Christians, and especially their bishops, this fact bestowed special authority on the Roman church. The popularity of the apocryphal accounts of the martyrdoms of Paul and Peter, therefore, made these texts powerful political tools of pro-Roman propaganda.

Far from being "hidden," then, the apocryphal acts served important functions in early Christianity. They served a critical role in the overall

8. Ibid., 97–107.

construction of Christian identity, in the development of Christian cultic practices, and in the relative balance of power among various Christian centers. Indeed, many key components in Christianity in antiquity owe their form and development to the apocryphal acts.

The Importance of This Volume for the Study of Peter and Paul

My research for *Paul the Martyr* involved careful analysis of the various literary accounts of Paul's death, and it became apparent to me that there is a noticeable gap in the scholarship on not only the Pauline martyrdom accounts, but also the Petrine ones. A brief survey of the most recent scholarship on the deaths of Peter and Paul demonstrates this point, for scholars have continued to draw almost exclusively on the Acts of Peter (text 1 in the current volume) and the Acts of Paul (text 5 in the current volume). References to the other accounts are rare and cursory, or simply nonexistent. In 1992 Richard Bauckham published "The Martyrdom of Peter in Early Christian Literature," the most important treatment to date of the literary traditions concerning Peter's martyrdom.[9] In this lengthy article Bauckham gathers references to the event from a number of patristic authors, but the only actual martyrdom account that he cites is the Acts of Peter. More recently, Marcus Bockmuehl has produced two volumes on the memory and reception of Peter in early Christianity: *The Remembered Peter* and *Simon Peter in Scripture and Memory*.[10] Both volumes include extensive citations from scriptural, rabbinic, and early Christian sources, yet only the Acts of Peter is discussed from among the available corpus of Petrine acts. George Demacopoulos's *The Invention of Peter*[11] stands out in this regard, for he at least includes two brief references to the Acts of the Holy Apostles Peter and Paul.[12]

---

9. Richard Bauckham, "The Martyrdom of Peter in Early Christian Literature," *ANRW* 26.1:539–95.

10. Marcus Bockmuehl, *The Remembered Peter in Ancient Reception and Modern Debate*, WUNT 1/262 (Tübingen: Mohr Siebeck, 2010); idem, *Simon Peter in Scripture and Memory: The New Testament Apostle in the Early Church* (Grand Rapids: Baker Academic, 2012).

11. George Demacopoulos, *The Invention of Peter: Apostolic Discourse and Papal Authority in Late Antiquity*, Divinations: Rereading Late Ancient Religion (Philadelphia: University of Pennsylvania Press, 2013).

12. This is text 10b in this volume, which Demacopoulos refers to as the Acts of Peter and Paul.

The picture is similar as it relates to Paul. In Dennis R. MacDonald's "Apocryphal and Canonical Narratives about Paul,"[13] the Acts of Paul is central but is accompanied by only a passing reference to another text, again the Acts of the Holy Apostles Peter and Paul (text 10b in the current volume). In 2007 Wayne Meeks and John T. Fitzgerald published an updated edition of *The Writings of St. Paul*, a collection of textual excerpts by and about the apostle from antiquity to the present.[14] However, the references to his death in this volume are confined to the Acts of Paul and a brief citation from 1 Clement. Harry W. Tajra's *The Martyrdom of St. Paul* is notable for its inclusion of references from a wider variety of apocryphal texts,[15] yet the excerpts are brief and presented out of context, such that it is difficult to use them to draw any wider conclusions.

The hegemony of the Acts of Peter and Acts of Paul is seen in other ways, as well. Collections of New Testament apocrypha, such as Hennecke-Schneemelcher's *New Testament Apocrypha* and J. K. Elliott's *The Apocryphal New Testament*, include full versions of the two primary texts but only summary paragraphs or even less for the other apostolic martyrdom accounts.[16]

A few exceptions are worth noting. Otto Zwierlein's *Petrus in Rom*[17] makes an important contribution in that it provides updated critical editions of the Acts of Peter and Acts of Paul, and elsewhere in the volume he discusses a handful of references to the *Martyrdom of Blessed Peter the Apostle* of Pseudo-Linus (text 2 in this volume) and the Passion of the Apostles Peter and Paul (text 11 in the current volume). Even here, though, these texts receive little treatment. A wider selection of the Pauline and Petrine martyrdom accounts appears in two Italian collections from the last century: Mario Erbetta's *Gli apocrifi del nuovo testamento: Atti e leggende*

---

13. Dennis R. MacDonald, "Apocryphal and Canonical Narratives about Paul," in *Paul and the Legacies of Paul*, ed. William S. Babcock (Dallas, Southern Methodist University Press, 1990), 55–70.

14. Wayne Meeks and John T. Fitzgerald, eds., *The Writings of St. Paul*, 2nd ed. (New York: Norton, 2007).

15. Harry W. Tajra, *The Martyrdom of St. Paul: Historical and Judicial Context, Traditions, and Legends*, WUNT 2/67 (Tübingen: Mohr, 1994).

16. Edgar Hennecke and Wilhelm Schneemelcher, eds., *New Testament Apocrypha*, trans. R. McL. Wilson, 5th ed., vol. 2 (Louisville: Westminster John Knox, 1992); J. K. Elliott, *The Apocryphal New Testament* (Oxford: Clarendon, 1993).

17. Otto Zwierlein, *Petrus in Rom: Die literarischen Zeugnisse*, 2nd ed., UALG 96 (Berlin: de Gruyter, 2010).

and Luigi Moraldi's *Apocrifi del Nuovo Testamento*.[18] Also significant is the two-volume set *Écrits apocryphes chrétiens*, which provides updated introductions and translations of nearly half of these texts for a Francophone audience.[19] However, even these more inclusive collections of martyrdom accounts are incomplete; in particular they tend to ignore the Syriac texts.

Thus, our picture of the early church's reception and conceptualization of the apostles has been hampered by a kind of myopia that focuses primarily on two texts and interprets them as exemplary for Christian antiquity, to the exclusion of other, sometimes variant voices, especially if those voices are not in Latin or Greek.

This volume brings together all these texts for the first time, in nearly every case providing the first English translation of the most updated edition. The volume is divided into four parts. Part 1 includes four martyrdom accounts that focus on Peter. In part 2 there are five accounts of Paul's martyrdom. Part 3 features six accounts of the joint martyrdoms of Peter and Paul, while part 4 includes more than forty references to the apostolic martyrdoms from early Christian literature. Each chapter is accompanied by an introduction that provides historical and literary background, and the commentary in the footnotes to the translations highlights important features and allusions to scriptural or other literature, including other texts within this volume.

The translations were produced to be accessible to a broad audience, so I have privileged readability (dynamic equivalence) over formal adherence to the grammar of the original languages (formal equivalence). Those with reading knowledge of the original languages will benefit from the presentation of the ancient texts on facing pages, which will facilitate more detailed analysis when desired. My general practice has been to reproduce the texts as they appear in the critical editions, but in some cases I have standardized the spelling and punctuation in order to aid the reader. In addition, many of these texts use masculine terms (e.g., *man*, *men*, *brothers*, *sons*) to refer to humanity in general or to mixed groups of (especially) Christians. I

18. Mario Erbetta, *Gli apocrifi del Nuovo Testamento: Atti e leggende*, 2nd ed. (Turin: Marietti, 1978); Luigi Moraldi, *Apocrifi del Nuovo Testamento*, vol. 2 (Turin: Unione, 1971).

19. François Bovon and Pierre Geoltrain, eds., *Écrits apocryphes chrétiens*, vol. 1, Pléiade 442 (Paris: Gallimard, 1997); Pierre Geoltrain and Jean-Daniel Kaestli, eds., *Écrits apocryphes chrétiens*, vol. 2, Pléiade 516 (Paris: Gallimard, 2005).

have employed inclusive language where appropriate but have maintained masculine terms in cases in which the context dictates it.

My next monograph will be dedicated to a detailed analysis of these texts. The goal of this volume, however, is to make these texts available to a broader audience, in hopes that our discussions about Paul and Peter in the early centuries of Christianity may be informed by a more complete picture of the memory, veneration, and reimagination of the apostles. In particular, I hope that more attention will be given to the role of the stories of their deaths in establishing Peter and Paul as Christianity's two greatest martyrs and the alleged twin founders of the Roman church.

Part 1. The Martyrdom of Peter

1. Martyrdom of the Holy Apostle Peter

CANT 190.iv / *BHG* 1483–1485

Contents

The texts of the New Testament do not provide details of Peter's later life or death. In the absence of good evidence, various stories arose of the apostle's later adventures and eventual martyrdom. The Martyrdom (or Passion) of Peter represents one such story. It is traditionally treated as the final section of a larger cycle of legends known as the Acts of Peter; chapters 1–12 of the Martyrdom of Peter correspond to chapters 30–41 of the Acts of Peter.

Prior to the beginning of the Martyrdom of Peter, Peter has already been in Rome for some time strengthening the church, which had been founded by the apostle Paul, against the destructive efforts of Simon the sorcerer (Simon Magus). The proofs of Peter's supernatural power have already included a talking dog, a resuscitated smoked fish, and several other miracles performed to show Peter's superiority over Simon. Peter's preaching is popular among aristocratic Romans, especially women. As the text opens, a wealthy matron named Chryse makes a sizable donation to support the poor.

Then the author turns the attention directly to the confrontation between Peter and Simon the sorcerer. Although Peter has continued healing in the name of Christ, Simon claims that Peter is preaching a false God. Therefore, Simon promises to prove his superiority by ascending into heaven. On the next day a large crowd gathers, and Simon begins to ascend into the sky. Peter prays, and Simon immediately falls and breaks his leg. The people are convinced that Peter is the true teacher, while Simon is abandoned by all of his followers and dies soon after.

Peter resumes his teaching, particularly his encouragement of sexual chastity, and four wives of the prefect Agrippa are convinced by Peter's preaching and refuse to sleep with their husband. Another woman named Xanthippe joins their number, and her husband Albinus becomes angry.

He joins forces with Agrippa in plotting Peter's demise, but Xanthippe overhears their plan and warns Peter. At first the apostle refuses to leave the city, as all the Christians are encouraging him to do, but finally he agrees to flee. As he is leaving Rome, he has an encounter with the risen Christ. Christ says he is going to Rome to be crucified again, and Peter understands that this is a prediction of his own impending martyrdom. The apostle returns to Rome and is arrested and sentenced to death by Agrippa. The crowd attempts to revolt against the prefect, but Peter calms them by saying that this is the Lord's will.

Once he arrives at the place of his crucifixion, Peter begins a monologue about the mystical nature of the cross and the mystery that it conceals. He is hung on the cross, upside down at his request, and states that his inverted crucifixion is symbolic of the distorted nature of the world. After more cryptic explanation of the cross and its mystery, he finally dies. A pious man named Marcellus buries the apostle in a lavish tomb. Nero receives word of what has happened and is angry, because he had hoped to torture the apostle for converting members of the imperial court. The emperor decides to kill all of Peter's disciples but receives a dire warning in a dream to leave them alone. The story ends with the believers in Rome rejoicing in the Lord.

Literary Background

The precise date of this text is unknown, but a date in the final quarter of the second century or the first quarter of the third century is most likely. Elements of the larger Acts of Peter appear in the third century in the Teaching of the Apostles (Didascalia Apostolorum), the writings of Origen of Alexandria, and the Pseudo-Clementine *Recognitions*. Some have suggested that the Acts of Paul, which could date from the very end of the second century, also depends on the Acts of Peter and provides proof of the early date of the Petrine text, but there is no consensus on this. The identity of the author is unknown, and the place of composition is disputed. Bithynia, Alexandria, Asia Minor, Syria, and Rome have all been suggested based on various factors.

As mentioned above, the Martyrdom of Peter is now attached to the Acts of Peter, but this was not always the case. Textual evidence suggests that this text also circulated on its own in some cases, for only the Martyrdom of Peter survives complete in Greek. The rest of the Acts of Peter, with the exception of a small fragment, is preserved first in a Latin translation

in a single manuscript of the sixth or seventh century. (This translation is known as the Vercelli Acts, because the manuscript is in a library in Vercelli, Italy.) In terms of how the Martyrdom of Peter was used, the fact that it survives as a unit in Syriac, Coptic, Armenian, Arabic, Ethiopic, Georgian, and Slavonic may suggest that it was consistently read in liturgical contexts.

Stories about Peter were seemingly in great demand by the second and third centuries, as texts like the Pseudo-Clementine literature and the Preaching of Peter also attest, but this is not a careful work of theology written by a "proto-orthodox" author. The esoteric nature of certain parts of the text, particularly Peter's monologue on the cross, has caused some scholars to suggest Gnostic influence. This perspective is not widely accepted, but Peter's prayer does display Platonic tendencies in its rejection of the perceptible world as being "not true" (§8). Evidence suggests that many in the early church were wary of this text. Perhaps the extreme asceticism advocated by Peter disturbed not just the dramatic characters Agrippa and Albinus, but also real-life bishops and other church leaders. Eusebius (*Hist. eccl.* 3.2.2) mentions a text called the Acts of Peter but specifies that it does not have ancient ecclesiastical authority. Active condemnation of the Acts of Peter by church leaders is attested at the end of the fourth century, when Philaster of Brescia claims that the Manichaeans and other "heretics" are reading this text (*Haer.* 88). This use by heretics resigned the text to second-class status among some ecclesiastical authorities, but the fact that elements of it appear so frequently in later martyrdom accounts suggests that it maintained much of its popularity.

Text

The Greek text survives in three manuscripts. Lipsius produced his critical edition based on a ninth-century manuscript from the library of the Monastery of St. John the Theologian in Patmos (ms. 48) and a tenth/eleventh-century manuscript from the monastery of Vatopedi on Mount Athos (ms. 79). In 1962 an eleventh-century manuscript containing chapters 4–12 was discovered in Ohrid, Macedonia (ms. 44), and this prompted a new edition of the text by Zwierlein.

The translation of chapters 1–3 is based on the edition by Lipsius. Zwierlein's edition begins at chapter 4, and the remainder of the translation is dependent on this edition, with a few modifications mentioned in the footnotes. Apart from Zwierlein's own translation into German, this is the only available translation based on the most recent edition of the text.

Select Bibliography

Baldwin, Matthew C. *Whose Acts of Peter? Text and Historical Context of the Actus Vercellenses*. WUNT 2/196. Tübingen: Mohr Siebeck, 2005.

Bremmer, Jan N., ed. *The Apocryphal Acts of Peter: Magic, Miracles, and Gnosticism*. SECA 3. Leuven: Peeters, 1998.

Elliott, J. K., trans. "Martyrdom of the Holy Apostle Peter." Pages 421–26 in *The Apocryphal New Testament*. Oxford: Clarendon, 1993.

Erbetta, Mario, trans. "Martirio del santo apostolo Petro." Pages 163–68 in *Atti e leggende*. Vol. 2 of *Gli apocrifi del Nuovo Testamento*. 2nd ed. Turin: Marietti, 1978.

Hennecke, Edgar, trans. "Martyrdom of the Holy Apostle Peter." Pages 311–17 in vol. 2 of *New Testament Apocrypha*. Edited by Edgar Hennecke and Wilhelm Schneemelcher. English trans. edited by R. McL. Wilson. 5th ed. Louisville: Westminster John Knox, 1993.

Lipsius, Richard A. and Max Bonnet, eds. Μαρτύριον τοῦ ἁγίου ἀποστόλου Πέτρου. Pages 78–103 in vol. 1 of *Acta apostolorvm apocrypha post Constantinvm Tischendorf*. Leipzig: Mendelssohn, 1891. Repr., Hildesheim: Olms, 1972.

Moraldi, Luigi, trans. "Martirio di san Pietro." Pages 1021–28 in vol. 2 of *Apocrifi del Nuovo Testamento*. Turin: Unione, 1971.

Poupon, Gérard. "Les Actes de Pierre et leur remaniement." *ANRW* 25.6:2363–83.

———, trans. "Martyre de saint Pierre apôtre." Pages 1041–46 and 1106–14 in vol. 1 of *Écrits apocryphes chrétiens*. Edited by François Bovon and Pierre Geoltrain. Pléiade 442. Paris: Gallimard, 1997.

Thomas, Christine M. *The Acts of Peter, Gospel Literature, and the Ancient Novel: Rewriting the Past*. New York: Oxford University Press, 2003.

Vouaux, Léon, ed. and trans. "Martyre de Pierre." Pages 398–467 in *Les Actes de Pierre: Introduction, textes, traduction et commentaire*. Paris: Letouzey et Ané, 1922.

Zwierlein, Otto, ed. and trans. Μαρτύριον τοῦ ἁγίου Πέτρου τοῦ ἀποστόλου μαρτυρήσαντος ἐν Ῥώμῃ. Pages 405–25 in *Petrus in Rom: Die literarischen Zeugnisse*. 2nd ed. UALG 96. Berlin: de Gruyter, 2010.

Μαρτύριον τοῦ ἁγίου Πέτρου τοῦ ἀποστόλου

1. κυριακῆς οὔσης, ὁμιλοῦντες τοῦ Πέτρου τοῖς ἀδελφοῖς, καὶ προτρέποντος εἰς τὴν τοῦ Χριστοῦ πίστιν, παρόντων πολλῶν συγκλητικῶν καὶ ἱππικῶν πλειόνων καὶ γυναικῶν πλουσίων <καὶ> ματρωνῶν καὶ στηριζομένων τῇ πίστει, μία τις ἔνθα οὖσα γυνὴ πάνυ πλουσία, ἥτις τὴν ἐπίκλησιν τοὔνομα Χρυσὴ εἶχεν, διὰ τὸ πᾶν αὐτῆς σκεῦος χρύσεον ὑπάρχειν — ἥτις γεννηθεῖσα οὔτε ἀργυρέῳ ποτὲ σκεύει ἐχρήσατο οὔτε ὑελῷ, εἰ μὴ μόνοις χρυσέοις — εἶπεν τῷ Πέτρῳ· Πέτρε, θεοῦ δοῦλε· εἰς ὄναρ ἐμοὶ παραστὰς ὃν λέγεις θεὸν εἶπεν· Χρυσή, Πέτρῳ τῷ διακόνῳ μου ἀποκόμισον μυρίους χρυσίνους· ὀφείλεις γὰρ αὐτῷ. ἐκόμισα οὖν φοβουνένη, μήτι κακὸν πάθω ὑπὸ τοῦ ὀφθέντος μοι, εἰς οὐρανὸν ἀπερχομένου. καὶ ταῦτα εἰποῦσα καὶ θεῖσα τὸ χρῆμα ἀπηλλάγη. ὁ δὲ Πέτρος ἰδὼν ἐδόξασεν τὸν κύριον, ὅτι ἤμελλον οἱ θλιβόμενοι ἀναψύχειν.

τινὲς οὖν τῶν παρόντων ἔλεγον αὐτῷ· Πέτρε, οὐ κακῶς ἐδέξω τὸ χρῆμα τοῦτο παρ' αὐτῆς; διαβέβληται γὰρ ἐν ὅλῃ <τῇ> Ῥώμῃ ἐπὶ πορνείᾳ, καὶ ὅτι οὐ προσέχει ἑνὶ ἀνδρί· μέχρι γὰρ καὶ τῶν ἰδίων νεανίσκων πρόσεισι. μὴ κοινώνει οὖν τῇ Χρυσῇ τραπέζῃ, ἀλλὰ πεμφθῇ ἐπ' αὐτὴν τὸ παρ' αὐτῆς.

ὁ δὲ Πέτρος ἀκουσὰς καὶ γελάσας εἶπεν τοῖς ἀδελφοῖς· αὕτη τίς μὲν ἔστιν τὸν ἄλλον βίον, οὐκ οἶδα. ὅτι δὲ τὸ χρῆμα τοῦτο ἐδεξάμην, οὐ μάτην ἐδεξάμην· παρείχεν γὰρ ὡς χρεώστρια τοῦ Χριστοῦ, καὶ δίδωσιν αὐτὸ τοῖς τοῦ Χριστοῦ δούλοις· αὐτὸς γὰρ αὐτῶν προενόησεν.

2. ἔφερον δὲ καὶ τοὺς κάμνοντας πρὸς αὐτὸν ἐν τῷ σαββάτῳ, δεόμενοι ὅπως ἀνασφάλωσιν τῶν νόσων. καὶ ἰῶντο πολλοὶ παραλυτικοὶ καὶ ποδαγρικοὶ καὶ

Martyrdom of the Holy Apostle Peter

1. When it was the Lord's day, and Peter was speaking to the brothers and sisters[1] and urging them to have faith in Christ, many of senatorial and equestrian rank and very many rich women and matrons were present and encouraged in the faith. One of them there was a very wealthy woman who had the nickname Chryse, because every vessel of hers was gold.[2] Since birth she had never used a vessel of silver or glass, but only gold. She said to Peter, "Peter, servant of God, in a dream the one whom you call God stood before me and said, 'Chryse, take ten thousand gold pieces to my servant Peter, for you owe them to him.' Because I was afraid I brought them, lest I suffer some evil from the one who appeared to me and went away into heaven." After saying these things, she put down the money and went away. Peter saw this and praised the Lord, because the oppressed were going to get relief.

Then some of those present said to him, "Peter, did you not wrongly accept this money from her? For she is known all over Rome for her promiscuity, and it is said that she does not have only one man, for she makes use even of her own servants. Have nothing to do, therefore, with the table of Chryse,[3] but let what came from her be sent back to her."

After he had heard these things and laughed, Peter said to the brothers and sisters, "Who she is in her other life I do not know. Because I have accepted this money, I have not accepted it in vain, for she offered it as a debtor to Christ and gives it to the servants of Christ. [Christ] has made provision for [the oppressed]."

2. They were bringing the sick to him on the Sabbath and begging for healing from their diseases. Many paralytics and people suffering

1. Literally "the brothers" here and elsewhere in the text, but it is clear throughout that Peter's followers are a mixed audience.

2. Chryse means "golden."

3. Or "the golden table."

ἡμιτριταῖοι καὶ τεταρτίζοντες, καὶ πάσης νόσου σωματικῆς ἰῶντο ἐν ὀνόματι Ἰησοῦ Χριστοῦ πιστεύοντες, καὶ πάνπολλοι εἰς τὴν τοῦ κυρίου χάριν καθ' ἑκάστην ἡμέραν προσετίθεντο. Σίμων δὲ ὁ μάγος τῷ ὄχλῳ ἡμερῶν ὀλίγων διελθουσῶν ὑπισχνεῖτο τὸν Πέτρον ἀπελέγξαι, μὴ πεπιστευκότα θεῷ ἀληθινῷ, ἀλλ' ἠπατημένῳ. πολλὰς οὖν φαντασίας ποιοῦντος αὐτοῦ οἱ ἤδη ἑδραῖοι τῶν μαθητῶν κατεγέλων αὐτοῦ. ἐν τρικλίνοις γὰρ ἐποίει πνεύματά τινα πρὸς αὐτοὺς εἰσάγεσθαι, φαινόμενα μόνον, οὐκ ὄντα δὲ ἀληθῶς. καὶ τί γὰρ λέγειν; διεληλεγμένου αὐτοῦ διὰ πολλῶν ἐπὶ μαγίᾳ, καὶ χωλοὺς ἐποίησεν φαίνεσθαι ὑγιεῖς πρὸς βραχὺ καὶ τυφλοὺς ὁμοίως, καὶ νεκροὺς ἅπαξ πολλοὺς ἔδοξε ζωοποιεῖν καὶ κινεῖσθαι, ὥσπερ καὶ τὸν Στρατόνικον. ταῦτα δὲ πάντα ὁ Πέτρος ἀκολουθῶν διήλεγχεν αὐτὸν πρὸς τοὺς ὁρῶντας.

καὶ δὴ ἀεὶ ἀσχημονοῦντος καὶ ἐγγελωμένου ὑπὸ τοῦ Ῥωμαίων ὄχλου καὶ ἀπιστουμένου ἐφ' οἷς ὑπισχνεῖτο ποιεῖν μὴ ἐπιτυγχάνοντος, ἐν τούτῳ τοῦτον πάντα εἰπεῖν αὐτοῖς· ἄνδρες Ῥωμαῖοι, νῦν δοκεῖτέ μου κατισχῦσαι τὸν Πέτρον ὡς δυνατώτερον καὶ μᾶλλον αὐτῷ προσέχετε; ἠπάτησθε. αὔριον γὰρ ἐγὼ καταλιπὼν ὑμᾶς ἀθεοτάτους καὶ ἀσεβεστάτους, ἀναπτήξομαι πρὸς τὸν θεόν, οὗ ἡ δύναμις ἐγώ εἰμι ἀσθενήσασα. εἰ οὖν ὑμεῖς πεπτώκατε, ἰδὲ ἐγώ εἰμι ὁ ἑστώς· καὶ ἀνέρχομαι πρὸς τὸν πατέρα καὶ ἐρῶ αὐτῷ· κἀμὲ τὸν ἑστῶτα υἱόν σου κατακλῖναι ἠθέλησαν· ἀλλὰ μὴ συνθέμενος αὐτοῖς εἰς ἐμαυτὸν ἀνέδραμον.

3. καὶ ἤδη τῇ ἐπιούσῃ ὁ ὄχλος πλείων συνήρχετο εἰς σάκραν βίαν, ὅπως ἴδωσιν αὐτὸν πετώμενον. ὁ δὲ Πέτρος ὅραμα θεασάμενος ἧκεν ἐπὶ τὸν τόπον, ὅπως αὐτὸν καὶ ἐν τούτῳ ἐλέγξῃ· ὅτε γὰρ εἰσίει εἰς τὴν Ῥώμην, ἐξέστησεν τοὺς ὄχλους πετώμενος. ἀλλ' οὔπω Πέτρος ὁ ἐλέγχων αὐτὸν ἦν ἐνδημῶν τῇ

from gout and malarian fevers[4] were healed, and those believing in the name of Jesus Christ were healed of every bodily disease. And very many were being added to the grace of the Lord each day. But after several days had passed, Simon the sorcerer promised the crowd that he would refute Peter for having believed not in a true god but a false one. Therefore, after [Simon] had performed many illusions, those among the disciples who were already steadfast were laughing at him. In the dining halls he was making some spirits appear to them, but they were only apparitions and did not truly exist. And what else is there to say? After he had been completely refuted in many ways concerning his magic, he made the lame and the blind briefly appear to be healed, and he seemed to make alive and move many who were once dead, even Stratonikos.[5] And Peter was following all these things and refuted him before those watching.

Because [Simon] was constantly being disgraced and mocked by the crowd of Romans and was distrusted because he was promising to do something he could not achieve, at last he said all these things to them, "Men of Rome, you now suppose that Peter has overcome me, as if he were more powerful, and you pay more attention to him. You are mistaken, for tomorrow I will leave behind you godless and impious people and fly up to God, whose power I am in weakened form. If, then, you have fallen, look, for I am[6] the one who stands. I am going up to the Father and will say to him, 'They wanted to bring down even me, the one who stands, your son. But I paid no heed to them and have returned to myself.' "

3. And already on the next day a large crowd came together on the Sacred Way,[7] in order to see him fly. Peter came to the place to see the spectacle, so that he might refute him even in this. For when [Simon] came to Rome, he astonished the crowds by flying. But Peter, who rebuked him, was not yet dwelling in Rome, the city that Simon deceived and misled so

4. Literally, "semi-tertian and quartan fevers." These are two varieties of malarian fevers distinguished by the frequency of the recurring onset of symptoms.

5. Earlier in the Acts of Peter, Simon had faked the resurrection of a certain Nicostratus. The Vercelli Codex of the Acts of Peter repeats that name here, instead of introducing the new figure Stratonikos.

6. Simon's use of the specific expression ἐγώ εἰμί links him to divinity through God's self-identification in the Hebrew Bible (e.g., Exod 3:14, Isa 52:6). Cf. Jesus's use of this phrase in e.g., John 8:24, 8:58, 9:9.

7. The *Via Sacra* (Sacred Way) was a main street through Rome that connected many of the city's most important religious sites and was part of the traditional route of the Roman Triumph.

Ῥώμῃ, ἥνπερ οὕτως πλανῶν ἐφάντασεν, ὡς ἐκστῆναί τινας ἐπ᾽ αὐτῷ. στὰς οὖν οὗτος ἐν τόπῳ ὑψηλῷ καὶ θεασάμενος τὸν Πέτρον, ἤρξατο λέγειν· Πέτρε, νῦν μάλιστα ὅταν ἀνέρχομαι κατέναντι τούτων πάντων θεωρουμένων λέγω σοι· εἰ σοῦ ὁ θεὸς δύναται, ὃν Ἰουδαῖοι ἀνεῖλον καὶ ὑμᾶς ἐλιθοβόλησαν τοὺς ὑπ᾽ ἐκείνου ἐκλελεγμένους, δειξάτω ὅτι θεοῦ ἐστιν ἡ πίστις αὐτοῦ, φανήτω ἐπὶ τούτῳ, εἰ ἀξία θεοῦ ἐστιν. ἐγὼ γὰρ ἀνελθὼν ἑαυτὸν ἐπιδείξω τῷ ὄχλῳ τούτῳ παντὶ ὅστις εἰμί. καὶ ἰδοὺ ἀρθέντος αὐτοῦ εἰς τὸ ὕψος καὶ πάντων ὁρώντων αὐτὸν εἰς ὅλην <τὴν> Ῥώμην, καὶ ὑπὲρ τοὺς ναοὺς αὐτῆς καὶ τὰ ὄρη ἠρμένον, ἀφεώρων οἱ πιστοὶ εἰς τὸν Πέτρον.

καὶ ὁ Πέτρος ἰδὼν τὸ παράδοξον τοῦ θεάματος ἐβόησεν πρὸς τὸν κύριον Ἰησοῦν Χριστόν· ἐὰν ἀφῇς τοῦτον ποιῆσαι ὃ ἐπεχείρησεν, νῦν πάντες οἱ εἰς σὲ πιστεύσαντες σκανδαλισθήσονται καὶ ἔσται ἃ δι᾽ ἐμοῦ ἔδωκας αὐτοῖς σημεῖα καὶ τέρατα ἄπιστα· τάχυνον κύριε τὴν χάριν σου, καὶ καταπεσόντος αὐτοῦ ἄνωθεν, ἐκλ<υθ>εὶς συστῇ καὶ μὴ ἀποθάνῃ, ἀλλὰ <κε>νωθῇ καὶ τὸ σκέλος κατεάξῃ ἐκ τριῶν τόπων. καὶ καταπεσόντος αὐτοῦ ἄνωθεν τὸ σκέλος κατέαξεν ἐκ τριῶν τόπων. τότε αὐτὸν λιθοβολήσαντες ἕκαστος εἰς τὰ ἴδια ἀνεχώρησαν, Πέτρῳ τὸ λοιπὸν πάντες πειθόμενοι.

εἷς δέ τις ἐλθὼν διὰ τάχους ἐξ ὁδοῦ τῶν φίλων τοῦ Σίμωνος, Γέμελλος ὀνόματι, παρ᾽ οὗ πολλὰ ἔλαβεν ὁ Σίμων, Ἑλληνίδα τινὰ γυναῖκα ἐσχηκώς, ἰδῶν αὐτὸν κατεάξαντα τὸ σκέλος εἶπεν· Σίμων, εἰ ἡ δύναμις τοῦ θεοῦ κατάσσεται, μὴ καὶ αὐτὸς ὁ θεός, οὗ δύναμις εἶ, τυφλωθήσεται; δραμὼν οὖν καὶ ὁ Γέμελος ἠκολούθει τῷ Πέτρῳ λέγων αὐτῷ· κἀγὼ τῶν ἐπὶ Χριστὸν πιστευόντων εὔχομαι εἶναι.

ὁ δὲ Πέτρος· τίς οὖν ὁ φθόνος, ἔφη, ἄδελφέ μου; ἐλθὲ καὶ παρέδρευε. ὁ δὲ Σίμων ἐν τῇ συμφορᾷ γενόμενος εὗρέν τινας τοὺς διακομίσαντας αὐτὸν νυκτὸς κραββάτῳ ἀπὸ Ῥώμης εἰς Ἀρικίαν· κἀκεῖ ἐπιμείνας ἀπηνέχθη πρός

much that some lost their senses because of him. Standing on an elevated place and looking at Peter, he began to say, "Peter, as I am now ascending in front of all these who are looking on, I say to you that if your God is powerful—the one who was killed by the Jews, who also stoned those of you who were called by this one—then let him show that faith in him is from God. Let it be shown in this case that this faith is worthy of God. For by ascending I will show to this entire crowd what kind of person I am." Behold, he was raised up into the air, and everyone saw him in the entire city of Rome being lifted up above its temples and hills. The faithful were looking at Peter.

And Peter saw this surprising spectacle and cried to the Lord Jesus Christ, "If you permit this man to do what he has set out to do, then now all those who have believed in you will be made to stumble, and the signs and wonders that you gave to them through me will be disbelieved. Hurry, Lord, to demonstrate your grace, and after he has fallen down, let him be manifestly broken to pieces but not die. Let him be destroyed, and let his leg break in three places." When Simon fell down, his leg broke in three places.[8] After they had stoned him, each person went back to his own house. After that everyone was convinced by Peter.

But a certain one of the friends of Simon named Gemellus[9] came quickly from the road. Simon had received many things through him, and he had a Greek wife. Seeing Simon's leg broken, Gemellus said, "Simon, if the power of God is broken, then will not God himself whose power you are be blinded?" Then Gemellus ran and followed Peter, saying to him, "I also pray to be among those who believe in Christ."

But Peter said, "What hindrance is there, my brother? Come and stay with us." But Simon, who was in misery, found some people to carry him by night on a bed out of Rome to Aricia.[10] After staying there he was taken to a certain Castor, who had been banished from Rome to Terracina on the

---

8. The Apostolic Constitutions state that Simon was thrown to the earth as he was flying "in an unnatural way" (Apos. Con. 2.3.14), while Arnobius of Sicca claims that Simon tried to fly in a fiery chariot. Thrown down by the words of Peter, he broke his legs and soon after committed suicide (*Adv. Nat.* 2.12).

9. In the other accounts of Peter's death, this figure is identified as Marcellus, a converted follower of Simon the sorcerer.

10. Cf. Pass. Apost. 11.

τινα Ῥώμης ἐξορισθέντα Κάστωρα εἰς Ταρακίνα<ν> ἐπ' αἰτίᾳ μαγικῇ· κἀκεῖ κατατεμνόμενος, τὸ πέρας τοῦ βίου ὁ τοῦ διαβόλου ἄγγελος ἔδωκεν Σίμων.

4. Πέτρος ὁ ἀπόστολος ἦν ἐν τῇ Ῥώμῃ ἀγαλλιώμενος μετὰ τῶν ἀδελφῶν ἐν τῷ κυρίῳ καὶ εὐχαριστῶν τῷ θεῷ νυκτός τε καὶ ἡμέρας ἐπὶ τῷ ὄχλῳ τῷ καθ' ἡμέραν προσαγομένῳ τῷ ὀνόματι τοῦ κυρίου Ἰησοῦ Χριστοῦ τῇ χάριτι τοῦ θεοῦ. συνήγοντο οὖν καὶ αἱ γυναῖκες τοῦ πραιφέκτου Ἀγρίππα πρὸς τὸν Πέτρον, τέσσαρες οὖσαι, Ἀγριππῖνα καὶ Ἰκαρία καὶ Εὐφημία καὶ Δῶρις. αὗται ἀκούσασαι τὸν τῆς ἁγνείας λόγον καὶ πάντα τὰ τοῦ κυρίου λόγια, κατενύγησαν τὰς ψυχάς, καὶ συνθέμεναι ἀλλήλαις ἁγναὶ τῆς Ἀγρίππα κοίτης διαμεῖναι ἠνοχλοῦντο ὑπ' αὐτοῦ ἑκάστης ἡμέρας. διαποροῦντος οὖν τοῦ Ἀγρίππα καὶ λυπουμένου περὶ αὐτῶν — καὶ ὅτι μάλιστα τούτων ἤρα — ἐπετηρεῖτο καὶ πέμψας ἰδεῖν ποῦ προέρχονται, μανθάνει ὅτι πρὸς τὸν Πέτρον. ἔλεγεν οὖν αὐταῖς ἐλθούσαις· μὴ συνεῖναί μοι ὁ Χριστιανὸς ἐκεῖνος ἐδίδαξεν ὑμᾶς· γινώσκετε ὅτι καὶ ὑμᾶς ἀπολέσω κἀκεῖνον ζῶντα κατακαύσω. αὗται μὲν οὖν πᾶσαν κακοπαθίαν ὑπὸ τοῦ Ἀγρίππα ὑπέμειναν, ἵνα μηκέτι μιαίνωνται, ἐνδυναμούμεναι ἐν τῷ κράτει Ἰησοῦ Χριστοῦ.

5. μία δέ τις καὶ μάλιστα εὐμορφοτάτη Ἀλβίνου φίλου τοῦ Καίσαρος γυνὴ ὀνόματι Ξανθίππη ἅμα ταῖς λοιπαῖς ματρώναις συνερχομένη πρὸς τὸν Πέτρον καὶ αὐτὴ τοῦ Ἀλβίνου ἀπέστη. 2 ἐκεῖνος οὖν μεμηνὼς καὶ ἐρῶν τῆς Ξανθίππης καὶ λυπούμενος ὅτι ἀποστρέφεται αὐτόν, ὡς θηρίον ἠγριαίνετο, βουλόμενος τὸν Πέτρον διαχειρίσασθαι· ἔγνω γὰρ αὐτὸν παραίτιον τοῦ χωρισμοῦ τῆς κοίτης γεγενῆσθαι.

πολλαὶ δὲ καὶ ἄλλαι γυναῖκες ἐρασθεῖσαι τοῦ λόγου τῆς ἁγνείας τῶν ἀνδρῶν ἐχωρίζοντο καὶ ἄνδρες τῶν ἰδίων αὐτῶν γυναικῶν διὰ τὸ ἁγνῶς καὶ σεμνῶς θέλειν αὐτοὺς θεοσεβεῖν. θορύβου οὖν ὄντος μεγίστου ἐν τῇ Ῥώμῃ καὶ τοῦ Ἀλβίνου δηλώσαντος τὰ κατ' αὐτὸν τῷ Ἀγρίππᾳ καὶ λέγοντος αὐτῷ ὅτι· ἢ σύ με, Ἀγρίππα, ἐκδίκησον ἀπὸ τοῦ χωρίσαντός μου τὴν γυναῖκα Πέτρου ἢ ἐμαυτὸν ἐκδικῶ, καὶ ὁ Ἀγρίππας ταὐτὰ ἔλεγεν πεπονθέναι ὑπ' αὐτοῦ. καὶ ὁ Ἀλβῖνος ἔφη· τί οὖν μέλλεις, Ἀγρίππα; συσχῶμεν αὐτόν, καὶ ὡς περίεργον ἄνδρα ἀνέλωμεν, καὶ ἐκδικήσωμεν ἑαυτούς, ὅπως σχῶμεν ἡμῶν τὰς γυναῖκας,

charge of sorcery. After undergoing surgery[11] there, Simon the messenger of the devil came to the end of his life.

4.[12] Peter the apostle was in Rome rejoicing with the brothers and sisters in the Lord and giving thanks to God night and day for the crowd being brought daily to the grace of God in the name of the Lord Jesus Christ. Even the wives of the prefect Agrippa were coming to Peter, four of them: Agrippina, Ikaria, Euphemia, and Doris. When they heard the teaching about chastity and all the sayings of the Lord, they were sorely pricked in their spirits. After they had agreed among themselves to remain pure from intercourse with Agrippa, they were harassed by him every day. Therefore, because Agrippa was at a loss and was grieved concerning them—because he truly loved them—he kept them under surveillance. He sent someone to see where they were going and learned that they were going to Peter. Then he said to them as they were coming back, "That Christian has taught you not to be with me. Know that I will destroy you and burn that man alive." They therefore endured every kind of suffering at the hands of Agrippa so that they might no longer be defiled, because they were empowered in the strength of Jesus Christ.

5. And a certain very beautiful woman named Xanthippe was the wife of Albinus, a friend of Caesar. She went together with the other matrons to Peter, and she withdrew from Albinus. Filled with fury and love for Xanthippe, he was grieved that she had pulled away from him. He was angry like a wild beast and wanted to kill Peter, for he knew that Peter was responsible for her withdrawal from intercourse.

Many other wives were enamored with the teaching about chastity and were separated from their husbands, and husbands also withdrew from their own wives, because they wished to worship God in a holy and reverent way. Then there was a great uproar in Rome, and Albinus reported his own situation to Agrippa and said to him, "Agrippa, either you take vengeance for me on Peter, who has separated my wife from me, or I will avenge myself." And Agrippa said that he had suffered the same things on account of Peter. Albinus said, "Then why are you hesitating, Agrippa? Let us arrest him and kill him as a meddlesome man. And let us avenge ourselves, so that we might have our wives back, and so that we might avenge

11. Literally, "being cut up," but I assume that Castor is trying to help Simon.

12. From this point the text follows the updated edition in Otto Zwierlein, *Petrus in Rom: Die literarischen Zeugnisse*, 2nd ed., UALG 96 (Berlin: de Gruyter, 2010), 404–24.

ἵνα κἀκείνους ἐκδικήσωμεν τοὺς μὴ δυναμένους ἑαυτοὺς ἐκδικεῖν, ὧν καὶ αὐτῶν ἀπέστρεψεν τὰς γυναῖκας.

6. ὡς δὲ ταῦτα ἐσκέπτοντο, γνοῦσα ἡ Ξανθίππη τοῦ ἀνδρὸς τὴν συμβουλίαν τὴν πρὸς Ἀγρίππαν, πέμψασα ἐδήλωσεν τῷ Πέτρῳ, ὅπως ἐξέλθῃ Ῥώμης. καὶ οἱ λοιποὶ δὲ ἀδελφοὶ ἅμα τῷ Μαρκέλλῳ παρεκάλουν αὐτὸν ἐξελθεῖν. ὁ δὲ Πέτρος ἔφη αὐτοῖς· δραπετεύωμεν, ἀδελφοί;

οἱ δὲ ἔλεγον αὐτῷ· οὐχί, ἀλλ' ὡς ἔτι σοῦ δυναμένου ὑπηρετεῖν τῷ κυρίῳ ἐπίμεινον ἐν σαρκὶ ἡμῶν χάριν.

πεισθεὶς δὲ τοῖς ἀδελφοῖς ὁ Πέτρος ἐξῆλθεν μόνος εἰπών· μηδεὶς ὑμῶν ἐρχέσθω σὺν ἐμοί, ἀλλ' ἐξέρχομαι μόνος, μεταμφιάσας τὸ σχῆμά μου. ὡς δὲ ἐξῄει τὴν πύλην, εἶδεν τὸν κύριον εἰσερχόμενον εἰς τὴν Ῥώμην. καὶ ὁ Πέτρος ἰδὼν εἶπεν αὐτῷ· κύριε, ποῦ ὧδε;[1]

καὶ ὁ κύριος εἶπεν αὐτῷ· εἰσέρχομαι εἰς τὴν Ῥώμην σταυρωθῆναι.

καὶ ὁ Πέτρος εἶπεν αὐτῷ· κύριέ μου, πάλιν σταυροῦσαι;

καὶ εἶπεν αὐτῷ ὁ κύριος· ναί, Πέτρε, πάλιν σταυροῦμαι.

καὶ ἐλθὼν εἰς ἑαυτὸν ὁ Πέτρος καὶ ἰδὼν τὸν κύριον εἰς οὐρανὸν ἀνελθόντα, ὑπέστρεψεν εἰς τὴν Ῥώμην ἀγαλλιῶν καὶ δοξάζων τὸν κύριον, ὅτι ἑαυτὸν εἶπεν πάλιν σταυροῦσθαι, ὃ εἰς τὸν Πέτρον προέλεγεν γίνεσθαι.

7. ἀναβὰς οὖν πρὸς τοὺς ἀδελφοὺς ἔλεγεν αὐτοῖς τὸ ὁραθὲν αὐτῷ· κἀκεῖνοι

1. Zwierlein: τί ὧδε, κύριε;

those who are not able to avenge themselves—those whose wives he has also turned away from them."

6. As they were pondering these things, Xanthippe learned her husband's scheme with Agrippa. She sent someone to tell this to Peter, so that he might leave Rome. The other brothers and sisters together with Marcellus begged him to leave. But Peter said to them, "Are we to run away, brothers and sisters?"

But they said to him, "No, but so that you are able to serve the Lord, stay in the flesh for our sake."

Having been persuaded by the brothers and sisters, Peter left alone, saying, "Let none of you go with me, but I will go out alone after changing my appearance." As he was going out the gate, he saw the Lord entering Rome. Seeing him Peter said to him, "Lord, where are you going?"[13]

And the Lord said to him, "I am going to Rome to be crucified."

And Peter said to him, "My Lord, you are being crucified again?"

And the Lord said to him, "Yes, Peter, I am being crucified again."[14]

Then Peter came to himself and saw the Lord ascending into heaven, and he went back into Rome rejoicing and praising the Lord, because he said that he would be crucified again—which was a prophecy of what would happen to Peter.

7. Then he went up to the brothers and sisters and told them what he saw. After they heard him, they began to grieve in their spirits, and weep-

---

13. Cf. Zwierlein's edition: "Lord, why are you coming here?" Zwierlein favors this reading found in an eleventh-century manuscript from Ohrid, Macedonia. It runs counter to the traditional reading, which I have maintained here because it is supported by the two other primary Greek textual witnesses (ninth–eleventh century) and the other accounts of the scene in this volume (Lin. *Mart. Pet.* 6; Abd. *Pass. Pet.* 19; Pass. Holy 61; Acts Pet. Paul 82; Pass. Apost. 12). Zwierlein (*Petrus in Rom*, 82–92) argues that the Ohrid reading makes more sense of Jesus's answer to Peter, "I am going to Rome to be crucified." Because Peter meets Jesus as Jesus is entering the city, it is obvious *where* Jesus is going—to Rome. Peter's question is *why* Jesus is in Rome, and the answer is crucifixion. In addition, Zwierlein claims that the account in Lin. *Mart. Pet.* 6 was altered based on John 13:36 and Acts 12:11 and may have influenced even some of the later Greek manuscripts of the Martyrdom of Peter. Zwierlein also notes that a Coptic manuscript, dating perhaps from the fifth century, includes both questions, "Lord, why are you here, and where are you going?" Perhaps in support of Zwierlein's attempts to problematize the dominant tradition, we should note that in the Hist. Shim. 3, the question to Jesus is not "Where?" but "Why?"

14. Origen (*Comm. Jo.* 20.12.91) cites this saying of Jesus but assigns it to the Acts of Paul. Cf. Ambrose, *Aux.* 13, who correctly connects the saying to Peter.

ἀκούσαντες αὐτοῦ ἐπένθουν τῇ ψυχῇ κλαίοντες καὶ ἔλεγον πρὸς αὐτόν· παρακαλοῦμέν σε, Πέτρε· ἡμῶν τῶν νεωτέρων ἐν τῇ πίστει φρόντισον.

καὶ ὁ Πέτρος αὐτοῖς εἶπεν ὅτι· ἐὰν ᾖ τοῦ κυρίου τὸ θέλημα, γενήσεται, κἂν ἡμεῖς μὴ θέλωμεν. ὑμᾶς δὲ δυνατὸς ὁ κύριος στηρίξαι ἐν τῇ πίστει αὐτοῦ καὶ θεμελιῶσαι ἐν αὐτῷ καὶ κρατῦναι, οὓς αὐτὸς ἐφύτευσεν· καὶ ὑμεῖς δὲ ἄλλους φυτεύσετε καὶ ζωογονήσετε δι' αὐτοῦ. ἐγὼ δέ, μέχρι θέλει με ὁ κύριος ἐν σαρκὶ εἶναι, οὐκ ἀντιλέγω· καὶ πάλιν θέλοντος αὐτοῦ με παραλαβεῖν, ἀγαλλιῶ καὶ εὐφραίνομαι. ταῦτα τοῦ Πετροῦ ὁμιλοῦντος καὶ τῶν ἀδελφῶν πάντων κλαιόντων φρουμεντάριοι[2] τέσσαρες αὐτὸν παραλαβόντες ἀπήγαγον τῷ Ἀγρίππᾳ. κἀκεῖνος διὰ τὴν νόσον αὐτοῦ ἐκέλευσεν αὐτὸν σταυρωθῆναι. συνέδραμεν οὖν τὸ πλῆθος τῶν ἀδελφῶν ὅλον πλουσίων τε καὶ πενήτων, ὀρφανῶν τε καὶ χηρῶν, ἀδυνάτων τε καὶ δυνατῶν, βουλομένων ἰδεῖν καὶ ἀφαρπάσαι τὸν Πέτρον.

τοῦ δὲ δήμου <θυμῷ> ἐκβοῶντος ἀκατασχέτῳ καὶ μιᾷ φωνῇ· τί ἠδίκησεν Πέτρος, Ἀγρίππα; τί σε κακὸν διέθηκεν; λέγε Ῥωμαίοις. στασιάζει Ῥώμη ἐὰν οὗτος ἀποθάνῃ.

Πέτρος ὁ ἀπόστολος γενόμενος ἐπὶ τὸν τόπον καὶ καταστείλας τὸν ὄχλον εἶπεν· ἄνδρες οἱ εἰς θεὸν στρατευόμενοι, ἄνδρες οἱ εἰς θεὸν ἐλπίζοντες, ἄνδρες οἱ ζωὴν ἐν Χριστῷ ἔχοντες, μέμνησθε ὧν εἴδετε δι' ἐμοῦ σημείων καὶ τεράτων, μέμνησθε τῆς συμπαθείας τοῦ θεοῦ, δι' ἡμᾶς πόσας ἰάσεις ἐποίησεν ἐν ὑμῖν καὶ ποίας. ὑπομείνατε οὖν αὐτὸν ἐρχόμενον καὶ ἀποδιδοῦντα ἑκάστῳ κατὰ τὰς πράξεις αὐτοῦ. καὶ νῦν πρὸς τὸν Ἀγρίππαν μὴ ἀγριαίνεσθε· διάκονος γάρ ἐστιν τῆς πατρικῆς οὐσίας αὐτοῦ καὶ ἐξουσίας καὶ συνεργίας, καὶ πάντως τοῦτο γίνεται τοῦ κυρίου φανερώσαντος ἐμοὶ τὸ συμβαῖνον. ἀλλὰ τί μέλλω καὶ οὐ πρόσειμι τῷ σταυρῷ;

8. προσελθόντος οὖν αὐτῷ καὶ παραστάντνος ἤρξατο λέγειν· ὦ ὄνομα σταυροῦ, μυστήριον ὅλον ἀπόκρυφον· ὦ χάρις ἀνέκφραστος ἐπ' ὀνόματι σταυροῦ εἰρημένη· ὦ φύσις ἀνθρώπου ἀπὸ σταυροῦ χωρισθῆναι μὴ δυναμένη· ἄρρητε φιλία καὶ ἀχώριστε, διὰ χειλέων ῥυπαρῶν ἐκφαίνεσθαι μὴ δυναμένη· βιάζομαι ἐμαυτὸν νῦν πρὸς τῷ τέλει τῆς ἐνθάδε συσχέσεως ὑπάρχων, ὅστις εἶ, ἄνθρωπε, δηλῶσαί, σε· οὐκ ἠρεμίσω τὸ πάλαι μεμυκὸς καὶ κρυπτόμενον τῇ ψυχῇ μου τοῦ σταυροῦ μυστήριον. μὴ τοῦτο ὑμῖν ἔστω τὸ φαινόμενον ὄνομα σταυροῦ, οἱ ἐπὶ

2. From the Latin *frumentarii*. These were soldiers specifically in charge of securing corn supplies for the military.

ing they said to him, "We beg you, Peter, think about those of us who are newer in the faith."

And Peter said to them, "If it is the will of the Lord, then it will be done, even if we do not wish it. But the Lord is able to establish you in faith in him, to set your foundations on him, and to strengthen those whom he has planted. And you will plant others and give life to them through him. But as for me, if the Lord wants me to remain longer in the flesh, I will not speak against it. But again, if he wants to take me, I will rejoice and be glad." While Peter was saying these things and all the brothers and sisters were weeping, four soldiers arrested and took him to Agrippa. Agrippa, on account of his illness,[15] ordered him to be crucified. Then the whole multitude of the brothers and sisters assembled—rich and poor, orphans and widows, the powerless and powerful—wishing to see Peter and snatch him away.

Then the people cried out uncontrollably and with one voice, "What has Peter done wrong, Agrippa? How has he done you any harm? Tell us Romans. Rome will rise in rebellion if this man dies."

The apostle Peter went up to the place, calmed the crowd, and said, "You who are being crucified to God, you who hope in God, you who have life in Christ, remember the signs and wonders that you saw through me. Remember the compassion of God, who performed so many and such great healings through us among you. Wait, therefore, for him to come and reward each one according to their deeds.[16] Do not be angry now toward Agrippa, for he is a servant of his father's essence and authority and conspiracy, and what is coming to pass is happening exactly as the Lord revealed it to me. But why do I delay and not go forth to the cross?"

8. After coming to the cross and standing beside it, he began to say, "Oh, name of the cross, a mystery completely hidden. Oh, grace inexpressible, spoken in the name of the cross. Oh, nature of humanity that cannot be separated from the cross. Oh, unspoken and inseparable love, which cannot be revealed through unclean lips. I am compelled now to begin revealing it and making it known to you, oh person, whoever you are, until the end of my imprisonment here. I will not conceal the mystery of the cross, which for a long time has been closed up and hidden in my soul. Do not let that which is visible be for you the name of the cross, oh you

15. That is, the sickness that resulted from being denied sex.

16. Matt 16:27; Rom 2:5–6; 2 Cor 5:10; Rev 22:12.

Χριστὸν ἐλπίζοντες· ἕτερον γάρ τί ἐστιν παρὰ τοῦτο τὸ φαινόμενον ὑμῖν. καὶ νῦν μάλιστα, ὅτε δύνασθε οἱ δυνάμενοι ἀκούειν ἐν ἐσχάτῃ ὥρᾳ καὶ, τελευταίᾳ τοῦ βίου ὑπάρχοντός μου, ἀκούσατε· παντὸς φαινομένου αἰσθητοῦ χωρίσατε ὑμῶν τὰς ψυχὰς μὴ ὄντος ἀληθοῦς· πηρώσατε ὑμῶν τὰς ὄψεις τῆς σαρκός, πηρώσατε ὑμῶν τὰς ἀκοὰς ταύτας τὰς ἐν τῷ φανερῷ [πράξεις], καὶ γνῶτε τὰ πάλαι ὑπὸ τοῦ Χριστοῦ γεγονότα καὶ τὸ ὅλον τῆς σωτηρίας μυστήριον τὸ πάντοτε λεγόμενον καὶ μηδ᾽ ὅλως ἀκουόμενον. ὥρα δέ σοι, Πέτρε, παραδοῦναι τὸ σῶμα τοῖς λαμβάνουσιν. ἀπολάβετε οὖν, ὧν ἐστιν τὸ ἴδιον. ἀξιῶ οὖν ὑμᾶς τοὺς δημίους, οὕτως με σταυρώσατε, ἐπὶ κεφαλὴν καὶ μὴ ἄλλως· καὶ διὰ τί, τοῖς ἀκούουσιν ἐρῶ.

9. ὡς δὲ ἀπεκρέμασαν αὐτὸν ὃν ἠξίωσεν τρόπον, ἤρξατο πάλιν λέγειν· ἄνδρες, ὧν ἐστιν ἴδιον τὸ ἀκούειν, ἐνωτίσασθε ἃ νῦν ἀναγγελῶ ὑμῖν ἀποκρεμάμενος. γινώσκετε τῆς ἁπάσης φύσεως τὸ μυστήριον καὶ τῶν ἁπασῶν φύσεων τὴν ἀρχὴν ἥτις ἦν. ὁ γὰρ πρῶτος ἄνθρωπος, ὁ γενόμενος ἐν εἴδει ὃ ἔχω ἐγώ, κατὰ κεφαλῆς ἐνεχθεὶς ἔδειξεν γένεσιν τὴν οὐκ οὖσαν πάλαι νεκράν, νεκρὰ γὰρ αὐτὴ ἡ φύσις, νεκρὰν τε καὶ κίνησιν ἔχει· κατελθὼν οὖν ἐκεῖνος καὶ τὴν ἀρχὴν τὴν ἑαυτοῦ εἰς γῆν ῥίψας, πρὸς ἑαυτὸν τὸ πᾶν τοῦτο τῆς διακοσμήσεως συνεστήσατο εἶδος, ἐν ᾧ τὰ δεξιὰ ἀριστερὰ ἔδειξεν καὶ τὰ ἀριστερὰ δεξιά, καὶ πάντα ἐνηλλάγη τῆς φύσεως αὐτῶν τὰ σημεῖα, ὡς καλὰ τὰ μὴ καλὰ νομισθῆναι καὶ τὰ ἐκ φύσεως ἀγαθὰ κακά· περὶ ὧν ὁ κύριος ἐν μυστηρίῳ λέγει· ἐὰν μὴ ποιήσητε τὰ δεξιὰ ὡς τὰ ἀριστερὰ καὶ τὰ ἀριστερὰ ὡς τὰ δεξιὰ καὶ τὰ κάτω ὡς τὰ ἄνω καὶ τὰ ὀπίσω

who hope in Christ, for it is something other than what is visible to you. And now especially, because you are able—you who are able—to hear me as I am in the last and final hour of life, listen. Separate your souls from everything that seems to be perceptible but is not true. Close the eyes of the flesh, and close your ears to these things done only in appearance. Know the things that were brought about by Christ long ago and the entire mystery of salvation, which was spoken everywhere but not completely heard. But the hour has come for you, Peter, to surrender your body to those taking it. Take it, then, for it is yours. I ask you executioners, crucify me in this way—with my head down and no other way.[17] I will say the reason to those who are listening."

9. Thus, they hung him up in the way that he had requested, and he began to speak again: "Oh men, whose duty it is to hear, pay attention to the things that I will now proclaim to you as I am hanging here. Understand the mystery of all nature and what was the beginning of all natures.[18] For the first man, who existed in the form that I now have and was brought forth with his head down, showed an origin that did not exist long ago.[19] For nature itself is dead, and it has dead movement. Therefore, because that one came down after casting down his own beginning to the earth, he framed for himself this entire form of the cosmos, in which he showed that the things on the right are on the left, and the things on the left are on the right. And all the signs of their nature were perverted, so that good things are considered not good, and the evil things that come from their nature are considered noble. Concerning these things the Lord says in a mystery, 'Unless you make the things on the right as things on the left, and the things on the left as things on the right, and the things below as the things

17. The inverted crucifixion of Peter was widely recounted by patristic authors (e.g., Eusebius, *Hist. eccl.* 3.1; Jerome, *Vir. ill.* 1) and has inspired numerous works of art, such as the famous paintings by Michelangelo and Caravaggio. Many authors also repeated Peter's motivations for this request, e.g., Ambrose, *Job* 1.1.2; Theodoret, *Car.* 1309–1310.

18. Sections 9.2–3 probably influenced the fourth-century Acts Phil. Mart. 19–34, which recounts Philip's inverted crucifixion and includes particular reference to "mystery." Imitation of this type was common in the apocryphal acts, especially in the Acts of Philip, as shown by François Bovon, "The Synoptic Gospels and the Noncanonical Acts of the Apostles," *HTR* 81.1 (1988): 25–29.

19. Zwierlein's inclusion of an additional *νεκράν* here renders the sentence virtually incomprehensible, so I favor the variant that omits this reading.

ὡς τὰ ἔμπροσθεν, οὐ μὴ εἰσέλθητε εἰς τὴν βασιλείαν τοῦ θεοῦ. ταύτην οὖν τὴν ἔννοιαν εἰς ἡμᾶς προάξας < ... >.

καὶ τὸ σχῆμα ἐν ᾧ ὁρᾶτέ με ἀποκρεμάμενον ἐκείνου διατύπωσίς ἐστιν τοῦ καταβεβηκότος καὶ εἰς γένεσιν ἐλθόντος ἀνθρώπου. ὑμᾶς οὖν, ἀγαπητοί μου, καὶ τοὺς νῦν ἀκούοντας καὶ τοὺς μέλλοντας ἀκούειν, λήξαντας τῆς πρώτης πλάνης ἐπαναδραμεῖν προσῆκεν πρὸς τὴν ἀρχαίαν πατρίδα, ἐπιβαίνειν οὖν τῷ τοῦ κυρίου σταυρῷ, ὅς ἐστι τεταμένος λόγος, εἷς καὶ μόνος, περὶ οὗ τὸ πνεῦμα λέγει· τί ἐστιν Χριστὸς ἀλλ' ἢ λόγος, ἦχος θεοῦ; ἵνα λόγος ᾖ τοῦτο τὸ εὐθύξυλον, ἐφ' οὗ ἐσταύρωμαι· ἦχος δὲ τὸ πλάγιόν ἐστιν, ἡ ἀνθρώπου φύσις· ὁ δὲ ἧλος ὁ συνέχων ἐπὶ τῷ ὀρθῷ ξύλῳ τὸ πλάγιον κατὰ μέσου, ἡ ἐπιστροφὴ καὶ ἡ μετάνοια τοῦ ἀνθρώπου.

10. ταῦτα οὖν μοι σοῦ γνωρίσαντος καὶ ἀποκαλύψαντος, λόγε ζωῆς, ξύλον νῦν ὑπ' ἐμοῦ εἰρημένον, εὐχαριστῶ σοι οὐ χείλεσι τούτοις οἷς προσηλωμένος λαλῶ, οὐδὲ γλώσσῃ, δι' ἧς τὸ ἀληθὲς, καὶ τὸ ψεῦδος προέρχεται, οὐδὲ λόγῳ τούτῳ τῷ ὑπὸ τέχνης φύσεως ὑλικῆς προερχομένῳ, ἀλλ' ἐκείνῃ φωνῇ σοι εὐχαριστῶ τῇ διὰ σιγῆς νοουμένῃ, τῇ μὴ δι' ὀργάνων σώματος προϊούσῃ, τῇ μὴ εἰς σαρκικὰ ὦτα πορευομένῃ, τῇ μὴ φύσει φθαρτῇ ἀκουομένῃ, τῇ μὴ ἐν κόσμῳ οὔσῃ καὶ ἐν γῇ ἀφιομένῃ καὶ ἐν βίβλοις γραφομένῃ, μηδὲ τινὶ μὲν οὔσῃ, τινὶ δὲ οὔ· ἀλλὰ ταύτῃ, Ἰησοῦ, εὐχαριστῶ σοι σιγῇ — φωνῇ τῇ σῇ — ᾗ τὸ ἐν ἐμοὶ πνεῦμά σε φιλοῦν καί σοι λαλοῦν καί σε ὁρῶν ἐντυγχάνει σοι, ὃς καὶ μόνῳ πνεύματι νοητός εἶ.

σύ μοι πατήρ, σύ μοι μήτηρ, σύ μοι ἀδελφός, σὺ φίλος, σὺ δοῦλος, σὺ οἰκονόμος, σὺ τὸ πᾶν καὶ τὸ πᾶν ἐν σοὶ ἕστηκεν καὶ οὐκ ἔστι σωτηρία ἐκτὸς

above, and the things behind as the things in front, you will not enter into the kingdom of God.'[20] Having presented this idea to us[21] [...].

"The form in which you see me hanging here is a perfect representation of that one who descended and came as a man at his own beginning. Therefore, you, my beloved—both those who hear now and those who are going to hear—having left off your earlier wandering, return, as it is fitting, to your ancient place of origin. Go upon the cross of the Lord, who is the word stretched out, the one and only, about whom the Spirit says, 'What is the Christ except the word, the sound of God?'[22] So the word is this upright tree on which I am being crucified, but the sound is the crossbeam, the nature of humanity. And the nail that holds the crossbeam on the upright tree across the middle is the turning and repentance of humanity.[23]

10. "Because you have made known and revealed these things to me, oh word of life and tree now being spoken about by me, I thank you—not with these lips with which I speak as I am nailed here, nor with this tongue through which both truth and falsehood go forth, nor with this word that goes forth by the skill of material nature. But I thank you with that voice which is perceived through silence, which is not heard aloud, which does not go forth through the organs of the body, which is not conveyed to fleshly ears, which is not heard by perishable nature, which is not in the world or spoken on the earth or written in books, which does not belong to a certain one but not to another. I thank you, Jesus, with this silence—with a voice that is yours—with which the spirit within me that loves you and speaks to you and sees you also appeals to you—you who are known to the spirit alone.

You are my father; you are my mother; you are my brother, my friend, my servant, my household manager. You are everything, and everything is

20. Cf. Gos. Thom. 22. This statement of Jesus overall seems to be an amalgam from multiple sources. On the use of otherwise unattested sayings in the acts, see Bovon, "Synoptic Gospels," 30–31. Wilhelm Schneemelcher has considered the possibility that these sayings could come from the lost Gospel of the Egyptians but finds the evidence lacking (*New Testament Apocrypha*, ed. Wilhelm Schneemelcher, trans. R. McL. Wilson, 5th ed. [Louisville: Westminster John Knox, 1993], 212–14).

21. Some manuscripts read " ... to you." The lacuna that follows in the text makes it difficult to determine the original reading.

22. The source of this statement is unknown.

23. This allegorical interpretation for inverted crucifixion is quite different from the explanation in other accounts of Peter's death, in which he does not feel worthy to die in the same way as his Lord.

σοῦ τινι. ἐπὶ τοῦτον οὖν, ἀδελφοί, καὶ ὑμεῖς καταφεύγοντες ἀνανεωθήσεσθε· ἐν αὐτῷ γὰρ μόνῳ τοῦτο ὑπάρχει τὸ ὑμᾶς μαθόντας ἐκείνων τεύξασθαι ὧν λέγει δοῦναι ὑμῖν· ἃ οὔτε ὀφθαλμὸς εἶδεν, οὔτε οὖς ἤκουσεν, οὔτε ἐπὶ καρδίαν ἀνθρώπου ἁμαρτωλοῦ ἀνέβη. δεόμεθα σοῦ, ἀμίαντε, περὶ ὧν ἡμῖν ὑπέσχου δοῦναι· αἰνοῦμέν σε εὐχαριστοῦντες καὶ δεόμενοι ἀνθομολογούμεθα, δοξάζοντές σε ἔτι ἀσθενεῖς ὄντες ἄνθρωποι, ὅτι σὺ εἶ ὁ σωτὴρ τῶν ψυχῶν ἡμῶν καὶ θεὸς καὶ πατὴρ καὶ δεσπότης μόνος καὶ οὐχ ἕτερος εἰ μὴ μόνος σὺ θεός, ᾧ ἡ δόξα καὶ νῦν καὶ εἰς τοὺς ἅπαντας αἰῶνας. ἀμήν.

11. ὡς δὲ ὁ παρεστὼς ὄχλος τὸ ἀμὴν μεγάλῃ τῇ φωνῇ ἅμα αὐτῷ ἀνέπεμψεν, καὶ ὁ ἀπόστολος Πέτρος παρέδωκε τὸ πνεῦμα. ὁ δὲ Μάρκελλος, μηδὲ γνώμην τινὸς λαβών, ὃ μὴ ἐξὸν ἦν, ἰδὼν ὅτι ὁ μακάριος Πέτρος ἀπέπνευσεν, ἰδίαις χερσὶν καθελὼν τὸ σῶμα ἀπὸ τοῦ σταυροῦ ἔλουσεν γάλακτι καὶ οἴνῳ. καὶ κόψας μαστίχης μνᾶς πεντήκοντα καὶ σμύρνης καὶ ἀλόης καὶ φύλλου ἄλλας μνᾶς πεντήκοντα ἐσμύρνισεν αὐτοῦ τὸ λείψανον καὶ γεμίσας μακρὰν σορὸν λιθίνην πολλοῦ τιμήματος μέλιτος Ἀττικοῦ κατέθετο αὐτόν.

ὁ δὲ ἀπόστολος Πέτρος νυκτὸς ἐπιστὰς τῷ Μαρκέλλῳ ἔλεγεν· Μάρκελλε, οὐκ ἤκουσας τοῦ κυρίου λέγοντος· ἄφετε τοὺς νεκροὺς θάπτειν τοὺς ἑαυτῶν νεκρούς;

τοῦ δὲ Μαρκέλλου εἰρηκότος· ναί.

εἶπεν αὐτῷ ὁ Πέτρος· ἐκεῖνα οὖν ἃ παρέσχου εἰς τὸν νεκρόν, ἀπώλεσας· σὺ γὰρ ζῶν ὑπάρχων ὡς νεκρὸς νεκροῦ ἐπεμελήσω. ὁ δὲ Μάρκελλος διυπνισθεὶς ἀνήγγειλεν τὸν ἐμφανισμὸν τοῖς ἀδελφοῖς τοῖς ὑπὸ Πέτρου στηριχθεῖσιν τῇ εἰς

in you, and there is no salvation apart from you.[24] You also, brothers and sisters, will be renewed if you take refuge in him. For in him alone exist, as you have learned, the things that have been prepared, which he says will be given to you: 'Things that neither eye has seen, nor ear has heard, nor has entered into the heart of sinful humankind.'[25] We ask you, undefiled one, for the things that you promised to give to us. We praise you by giving thanks, acknowledge you by making petition, and glorify you, although we are only weak people, because you are the savior of our souls and none other than God alone, to whom be the glory both now and throughout all ages. Amen."

11. As the crowd standing nearby offered up the "amen" in a loud voice together with him, the apostle Peter gave up his spirit.[26] But Marcellus, who had not received this idea from anyone—and this was not allowed—saw that the blessed Peter had died, and after taking the body off the cross with his own hands, he washed it with milk and wine.[27] After he cut up fifty minas of mastic and myrrh and aloe, and another fifty minas of silphium,[28] he embalmed his remains. And after filling a great stone coffin with a large amount of expensive Attic honey, he placed Peter in it.

But the apostle Peter visited Marcellus by night and said, "Marcellus, did you not hear the Lord say, 'Leave the dead to bury their own dead'?"[29]

Then Marcellus said, "Yes."

Peter said to him, "Therefore, those things that you offered for the dead, you have lost, for you who are alive took care of the dead as if you were dead." But Marcellus awoke and recounted this appearance to the brothers and sisters who had been strengthened in their faith in Christ by

24. Cf. Acts 4:12.

25. Cf. 1 Cor 2:9; Gos. Thom. 17. On the possibility that the Testament of Jacob could be the common source of these related sayings, see Eckhard von Nordheim, "Das Zitat des Paulus in 1 Kor 2,9 und seine Beziehung zum koptischen Testament Jakobs," *ZNW* 65 (1974): 112–20.

26. Cf. John 19:30.

27. Marcellus's offense was apparently removing the body from the cross. Condemned criminals were often left on the cross and denied proper burial.

28. This rare plant from Cyrene was highly valued by the Romans until it became extinct due to overharvesting (Pliny the Elder, *Nat.* 19.15).

29. Matt 8:22; Luke 9:60.

τὸν Χριστὸν πίστει, στηριζόμενος καὶ αὐτὸς ἔτι μᾶλλον μέχρι τῆς ἐπιδημίας Παύλου τῆς εἰς Ῥώμην.

12. ὁ δὲ Νέρων γνοὺς ὕστερον τὸν Πέτρον ἀπαλλαγέντα τοῦ βίου, ἐμέμψατο τὸν πραίφεκτον Ἀγρίππαν, ὅτι μὴ μετὰ γνώμης αὐτοῦ ἀνῃρέθη. ἐβούλετο γὰρ αὐτὸν μᾶλλον περισσοτέρως κολάσαι καὶ μειζόνως τιμωρήσασθαι· καὶ γάρ τινας τῶν πρὸς χεῖρα αὐτοῦ ὁ Πέτρος μαθητεύσας ἀποστῆναι αὐτοῦ ἐποίησεν· ὥστε ὀργίλως διακεῖσθαι τὸν Νέρωνα καὶ χρόνῳ ἱκανῷ τῷ Ἀγρίππᾳ μὴ λαλῆσαι.

ἐζήτει οὖν ὁ Νέρων πάντας τοὺς ὑπὸ Πέτρου μαθητευθέντας ἀδελφοὺς ἀπολέσαι. καὶ ὁρᾷ τινα νυκτὸς μαστίζοντα αὐτὸν καὶ λέγοντα· Νέρων, οὐ δύνασαι νῦν τοὺς τοῦ Χριστοῦ δούλους διώκειν ἢ ἀπολλύειν· ἔπεχε ἀπ' αὐτῶν τὰς χεῖρας. καὶ οὕτως ὁ Νέρων περίφοβος γενόμενος ἐκ τῆς τοιαύτης ὀπτασίας ἀπέστη τῶν μαθητῶν ἐν ἐκείνῳ τῷ καιρῷ, καθ' ὃν ὁ Πέτρος τοῦ βίου ἀπηλλάγη. καὶ ἦσαν τὸ λοιπὸν οἱ ἀδελφοὶ ὁμοθυμαδὸν εὐφραινόμενοι καὶ ἀγαλλιῶντες ἐπὶ τῷ κυρίῳ, δοξάζοντες πατέρα καὶ υἱὸν καὶ ἅγιον πνεῦμα, ᾧ ἡ δόξα εἰς τοὺς αἰῶνας τῶν αἰώνων. ἀμήν.

Peter. And he himself was strengthened even more until the arrival of Paul in Rome.[30]

12. When Nero finally learned that Peter had departed this life, he was angry at the prefect Agrippa, because he had killed him against his will. For Nero wanted to punish him more extensively and exact even greater revenge upon him, because Peter had made disciples of some of those close to him, who had then left him. Thus, Nero remained angry and for a long time did not speak to Agrippa.

Nero therefore wanted to kill all the brothers and sisters who had been made disciples by Peter. One night he saw a certain figure whipping him and saying, "Nero, you are now not able to persecute or kill the servants of Christ. Keep your hands off them."[31] And Nero was so frightened by this vision that he kept away from the disciples in that time after Peter departed this life. After that the brothers and sisters were with one accord delighting and rejoicing in the Lord, glorifying the Father and the Son and the Holy Spirit, to whom be glory forever and ever. Amen.

---

30. This was Paul's anticipated return to Rome, for he had previously been evangelizing in the city according to Acts Pet. 1–4.

31. This anonymous figure is identified as Peter in Lin. *Mart. Pet.* 17.

2. Pseudo-Linus, *Martyrdom of Blessed Peter the Apostle*

CANT 191 / *BHL* 6655

Contents

At its core this is primarily a Latin revision of the Greek Martyrdom of Peter. The text includes many of the same elements we find in the earlier Greek text. Peter's preaching of chastity reaches the aristocratic women of Rome, including four concubines (not "wives" as in the Greek Martyrdom of Peter) of the prefect Agrippa and Xanthippe, the wife of Albinus. The sexually frustrated husbands plot against Peter, but Xanthippe alerts Peter to the impending threat. The believers plead with Peter to flee Rome, and he finally agrees. However, he meets Christ on the road and understands that Christ's reference to being crucified again is a prediction of Peter's own demise. He returns to the city, is arrested, and is sentenced to crucifixion by Agrippa. An angry mob protests, but Peter calms the crowd and goes passively to his execution. Once at the cross, he extols the hidden mystery of salvation that the cross represents and bemoans the distortion of affairs in the natural world. After his death, Peter is buried in an expensive tomb by Marcellus but returns to visit and admonish Marcellus in a dream. Nero is angry that Agrippa's actions have denied him the opportunity to torture Peter, and he decides to persecute Peter's followers. A dream warns the emperor against this course of action, and he relents. The believers in Rome rejoice and exult in the Lord.

This list of similarities between these texts, however, risks overshadowing the significant differences, which can be summarized in two broad categories.

(1) Literary and dramatic expansions. The author of this Latin text includes extensive details that are not in the Greek. For example, in the Greek Martyrdom of Peter the plot against Peter's life is confined to

Agrippa and Albinus. But in this text, the Roman Senate becomes involved. Multiple Senators rise up in the assembly and condemn the perversion that Peter has introduced into their marriages. Thus, Peter is being opposed not just by two sexually deprived husbands, but by the Senate itself. Also, the Greek text states that Xanthippe and the other believers were begging Peter to leave the city. But here Peter is accosted by a series of different constituencies concerned about his well-being. After "the brothers" have appealed to him, the young men come to him, crying and wailing. Then come the matrons, throwing dust on their heads and doing their best to sway Peter with guilt. Even Peter's guards, who here are named, appeal to him to go away. Finally, the widows, orphans, and elderly come to Peter, beseeching him to leave. Yet another example occurs after Peter has returned to the city. The author of this text inserts a dialogue between Agrippa and Peter. Agrippa attacks Peter for destroying marriages, and Peter, with his face shining like the sun, responds with a list of insults, even calling Agrippa the "habitation of Satan." Such dramatic flourishes occur throughout this text.

(2) Liturgical and theological insertions. Peter's manner of speaking in this text, particularly in his prayers, suggests a strong liturgical influence. This is most clearly seen in the scene of his death. After arriving at the scene of his execution, Peter breaks out in no less than five prayers. Every time it appears that he is about to die, he launches into a new, theologically dense soliloquy. As he is praying ostensibly to God, he is teaching theology to those around him. Important themes include remaining constant in the face of persecution, the significance of the Incarnation, and the role of Christ as the second Adam. Peter appears to be particularly familiar with the Pauline epistles, for he alludes to them on multiple occasions, and he is presented as anticipating the language of the fourth-century creeds of Nicea (325) and Constantinople (381). Indeed, Peter's prayers in this text seem more at home in a liturgical commemoration of his death than they do in any realistic scene of the death itself. Notably, the Platonic dualism in Peter's address to the cross in the Greek Martyrdom of Peter is softened here by a more universalizing message, thus making Peter sound more "orthodox" in his final moments.

Literary Background

The date of the text is uncertain. The explicit references to the doctrinal formulations of the fourth century make a date earlier than the last quarter of that century unlikely. The account of Peter's encounter with Jesus

outside Rome ("Lord, where are you going?") is very similar to that in late fourth-century texts by Pseudo-Hegesippus (ca. 370–375 CE) and Ambrose of Milan (385 CE).[1] However, it is impossible to prove literary dependence in any direction that would establish the dating of Pseudo-Linus *Martyrdom of Peter*, and Gérard Poupon has suggested a common source for these texts. At the same time, the references to the Mamertine prison and the baptisms of Processus and Martinianus have caused some to push the date as late as the first half of the sixth century. The Mamertine prison, at the foot of the Capitoline Hill, had previously been known as the Tullianum. The first evidence of the new title (perhaps apart from this text) comes from the fifth century, and the name may not have been used more broadly until the sixth. As for Processus and Martinianus, soldiers with those names are the subject of a martyrdom story set in the time of the emperor Diocletian (285–305 CE). There was a church dedicated to them in Rome by the end of the fourth century, but when bishop Gregory I (590–604 CE) preached a homily in their honor, he failed to identify them as Peter's guards. This could be an indication that the connection to Peter does not occur until after Gregory's time, but such an assumption is also problematic, for the author of the sixth-century Acts of Nereus and Achilleus appears to know Pseudo-Linus's *Martyrdom of Peter*. Thus, overall a date later than the middle of the sixth century is unlikely. A middle way has been proposed by Poupon, who believes the problematic passages about the Mamertine prison and the names of the guards were later interpolations. If Poupon is correct, then a date at the end of the fourth or in the fifth century remains possible.

Tradition ascribes this text to Linus, Peter's successor as the bishop of Rome in some accounts. Poupon has suggested that Linus was first attached to the text due to the misinterpretation of a reference in the Acts of Nereus and Achilleus to a writing from Linus to the churches of the East. No matter how Linus's name became attached to this text, he cannot have been its author for the chronological reasons discussed above, and even his identification as the second bishop of Rome is not universally supported in all the ancient sources.[2] Based upon the author's detailed knowledge of the Roman context (e.g., the precise location of Peter's death) and strong focus

1. Pseudo-Hegesippus, *Exc. Hier.* 3.2; Ambrose, *Aux.* 13.

2. Support for Linus as the second bishop of Rome comes from the Liberian Catalog of 354 CE (*Chronica minora saec. IV. V. VI.VII.*, ed. T. Mommsen, MGH.AA 9 [Berlin: Weidmann, 1892], 73); Irenaeus (*Haer.* 3.3.3); Eusebius (*Hist. eccl.* 5.6.1); and

on the preeminent position of Rome, Rome is the most likely location for the text's production.

This author is concerned with producing a text that is not only more literarily dramatic and theologically informed, but also more rhetorically sophisticated than the Greek Martyrdom of Peter. Indeed, the lengthy opening sentence of this text, which poses a challenge for any translator wishing to render it in a comprehensible way, has no parallel in the Greek text. Overall, we may describe this as a "new and improved" Roman version of the Greek Martyrdom of Peter.

It should be noted that although Pseudo-Linus's *Martyrdom of Paul* (translated in ch. 6 of this volume) is also traditionally credited to Linus, there is no reason to link the dates or authors of Pseudo-Linus's *Martyrdom of Peter* and Pseudo-Linus's *Martyrdom of Paul*. The shared ascription may simply be a function of the fact that they were frequently copied together in manuscripts, and there is no other apparent stylistic or historical connection between them.

Text

The text survives in twenty-two known manuscripts, and this translation, the first ever produced in English, is based on the edition of Lipsius. Salonius and Poupon have produced subsequent editions—the most recent being Poupon's unpublished master's thesis from 1975. But these texts offer no notable updates to Lipsius, and Poupon even notes that his edition diverges from Lipsius in only "a few minor variants."[3]

Select Bibliography

Erbetta, Mario, trans. "La Passione di Pietro dello Ps. Lino." Pages 169–77 in *Atti e leggende*. Vol. 2 of *Gli apocrifi del Nuovo Testamento*. 2nd ed. Turin: Marietti, 1978.

Flamion, J. "Les Actes de Pierre." *RHE* 11 (1910): 19–28.

Teach. Shim. 6. Cf. Abd. *Pass. Pet.* 3.15; the apocryphal Epistle of Clement to James 2; and Tertullian, *Praescr.* 32, where Clement is identified as the second bishop of Rome.

3. Gérard Poupon, "Passion de Pierre (dite du pseudo-Linus)," in *Écrits apocryphes chrétiens*, ed. Pierre Geoltrain and Jean-Daniel Kaestli (Paris: Gallimard, 2005), 2:715. Poupon has clarified via personal correspondence that his edition offers significant contributions to the critical apparatus but not to the text itself.

Lipsius, R. A. Pages 2.1:84–142 in *Die apokryphen Apostelgeschichten und Apostellegenden*. Braunschweig: Schwetschke, 1887.

Lipsius, Richard A. and M. Bonnet, eds. "Martyrium beati Petri apostoli a Lino episcopo conscriptum." Pages 1–22 in vol. 1 of *Acta apostolorvm apocrypha post Constantinvm Tischendorf*. Leipzig: Mendelssohn, 1891. Repr., Hildesheim: Olms, 1972.

Poupon, Gérard, trans. "Passion de Pierre (dite du pseudo-Linus)." Pages 709–34 in vol. 2 of *Écrits apocryphes chrétiens*. Edited by Pierre Geoltrain and Jean-Daniel Kaestli. Pléiade 516. Paris: Gallimard, 2005.

———, ed. and trans. "La passion de saint Pierre apôtre: Introduction, texte et traduction." Master's thesis, Université de Genève, 1975.

Salonius, A. H. "Martyrium beati Petri apostoli a Lino episcopo conscriptum," Pages 22–58 in *Societas scientiarum fennica—Commentationes humanarum litterarum* 1.6. Helsinki: Helsingfors, 1926.

Verrando, G. N. "Osservazioni sulla collocazione cronologica degli apocrifi Atti di Pietro dello Pseudo-Lino." *VetChr* 20 (1983): 391–426.

Martyrium beati Petri apostoli a Lino episcopo conscriptum

1. Post multimoda et multifaria uiae uitaeque salutaris documenta et eximia atque celeberrima miraculorum ostenta, seu aduersa immo diuersa cum Symone mago aliisue quam plurimis Antichristi praeconibus pro nomine ueri Christi certamina; post passionum quoque multiplicium et flagellorum acerbitatem et carcerum squalorem horrificum, cum esset exultans in Domino beatus Petrus et gratias agens nocte ac die cum fratribus, in turba uenientium ad fidem Domini nostri Iesu Christi, intentus orationibus et doctrinae caeterisque diuinae pietatis officiis, praecipue caritatis et castitatis gratiam audientium pectoribus inserebat, adhortans credentes in Christum ut pudice et continenter se gererent. nimis enim abundanter et supereminenter urbs orbi praelata, mente se in fastum elationis extulerat et idcirco, ut solet in opulentia et inerti securitate, indecenti fluxu dominabatur. persaepe namque ubi est elatio mentis sequitur contumelia carnis. unde factum est ut beati Petri sermonibus magnus pudicitiae apud multas diuersae aetatis ac potestatis seu nobilitatis feminas amor exarserit, ita ut pleraeque etiam Romanorum matronae a commixtione uirilis thori[1] seruare munda corda simul et corpora, quantam ex ipsis erat, diligerent.

2. sed cum iam tempus appropinquaret quo fides beati apostoli et labores remunerari deberent, praeueniens perditionis caput scilicet antichristus Nero, consummata iniquitas, artari eum et in custodia squalidissima compedibus uinciri iussit. ubi coeperunt frequentare illum quatuor

1. *Thorus*, a transliteration of the Greek θορός, refers to the male genitalia and is used in this text in multiple expressions (often with *commixtio*) for sexual intercourse.

Martyrdom of Blessed Peter the Apostle Written by Linus the Bishop

1. After various and multifarious proofs of the way and life of salvation and numerous and very famous demonstrations of miracles; and after conflicts and various struggles on behalf of the name of the true Christ had taken place against Simon the sorcerer and so many other heralds of Antichrist; and after numerous sufferings, the harshness of whips, and the terrible squalor of prisons, the blessed Peter was exulting in the Lord, giving thanks both night and day with his brothers and sisters[1] in a crowd of those who had come to faith in our Lord Jesus Christ. He was being attentive to prayers, to other matters of teaching, and to the duties of divine piety. First and foremost, he was introducing the grace of charity and chastity into the hearts of those hearing him, and he was exhorting those that believed in Christ to conduct themselves chastely and temperately. The city, the greatest in the world, had become far too fully and overwhelmingly puffed up in mind[2] and in the arrogance of pride, so that it was accustomed to opulence and idle carelessness and was dominated by a despicable laziness. Indeed, very often where there is arrogance of mind, the abuse of fleshly indulgence[3] follows. It then came about through the blessed Peter's preaching that great love of chastity burned brightly among many women of different ages and social status, even from among the nobility. As a result, very many Roman matrons were eagerly striving to keep their hearts and their bodies, as much as they could, pure from intercourse with a man.

2. But when the time arrived that the faith and labors of the blessed apostle should have been rewarded, the chief of perdition—obviously the Antichrist Nero, wickedness in its highest form—prevented this and ordered Peter to be bound and fettered with shackles in the foulest prison.

1. Literally, "brothers." At points in this text it is clear that the group of Peter's disciples is mixed, so inclusive language will be used in those cases. In other cases, however, the group is clearly set off as all male.

2. Cf. Col 2:18.

3. Literally, "the abuse of the flesh."

concubinae praefecti Agrippae, quarum erant uocabula Agrippina, Eucharia, Eufemia, et Dionis. quae audientes ab eo castitatis sermonem et omnia Domini nostri Iesu Christi mandata, tabescebant et molestabantur esse sub thoro Agrippae. unde castitati se deuouentes pactum consilii alterutrum inierunt et confortatae a Domino Iesu Christo nullo modo ei obsequio concubitus adquiescere ulterius decreuerunt. subtrahentibus autem se isdem non solum a complexu uerum et ab omnimoda coniunctione Agrippae, coepit idem super hoc ualde taedere et maestus esse.

mittensque sollicitos ac sollertes exploratores didicit eas studiosissime ad beatum Petrum prorumpere. quibus ad se reductis dixit uehementissima amoris captus insania: scio unde uenitis. ille Christianus uos docuit mecum non coire et a debito thoro subtrahere. sed certus sum quia suis magicis artibus amorem erga me uestrum non poterit infirmare. quae multis blanditiis delinitae nec uerbo amatorio adquieuerunt nec intento oculo libidinis fomitem respexerunt, quia apostolico sermone fundatae erant. uidens autem Agrippa praefectus quod Petri doctrinam sequentes libidinem eius unanimiter spernerent et ipsius blanditiis minime adquiescerent, coepit eis minas intentare horrificas, iurans quod et illas uiuas incendio concremaret et Petrum grauissimis afflictum suppliciis ab hominum de sub caelo memoria perderet. sed numquam potuit eas ad inquinamentum commixtionis inflectere, dicentes amabilius sibi esse omnibus tormentis pro castitate succumbere, quam Christum cui deuouerant castimoniam recusare. indignabatur itaque Agrippa praefectus maxime in apostolum et fremebat super eum dentibus, quaerens occasionem ut eum quasi rationabiliter potuisset occidere.

3. interea uxor Albini, Caesaris amicissimi, nomine Xandips, cum aliis pluribus nobilissimis matronis uenit ad Petrum. a quo uerbum percipiens castae uitae, repudiauit non modo uirile conubium, quin estiam et omne uitae huius delectamentum. qua de re Albinus nimio maerore

There four concubines of the prefect Agrippa, whose names were Agrippina, Eucharia, Eufemia, and Dionis, began to visit Peter frequently.[4] Hearing from him the teaching about chastity and all the commands of our Lord Jesus Christ, they were wasting away and distressed to be subject to the sexual passions of Agrippa. As a result, they devoted themselves to chastity and entered into a pact with one another. Greatly strengthened by the Lord Jesus Christ, they resolved that they would no longer agree to share his bed. After they had withdrawn not only from his embrace but indeed from any manner of relation with Agrippa, he became extremely vexed at this and was full of sadness.

Sending careful and clever spies, he learned that the women were rushing most eagerly to the blessed Peter. When they were brought back to him, he was seized by a violent frenzy of lust and said, "I know where you have been. That Christian is teaching you not to have sex with me, but rather to withdraw from your sexual duty to me. But I am certain that by his magical arts he has not been able to weaken your love for me." These women, although enticed by many flatteries, neither yielded themselves to his amorous speech nor paid heed to the kindling of desire in his lustful look, because they had been grounded in apostolic teaching. The prefect Agrippa saw that they were following the teaching of Peter, unanimously spurning Agrippa's sexual desires and not at all yielding themselves to his flatteries. He then began to make terrible threats against them, swearing that he would burn them alive with fire and would obliterate Peter from the memory of those under heaven by subjecting him to the most extreme torments. However, he was in no way able to pervert them to the filth of intercourse. They said that it was better for them to undergo all kinds of tortures for chastity than to reject Christ, to whom they had vowed moral purity. So Agrippa the prefect greatly despised the apostle and was gnashing his teeth at him,[5] seeking an opportunity to be able to kill him in a way that would seem justified.

3. In the meantime a woman named Xanthippe, the wife of Albinus—who was a close friend of the emperor—went to Peter along with many others of the noblest matrons. After receiving from Peter the teaching about a chaste life, she spurned not only sex with her husband, but also every pleasure of this life. As a result, Albinus, greatly overcome by grief,

4. With the account of Agrippa's concubines, this version picks up Mart. Pet. 4 and generally follows the same storyline until the end.

5. Cf. Acts 7:54, where the members of the crowd gnash their teeth at Stephen.

affectus comminabatur multa se Petro illaturum tormenta, Xandippem uero uxorem suam uerbis iniuria plenis indeque delinimentis a coepto conamine refragari temptabat. mittensque ad Agrippam praefectum sibi amicitia copulatum mandauit ei omnia quae agente Petro de uxore sua patiebatur, deprecans ut si ei secundum suam fiduciam esset amicus, ulcisceretur eum de Petro: alioquin ipse se uindicaret. Agrippa quoque reddidit ei mandatum, se eadem, adhuc etiam duriora per eum pati. unde factum est ut cum Albinus cubitum iret et Xandippem sibi adduci fecisset, suaeque delectationis commixtionem apud eam nec blanditiis nec terroribus obtinere potuisset, consiliaretur quatinus una cum Agrippae manu uelut auem laqueo Petrum caperet et ut maleficum pessumdaret.

Xandips autem, Albini uxor, haec audiens misit fidelissimum nuntium ad Petrum, ut Roma exiret et insidias paene ineuitabiles declinaret. Marcello nihilominus, Marci praefecto filio, qui postquam Symonis magi pestiferam doctrinam auerterat, apostolo fideliter et utiliter in cunctis adhaeserat, seu et fratribus conspirationem uiri sui et praefecti Agrippae innotuit.

was threatening to inflict many torments on Peter and was attempting to dissuade his wife Xanthippe from the struggle she had undertaken[6]—first by insulting words, and then by charming ones. Sending word to Agrippa the prefect, who was joined to him in friendship, he confided in him all the things that he was suffering from his wife because of Peter. He begged Agrippa to avenge him concerning Peter, if he was truly a faithful friend. Otherwise, he would take revenge himself.[7] Agrippa sent word back to him that he himself had suffered the same things, and even worse, on account of Peter. Thus it came about that when Albinus went to bed and had Xanthippe brought to him, he was not able by flattery or threats to convince her to have intercourse for his pleasure. He thus pondered how with the help of Agrippa he might capture Peter, like a bird in a trap, and might destroy him for being a sorcerer.[8]

However, Xanthippe, the wife of Albinus, heard these things and sent a very faithful messenger to Peter, so that he might leave Rome and escape the almost unavoidable plots. She also revealed the conspiracy of her husband and the prefect Agrippa to the brothers[9] and to Marcellus, who was the son of the prefect Marcus[10] and clung to the apostle faithfully and profitably in all things after he turned from the pestilent teaching of Simon the sorcerer.

---

6. That is, the discipline of a life of chastity.

7. The mention of friendship, combined with Albinus's appeal to Agrippa for help, suggests that their relationship is based on patronage. Albinus, the less powerful client, is calling upon his more powerful patron, Agrippa, to aid him in the matter of his wife. The use of friendship language was common in patronage relationships and did not mitigate the power differential between the parties involved. On inequality among friends, see Richard P. Saller, *Personal Patronage under the Early Empire* (Cambridge: Cambridge University Press, 1982), 11–13; David Konstan, *Friendship in the Classical World* (Cambridge: Cambridge University Press, 1997), 93–98, 105–6, 135–37; idem, "Patrons and Friends," *CP* 90 (1995): 328–42.

8. *Maleficus* is a general term for a troublemaker or wicked person, but it can have specific connotations of magic. Agrippa above had already accused Peter of seducing women with magic, and Albinus believes that such a charge may be the best way to eliminate the apostle.

9. In this section of the text I preserve the term "brothers," because the author places Peter's female disciples in a separate group (§4).

10. The identity of this Marcus is unknown. Josephus refers to a Marcus Ambivius, who was prefect of Judea from 9–12 CE (*Ant.* 18.2.2), and the case of Agrippa shows that prefects of Judea could be "transplanted" to Rome in these martyrdom stories. However, there is no reason to connect the father of Marcellus to any historical figure.

in crastina quoque surrexerunt quidam ex senatoribus in conuentu senatus et dixerunt: suggerimus amplitudini uestrae, nobiles uiri, quod ad peruersionem urbis aeternae Petrus conubia diuortiis mancipat, uxores nostras a nobis disiungit et nescimus quam nobis nouam et inauditam legem inducit. et haec dicentes incitabant etiam alios ad tumultum et appellationem. tunc Agrippa gratulatus est, quia quod de Petro optauit sub occasione senatus inuenit. sed et hoc Petrum et fratres non latuit. innotuerant siquidem hoc eis celeri nuntio qui fuerant ex senatoribus illuminati per Petrum a Domino.

4. quapropter Marcellus et fratres deprecabantur Petrum ut secederet. Petrus uero ait: non oportet, fratres et filii, fugere propter Christum Dominum passiones, cum ipse se ultro pro nostra salute morti obtulerit.

Marcellus autem et fratres nimio cum fletu aiunt: miserere, pater misericors, iuuenum et eorum qui sunt in fide rudes: ne nos ac illos inter infidelium turbines destitutos relinquas.

tunc Petrus rogantibus se ait: fugiendum suadetis et iuuenum atque infirmorum cordibus exemplo nostro metum passionis incutere, cum uerbum Dei constanter debeamus asserere et sancta castimoniae fundamenta quae iecimus conseruare. fugiendum putatis ut mortem declinemus, quam multis suspiriis et gemitibus diuturnis ut ingressum uitae expetimus, qua etiam secundum illius reuelationem Dominum clarificare debemus.

fratres uero haec audientes leuauerunt planctum dicentes: o pater ueracissime, ubi sunt uerba modo quibus dicebas, quoniam pro uita nostra morti esses paratus succumbere? et nunc impetrare non possumus ut pro nostra salute, donec corroboremur, patriaris aliquantulum uiuere.

adolescentes quoque, quos ipse sollicite custodiens in fide et castitate sedulo educabat, manus protendentes in caelum et porrecti ante faciem illius uelut subito mortui, cadentes in terram uociferabantur, nimio eiulatu clamantes: o bone Petre, pater et pastor, post tuum Dominum in clementia singularis, cur nos affectu materno nouiter per sacrum fontem Domino

On the next day certain Senators rose up in the assembly of the Senate and said, "We bring to the attention of your greatness, noble men, that to the perversion of the eternal city, Peter is making marriages into divorces. He has separated our wives from us and has introduced among us we do not know what new and unheard of law." Saying these things, they stirred others into an uproar and secured an injunction [against Peter]. Then Agrippa rejoiced, because with the favor of the Senate he got what he wanted concerning Peter. But this was not unknown to Peter and the brothers. Certain men, who were among the Senators and had been enlightened by the Lord through Peter, made this known to them by a swift messenger.

4. Therefore, Marcellus and the brothers pleaded with Peter to depart. Peter said, "It is not proper, brothers and children,[11] to flee sufferings for the sake of Christ the Lord, after he offered himself unto death for our salvation."

But Marcellus and the brothers said with much weeping, "Have pity, merciful father, on the young and on those who are new in the faith. Do not leave us and them abandoned among the whirlwinds of faithless ones."

Then Peter said to those begging him, "You are urging me to flee and instill fear of suffering in the hearts of the young and weak by our example, but we should constantly sow the word of God and preserve the holy foundations of chastity that we have established. You think we should flee to avoid death, which with many sighs and long groans we have longed for as the entrance to life. For by death, according to his revelation, we ought to glorify the Lord."[12]

Hearing these things, the brothers lifted up their lamentation, saying, "Oh, truest father, what about the words that you said only recently, that you were prepared to suffer death for our life? And now we are not able to convince you to live a little longer for the sake of our salvation, until we are strengthened."

The young men also, whom Peter watched over diligently and educated carefully in the faith and in chastity, thrust their hands into heaven and stretched out before him as if suddenly dead. They fell to the ground and cried out, calling out with great wailing, "Oh, good Peter, father and shepherd, one of a kind in mercy after your Lord, why did you recently beget us for the Lord with maternal affection through the sacred font? And

11. Literally "sons," but we know from the narrative that women are among the crowd he is addressing.

12. This statement by Peter is a declaration of the evangelistic function of martyrdom.

peperisti, quos tam immaturo solatio et animo crudeli, qui te numquam antea attigerat, immanissimorum morsibus luporum exponis?

clamabant autem et matronae puluere conspersis capitibus: haeccine est misericordia quam de saluatore tuo praedicare solebas, qui tuis lacrimis se quem ad tempus negaueras, in aeternum pietate motus indulserat? et tu tantis lacrimarum fluminibus te uel paruo tempore non concedis, praesertim cum et Domino possis ministrare in carne et tibi reseruatam coronam adipisci perpetuam?

5. sed et custodes carceris, Processus et Martinianus, cum reliquis magistrianis et ex officio iunctis postulabant eum, dicentes: Domine, quo uis abscede, quia imperatorem oblitum tui iam credimus. sed iste iniquissimus Agrippa paelicum amore et intemperantia suae libidinis inflammatus perdere te festinat. si enim regis iussio te impeteret, Paulini, uiri clarissimi, cui te commendatum nos custodiendum suscepimus, de tua nece sententiam haberemus. nam postquam nos credentes in hac uicina Mamertini custodia, fonte precibus et ammirabili signo crucis de rupe producto, in sanctae trinitatis nomine baptizasti, licentiose quo libuerat perrexisti et nemo tibi fuit molestus, nec modo esset, nisi incendium daemoniale quod urbem stimulat Agrippam acrius peruasisset. quapropter oramus te, salutis nostrae minister, hanc nobis digneris recompensare uicissitudinem,

yet now, for a premature consolation and with a cruel spirit, which you had never shown before, you expose us to the bites of monstrous wolves?"

The matrons were also crying out, their heads covered with dust, "Is this the compassion that you used to praise in your Savior, who showed it to you, moved by your tears at the time that you had denied, and who is also moved by pity? But you, despite such a great flow of tears, do not permit yourself even a little more time, even though you are able both to minister for the Lord in the flesh and obtain the eternal crown reserved for you?"[13]

5. But the guards of the prison, Processus and Martinianus, together with the other magistrates and those associated by way of their office, appealed to him, saying, "Lord, go where you wish, because we believe that the emperor has now forgotten about you. But that most wicked Agrippa, enflamed by lust for his concubines and the intemperance of his passion, is eager to destroy you. If an order from the king were accusing you, then we would have a command concerning your execution from Paulinus—a very prominent man to whom you were handed over and from whom we received the order to guard you. After we believers in this region of the Mamertine prison[14] were baptized in the name of the Holy Trinity[15] in a spring brought forth from stone by prayers and the glorious sign of the cross, you went around as freely as you pleased. No one bothered you or would be doing so now, if the demonic fire that troubles the city had not taken over Agrippa so violently. For this reason we beg you, minister of our salvation, to do us this favor in return. Because you freed us from the

---

13. The matrons are levying a charge of hypocrisy against Peter. A weeping Peter had received mercy from Jesus following his denials, but now Peter is callously ignoring the tearful supplications of his own followers. The idea that Peter wept before Jesus may be derived from the restitution scene of John 21:15–19, where Peter is described as "grieved." A reference to that scene is significant here, for that Johannine passage also includes a foreshadowing of Peter's death "to glorify God."

14. The connection with the Mamertime prison first appears in this text. This was Rome's most famous prison and had housed enemies of the empire such as Jugurtha, Vercingetorix, and the members of the Second Catilinarian Conspiracy. The author places Peter here in order to emphasize that the apostle was among Rome's most illustrious prisoners.

15. This reference to the concept of the "Holy Trinity" is a clear anachronism. The earliest evidence for the use of the Latin *Trinitas* in this technical sense is Tertullian, *Prax.* 2 (ca. 208–209 according to Timothy David Barnes, *Tertullian: A Historical and Literary Study*, 2nd ed. [Oxford: Clarendon, 1985], 47, 55).

ut quia nos a peccatorum et daemonum uinculis absoluisti, a carcerali et compedum nexibus, quorum nobis est commissa immanitas, nostra non tantum permissione quam deprecatione liber in saluationem tantae plebis abscedas.

uiduae quoque et orphani ac senio ualde affecti capillos sibi trahentes genasque scindentes et pectora denudantes dicebant: alios quorum ministerio fouebamur, a diuersis languoribus sanasti et de ipsa etiam morte resuscitasti, et te nobis, pater piissime, subtrahis? uel ante te nos omnes praemitte, ne tuae institutionis doctrina destitutae animae pereant, et corpora ministrationis tuae solatio desolata intereant; et sic, quo ire desideras accelera festinare, ne uitam nostram post Dominum mori uidentes, remanentes in uita miseri moriamur.

6. tunc Petrus haec undique audiens, qui ultra humanum modum misericors, lacrimas afflictorum sine lacrimis umquam praeterire non poterat, deuictus tantis fletibus ait: nemo uestrum ueniat mecum; ego solus mutato scemate[2] pergam. proxima namque nocte celebrata oratione ualedicens fratribus et cum benedictione illos Deo commendans profectus est solus.

et dum pergeret, ceciderunt illi fasciamenta ex crure demolita a compede. ut autem portam ciuitatis uoluit egredi, uidit sibi Christum occurrere. et adorans eum ait: Domine, quo uadis?

respondit ei Christus: Romam uenio iterum crucifigi.

et ait ad eum Petrus: Domine, iterum crucifigeris?

et dixit ad eum Dominus: etiam, iterum crucifigar.

Petrus autem dixit: Domine, reuertar et sequar te. et his dictis Dominus ascendit in caelum. Petrus autem prosecutus est eum multo intuitu atque dulcissimis lacrimis. et post haec rediens in se ipsum intellexit de sua

2. *Scema* (*schema* in earlier Latin) from the Greek σχῆμα.

chains of sin and demons, now depart free from prison and being fettered with chains—a cruelty that we are charged to enforce—not just with our permission but at our request, for the salvation of so great a multitude."[16]

Also the widows, orphans, and those greatly weakened by old age were pulling out their hair, tearing their cheeks, and baring their breasts, saying, "You have healed some of us of various diseases and even raised from death itself others by whose aid we were comforted, but now you yourself are leaving us, most benevolent father? Rather, send us all ahead of you, lest our souls perish, deprived of the teaching of your instruction, and our bodies waste away, abandoned by the consolation of your service. Hurry, therefore, to go where you wish, lest by seeing our life after our master dies, those of us remaining alive should die miserable."

6. Then Peter heard these things, he who was merciful beyond all human measure and never able to ignore the tears of the afflicted without shedding his own tears. He was overcome by such great wailing and said, "Let none of you come with me. After changing my appearance I will go alone." And so on the next night, after offering prayer he bid farewell to the brothers and sisters,[17] committed them to God with a blessing, and set out alone.

While he was going, the bandages fell from his leg, which had been damaged by the shackle. Just as he was about to pass through the gate of the city, he saw Christ coming to meet him. He worshiped him and said, "Lord, where are you going?"

Christ responded to him, "I am going to Rome to be crucified again."[18]

And Peter said to him, "Lord, you will be crucified again?"

And the Lord said to him, "Yes, I will be crucified again."

But Peter said, "Lord, I will turn back and follow you." After these words the Lord ascended into heaven. Peter followed him with an intent look and very sweet tears. After these things Peter came back to himself and realized that Christ had spoken about his passion, because the Lord

---

16. Unlike the prison guard of Acts 16, who is prepared to take his own life when he believes that Paul and Silas had escaped, these guards seem eager to release Peter out of gratitude for their salvation.

17. The use of "brothers" appears to apply to a mixed group here and for the remainder of the text.

18. Origen (*Comm. Jo.* 20.12.91) cites this saying of Jesus but assigns it to the Acts of Paul. Cf. Ambrose, *Aux.* 13, who correctly connects the saying to Peter.

dictum passione, quod in eo Dominus esset passurus, qui patitur in electis misericordiae compassione et glorificationis celebritate.

7. conuersusque in urbem rediit cum gaudio, glorificans deum et narrans fratribus quod ei obuius fuisset Dominus, et declarasset ei quod in ipso esset iterum crucifigendus. qui cum manifestasset passionem suam, fletum omnes et ululatum emiserunt. dolebant enim uniuersi et lacrimas profundebant dicentes: considera oues tuas, pastor bone, sustenta eos quorum fides infirmior tuo expetit roborari sermone. considera corda titubantia quae per te stabilienda noscuntur.

quibus Petrus ait: facile est Domino ut seruorum suorum corda etiam sine meae humilitatis ammonitione corroboret. quos enim plantauit ad hoc faciet adolescere, ut et alios possint plantare. ego autem quasi seruus necesse est ut Domini exequar uoluntatem. quapropter si me adhuc in carne morari disponit propter uos, non contradico. et si me pati pro nomine suo decreuerit, et per passionem meam dignatur suscipere, exulto et laetor in gratia ipsius.

8. cum igitur his et aliis multis uerbis fratrum animos consolaretur, et illi lacrimas tenere non possent, superuenit Hieros cum quatuor apparitoribus et aliis decem uiris, qui eum comprehendentes rapuerunt de medio fratrum et statuerunt uinctum Agrippae praefecti urbis obtutibus. cui ait Agrippa: multa tibi est fiducia, scelerate, in plebibus quas circumuenis, atque in feminis quae tua persuasione a maritali thoro discedunt. ausus es

was going to suffer in him—the Lord who suffers in the elect by the compassion of his mercy and the celebration[19] of their glorification.

7. Peter turned around and reentered the city with joy, glorifying God and telling the brothers and sisters that the Lord had met him on the way and had declared to him that he (Christ) would be crucified again in him (Peter). When he had revealed his impending passion, they all broke out in weeping and wailing. All were grieving and pouring forth tears, saying, "Consider your sheep, good shepherd. Uphold those whose rather feeble faith longs to be strengthened by your teaching. Consider the wavering hearts that know they must be stabilized through you."

Peter said to them, "It is easy for the Lord to strengthen the hearts of his servants even without my humble admonition. Those whom he planted he will make grow to the point that they may be able to plant others.[20] But I, as a servant, must carry out the will of the Lord. Therefore, if he sends me back to remain in the flesh for your sake, then I will not resist. But if he has decided that I should suffer for his name and sees fit to receive me through my passion, then I exult and rejoice in his grace."[21]

8. Therefore, after with these and many other words he had consoled the spirits of the brothers and sisters, and they had been unable to hold back their tears, Hieros arrived with four deputies and ten other men. They seized Peter, taking him from the midst of the brothers and sisters, and led him in chains before Agrippa, the prefect of the city.[22] Agrippa said to him, "You wicked man, you have great confidence in the common people you deceive and in the women who have withdrawn under your influence from intercourse with their husbands. You have even dared, to the detriment

---

19. This may refer both to the actual day of a martyr's death and the subsequent celebrations of the martyr's festival.

20. Cf. 1 Cor 3:5–9. From this point on in the text, Peter frequently speaks with the words of Paul. See David L. Eastman, "Confused Traditions? Peter and Paul in the Apocryphal Acts," in *Forbidden Texts on the Western Frontier: Christian Apocrypha in North American Perspectives*, edited by Tony Burke and Brent E. Landau (Eugene, OR: Cascade, forthcoming).

21. This tension between dying for Christ or living for the sake of the community recalls Paul's words in Phil 1:20–26.

22. On ancient sarcophagi the predominant iconographical image of Peter's martyrdom represents this scene of his arrest, rather than his actual execution. This may result from the desire to draw parallels between the deaths of Christ and Peter. On the famous sarcophagus of Junius Bassus (359 CE), for example, the arrest of Peter on the viewer's left is balanced on the right by the arrest of Christ.

etiam in deorum iniuriam nescio quem Christum inducere et contra sanctum ritum Romanum et contra urbis aeternae deuotionem nescio quae inepta et uana docere.

tunc facta est facies apostoli sicut sol splendida, et aperiens os suum dixit ad eum: uideo quo tendis, dux libidinum, amator pollutionis, atrocitatis inuentor, innocentium persecutor, deceptorum fautor, fallaciae conditor, habitaculum satanae. ignoras namque gloriam in qua glorior, et ideo dicis quod in uiris et mulieribus sit mihi fiducia.

et ait ad eum Agrippa: quia scis me ignorare in quo gloriaris, fac cito me nosse.

et ait ad eum Petrus: nulla sit mihi gloria nisi crux Domini mei Iesu Christi, cuius ego sum seruus.

et ait Agrippa: uis ergo, ut crucifigaris sicut Deus tuus est crucifixus?

Petrus quoque respondit: non sum dignus recta cruce mundum testem facere passionis meae; sed per quaelibet supplicia opto et desidero eius sequi uestigia passionis. tunc praefectus, morbo incontinentiae suae praetendens superstitionis accusationem, crucifigi iussit apostolum.

9. et ecce ingens subito concursus factus est diuersae aetatis et sexus, diuitum pauperum, uiduarum pupillorum, imbecillium atque potentum, qui summa uoce clamabant: ut quid occiditur Petrus? quid admisit criminis? in quo laesit urbem? nec innocentem dampnare fas est. nonne timendum est, ne talis ac tanti uiri necem Deus uindicet et nos omnes perire praecipiat? et coeperunt in Agrippam saeuire populi, molientes illaesum rapere et conseruare Petrum; et inconditis uocibus plebis innumerae confundebatur Roma.

of the gods, to introduce I do not know what Christ and to teach I do not know what foolish and vain things against the sacred rite of the Romans and the piety of the eternal city."

Then the face of the apostle was made brilliant like the sun,[23] and opening his mouth he said to Agrippa, "I see what you are aiming at, you chief of lusts, you lover of impurity, you creator of cruelty, you persecutor of the innocent, you supporter of deceivers, you author of deceit, you habitation of Satan. For you do not know the glory in which I boast, and therefore you say that my boldness rests in men and women."

And Agrippa said to him, "Because you know that I do not know the glory in which you boast, make me know it now."

And Peter said to him, "I have no glory except the cross of my Lord Jesus Christ, whose servant I am."[24]

And Agrippa said, "Do you wish, therefore, to be crucified just as your God was crucified?"

Peter responded, "I am not worthy to make the testimony of my passion to the world on an upright cross, but through whatever kinds of entreaties are necessary, I wish and desire to follow in the footsteps of his passion."[25] Then the prefect, prompted by the sickness of his own incontinence, put forth a charge of superstition[26] and ordered the apostle to be crucified.

9. And behold, suddenly there was formed a great assembly of people of different ages and sex, of rich and poor, of widows and orphans, of weak and strong, who were crying out with a loud voice, "Why is Peter being killed? What crime did he commit? How did he harm the city? It is not proper to condemn an innocent man. Should we not fear that God may avenge the death of so great a man as this and may cause us all to perish?" The people began to rage against Agrippa, striving to seize and protect Peter unharmed, and Rome was thrown into disorder by the cacophony of voices of the enormous crowd.

---

23. Matt 17:2; Rev 1:16.

24. Cf. Gal 6:14.

25. Peter is determined to die by crucifixion, so that Christ might be "crucified again" through him, although he does not feel worthy to die in the same position, as the author explains later.

26. Both Tacitus (*Ann.* 15.44) and Suetonius (*Nero* 16) state that Christians were accused of superstition as early as the Neronian persecution.

tunc Petrus restitit modicum et ascendens editiorem locum nutuque ad silentium prouocans populum ait: o uiri et fideles Dei, qui Christo militatis! o omnes, qui in Christo speratis! si caritas uestra in me uera est et uiscera integra in me pietatis ostenditis, nolite reuocare euntem ad Dominum, nolite impedire properantem ad Christum. state ergo quieti, gaudentes et laeti, ut hostiam meam cum hilaritate Domino offeram. hilarem enim datorem diligit Deus. et his dictis uix est sedata seditio et praefecti disceptatio. poterant enim et inhianter optabant multi populi praefectum euertere; sed timebant apostolum contristare, qui magistri sui sequebatur exemplum dicentis: possum mihi nunc, si uolo, plus quam duodecim legiones angelorum exhibere.

10. peruenit denique una cum apostolo et apparitoribus populus infinitus ad locum qui uocatur Naumachiae[3] iuxta obeliscum Neronis in montem. illic enim crux posita erat. et respiciens flentem populum et iterum seditionem excitare uolentem, ait uoce clara: nolite, obsecro uos fratres, oblationem meam impedire, nolite aduersus Agrippam saeuire et amaro animo in eum esse. ille enim minister est alienae operationis. nam

3. From the Greek *ναυμαχία*.

Then Peter stopped for a moment and climbed to a high place. With a gesture he silenced the people and said, "Oh, faithful ones of God,[27] you who are soldiers in Christ! Oh, all of you who hope in Christ! If your affection for me is sincere, and if you demonstrate toward me hearts full of piety, then do not call back one going to the Lord, and do not hinder one hastening to Christ.[28] Remain calm, therefore, rejoicing and being happy, so that I may offer my sacrifice to the Lord with gladness, for God loves a cheerful giver."[29] By these words a riot was narrowly averted, as was the dispute with the prefect. The crowds had the ability to overthrow the prefect, and indeed many people eagerly wanted to do so. However, they were afraid to sadden the apostle, who was following the example of his master, who had said, "I am able now, if I wish, to produce for myself more than twelve legions of angels."[30]

10. A great multitude then went together with the apostle and the deputies to a place called the Naumachia, next to the obelisk of Nero on the mountain,[31] for there a cross had been placed. Observing the people weeping and sensing their desire to stir up unrest again, Peter said in a loud voice, "I implore you, brothers and sisters, not to stand in the way of my offering. Do not rage against Agrippa and hold bitter feelings toward him. He is just the servant of the work of another. For the devil is the author

---

27. The text also refers to them as "men," but this is obviously a mixed group.

28. Cf. Ignatius *Rom.* 2, where Ignatius of Antioch asks the Roman Christians not to intervene to prevent his martyrdom.

29. 2 Cor 9:7.

30. Matt 26:53.

31. The term *naumachia* refers to a mock sea battle or to the place where mock sea battles were staged. Nero was apparently the first emperor to put on such an event in an amphitheater (as opposed to a dug basin) in 57 CE. He constructed this building on (or at least very near) the Field of Mars, opposite the Vatican hill (Suetonius, *Nero* 12.2–6; Cassius Dio, *Hist.* 61.9.5). Cassius Dio (*Hist.* 62.15.1) records that Nero staged a battle there in 64 CE, preceded by animal hunts and gladiatorial shows. Its exact location is unknown, but it is possible that the amphitheater and the place at which it was located could have taken on the name of the spectacles staged there. Archaeologists have identified a structure on the Vatican hill close to the Circus of Nero (where the obelisk stood) that may have been constructed for *naumachia* and was dedicated by Trajan in 109 CE. See Eva Margareta Steinby, ed., *Lexicon topographicum urbis Romae*, 5 vols. (Rome: Quasar, 1996), 3:338–39. This location is now the site of the Church of San Pellegrino in Vaticano (formerly San Pellegrino in Naumachia). If the topographical allusion in this text is taken to refer to the Trajanic structure, then this would be a clear anachronism.

dampnationis meae secundum corporis qualitatem diabolus auctor est, dominica abutens permissione, quia dolet uasa contumeliae per me sibi sublata esse et facta esse diuersoria continentiae, templa Christi, domicilia honoris et gratiae.

itaque, fratres mei et filii, obedientes estote, quia per reuelationem a Domino Iesu Christo proditum est mihi quod ita esset uenturum. non ergo est discipulus super magistrum, nec seruus super Dominum suum. festino itaque ut carne exutus assigner Domino. nunc enim tempus est in quo et meam offeram hostiam. mementote signorum et prodigiorum atque sanitatum, quae Christo operante et me ministrante uidistis et sensistis. ideo enim plurimorum infirmitates curatae sunt ut omnium animae saluarentur. ideo mortua corpora suscitata sunt ut animae mortuae reuiuiscerent. sed quid iam moras patior et non appropinquo cruci? ualete, fratres et patientes estote et seruate quae audistis. commendo uos Domino Iesu Christo.

11. accedens autem et astans cruci dixit: o nomen crucis, occultum mysterium! o gratia ineffabilis! in nomine enim crucis pax. o crux, quae Deo hominem coniunxisti, et a dominio diabolicae captiuitatis magnifice segregasti! o crux, quae humano generi passionem saluatoris mundi et redemptionem captiuitatis humanae uera comitante fide semper repraesentas incolumem! o crux, quae cotidie carnes immaculati agni fidelibus diuidis populis et dira serpentis uenena poculo salutari depellis atque rumphaeam[4] paradisi ignitam credentibus sine intermissione restinguis! o crux, quae pacem cotidie terrenis cum caelestibus operaris et mediatoris mortem, qui a mortuis resurrexit et iam non moritur, aeterno patri,

4. From the Greek *ῥομφαία*.

of my condemnation in the body. He is abusing the Lord's permission,[32] because it grieves him that the vessels of reproach have been exalted over him through me and have been made dwelling places of continence, temples of Christ, and habitations of honor and grace.[33]

"Thus, my brothers and sisters and children, remain obedient, because what is about to happen was revealed to me through a revelation from the Lord Jesus Christ. A disciple is not above his teacher, nor a servant above his master.[34] I hasten, then, to put aside the flesh and commit myself to the Lord. Now is the time for me to offer my sacrifice. Remember the signs, wonders, and healings that you have seen and perceived, which Christ performed but I administered. For this reason the illnesses of many were healed, so that the souls of all may be saved. For this reason dead bodies were resuscitated, so that dead souls may be given new life. But why do I now allow these delays and not approach the cross? Farewell, brothers and sisters. Be steadfast, and preserve the things that you have heard.[35] I entrust you to the Lord Jesus Christ."

11. Peter approached and stood next to the cross, then said, "Oh name of the cross, hidden mystery! Oh, unspeakable grace! In the name of the cross there is in fact peace. Oh cross, you have joined humanity to God and have admirably removed humanity from the dominion of diabolical captivity! Oh cross, you always represent for the human race the passion of the Savior of the world and the complete redemption of human captivity, when true faith is present! Oh cross, every day you distribute to faithful peoples the flesh of the spotless lamb, and drive out the terrible venom of the serpent by the life-giving cup, and extinguish for those who believe the sword of paradise that burns without ceasing![36] Oh cross, you daily bring about peace between earthly and heavenly things! And the death of the mediator, who rose from the dead and now is dead no longer, you present with care

32. This may be a reference to the story of Job, in which the Satan is given freedom by God to attack Job's body.

33. Through Peter's preaching of chastity, the physical bodies of the believers have been exalted to holiness and are no longer "vessels of reproach."

34. Matt 10:24.

35. 2 Thess 2:15.

36. The cross thus reverses the curse of Gen 3:24, where God places a fiery sword to block the way back to the garden and the tree of life.

ecclesia pro filiis agente, sedulo reparas et legatione felicissima renouas et reformas.

uim patior tui causa, et iam nunc, in finitima absolutione existens, non quiescam manifestare de cruce occultum Dei mysterium, quod olim clamauit anima mea. o qui in Christum creditis, non istud sit uobis crux quod apparet; aliud enim quiddam est mysticum in hoc quod apparet uobis. et nunc maxime, qui potestis audire, in nouissima hora uitae huius existente me, omnes sensus segregate et animas uestras ab omni quod apparet, ad illud quod inuisibile est! et scietis quod in Christo per crucem factum est salutis mysterium. debitum est tibi, Petre, reddere terrae corpus acceptum per eos quibus est corpus occidere proprium.

12. ait autem ad magistros carnificum: quid est quod tricatis? quid, apparitores, innecti moras mihi patimini? implete quod uobis est iussum. exuite me mortali tunica, ut spiritu adhaeream Domino. Petiit sane et ita ministros carnificum alloquens exorauit: precor uos, boni salutis meae ministri, ut crucifigentes me caput deorsum ponatis et pedes sursum. non enim decet me seruum ultimum ita crucifigi, ut Dominus uniuersitatis pro salute totius mundi dignatus est pati, quem passione mea constat glorificari. est etiam ut mysterium crucis intento uultu semper possim conspicere, quo facilius quid inde dixero a circumstantibus possit audiri.

to the eternal Father and renew and transform by your most blessed delegation, with the church[37] leading the way on behalf of its children.

"I am suffering greatly for your sake, and now, at the point of consummation, I will not cease to make known the hidden mystery of God concerning the cross—the mystery that my soul once proclaimed. Oh, you who believe in Christ, may the cross not be for you what is visible, for there is another, mystical meaning in what is visible to you. And now, most of all, you who are able to hear as I pass the very last hour in this life, separate all your affections and your souls from everything that is visible [and direct them] toward that which is invisible. You know that in Christ the mystery of salvation has been accomplished through the cross. As for you, Peter, through those whose task is to kill the body you must give back to the earth the body you received."

12. To the chiefs of the executioners, however, he said, "Why are you hesitating? Why do you permit these delays for me, deputies? Carry out the order given to you. Strip me of this mortal garment, so that I may join with the Lord in spirit." He also entreated the masters of the executioners, speaking to them and prevailing upon them, "I beg you, noble ministers of my salvation, that when you crucify me, position me with my head downward and my feet upward.[38] It is not proper that I, the least of all servants,[39] should be crucified in the same way as the Lord of the universe deemed worthy to suffer for the salvation of the whole world, for he should be glorified by my passion. This is also so that I may always be able to contemplate with a focused gaze the mystery of the cross, and so that what I say from the cross may be more easily heard by those standing around me.[40]

---

37. The church is thus brought into the center of the salvation story along with God, Christ, and the cross, for it serves an additional mediation function.

38. Matthew C. Baldwin argues that the earliest reference to Peter's inverted crucifixion is found in Eusebius of Caesarea's reference (*Hist. eccl.* 3.2) to the third book of Origen's *Commentary on Genesis*. See Matthew C. Baldwin, *Whose Acts of Peter? Text and Historical Context of the Actus Vercellenses*, WUNT 2/196 (Tübingen: Mohr Siebeck, 2005), 71–73. This passage is translated in ch. 15 of this volume.

39. Cf. 1 Cor 15:9; Eph 3:8.

40. The inverted crucifixion of Peter was widely recounted by patristic authors (e.g., Eusebius, *Hist. eccl.* 3.1; Jerome, *Vir. ill.* 1) and has inspired numerous works of art, such as the famous paintings by Michelangelo and Caravaggio. Many authors also repeated Peter's motivations for this request, e.g., Ambrose, *Job* 1.1.2; Theodoret, *Car.* 1309–1310.

quod cum factum fuisset, adorsus est Petrus flentem populum de cruce consolari et alloqui mirabiliter dicens: grande et profundum est mysterium crucis, et ineffabile atque inseparabile uinculum caritatis. per crucem ad se trahit omnia Deus. hoc est lignum uitae quo destructum est mortis imperium. hoc mihi tu aperuisti, Domine; aperi et omnium istorum oculos, ut uideant consolationem uitae aeternae. et his dictis aperuit Deus oculos eorum qui lugebant et lacrimas fundebant in passione eius, et uiderunt angelos stantes cum coronis de floribus rosarum et liliorum et in uertice crucis erectae stantem Petrum et librum a Christo accipientem et ea uerba quae loquebatur inde legentem. quod uidentes ita coeperunt laetari et gaudere in Domino, ut illi ipsi increduli et carnifices, uidentes eos exultare et laetari quos prius tristes uiderant et plangentes, subito delitescerent et uelut fumus euanescerent.

13. uidens autem Petrus quod demonstrata esset multis antea flentibus gloria eius, gratias egit Domino Iesu Christo dicens: digne tu solus, Domine, in altum porrecto uertice crucifixus es, qui totum mundum a peccato redemisti. te imitari etiam in passione optaui; sed rectus crucifigi non usurpaui, quia nos ex Adam puri homines et peccatores nati sumus, tu uero ex Deo Deus, et lux uera de uero lumine ante omnia saecula, in fine saeculorum pro hominibus homo sine contagione hominis fieri dignatus, redemptor hominis gloriosus existis. tu semper rectus, tu semper

When this was done, Peter began to offer the weeping crowd comforting words about the cross and to address them in an amazing way, saying, "Great and profound is the mystery of the cross, and unspeakable and inseparable is the bond of love. Through the cross God draws all things to himself. This is the wood of life by which the empire of death has been destroyed. You have revealed this to me, Lord. Open also all of their eyes, so that they may perceive the consolation of eternal life." After these words, God opened the eyes of those who were mourning and shedding tears for Peter's passion. They saw angels standing with crowns made of roses and lilies and Peter standing at the top of the raised cross, receiving a book from Christ and reading from it the words that it was saying.[41] Seeing this, they began to rejoice and exult in the Lord, so that the unbelievers and the executioners saw them exulting and rejoicing—the same people whom they had previously seen sad and mourning—and suddenly they skulked away and vanished like the mist.

13. Peter saw that his glory had been revealed to the many who had previously been weeping, and he gave thanks to the Lord Jesus Christ, saying, "You alone, Lord, were worthily crucified with your head raised on high, you who redeemed the whole world from sin. I have sought to imitate you also in my passion. But I did not presume to be crucified upright, because we who were born from Adam are only human beings and were born sinners, while you indeed are God from God and true light from true light before all ages.[42] At the end of the ages you lowered yourself to become human for humanity but without the contamination of being human,[43] and you are the glorious redeemer of humanity. You are always

---

41. This description of Peter's receiving a crown from an angel and a book from Christ combines two iconographical traditions of antiquity that were meant to symbolize the apostolic authority of Peter and Paul. In the one, Peter is presented (typically with Paul) receiving a martyr's crown from Christ. In the other, known as the *Traditio legis* ("handing over of the law"), Christ hands to Peter (and often to Paul) a scroll or book that contains the "law of Christ." See e.g., Eastman, *Paul the Martyr*, 79–81; Bas Snelders, "The *Traditio legis* on Early Christian Sarcophagi," *AnTard* 13 (2005): 321–33; Robin Margaret Jensen, *Understanding Early Christian Art* (New York: Routledge, 2000), 107–14.

42. This imagery appears in the Christological passages in Niceno-Constantinopolitan Creed of 381, which, unlike the Nicene Creed of 325, emphasizes both the eternal beginning of Christ and his never-ending reign.

43. Cf. Phil 2:6–8.

excelsus, tu semper altus. nos secundum carnem primi hominis filii sumus, qui principale suum demersit in terram. cuius lapsus significatur specie generationis humanae: sic enim nascimur ut proni uideamur in terram effundi, et quod ad dexteram est hoc ad sinistram sit, et quod ad sinistram hoc ad dexteram fiat, eo quod in auctoribus huius uitae mutata conditio est. hoc enim putat mundus iste dextrum quod est sinistrum, in quo tu nos, Domine, sicut Niniuitas inuenisti, et perituros tua sancta praedicatione liberasti.

14. uos uero, fratres, quibus est proprium audire, aures cordis apponite, et nunc quae annuntianda sunt uobis cognoscite, scilicet omnis naturae mysterium et omnis factae constitutionis initium. nam primus homo, cuius genus in specie ego habeo, misso deorsum capite ostendit olim perditam generationem. mortua enim erat generatio eius et nec uitalem habebat motum. sed tractum misericordia sua principium uenit in mundum per corporalem substantiam ad eum quem iusta sententia in terram proiecerat, et suspensum in cruce per speciem huius honorandae uocationis uidelicet crucis restituit, et constituit nobis ea quae antea hominum iniquo

upright,[44] always exalted, always on high. We are according to the flesh children of the first man, who let go of[45] his original purpose on the earth. His fall is illustrated by the form of human birth, for we are born so that we appear to be inclined toward going down to the earth.[46] What is on the right is on the left, and what is on the left is on the right, because the condition that existed for the originators of this life has been distorted.[47] Indeed, what is on the right is considered to be on the left in this world in which you, oh Lord, found us like the Ninevites, and by your holy preaching you freed those who were about to perish.[48]

14. "And you, brothers and sisters, who have the chance to hear me, apply the ears of your heart and understand now the things that must be proclaimed to you, namely the mystery of all nature and the beginning of everything that has been made. The first man,[49] whose race I have in form, with his head directed downward displays a generation that was lost at one time. Indeed, this generation was dead and had no movement of life. However, moved by his mercy, the Progenitor came into the world in corporeal form to the one whom he had cast to the earth by a just sentence. Hanging on a cross, he restored and established for us through the appearance of this calling that must be honored—namely the cross—the things that formerly had been altered by the regrettable error of humans, namely, the

44. Or "just." The author is likely appealing to the multiple meanings of *rectus*, which can mean "upright" (a reference to Jesus's physical position on the cross) and "just" (a reference to his moral attributes).

45. Literally, "caused to sink" or "buried."

46. This is a theological and allegorical explanation for the technique of childbirth. Women in antiquity delivered in an upright position, such that the head of the child (except in the case of breach) would come out pointed toward the ground, like the head of Peter himself on his cross. This position during childbirth is attested by ancient imagery and literary accounts, while the contemporary western practice of delivering while lying on a bed seems to have been unknown. See e.g., Soranus of Ephesus, *Gyn.* 39–41; Donald Todman, "Childbirth in Ancient Rome: From Traditional Folklore to Obstetrics," *ANZJOG* 47.2 (2007): 82–85; Valerie French, "Midwives and Maternity Care in the Roman World," *Helios* 13.2 (1986): 69–84.

47. Because of the fall of Adam, human perception has been distorted, even something as simple as telling right from left. The fact that a child is born upside down illustrates that this disorientation begins at birth.

48. Christ's mission is compared to that of Jonah, who went and preached a message of repentance to a people who were about to be destroyed on account of their wickedness (Jonah 1:1–2; 3:1–10) and could not tell their right hand from their left (4:11).

49. For the imagery in this passage, see 1 Cor 15:20–23, 45–49; Rom 5:12–21.

errore immutata fuerunt, praesentia uidelicet pro sinistra et quae pro sinistra ducebantur aeterna. siquidem dextera glorificans omnia signa ad propriam mutauit naturam, sicut bona intellegens quae non putabantur bona, et reuera benigna quae maligna aestimabantur.

unde Dominus in mysterio dixerat: si non feceritis dexteram sicut sinistram et sinistram sicut dexteram, et quae sursum sunt sicut deorsum, et quae ante sicut quae retro, non cognoscetis regnum Dei. istam ergo sententiam in me produxi, fratres; et haec est figura qua me pendentem oculi carnales conspiciunt. scema est enim primi hominis. uos uero, dilecti mei, haec audientes et quae auditis ad perfectionem conuertendo et conuersando ducentes, sicut de primo uestro errore ad certissimam fidei stationem redistis, ita perseuerate currentes et ad quitem supernae uocationis tendite bene conuersantes. uia enim qua illuc iter agere debetis, Christus est.

oportet igitur cum Iesu Christo Deo uero superascendere crucem, qui est constitutus nobis sermo unus et solus. unde et Spiritus dicit: Christus est uerbum et uox Dei. uerbum siquidem significat istud rectum lignum in quo crucifigor. et quia uox proprie corporis est, quod liniamenta recipit quae diuinitati non imputantur, lateralia crucis humanam praetendere noscuntur naturam, quae immutationis errorem in primo homine passa est, sed per deum et hominem ueram intelligentiam recuperauit. ipsa

temporary things clearly on the left and the eternal things that are considered to be on the left. Since in glorifying things on the right, he has altered all the signs to their proper nature, it is as if he considers good the things that were not being considered good, and considers favorable the things that were being counted evil.[50]

"Concerning this the Lord said in a mystery, 'Unless you make the right as the left and the left as the right, and the things that are upwards as the things that are downwards, and the things that are in front as the things that are behind, then you will not comprehend the kingdom of God.'[51] I have presented this same idea in myself, brothers and sisters, and this is the form in which your carnal eyes perceive me hanging. This is indeed the form of the first man.[52] You, my beloved ones, because you hear these things and consider the things that you hear for your own perfection by turning back and turning around, just as you returned from your former error to the most certain standing of faith—keep running and in turning around stretch vigorously toward the rest of your heavenly calling.[53] Indeed, Christ is the road on which you ought to make your journey.[54]

"It is necessary, therefore, to mount the cross with Jesus Christ, the true God, who was placed among us as the one and only proclamation. Therefore the Spirit says, 'Christ is the word and voice of God.'[55] Indeed, this upright beam on which I am crucified stands for the word. Since the voice is particular to a body, which receives the features that are not ascribed to divinity, the crossbeams of the cross are understood to stand for human nature, which suffered the error of alteration in the first man but has recovered its true understanding through the one who is God and human.[56] For

---

50. This confusing exposition on left and right may be a reference to the final judgment passage in Matt 25:31–46, where the sheep are placed on the right side and the goats on the left. Admittedly, connecting this passage to Matthew does little to explain the peculiarity of this section.

51. The source of this saying is unknown, although Wilhelm Schneemelcher (*New Testament Apocrypha*, trans. R. McL. Wilson, 5th ed., 2 vols. [Louisville: Westminster John Knox, 1990], 1:213) has compared it to some other inversion statements ascribed to Jesus and has suggested a possible connection to the *Vorlage* of the Gospel of the Egyptians.

52. That is, with his head toward the earth.

53. Phil 3:14.

54. Cf. John 14:6.

55. The source of this reference is unknown.

56. This perhaps may be read: "Through God and the second man (i.e., the second

namque disciplinae clauis[5] in medio astricta est, conuersione uidelicet et conuersatione atque cum fide paenitentia hominis.

15. et haec dicens alacri uultu et facie serena sic exclamauit in orationem erumpens: ista tu mihi, Domine Iesu Christe uerbum uitae, nota fecisti, et reuelanti tibi quae dixeram de ligno a me praedicato gratias ago. non corde cui saepe indecens quiddam subrepit, non labiis istis confixis, nec lingua per quam uerum et falsum procedit, neque uerbo articulata et materiali natura producto, sed illa uoce gratias ago tibi, rex bone, quae per silentium intellegitur, quae non in manifesto auditur, quae non per organa oris corruptibilis procedit, quae non carnales aures percutit, quae non a natura corruptibili percipitur, quae nec est terrea nec in terra dimittitur, quae in libris materialibus non scribitur, neque quemquam materialiter patitur moueri, neque materialiter existit. illo inquam spiritu, Iesu Christe Domine et magister meus, gratias ago tibi, quo te credo, quo te intellego, quo te diligo, quo te teneo, et uoce qua te alloquor, qua te interpello, quia tu toto et modesto tantum spiritu intelligibilis es.

tu mihi, Domine, pater et amicus, auctor et perfector salutis, tu desiderium, tu refrigerium et tu satietas. tu mihi omnia es, et omnia mihi in te sunt. tu mihi totum es, et totum quod est tu mihi es. tu es enim mihi omnia. in te uiuimus, mouemur et sumus. et ideo te ut omnia habere debemus ut tu des nobis illa quae promisisti, quae nec oculus uidit nec auris audiuit nec in cor hominis ascenderunt, quae praeparasti his qui diligunt te. haec custodi seruis tuis, haec tribue atque largire, quia tu es pastor aeternus et summe bonus, uerus filius Dei. tibi commendo oues quas tradidisti mihi. tu eas in ouile tuum aggrega et conserua, quia tu

5. *Clauus* (nail) would seem more logical here than *clauis* (key), and a mistake of this type in transmission would be easy to make. However, the participial form *astricta* requires a feminine noun. Thus, either *clauis* is the correct reading, or *clauus* was changed to *clauis* at some point, and the participle was correspondingly altered from masculine to feminine. There are no variants in the manuscripts to suggest such a change, so I have opted to retain the feminine noun *clauis*.

the key of discipline is nailed in the middle of the cross, certainly by the conversion and good conduct and repentance of humanity by faith."

15. After saying these things with a joyful face and a peaceful countenance, he broke out in prayer and exclaimed, "You made these things known to me, Lord Jesus Christ, the word of life, and I give you thanks for revealing by my preaching the things that I have said from the cross. I thank you not with this heart that often sneaks away toward some shameful thing, nor with these lips that are closed tight, nor with this tongue that produces both truth and falsehood, nor with a word produced by an articulate and material nature. Instead, I thank you, oh good King, with that voice that is understood through silence, that is not heard openly, that proceeds not from the organ of a corruptible mouth, that does not pass through carnal ears, that is not perceived by a corruptible nature, that is neither earthly nor sent forth on the earth, that is not written in material books. No one experiences it materially, nor does it exist materially. But I say that I thank you, Jesus Christ, my Lord and master, by that spirit through which I trust you, know you, love you, and hold fast to you, and with that voice with which I speak to you and address you, because you are understood by a spirit that is whole and humble.

"You, oh Lord, are my father and friend, the author and perfecter of salvation.[57] You are my desire, my consolation, and my sufficiency. You are everything to me, and everything for me is in you. You are my all in all, and you are to me everything that is. Indeed, you are everything to me. In you we live, move, and exist.[58] Therefore, we ought to have you as our everything, so that you may give to us those things that you have promised—things which neither eye has seen nor ear has heard nor have entered into the heart of humanity, things which you have prepared for those who love you.[59] Guard these things for your servants. Grant and bestow them, because you are the eternal shepherd and the highest good, the true Son of God. I entrust to you the sheep that you gave to me.[60] Bring them into your sheepfold and protect them, because you are the door of the sheepfold

Adam)." Alternatively, it could be a reference to the dual natures of Christ: "Through the one who was both God and human."

57. Heb 12:2.

58. Acts 17:28.

59. 1 Cor 2:9.

60. Cf. John 17:6–12.

ostium ouilius et ostiarius, tu pascua, tu aeternae uitae refectio. tibi gloria cum Patre et Spiritu Sancto nunc et in omnia saecula saeculorum.

16. et mox ut omnis plebs magna uoce amen reddidit, Petrus spiritum tradidit. statimque Marcellus nullius expectauit sententiam, sed uidens quia beatus expirauit apostolus, propriis manibus deposuit corpus sanctum de cruce et lauit illud lacte et uino optimo, terensque masticae et aloës minas mille quingentas et myrrae ac folii, atque stacten[6] cum caeteris uariis aromatibus alias minas mille quingentas, condiuit eum diligentissime. melle quoque Attico nouum repleuit sarcophagum et in eo corpus aromatibus perlitum collocauit.

in ipsa autem nocte cum Marcellus ad sepulchrum ipsius uigilaret, et ardenti eius desiderio fleret—statuerat enim in uita sua non separari a doctoris sui amantissimi sepultura—uenit ad eum beatus Petrus. quem uidens Marcellus et contremiscens illi uelociter assurrexit stetitque ante eum. cui ait beatus apostolus: frater Marcelle, non audisti uocem Domini dicentis: relinque mortuos sepelire mortuos suos?

et Marcellus ait: care magister, audiui.

tunc Petrus ad eum: ne ergo quasi mortuus mortuum uidearis sepelisse et flere, sed quasi uiuus uiuenti et gaudenti melius collaetari, relinque mortuos sepelire mortuos suos. tu autem, ut per me didicisti, uade, annuntia regnum Dei.

quod cum gratia multa cunctis fratribus Marcellus indicauit, et meritis sancti Petri ex omni parte fides credentium a Deo Patre confirmata est in nomine Domini nostri Iesu Christi et in sanctificatione Spiritus Sancti.

17. Nero autem comperiens beatum Petrum obisse, quem artare non interficere iusserat, misit ut comprehenderetur Agrippa praefectus, quoniam Petrum non cum sua sententia interfecerat, quem disponebat per uaria punire supplicia. querebatur enim se ipsius praestigiis desolatum Symone suae salutis praesule, et dolebat pro tanti amici casu qui sibi et reipublica, ut fatebatur, commoda praestabat innumera. Agrippa uero interuenientibus

6. From the Greek στακτή.

and the doorkeeper;[61] you are the pasture; and you are the refreshment of eternal life. Glory to you with the Father and the Holy Spirit now and forever and ever."

16. As soon as all the people pronounced the "Amen" with a loud voice, Peter surrendered his spirit.[62] Immediately Marcellus did not at all wait for permission, but seeing that the blessed apostle had expired, he took down the holy body from the cross with his own hands and washed it with milk and the best wine. Rubbing it with 1500 minas of mastic, aloe, myrrh, and aromatic leaves, along with another 1500 minas of myrrh oil and various other spices, he embalmed Peter with the greatest care. He also filled a new sarcophagus with Attic honey and placed the body in it coated with spices.

On that same night, when Marcellus was keeping a vigil at Peter's tomb and weeping out of his severe grief—for he had decided not to be separated in his own lifetime from the tomb of his most beloved teacher—the blessed Peter came to him. Seeing him and beginning to shake, Marcellus rose quickly and stood in front of him. Blessed Peter said to him, "Brother Marcellus, did you not hear the voice of the Lord, who said, 'Leave the dead to bury their own dead'?"[63]

And Marcellus said, "I heard him, dear master."

Then Peter said to him, "Therefore, do not seem to bury and weep for the dead as if you were dead, but rather as one who is alive, delight in living and rejoicing, and leave the dead to bury their own dead. But as for you, as you learned from me, go and proclaim the kingdom of God."[64]

With great gratitude Marcellus told this to all the brothers and sisters, and by the merits of holy Peter, the faith of the believers was completely confirmed by God the Father in the name of our Lord Jesus Christ and in the sanctification of the Holy Spirit.

17. Nero learned that the blessed Peter had died—the one whom he had ordered to have arrested but not killed. He sent for the prefect Agrippa to be arrested, because Agrippa had killed without his approval the one he had decided to punish with various tortures. [Nero] was lamenting that he had been deprived of the spells of Simon, the patron of his salvation, and he was grieving for the sake of so great a friend, who, he claimed, had performed numerous favors for himself and the republic. Agrippa, with

61. John 10:1–9.
62. Cf. John 19:30 (Vulgate).
63. Matt 8:22; Luke 9:60.
64. Luke 9:60.

amicis obtinuit ut praefectura carens priuatus et contemptus domo propria degeret. sicque furorem Caesaris declinauit, sed ultionem diuini iudicii non euasit, quam mox terribiliter expertus interiit.

denique conuertit crudelissimus Nero animum ad persecutionem eorum quos didicit beato Petro familiarius adhaesisse, ut uel eorum poenis de Petro satiaretur. beatus uero apostolus fratribus hoc per reuelationem innotuit et qualiter feram bestiam declinarent insinuauit. Nero siquidem uidit per uisum sibi sanctum astare Petrum et dirissime a quodam iussu ipsius flagellatus audiuit: contine manus, impiisime, a seruis Domini nostri Iesu Christi, quos nunc tenere non poteris. unde parum pauefactus quieuit.

erant quoque fratres simul laetantes et exultantes in Domino, confortati saepe uisione beati Petri apostoli, glorificantes Dominum Deum Patrem omnipotentem et Dominum Iesum Christum cum Spiritu Sancto, cui est gloria, uirtus et adoratio in saecula saeculorum. amen.

the help of his friends, arranged to spend time at his own house, deprived of the prefecture, out of public affairs, and despised. In this way he avoided the wrath of Caesar, but he did not evade the vengeance of divine judgment, for very soon he died in terrible suffering.

Then the very cruel Nero set his mind on the persecution of those whom he learned had been close to the blessed Peter, so that his wrath toward Peter might be satisfied by their punishments. But the blessed apostle made this known to the brothers and sisters through a revelation and recommended that they avoid Nero like a wild beast. Nero, in fact, saw in a vision the holy Peter standing by him. After being scourged brutally at [Peter's] command, he heard, "Most impious one, withdraw your hands from the servants of our Lord Jesus Christ, whom you will no longer be able to bind." Frightened by this, Nero calmed down a little from that point on.

As for the brothers and sisters, they were rejoicing and exalting together in the Lord, comforted often by a vision of the blessed apostle Peter. And they glorified the Lord God the omnipotent Father and the Lord Jesus Christ, together with the Holy Spirit, to whom is glory, strength, and adoration forever and ever. Amen.

3. Pseudo-Abdias, *Passion of Saint Peter*

CANT 195 / *BHL* 6663–6664

Contents

This Latin text is part of a larger cycle recounting the lives and deaths of the apostles. The section on Peter is always first in the sequence and begins with a retelling of selected stories from the Gospels. It then moves to an account of a conflict in Caesarea Maritima between Peter and Simon the sorcerer that eventually leads Peter to Rome and his martyrdom. This is the point at which this translation joins the story.

Simon has been actively trying to undermine Peter and finally proposes a public debate. A crowd of Simon's followers joins the sorcerer in the courtyard of Zacchaeus, the leading man of Caesarea. Peter opens by exhorting the crowd to avoid divine judgment by working for justice and offers peace to all those present. Simon rejects Peter's offer of peace and declares himself the "first power," as evidenced by his many mighty deeds. He claims to be the son of God—unlike Peter's master, who was a crucified sorcerer. Peter responds that if they go to Simon's house, he will prove that Simon is the sorcerer. The crowd turns on Simon and drives him out, leaving him with only one follower.

On the next day that follower comes to Peter begging for forgiveness. He recounts that Simon had decided to destroy the evidence of his sorcery and convinced this man to carry the foul paraphernalia down to the sea, where he threw it into the water. Simon then promised him great honors if he would remain loyal and travel with him to Rome. The man then saw Simon for what he truly was, refused to go to Rome, and came back to Peter immediately to beg for mercy. Peter then presents him to the crowd as proof of Simon's witchcraft.

After the insertion of a story, taken from the Pseudo-Clementine *Recognitions* and *Homilies*, of the reunion of Clement's family, the account rejoins Peter as he arrives in Rome. One of his first actions is to ordain

Clement as his successor, bestowing upon him the power of "binding and loosing" (Matt 16:19). Paul soon comes to Rome, and the faith grows dramatically through their teaching and works of power. At this point Nero enters the story. He had fallen under the influence of Simon through the sorcerer's deceptive acts, and because the apostles stood against Simon, he actively began to oppose the apostles. Simon had, among other things, claimed that he could raise the dead, so when a young relative of Nero fell sick and died, the opportunity presented itself to determine whether Simon or Peter truly had divine power. Simon momentarily deceives the onlookers by appearing to make the head of the dead youth move, but Peter counters that Simon had deceived everyone. Peter then raises the young man in the name of Jesus Christ, and the mob turns on Simon, intending to stone him.

Simon runs to Nero, complaining of his treatment at the hands of Peter. The apostle proposes yet another contest between the two, this one involving the discernment of the opponent's inner thoughts, and once again Peter bests Simon. Now desperate, the sorcerer declares that he will ascend into heaven as the final proof of his divine power. Peter prays to God, and Simon is struck down from the sky. Simon soon dies, and Nero begins actively seeking to kill Peter. The apostle is convinced to leave the city but turns back after having a vision of Christ. He is hung on the cross upside down and praises the mystery of the cross (although in a much shorter form than in the Martyrdom of Peter and Pseudo-Linus's *Martyrdom of Peter*). After Peter's death Marcellus takes his body, embalms it, and buries it at the Vatican, where it is honored by all the people in Rome.

Literary Background

The text is generally dated to the end of the sixth century, because it seems to come from the same literary context as the works of Gregory of Tours (ca. 538–594 CE), Venantius Fortunatus (ca. 530–600 CE), and a recension of the Martyrology of Jerome traced to southern Gaul. Lipsius proposed the theory that an earlier text contained only accounts of the passions of the apostles, and additional elements (including summaries of other gospel stories) were added to produce this fuller cycle of apostolic lives. The strong Gallic connections point to Gaul as the likely place of production and Latin as the original language.

In the Middle Ages the author was identified as Abdias, bishop of Babylon, but this was probably due to a misunderstanding of a notation in the

final part of the cycle. In the Passion of Simon and Jude, who according to tradition had ordained Abdias, there is a reference to the writing of the acts of the holy apostles by Abdias. This is probably meant to create the appearance of historical veracity for the Simon and Jude account, because the author had allegedly witnessed the events, but at a later date this ascription to Abdias was placed at the beginning of the cycle and taken to apply to its entirety. The convention has been to refer to the unknown author as Pseudo-Abdias.

The author freely depends on the third- and fourth-century Pseudo-Clementine *Recognitions* and *Homilies* and the writings of Pseudo-Hegesippus (ca. 370–375 CE).[1] This shows familiarity with earlier, apocryphal Petrine traditions and explains the patchwork nature of the text.

Text

The text survives in numerous manuscripts dating back to the ninth century, and the quantity of manuscripts attests to its popularity in Europe in the Middle Ages. The translation is based upon the publication by Fabricius, which remains the standard edition of the text and was reproduced by Giles in the nineteenth century.

Select Bibliography

Alibert, Dominique. "Vision du monde et imaginaire dans quelques textes de la collection dite du Pseudo-Abdias." *Apocrypha* 11 (2000): 207–26.

Alibert, Dominique, Gisèle Besson, Michèle Brossard-Dandré, and Simon C. Mimouni. "Actes latins des apôtres." Pages 735–46 in vol. 2 of *Écrits apocryphes chrétiens*. Edited by Pierre Geoltrain and Jean-Daniel Kaestli. Pléiade 516. Paris: Gallimard, 2005.

Duchense, Louis. "Les Anciens Recueils dans légendes apostoliques." Pages 69–79 in *Compte rendu du troisième congrès scientifique international des catholiques*. Brussels: Société belge de librairie, 1895.

Erbetta, Mario, trans. "Atti e Martirio di Pietro dello Ps. Abdia." Pages 199–210 in *Atti e leggende*. Vol. 2 of *Gli apocrifi del Nuovo Testamento*. 2nd ed. Turin: Marietti, 1978.

1. Pseudo-Hegesippus, *Exc. Hier.* 3.2.

Giles, John Allen, ed. Pages 270–77 in *The Uncanonical Gospels and Other Writings, Referring to the First Ages of Christianity, in the Original Languages: Collected together from the Editions of Fabricius, Thilo, and Others*. London: Nutt, 1852.

Lipsius, Richard A. Pages 1:117–78, 2.1:384–90, and Ergänzungsband 5–11 in *Die apokryphen Apostelgeschichten und Apostellegenden*. Braunschweig: Schwetschke, 1883–1890.

Malan, Solomon C., trans. "The Conflict of S. Peter." Pages 1–10 in *The Conflicts of the Apostles: An Apocryphal Book of the Early Eastern Church*. London: Nutt, 1871.

Migne, J.-P., trans. "Histoire de saint Pierre d'après l'Histoire apostolique d'Abdias, liv. Ier." Pages 701–16 in vol. 2 of *Dictionnaire des apocryphes*. Paris: Migne, 1858.

Moraldi, Luigi, trans. "La splendida attività del Beato Pietro, primo degli apostoli." Pages 1441–59 in vol. 2 of *Apocrifi del Nuovo Testamento*. Turin: Unione, 1971.

De rebus a beato Petro auctore Abdia

6. His ita gestis, surrexit quidam Simon Samareus genere, qui dudum uisis miraculis Petri, pecunia comparare uoluit donum spirituale, qui se magnum et perpetuo aliter stantem esse dicebat: promittens eos qui in se crederent, prorsus dissolui non posse. hic etiam Petri cupiens euertere uias, et ea, quae docebat, ad irritum reuocare, diem constituit, in quo conuenientibus turbis ad disputandum cum Petro, praesens adesset. erat autem tunc Petrus apud Caesaream Stratonis.

igitur illucescente statuta die, Zachaeus, qui erat prior ciuitatis, adstitit Petro dicens: tempus est ut procedas ad disputandum, Petre. turba autem in medio atrii congregata opprimitur, te opperiens, quorum in medio multis fultus adseclis constitit Simon.

tum Petrus ut haec audiuit, orationis gratia secedere aliquos iubens; qui nondum erant diluti a peccatis, quae in ignorantia commiserant, ait ad reliquos: oremus fratres, ut Dominus per Christum filium suum pro inef-

Concerning the Things Done by Blessed Peter, Written by Abdias

6. After these things occurred, a certain Simon arose.[1] He was a Samaritan by race and at one time had seen the miracles of Peter and wanted to purchase the spiritual gift with money.[2] He was saying that he was great and would abide forever, and he promised those who believed in him that they certainly would not be able to die. Seeking to undermine the ways of Peter and to bring to nothing the things that Peter was teaching, he set a day on which crowds would be gathered together and he would come to debate with Peter.[3] At that time Peter was at Caesarea of Straton.[4]

Therefore, when the designated day had dawned, Zacchaeus,[5] who was the leading man of the city, came to Peter and said, "It is time for you to go out for your debate, Peter. A crowd has gathered in the middle of the courtyard and is pressed together waiting for you. Simon stands in the middle of them, supported by many followers."

When he heard these things, Peter ordered some to depart for the sake of his prayer—that is, those who were not yet washed clean from sins that they had committed in ignorance.[6] To those remaining he said, "Let us

1. The conflict between Peter and Simon is one of the primary elements in this text taken from the Pseudo-Clementine *Homilies* and *Recognitions*. On this dynamic see Dominique Côté, *Le thème de l'opposition entre Pierre et Simon dans les Pseudo-Clémentines*, Études Augustiniennes, Série Antiquités 167 (Paris: Institut d'Études Augustiniennes, 2001); Nicole Kelley, *Knowledge and Religious Authority in the Pseudo-Clementines: Situating the 'Recognitions' in Fourth Century Syria*, WUNT 2/213 (Tübingen: Mohr Siebeck, 2006), esp. 147–78.

2. Acts 8:9–24.

3. Sections 6–8 closely follow Pseudo-Clement, *Recog.* 2.19–23.

4. That is, Caesarea Maritima.

5. Zacchaeus also appears in the Pseudo-Clementine *Recognitions*, where he hosts Peter upon his arrival in Caesarea (1.73) and is later ordained the first bishop of the city (3.66). He is perhaps meant to be the diminutive tax collector from Jericho who is converted by the teachings of Jesus (Luke 19:1–10).

6. Peter asks the unbaptized to leave before he prays, thus reflecting the early Christian practice of allowing the unbaptized to be present for only parts of the liturgy.

fabili misericordia sua adiuuet me, exeuntem pro salute hominum qui ab ipso creati sunt. et haec quum dixisset, oratione facta, processit ad atrium domus, in quo erat multitudo plurima populi congregata. quos ubi omnes summo cum silentio esse attentos uideret, et Magum Simonem in medio eorum uelut signiferum, statim hoc modo coepit:

7. pax uobis omnibus, qui parati estis dare dextras ueritati. quicunque enim obediunt ei, uidentur quidem sibi aliquid gratiae conferre Domino; porro autem ipsi ab eo donum summi muneris consequuntur, iustitiae eius semitas incedentes. propter quod et primum est omnium, iustitiam Domini, regnumque inquirere eius. iustitiam quidem, ut recte agere doceamur: regnum uero, ut quae sit merces posita laborum et patientiae, nouerimus. in quo est bonis quidem aeternorum bonorum remuneratio: his autem, qui contra uoluntatem eius egerint, pro uniuscuiusque gestis poenarum digna restitutio. hic ergo, hoc est, in praesenti uita positos oportet uos agnoscere uoluntatem Domini, ubi et agendi locus est. nam, si quis uelit, antequam actus suos emendet de his requirere, quae non potest inuenire, stulta et inefficax erit huiuscemodi inquisitio. tempus enim breue est, et iudicium gestorum causa agetur, non quaestionum. ideoque ante omnia hoc quaeramus, quod nos, aut qualiter agere oporteat, ut aeternam uitam consequi mereamur. mea ergo ista sententia est, sicut et uero prophetae uisum est: ut primum de iustitia requiratur, ab his maxime qui Dominum

pray, brothers and sisters,[7] that the Lord may help me through Christ his Son on account of his unspeakable mercy, as I go forth for the salvation of men who were created by him." After he had said these things and offered a prayer, he proceeded to the atrium of the house, in which a great multitude of people was gathered. When he saw that they were all waiting there in total silence and that Simon the sorcerer was in the middle of them like a standard-bearer, he immediately began to speak in this way:

7. "Peace to all of you who are ready to give your right hands to the truth. Those who obey it seem to themselves to confer some kind of favor to the Lord, but thereafter they obtain from him the gift of greatest of blessing as they march along the paths of his justice. Therefore, the most important thing of all is to seek the justice of God and his kingdom[8]—his justice, so that we may be taught to act rightly, and his kingdom, so that we may know what reward has been set aside for our labors and perseverance. In the kingdom there is a reward of eternal benefits for the good; but for those who have acted against his will, there is a worthy payback of punishments for the deeds of every person.[9] Here, therefore—that is, in this present life—it is necessary that you discover the will of the Lord and when it is time to act. For if, before he changes his actions, one wishes to search for the things he is not able to find, then an inquiry of this sort will be foolish and useless. The time is short,[10] and the judgment will be made on the basis of deeds, not questions.[11] Therefore, above all let us seek to be found worthy to reach eternal life, no matter what we must do. This is my opinion, which is the same as that of the true prophet,[12] that first of all justice

---

See e.g., Augustine, *Ennarat. Ps.* 103.1.4: "What is it that is hidden in the church and not open to everyone? The sacrament of baptism and the sacrament of the Eucharist."

7. The text says "brothers" throughout, but it is clear that the group is not uniquely male.

8. Matt 6:33.

9. Matt 16:27; Rom 2:5–6; 2 Cor 5:10; Rev 22:12.

10. 1 Cor 7:29.

11. Ethical change must precede the discovery of profound theological truths, and faith will be proven by actions.

12. This term is used in reference to Christ in Pseudo-Clement, *Recog.* 1.16, 1.40–41, 1.45, 1.48, 5.10, 8.59, 10.51. Nicole Kelley (*Knowledge and Religious Authority*, 135–78) has convincingly argued that its role there is to establish a line of succession from Christ (the True Prophet) to Peter and Clement, who therefore represent legitimate prophetic knowledge over and against their opponents. Kelley's argument seems equally applicable to the use of the term in this text. J.-P. Migne suggests that this

se nosse confitentur. si ergo habet aliquis, quod esse rectius putet, dicat. et quum dixerit, audiat sed cum patientia et quiete. propter hoc enim ab initio, salutationis specie, pacem cunctis imprecatus sum.

8. ad haec Simon respondit: nos pace tua opus non habemus. si enim pax et concordia sit, ad inueniendam ueritatem nihil proficere poterimus, habent enim pacem inter se et latrones, et scortatores, et omnis nequitia cum semetipsa concordat. et nos ergo si ob hoc conuenimus, ut pacis causa omnibus quae dicuntur praebeamus assensum, nihil auditoribus conferemus, sed e contrario inlusis eis, nos amici discedimus. propter quod noli inuocare pacem, sed magis pugnam et si potes expugnare errores, ne requiras amicitiam, iniustis assentationibus partam. hoc enim te ante omnia scire uolo, quia duobus inter se dimicantibus, tunc erit, quum alter ceciderit superatus.

et Petrus ait: quid times crebro audire pacem? an ignoras, quia perfectio legis est pax? ex peccatis enim bella nascuntur, et certamina. ubi autem peccatum non fit, pax in disputationibus, ueritas in operibus inuenitur.

et Simon: nihil momenti continent haec uerba, quae loqueris. sed nunc ostendam uirtutis ac diuinitatis meae potentiam, ut repente procidas, et adores me.

9. ego sum prima uirtus, qui semper et sine initio sum. ingressus autem in uterum Rachel natus sum ex ea, ut homo, quo ab hominibus uideri

must be sought, especially by those who confess that they know the Lord. Therefore, if anyone has something that he believes to be more correct, let him say it. And after he proclaims it, let him listen, but with patience and peace. For this reason from the outset, in the form of my greeting, I invoked peace for all."

8. Simon responded to these things, "We have no need of your peace. If indeed there were peace and concord, then we could make no progress toward finding the truth. Even robbers and fornicators have peace among themselves, and every form of wickedness is at peace with itself. Therefore, if we gather so that for the sake of peace we agree with everything that is said, then we will do nothing for our listeners. On the contrary, after making sport of them, we depart friends. Therefore, do not invoke peace, but conflict. If you are able to refute errors, then you should not seek friendship that is based on false flatteries. First of all, then, I want you to know that there will be [peace] between two combatants only when one overcomes and cuts down the other."

And Peter said, "Why are you afraid to hear often about peace? Or do you not know that the perfection of the law is peace?[13] From transgressions wars and conflicts are born; however, where there is no sin, peace is found in discussions, and truth is found in deeds."

And Simon said, "These words that you are saying are useless. But now I will show you the power of my strength and divinity, and as a result you will suddenly fall down and worship me.

9. "I am the first power,[14] who is forever and without beginning. However, I entered the uterus of Rachel and was born from her, so that I might

---

title reflects "a trace of the doctrines of the Ebionites, who, refusing to recognize the divinity of the Savior, willingly called him the true or unique prophet" (*Dictionnaire des apocryphes* [Paris: Migne, 1858], 2:701–702 n. 679). Jarl E. Fossum follows Migne in assigning Ebionite associations to the term and adds that it was also a "Samaritan savior epithet" (*The Name of God and the Angel of the Lord*, WUNT 1/36 [Tübingen: Mohr, 1985], 59).

13. Cf. Ps 119:165.

14. Cf. Pseudo-Clement, *Recog.* 3.47. The language of "first power" has multiple possible resonances. According to Irenaeus, Simon's successor, Menander, affirmed the existence of a "first power that is unknown to all, but he himself is the one who was sent by the invisible ones as a savior for the salvation of people" (*Haer.* 1.23.5). This connection of the "first power" to a divine incarnation is also seen in the Pistis Sophia, where Jesus claims that he visited Mary in the form of Gabriel and then "cast into her the first power that I had received from Barbēlō—that is, the body that I had on high"

possim. ego per aerem uolaui, igne commixtus unum corpus effectus sum: statuas moueri feci, animaui exanima, lapides panes feci, de monte uolatu transmeaui, manibus angelorum sustentatus, ad terram descendi. haec non solum feci, sed et nunc facere possum ut rebus ipsis probem omnibus, quia ego sum filius Domini, stans in aeternum et credentes mihi similiter in perpetuo stare faciam. tua autem uerba uana sunt omnia, nec ullum potes opus ostendere ueritatis sicut et ille qui misit te magus, qui nec se ipsum potuit liberare de crucis poena.

possum enim facere, ut uolentibus me comprehendere, non appaream, et rursum uolens uideri, palam sim. si fugere uelim, montes perforem, et saxa quasi lutum pertranseam. si me de monte excelso praecipitem dedero, tanquam subuectus, in terram illaesus deferar. uinctus memetipsum soluam, eos uero, qui uincula iniecerint, uinctos reddam. in carcere conligatus, claustra sponte patefieri faciam. statuas inanimatas reddam ita, ut putentur ab his, qui uident, homines esse. nouas arbores subito oriri faciam, et repentina uirgulta producam. igni meipsum iniiciam, ut non ardeam. uultum meum commuto ut non cognoscar. sed et duas facies habere me possum hominibus ostendere, ut ouis, ut capra efficiar, puer paruus, barbam producam. In aere uolando inuehar, aurum plurimum

be able to be seen by people as a man.[15] I flew through the air mixed with fire, and I was constituted as one body. I caused statues to be moved; I reanimated the dead;[16] I made stones into loaves of bread;[17] down from a mountain I crossed over in flight, supported by the hands of angels, and descended to the earth. Not only did I do these things, but I am able to do them even now, so that I may prove to everyone by these things that I am the son of God who stands in eternity and can make those who believe in me stand forever, as well. All your words are empty, however, and you are not able to demonstrate any true deed—just like the one who sent you was a sorcerer who was not able to free himself from the penalty of the cross.[18]

"I can disappear from those wanting to seize me but appear again when I want to be seen.[19] If I wanted to flee, then I would bore through the mountains and pass through stones like clay. If I throw myself headlong from a high mountain, I will bring myself to the earth unhurt, as if I were carried down.[20] If chained, I will free myself and send back in chains those who had enchained me. If bound in prison, I will cause the bars to be opened spontaneously. I will make inanimate statues appear to be men to those who look at them. I will cause new trees to grow suddenly and will produce bushes out of nowhere. I will cast myself into the fire but not be burned. I can alter my appearance, so that I may not be recognized. I am also able to have two faces to display to men, so that I can show myself as a sheep and as a goat, or as a young boy or a man with a beard. I can be carried flying into the air and reveal a great amount of gold.[21] I will set

---

(Pist. soph. 1.8). Elsewhere in Gnostic literature, the Barbēlō itself is described as the "first power" (Ap. John 4), and there is another, apparently destructive figure called the "first power of darkness" (Dial. Sav. 3). The title in our text may also relate to Acts 8:10, where the people are calling Simon the "Great Power of God." On the association of "Great Power" language with Samaritanism and later Gnosticism, see Fossum, *Name of God*, 162–91.

15. Pseudo-Clement, *Recog.* 2.14.

16. Simon thus rivals Jesus's power as displayed in the raising of Lazarus (John 11:1–44).

17. Cf. Matt 4:3. The fourteenth-century Byzantine chronicle of Nicephorus Callistus Xanthopulus (*Hist. eccl.* 2.27) closely repeats this list.

18. Cf. Mark 15:31 and parallels.

19. Pseudo-Clement, *Recog.* 2.9.

20. Cf. the temptation of Jesus in Matt 4:5–7.

21. Cf. Pseudo-Clement, *Hom.* 2.32.

ostendam. reges faciam, adorabor ut Dominus. publice diuinis donabor honoribus, ita ut simulacrum mihi statuentes, tanquam Dominum colant, et adorent. et quid opus est multa dicere? quidquid uoluero, facere potero. multae enim iam mihi experimento causae consummatae sunt. denique aliquando, inquit, quum mater mea Rachel iuberet me exire ad agrum, ut meterem ego falcem uidens positam, praecepi ei, ut iret et meteret. messuit decuplo amplius caeteris. multa iam noua uirgulta produxi de terra, et comare ea ego feci, et sub momento temporis apparere. et montem proximum ego secundo perforaui.

10. his dictis a Simone, Petrus respondit: ne aliis aliena. tu enim quod sis Magus, ex ipsis quae gessisti confessus es, et manifestatus. noster autem magister, qui est filius Domini et hominis, manifeste bonus est. quod autem uere sit Domini filius, quibus oportuit dictum est, et dicitur. tu autem si non uis confiteri quod magus es, cum omni hac turba pergamus ad domum tuam, et tunc apparebit quis sit magus.

haec autem Petro dicente, Simon blasphemiis et maledictis agere coepit, et, seditione facta, perturbatis omnibus, argui non potuit. et Petrus, ne quasi blasphemiae causa secedere uideretur, perstitit immobilis, et arguere eum uehementius coepit. tum populus indignatus, Simonem de atrio eiectum extra ianuas domus repulit: eoque depulso, unus sequutus est solus.

facto autem silentio, Petrus alloqui populum hoc modo coepit: patienter, fratres, malos ferre debetis, scientes quia Dominus quum possit eos excidere, patitur tamen durare usque ad praesitutam diem in qua de omnibus iudicium fiet. quomodo ergo nos non patiemur, quos patitur Dominus, cui subsunt et obediunt coeli, et terrae? uos ergo qui ad Dominum conuertimini per poenitentiam, curuate ei genua. haec quum dixisset,

up kings[22] and be worshiped as the Lord. In public I will be given divine honors, such that those standing before my image will worship me, just as they honor the Lord.[23] What need is there to recount these many things? I will be able to do whatever I want to do. Indeed, many things have already been accomplished that have proven my power. In addition," he said, "once when my mother Rachel ordered me to go out to the field to reap, I saw a sickle placed there. I commanded it to go and reap, and it harvested tenfold more than the others. I have already produced many new bushes from the earth, and I have made them produce leaves that appear suddenly. Also, I have pierced through a mountain very near to here."

10. After Simon said these things, Peter responded,[24] "Do not divert attention to other things. You have admitted and shown by the things that you have done that you are a sorcerer. Our master, however, who is son of the Lord and son of man, is manifestly good. That he is truly the son of the Lord was declared and is declared to those who deserve it. As for you, however, if you do not wish to admit that you are a sorcerer, then let us go with this entire crowd to your house, and then it will be clear who is the sorcerer."

After Peter had said these things, Simon began to assault him with blasphemies and curses. Because discord had been stirred up and everyone had been provoked into a tumult, it was not possible to refute Simon. Peter did not retreat in the face of this blasphemy, but stood firm and began to accuse Simon more vigorously. Then the people were angry and drove Simon from the atrium to a place outside the doors of the house. After he had been driven out, only one man followed him.

Peace was restored, and Peter began speaking to the people in this way, "You ought to bear patiently with evil ones, brothers and sisters, knowing that the Lord—although he is able to destroy them—nevertheless patiently bears with them until the appointed day. On that day there will be judgment for all. How, then, can we not endure those whom the Lord endures, since the heavens and the earth are under him and obey him? You, therefore, who have turned to the Lord through repentance, bend your knees to

22. Cf. Ps 75:7; Dan 2:21.

23. Cf. Justin Martyr, *1 Apol.* 26, where Justin famously misreads an inscription in Rome to say "To Simon the holy God" (*Simoni deo sancto*), instead of the correct reading "To the god Semo Sancus" (*Semoni Sanco deo*). See e.g., Otto Zwierlein, *Petrus in Rom: Die literarischen Zeugnisse*, 2nd ed., UALG 96 (Berlin: de Gruyter, 2010), 129–34.

24. Pseudo-Clement, *Recog.* 3.48–50.

omnis multitudo genua flexit Domino. et Petrus respiciens ad coelum, cum lachrymis orabat super eos, ut Dominus pro sua bonitate suscipere eos dignaretur, confugientes ad se. et postquam orauit, et praecepit ut die postera maturius conuenirent, sacrificium fecit. tum deinde secundum consuetudinem quieuit.

11. mane autem facto, ueniens quidam ex discipulis Simonis, clamabat dicens: obsecro te, Petre, suscipe me miserum, et a magno Simone deceptum, cui ego uelut coelesti Domino intendebam, pro his quae ab eo fieri mirabilibus uidebam: auditis tamen sermonibus tuis, coepit iam homo mihi uideri, et quidem malus. ueruntamen quum hinc exisset, ego eum subsequutus sum solus: nondum enim ad liquidum impietates eius agnoueram. quum autem uidisset me subsequentem, beatum me dicens, perduxit me in domum suam. circa medium uero noctis ait ad me, omnibus te hominibus faciam meliorem, si uolueris usque ad finem perseuerare mecum. cui quum promisissem, exegit a me sacramentum perseuerantiae: eoque accepto imposuit super humeros meos polluta quaedam et execrabilia secreta sua, ut portarem, et sequutus est me. ubi uero uentum est ad mare, nauigium, quod forte aderat, ingressus, sumit a ceruicibus meis, quod portare me iusserat. et paulo post egressus, nihil extulit: certum quod in mare id deiecerat. rogabat ergo me cum ipso ut proficiscerer, dicens se Romam petere. ibi enim se in tantum placiturum, ut Dominus putetur, et diuinis publice donetur honoribus. tunc, inquit, te omnibus diuitiis repletum, si huc redire placuerit, pluribus fultum ministeriis remittam.

haec ego audiens, nihil in eo secundum hanc professionem uidens sed magum et deceptorem eum intelligens, respondi, quaeso te ignosce mihi, quia pedes doleo, et propterea exire Caesaream non ualeo. praeterea est mihi uxor, sunt paruuli liberi, quos relinquere omnino non possum. at ille

him." When he had said these things, the whole multitude bent their knees to the Lord. Peter looked up into heaven and with tears prayed for them that the Lord, because of his goodness, would see fit to receive those who were taking refuge in him. After he prayed and instructed them to gather together early on the next day, he offered the sacrifice.[25] Then he rested, according to his custom.

11. When dawn came,[26] a certain one of the disciples of Simon came and cried out, saying, "I beg you, Peter, to receive me, a miserable man who was deceived by that great Simon, whom I regarded as the heavenly Lord because of the amazing things that I saw done by him. However, after I heard your teaching, I began to regard him as just a man—an evil man,[27] in fact. Nevertheless, when he left here, I alone followed him, for I did not yet clearly understand his impieties. When he saw me following, he called me blessed and led me to his house. Around the middle of the night he said to me, 'I will make you greater than all other men, if you commit to stay with me to the end.' After I had promised this, he demanded from me an oath of allegiance. When I agreed, he placed in my arms certain foul things and his own accursed secret things for me to carry, and he followed me. When we came to the sea, he boarded a ship that happened to be there, and he took from me what he had ordered me to carry. Shortly afterward he came out and was carrying nothing. It was certain that he had thrown it into the sea.[28] He asked me to depart with him, saying that he was traveling to Rome, where he would be held in high esteem as the Lord and given divine honors in public. 'Then,' he said, 'I will heap all kinds of riches upon you, and if you wish to return here, I will send you back being carried by many servants.'

"When I heard these things and saw that this promise was empty, I realized that he was a sorcerer and deceiver and responded, 'I ask you to forgive me, because I have pain in my feet and am therefore unable to leave Caesarea. Besides, I have a wife and small children whom I am not able to

---

25. That is, he celebrated the Eucharist. Cf. Pseudo-Clement, *Recog.* 3.50, where Peter "offered the mass" (*missam fecit*).

26. Pseudo-Clement, *Recog.* 3.63–64.

27. Migne (*Dictionnaire des apocryphes* 2:705) suggests that the correct reading should be *magus* ("sorcerer"), instead of *malus* ("evil"), and ascribes the change to an error by a copyist. However, the Pseudo-Clementine *Recognitions* have *malus*, and there is no evidence of the proposed variant in the manuscript tradition.

28. Simon therefore destroyed the evidence that Peter had threatened to take the crowd to his house to discover.

haec audiens, et ignauiae me incusans, profectus est Romam dicens, quum audieris quanta mihi gloria in urbe Roma erit, poenitebit te. et post haec ipse quidem ut aiebat, Romam petiit. ego autem confestim redii huc, orans ut me suscipias ad poenitentiam, quia ab eo deceptus sum.

12. quum haec dixisset is qui a Simone regressus est, iussit eum Petrus in atrio residere. procedens autem ipse, et turbas uidens multo plures quam superioribus diebus, stetit in loco solito, et ostendens eum, qui a Simone uenerat, ait: iste, fratres, quem uidetis, paulo ante uenit ad me, de Simonis mihi malis artibus nuncians, quomodo ipsam sceleris sui officinam proiecerit in profundum, non quasi poenitentia ductus, sed metuens ne deprehensus publicis legibus subiaceret. haec dicente Petro, populus uidens hominem qui uenerat a Simone, stupebat.

15. post haec autem Petrus Romam ueniens, in ipsis diebus sibi finem uitae imminere praesensit. in conuentu ergo fratrum positus, adprehensa Clementis manu repente consurgens in auribus totius ecclesiae haec protulit uerba: audite me fratres, et conserui mei: quoniam sicut edoctus sum ab

abandon.' After hearing these things and accusing me of laziness, he set out for Rome, saying, 'When you hear how great my glory is in the city of Rome, then you will be sorry.' After these things he set out for Rome, as he had said. But I returned here immediately, praying that you would receive me into repentance, because I was deceived by him."

12. After the one who had returned from Simon said these things, Peter ordered him to remain in the atrium. Then Peter went out and saw crowds that were much larger than they had been in previous days. He stood in his usual place, and pointing to the one who had come from Simon, he said, "This one whom you see, brothers and sisters, came to me a little while ago and told me about the evil stratagems of Simon, how he hurled into the deep the instruments of his wickedness—not as though prompted by penance, but fearing that he would be arrested and punished under the laws of the republic."[29] When Peter said these things, the people saw the man who had come from Simon and were amazed.

The author then includes the story of the reunion of Clement with his family, taken from the Pseudo-Clementine Recognitions *and* Homilies. *This translation picks up the story again when Peter arrives in Rome.*

15. After these things Peter came to Rome, and in these days he sensed that the end of his life was near. When he was in a meeting of the brothers and sisters, he got up suddenly, seized the hand of Clement,[30] and offered these words in the hearing of the whole church, "Listen to me, my brothers and sisters and fellow servants, because as I have learned from the one who

---

29. Practitioners of magic (including sorcery, divination, astrology, etc.) were subject to punishment under Roman law as early as the Twelve Tables and into the imperial period, even before the arrival of Christianity. They were, for example, expelled from the city in 139 BCE, 33 BCE, and 19 CE. On the tenuous status of magicians in Rome, see Mary Beard, John North, and Simon Price, *Religions of Rome: Volume 1: A History* (Cambridge: Cambridge University Press, 1998), 231–36; Matthew Dickie, *Magic and Magicians in the Greco-Roman World* (London: Routledge, 2001), 137–241; Clyde Pharr, "The Interdiction of Magic in Roman Law," *TAPA* 63 (1932): 269–95.

30. This account of Clement's ordination is taken from the apocryphal Epistle of Clement to James (§2). Tertullian (*Praescr.* 32) also claims that Clement was ordained by Peter, while Irenaeus (*Haer.* 3.3.3) and Eusebius (*Hist. eccl.* 5.6.1–2) place Clement fourth in the line of Roman bishops, and the Liberian Catalog lists him third (*Chronica minora saec. IV. V. VI.VII.*, ed. T. Mommsen, MGH.AA 9 [Berlin: Weidmann, 1892], 73).

eo qui me misit Domino et magistro Iesu Christo, dies mortis meae instat, Clementem hunc episcopum uobis ordinabo, cui soli meae praedicationis et doctrinae cathedram credo, qui mihi ab initio usque ad finem comes in omnibus fuit, et per hoc ueritatem totius meae praedicationis agnouit. qui in omnibus tentationibus meis socius extitit fideliter perseuerans: quem prae caeteris expertus sum, Dominum colentem, homines diligentem, castum, discendi studiis deditum, sobrium, benignum, iustum, patientem, scientem ferre nonnullorum etiam ex his, qui in uerbo Domini instruuntur, iniurias. propter quod ipsi trado a Domino mihi datam potestatem ligandi et soluendi, ut de omnibus quibuscunque decreuerit in terris, hoc decretum sit et in coelis. ligabit enim quod oportet ligari, et soluet quod oportet solui. et haec quum dixisset, manus ei imposuit, eumque in cathedra sua sedere compulit, multum eum instruens, qualiter aut ecclesiam sibi commissam regeret, aut oues susceptas aleret.

16. tunc et Paulus apostolus Romam ueniens, Christum Dominum praedicabat. tempore igitur Neronis Caesaris, erant Romae salutiferi doctores Christianorum Petrus et Paulus apostoli, per quos dum fides Domini Iesu Christi in omnium cresceret mentes, et religionis propagarentur augmenta, quia essent sublimes operibus, clari magisterio ob uirtutem diuinae gratiae.

Nero per magum Simonem uehementer aduersari coepit apostolis: quia diuersis illusionibus daemonum ita magus Caesaris animum obtinuerat, ut eum salutis suae praesulem, uitaeque custodem, remota ambiguitate confideret. nam et bellorum uictorias, et subiectiones gentium, et prosperitatem rerum se per eum in omnibus habiturum esse credebat. sed

sent me—namely, our Lord and master Jesus Christ—the day of my death is near.[31] I will ordain for you this man Clement as your bishop. I entrust to him alone the seat of my preaching and teaching, for he was my companion in all situations from the beginning up to the end, and for this reason he knows the truth of my entire message. He proved to be a partner in all my trials by faithfully persevering. I have found him above all others to be a worshiper of God, a lover of men, chaste, dedicated to study and learning, sober, kind, just, patient, and understanding of how to endure injuries from others, even from those who are instructed in the word of the Lord. For this reason I hand over to him the power of binding and loosing that was given to me by the Lord,[32] so that whatever he decrees on earth will also be decreed in heaven. He will bind what is necessary to bind and loose what is necessary to loose." After Peter had said these things, he placed his hands on [Clement] and brought him to sit in his seat.[33] He taught him much about how he should govern the church that had been commissioned to him and how he should nourish the sheep whom he had received.[34]

16. Then the apostle Paul came to Rome and was preaching Christ the Lord. Therefore, at the time of Nero Caesar,[35] there were in Rome the salvation-bearing teachers of the Christians, the apostles Peter and Paul. Through them the faith of the Lord Jesus Christ was growing in the minds of all, and the growth of religion was being spread, because they were distinguished in their deeds and famous in their teaching by the strength of divine grace.

Nero, however, began to oppose the apostles vehemently under the influence of Simon the sorcerer. Through various illusions of demons, the sorcerer had gained control of the mind of Caesar to the extent that Nero without hesitation placed confidence in Simon as the author of his salvation[36] and the guardian of his life. For he believed that he would enjoy victories in war, the conquest of nations, and prosperity in all his affairs

31. John 21:18–19.

32. Matt 16:19, 18:18.

33. The term *cathedra* was regularly used to refer to the bishop's seat both figuratively and literally. See e.g., Cyprian, *Unit. eccl.* 4, 10; *Laps.* 6; *Ep.* 3.1.1, 17.2.1, 43.5.2, 52.1.2, 55.8.4; and Optatus of Milev, *Adv. Donat.* 1.10.5, 1.15.1–3, 1.17.2, 1.19.3, 2.2.1–2.

34. John 21:15–17.

35. Sections 16–19 closely follow Pseudo-Hegesippus, *Exc. Hier.* 3.2.

36. Cf. Heb 5:9.

Petrus apostolus uanitates eius et flagitia uniuersa detexit, quia ueritatis lux, et uerbi diuini claritas, quae ob salutem hominum nuper obfulserat, totius mendacii caligine de humanis mentibus discussa per apostolos, ignorantiae tenebras effugabat. tunc Simon magus ueri luminis fulgore perculsus caecitatem[1] continuo male sanae mentis incurrit, quippe qui iam in Iudaea per apostolum Petrum de his quae egerat sceleribus confutatus, transmarinam ingressus est fugam. et qui in aliis terrarum partibus Petri expertus erat potentiam, tamen praeueniens Romam, ausus est se iactare, quod posset mortuos suscitare.

illo ipso tempore erat quidam defunctus adolescens nobilis propinquus Caesaris. ubi, quum multa turba propinquorum conuenisset, sciscitabantur in uicem, si esset aliquis qui posset mortuum excitare. celeberrimus scilicet et tunc Petrus in his operibus habebatur, sed apud gentiles nulla huius firmabatur fides. dolor tamen exegit inquiri remedium: perrectum est ad Petrum. fuerunt equidem qui etiam Simonem accersendum putarent, ut uterque adesset. tum Petrus ad cognatos defuncti ait, ut Simon, qui de sua se iactabat potentia, prior, si posset, mortuum suscitaret. sin ille nequiuisset, sibi non ambiguum, quin Christus opem ferret defunto. ibi Simon, qui putabatur apud gentiles magnae esse pontentiae, conditionem interposuit, ut si ille mortuum suscitaret, Petrus occideretur, qui tantae potestati uerbis audacibus lacessendo irrogasset iniuriam. si uero illo nihil agente, Petrus mortuum suscitasset, magus sententiae, quae in apostolum data fuerat, subiaceret. talis quum esset interiecta conditio, quieuit Petrus.

exorsus est autem Simon, et accedens ad lectulum defuncti, incantare atque immurmurare dira clam carmina coepit. uisumque est circumstantibus, caput agitari defuncti. itaque clamor gentilium ingens attollitur, quod

1. MS *coecitatem*.

because of him. But the apostle Peter exposed his deceptions and all his shameful acts, because the light of truth and the clarity of the divine word, which had recently shone for the salvation of men, were driving out the shadows of ignorance, while through the apostles the fog of all deception was being dispersed from human minds. Then Simon the sorcerer, struck blind by the bright flash of the true light, immediately fell into a poor state of mind. In fact, already in Judea he had been thwarted by the apostle Peter from the wicked things he was doing[37] and had fled across the sea. He had also experienced the power of Peter in other parts of the world. Nevertheless, when he came to Rome, he dared to boast that he was able to raise the dead.

At that very time a certain young man who was from a noble family and related to Caesar died.[38] When a large crowd of relatives had gathered there, they were asking each other if there was anyone who was able to raise the dead. Peter was very famous at that time because of the things he had done, but the unbelievers[39] had no faith in him. Nevertheless, pain forced them to seek for a remedy, so they hastened to Peter. There were others, however, who thought they should call Simon, so both came. Then Peter said to the relatives of the dead youth that Simon, who was boasting about his power, should raise the dead man first, if he was able. If Simon were unable, then he had no doubt that Christ would perform this deed for the dead youth. Then Simon, who was thought by the unbelievers to have great power, proposed the condition that if he raised the dead, then Peter should be killed, because he had inflicted harm on one of such great power by exasperating him with his bold words. If he was able to do nothing and Peter raised the dead, then the sorcerer should suffer the sentence that had been established for the apostle. After this condition had been proposed, Peter agreed.

Simon began. Approaching the bed of the dead youth, he began to chant and whisper horrible, incomprehensible incantations. And it seemed to those standing around that the head of the dead moved, so a great cry arose from the unbelievers that he was now alive and was speaking with

37. Acts 8:9–11.

38. Here the narrative is parallel to Pass. Apost. 8–12.

39. Literally, the "gentiles" or the "nations." The Christian use of "gentiles" to indicate unbelievers is seen as early as 1 Cor 5:1, 12:2. I have avoided the use of the problematic term "pagans" here.

iam uiueret, quod cum Simone loqueretur. miraque indignatio in Petrum esse omnium coepit, eo quod esset ausus se tantae potestati conferre.

tum Petrus fieri silentium postulat, et ait: si uiuit defunctus, loquatur: si suscitatus est, surgat et ambulet, atque fabuletur. ego uero phantasma hoc, non ueritatem esse, quod cernitis motum caput defuncti, docebo. denique (inquit) separetur magus a lectulo, et ad plenum figmenta diaboli denudabuntur. abducitur itaque Simon a lectulo, et sine ulla spe uitae manet defunctus immobilis. adstitit Petrus a longe, et intra se orationi paulisper intentus, cum magna uoce ait: adolescens, tibi dico surge. sanat te Dominus noster Iesus Christus. et statim surrexit adolescens, et loquutus est, et ambulauit, et dedit eum Petrus matri suae uiuentem. quae quum remunerare beatum apostolum uellet: secura, inquit, esto mater de filio, et non uerearis. habet enim custodem suum.

17. et quum uellet populus magum Simonem lapidare, ait Petrus: satis est ad poenam eius, quod agnoscit se in suis actibus superatum. uiuat et regnum Christi crescere uideat, uel inuitus. torquebatur interea magus, et apostolica perculsus gloria ad Neronem Caesarem currit, nouamque Petro iniuriam molitus, obtinuit ut Petrum uocaret.

itaque quum uterque coram imperatore staret, prior Simon: miror te, inquit, Caesar, hunc te alicuius momenti hominem existimare, imperitum piscatorem, mendacissimum, et nec in uerbo nec in re aliquia praeditum potestate. sed ne diutius hunc patiar inimicum, praecipiam modo angelis meis, ut ueniant, et uindicent me de isto.

ad quae Petrus: non equidem timeo angelos tuos, qui me coguntur timere, et in uirtute, et in confidentia huius Christi Domini mei, quem te esse mentiris. nam si diuinitas in te est, quae cordis arcana rimatur, dic mihi nunc, Simon, quid cogitem, uel quid facturus sim. quam cogitationem meam, antequam tibi mentiatur magus, Caesar optime, auribus tuis insinuabo, ut non possit mentiri quid cogitem.

tum Nero: accede huc, et dic mihi quid cogites.

Simon. Great anger against Peter began to arise among all, because he had dared to present himself as being so powerful.

Then Peter asked for silence and said, "If the dead man is living, then let him speak. If he has been raised, then let him get up, walk around, and talk. I will show you that it is an illusion, not the truth, that you see the head of the dead move." Then he said, "Let the sorcerer be separated from the bed, and the deceptions of the devil will be completely laid bare." So Simon was led away from the bed, and the dead youth remained immobile, without any hope of life. Peter stood at a distance, and having focused inwardly in prayer for a little while, he said with a loud voice, "Young man, I say to you, 'Get up!' Our Lord Jesus Christ heals you!" Immediately the young man got up, spoke, and walked around, and Peter gave him to his mother alive.[40] When she wanted to pay the blessed apostle,[41] he said, "Be at peace, mother, concerning your son, and do not fear. He has his own guardian."

17. When the people wanted to stone Simon the sorcerer, Peter said, "It is enough of a punishment for him to know that he was defeated in his deeds. Let him live and see the kingdom of Christ grow against his will." Meanwhile the sorcerer was being tormented and beaten down by the apostolic glory, so he ran to Nero Caesar. He contrived a new attack on Peter and managed to get Nero to summon Peter.

When both of them stood in the presence of the emperor, Simon spoke first, "I am amazed at you, Caesar," he said, "that you consider this man of any importance—an ignorant fisherman, the greatest liar, and endowed with power neither in word nor in deed. I will no longer endure this enemy but will now instruct my angels to come and avenge me on this man."

Peter responded, "I do not at all fear your angels, who will be forced to fear me in the power and the confidence of my Lord Jesus Christ—the one you lie and say that you are. If there is divinity in you that can probe the secrets of the heart, then tell me now, Simon, what I am thinking, or what I am about to do. I will whisper into your ears, greatest Caesar, what I am thinking before this sorcerer lies to you, so that he is not able to lie about what I am thinking."

Then Nero said, "Come here, and tell me what you are thinking."

40. Cf. Luke 7:15.

41. The mother's attempt to pay Peter is a divergence from the Pseudo-Hegesippus account.

Petrus dixit: iube mihi adferri hordeaceum panem, et occulte dari. quumque hoc iussum fuisset, Petrus ait: dicat nunc ergo Simon, quid cogitatum, quid dictum, quidue sit factum a me.

tum Nero: quid dicis, Simon?

respondet Simon: imo Petrus dicat quid ego cogitauerim, uel quid fecerim.

tum Petrus: quid cogitet Simon, me scire docebo, si tamen ipse prius dixerit, quid ego cogitauerim.

quae quum audiuisset Simon: hoc, inquit, scias, bone imperator, quia cogitationes hominum nemo nouit, nisi solus Deus. caeterum Petrus mentitur.

ad quae iterum Petrus: tu uero, qui filium Dei te esse dicis, dic quid cogitem, et quid fecerim modo in occulto, si potes, exprime. Petrus autem benedixerat panem hordeaceum, quem acceperat, et fregerat, et in dextra atque sinistra manica sua collocauerat.

18. tunc Simon indignatus, quod dicere non posset secretum apostoli, exclamauit dicens: procedant canes magni, et deuorent eum in conspectu Caesaris. et quum haec dixisset, apparuerunt canes mirae magnitudinis, et impetum fecerunt in Petrum. Petrus uero extendens manus in orationem, ostendit canibus, quem benedixerat panem. quem ut uiderunt canes, subito nusquam comparuerunt.

tum conuersus Petrus ad Caesarem: ecce ostendi tibi, imperator, quid cogitarit Simon, non uerbis, sed factis. nam qui angelos promiserat contra me esse uenturos, canes exhibuit ut se ostenderet non diuinos angelos, sed caninos habere. quare indignatus magus, sese ad omnem excitare coepit carminum suorum potentiam. congregatque populum, ac offensum se dicit a Galilaeis relicturum se urbem, quam tueri soleret. denique diem statuit,

Peter said, "Order a barley loaf to be brought and given to me secretly." When this had been commanded, Peter said, "Now let Simon say what I thought, said, and did."

Then Nero said, "What do you say, Simon?"

Simon responded, "On the contrary, let Peter say what I thought or did."

Then Peter said, "I will show that I know what Simon is thinking, if he first says what I was thinking."

When Simon heard these things, he said, "Know this, good emperor, that no one knows the thoughts of men except God alone.[42] But Peter is lying."

Then Peter said again, "You who say that you are the son of God, say what I am thinking and what I just did in secret. If you are able, say it." Peter, however, had blessed the barely loaf that he had received, broken it, and placed it under his sleeves in his right and left hand.

18. Then Simon was indignant that he was not able to tell the secret of the apostle and cried out, saying, "Let great dogs come and devour him in the sight of Caesar!" And when he had said these things, dogs of amazing size appeared and attacked Peter.[43] But Peter extended his hands in prayer and showed the dogs the bread that he had blessed. When the dogs saw it, they suddenly disappeared.

Then Peter turned to Caesar [and said], "Look, I have shown you, emperor, what Simon was thinking, not with words but with deeds. For he had promised that his angels would come against me, but he produced dogs. Thus, he demonstrated that he has angels that are not divine, but canine." Therefore, the indignant sorcerer began to incite himself to use the full power of his incantations. He gathered together the people and said that he had been insulted by the Galileans and would leave the city that he was accustomed to protect.[44] Then he set a day on which he boastingly promised

---

42. Cf. 1 Cor 2:11.

43. Cf. Pass. Apost. 7, where Paul is also included in this scene. Several medieval legends state that Simon was known to own a large, ferocious dog (e.g., Jacobus de Voragine [*Leg. aur.* 89], Nicephorus Callistus Xanthopulus [*Hist. eccl.* 11.27]), but it is unclear if there is a direct connection. For an explanation of this peculiar canine incident, see Alberto Ferreiro, "Simon Magus, Dogs, and Simon Peter," in *Simon Magus in Patristic, Medieval, and Early Modern Traditions*, ed. Alberto Ferreiro (Leiden: Brill, 2005), 147–200.

44. Simon identifies himself as the patron and protector of Rome, a role ascribed by Christians to Peter and Paul, Rome's martyr-patrons. See David L. Eastman, *Paul the Martyr: The Cult of the Apostle in the Latin West*, WGRWSup 4 (Atlanta: Society of Biblical Literature, 2011), 87–89.

quo se per uolatum supernis sedibus satis iactanter promittebat inuehendum, ueluti quando uellet coelum petiturus, in sua potestate consisteret.

statuo igitur die montem Capitolinum ascendit, ac se de rupe deiiciens, uolare coepit. mirari populus ac uenerari. plerique etiam dicebant dei hanc esse potentiam, non hominis, qui ita corpore uolaret ad coelum. nihilque tale Christum fecisse, multi asseuerabant. tunc Petrus, stans in medio, inquit: Domine Iesu, ostende uirtutem tuam, et ne permittas his uanis artibus decipi populum, qui tibi est crediturus. sic decidat Domine (inquit) ut uiuens se contra tuam potentiam nihil potuisse cognoscat. quumque haec cum lachrymis orasset apostolus, ait: adiuro uos in nomine Iesu Christi, qui eum fertis, ut nunc demittatis. et statim ad uocem Petri demissus a daemonibus, implicitis remigiis alarum quas sumpserat, corruit. nec statim exanimatus est, sed totus fractus corpore, debilitatisque cruribus, post paucarum horarum spatium inibi expirauit. quod ubi Neroni compertum est, deceptum se ac destitutum dolens, sublatumque sibi uirum utilem ac necessarium reipublicae indignatus, quaerere coepit causas, quibus Petrum occideret.

19. itaque datur a Nerone praeceptum, ut Petrus comprehenderetur. et quum ab omnibus ante fuisset rogatus, ut se alio conferret, ille semper resistebat, dicens: nequaquam hoc se esse facturum, ut tanquam metu mortis territus fugeret. quippe quum sciret, et sibi et omnibus pro passione Christi, immortalitatis gloriam prouenire. quumque haec et talia Petrus

that he would fly on celestial thrones, because whenever he wanted to go into heaven, it was in his power to do so.

Therefore, on the established day he ascended the Capitoline hill, and throwing himself down from the cliff, he began to fly.[45] The people were amazed and worshiped him. Many were indeed saying that this was the power of a god, not of a man, who was flying with a body into heaven. And many said that Christ had never done anything like this. Then Peter stood in the midst of them and said, "Lord Jesus, show your power, and do not allow the people who are going to believe in you to be deceived by these empty tricks. Let him fall, Lord," he said, "so that while he is still alive he may know that he can do nothing against your power." After the apostle had prayed these things with tears, he said, "You who are carrying him, I order[46] you in the name of Jesus Christ to drop him right now." As soon as Peter spoke, [Simon] was dropped by the demons, and when the wings[47] that he had taken became entangled, he fell.[48] He did not die right away, but his whole body was broken, and his legs were crippled. After a few hours he died in that very place. When Nero learned this, he was angry that he had been deceived and disappointed and was indignant at being deprived of a man useful to himself and necessary for the republic. He then began to seek reasons to kill Peter.

19. And so an order was given by Nero that Peter be arrested. When Peter had been asked by everyone to escape to another place, he always resisted, saying that he would never flee as if he were terrified by the fear of death. For he knew that, just as with the suffering of Christ, the glory of immortality was shining forth for him and for all. Peter hid these and

---

45. In other versions of this story, Simon jumps from a tower that Nero had constructed for him.

46. Cf. Lactantius, *Inst.* 2.16, where the verb *adjuro* is also used specifically in the context of exorcism.

47. Literally, "the oars of wings." This suggests that he was employing a rowing motion as he flew and had constructed some type of artificial wings to aid his flight. Cf. Arnobius, *Adv. nat.* 2.12, where the people of Rome "even saw the chariot [*currum*, although a variant offers *cursum*, 'journey'] of Simon the sorcerer and his fiery team of horses, which were blown apart by the prayer of Peter and vanished at the mention of Christ's name."

48. The Apostolic Constitutions state that Simon was thrown to the earth as he was flying "in an unnatural way" (Apos. Con. 2.3.14), while Arnobius of Sicca claims that Simon tried to fly in a fiery chariot. Thrown down by the words of Peter, he broke his legs and soon after committed suicide (*Adv. nat.* 2.12).

obtexisset, plebs lachrymans, ne se relinqueret, ne imminente procella Christianorum, despiceret tot bonorum lachrymas. uictus tandem populorum fletibus adquieuit, promisitque se urbem egressurum.

proxima igitur nocte salutatis fratribus, celebrataque oratione, proficisci solus coepit. ubi uentum erat ad portam, uidit Christum sibi occurrere. quem adorans ait: Domine, quo uadis?

cui Dominus: uenio Romam iterum crucifigi.

quod quum audisset, intellexit apostolus, de sua hoc passione dictum, in quo scilicet passurus uideretur Christus, quem pati constabat in singulis, non dolore corporis, sed misericordiae contemplatione, et pietatis affectu. itaque Petrus ad urbem rediit, captusque a custodibus, mox cruci adiudicatus est.

quo audito, ingens subito populi concursus factus est, ita ut plateae non reciperent homines utriusque aetatis, et sexus, qui summa uoce clamabant dicentes: cur occiditur Petrus? quid admisit criminis? quid laesit urbem? innocentem damnare nefas est. et metuendum est, ne in tanti uiri nece ulciscatur Christus, et nos omnes pereamus.

20. at uero Petrus mulcebat plebis animos, ne aduersus principem desaeuirent, dicens eis: uiri Romani, qui in Christo creditis, et in illo solo speratis, in mente habetote eius patientiam, et consolationem in his signis quae uidistis facta per me. sustinete itaque eum aduenientem, et retribuentem unicuique secundum opera sua. hoc autem quod nunc in me uidetis fieri, iam antea mihi a Domino est proditum, non esse discipulum supra magistrum nec seruum supra dominum. quare scitote, ad hoc ipsum me

other such things, but the people were tearfully entreating him not to leave or ignore the tears of so many good people at a time when a storm was coming against the Christians. Finally, convinced by the weeping of the people, he agreed and promised that he would leave the city.

Therefore, on the next night, after saying farewell to the brothers and sisters and offering prayer, he began to set out alone. When he came to the gate [of the city], he saw Christ hurrying toward him. Peter worshiped him and said, "Lord, where are you going?"

The Lord said to him, "I am coming to Rome to be crucified again."[49]

When he heard this, the apostle knew that he was speaking about his own suffering and that Christ would clearly be seen to suffer in him, because it was known that Christ suffers in each one [of the martyrs]—not in the pain of the body but by the consideration of his mercy and the affection of his love.[50] So Peter returned to the city. He was arrested by the guards and soon sentenced to be crucified.

When this became known, a large mob of people suddenly rushed together, and the streets could not contain the people of every age and sex who were crying out with a loud voice, saying, "Why is Peter being killed? What crime did he commit? What harm did he do to the city? It is wrong to condemn an innocent man, and we should fear that Christ might avenge the murder of such a great man and we would all perish."

20. But Peter calmed the minds of the people, so they would not rage against their leader,[51] and said to them, "You men of Rome who believe in Christ and hope in him alone, keep in mind his patience, and take comfort in these signs that you saw performed through me. Thus, wait for him to arrive[52] and repay each one according to his deeds.[53] However, that which you see being done to me now was already revealed to me by the Lord, because a student is not above his teacher, nor is a servant above his

49. Origen (*Comm. Jo.* 20.12.91) cites this saying of Jesus but assigns it to the Acts of Paul. Cf. Ambrose, *Aux.* 13, who correctly connects the saying to Peter.

50. The Latin text here is obscure and perhaps corrupt.

51. Cf. 1 Pet 2:13–17, where Christians are instructed to honor government authorities. Perhaps the Petrine tradition, in the eyes of the author of this martyrdom, could not support overt anti-imperial activity.

52. The verb used is directly connected to the term *adventus*, which was the word used to describe the arrival of a victorious emperor or dignitary. Thus, Christ's return is being described with imperial overtones.

53. Matt 16:27; Rom 2:5–6; 2 Cor 5:10; Rev 22:12.

festinare, ut carne exutus Domino adsistam. sed quid moror, inquit, et non accedo ad crucem? teneant persequutores corpus, ego Domino meo spiritu adhaerebo. et accedens ad crucem, rogauit, ut cruci inuersis uestigiis figeretur. ea reuerentia, ne ita seruus crucifigi uideretur, ut Dominus.

quod ubi factum est, coepit de cruce ad populum loqui: o ineffabile ac profundum mysterium crucis, o inseparabile uinculum caritatis. istud est lignum uitae, in quo Dominus Iesus exaltatus, omnia traxit ad se. istud est lignum uitae, in quo crucifixum est corpus Domini Saluatoris. at in eo confixa est mors, et mundus totus aeternae mortis est uinculis absolutus. o gratia incomparabilis, et amor crucis irrecessibilis. gratias itaque tibi, Domine Iesu fili Dei uiui, non solum uoce et corde ago, sed etiam spiritu, quo te diligo, quo te loquor, quo te interpello, quo te teneo, quo te intelligo, quo te uideo. tu mihi omnia, et in omnibus tu mihi totum, et nihil mihi aliud praeter te solum. qui es bonus et uerus Dei filius, et Deus, cui cum aeterno Patre et Spiritu sancto honor et gloria est, in cuncta semper secula seculorum. et quum magna uoce omnis populus respondisset: amen, emisit spiritum.

cuius corpus Marcellus, unus ex discipulis eius, nullius expectans sententiam, propriis manibus de cruce deposuit, et pretiosissimis aromatibus conditum in suo ipsius sarcophago collocauit, in loco qui dicitur Uatica-

master.[54] Therefore, know that I am hastening to him, so that I may stand before the Lord after laying aside the flesh.[55] But why do I delay," he said, "and not go to the cross? Let the persecutors keep my body, but I will cling to my Lord in spirit."[56] Approaching the cross, he asked to be put on the cross upside-down. This he did out of reverence, lest the servant seem to be crucified as his Lord was.[57]

After this was done, he began to speak to the people from the cross, "Oh, unspeakable and profound mystery of the cross. Oh, unbreakable chain of love. This is the wood of life on which the Lord Jesus was lifted up and drew all things to himself.[58] This is the wood of life on which the body of our Lord and Savior was crucified. But on it[59] death was crucified, and the whole world was freed from the chains of eternal death. Oh, incomparable grace and unconquerable love of the cross. I thank you, Lord Jesus, Son of the living God, not only with my voice and heart but also with my spirit, by which I love you, speak to you, address you, cling to you, know you, and see you. You are everything to me, and in all things you are my all in all. There is nothing for me but you alone—you who are the good and true Son of God and also God, to whom be honor and glory, together with the eternal Father and the Holy Spirit, always and forever and ever." When all the people with a loud voice had responded, "Amen," he gave up his spirit.[60]

Marcellus, one of his disciples, did not wait for anyone's permission but took down his body from the cross with his own hands. After embalming it with the most precious spices, he placed it in his own sarcophagus in a

54. Matt 10:24; Luke 6:40; John 13:16, 15:20.

55. Cf. Phil 1:22–24.

56. Notable here is the strong flesh-spirit dichotomy, reminiscent of Pauline theology. On the ascribing of Pauline words and concepts to Peter, see David L. Eastman, "Confused Traditions? Peter and Paul in the Apocryphal Acts," in *Forbidden Texts on the Western Frontier: Christian Apocrypha in North American Perspectives*, edited by Tony Burke and Brent E. Landau (Eugene, OR: Cascade, forthcoming).

57. The inverted crucifixion of Peter was widely recounted by patristic authors (e.g., Eusebius, *Hist. eccl.* 3.1; Jerome, *Vir. ill.* 1) and has inspired numerous works of art, such as the famous paintings by Michelangelo and Caravaggio. Many authors also repeated Peter's motivations for this request, e.g., Ambrose, *Job* 1.1.2; Theodoret, *Car.* 1309–1310.

58. John 12:32.

59. Or "in him."

60. The author reproduces the Vulgate of Matt 27:50: *emisit spiritum*.

nus, iuxta uiam triumphalem, ubi totius urbis ueneratione celebratur in pace.

place that is called the Vatican, next to the triumphal way, where it is honored in peace by the veneration of the entire city.[61]

61. This final line is reminiscent of the text of Jerome, *Vir. ill.* 1: *Sepultus Romae in Vaticano, iuxta viam triumphalem, totius orbis veneratione celebratur*. Textual variants offer the reading "the entire world" (*totius orbis*) or "the entire city" (*totius urbis*). Ernest C. Richardson chose the former in his critical edition (*Hieronymus Liber de viris inlustribus*, TUGAL 14 [Leipzig: Hinrichs, 1896], 7), but the author of this martyrdom account reflects the latter. The reference to the triumphal way likely reflects the Christian reappropriation of Roman space, such that the Basilica of St. Peter now marked the beginning of the new *via triumphalis*. See e.g., Raymond Van Dam, *Remembering Constantine at the Milvian Bridge* (Cambridge: Cambridge University Press, 2011), 211–15.

4. History of Shimeon Kepha the Chief of the Apostles

CANT 200 / *BHO* 935

Content

Our translation picks up the story of Peter, also identified by his Aramaic name Shimeon Kepha, at the point of the apostle's successful preaching in Rome. The reference to his strengthening of the churches there serves to establish Peter as the de facto founder of Roman and Italian Christianity.

Shimeon's preaching attracts members of the imperial household and various aristocratic women, including two wives and two concubines of the prefect. His message of sexual renunciation causes them to withdraw from Agrippa's bed, despite the prefect's violent threats. Then Xanthippe, the wife of Albinus, is swayed by the apostolic preaching such that finally Agrippa and Albinus conspire to kill Shimeon. Meanwhile, the apostle (here again called Peter) senses that his death is imminent and does not want to leave Rome. He is at last persuaded by the believers and sets out alone. He is met on the road by a vision of Christ carrying a cross, a model for how Peter was to die. Christ rebukes him for the weakness of his nature, and a sense of guilt causes him to turn back to the city. He is arrested and thrown into prison by the emperor, despite the protests of a large crowd, and there he stays for an unspecified period of time.

The author then states that Peter oversaw the administration of the Roman church for twenty-five years. Just before his death he ordained Linus and instructed him to continue his preaching. Shimeon is crucified upside down, so that he may symbolically kiss the place of Jesus's feet, and after his death Marcellus buries him in an expensive tomb.

A postscript identifies the author of the text as Clement, a disciple of Peter who had bested Simon the sorcerer and translated a "letter of the

Hebrews" into Greek. He also wrote other books but wrongly desired to be bishop. The text closes with an appeal for prayer on behalf of the scribe.

Literary Background

The History of Shimeon Kepha the Chief of the Apostles is the first in a cycle of Syriac Acts of the Martyrs and Saints. Earlier sections of the Petrine account not translated here show dependence on several other works, including the Acts of the Apostles, the Pseudo-Clementine *Homilies* and *Recognitions* (third and fourth century, respectively), the lost Syriac translation of the Acts of Peter (uncertain date), and the Syriac Teaching of Shimeon Kepha in Rome (fifth or sixth century—the end of which appears as ch. 13 in this volume). The text as we have it may date from the sixth or seventh century, and the author and place of origin are unknown.

The Petrine martyrdom section of this history is largely a resume of earlier renditions of Peter's passion, especially the Martyrdom of Peter. The primary elements of ascetical preaching, angry and scheming husbands, and eventual crucifixion are present. The text does contain some interesting characteristics of its own, however.

(1) The first of these is the apostle's name. There is a preference for identifying him as Shimeon Kepha, instead of Peter. Martyrdom accounts in Greek and Latin tend to avoid Peter's other biblical name, Simon, probably because his primary antagonist in many of these texts is another Simon, Simon the sorcerer. In Syriac, the two can be distinguished by the use of the letter *Shin* ("sh") for Shimeon, but *Semkat* ("s") for Simon. Indeed, in the postscript of this text we see the magician's name with *Semkat* (ܣܝܡܘܢ).

(2) Another notable detail is the use of the term "Christian." Xanthippe is explicitly called a Christian, and the conspiracy against Shimeon is hatched because he had provoked sexual renunciation *and* because "he had made all of Rome Christian" (§30). This designation does not appear in many other versions of the story.

(3) The author also expands on the famous scene of Shimeon's vision of Christ. While other accounts typically provide a brief dialogue—Peter asks Jesus where he is going, and Jesus responds that he is going to Rome to be crucified again—here Jesus speaks at length about the centrality of suffering. This is what Shimeon must primarily do in Jesus's place, if he can overcome his weak nature.

(4) The author interrupts the climactic part of the story after Shimeon's arrest by inserting the ordination and teaching of Linus as the apostle's successor, thus establishing the line of episcopal authority. This requires the assumption of a chronological gap between Shimeon's imprisonment and execution that is not evident in other accounts.

(5) The Clementine postscript includes some intriguing claims about Clement's connection to Peter and Simon, his alleged authorial and translation work (the suggestion of his authorship is a clear anachronism), and his allegedly misguided desire to be bishop of Rome. In Pseudo-Abdias, *Pass. Pet.* 15, by contrast, Clement is specifically identified as Peter's legitimate successor.

This text is the work of the same hand that produced the Syriac History of the Holy Apostle Paul (ch. 8 in this volume), for the style is consistent and the two works are transmitted together in the manuscripts. Unfortunately, the Pauline text provides no further clues to a more precise date or place of production, and the fact that there is no reference to Clement at the end of that text is further indication of the imprecise nature of traditions about authorship.

Text

The version of the text translated here is attested by a single manuscript from Kirkūk, Iraq, perhaps from the Monastery of Mār Thomas. Because the East Syrian Christians of Kirkūk in the eighteenth and nineteenth centuries were reportedly Nestorians, this text is sometimes called a "Nestorian" text in the secondary literature; but there is nothing distinctly "Nestorian" about it. It was made available by Archbishop Khayyāt of Diyarbekh to Ignazio Guidi, who in turn permitted Paul Bedjan to publish an edition of the text.

The translation is from the Bedjan edition, supplemented by Guidi, who later published several additions based on his reading of the manuscript. These additions are printed in italics in the translation and marked off with double square brackets in the Syriac text. This is the first translation available in any modern language. Another English translation is anticipated from F. Stanley Jones but has not yet appeared.

There exists another unedited Syriac text that could be confused with the History of Shimeon Kepha, because it has been identified by a similar title. It is preserved in two manuscripts in the British Museum (Add. 12172 and Add. 14732), and a French translation was published in 1898 by

François Nau. According to Jones, it is the martyrdom section of the Syriac translation of the Acts of Peter.[1]

Select Bibliography

Baumstark, Anton. Pages 40–44 in *Die Petrus- und Paulusacten in der litterarischen Überlieferung der syrischen Kirche.* Leipzig: Harrassowitz, 1902.

Bedjan, Paul, ed. "History of Shimeon Kepha the Chief of the Apostles" (in Syriac). Pages 29–33 in *Acta martyrum et sanctorum.* Leipzig: Harrassowitz, 1890.

Guidi, Ignazio. "Bemerkungen zum ersten Bande der syrischen Acta Martyrum et Sanctorum," *ZDMG* 46 (1892): 744–46.

Jones, F. Stanley, trans. "History of Simon Cephas, the Chief of the Apostles." In *New Testament Apocrypha: More Noncanonical Scriptures.* Edited by Tony Burke and Brent E. Landau. Grand Rapids: Eerdmans, forthcoming.

Peeters, Paul. "Notes sur la légende des apôtres S. Pierre et S. Paul dans la littérature syrienne." *AnBoll* 21 (1902): 121–40.

1. François Nau, "La version syriaque inédite des martyres de S. Pierre, S. Paul et S. Luc d'après un manuscrit du dixième siècle," *ROC* 3 (1898): 39–57.

ܠܣܗܕܘܬܐ ܕܫܡܥܘܢ ܒܪܨܒܥܐ ܪܫܐ ܕܟܗ̈ܢܐ[1]

29. [29] ܘܐܬܬܚܕܘ ܣܓܝ̈ܐܐ ܡܢ ܡܕܝ̈ܢܬܐ ܘܡܢ ܚܩ̈ܠܐ. ܘܟܕ (ܫܡܥܘܢ ܒܪܨܒܥܐ) ܚܒܝܫܐ ܒܬܪܘܢܘܬܐ
ܘܒܠܒܗ ܐܝܟܢܐ. ܘܗܟܢ ܠܘܩܒܠ ܟܠܐܙܐ ܕܡܘܬܐ: ܐܦ ܣܓܝ̈ܐܐ ܡܢ ܒܠܥܕ ܕܫܡܗ: [30] ܘܡܢܗ
ܒܡܠܟܘܬܗ ܕܡܪܢ. ܒܬܪ ܗܠܝܢ ܐܬ̈ܐ ܠܐܬܪ̈ܝܢ ܢܦܩܘܢ ܘܐܬܪܘܦܣܘ ܗܓܡܘܢܐ ܘܐܬܪܝܢ ܕܪܘܚܗ. ܗܠܝܢ
ܡܫܡ̈ܫܢܐ: ܐܬܪܘܦܣܐ ܘܡܢܕܪܢܐ [ܘܡܢܕܪܘܣܐ؟]: ܘܐܦܠ ܘܪܘܙܚܝܐ. ܘܗܡܢ ܒܡܪܢ ܡܫܝܚܐ: ܘܐܝܟ
ܢܗܘܘܢ ܒܚܝܡܢܘܬܐ. [[ܘܗܘܢ ܒܪܚܡܬܗܘܢ ܘܠܐ ܢܫܒܘܩ ܠܘܬ ܠܒܪܗܘܢ ܕܗܓܡܘܢܐ.[2]]] ܘܡܪܝ ܪܒܐ ܗܘܐ
ܠܗܘܢ ܘܡܒܝܢ ܗܘܐ ܠܗܘܢ. ܘܩܡ ܠܡܩܒܠܘܗܝ ܕܝܠܗ ܠܐܬܪܐ ܐܪ̈ܥܬܐ ܘܐܬܐ. ܘܡܛܠ ܕܟܠܐ ܫܡܥܘܢ ܐܪ̈ܥܬܐ.
ܘܐܪܙ ܐܝܟ ܗܓܡܘܢܐ ܘܠܐ ܠܘܬ ܢܐܪ̈ܥܬܐ ܟܠܐ ܗܘ ܒܪܫܝܬܐ. ܡܛܠ ܕܐܦ ܐܫܡܥ ܘܠܘܬ ܐܪ̈ܥܬܐ ܟܠܐܘ:
ܟܡܢ ܐܬܛܠܒ: ܘܟܠܗ ܒܡܘܙܐ ܐܘܡܝ. ܗܢܝܢ ܕܝܢ ܡܫܡܫܢ̈ܐ ܗܘܝܢ ܒܡܪܢ: ܘܗܡ ܟܠܟܘܢ ܕܢܫܡܥܘܢ ܟܠ
ܕܐܬܐ ܟܠܗܘܢ: ܘܠܘܬ ܠܐ ܢܗܘܘܢ ܒܫܡܗ.

30. ܘܠܘܬ ܐܢܫܐ ܕܫܡܥܘ ܒܫܡܠܦܐ ܐܢܫܐܬܐ ܘܐܘܟܠܝܢܘܗ [ܘܐܟܠܝܢܘܗ؟] ܘܫܡܥܘ ܕܡܢ: ܐܪܟܢ
ܟܠܐ ܫܡܥܘܢ ܒܪܨܒܥܐ ܒܡ ܡܠܘܬܐ ܐܡܝܢܬܐ: ܕܢܫܒܘܩ ܡܢܗ ܡܟܠܐ ܕܟܠܗ. ܐܦ ܗܘ ܫܡܠ ܠܗ ܒܚܝܡܢܘܬܐ.
ܘܐܬܡܟܟ ܒܟܠܗ ܣܡܠܐ: ܘܟܕ ܠܫܡܠܗ ܠܫܡܥܘܢ ܡܛܠ ܐܢܫܐ ܕܗܘܐ ܒܪܫܝܬܐ. ܐܦ ܓܒܪܐ

1. Single brackets and parentheses are reproduced from the Bedjan edition, and the superscript numbers in brackets indicate the page numbers in that edition. The double square brackets indicate additions by Guidi.

2. From Greek ἡγεμών.

History of Shimeon Kepha the Chief of the Apostles

29. Many of the Jews and gentiles became disciples, and Shimeon Kepha built churches in Rome and in all of Italy. He multiplied the teaching in the region of Rome, and many from the household of Caesar also believed in the teaching of our Lord. After them came two wives of Agrippinus[1] the prefect and two of his concubines. They were named Agrippina, Charithna,[2] Aphia,[3] and Darousina.[4] They believed in our Lord Jesus, and Shimeon captured their souls with holiness[5] *and established in their mind that they would not go up again to the bed of the prefect.* Agrippinus began persecuting and harassing them, and he ordered his servants to see where they were going to and coming from. He learned that they were going unto Shimeon, and the prefect warned them not to go to that Christian again, "Because if I hear that you are going to him again, I will kill you and burn him with fire." But they were strengthened in our Lord, and the Lord put it in their hearts that they could endure anything that might happen to them. And still they were not living with Agrippinus.

30. And also a woman named Xanthippe, the wife of Albinus—a friend of Caesar—went to Shimeon Kepha with the other noble women, so that they might hear from him the word of God. And she also remained with him in holiness.[6] Her husband was filled with rage and sought to kill Shimeon, because his wife was a Christian.[7] Many men with their wives

1. He is called Agrippa in the other texts in this volume.

2. Bedjan adds "(or Charithounia?)." This is one of several places in the edition where Bedjan proposes an alternative Syriac form of the name, and in each case I will note the alternative in a footnote. This name is given as Ikaria in Mart. Pet. 1.4 and Eucharia in Pseudo-Linus, *Mart. Pet.* 2.2.

3. Euphemia/Eufemia in Mart. Pet. 1.4; Pseudo-Linus, *Mart. Pet.* 2.2.

4. Doris in Mart. Pet. 1.4; Dionis in Pseudo-Linus, *Mart. Pet.* 2.2.

5. That is, sexual chastity.

6. Again, sexual chastity from her husband is implied.

7. Notable here is the direct correlation between Xanthippe's renunciation of sex and her identity as a Christian.

ܗܫܬܐ ܟܕ ܢܫܐ ܐܬܐܡܪܘ ܗܘܘ ܡܢ ܙܘܥܐ ܕܢܦܩܘܢ ܠܠܒܪ. ܘܐܬܐܙܝ ܐܘܠܟܣܘܣ ܟܕ ܦܛܪܘܣ ܕܐܬܡܪܢܝ ܠܡܦܩ: ܘܢܦܩܘܗܝ ܠܫܡܥܘܢ. ܟܕ ܕܝܢ ܕܢܦܩ ܠܬܪܥܐ ܕܡܕܝܢܬܐ ܕܪܗܘܡܝ: ܚܙܐ ܐܝܟ ܠܡܪܢ ܡܫܝܚ. ܘܡܗܠܟ ܒܫܒܝܠܐ ܘܐܘܪܥܗ ܠܫܡܥܘܢ؛ ܘܟܕ ܠܐ ܡܛܝܐ ܐܢܬ: ܐܡܪܐ ܡܪܝ ܐܢܬ: ܠܐܝܟܐ ܕܐܙܠ؟

31. [31] ܬܘܒ ܕܝܢ ܦܛܪܘܣ ܐܙܠ ܕܢܦܩ ܘܚܙܐ ܕܗܘ ܢܚܬ ܠܒܪ ܡܢ ܟܘܒܐ ܕܢܦܩܘܢ ܘܐܡܪ ܠܬܠܡܝܕܘܗܝ: ܐܚܝ ܠܐ ܗܘܐ ܠܝ ܕܐܙܠ. ܟܕ ܡܠܟܘܗܝ ܘܐܦܝܣܘܗܝ ܘܟܝܣܘܗܝ ܗܝܢ: ܩܡ ܘܢܦܩ ܠܒܪܩܘܗܝ ܘܢܦܩ ܠܗ ܒܟܢܘܫܬܗ. ܘܐܦ ܠܐ ܐܘܪܚ ܠܗ: ܡܫܝܚ ܕܡܪܢ ܕܟܠܗ ܐܬܚܘܝ ܗܘܐ.

ܘܐܬܚܙܝ ܠܗ ܕܡܘܬܗ ܕܦܛܪܘܣ ܕܟܪܝܢ ܕܐܬܐ ܠܡܣܒܠܗ: ܘܫܡܥ ܟܠ ܡܠܘܗܝ ܡܢܗܐ: ܟܕ ܗܘܐ ܛܘܦܣܐ[3] ܕܗܘ ܐܙܕܩܦ ܡܢ ܡܬܩܝܢܐ. ܘܐܬܬܙܝܥ ܫܡܥܘܢ ܘܢܦܠ ܠܗ ܟܠ ܐܦܘܗܝ ܟܕ ܙܐܬ ܘܐܡܪ ܠܗ: ܡܪܝ ܗܘ ܠܐܝܟܐ ܕܟܕ ܡܢ ܡܛܝܐ ܕܐܢܬ ܡܬܕܒܪ ܐܢܬ: ܕܡܘܬܐ ܗܘܐ ܕܡܬܚܙܝܐ ܠܟ ܐܘܪܚܐ ܡܛܝܐ ܐܢܬ؟

ܘܐܡܪ ܠܗ ܡܪܢ ܠܫܡܥܘܢ: ܕܐܢܐ ܡܢܟ ܩܘܪܒܐ ܕܟܠ ܡܘܬܐ ܕܙܕܩܐ ܡܫܒܚܐ: ܘܗܘ ܥܒܕܐ ܘܡܘܬܗ ܠܗܘܢ ܛܘܦܣܐ. ܕܐܡܪܐ ܕܟܕ ܠܐ ܚܙܐ ܐܢܐ ܡܬܟܠܡ ܚܝܐ ܕܝܠܟܘܢ: ܕܐܦ ܐܢܬܘܢ ܠܡܛܠܗܘܢ ܢܫܡܥܘܢ ܠܚܝ̈ܐ ܚܕܬܐ ܕܡܬܡܠܟܝܢ. ܗܘܐ ܕܝܢ ܡܫܝܚ ܕܚܝܠܬܗ ܘܕܡܬܝܠ ܒܡܫܝܚܘܬܐ ܕܟܠܐ ܐܚܝܕܬܗܘܢ: ܘܠܐ ܐܬܚܫܒܬܘܢ ܟܕ ܚܝܝܢ ܕܐܬܬܥܝܪܘܢ ܚܝܐ ܕܚܝܠ ܗܟܢ ܠܡܫܝܚܐ: ܐܬܬܐ ܕܪܘܚܐ ܕܐܬܝܠܕ ܐܚܕ. ܕܟܕ ܐܬܬܥܝܪܘܢ ܘܠܐ ܐܬܚܫܒܘܢ ܡܢ ܚܝܐ ܕܚܠܦ.

ܟܕ ܗܟܢ ܫܡܥ ܦܛܪܘܣ ܪܒܐ ܐܬܐܘܢ: ܘܠܡܪܢ ܡܫܒܚ ܗܘܐ ܘܐܡܪ: ܡܫܝܚ ܕܡܠܟܐ ܫܡܝܐ

3. From Greek τύπος.

were also sanctified from sexual relations,[8] so that they might serve God. And Albinus conspired with the prefect that they would speak to Caesar and kill Shimeon, because, "He has made all of Rome Christian, and has separated our wives from us." But Xanthippe heard this and made it known to Shimeon, "Unless you depart, how will you preach the word of God?"

31. But the blessed Peter perceived that the time had come at which he [Peter] would depart to our Lord by death on account of him [Christ].[9] He said to his disciples, "My brothers and sisters,[10] it is not fitting that I should flee." But after they exhorted and persuaded and prevailed upon him greatly, he arose, changed his clothes, and set out alone. And he did not notice that anyone was with him, because it was the dead of night.

Then the likeness of our Savior, as he had been in the flesh, appeared to him and came before him. He was carrying a cross upon his shoulder, indicating how he had been crucified by the Jews. Shimeon was disturbed and fell down on his face before him. Trembling, he said to him, "Why have you been led from the right hand of God[11] to manifest this humble form on earth?"[12]

Our Lord said to Shimeon, "I endured death by crucifixion for the salvation of all. In this I perfected and gave to you (pl.) a model, so that just as I, although not guilty, accepted the pain of the cross, you (pl.) also may perfect your souls by sufferings for the sake of the truth of my teaching. But because I have seen that you are still limited by the weakness of your nature and did not learn by my sufferings that you will be perfected by sufferings on behalf of divine things, I have come to suffer a second time. Perhaps you (pl.) will be perfected and will not become weary from the sufferings for my sake."

When the great Peter heard these things, he repented, and entreating our Lord he said, "Because I learned from you that this is your will, I will

8. The term can also mean *marriage*, but the issue is clearly that they are giving up sexual activity even within the context of marriage.

9. The Syriac here is somewhat obscure. This passage may indicate that through Peter's death the Lord would die again. Here Peter may be anticipating his role as the stand-in for Christ's second death, unlike other texts in which Peter realizes this only after Christ speaks to the apostle as he is fleeing the city. Cf. e.g., Mart. Pet. 1.6; Pseudo-Linus, *Mart. Pet.* 2.6; Pseudo-Abdias, *Pass. Pet.* 3.19.

10. The text states "brothers," but the context makes it clear that the group includes both men and women.

11. Cf. Rom 8:34; Eph 1:19–21.

12. Cf. Phil 2:6–8.

ܕܗܘ ܙܟܝܢ: ܚܣܕܘܬܐ ܐܚܝܕ ܢܦܫ ܣܠܩܝܢ. ܘܫܘܒܚܐ ܕܫܘܒܚ ܪܒܐ ܕܫܘܠܛ ܠܟܠܗܘܢ: ܒܥܠܡܐ ܕܡܪܝܐ ܚܣܩܐ ܕܣܠܩܝܢ ܦܢܐ ܐܢܐ. ܘܡܚܣܕܐ [32] ܕܡܘܬܐ ܗܘ ܠܐܦܝ ܥܡܐ ܡܬܟܒܐ ܗܘܐ.

ܘܦܢܝܘܗ ܠܘܬ ܟܠܐ ܐܢܫܐ. ܘܐܬܬܟܝܢ ܟܠܗܘܢ ܡܢܝܢ ܘܚܕܐ ܘܫܡܥܘ. ܘܟܪܙܘ ܟܠܗܘܢ ܠܐܢܫܐ ܛܒ. ܐܡܪ ܠܗܘܢ: ܠܐ ܬܬܪܐ ܠܟܘܢ ܐܢܫ: ܙܟܝܢ ܕܡܪܢ ܝܫܘܥ. ܐܠܐ ܕܝܢ ܐܬܬܪܥܘ ܒܗܝܡܢܘܬܐ ܗܘܐ ܕܡܫܠܡܝܢ: ܘܠܐ ܬܬܪܥܘܢ.

32. ܗܝܕܝܢ ܐܬܐ ܐܘܟܠܐ ܕܥܡܡ̈ܐ: ܘܐܚܕܘܗܝ ܠܫܡܥܘܢ ܘܐܫܠܡܘܗܝ ܠܘܬ ܩܣܪ. ܘܦܪܣܘ ܥܠܘܗܝ ܠܝܬܐ ܘܡܫܩܠܐ ܘܩܡ ܗܘܘ ܘܐܡܪܝܢ: ܡܢܐ ܐܚܪܢܐ ܗܘܐ ܫܡܥܘܢ ܥܒܕܘ ܕܠܐܠܗܐ? ܘܡܢܐ ܒܫܡܐ ܗܢܐ ܥܒܕ ܒܡܒܝܢܘܬܐ ܗܘܐ? ܗܝܕܝܢ ܡܪܢ ܫܡܥܘܢ ܒܫܡܥܬܗ ܐܘܪܚ ܐܝܟܘ ܘܫܠܡ ܐܢܘܢ: ܘܡܪܐ ܐܢܘܢ ܐܝܟ ܟܠܡܐ. ܗܝܕܝܢ ܐܘܟܠܘܗܝ ܠܫܡܥܘܢ ܘܢܣܒܘܗܝ ܒܝܬ ܐܣܝܪ̈ܐ.

33. ܒܝ ܫܡܫ ܡܕܒܪܢܘܬܐ ܕܦܘܪܩܢܐ ܒܬܪܥܘܬܐ ܡܕܝܢܬܐ ܒܥܙܝܙ ܘܫܡܥ ܗܢܝ: ܘܟܕ ܐܪܟܘܢ ܕܡܪܝܐ ܕܥܡܘܬܐ ܕܙܟܝܐ ܢܦܫ ܠܐܠܗܐ: ܒܝܘܡ ܗܢܐ ܠܠܝܐ ܡܫܡܫܢܐ: ܘܟܒܪ ܐܦܣܩܘܐ ܣܠܩܘܗܝ ܒܬܪܥܘܬܐ. ܘܪܗܛܘ ܘܦܩܕܘ: ܕܢܦܩ ܒܝܕܐ ܡܠܟܝܢ ܕܫܡܥܘܢ ܡܢܗ ܕܡܠܟ ܗܘܐ.

34. ܗܝܕܝܢ ܢܛܪܝ ܩܣܪ ܗܘܐ ܐܦܘܦܣܝܣ[4] ܠܟܠܗܘܢ ܕܥܡܘܬܐ ܕܪܘܡܝܐ ܢܒܘܐ. ܘܟܕ ܐܦܣܩܘܗܝ ܘܐܝܬܘܗܝ ܩܕܡܐ ܠܥܡܘܕܘ: ܚܝܢ ܘܐܘܕܝ ܠܡܪܢ. ܘܫܡܥܘܢ ܗܘܐ ܠܡܦܩܘܗܝ ܘܐܡܪ: ܒܟܠܐ ܡܢܝܢ ܕܐܝܬ ܕܙܟܐ ܐܢܐ: ܗܟܢܐ ܢܦܩܘܢ. ܘܠܐ ܒܗܘ ܢܚܐ ܙܒܐ ܕܡܪܢ: ܕܐܙܕܩܦ ܥܡ ܬܪܝܬܐ. ܡܛܠ [33] ܗܘ ܠܟ:

4. From Greek ἀπόφασις.

joyfully lay down my life for your sake. The debt of your love is clearly great forever, and how much can I repay in these sufferings for your sake?" Immediately the likeness was taken up toward heaven.

Peter returned to the brothers and sisters and told them what he had seen and heard, and the brothers and sisters were exceedingly sad. He said to them, "Do not feel sorrow, my brothers and sisters. Let the will of our Lord be done. But be strong in this faith that you have received, and you will not fall away."

32. Then four men came and arrested Shimeon, so that they might take him to Caesar. And all the people hastened, rich and poor, and cried out, saying, "What offense did Shimeon, the servant of God, commit? And what evil did he do in this city?" Then my lord[13] Shimeon raised his hand gently and silenced them. And he sent them away, each one to his home.[14] Then they took Shimeon and threw him into prison.

33. He had administered the oversight of salvation in the city of Rome for twenty-five years. When he perceived that he would soon glorify God by death on a cross, he summoned Linus the deacon and made him bishop of Rome in his place.[15] He admonished and ordered him to teach in the church everything that he had heard him teaching.

34. Then Nero Caesar pronounced a sentence upon him that he would die by death on a cross. When they brought forth and prepared the cross to crucify him, he rejoiced and praised our Lord. He beseeched his crucifiers and said, "I ask of you that, as I wish, they may crucify me in this way, and not in the great sign of my Lord, for he was crucified upright.[16] I fear that if I am nailed on a cross like he was, by the similarity I might presumptuously

---

13. The term *marí* ("my lord") is frequently used in Syriac literature to refer to holy people.

14. Cf. John 7:53.

15. This passage provides a foundation story for the Roman episcopate and its claims to apostolic succession. The ordination of Linus by Peter is also recounted in the Liberian Catalog from 354 CE (*Chronica minora saec. IV. V. VI. VII.*, ed. T. Mommsen, MGH.AA 9 [Berlin: Weidmann, 1892], 73); Irenaeus (*Haer.* 3.3.3)—although Irenaeus states that Peter and Paul together ordained Linus; Eusebius (*Hist. eccl.* 5.6.1); Hist. Paul 12; and Teach. Shim. 6. Cf. Pseudo-Abdias, *Pass. Pet.* (§15); the apocryphal Epistle of Clement to James (§2); and Tertullian (*Praescr.* 32), where Clement is identified as the one ordained by Peter as the second bishop of Rome.

16. The upright cross is identified by Peter as the sign of the Lord.

ܕܕܡ ܒܐܬܘܬܗ ܕܡܫܝܚܐ ܐܠܗܢ: ܡܫܝܚܐ ܐܬܚܙܝ ܡܢ ܫܡܝܐ ܘܒܗ ܒܝܘܡܐ. ܐܠܐ[5] ܟܕ ܒܠܒܪ ܙܒܢ ܡܬܕܡܪܬܐ: ܡܠܟܘܬܗ ܐܬܐ ܠܫܡܝܐ ܘܫܠܡ. ܘܫܡܥܘ ܘܟܢܫܘ ܫܡܥܘܢ ܠܒܘܣܡܐ ܕܪܐܙܐ ܕܒܗܘܢ ܩܛܠܐ ܕܫܦܝܪܐ ܕܠܗܐ ܡܠܟܐ ܐܠܗܢ. ܩܕܡܝܐ ܕܝܢ ܒܗܝܢ ܠܗ ܐܝܟ ܕܝܠܐ: ܟܕ ܚܙܝܢ ܕܗܘܝܐ ܡܠܟܘܬܗ ܥܡܪ ܕܚܝܠ.

35. ܘܟܕ ܫܠܡܬ ܢܦܫܗ ܕܫܡܥܘܢ: ܡܢ ܗܘܐ ܡܪܩܠܠܘܣ: ܟܕ ܟܬܒ ܠܐ ܐܬܡܠܟ: ܘܐܚܬܗ ܠܦܓܪܗ ܡܢ ܙܩܝܦܐ: ܘܐܣܚܝܗ. ܘܡܫܚܗ ܚܢܘܛܬܐ ܕܡܘܪܐ[6] ܘܒܠܣܡܐ: ܣܡܗ. ܘܣܡܗ ܒܓܘܪܢܐ[7] ܕܟܐܦܐ ܢܨܝܒܬܐ: ܘܟܪܟܗ ܒܥܛܦܐ ܫܦܝܪܐ. ܘܣܡܗ ܒܒܝܬ ܩܒܘܪܐ ܕܝܠܗ.

36. ܘܗܘܝܐ ܐܬܬܣܝܡ ܒܚܠܠܗ ܕܓܘܦܐ ܡܢ ܗܫܐ: ܒܟܪܟܐ ܕܪܘܡܝ̈ܐ: ܟܕ ܓܒܠܘܗ ܕܡܫܝܚܐ ܡܪܢ. ܕܠܗ ܫܘܒܚܐ: ܘܥܠܝܗ ܬܫܒܘܚܬܐ ܠܥܠܡ ܥܠܡܝܢ. ܐܡܝܢ.

37. [[ܡܠܟܘܬܐ ܕܝܢ ܕܐܠܗܐ ܘܦܛܪܘܣ ܐܬܓܠܝܬ ܗܘܐ. ܘܗܘ ܕܝܢ ܟܕ ܫܡܥܘܢ ܘܫܩܠܗ. ܘܗܘ ܥܡ ܐܚܘܗܝ ܕܒܥܬܐ. ܡܢ ܒܬܪ ܟܠ ܫܢܝܐ.[8] ܘܗܘ ܐܬܠܝܘ ܠܡܫܝܚܐ ܕܐܬܩܛܠ ܡܫܝܚܐ. ܘܡܫܒܚܝܢ ܘܐܡܪܝܢ.

5. From Greek ἀλλά.

6. From Greek μύρρα.

7. From Greek γοῦρνα.

8. Guidi incorrectly produces the form as ܚܡܘܣܐ.

claim some equality to him.[17] But if I am crucified with my head downward, then I will remember his sufferings for my sake. My mouth and my eyes will kiss the places of the nails with which the feet of the body of God the Word were crucified.[18] Then the crucifiers did to him as he wished and rejoiced that he had thus doubled his sentence.[19]

35. When the soul of the holy man went up, Marcellus approached, although he had not consulted with anyone. He took Shimeon down from the cross and washed him. Then he prepared a mixture of spices of myrrh and aloe and embalmed him. He placed him in a splendid stone coffin[20] purchased at a high price and laid him in his own burial place.

36. Thus was fulfilled the crowning of my lord the blessed Shimeon, the firstborn of the apostles, through the blessing of Christ our Lord. Let there be glory to him and upon us who love him forever and ever. Amen.

37. *But Clement was a disciple of Peter, and he debated with Simon and defeated him.*[21] *And he translated the letter of the Hebrews from Hebrew into Greek.*[22] *He also wrote histories of the twelve apostles*[23] *and of the seventy-two,*[24] *and he composed many books,*[25] *although he erred in his desire for the*

---

17. That is, Peter fears that even being crucified in the same form as Christ will be presumptuous.

18. This imagery suggests that Peter wanted to be crucified not only upside down but also with his face turned toward the cross, instead of facing out.

19. The Syriac here is somewhat unclear, but it appears that the crucifiers are rejoicing that Peter has increased his suffering by being crucified upside down.

20. Literally, a "vessel" or "urn."

21. Direct conflict between Clement and Simon Magus is not otherwise attested.

22. The tradition that Paul wrote Hebrews in Hebrew and had it translated into Greek by Luke or Clement goes back at least as early as Origen of Alexandria, according to Eusebius of Caesarea (*Hist. eccl.* 6.25). Eusebius considers Clement the more likely translator, based on similarities in style and content between Hebrews and 1 Clement (*Hist. eccl.* 3.38).

23. It is unclear if the author of this postscript counts among these "histories" the larger cycle of apostolic "histories" of which this Petrine text is the first part.

24. In Luke 10:1, Jesus sends out seventy or seventy-two disciples to preach the gospel. The Greek manuscripts offer both variants. The Syriac Peshitta gives the number as seventy, while Jerome favored seventy-two in the Latin Vulgate. Various authors attempted to construct the list of names, including the third or fourth-century author of the Pseudo-Hippolytan *On the Seventy Apostles*. In the thirteenth century, Solomon of Basra (*Lib. apis* 49) gives a list of the seventy names and notes that Luke and Mark were chosen from among them to write gospels.

25. Early Christian texts ascribed to Clement include 1 and 2 Clement, two letters

ܘܡܠܐ̈ܟܐ ܣܓܝ̈ܐܐ ܗܘܘ ܐܦ ܐܬܚܙܝܘ ܒܪܘܡܐ ܪܘܡܝܐ܀ ܡܫܒܚܝܢ ܠܡܫܝܚܐ ܘܝܕܥܝܢ ܦܛܪܘܣ ܡܫܝܚܐ.
ܘܢܬܠܘܢ ܟܠ ܬܫܒܘܚܬܐ ܚܝܐ ܩܕܝܫܐ ܐܒܘܗܝ. ܐܡܝܢ.]]

episcopacy. His history of the glorious Peter the apostle has come to an end. May his prayer be upon the scribe, the presbyter Abraham, a sinner. Amen.

---

addressed to virgins, and the *Homilies* and *Recognitions*. None of these texts, however, can be historically linked to a first-century disciple of Peter.

Part 2. The Martyrdom of Paul

5. Martyrdom of the Holy Apostle Paul in Rome

CANT 211.v / *BHG* 1451–1452

Contents

The story opens with Luke and Titus, two of Paul's closest disciples, waiting for him in Rome. Upon arrival, Paul rents a dwelling outside the city and begins preaching freely. This is presumably meant to connect this text with the end of Acts (28:16–31), where a similar story is told. The apostle's preaching attracts large crowds, including a young man named Patroclus, a servant of the Emperor Nero. Like the young man Eutyches in Acts 20, Patroclus falls asleep while listening to Paul's preaching and plummets from an open window to his death. Nero hears of this tragic event and is greatly grieved. Meanwhile, Paul has already raised Patroclus from the dead, and the young man returns to the service of the emperor. Nero asks how this came about, and Patroclus says that he was raised by Jesus Christ, the king of all the ages. Nero is outraged that Patroclus would follow a rival and soon discovers that several of his chief bodyguards are also followers of that eternal king. He therefore orders the Christians to be rounded up and killed.

Paul is among those arrested. Nero quickly recognizes that he is the leader among the Christians, and he accuses Paul of being a traitor by recruiting soldiers for a rival king. Paul confirms that he follows Christ as the true king and is condemned to death by beheading. Many Christians are killed, and finally a crowd of Romans gathers before the imperial palace to call upon Nero to stop these executions. The apostle, however, still must face his fate. Before going to his death, he promises Nero that he will come back from the dead to prove that he is still alive in his king Jesus Christ. Two soldiers named Longinus and Cescus offer to free Paul in exchange for their salvation, but Paul refuses to be a deserter. Two other soldiers arrive from Nero to ensure that Paul is dead. They are foils to Longinus and Cescus, for their response to Paul's preaching is cynicism.

For Longinus and Cescus, however, Paul tells them to come to his tomb the next day and meet Titus and Luke, who will baptize them. Paul says a brief prayer in Hebrew and is then decapitated.

Nero hears this news, but while he is still pondering it in the presence of members of his court, Paul appears to them. He pronounces the judgment of God in retaliation for Nero's cruelty and the spilling of Christian blood. The emperor immediately releases all the Christian prisoners, including Patroclus.

At dawn the next morning, Longinus and Cescus come to the tomb of Paul and see Titus and Luke with Paul praying in the midst of them. They are taken aback by this sight, and Titus and Luke begin to flee in fear of their lives. However, the soldiers explain why they are there, and the two disciples of Paul give them the seal in Christ.

Literary Background

Paul's letters and the information in the Acts of the Apostles do not address the end of the apostle's life. The passing reference in 2 Tim 4:6–8 that Paul is "already being poured out as a drink offering" offers no additional help. Many critical scholars doubt that 2 Timothy is the work of the apostle, and even if it was written by a close disciple of Paul, the epistle still tells us nothing about Paul's actual death. Later traditions and legends would serve to fill in this gap in the evidence. The Martyrdom of Paul is one of the earliest examples of this. The text circulated independently but is also transmitted as the final act in the broader Acts of Paul. The Martyrdom of Paul is thus equivalent to Acts of Paul 14, although Glenn Snyder[1] has argued that the Martyrdom of Paul may (and he argues should) be studied on its own.

The precise date of this text is unknown, and here the connection of the Martyrdom of Paul to the larger Acts of Paul becomes important. The Acts of Paul is typically dated to the end of the second century based upon two main factors. First, many scholars consider the relation of the Acts of Paul to the Acts of Peter. Some argue that parts of the Acts of Paul outside the martyrdom account are dependent on the Acts of Peter. Since the late second century seems the earliest possible date for the latter text, it is also

1. Glenn Snyder, *Acts of Paul: The Formation of a Biblical Canon*, WUNT 2/352 (Tübingen: Mohr Siebeck, 2013).

the earliest possible date for the former. Second, Tertullian refers to a text called the Acts of Paul around the year 200. He states that a presbyter in Asia Minor had written a spurious work of this title out of love for Paul, but then this presbyter lost his position because the work had been used to justify the practice of women baptizing (*Bapt.* 17.5). This detail suggests that Tertullian has in mind a scene from another part of the Acts of Paul, namely the Acts of Paul and Thecla, in which Thecla baptizes herself in an arena. However, if we treat the Martyrdom of Paul as an independent text, then neither possible literary dependence on the Acts of Peter nor the reference in Tertullian is determinative of the date. Snyder has suggested a date for the martyrdom account as early as the reign of the Emperor Trajan (98–117 CE) based upon the anti-Neronian polemic, while Willy Rordorf et al.—who, it must be noted, treat the Martyrdom of Paul as part of the Acts of Paul—suggest a date around 150.

The author and location are also difficult to determine. Tertullian's presbyter likely has nothing to do with this text (*pace* Rordorf), but Asia Minor may still be its place of production. Indeed, Snyder has favorably compared the anti-imperial rhetoric in the Martyrdom of Paul to 1 Peter and Revelation, two texts connected to this region.

Like the Martyrdom of Peter, the Martyrdom of Paul was likely used for liturgical celebrations of the apostle's death based on its preservation in Latin, Syriac, Coptic, and Ethiopic translations. Beyond that it is difficult to say much about its early use and reception, except that as other texts in this volume attest, this account had significant influence over later traditions about Paul's execution.

Text

The Greek text survives in two papyrus fragments and three manuscripts. The papyri are Hamburg Pap. bil. 1 (ca. 300 CE) and Barcelona Palau-Ribes 18 (fifth century). The manuscripts are from the Monastery of St. John the Theologian in Patmos (MS 48; ninth century), the monastery of Vatopedi on Mount Athos (MS 79; tenth/eleventh century), and the municipal library in Ohrid, Macedonia (MS 44; eleventh century). This last text was discovered in 1962 and prompted a recent edition by Otto Zwierlein that incorporates all five textual witnesses and replaces the edition by Richard A. Lipsius. The translation is based upon this Zwierlein edition, and apart from Zwierlein's own translation into German, this is the only available translation based on the most recent edition of the text.

There is reportedly an edition by Rordorf in process for the Corpus Christianorum Series Apocryphorum, but it has not yet appeared.

Select Bibliography

Bremmer, Jan N., ed. *The Apocryphal Acts of Paul and Thecla*. Kampen: Kok Pharos, 1996.

Eastman, David L. *Paul the Martyr: The Cult of the Apostle in the Latin West*. WGRWSup 4. Atlanta: Society of Biblical Literature, 2011.

Elliott, J. K., trans. "Martyrdom of the Holy Apostle Paul." Pages 385–88 in *The Apocryphal New Testament*. Oxford: Clarendon, 1993.

Erbetta, Mario, trans. "Gli Atti di Paolo: Martirio." Pages 285–88 in *Atti e leggende*. Vol. 2 of *Gli apocrifi del Nuovo Testamento*. 2nd ed. Turin: Marietti, 1978.

Hennecke, Edgar, trans. "Martyrdom of the Holy Apostle Paul." Pages 260–63 in vol. 2 of *New Testament Apocrypha*. Edited by Wilhelm Schneemelcher. English trans. edited by R. McL. Wilson. 5th ed. Louisville: Westminster John Knox, 1993.

Lipsius, Richard A. and Max Bonnet, eds. Μαρτύριον τοῦ ἁγίου ἀποστόλου Παύλου. Pages 104–17 in vol. 1 of *Acta apostolorvm apocrypha post Constantinvm Tischendorf*. Leipzig: Mendelssohn, 1891. Repr., Hildesheim: Olms, 1972.

MacDonald, Dennis R. *The Legend and the Apostle: The Battle for Paul in Story and Canon*. Philadelphia: Westminster John Knox, 1983.

Moraldi, Luigi, trans. "Martirio di san Paolo apostolo." Pages 1125–30 in vol. 2 of *Apocrifi del Nuovo Testamento*. Turin: Unione, 1971.

Rordorf, Willy, Rodolphe Kasser, and Pierre Cherix, trans. "Actes de Paul." Pages 1115–25 and 1172–77 in vol. 1 of *Écrits apocryphes chrétiens*. Edited by François Bovon and Pierre Geoltrain. Pléiade 442. Paris: Gallimard, 1997.

Snyder, Glenn. *Acts of Paul: The Formation of a Biblical Canon*. WUNT 2/352. Tübingen: Mohr Siebeck, 2013.

Tajra, Harry W. *The Martyrdom of St. Paul: Historical and Judicial Context, Traditions, and Legends*. WUNT 2/67. Tübingen: Mohr Siebeck, 1994.

Vouaux, Léon, trans. "Séjour à Rome. Martyre." Pages 278–314 in *Les Actes de Paul et ses lettres apocryphes: Introduction, textes, traduction et commentaire*. Paris: Letouzey et Ané, 1913.

Zwierlein, Otto, ed. and trans. Μαρτύριον τοῦ ἁγίου Παύλου τοῦ ἀποστόλου ἐν Ῥώμῃ. Pages 426–49 in *Petrus in Rom: Die literarischen Zeugnisse*. 2nd ed. UALG 96. Berlin: de Gruyter, 2010.

Μαρτύριον τοῦ ἁγίου Παύλου τοῦ ἀποστόλου ἐν Ῥώμῃ

1. ἦσαν δὲ περιμένοντες τὸν Παῦλον ἐν τῇ Ῥώμῃ Λουκᾶς ἀπὸ Γαλλιῶν καὶ Τίτος ἀπὸ Δελματίας. οὓς ἰδὼν ὁ Παῦλος ἐχάρη, ὥστε ἔξω Ῥώμης ὅρριον μισθώσασθαι, ἐν ᾧ μετὰ τῶν ἀδελφῶν ἐδίδασκε τὸν λόγον τῆς ἀληθείας. διαβόητος δὲ ἐγένετο, καὶ ψυχαὶ πολλαὶ προσετίθεντο τῷ κυρίῳ, ὡς ἦχόν τινα ἐν τῇ Ῥώμῃ γενέσθαι καὶ προσιέναι αὐτῷ πλῆθος πολὺ ἐκ τῆς Καίσαρος οἰκίας καὶ πιστεύειν εὐθέως τῷ λόγῳ, ὡς εἶναι μεγάλην χαρὰν τῷ Παύλῳ καὶ τοῖς ἀκούουσιν. καί τις οἰνοχόος τοῦ Καίσαρος ὀνόματι Πάτροκλος ὀψίας πορευθεὶς εἰς τὸ ὅρριον οὐκ ἴσχυσεν εἰσελθεῖν πρὸς τὸν Παῦλον διὰ τὸν ὄχλον, ἀλλὰ καθίσας ἐπί τινα θυρίδα ὑψηλὴν ἤκουεν τὸν λόγον τοῦ θεοῦ. τοῦ δὲ πονηροῦ διαβόλου ζηλοῦντος τὴν ἐν κυρίῳ ἀγάπην καὶ τὴν τῶν ἀδελφῶν σωτηρίαν ὁ Πάτροκλος

Martyrdom of the Holy Apostle Paul in Rome

1. Luke, who had come from Gaul,[1] and Titus, who had come from Dalmatia, were awaiting Paul in Rome.[2] When Paul saw them he rejoiced and rented a barn outside Rome in which he was teaching the word of truth with the brothers and sisters.[3] He became famous, and many souls were being added to the Lord, so there was a certain sound going out in Rome. And a great crowd came out to him from the house of Caesar and immediately believed in the word,[4] so that there was great joy for Paul and those hearing. A certain cupbearer of Caesar, named Patroclus, came to the barn one evening but was not able to go in to Paul because of the crowd.[5] After sitting on a certain high window, he was hearing the word of God. But because the wicked devil was jealous of the love in the Lord and the salvation of the brothers and sisters, Patroclus dozed off, fell down from the

---

1. The connection between Paul's missionary circle and Gaul is probably related to the perceived ambiguity in 2 Tim 4:10, where Titus went to Dalmatia and Crescens went εἰς Γαλατίαν. The name Γαλατία (Galatia) was used in antiquity to refer to both Galatia, the eastern region of Paul's first missionary activity, and to Gaul. Some patristic authors assumed it meant the latter, and some manuscripts of 2 Timothy include the variant εἰς Γαλλίαν (Gallia)—no doubt meant to clarify that Crescens was in fact in Gaul. Ironically the strongest textual evidence and interpretative support for Crescens's Gallic mission come from the Greek East, not the Latin West. For more discussion of this debate, see David L. Eastman, *Paul the Martyr: The Cult of the Apostle in the Latin West*, WGRWSup 4 (Atlanta: Society of Biblical Literature, 2011), 124–26. The three primary manuscripts of our text all read ἀπο Γαλλιῶν *(from the Gallians* = Gaul). While the Latin translation (Pseudo-Linus, *Mart. Paul* 1) and one Coptic manuscript preserve the potentially ambiguous *Galatia*, there is no such ambiguity with the term *Gallia*.

2. Cf. 2 Tim 4:10–11.

3. Cf. Acts 28:16. The text literally says, "Men and brothers," but Paul is speaking to a mixed audience.

4. Phil 4:22.

5. Cf. Mark 2:4.

νυστάξας ἀπὸ τῆς θυρίδος, ἔπεσεν κάτω καὶ ἀπέπνευσεν, ὡς ἀποθανόντα αὐτὸν ταχέως ἀναγγελθῆναι τῷ Νέρωνι ὑπὸ τῶν οἰκετῶν.

συνιδὼν δὲ τῷ πνεύματι ὁ Παῦλος εἶπεν· ἄνδρες ἀδελφοί, ἔσχεν ὁ πονηρὸς τόπον, ὅπως ἡμᾶς πειράσῃ· ὑπάγετε ἔξω, καὶ εὑρήσετε παῖδα πεπτωκότα μέλλοντα ἐκπνέειν. τοῦτον ἐνέγκατε πρός με. καὶ ἀπελθόντες ἤνεγκαν αὐτῷ τὸν παῖδα. ἰδόντες δὲ οἱ ὄχλοι ἐταράχθησαν. καὶ εἶπεν ὁ Παῦλος· νῦν ἡμῶν ἡ πίστις φανήτω· δεῦτε πάντες, κλαύσωμεν πρὸς τὸν κύριον ἡμῶν Ἰησοῦν Χριστόν, ἵνα ζήσῃ οὗτος καὶ ἡμεῖς ἀνενόχλητοι μείνωμεν. καὶ πάντων εὐξαμένων πρὸς κύριον ἀνέστη ὁ παῖς καὶ ἀνέλαβεν τὸ πνεῦμα αὐτοῦ· καὶ καθιστάντες αὐτὸν ἀποπέμπουσιν μετὰ τῶν ἄλλων τῶν ἀπὸ τῆς οἰκίας τοῦ Καίσαρος.

2. ὁ δὲ Καῖσαρ ἀκούσας τὸν θάνατον τοῦ Πατρόκλου μεγάλως ἐλυπήθη καὶ ἐλθὼν ἀπὸ τοῦ βαλανείου ἄλλον ἐκέλευσεν στῆναι, ἐπὶ τοῦ οἴνου. οἱ δὲ παῖδες εἶπον αὐτῷ· Καῖσαρ, Πάτροκλος ζῇ καὶ ἕστηκεν ἐπὶ τῆς τραπέζης.

καὶ ὁ Καῖσαρ ἐκέλευσεν αὐτὸν εἰσελθεῖν. καὶ εἰσελθόντος αὐτοῦ εἶπεν· Πάτροκλε, ζῇς;

ὁ δὲ εἶπεν· ζῶ.

καὶ ὁ Καῖσαρ εἶπεν· καὶ τίς ὁ ποιήσας σε ζῆσαι;

φρονήματι δὲ πίστεως φερόμενος ὁ Πάτροκλος εἶπεν· Ἰησοῦς Χριστὸς ὁ βασιλεὺς τοῦ σύμπαντος κόσμου καὶ τῶν αἰώνων.

ὁ δὲ Καῖσαρ ἐταράχθη καὶ εἶπεν· ἐκεῖνος οὖν μέλλει βασιλεύειν τῶν αἰώνων, καὶ καταλύειν πάσας τὰς βασιλείας τὰς ὑπὸ τὸν οὐρανόν;

καὶ ἀποκριθεὶς ὁ Πάτροκλος εἶπεν· ναί, καὶ γὰρ αὐτὸς βασιλεύει ἐν οὐρανῷ καὶ ἐπὶ γῆς, Ἰησοῦς Χριστὸς, καὶ οὐ μόνον τὰς βασιλείας τὰς ὑπὸ τὸν οὐρανὸν καταλύει, ἀλλὰ πᾶσαν ἀρχὴν σκότους καὶ ἐξουσίαν θανάτου καὶ δύναμιν πονηράν. καὶ αὐτός ἐστι μόνος οὗ τῆς βασιλείας οὐκ ἔσται τέλος εἰς τοὺς αἰῶνας, καὶ οὐκ ἔστιν βασιλεία ἥτις διαφεύξεται αὐτόν.

ὁ δὲ ῥαπίσας εἰς τὸ πρόσωπον αὐτοῦ εἶπεν· Πάτροκλε, καὶ σὺ στρατεύει τῷ βασιλεῖ τούτῳ;

καὶ εἶπεν· ναί, καὶ γὰρ αὐτός μέ ἤγειρεν τεθνεῶτα.

window, and died.[6] It was quickly reported to Nero by his household servants that he had died.

Paul perceived it in his spirit and said, "Brothers and sisters, the evil one has had an opportunity to test us. Go outside, and you will find a youth who has just fallen and died. Bring him to me." They went out and brought the youth to him. Seeing this the crowds were troubled, but Paul said, "Now let our faith be seen. All of you come, and let us cry out to our Lord Jesus Christ, so that this youth may live and we may remain undisturbed." After they had all prayed to the Lord, the youth arose and regained his breath. They set him on a beast and sent him away with the others from the house of Caesar.

2. When Caesar heard about the death of Patroclus, he was deeply grieved. Having come back from the bath, he ordered another to take charge of the wine. But his servants said to him, "Caesar, Patroclus is alive and is standing at the table."

Caesar ordered him to come, and after he had come, he said, "Patroclus, are you alive?"

And Patroclus said, "I am alive."

Caesar said, "Who made you alive?"

Empowered by the strength of his faith, Patroclus said, "Jesus Christ, the king of the whole world and the ages."[7]

Caesar was troubled and said, "Is that one, then, going to rule throughout the ages and destroy all the kingdoms under heaven?"[8]

Patroclus answered and said, "Yes, for he rules in heaven and on earth, namely Jesus Christ. He destroys not only the kingdoms under heaven, but also every empire of darkness and the power of death and wicked authority.[9] He alone is the one whose kingdom will have no end forever, and there is no kingdom that will escape him."

But Nero struck him on the face and said, "Patroclus, are you also a soldier[10] of that king?"

And he said, "Yes, for he raised me from the dead."

---

6. This story has obvious connections to the account of Eutychus in Acts 20:7–12.

7. 1 Tim 1:17.

8. Cf. Dan 7:27.

9. 1 Cor 15:24–26.

10. The use of military language may be inspired by texts such as 1 Tim 1:18; 2 Tim 2:3, 4:7. See also Adolf von Harnack, *Militia Christi: Die christliche Religion und der Soldatenstand in den ersten drei Jahrhunderten* (Tübingen: Mohr, 1905).

τότε Ἰοῦστος ὁ πλατύπους καὶ Ὠρίων ὁ Καππάδοξ καὶ Ἥφαιστος ὁ Γαλάτης, οἱ πρῶτοι σωματοφύλακες Νέρωνος, εἶπον· καὶ ἡμεῖς ἐκείνῳ στρατευόμεθα τῷ αἰωνίῳ βασιλεῖ. ὁ δὲ Καῖσαρ συνέκλεισεν αὐτοὺς καὶ ἐβασάνισεν, οὓς ἐφίλει λίαν, καὶ ἔπεμψεν ζητεῖσθαι τοὺς τοῦ μεγάλου βασιλέως στρατιώτας καὶ προέθηκεν διάταγμα τοιοῦτον, ὥστε πάντας τοὺς εὑρισκομένους Χριστιανοὺς ἀναιρεῖσθαι.

3. καὶ δὴ ἐν τοῖς πολλοῖς ἄγεται καὶ ὁ Παῦλος δεδεμένος· ᾧ πάντες οἱ συνδεθέντες προσεῖχον, τί ἄρα ὁ Παῦλος ἀποκρίνεται, ὥστε νοῆσαι τὸν Καίσαρα, ὅτι ἐπὶ τῶν στρατοπέδων ἐστὶν αὐτός. καὶ εἶπεν αὐτῷ ὁ Νέρων· ἄνθρωπε τοῦ μεγάλου βασιλέως καὶ στρατοπεδάρχα, τί σοι ἔδοξεν λάθρα εἰσελθεῖν εἰς τὴν Ῥωμαίων ἡγεμονίαν καὶ στρατολογεῖν ἐκ τῆς ἐμῆς βασιλείας;

καὶ εἶπεν ὁ Παῦλος ἔμπροσθεν πάντων· Καῖσαρ, οὐ μόνον ἐκ τῆς σῆς ἡγεμονίας στρατολογοῦμεν, ἀλλὰ καὶ ἐκ τῆς οἰκουμένης ὅλης. τοῦτο γὰρ διατέτακται ἡμῖν, μηδένα ἀποκλεισθῆναι θέλοντα στρατεύεσθαι τῷ ἐμῷ βασιλεῖ. ὅθεν καὶ σύ, εἰ φίλον ἐστίν σοι, στράτευσαι αὐτῷ· οὐ γὰρ πλοῦτος καὶ τὰ νῦν ἐν βίῳ λαμπρὰ σώσει σε, ἀλλ᾽ ἐὰν πιστεύσῃς τῷ ἐμῷ βασιλεῖ Ἰησοῦ Χριστῷ, αὐτὸς σώσει σε. μέλλει γὰρ ἐν μιᾷ ἡμέρᾳ τὸν κόσμον κρίνειν ἐν δικαιοσύνῃ.

καὶ ταῦτα ἀκούσας ὁ Καῖσαρ ἐκέλευσεν πάντας τοὺς δεθέντας πυρὶ κατακαῆναι, τὸν δὲ Παῦλον τραχηλοκοπηθῆναι τῷ Ῥωμαίων νόμῳ. ὁ δὲ Παῦλος ἦν μὴ σιωπῶν ἀλλὰ καταγγέλλων πᾶσιν τὸν λόγον τοῦ θεοῦ, ἀνακοινούμενος καὶ τῷ πραιφέκτῳ Λογγίνῳ καὶ τῷ ἑκατοντάρχῳ Κέσκῳ. ἦν δὲ ὁ Νέρων ἐν τῇ Ῥώμῃ πολλῇ ἐνεργείᾳ τοῦ πονηροῦ κινούμενος, ὡς πολλοὺς Χριστιανοὺς ἀνελεῖν καὶ λοιπὸν τοὺς Ῥωμαίους ἐπὶ τοῦ παλατίου σταθέντας βοῆσαι· ἀρκεῖ, Καῖσαρ, οἱ γὰρ ἄνθρωποι ἡμέτεροί εἰσιν· αἴρεις τὴν Ῥωμαίων δύναμιν. καὶ ἐπὶ τούτοις ἐπαύσατο θεὶς διάταγμα μηδένα ἅπτεσθαι τῶν Χριστιανῶν, μέχρις ἂν διαγνῷ τὰ περὶ αὐτῶν.

Then Justus the flat-footed, Orion the Cappadocian, and Hephaestus the Galatian, the chief bodyguards of Nero, said, "We are also soldiers of that eternal king." Caesar locked them in prison and tortured them—the ones whom he used to love very much. He also sent word that the soldiers of the great king should be sought out, and he issued an edict to the effect that all those found to be Christians should be killed.

3. Among the many, Paul was also brought in chains. All his fellow prisoners paid attention to him and to what Paul answered, so Caesar understood that he was the leader of the armies. Nero said to him, "Oh, man of the great king and military commander, why did it seem good to you to enter secretly into the empire of the Romans and enlist soldiers from my kingdom?"

And Paul said in front of everyone, "Caesar, we levy soldiers not only from your kingdom but also from the entire world. For this has been ordained for us, that no one wishing to be a soldier for my king should be excluded. Thus, even you, if it pleases you, can be his soldier, for wealth and the splendid things now in this life will not save you. But if you believe in my king Jesus Christ, he will save you, for he will come one day to judge the world in righteousness."[11]

After he heard these things, Caesar ordered all those in chains to be burned with fire,[12] but Paul to be beheaded according to the law of the Romans. Paul was not silent but was proclaiming to all the word of God, preaching even to the prefect Longinus and the centurion Cescus.[13] But Nero, roused by the evil one,[14] was acting in Rome with great force, such that he killed many Christians. Finally, the Romans stood in front of the palace and cried out, "Enough is enough, Caesar, for these people are ours! You are destroying the power of the Romans!"[15] Because of these people he relented and established an edict that none of the Christians should be set on fire[16] unless he passed judgment on the affairs concerning them.

---

11. Acts 10:42, 17:31; 2 Tim 4:1.

12. Tacitus, *Ann.* 15.44.

13. Other manuscripts give the name as Cestus, while the Latin translations have Acestus or Egestius.

14. Or, "by wickedness."

15. That is, Nero is hurting Rome by killing so many Romans.

16. The verb ἅπτεσθαι can also mean "arrested," but the context suggests that the Christians in question had already been arrested and were being killed without a trial. These executions without trial are what the new edict addresses.

4. καὶ προσαχθέντος αὐτῷ τοῦ Παύλου μετὰ τὸ διάταγμα ἐνέμεινεν λέγων· τοῦτον τραχηλοκοπήσατε, ἵνα μὴ τὰ ἀλλότρια ὡς ἴδια λαμβάνῃ. καὶ ὁ Παῦλος εἶπεν· Καῖσαρ, οὐ πρὸς ὀλίγον καιρὸν ἐγὼ ζῶ τῷ βασιλεῖ μου· τοῦτο δὲ γίνωσκε· κἄν με τραχηλοκοπήσῃς, τοῦτο ποιήσω· αὖθις ἐγερθεὶς ἐμφανισθήσομαί σοι, εἰς τὸ γνῶναί σε ὅτι οὐκ ἀπέθανον, ἀλλὰ ζῶ τῷ ἐμῷ βασιλεῖ Ἰησοῦ Χριστῷ, τῷ κρινοῦντι πᾶσαν τήν οἰκουμένην.

ὁ δὲ Λογγῖνος καὶ ὁ Κέσκος εἶπαν τῷ Παύλῳ· πόθεν ὑμεῖς ἔχετε τὸν βασιλέα τοῦτον, ἵνα αὐτῷ οὕτως πιστεύητε μὴ βουλόμενοι μεταβαλέσθαι ὥστε καὶ θάνατον καταφρονεῖτε;

καὶ εἶπεν αὐτοῖς ὁ Παῦλος· ὑμεῖς οἱ ὄντες ἐν τῇ ἀγνοίᾳ καὶ πλάνῃ, μεταβάλεσθε καὶ σωθῆτε ἀπὸ τοῦ πυρὸς τοῦ ἐρχομένου ἐφ' ὅλην τὴν οἰκουμένην. οὐ γάρ, ὡς ὑμεῖς ὑπονοεῖτε, βασιλεῖ ἐπιγείῳ στρατευόμεθα, ἀλλὰ οὐρανίῳ ζῶντι θεῷ καὶ μένοντι εἰς τοὺς αἰῶνας, ὃς διὰ τὰς ἀνομίας τὰς γενομένας ἐν τῷ κόσμῳ ἔρχεται κριτὴς ζώντων καὶ νεκρῶν. μακάριος ἀνὴρ ἐκεῖνος ὁ πρὸ τῆς παρουσίας αὐτοῦ πιστεύσας εἰς αὐτόν· οὗτος ζήσεται εἰς τὸν αἰῶνα, ὅταν ἐκεῖνος ἔλθῃ καθαίρων καὶ κατακαίων τὴν οἰκουμένην.

ὁ δὲ Λογγῖνος καὶ ὁ Κέσκος ἔλεγον· παρακαλοῦμέν σε, βοήθησον ἡμῖν, καὶ ποίησον ἡμᾶς τοιούτους γενέσθαι, καὶ ἀπολύομέν σε.

καὶ εἶπεν ὁ Παῦλος· οὔκ εἰμι δραπέτης, ἵνα μοι τοῦτο χαρίσασθε, ἀλλ' ἔννομος στρατιώτης εἰμὶ τοῦ Χριστοῦ. καὶ γὰρ εἰ ᾔδειν ὅτι ἀποθνήσκω, Λογγῖνε καὶ Κέσκε, ἔφυγον ἄν, ἀλλ' ἐπειδὴ οἶδα ὅτι ζῶ τῷ ἐμῷ βασιλεῖ Χριστῷ,

4. When Paul was brought to him in accordance with the edict, he stood by his sentence, saying, "Decapitate this man, lest he should take on strange ideas as his own." And Paul said, "Caesar, it is not for a short time that I live for my king. Know that even if you cut off my head, I will do this: I will appear to you after I have been raised again, so that you may know that I did not die but am alive in my king Jesus Christ,[17] who judges the entire world."

But Longinus and Cescus said to Paul, "How did you come to have this king, such that you believe in him in this way and are not willing to be swayed, but even look at death with disdain?"

And Paul said to them, "You who are in ignorance and error, repent and be saved from the fire that is coming upon the whole world.[18] For we do not take the field, as you suppose, for an earthly king but a heavenly one, the living God, who remains forever and who, because of the lawless things that have been done on earth, comes as judge of the living and the dead.[19] Blessed is the one who has believed in him before his appearance.[20] Such a person will live forever,[21] when he comes purifying and completely consuming the world with fire."

But Longinus and Cescus were saying, "We ask you to help us and make us become such men, and we will free you."

And Paul said, "I am not a deserter[22] that you should grant this favor to me, but I am a lawful soldier of Christ. For if I knew that I were going to die, Longinus and Cescus, then I would flee, but since I know that I live for

---

17. Cf. Rom 14:8.

18. Cf. Luke 12:49.

19. 2 Tim 4:1; 1 Pet 4:5.

20. This is the appearance of Christ (Greek *parousia*) at the second coming, e.g. Matt 24:3; 1 Cor 15:23; 1 Thess 2:19.

21. Cf. John 11:26, where Jesus also employs the expression εἰς τὸν αἰῶνα.

22. We may detect here subtle anti-Petrine polemic. Paul claims that he is not a δραπέτης (deserter), while in Mart. Pet. 6.2, when Peter is being pressured to flee from Rome, he asks, δραπετεύωμεν ἀδελφοί? ("Are we to run away, brothers?"). The Roman believers convince Peter to do just that, and only his encounter with Christ at the city gate prompts him to return and face death. Peter, then, is a δραπέτης and initially retreats from a lethal battle for the cause of Christ, but Paul refuses this same opportunity when it is offered to him. There is good reason to think that the author of this text knows the Martyrdom of Peter, so Paul's specific word choice is notable.

χαιρόμενος ὑπάγω πρὸς αὐτόν, ἵνα κἀγὼ ἔλθω μετ' αὐτοῦ ἐν τῇ δόξῃ τοῦ πατρὸς αὐτοῦ.

λέγουσιν αὐτῷ· καὶ πῶς τραχηλοκοπηθέντος σοῦ ἡμεῖς ζήσομεν ἐπ' αὐτῷ;

5. ἔτι δὲ αὐτῶν ταῦτα λαλούντων πέμπει ὁ Νέρων Παρθένιον καὶ Φέρητα ἰδεῖν εἰ ἤδη τετραχηλοκόπηται ὁ Παῦλος· καὶ εὗρον αὐτὸν ἔτι ζῶντα. καὶ προσκαλεσάμενος αὐτοὺς ὁ Παῦλος εἶπεν· πιστεύσατε τῷ ζῶντι, θεῷ, τῷ κἀμὲ καὶ τοὺς πιστεύσαντας αὐτῷ ἐκ νεκρῶν ἐγείροντι.

οἱ δὲ εἶπον αὐτῷ· ὑπάγομεν πρὸς Νέρωνα τέως· καὶ ὅταν ἀποθάνῃς καὶ ἐγερθῇς, πιστεύομεν τότε τῷ θεῷ σου.

τοῦ δὲ Λογγίνου καὶ τοῦ Κέσκου δεομένων περὶ τῆς σωτηρίας αὐτῶν εἶπεν ὁ Παῦλος· ταχέως πορευθέντες ἐπὶ τὸν τάφον μου εὑρήσετε δύο ἄνδρας προσευχομένους, Τίτον καὶ Λουκᾶν· κἀκεῖνοι ὑμῖν δώσουσιν τὴν ἐν Χριστῷ σφραγῖδα. καὶ στραφεὶς ὁ Παῦλος πρὸς ἀνατολὰς ἐκτείνας τὰς χεῖρας ηὔχετο ἐπὶ πολὺ τῇ Ἑβραΐδι διαλέκτῳ. καὶ καταπαύσας τὴν προσευχὴν ἐκοινώνησεν αὐτοῖς τὸν λόγον καὶ εἰπὼν τὸ ἀμὴν προέτεινεν τὸν τράχηλον τοῦ ἀποτμηθῆναι. σιγῶντος δὲ αὐτοῦ καὶ μηκέτι λαλοῦντος ἀπετίναξεν αὐτοῦ τὴν κεφαλὴν ὁ στρατιώτης. ὡς δὲ ἀπετμήθη ἡ κεφαλὴ αὐτοῦ γάλα ἐπύτισεν εἰς τοὺς χιτῶνας τοῦ στρατιώτου. καὶ ἰδόντες οἱ παρεστῶτες ὄχλοι ἐθαύμασαν καὶ ἐδόξασαν τὸν θεὸν τὸν δόντα τοιαύτην χάριν τῷ Παύλῳ. ἀπελθόντες δὲ ἀπήγγειλαν τῷ Νέρωνι τὰ γεγονότα.

6. θαυμάζοντος δὲ καὶ διαποροῦντος τοῦ Καίσαρος, ἦλθεν ὁ Παῦλος ὡς περὶ ὥραν ἐνάτην ἑστώτων πολλῶν μετὰ τοῦ Καίσαρος φιλοσόφων τε καὶ ἀρχόντων καὶ πλουσίων καὶ ἐπισήμων, συμπαρόντος καὶ τοῦ ἑκατοντάρχου. καὶ πᾶσιν φανεὶς ὁ Παῦλος εἶπεν· Καῖσαρ, ἴδε ὅτι ὁ τοῦ θεοῦ στρατιώτης οὐκ ἀπέθανεν, ἀλλὰ ζῇ. σοὶ δὲ ἔσται πολλὰ κακά, ἀνθ' ὧν αἷμα πολλῶν δικαίων ἐξέχεας, καὶ οὐ

Christ my king, I go away to him rejoicing, so that I may also come with him in the glory of his Father."[23]

They said to him, "And how, after you have been beheaded, will we live in him?"

5. While they were still saying these things, Nero sent Parthenius and Pheres to see if Paul had already been decapitated, and they found him still alive. Paul called them to him and said, "Believe in the living God, who will raise from the dead both me and those who have believed in him."[24]

But they said to him, "We are going back to Nero in the meantime, but after you die and rise, then we will believe in your God."

Because Longinus and Cescus were inquiring about their salvation,[25] Paul said, "Go quickly [at dawn][26] to my tomb, and you will find two men praying—Titus and Luke. They will give you the seal in Christ." After turning to the east and stretching out his hands, Paul prayed for a long time in the Hebrew language.[27] He ended his prayer and shared the word with them. Then he said the "amen" and stretched out his neck to be severed. When he was silent and no longer speaking, the soldier[28] cut off his head. As his head was cut off, milk spurted onto the clothes of the soldier. After they saw this, the crowds standing there were amazed and glorified God, who had given such grace to Paul.[29] They went away and reported to Nero the things that had happened.

6. While Caesar was still amazed and at a loss, Paul came at around the ninth hour,[30] when many philosophers and leaders—both rich and distinguished—were standing with Caesar, and when the centurion was present. Appearing to them all, Paul said, "Caesar, see that the soldier of God did not die but lives. There will be great evil for you on account of the many

---

23. Mark 8:38; Matt 16:27; Luke 9:26. The natural human reaction is to avoid death, but Paul does not fear the sword, because physical execution does not truly bring death.

24. Rom 8:11.

25. Cf. 1 Pet 1:10.

26. Some manuscripts insert ὄρθρου here.

27. On Paul's ability to speak Hebrew (or perhaps Aramaic), see Acts 21:40, 22:2, 26:14.

28. Some manuscripts read σπεκουλάτωρ ("executioner"), a loanword from the Latin *speculator*. The presence of a loanword from Latin is a likely indication that these manuscripts represent later textual traditions.

29. Cf. Matt 9:8.

30. That is, around 3:00 p.m.

μετὰ πολλὰς ἡμέρας ἔσται σοι ταῦτα. ὁ δὲ Νέρων ταραχθεὶς ἐκέλευσεν λυθῆναι πάντας τοὺς δεσμίους, τόν τε Πάτροκλον καὶ τοὺς λοιποὺς ἅπαντας.

7. καὶ ὡς ἐτάξατο ὁ Παῦλος, ὄρθρου πορευθεὶς ὁ ἑκατόνταρχος καὶ οἱ σὺν αὐτῷ μετὰ φόβου καὶ δειλίας προσήρχοντο τῷ τάφῳ Παύλου. καὶ ἐγγίσαντες εἶδον ἄνδρας προσευχομένους, Τίτον καὶ Λουκᾶν καὶ μέσον τὸν Παῦλον ἑστῶτα, ὥστε ἐκπλαγῆναι αὐτοὺς ἰδόντας. Τίτος δὲ καὶ Λουκᾶς ἄνθρωποι ὄντες καὶ φοβηθέντες ἔφυγον. τῶν δὲ διωκόντων καὶ καταλαβόντων αὐτοὺς εἶπον· οὐκ εἰς θάνατον ὑμᾶς διώκομεν, δοῦλοι τοῦ Χριστοῦ, ἀλλ' ἵνα ζωὴν αἰώνιον δῶτε ἡμῖν, καθὼς ἐνετείλατο ἡμῖν Παῦλος ὁ μεθ' ὑμῶν πρὸ μικροῦ μέσος προσευχόμενος. καὶ ταῦτα ἀκούσαντες ἀπεδέξαντο αὐτοὺς καὶ ἐδόξασαν τὸν θεὸν καὶ ἔδωκαν αὐτοῖς τὴν ἐν Χριστῷ σφραγῖδα χάριτι τοῦ κυρίου ἡμῶν Ἰησοῦ Χριστοῦ, ᾧ ἡ δόξα εἰς τοὺς αἰῶνας. ἀμήν.

righteous people whose blood you spilled, and these things will happen to you after not many days." Nero was troubled and ordered that all the prisoners be set free, including Patroclus and all those remaining.

7. As Paul had ordered, at dawn the centurion and those with him went with fear and hesitation and approached the tomb of Paul. They drew near and saw men praying—Titus and Luke—and Paul standing in their midst. They saw this and were astounded. Titus and Luke, being men and fearful, started to flee. But after they pursued and laid hold of them, they said, "We pursue you not to kill you,[31] servants of Christ, but so that you may give us eternal life, just as Paul—the one who was praying in your midst just a little bit ago—commanded us." After they heard these things, Titus and Luke received them, glorified God, and gave them the seal in Christ, by the grace of our Lord Jesus Christ, to whom be glory forever. Amen.[32]

31. Literally, "not for death."

32. Cf. Rom 11:36, 16:27; Gal 1:5; Eph 3:21; Phil 4:20.

6. Pseudo-Linus, *Martyrdom of the Blessed Apostle Paul*

CANT 212 / *BHL* 6570

Contents

This is primarily a Latin revision and expansion of the Greek Martyrdom of the Holy Apostle Paul in Rome, so many of the same elements are present. Paul is preaching unfettered in a barn outside Rome, and crowds are coming out to him, including some from the household of Caesar. Nero's cupbearer, Patroclus, goes out to listen to Paul but has to sit in a window because of the large crowd. Sleep eventually overtakes him, and he dies after falling from the window. Nero hears of this and is deeply grieved, but he does not know that Paul has already raised Patroclus from the dead. The revivified Patroclus returns to the emperor and declares that he was raised by the power of Jesus Christ, the King of all the ages. Nero discovers that he has other followers of this king in his household, so he issues a decree that all the soldiers of Christ are to be arrested and tortured without a trial.

Paul is arrested and comes to Nero's attention as the leader of the Christians, and the two engage in verbal combat until Nero sentences him to death. A crowd of Romans rises up against Caesar because of his violent treatment of the Christians, and he slows the persecution. Before his death Paul promises Nero a posthumous visit, and even on the way to his execution he continues to preach and spurns any opportunity of escape. Soldiers favorable to his message ask how they may receive salvation, and Paul tells them to visit his tomb on the following morning. Paul is beheaded and soon after visits Nero and his entourage in the middle of the day. He threatens divine punishment on the emperor, who out of fear releases all his Christian prisoners. The soldiers come to Paul's tomb the next morning to find Titus and Luke, who are accompanied by a vision of Paul himself, and the disciples of Paul baptize the soldiers in the name of Christ.

Like the other Pseudo-Linus text in this volume (*Martyrdom of Blessed Peter the Apostle* in ch. 2), this adaptation displays some significant differences from its Greek predecessor. First of all, it contains numerous literary flourishes and expansions. At the beginning of the text, for example, the Greek Martyrdom of Paul simply states that Paul is preaching and then moves into the Patroclus story. Here, however, the author adds the detail that Paul had already gained a reputation among the Romans for his ability to perform signs and wonders. He is also renowned for the greatness of his teaching. Not only servants from the imperial household are attracted by Paul's wisdom—one of Paul's close friends is actually the teacher of the emperor. He used to exchange letters with Paul and read them in the presence of Nero himself, because they were full of such admirable wisdom. Even the philosophers of Rome and the Senate are being convinced by Paul's teaching. In this Latin version, therefore, Paul is already something of a celebrity based upon his preaching. Another example comes in the Patroclus scene. The young man does not just fall asleep; he is actually the victim of an attack from the devil himself, who is angered by the success of the apostle's preaching. Later, when Nero pronounces judgment on Paul, the narrator tells us that the apostle is not the victim of just Nero's wrath. The Senate itself, which earlier had held Paul in such high regard, issues the decree against Paul as if he were a traitor. Before his death Paul has not one, but two confrontations with Nero; he converts not two soldiers, but three; and the drama of the apostle's execution is heightened by his miraculous use and return of a scarf to a pious woman named Plautilla.

The other primary difference from the Greek Martyrdom of Paul is a lengthy theological insertion as Paul is on his way to die. His words to the soldiers and those around him are few in the earlier text, but here he delivers an extended sermon explaining the primary points of the gospel and calling the crowds to repentance for following their gods of wood and stone. The outcome is reminiscent of Peter's sermon on the day of Pentecost in Jerusalem (Acts 2:1–41). The people cry out in repentance for their errors and ask what they can do to avoid the ultimate judgment. Paul tells them to be baptized and to persevere, and then he admonishes them with other allusions to Pauline epistles. Even after his head is removed from his body, it delivers one last proclamation of the gospel, calling out the name of the Lord Jesus Christ. Overall, there is much more explicit theology in this text than we find in the Greek Martyrdom of Paul. This fact argues against the theory of Richard A. Lipsius that one of the sources for Pseudo-Linus's

Martyrdom of Paul was a gnostic text of the late second century. This text is more explicitly "orthodox" than the Greek Martyrdom of Paul, not less.

In these ways the additions mirror those in Pseudo- Linus, *Martyrdom of Peter*, but the styles of the two Pseudo-Linus authors are demonstrably different. The common ascription to Linus may result from the fact that these two texts were usually copied together in manuscripts and were likely used together on the joint festival day of the apostles (June 29).[1]

Literary Background

The date of this text is difficult to establish precisely. While it does not reveal direct dependence on Pseudo-Linus's *Martyrdom of Peter*, it is possible that this Pseudo-Linus takes his inspiration from the Petrine example. If this is correct, then a date in the fifth or sixth century is likely. As a number of texts in this volume attest, this was a popular period for the production of martyrdom accounts about the apostles, but it is impossible to establish this date with any certainty.

Linus, traditionally identified as the second bishop of Rome,[2] cannot be the author of this text. In the Acts of Nereus and Achilleus, there is a reference to a text addressed from Linus to the churches in the East. Gérard Poupon argues that this passage was incorrectly applied to this text and to Pseudo-Linus's *Martyrdom of Peter*,[3] so there is in fact no historical reason to connect this text with even an author posing as Linus.

Rome is the likely place of production due to details like the author's inclusion of the Roman Senate in the narrative; but nothing in the text would specifically eliminate other locations in the Latin West as a possibility.

---

1. As Christine M. Thomas has stated, "The proximity of these two martyrdom accounts expresses the harmony between Peter and Paul so important to the self conception of the early church (*The Acts of Peter, Gospel Literature, and the Ancient Novel: Rewriting the Past* [New York: Oxford University Press, 2003], 24).

2. Linus is not universally recognized in antiquity as the second bishop of Rome. This is the account in the Liberian Catalog of 354 CE (*Chronica minora saec. IV. V. VI. VII.*, ed. T. Mommsen, MGH.AA 9 [Berlin: Weidmann, 1892], 73); Irenaeus (*Haer.* 3.3.3); Eusebius (*Hist. eccl.* 5.6.1); and Teach. Shim. 6. However, Pseudo-Abdias (*Pass. Pet.* 15), the apocryphal Epistle of Clement to James (§2), and Tertullian (*Praescr.* 32) name Clement as the second bishop of Rome.

3. Gérard Poupon, "Passion de Pierre (dite du pseudo-Linus)" in *Écrits apocryphes chrétiens*, ed. Pierre Geoltrain and Jean-Daniel Kaestli, Pléiade 516 (Paris: Gallimard, 2005), 2:714–15.

Text

The text survives in numerous manuscripts dating from as early as the tenth century. The translation is based on the critical edition of Lipsius and is the first produced in English.

Select Bibliography

Eastman, David L. *Paul the Martyr: The Cult of the Apostle in the Latin West.* WGRWSup 4. Atlanta: Society of Biblical Literature, 2011.

Erbetta, Mario, trans. "La Passione di Paolo dello Ps. Lino." Pages 289–96 in *Atti e leggende.* Vol. 2 of *Gli apocrifi del Nuovo Testamento.* 2nd ed. Turin: Marietti, 1978.

Lipsius, Richard A. Pages 2.1:84–109, 142–73 in *Die apokryphen Apostelgeschichten und Apostellegenden.* Braunschweig: Schwetschke, 1887.

Lipsius, Richard A. and Max Bonnet, eds. *Martyrium beati Petri apostoli a Lino episcopo conscriptum.* Pages 23–44 in vol. 1 of *Acta apostolorvm apocrypha post Constantinvm Tischendorf.* Leipzig: Mendelssohn, 1891. Repr., Hildesheim: Olms, 1972.

Migne, J.-P., trans. "Passion de saint Paul." Pages 665–74 in vol. 2 of *Dictionnaire des apocryphes.* Paris: Migne, 1858.

Peebles, Rose Jeffries. *The Legend of Longinus in Ecclesiastical Tradition and in English Literature.* Baltimore: Furst, 1911 (esp. pp. 5–31).

Tajra, Harry W. *The Martyrdom of St. Paul: Historical and Judicial Context, Traditions, and Legends.* WUNT 2/67. Tübingen: Mohr Siebeck, 1994.

Martyrium Pauli apostoli a Lino conscriptum

1. Cum uenissent Romam Lucas a Galatia, Titus a Dalmatia, expectauerunt Paulum in urbe. quos cum adueniens Paulus uidisset, laetatus est ualde et conduxit sibi extra urbem horreum publicum, ubi cum his et allis fratribus de uerbo uitae tractaret. coepit interea colligere multitudinem maximam, adiciebanturque per eum fidei multae animae operante gratia Dei, ita ut per totam urbem sonus praedicationis et sanctitatis ipsius fieret, et exiret fama per uniuersam circa regionem de illo. iam enim admodum innotuerat orbi Romano signis et prodigiis et doctrina multa atque mirabili sanctitate.

concursus quoque multus de domo Caesaris fiebat ad eum credentium in dominum Iesum Christum et augmentabatur cotidie fidelibus gaudium magnum et exultatio. sed et institutor imperatoris adeo illi est amicitia copulatus, uidens in eo diuinam scientiam, ut se a colloquio illius temperare uix posset, quatinus si ore ad os illum alloqui non ualeret, frequentibus datis et acceptis epistolis ipsius dulcedine et amicali colloquio atque consilio frueretur, et sic eius doctrina agente Spiritu Sancto multiplicabatur et amabatur, ut licite iam doceret et a multis libentissime audiretur. disputabat siquidem cum ethnicorum philosophis et reuincebat eos, unde et plurimi eius magisterio manus dabant. nam et scripta illius quaedam magister Caesaris coram

Martyrdom of Paul the Apostle Written by Linus

1. After Luke had come to Rome from Galatia,[1] and Titus from Dalmatia, they waited for Paul in the city. When Paul came and saw them, he rejoiced greatly and rented a barn for himself outside the city, where he held discussions concerning the word of life with these and other brothers and sisters.[2] Meanwhile he began to assemble a very great multitude, and by the grace of God many souls were being added to the faith through him, so that the sound of his preaching and sanctity rose through the whole city, and his fame went out through the entire region. Now indeed he became well known to the Roman world with signs and wonders and great teaching and extraordinary sanctity.

A great throng of those believing in the Lord Jesus Christ was also coming to him from the house of Caesar, and great joy and gladness were daily growing among the faithful. But the teacher of the emperor was joined closely to Paul in friendship, seeing in him divine knowledge, such that he was scarcely able to restrain himself from conversation with Paul. Thus, if he was not able to speak to him face-to-face, he took delight in his pleasantness and friendship, and in his conversation and counsel, through letters frequently sent and received.[3] By the action of the Holy Spirit, Paul's teaching was being widely disseminated and well received, so that now he was teaching legally and was being heard freely by many people. He was debating with the philosophers of the unbelievers and convincing them, so that very many of them were giving themselves to his teaching. A teacher of Caesar read certain of his writings in the emperor's presence and showed

1. See ch. 5 n. 1 (Mart. Paul 1) on the question of whether Luke is presented as coming from Galatia or Gaul.

2. Literally, "brothers."

3. The author is likely referring to the correspondence between Paul and Seneca the Younger, Nero's tutor and later advisor. On these spurious letters, see Richard I. Pervo, *The Making of Paul: Constructions of the Apostle in Early Christianity* (Minneapolis: Fortress, 2010), 110–16.

eo relegit et in cunctis admirabilem reddidit. senatus etiam de illo alta non mediocriter sentiebat.

2. quadam denique die, cum Paulus doctrinae inseruiens circa uesperam in cenaculo editiori turbas alloqueretur, quidam Patroclus, deliciosus et pincerna regis, ipsius se subducens aspectibus abiit ad horreum ubi Paulus hospitabatur, ut audiret documenta uitae perpetuae. inuitatus enim ad hoc et animo ductus iam fuerat a consodalibus suis et Caesaris amicissimis, qui de eius familiari obsequio Pauli monita sectabantur. sed cum prae multitudine populi ad eum introire non posset, ascendit ad fenestram excelsiorem, et secus eam sedit ut uerbum Dei commodius posset audire desiderabat namque feruenti animo Pauli sermone refici. sed cum Paulus in longum protraxisset sermonem et iuuenis somno fatigaretur, diaboli maligni inuidia dolens super dilectionem uerbi Dei et ipsius apostoli quam studiosius adolescens habebat, fecit iuuenem paululum dormitare; cadensque de fenestra satis excelsa spiritum exalauit.

quod cum mox Neroni reuertenti a balneo fuisset nuntiatum, qui multa frequentia dilectum sibi iuuenem requirebat, contristatus est rex usque ad animam super mortem Patrocli, statuitque alium pro eo ad uini officium, ut ei porrigeret poculum.

3. Paulus uero statim cognoscens quod gestum erat per spiritum, dixit ad plebem: uiri fratres, inuenit locum malignus ut uos temptaret. sed dominus Iesus Christus more solito eius nequitiam conuertet ad suam gloriam. ite igitur foras, et inuenietis iuuenem Caesaris delicatum ex alto cecidisse et iam nunc iacere exanimem. quem leuantes ad me huc afferre satagite.

illi uero concito gradu pergentes confestim iuuenem mortuum attulerunt. mirabantur autem turbae, quomodo Paulus rem gestam ex ordine cognouisset sibi nemine nuntiante. dixit itaque Paulus ad turbas: nunc fides uestra parebit erga dominum Iesum Christum. tempus est enim, ut semen aeternae uitae in bonam terram deueniens centuplicata satione

him to be admirable in all things. Even the Senate had a particularly high opinion of him.[4]

2. Then on a certain day, when Paul was devoted to teaching, at around evening he was speaking to crowds in an upper room. A certain Patroclus, one dear to the emperor and his cupbearer, withdrew from the emperor's presence and went out to the barn where Paul was lodging, so that he might hear the instructions of eternal life. He had been invited to this barn and led in his soul by his companions and very close friends of Caesar, who were eagerly following the teachings of Paul out of their close allegiance to him. But when Patroclus was not able to go in to Paul because of the multitude of people, he climbed to a very high window and sat in it, so that he could better hear the word of God. Because his soul was burning, he desired to be made new by the preaching of Paul. But when Paul kept preaching for a long time, and the young man became weary and sleepy, the jealousy of the wicked devil was grieved at how zealously the young man showed his love for the word of God and the apostle himself. He made the young man sleep just a little, and Patroclus fell from this very high window and breathed out his spirit.

Immediately after Nero returned from the bath, this was announced to him, for he very often asked this beloved youth to come to him. The emperor was deeply saddened in his soul because of the death of Patroclus and installed another to take his place as the wine servant, so that this one could hand him the goblet.

3. Paul immediately knew through the Spirit what had occurred and said to the people, "Brothers and sisters,[5] the evil one has found an occasion to test you, but the Lord Jesus Christ, in his usual way, will turn wickedness to his own glory. Go outside, therefore, and you will find a young man, beloved of Caesar, who fell from a height and now lies dead. Lift him up and quickly bring him here to me."

They went out quickly and immediately brought the dead youth. The crowds were amazed, however, at how Paul knew the affair in detail, although no one had told him about it. Paul said to the crowds, "Now your faith in the Lord Jesus Christ will be made manifest. It is indeed time that the seed of eternal life, which has fallen onto good soil, should bear fruit a

---

4. These claims about Paul's high standing with Caesar's teacher and the Senate are not present in the Greek Martyrdom of Paul, on which most of this story otherwise depends.

5. Literally, "Men and brothers," but Paul is speaking to a mixed audience.

fructificet. accedite ergo plena fide ad dominum Deum nostrum, et deprecemur illum ut restituatur anima eius in istud iuuenile cadauer, uiuatque melius quam uixisset. et cum ingemuissent uniuersi procumbentes orationi, ait Paulus: adolescens Patrocle, surge et narra quanta tibi fecerit Deus. ad quam uocem mox Patroclus tamquam a somno surrexit et coepit glorificare deum, qui dedit potestatem talem hominibus. dimisitque eum Paulus cum caeteris qui erant ex domo Caesaris, et abibant laetantes et gaudentes omnes in domino, qui facit uoluntatem timentium se et deprecationes eorum exaudit.

4. cum autem lamentaretur Nero Patroclum et immensitate absorberetur tristitiae dixerunt circumstantes ad Caesarem: non, domine, magnanimitas uestra grauetur molestia super mortem adolescentis. nam uiuit et adest pro foribus. Caesar uero cum audisset Patroclum uiuere quem paulo ante didicerat mortuum, expauit corde et recusabat eum introire et adstare suo conspectui. sed cum persuasum illi fuisset ab amicis perplurimis, iussit eum introire.

et uidens eum uegetum et nulla mortis signa habentem, obstupuit et ait ad eum: Patrocle, uiuis?

at ille respondit: Caesar, uiuo.

Nero dixit: quis te fecit uiuere?

cui Patroclus exhilaratus corde et accensus calore fidei dixit: dominus Iesus Christus, rex omnium saeculorum.

et Nero conturbatus de nomine uirtutis Dei dixit ad iuuenem: ille ergo debet regnare in saecula et resoluere omnia regna mundi?

et Patroclus ait: etiam, Caesar, destruet omnia regna quae sub caelo sunt, et uniuersa quae sub caelo sunt seruient ei; et ipse est solus rex regum et dominus dominantium.

hundredfold from what was planted.[6] Draw near, therefore, to the Lord our God with full faith,[7] and let us entreat him so that the spirit in that young man's corpse may be restored, and he may live better than he had lived." When everyone had fallen down and cried out in prayer, Paul said, "Young Patroclus, get up and declare how much God has done for you." At the sound of Paul's voice, Patroclus immediately rose up as if from sleep and began to glorify God, who had given such great power to people.[8] Paul sent him away with the others who were from the house of Caesar, and they all went out rejoicing and exulting in the Lord, who does the will of those who fear him and hears their prayers.[9]

4. While Nero was lamenting Patroclus and was overwhelmed with the depth of his sadness, they[10] came before Caesar and said, "Lord, let your greatness not be weighed down by distress over the death of the young man, for he is alive and is in front of your doors." When Caesar heard that Patroclus was alive—the one he learned was dead just a little earlier—he was terrified in his heart and was reluctant to let him enter and stand in his presence. But when he had been persuaded by his many friends, he ordered him to enter.

Seeing him fully alive and having no signs of death, he was amazed and said to him, "Patroclus, are you alive?"

And he responded, "Caesar, I am alive."

Nero said, "Who made you alive?"

Enlivened in heart and kindled by the heat of his faith, Patroclus said to him, "The Lord Jesus Christ, the King of all the ages."

Nero was troubled by the name of the power of God and said to the young man, "He, therefore, is to reign throughout the ages and abolish all the kingdoms of the world?"[11]

Patroclus said, "Yes, Caesar, he will destroy all the kingdoms that are under heaven, and all the kingdoms that are under heaven will serve him. He is the only King of kings and Lord of lords."[12]

---

6. Matt 13:8; Luke 8:8.

7. Heb 10:22.

8. Matt 9:8.

9. Ps 145:19.

10. The believers from Caesar's house.

11. Cf. Dan 7:27.

12. Rev 17:14, 19:16. These titles are used for God (the Father) in 1 Tim 6:15. Cf. Deut 10:17: "God of gods and Lord of lords."

Nero autem dedit ei alapam dicens: ergo militas illi regi?

et Patroclus exultans ait: etiam, nam excitauit me a mortuis.

5. tunc Barnabas et Iustus et quidam Paulus et Arion Cappadocus et Festus Galatha, qui erant ministri Caesaris et ei iugiter assistebant, dixerunt Neroni: cur, Caesar, recta sapientem et prudentissime atque ueracissime respondentem percutis iuuenem? nam et nos illi militamus regi inuicto, Iesu Christo domino nostro. Nero autem cum audisset uno sensu eodemque sermone dicere illos inuictum regem Iesum, retrusit eos in carcerem , ut nimium illos torqueret quos nimis ante amauerat. et iussit requiri magni illius regis famulos posuitque edictum, ut sicubi fuissent inuenti, sine interrogatione omnes Christi milites per tormenta uaria punirentur. unde multa scrutatione a ministris reipublicae et apothecae malignitatis fautoribus serui Dei quaesiti et inuenti, quam plurimi perducti sunt ad praesentiam Caesaris.

6. inter quos et Paulus, consuetudinarias sibi pro Christi nomine gestans cathenas, ductus est uinctus. quem omnes simul uincti adeo intendebant, ut sine alicuius inditio facile potuerit Nero cognoscere, ipsum magni regis militibus praesidere. intellegensque illum ducem et Christi seruorum magistrum, ait ad eum: o homo, magni regis seruus, mihi autem uinctus, quid tibi uisum est introire latenter in regnum Romanorum, et mihi subtrabere, illi autem colligere milites de meae militiae principatu?

Paulus autem repletus Spiritu Sancto constanter in aure omnium qui poterant adesse dixit ad Caesarem: Nero, non solum de tuo angulo colligimus milites, sed etiam de toto orbe terrarum. hoc enim praeceptum est mihi ut neminem ex omni gente militare uolentem aeterno regi meo repellam. potens est enim omnium dominus cunctis larga manu secundum cuiusque meritum dona ditissima dispensare. si enim et tibi uisum fuerit in illum credere et ei fideliter obedire, non te paenitebit. caeterum

Nero struck him on the cheek and said, "Are you therefore a soldier of that King?"

Patroclus rejoiced and said, "Yes, for he raised me from the dead."

5. Then Barnabas, Justus, a certain Paul, Arion the Cappadocian, and Festus the Galatian,[13] who were servants of Caesar and constantly attended him, said to Nero, "Why, Caesar, do you strike this young man, who judges rightly and responds most prudently and truthfully? For we are also soldiers of that unconquered King, Jesus Christ our Lord." When Nero heard them say with one accord and the same profession that Jesus was the unconquered King, he sent them to prison in order to torture greatly those he had previously loved greatly. He ordered the servants of that great King to be found, and he issued an edict that wherever they were found, all the soldiers of Christ should be punished through various tortures without any questioning.[14] Thus, through extensive searching by the servants of the republic, and with the help of the storehouse of wickedness,[15] the servants of God were sought and found. How many of them were led into the presence of Caesar!

6. Among these Paul was brought and bound, bearing his usual chains for the name of Christ. All those bound were looking toward him at the same time, such that without any other indication Nero was easily able to discern that he presided over the soldiers of the great King. Knowing that Paul was the leader and chief of the servants of Christ, Nero said to him, "You, oh man, who are a servant of the great King but have been captured by me, why did it seem good to you to enter the kingdom of the Romans in secrecy, undermine me, and gather soldiers for that King from among the best of my army?"

Paul, however, was constantly filled with the Holy Spirit and said to Caesar in the hearing of all those who were able to be present, "Nero, we gather soldiers not only from your region, but also from the entire world. I was ordered not to reject anyone from any nation who wishes to be a soldier for my eternal King. The Lord of all is able to give the most lavish gifts to all from his generous hand[16] according to the merit of each one. If indeed it also seems good to you to believe in him and obey him faithfully,

13. Or Festus the Gaul. The list in Mart. Paul 2 does not include Barnabas or the other Paul, and the name Orion appears in place of Arion.

14. In other words, these Christians were being denied a legal process.

15. This is presumably a reference to Satan.

16. Ps 145:16.

noli putare, quia diuitiae huius saeculi, splendor aut gloria saluare te debeant; sed si subiectus illi fueris, in perpetuum saluus eris. cum enim uenerit iudicare uiuos et mortuos, deuastabit huius mundi figuram per ignem, et ante mundi constitutionem parata et a saeculis occulta militibus suis donatiua, quae numquam deficient et quae omnem excludent indigentiam, largietur.

7. haec audiens Nero et ira succensus, quia mundi figuram per ignem Paulus dixerat resoluendam, iussit omnes Christi milites igne cremari, Paulum autem senatus consultu tamquam maiestatis reum capite secundum Romanas leges truncari; tradiditque eum Longino et Megisto praefectis atque Acesto centurioni, ut illum extra urbem ducentes et populo spectaculum de eius occisione praebentes decollari praeciperent. quibus Paulus sine intermissione uerbum praedicabat salutis.

ministros etiam et apparitores per omnem ciuitatem et circa regionem cum uelocitate Nero diaboli exagitatus operatione direxit, qui summa diligentia perscrutarentur latitantes et manifestos simul interficerent Christianos. unde tam multiplex occisa est turba Christianorum, ut populus Romanus palacium uirtute irrumperet et seditionem contra Caesarem excitare moliens proclamaret: pone modum, Caesar, iniustissimae ius-

then he will not disappoint you.[17] Do not think that anything else—the riches of this world, splendor, or glory—is necessary to save you. But if you will be subject to him, you will be saved for eternity. When he comes to judge the living and the dead,[18] he will destroy the form of this world by fire.[19] Before the foundation of the world,[20] the lavish gifts that he will give to his soldiers were prepared and hidden from the world. They will never waste away[21] and will eliminate all want."

7. Hearing these things Nero was inflamed with anger. Because Paul had said that the form of the world must be destroyed through fire, he ordered that all the soldiers of Christ be consumed by fire.[22] But as for Paul, by the decree of the Senate, and as if it were a case of treason,[23] Nero ordered that his head be cut off according to the Roman laws. He handed Paul over to the prefects Longinus[24] and Megistus and the centurion Acestus, so that they could lead him outside the city and make a spectacle of his death for the people by having him decapitated. Paul was preaching the word of salvation to them without interruption.

But Nero, who had been roused by the agency of the devil, quickly sent agents and deputies throughout the entire city and around the region. With the utmost diligence they were seeking out the Christians who were hidden and killing those who were found. Thus, so great a multitude of Christians was killed that the Roman people rushed into the palace by force, and attempting to incite an uprising against Caesar they cried out,

---

17. Rom 10:11.

18. Acts 10:42; 2 Tim 4:1; 1 Pet 4:5.

19. 2 Pet 3:7–13.

20. Eph 1:4.

21. Matt 6:19–20; 1 Pet 1:4.

22. Tacitus (*Ann.* 15.38–44) states that Christians were killed on the charge of arson, because Nero was attempting to deflect the blame for the devastating fire in Rome in 64 CE.

23. Most scholars agree that the charge against Paul was probably *maiestas* (treason). See e.g., Richard J. Cassidy, *Paul in Chains: Roman Imprisonment and the Letters of St. Paul* (New York: Crossroad, 2001), 55–67; Harry W. Tajra, *The Trial of St. Paul: A Judicial Exegesis of the Second Half of the Acts of the Apostles*, WUNT 2/35 (Tübingen: J.C.B. Mohr, 1989), 36–42.

24. According to Rose Jeffries Peebles, in later Christian tradition this name would also be applied to the centurion responsible for the crucifixion of Jesus (*The Legend of Longinus in Ecclesiastical Tradition and in English Literature* [Baltimore: Furst, 1911], 30–31).

sioni! tempera furorem irrrationabilem! sufficiat saeuitiae quod crudelitatis metas transcenderit. nostrates homines sunt quos perdis, Romanum tuentur imperium. aufers, Caesar, Romanam uirtutem, quae militum tantorum frequentia terribilis cunctis gentibus existebat. tunc Nero clamores populi expauescens aliud edictum proposuit, ut nemo auderet contingere Christianos nec quicquam eis inferre molestiae, donec relatio plenissimae cognitionis ex delatione cuiusque referretur ad Caesarem.

8. quapropter Paulus iterum eius est oblatus aspectibus. Nero autem ut eum uidit, uehementissime exclamauit dicens: tollite, tollite maleficum, decollate impostorem, nolite sinere uiuere carminatorem, perdite sensuum alienatorem, auferte de superficie terrae mentium immutatorem!

ad quem Paulus ait: Nero, tempore modico patiar ego; sed uiuam in perpetuum Deo meo et regi aeterno domino Iesu Christo, qui uenturus est iudicare orbem terrae in conflagratione ignis.

Nero dixit Longino, Megisto et Acesto: auferte celerius ab illo caput, et sic sibi de uita perpetua blandiatur sentiatque me regem inuictum, qui eum uinxi et occidendo deuici.

Paulus uero ait: ut scias, Nero, me post decollationem meo regi inuicto aeternaliter uiuere, te autem uictum qui nunc putas te uincere, cum mihi caput abscisum fuerit, uiuus tibi apparebo, et cognoscere poteris quia mors et uita famulantur domino meo Iesu Christo, cuius est omne regnum et cui uoluerit dabit illud et omnis uictoria est illius et quem uult uincere facit magnifice triumphare, et ipse solus inuictus est rex in aeternum. et his dictis ductus est Paulus ad supplicium.

9. cum autem duceretur, Longinus et Megistus atque Acestus dixerunt ad illum: Dic nobis, Paule, ubi est rex ille et ubi apparuit uobis et qualiter cognouistis eum et quid uobis contulit aut conferet boni, quod sic ardentissime eum diligatis uos Christiani, quatinus nullo pacto religioni nostrae uelitis accommodare assensum, ut uiuatis ac bonis huius uitae fruamini, sed potius omni delectamento iocundius pro illo mori uariis tormentis

"Put an end, Caesar, to this most unjust command! Restrain your irrational fury! Let your wrath be satisfied, because this goes beyond the limits of cruelty. The ones whom you kill are our own, and they defend the Roman Empire. Caesar, you are undermining Roman strength, which was terrifying to all nations based on the vast number of soldiers." Then Nero was frightened by the cries of the people and published another edict, so that no one would dare to seize Christians or inflict any harm on them, until a full report concerning the accusation against each one was sent to Caesar.

8. For this reason Paul was once again brought into his presence. However, as Nero saw him, he cried out loudly and said, "Take him away! Take away this evildoer! Cut off the head of this imposter! Do not permit this enchanter to live! Destroy this distorter of the senses! Remove this changer of minds from the surface of the earth!"

Paul said to him, "Nero, I will suffer for a short time, but I will live forever with my God and the eternal King, the Lord Jesus Christ, who will come to judge the earth with fire."

Nero said to Longinus, Megistus, and Acestus, "Remove his head quickly. Let him delude himself about eternal life but understand that I am the unconquered king—I who chained him and conquered him by striking him down."

Paul said, "Nero, so that you may know after my decapitation that I live eternally with my unconquered King, but that you have been conquered—you who now think that you are the conqueror—I will appear to you alive after my head has been cut off. And you will be able to understand that death and life are subservient to my Lord Jesus Christ. Every kingdom belongs to him, and he will give it to whomever he wishes. Every victory is his, and he causes to triumph greatly whomever he wants to be victorious. He alone is the unconquered King forever." With these words Paul was led away to punishment.

9. When he was being led away, Longinus, Megistus, and Acestus said to him, "Tell us, Paul, where is that King, and where did he appear to you?[25] And how do you know him? And what good did or will he confer upon you, because you Christians love him so fervently that you are willing to give your assent to no part of our religion, although this would allow you to live and enjoy the good things of this life? Instead, with total delight you

25. The forms of "you" in this passage are all plural, suggesting that they are asking Paul to speak on behalf of Christians in general.

ducatis. magnus enim nobis uidetur error iocunditatem odisse ac uitam, et toto desiderio paenas amplecti ac mortem.

10. Paulus uero ait: o uiri cordati atque sensu bono uigentes, relinquite tenebras ignorantiae et erroris, quarum caligine obnubilatur intelligentia uestrae nobilitatis ne uerum quod in uobis latet uidere possitis, et conuertite mentis oculos ad aeternam et ueram lucem, ut ualeatis prius uos ipsos cognoscere, et sic ad cognitionem regis illius cum laetitia peruenire atque ab igne uniuerso orbi superuenturo salui et illaesi permanere. non enim, sicut uos putatis, alicui terreno regi militamus, sed Deo uiuo, regi caelorum et omnium saeculorum, qui propter iniquitates quae fiunt in hoc mundo ueniet iudex et iudicabit illum per ignem. felix autem erit homo qui crediderit in eum: habebit enim uitam aeternam et uiuet in omnia saecula. et infelicissimus ille quo non infelicior ullus, qui contempnens diuitias bonitatis et longanimitatis ipsius non conuertitur ad eum: nam periet in aeternum.

propter hoc namque de caelo in terram descendit qui caelum et terram fecit, et ad hoc factus est homo qui fecit hominem, ut homo conuersus ab iniquitate sua, relinquens uana et simulacra muta quae nefandissime satis pro Deo colit, seruiat ei qui fecit illum et adoret eum quem tremunt angeli et omnes caelorum potestates adorant quod cum factum fuerit, faciet illum uerum adoratorem atque cultorem suum consortem et socium angelorum suorum, spirituum uidelicet sanctorum ac beatorum. nec inmerito, quia spiritus est Deus, et eum qui illum in spiritu et ueritate colit et adorat sanctis spiritibus socium faciet; illum uero qui in eum credere recusauerit, socium et complicem reddet iniquorum daemoniorum in tormento et aeterni incendii concrematione: ad quem ignem perpetuum transmittet illum refugam, id est ignem uenturum, per quem Deus est orbem iudicaturus.

11. quapropter, uiri sapientes, apud se prudentia uestra diiudicet quis fecit mundum, quoniam sine factore non prodiit. perpendite quis fecit hominem, quia ut diuina testantur oracula non ipse se fecit. attendite quia

consider it more joyful to die for him by various torments. It seems to us a great mistake to spurn joyfulness and life, but to embrace punishments and death with the utmost desire."

10. Paul said, "Oh you who are wise and living by good sense, abandon the shadows of ignorance and error, by whose fog the discernment of your nobility is obscured, so that you are unable to see the truth that is concealed within you. Turn the eyes of your mind to the eternal and true light, so that you may first be able to know yourselves, and thus with gladness come to the knowledge of that King and preserve yourselves safe and unhurt from the fire that is coming upon the whole earth.[26] We are not, as you suppose, soldiers of another earthly king, but of the living God, the King of the heavens and all ages. Because of the injustices that occur in this world, he will come as a judge and judge it through fire.[27] Happy will be the one who has believed in him. He will have eternal life and will live forever. But most unhappy, and more unhappy than anyone else, will be the one who despises the riches of his goodness and patience and does not turn to him, for he will perish for eternity.

"It was for this reason that the one who made heaven and earth came down to the earth. And the one who made humankind was made human, so that humankind might turn from its iniquity, abandon the vain and mute images that it very foolishly worships in place of God,[28] serve the one who made it, and worship the one before whom the angels tremble and whom all the powers of the heavens worship. When this is done, Christ will make that true adorer and worshiper his own companion and the friend of his angels, as well as of his holy and blessed souls. And this is right, because God is spirit, and he will make a friend to the holy spirits the one who worships and adores him in spirit and in truth.[29] But the one who refuses to believe in him he will hand over as a friend and companion of the wicked demons for torment and the eternal burning of fire. He will send that fugitive into the eternal fire—that is, the coming fire through which God is going to judge the world.

11. "Therefore, wise ones, let your discernment determine for you who made the world, because it did not come about without a creator. Consider who made humankind, because as the divine oracles attest, it did not make

26. Cf. Luke 12:49.

27. 1 Cor 3:13; 2 Pet 3:7–12.

28. Ps 115:4–8; Isa 46:7; Jer 10:5; Hab 2:18–19; 1 Cor 12:2.

29. John 4:24.

simulacra uana non sunt dii sed hominum factura et daemonia in eisdem facturis latentia. quae licet in hoc concordari uideantur quia unanimiter perditionem humani generis cupiunt, sibi tamen inuicem modis diuersissimis dissident. non est enim pax impiis, dicit dominus. in causa namque est illud, cur homines festinant perdere et sibi socios in paenis habere, quia sciunt in caelestem habitationem homines ascensuros per Dei gratiam, unde ipsi spiritus ceciderunt per superbiam. uiri urbani, sensu cognoscite quia deitatis nomen per plures nequaquam diuiditur, quoniam unus Deus a quo omnia, et unus dominus Iesus Christus per quem sunt omnia, et unus Spiritus Sanctus in quo consistunt uniuersa, cui fideliter fidelia obtemperant omnia, et non est scisma in diuinitate quia caret pluralitate.

attendite, ciues Romani, unde discordia nata fuerit, et qua ratione accrescens sic longe lateque miserabiliter adoleuerit, et cur tam multiplicia non numina sed miserabilia emerserint deorum portenta, uidelicet quia multi coeperunt uelle fieri principes ac tyranni et dominatores, non uitiorum sed hominum suae naturae consortium, unde ignorantiae tempestate demersi et baratro elationis suae deiecti unusquisque potestatis suae deum aut mutuauit aut statuit. unde et dicitur, quia primus in orbe timor creauit deos. ad tantam miseri homines peruenerunt dementiam ut sic miserrimos homines sibi deos constituerent, quibus fierent similes ut mortem pessimam deuitarent. sed et quidam eorum, quoniam non probauerunt deum habere in notitiam, traditi sunt in uoluntates suas, ut exercerent illa opera quae leges Romanae puniunt cum execratione, et impletum est in

itself. Give attention to the fact that those worthless images are not gods but the creations of human beings, and demons are concealed in these creations.[30] It is possible that these demons may seem to be of one accord, because they all seek the destruction of the human race; however, they are at odds with each other in a great variety of ways. 'There is no peace for the wicked, says the Lord.'[31] This, then, is the reason why people rush to die and to have their friends with them in these punishments, because they know that people will ascend through the grace of God into the heavenly abode, from which those [evil] spirits fell because of their pride.[32] Learned ones, know by discernment that the name of the Godhead is in no way divided among many, because there is one God by whom all things were made, and one Lord Jesus Christ through whom all things exist,[33] and one Holy Spirit in whom all things have their existence and to whom all faithful things comply faithfully. There is no division in the Godhead, because it is free from plurality.[34]

"Pay attention, Roman citizens, to where discord was born; and to why it increased so deeply and so widely and unfortunately expanded; and to why so great a number of not divinely-willed, but wretched, portents of the gods have emerged. Obviously it is because many have begun to wish to become leaders and tyrants and rulers, not of their vices but of those who share in their own nature. As a result they are submerged in a storm of ignorance and hurled down into the abyss of their own exaltation. Each one has either borrowed or established a god by his own power. Thus it is said, 'The first one to create gods in the world was fear.'[35] Wretched people arrived at such a level of folly that they set up the most wretched people as their gods, and they became like them, so that they might avoid the worst death. But certain ones of them, because they did not show that they held God in esteem, were handed over to their own desires,[36] so that they were carrying out those deeds that the Roman laws punish with a curse.

30. 1 Cor 10:19–20.

31. Isa 48:22.

32. Isa 14:12–15; Ezek 28:13–18; Jude 6; *Vita Ad. Ev.* 12.1–16.3.

33. 1 Cor 8:6.

34. This technical Trinitarian language is an important clue to the date of the text. On the language for the Holy Spirit, see e.g., Origen, *Princ.* 1.3.1–4.

35. Caecilius Statius, *Theb.* 3.661: *Primus in orbe deos fecit timor.* Statius was later quoted by Petronius Arbiter (frag. 27), a contemporary of Paul. Here Paul is presented as quoting a pagan poet, as in Titus 1:12.

36. Rom 1:28.

illis, quod dictum est uerbis sanctissimis: similes illis, inquit, fiant qui faciunt ea. fecerunt enim sibi deos miseros et facti sunt ipsi miseri atque ad tantam sunt insaniam deuoluti ut trunco ligni dicant: deus noster es, et lapidi: adiuua nos, stipitemque fabrefactum adorent, qui eius sunt astulis calefacti.

12. ad haec multae audientium turbae eleuantes uocem in planctum dixerunt: errauimus, peccauimus, inique egimus, doctor salutis ac ueritatis et aeternae uitae ostensor, miserere nostri, ut eruamur a laqueis peccatorum et possimus euadere ignem, quo exuretur mundus et quisque cruciabitur infidelis et pessimus.

tunc Paulus ait: o uiri fratres, quorum Deus cor suo Spiritu tetigit, state uiriliter in fide. nam ministri aeternae salutis aderunt a quibus baptizabimini, et bene perseuerantes in caritate domini nostri Iesu Christi salui eritis in aeternum.

Longinus quoque et Megistus et Acestus secretius alloquentes apostolum dixerunt: rogamus te, domine, fac nos adscribi in militia regis aeterni, ut possimus uenturum ignem euadere et regni perpetui participes fieri: et dimittemus te, uel quocunque potius decreueris pergere, erimus tibi itineris comites et usque ad mortem parentes.

quibus Paulus dixit: fratres mei, non sum profugus sed miles legitimus regis mei. si enim scirem quia morerer et non potius ad uitam et gloriam per hanc mortem peruenirem, non solum facerem quae rogatis, sed ego hoc a uobis deposcerem. nunc autem non in uacuum cucurri per multas passiones, nec sine causa patior. nam restat mihi corona iustitiae, quam reddet mihi cui credidi et de quo certus existo quoniam ad illum uado et cum ipso ueniam in claritate sua et Patris ac sanctorum angelorum iudicare orbem terrarum. propterea mortem istam contempno et uestram petitionem ut abscedam non obaudiam neque faciam.

And in them is fulfilled what is said in the most holy writings, 'Let those who make them become like them.'[37] Indeed, they made for themselves wretched gods and were themselves made wretched, and they fell headlong to such insanity that they would say to a chunk of wood, 'You are our god,' and to a stone, 'Help us.'[38] Those who worship a hewn log are also warmed by its splinters."

12. In response to these things, great crowds of those listening raised their voice in lamentation and said, "We have erred! We have sinned! We have acted unjustly! Oh, teacher of salvation and truth, revealer of eternal life, have mercy on us, so that we may be rescued from the snares of sin and may be able to escape the fire by which the world will be consumed and each faithless and very wicked person will be tormented."

Then Paul said, "Brothers and sisters, whose God has touched your hearts by his Spirit, stand strong in the faith, for there will be ministers of eternal salvation by whom you will be baptized. And if you persevere well in the love of our Lord Jesus Christ, then you will be saved for eternity."

Longinus, Megistus, and Acestus spoke to the apostle separately and said, "We entreat you, sir, to enlist us in the army of the eternal King, so that we may be able to escape the coming fire and may be participants in the eternal kingdom. We will release you wherever you decide it is best to go and will be your traveling companions and servants until death."

Paul said to them, "My brothers and sisters, I am not a deserter but am a faithful soldier of my King. If I knew that I would die and would not go on to life and glory through this death, then not only would I do what you ask, but I would beg this from you. Now, however, I did not run in vain[39] through many sufferings, nor do I suffer for no reason. There remains for me a crown of justice, which the one in whom I have believed, and about whom I remain certain, will give to me.[40] I am going to him and will come with him in his splendor, and in the splendor of his Father and the holy angels, to judge the world.[41] Therefore, I have no concern for this death and will not obey or carry out your request that I flee."

---

37. Ps 115:8; 135:18. Cf. Isa 44:9–11.
38. Cf. Jer 2:27.
39. Gal 2:2.
40. 2 Tim 4:7–8.
41. 1 Cor 6:2.

illi uero flentes dixerunt ei: quid ergo acturi sumus? quomodo te punito uiuemus et ad illum in quo nos credere persuades peruenire ultra ualebimus?

13. et cum haec inter se loquerentur et populus multus uoces in altum ederet, misit Nero Parthenium quendam et Feritam milites, ut uiderent, si iam Paulus esset occisus. qui aduenientes reppererunt eum adhuc uiuentem et turbas diutissime alloquentem. quos Paulus ad se euocans dixit: uiri, credite in deum uiuum, qui et me et omnes, qui in eum credunt, a mortuis suscitabit.

at illi respondentes dixerunt: ad Caesarem prius ibimus renuntiantes, et cum perfectum fuerit pro quo missi sumus, et cum mortuus fueris et resurrexeris, tunc credemus tuo regi. tu autem explica moras quibus iussionem differs, et uade ad destinatum locum ubi sententiam merito dictatam suscipias.

Paulus quoque dixit eis: commoratione mea in carne plus uos indigetis, si credere uultis, quam ego qui ad uitam per mortem uado. sed iam pergamus exultantes in nomine domini nostri Iesu Christi.

14. cumque ad locum pergerent passionis comitantibus populorum turbis innumeris, uenit ad portam urbis Romae. ubi habuit obuiam nobilissimam matronam, nomine Plautillam, apostolorum feruentissimam dilectricem et religionis diuinae cultricem, quae flens eius se coepit orationibus commendare. ad quam Paulus ait: uale, Plautilla, aeternae salutis filia! commoda mihi pannum quo caput tegis, et secede paululum in partem propter plebis impedimentum, me hic expectans donec reuertar ad te et tibi restituam beneficium. ligabo enim mihi oculos uice sudarii et tuae dilectioni amoris mei pro Christi nomine pignus ad illum pergens relinquam. quae festinato pannum porrexit et ut apostolus iusserat oboediuit.

insultabant autem ei Parthenius et Feritas dicentes: quid credis impostori et mago? cur perdis pannum optimum, non tantum per eum in saeculo lucratura?

Paulus uero dixit ad eam: etiam, filia, hic praestolare aduentum meum, et signa mortis meae in panniculo tibi afferam cum Christo uicturus.

Weeping, they said to him, "What are we going to do? How will we live after you have been punished? And will we any more be able to come to the one in whom you persuade us to believe?"

13. While they were saying these things among themselves and a great number of people was yelling loudly, Nero sent soldiers—a certain Parthenius and Feritas—to see if Paul had already been killed. When they arrived they found him alive and speaking at length to the crowds. Paul summoned them to himself and said, "Men and women, believe in the living God, who will raise from the dead both me and all who believe in him."

But they responded to him and said, "First we will go and report back to Caesar. After the task for which we were sent has been completed, and after you are dead and have been resurrected, then we will believe in your king. You, however, explain the delays by which you are deferring this order, and go to the designated place where you will suffer the sentence that has been rightly prescribed."

And Paul said to them, "If you wish to believe, then you need me to remain longer in the flesh than I do, but I am going to life through death. Now let us go, rejoicing in the name of our Lord Jesus Christ."

14. When they were proceeding to the place of his passion accompanied by countless crowds of people, he came to the gate of the city of Rome. There he met a matron of the highest nobility named Plautilla, a most zealous lover of the apostles and supporter of the divine religion.[42] She was weeping and began to entrust herself to his prayers. Paul said to her, "Greetings, Plautilla, daughter of eternal salvation. Give me the scarf with which you cover your head, and back away a little because of the hindrance of the people. Wait for me here until I return to you and repay your kindness. I will bind my eyes in the manner of a shroud, and I will leave behind a token of your love for me in the name of Christ as I am going to him. She quickly offered the scarf and did as the apostle had ordered.

However, Parthenius and Feritas were insulting her, saying, "Why do you believe this imposter and sorcerer? Why do you give away this very expensive scarf, for you will not profit much through him in this world?"

Paul said to her, "Daughter, wait here for my arrival, and I will bring you signs of my death in this little cloth when I am victorious in Christ."

42. See similar stories in Acts Pet. Paul 80–84, where she is named Perpetua, and Pseudo-Dionysius, *Ep. Tim.* 8, where she is called Lemobia.

15. interea Longinus Megistus et Acestus dum instarent obnixius pro salute sua, inquirentes modum qualiter ad ueram uitam possent pertingere, audierunt a beato apostolo: fratres et filii mei, mox ut ego fuero decollatus et uos ac caeteri ministri interfectionis meae a loco in quo me dominus uocare dignabitur recesseritis, uiri fideles rapient et sepelient corpus meum. uos autem notate locum sepulchri mei, et cras ualde diluculo illuc uenite, ibique inuenietis duos uiros orantes, Titum et Lucam: quibus dicetis qua de causa uos misi; et illi uobis dabunt signum salutis in domino. nolite igitur dubitare exequi quod uobis imperatum est, quoniam statim ut credentes sacro fonte fueritis intincti et diuinorum mysteriorum uiuificatione sacrati, ab omnibus peccatorum contagiis et ab hoc etiam quod reueremini in me perpetrato scelere incunctanter purgati eritis et super niuem dealbati, in serie Christi militum adscripti et caelestis regni efficiemini cohaeredes.

16. et his dictis peruenit ad passionis locum: ubi ad orientem uersus tensis in caelum manibus diutissime orauit cum lacrimis Hebraice et gratias egit Deo. cumque patrio sermone consummasset orationem, ualedicens fratribus benedixit eos, et ligans sibi de Plautillae maforte[1] oculos, in terram utrumque genu fixit et collum tetendit. spiculator uero bracchium in altum eleuans cum uirtute percussit et caput eius abscidit. quod postquam a corpore praecisum fuit, nomen domini Iesu Christi Hebraice clara uoce personuit; statimque de corpore eius unda lactis in uestimento militis exiliuit et postea sanguis effluxit. stola uero qua sibi ligauerat oculos, cum eam quidam uellent rapere, non comparuit: tanta etiam lucis immensitas et odoris suauitas in momento illius decollationis caelitus ibi emicuit, ut mortalium oculi splendorem illum sufferre et humana lingua odorem narrare nequiuerit. uidentes autem omnes qui aderant gratiam Dei in

1. From the Greek μαφόρτης.

15. Meanwhile when Longinus, Megistus, and Acestus were earnestly inquiring about their salvation and asking how they might attain true life, they heard from the blessed apostle, "My brothers and sons, as soon as I am decapitated, and you and the other agents of my death have retired from the place in which the Lord deems it worthy to call me, faithful people will take and bury my body. You, however, note the location of my grave, and come there tomorrow right at dawn. There you will find two men praying, Titus and Luke. Tell them why I sent you, and they will give you the sign of salvation in the Lord.[43] Do not hesitate to carry out what was commanded to you, because as soon as you who believe are dipped in the sacred fountain and consecrated by the life-giving power of the divine mysteries, you will immediately be purified from all the contagions of sin, and even from this evil deed committed against me, which you fear. You will be purified whiter than snow,[44] added to the rank of the soldiers of Christ, and made coheirs of the heavenly kingdom."[45]

16. After saying these things he arrived at the place of his passion. Turning toward the east with his hands raised into heaven, he prayed in Hebrew[46] for a very long time with tears and gave thanks to God. When he had finished his prayer in the language of his fathers, he greeted the brothers and sisters and blessed them. Then binding his eyes with the veil of Plautilla, he placed both knees on the ground and stretched out his neck. The executioner raised his arm high into the air. He struck with force and cut off Paul's head. After it had been severed from the body, it called out the name of the Lord Jesus Christ in Hebrew in a clear voice. Immediately a stream of milk splashed out of his body onto the cloak of the soldier, and after that blood flowed out. The stole with which he had bound his eyes could not be found when certain people wanted to take it. In fact, such an immensity of light and sweetness of scent poured forth from heaven to that place at the moment of his decapitation, that the eyes of mortals were unable to bear that splendor, and human tongues could not describe the smell.[47] All those who were there saw the grace of God in the blessed

43. That is, baptism.

44. Ps 51:7.

45. Rom 8:17; Gal 3:29, 4:7.

46. On Paul's ability to speak Hebrew (or perhaps Aramaic), see Acts 21:40, 22:2, 26:14.

47. Reports of sweet smells surrounding the deaths of holy people are ubiquitous in early Christian texts. See e.g., Mart. Pol. 15.2; Susan Ashbrook Harvey, *Scenting Salvation: Ancient Christianity and the Olfactory Imagination* (Berkeley: University of

beato apostolo, admirati sunt ualde, laudantes et confitentes in multam horam dominum Iesum Christum, aeternum et inuictum regem, quem praedicauerat magnificus doctor et magister gentium.

17. reuertentes uero qui missi fuerant accelerare interfectioem eius, peruenerunt ad portam ciuitatis, ubi inuenerunt Plautillam laudantem et glorificantem dominum in omnibus quae audiuit et uidit per eius sanctum apostolum. et interrogauerunt eam cum irrisione, cur caput suum non operiret de maforte quam praestiterat suo Paulo. quae accensa calore fidei cum magnanimitate respondit: o uani et miseri, qui credere nescitis, quae oculis uidetis et manibus attrectatis! uere habeo eundem quem illi porrexeram pannum, de infusione gloriosi sui sanguinis preciosum. nam de caelo ueniens innumerabilium candidatorum caterua comitatus illum mihi ueracissime rettulit, et rependens gratiam pro benignitate in eum habita dixit: tu mihi Plautilla in terris obsequium praestitisti; ego te quantocius ad caelestia regna pergentem deuotissime obsequar. in proximo namque pro te reuertar et tibi inuicti regis gloriam demonstrabo. et extrahens Plautilla pannum a sinu roseo perfusum sanguine illis ostendit: qui nimio pauore correpti gressu concito perrexerunt ad Caesarem, quae uiderant et audierant nuntiantes.

18. at ille cum audisset miratus est horrifice, et ingenti stupore attonitus coepit de his quae nuntiata sunt ei cum philosophis et amicis atque ministris reipublicae, seu et cum his quos habere poterat ex senatu conicere, atque confabulationis sermonem cum timore et confusione sensus habere.

dumque haec inuicem mirarentur et secum quaererent, uenit Paulus circa horam nonam ianuis clausis stetitque ante Caesarem et ait: Caesar, ecce ego Paulus, regis aeterni et inuicti miles; uel nunc crede, quia non sum

apostle and were greatly amazed. For a long time they praised and confessed the Lord Jesus Christ, the eternal and unconquered King, whom the magnificent teacher and master of the gentiles had made known through his preaching.

17. Those who had been sent to speed along Paul's death turned back and came to the gate of the city, where they met Plautilla, who was praising and glorifying the Lord for all the things she heard and saw through his holy apostle. They asked her mockingly why she was not covering her head with the veil that she had given to Paul. Kindled by the heat of faith, she answered with greatness of spirit, "Oh, worthless and wretched men, who do not know enough to believe the things that you see with your eyes and touch with your hands! Truly I have that very same scarf that I had given to him, made precious by the soaking of his glorious blood. Coming from heaven and accompanied by a crowd of countless figures clothed in white, he truly returned it to me. He gave thanks for the mercy contained in it and said, 'You, Plautilla, offered your service to me in earthly affairs. I will most devotedly offer service to you very soon as you enter into the heavenly kingdom, for in a very short time I will return for you and show you the glory of the unconquered King.'" And pulling out from her reddened bosom the scarf stained with blood, Plautilla showed it to them.[48] They were seized by great trembling and with a quickened pace hurried to Caesar and told him the things that they had seen and heard.

18. When Nero heard this, he was greatly amazed and terrified. Stunned and in a great stupor, he began to talk about these things that had been reported to him with philosophers, friends, and officials of the republic, as well as with those he was able to gather from the Senate. Their conversations were marked by a sense of fear and confusion.

While they were marveling at these things and contemplating them with each other, Paul came at around the ninth hour,[49] although the doors were closed, and stood before Caesar and said, "Caesar, look, I am Paul, the soldier of the eternal and unconquered King. Now believe that I am

California Press, 2006); David L. Eastman, "The Matriarch as Model: Sarah, the Cult of the Saints, and Social Control in a Syriac Homily of Pseudo-Ephrem," *JECS* 21 (2013): 248–49.

48. See e.g., Guy Caesar Bauman, "The Miracle of Plautilla's Veil in Princeton's Beheading of Saint Paul," *Record of the Art Museum, Princeton University* 36.1 (1977): 2–11.

49. That is, around 3:00 p.m.

mortuus, sed uiuo Deo meo. tibi autem, miser, non post multum tempus mala ineffabilia imminent et supplicium maximum, atque aeternus restat interitus pro eo quod inter caetera flagitia pessima multum sanguinem iustorum effudisti iniuste. et haec dicens repente disparuit.

Nero siquidem his auditis ultra quam dici possit timore perculsus et uelut amens effectus, ignorabat quid agere potuisset. suadentibus uero amicis iussit Patroclum ac Barnabam et eos qui uincti erant cum illis soluere atque quo uellent abire.

19. Longinus denique, Megistus et Acestus, sicut eis constituerat Paulus, primo mane uenientes ad sepulchrum eius, uiderunt duos uiros orantes et in medio eorum stantem Paulum. qui pertimescentes in uisu admirabili horruerunt et reueriti sunt accedere propius. Titus autem et Lucas in se ab extasi orationis reuersi, uidentes praefectos atque centurionem qui ministri fuerant necis Pauli ad se properantes, humano timore subrepti in fugam uersi sunt. et Paulus euanuit ex oculis eorum. illi uero post eos clamauerunt dicentes: non, ut suspicamini, beati Dei homines, ideo uenimus, ut uos persequamur ad mortem, sed ut nos credentes per aquam baptismatis ad uitam transferatis aeternam, sicut nobis uerus doctor Paulus promisit, quem ante modicum in medio uestri stantem et orantem conspeximus. haec namque audientes ab eis Titus et Lucas steterunt cum multa laetitia et gaudio spirituali, imponentes eis mox manus et dantes signaculum sanctificationis perpetuae, sicque ieiunio usque ad uesperam percurrente baptizati sunt in nomine domini nostri Iesu Christi, cui cum Patre in unitate Spiritus Sancti est honor et gloria, uirtus et imperium in omnia saecula saeculorum. amen.

not dead but live in my God. As for you, wretched man, unspeakable evils and the greatest punishment will come upon you very soon. And eternal destruction awaits because, among other terrible crimes, you have unjustly spilled a large amount of blood of the righteous." After saying these things he suddenly disappeared.

When he heard these things, Nero was struck with fear even more than can be expressed, and he became like one who has lost his senses and did not know what to do. At the urging of his friends he ordered the release of Patroclus, Barnabas, and those who had been arrested with them, and that they should depart to wherever they wished.

19. Then Longinus, Megistus, and Acestus, just as Paul had ordered them, came at first light to his grave. They saw two men praying and Paul standing in the middle of them. Frightened by this amazing sight, they trembled and were afraid to go any closer. But Titus and Luke, having returned to themselves from the ecstasy of prayer, saw the prefects and the centurion who had been the agents of Paul's death hurrying toward them. Seized by human fear, they turned to flee, and Paul disappeared from their sight. But those men cried out to them, saying, "Blessed men of God, we have not come to persecute you to death, as you suspect. Rather, we have come so that you might transfer us believers through the water of baptism into eternal life, as the true teacher Paul promised us—the very one whom we saw a little bit ago standing and praying in your midst." Hearing these things from them, Titus and Luke stood up with great gladness and spiritual joy. They immediately placed their hands on them and gave them the sign of eternal sanctification. After fasting until evening, they were baptized in the name of our Lord Jesus Christ, to whom, together with the Father in the unity of the Holy Spirit, be honor, glory, power, and dominion forever and ever.[50] Amen.

50. Rev 5:13.

7. Pseudo-Abdias, *Passion of Saint Paul*

CANT 213 / *BHL* 6574–6577

Contents

This text was produced and transmitted as part of a cycle of apostolic lives and martyrdom accounts. It is consistently second in the series, following a version of the life and death of Peter (Pseudo-Abdias's *Passion of Peter*). The opening chapters are largely taken from the Acts of the Apostles and recount the stories of Paul's call and preaching up to the time he was taken to Rome. Our translation picks up the account as the apostle is sailing across the Mediterranean.

Paul miraculously survives a snake bite on the island of Malta and then travels to Rome and remains in free custody, which is where Luke leaves him at the end of Acts. The narrator tells us that Peter has already been crucified on account of his conflict with Simon the sorcerer, but God has spared Paul from martyrdom for the time being so that he may continue to preach the gospel. Paul has a conversation with some of the prominent Jewish leaders in Rome and otherwise preaches the gospel of Jesus Christ freely and openly.

Paul comes to Nero's attention because he is accused of teaching a new superstition and inciting rebellion. Paul tells the emperor that he has been preaching not rebellion but peace and love. By making multiple allusions to his own letters, Paul provides a lengthy list of groups whom he has taught to be obedient, temperate, and respectful of authority. At first Nero is simply amazed, yet he still decides that Paul must die by decapitation. The emperor sends two soldiers to arrest Paul, and the apostle responds by inviting them to salvation. They say that first they must oversee his death, but then they hope he will pray for them so that they may believe in God. Paul tells them to go to his sepulcher on the following day and look for Titus and Luke. The apostle bends his neck before the executioner, and milk comes out of his body instead of blood. All are amazed, and a pious

woman named Lucina takes his body and buries it on her own property on the Ostian Road outside Rome. The author specifies that Paul died on the same date as Peter but two years later.

Literary Background

This text has clear stylistic similarities to writings from Gaul in the sixth century, specifically the works of Gregory of Tours (ca. 538–594 CE), Venantius Fortunatus (ca. 530–600 CE), and a recension of the Martyrology of Jerome traced to southern Gaul. Richard A. Lipsius theorized that an earlier collection of apostolic martyrdom accounts lay behind the Pseudo-Abdias cycle, but in the sixth century additional elements, such as stories from the canonical Gospels, were added to supplement the cycle. Because of the strong comparisons to other writings from Gaul, that region is the most likely place of production for this Latin text.

Abdias, the bishop of Babylon, was identified in the Middle Ages as the author. However, this ascription is probably the result of a misunderstanding. The Passion of Simon and Jude is the final story in the apostolic cycle. Tradition says that they had ordained Abdias, who is credited in the text with producing their acts. In all likelihood, this detail is meant to give the appearance of historical reliability to the Simon and Jude story, as if it had been written by an eyewitness. However, in the Middle Ages the reference to Abdias was applied to the entire apostolic cycle, including the Pauline text. Thus, the author has traditionally been identified as Pseudo-Abdias, but his true identity is unknown.

The author is dependent on the Acts of the Apostles and other accounts in this volume, which he generally follows in the primary elements of the plot. The opening stories follow Acts, and subsequent details line up well with the earlier Martyrdom of Paul and Pseudo-Linus's *Martyrdom of Paul*. However, the author also provides some additional material. His account of the events on Malta includes the story of a leader named Publius, whose dying father is healed by Paul. Paul then performs many other healings and is sent on his way to Rome with many honors. I have already referred above to the long list of groups who, according to Paul before Nero, were taught to live peaceful and obedient lives by the apostle. This series takes on the tone of liturgical repetition and might suggest that the text was produced for a liturgical context. It is combined with a traditional Roman household code such as we find several places in the Pauline corpus. The reference to Lucina at the end of the text situates it among a number of martyrdom

accounts from late antiquity in which this pious matron (also sometimes called Lucilla) cares for the bodies of the saintly dead.[1]

Text

Numerous manuscripts dating back as early as the ninth century include this text, and the quantity of textual witnesses is proof of its popularity in medieval Europe. This translation is based upon the edition produced by Johann Fabricius and reproduced by Giles, which remains the standard edition of the text.

Select Bibliography

Alibert, Dominique, Gisèle Besson, Michèle Brossard-Dandré, and Simon C. Mimouni. "Actes latins des apôtres." Pages 735–46 in vol. 2 of *Écrits apocryphes chrétiens*. Edited by Pierre Geoltrain and Jean-Daniel Kaestli. Pléiade 516. Paris: Gallimard, 2005.

Duchense, Louis. "Les Anciens Recueils dans légendes apostoliques." Pages 69–79 in *Compte rendu du troisième congrès scientifique international des catholiques*. Brussels: Société belge de librairie, 1895.

Erbetta, Mario, trans. "La Passione di Paolo dello Ps. Abdia." Pages 297–301 in *Atti e leggende*. Vol. 2 of *Gli apocrifi del Nuovo Testamento*. Edited by Mario Erbetta. 2nd ed. Turin: Marietti, 1978.

Giles, John Allen, ed. Pages 1:281–85 in *The Uncanonical Gospels and Other Writings, Referring to the First Ages of Christianity, in the Original Languages: Collected together from the Editions of Fabricius, Thilo, and Others*. London: Nutt, 1852.

Lipsius, Richard A. Pages 1:117–78, 2.1:384–90, and Ergänzungsband 5–11 in *Die apokryphen Apostelgeschichten und Apostellegenden*. Braunschweig: Schwetschke, 1883–1890.

Malan, Solomon C., trans. "The Conflict of S. Paul." Pages 11–14 in *The Conflicts of the Apostles: An Apocryphal Book of the Early Eastern Church*. London: Nutt, 1871.

1. See e.g., David L. Eastman, *Paul the Martyr: The Cult of the Apostle in the Latin West*, WGRWSup 4 (Atlanta: Society of Biblical Literature, 2011), 107–10.

Migne, J.-P., trans. "Histoire de saint Paul d'après l'Histoire apostolique d'Abdias, lib. II." Pages 660–64 in vol. 2 of *Dictionnaire des apocryphes*. Paris: Migne, 1858.

Moraldi, Luigi, trans. "Gesta del beato Paolo apostolo e dottore delle genti, compiute in diversi luoghi." Pages 1460–66 in vol. 2 of *Apocrifi del Nuovo Testamento*. Turin: Unione, 1971.

[Passio sancti Pauli auctore Abdia]

5. Post haec Paulus, adscensa naui, uenit in insulam quae dicitur Miletus. barbari uero praestabant non modicam humanitatem nobis, et accensa pyra reficiebant nos omnes propter imbrem qui imminebat, et frigus. quumque congregasset Paulus sarmentorum aliquantam multitudinem, et imposuisset super ignem, uipera a calore prorupit, inuasitque manum eius. ut uero uiderunt barbari pendentem bestiam de manu eius, ad inuicem dicebant: utique homicida est homo hic, qui quum euaserit de mari, ultio non permittit eum uiuere. et ille quidem, excutiens bestiam in ignem, nihil mali passus est. at illi existimabant eum in tumorem conuertendum, et subito casurum, ac moriturum. quum autem illis sperantibus et uidentibus, Paulo nihil mali fieret, conuertentes se, dicebant eum esse deum.

in locis autem illis erant praedia principis, nomine Publii, qui nos suscipiens triduo benigne exhibuit. contigit autem patrem Publii febribus et dysenteria uexatum, iacere. ad quem Paulus ingressus, quum orasset, et imposuisset ei manus, saluauit eum. quo facto omnes qui in insula habebant infirmitates, accedebant et curabantur ab eo. qui etiam multis honoribus Paulum sunt prosequuti. exinde nauigans uenit Romam, ibique solutus a uinculis mansit biennio toto in conducto suo, et suscipiebat omnes qui ingrediebantur ad eum, praedicans subinde regnum Dei, et docens quae sunt de domino Iesu Christo.

6. post crucem uero Petri et elisionem Simonis magi, in urbe adhuc libera manebat custodia: qui a corona etiam martyrii eadem die dispensa-

[Passion of Saint Paul by Pseudo-Abdias]

5. After this Paul boarded a ship and came to the island called Malta.[1] The barbarians showed us no small measure of humanity and rebuilt a burning pyre for us all, on account of the rain and cold that were all around us. After Paul had gathered some sticks and placed them on the fire, a viper rushed out from the heat and seized his hand. When the barbarians saw the beast hanging from his hand, they said to each other, "Certainly this man is a murderer, and although he escaped it by sea, vengeance does not permit him to live." And Paul shook off the beast into the fire and suffered no harm. They supposed that he would swell up and suddenly fall down and die. When, however, they had looked on expectantly but seen that no harm would come to Paul, they changed their minds and said that he was a god.

In those places there were estates of the prince, named Publius, who received us and treated us kindly for three days. It happened that the father of Publius was lying ill, distressed by fevers and dysentery. Paul went in to him, and after he had prayed and laid hands on him, he healed him. After this was done, all those on the island who had illnesses came and were healed by him. They even accompanied Paul with many honors. Sailing from there he came to Rome, and there he remained free from chains for two years in his own rented lodging. He received all who came to him, preaching repeatedly the kingdom of God and teaching the things about the Lord Jesus Christ.[2]

6. After the crucifixion of Peter and the elimination of Simon the sorcerer, Paul remained in the city in free custody.[3] He had been spared from

1. Acts 28:1–10.

2. Acts 28:30–31a.

3. Cf. Acts 28:16, where Paul is allowed to live in a private dwelling but is guarded by a soldier (military custody). On the different categories of imprisonment, see Richard J. Cassidy, *Paul in Chains: Roman Imprisonment and the Letters of St. Paul* (New York: Crossroad, 2001), 37–43. Richard I. Pervo (*Acts: A Commentary*, Hermeneia [Minneapolis: Fortress, 2009], 678 n 80) has suggested that Luke's rendition affords to

tione diuina subtractus fuerat, ut per eum omnes gentes euangelii praedicatione implerentur. itaque quum Romam a Iulio centurione Paulus fuisset perductus, sub unius militis duntaxat custodia constitutus.

post tertium diem conuocauit primores Iudaeorum; quumque conuenissent in hospitium eius, loquebatur illis: ego, uiri fratres (inquit) nihil aduersus plebem faciens, aut consuetudinem maiorum, uinctus ab Hierosolymis traditus sum in manus Romanorum. qui quum inquisitionem de me habuissent, constituerant me primo dimittere, eo quod nulla esset causa mortis in me. contradicentibus autem Iudaeis, coactus sum appellare Caesarem. quam ob causam quum essem in itinere, rogaui uos uidere et alloqui: propter spem enim Israelis hac sum catena circumdatus.

at illi dixerunt ad eum: nos neque literas accepimus de te a Iudaea, neque adueniens aliquis fratrum adnunciauit nomen et conditionem tuam. cupimus autem nunc ex te audire, quae sentis. nam de secta hac notum est nobis, quia ubique ei contradicitur. igitur constituto die uenerunt ad eum plurimi in hospitium ex Iudaeis. quibus exponebat ille scripturas, testificans regnum Dei, suadensque eis ex lege Moysi et Prophetis, a mane usque ad uesperam docebat.

sed quum non omnes crederent in Iesum, dixit Paulus ad eos: Spiritus Sanctus recte per Esaiam loquutus est, uade ad populum istum, et dicas, aure audietis, et non intelligetis, et uidentes uidebitis, et non poteritis perspicere. incrassatum est enim cor populi huius, et oculos compresserunt, ne

the crown of martyrdom on that same day by divine provision,[4] so that through him all nations might be filled with the preaching of the gospel. After Paul had been led to Rome by the centurion Julius, he was placed in the custody of only one soldier.

After the third day he gathered the leaders of the Jews.[5] When they had come together in his lodging, he was saying to them, "I, men and brothers,[6] who am doing nothing against the people or the custom of our ancestors, was chained and given over from Jerusalem into the hands of the Romans. After they had held an inquiry concerning me, they first decided to release me, because there was no reason for death in my case. However, because some Jews contradicted them, I was forced to appeal to Caesar. For this reason when I was on my journey, I asked to see and speak to you, because I am wrapped in this chain on account of the hope of Israel."

But they said to him, "We have received no letters about you from Judea, nor has any one of the brothers coming here made known your name and situation. Now we, however, wish to hear from you what you think, for concerning this sect we know that it is spoken against everywhere." And so on the appointed day a great number of the Jews came to him in his lodging. He explained to them the scriptures, bearing witness to the kingdom of God. He persuaded them from the law of Moses and the prophets and taught from dawn until evening.

But when not all believed in Jesus, Paul said to them, "The Holy Spirit spoke rightly through Isaiah, 'Go to that people and say, "You will hear with your ear but not understand, and seeing you will see but not be able to perceive. The heart of this people has grown fat, and they have closed

---

Paul more liberty than he could have actually enjoyed and may be modeled on Josephus's account of Agrippa's situation in *Ant.* 18.188–237.

4. Cf. the tradition that Peter and Paul died on exactly the same day, as stated by Jerome (*Vir. ill.* 5; *Tract. Ps.* 96.10) and Maximus of Turin (*Serm.* 1.2; 2.1; 9.1), and implied by Dionysius of Corinth (Eusebius, *Hist. eccl.* 2.25.8). A passage linking this opinion to Damasus of Rome is spurious, as demonstrated in *Ecclesiae occidentalis monumenta iuris antiquissima*, ed. Cuthbert H. Turner (Oxford: Clarendon: 1899–1939), 1.2:157

5. The text now follows Acts 28:17–31. Although the author had just above referred to the end of Acts 28 concerning Paul's stay in Rome, the author now goes back to 28:17 and recounts Paul's encounter with some of the Jews in the city. The author actually ends up citing Acts 28:30–31 again at the end of this section.

6. Leaders of a first-century Jewish community in Rome would have been all male, so I have preserved the language of the original.

forte uideant oculis, et auribus audiant et corde intelligant, et conuertantur, et sanem eos. notum ergo cupio esse uobis, et gentibus missum esse hoc salutare Dei et ipsos ab salutem uenturos. et quum hoec dixisset, exierunt ab eo Iudaei, magnas inter se concertationes agitantes. ipse autem Paulus mansit Romae toto illo biennio, in conducto suo, et suscipiebat omnes qui ingrediebantur ad eum, praedicans regnum Dei, et docens quae sunt de domino Iesu Christo, cum omni fiducia, sine impedimento.

7. haec dum Romae apostolus faceret, interea apud Neronem Caesarem defertur, quod non solum nouam superstitionem inueheret, uerum etiam aduersus imperium seditiones excitaret. accersitus igitur, et interrogatus a Nerone, ut rationem doctrinae suae redderet, ita coram Caesare loquutus est: de doctrina quidem Magistri mei, de qua interrogasti me, non eam capiunt, nisi qui fidem mundo pectore adhibuerint. quae enim pacis sunt et caritatis, docui, et per circuitum ab Hierusalem usque in Illyricum repleui uerbum pacis. docui, ut inuicem se honore praeueniant. docui sublimes et diuites, se non extollere, et sperare in incerto diuitiarum, sed in Deum ponere spem suam. docui mediocres, in uictu et uestimento contentos esse. docui pauperes, in sua egestate gaudere. docui patres, filios

their eyes, lest by chance they would see with their eyes, hear with their ears, understand with their hearts, and turn, and I would heal them.”’[7] Therefore, I wish it to be known to you that this salvific message of God is being sent also to the gentiles, and I am going to them for their salvation.”[8] When he had said these things, the Jews went out from him and had great disagreements among themselves.[9] Paul, however, remained in Rome for two entire years in his own rented lodging. He received all those who came to him, preaching the kingdom of God and teaching the things about the Lord Jesus Christ with total confidence and without hindrance.

7. While the apostle was doing these things in Rome, it was reported in the presence of the emperor Nero that not only was Paul bringing a new superstition, but in fact he was inciting rebellions against the empire. Therefore, he was summoned and questioned by Nero, so that he could give an explanation of his teaching. In the presence of Caesar he spoke thus:[10] “Concerning the teaching of my master about which you asked me, indeed no one can understand it except those who accept faith with a pure heart.[11] For whatever things contribute to peace and love, I have taught them. Throughout my journey from Jerusalem as far as Illyricum,[12] I have spread the word of peace. I have taught them to outdo one another in showing honor. I have taught the lofty and the rich not to elevate themselves and hope in the uncertainty of riches, but to place their hope in God.[13] I have taught those with ordinary food and clothing to be content.[14] I have

---

7. Isa 6:9–10.

8. The author omits Paul’s final insult directed at the Jews, “They will listen” (Acts 28:28), perhaps because we soon find out that gentiles like Nero did not in fact listen.

9. This reference to disagreements among the Jews is an expansion in some of the Greek manuscripts of Acts and is designated Acts 28:29. This change appears first in the Western Greek text (D-text) and was later adopted by the Byzantine text. See Bruce M. Metzger, *A Textual Commentary on the Greek New Testament*, 2nd ed. (New York: United Bible Societies, 1994), 444; Pervo, *Acts*, 685–86. The author may, of course, be depending primarily on the Old Latin and/or the Vulgate instead of a Greek manuscript. The details of that dependence are difficult to establish, however, because not all editions of the Vulgate reflect this variant, and a critical edition of the Old Latin is reportedly still in process.

10. Paul’s speech is taken nearly verbatim from Pseudo-Marcellus, *Pass. Holy* 36–38.

11. 1 Tim 1:5; 2 Tim 2:22.

12. Rom 15:19.

13. 1 Tim 6:17.

14. 1 Tim 6:8.

suos docere disciplinam timoris Dei. docui filios, obtemperare parentibus, et monitis salutaribus. docui possidentes, reddere tributum sollicitudine. docui negotiatores, reddere uectigalia ministris Reipublicae. docui uxores, diligere uiros suos, et timere eos quasi dominos. docui uiros, fidem seruare coniugibus, sicut illi seruari sibi pudorem omnibus modis uolunt. quod enim punit maritus in uxore adultera, hoc punit in marito adultero ipse pater et conditor rerum Deus. docui praeterea dominos, ut mitius cum seruis suis agant. docui seruos, ut fideliter, et quasi Deo, ita seruiant dominis suis. docui ecclesiam credentium, unum et omnipotentem, inuisibilem et incomprehensibilem colere Deum. haec autem mihi doctrina non ab hominibus, neque per hominem aliquem data est, sed per Iesum Christum, et Patrem gloriae, qui mihi de coelo loquutus est. et dum me mitteret ad praedicationem dominus meus Iesus Christus, dixit mihi: uade, ego ero tecum, spiritus uitae omnibus credentibus in me: et omnia quaecunque dixeris, aut feceris, ego iustificabo.

8. haec quum dixisset Paulus, Nero imperator obstupuit: indignatusque postea, sententiam in eum mortis pronunciauit, ut capite afficeretur. et quum ei de morte illius tardius nunciaretur, misit duos ex armigeris suis Nero, Feregam et Parthemium: qui euntes inuenerunt Paulum cum omni fiducia et libertate uniuersum populum de Christi mirabilibus

taught the poor to rejoice in their poverty.[15] I have taught fathers to teach their children the discipline of the fear of God.[16] I have taught children to obey their parents and the admonitions that bring salvation.[17] I have taught those who have possessions to pay tribute with care. I have taught merchants to pay taxes to the servants of the republic.[18] I have taught wives to love their husbands and fear them as their masters.[19] I have taught husbands to be faithful to their wives, just as they wish to keep themselves blameless in every way.[20] That which a husband punishes in an adulterous wife, the Father and maker of all things, God himself, punishes in an adulterous husband. I have meanwhile taught masters to deal mildly with their servants.[21] I have taught servants to serve their masters faithfully and as if working for God.[22] I have taught the assembly[23] of believers to worship the one omnipotent, invisible, incomprehensible God. This teaching was given to me not by a human source, nor through another person, but through Jesus Christ and the Father of glory, who spoke to me from heaven.[24] And when my Lord Jesus Christ sent me to preach, he said to me, 'Go, and I will be with you, as the spirit of life for all those who believe in me. And I will forgive whatever things you may have said or done.' "[25]

8. When he had said these things, the emperor Nero was amazed. But afterward he was angered and pronounced a sentence of death against Paul, namely that he should have his head cut off. When Nero heard later about the death of Paul, he sent two of his own armed men, Ferega and Parthenius.[26] They went and found Paul teaching all the people about the

15. Cf. 2 Cor 6:10; Jas 1:9.

16. Eph 6:4.

17. Col 3:20; Eph 6:1.

18. Rom 13:5–7.

19. Even among the disputed Paulines no such command is given.

20. Col 3:18–19; Eph 5:22–28.

21. Phlm; Col 4:1; Eph 6:9.

22. Col 3:22–24; Eph 6:5–6.

23. Or "church."

24. Gal 1:11–12.

25. The source of this quotation ascribed to Jesus is unknown.

26. Cf. Mart. Paul 5 and Pseudo-Linus, *Mart. Paul* 13–16. In Martyrdom of Paul these soldiers are called Parthenius and Pheres. They are sent by Nero to confirm Paul's death and respond sarcastically to the apostle's appeal for them to believe. In that text two other soldiers, Longinus and Cescus, desire salvation. In Pseudo-Linus's *Martyrdom of Paul*, Pheres (there called Feritas) and Parthenius treat both Paul and

instruentem. hos quum uidisset Paulus se accedentes, hortabatur eos, dicens: uenite, filii, et uos credite in Deum, ut saluentur animae uestrae, qui me et omnes credentes sibi per aduentum unigeniti filii sui suscitauit, et in regno suo, quod aeternum est, collocauit.

qui responderunt, dicentes: nos quidem, Paule, prius ibimus ad Neronem, nunciantes ei finem mortis tuae. tu autem ora pro nobis, ut credamus illi, quem tu praedicas Deum. rogabant enim Paulum pro salute sua, ut baptizarentur.

tum rursus apostolus: post paululum, filii, uenite huc ad sepulchrum meum, et inuenietis duos uiros orantes, Titum et Lucam: ipsi post me dabunt signum salutis. et quum haec dixisset, superuenerunt milites, qui correptum eum foras, extra ciuitatem duxerunt. Paulus uero quum uenisset ad locum supplicii, conuertit se contra Orientem: et eleuatis manibus ac oculis suis ad coelum, diutissime orauit. et completa oratione, dedit pacem fratribus qui eum sequuti fuerant: et ualefaciens eis, flexis genibus, crucisque se signo muniens, ceruicem praebuit percussori. e cuius gladio, desecto capite, pro sanguine lac cucurrit, ita ut percussoris dextram lactea unda perfunderet. quod quum circumstantibus uisum fuisset, obstupefacti omnes magnificauerunt Deum, qui tantam gloriam donauerat apostolo suo. cuius corpus Lucina Christi famula, secundo ab urbe milliario, uia Ostiensi, in proprio praedio, differtum aromatibus sepeliuit. passus est

miracles of Christ with all boldness and freedom. When Paul saw them coming toward him, he spoke to them, saying, "Come, my sons, and believe in God, so that your souls may be saved. God has raised up me and all those who believe in him through the coming of his only begotten Son, and he has placed us in his kingdom, which is eternal."

They responded, saying, "First, Paul, we will go to Nero and announce the finality of your death. But you pray for us, so that we may believe in the God whom you preach." They were beseeching Paul for their own salvation, so that they might be baptized.

Then the apostle turned back and said, "After a little while, sons, come here to my sepulcher, and you will find two men praying, Titus and Luke. They will give you the sign of salvation after me." When he had said these things, the soldiers came and led him bound outside and out of the city. When Paul had come to the place of punishment, he turned toward the east. With his hands and eyes raised to heaven, he prayed for a very long time. When his prayer was over, he gave peace to the brothers and sisters[27] who had followed him. He said good-bye to them and, on bended knees, protected himself with the sign of the cross. Then he offered his neck to the executioner. After the head had been severed by his sword, milk rushed out instead of blood, and the milky surge drenched the right hand of the executioner. When this was seen by those standing around, all were amazed and glorified God, who had given such glory to his apostle. Lucina, a servant of Christ, packed his body with spices and buried it at the second milestone from the city on the Ostian Road on her own estate.[28] He suffered on the

---

a noble matron named Plautilla with disdain, as opposed to the believing soldiers Longinus, Megistus, and Acestus.

27. The text says "brothers," but the group present at the execution was likely mixed.

28. This detail is consistent with Lib. pontif. 22. Lucina also appears in many other texts, e.g., Pass. Sebast. 88. On the presence of Lucina as a clear sign of hagiography, see David L. Eastman, *Paul the Martyr: The Cult of the Apostle in the Latin West*, WGRWSup 4 (Atlanta: Society of Biblical Literature, 2011), 107–10. The so-called "Crypt of Lucina" is among the most ancient parts of the Catacomb of St. Callistus, but it is on the Appian Road, not the Ostian Road. Ancient accounts of Paul's martyrdom and burial locate these events in different places in Rome (see ibid., 62–69, 94–114), so the confusion here is not surprising. Archaeologists date the St. Callistus catacomb to the second century at the earliest, so there are multiple reasons not to take this account as historical. Giovanni B. de Rossi suggests that Lucina should be identified with Pomponia Graecina, wife of Aulus Plautius, the first Roman governor of Britain. Tacitus (*Ann.* 13.32) says that Pomponia was accused of following a "foreign superstition"

autem IIIo kalendas Iulias, duobus iam a passione Petri elapsis annis, regnante domino nostro Iesu Christo, cui est apud aeternum Patrem et Spiritum Sanctum honor et gloria, in secula seculorum. amen.

third calends of July (June 29) two years after the passion of Peter,[29] during the reign of our Lord Jesus Christ.[30] To him, along with the eternal Father and the Holy Spirit, be honor and glory forever and ever. Amen.

---

but acquitted in a trial. De Rossi reads this as a veiled reference to her conversion to Christianity, at which time she took the name Lucina (Giovanni B. de Rossi, *La Roma sotterranea cristiana* [Rome: Litografia Pontificia, 1864–1877], 1:319; 2:282, 362–63). De Rossi's bold conjecture finds little support in the evidence, however.

29. On the belief that the apostles died on the same day, see n. 4 above. Cf. also Ambrose of Milan (*Virginit.* 19.124), Augustine (*Serm.* 295.7; 381.1), Prudentius (*Perist.* 12.5, 21–22), Gregory of Tours (*Glor. mart.* 28), and Arator (*Act. apost.* 2.1247–49), who record that the apostles died on the same date but a year apart.

30. It was standard Roman practice to date events by the tenure of the consuls or the emperor, but here the author emphasizes that Christ, not Nero, was actually reigning at that time.

8. History of the Holy Apostle My Lord Paul

BHO 889

Content

The first seven chapters of this history of Paul are a resume of the material in the Acts of the Apostles. The author acknowledges as much and states that he had quickly passed over those stories, because Luke had accurately portrayed them. We pick up the story in the period after Paul's initial defense before the emperor Nero. The apostle is released and reaches his goal of going to Spain to preach the gospel. Ten years later Paul hears of the death of Shimeon (Peter) in Rome and returns to encourage the Christians there. He converts many along the way, including thousands in Rome and many from Nero's household.

A prefect named Tertullus complains to Nero that Paul is making all of Rome into Christians. Nero realizes that many of his close associates have changed their lifestyles and even left his court in order to follow Paul's preaching, so he becomes angry and has the apostle arrested. Paul foresees that he is about to die and writes a letter to Timothy predicting his demise. Nero arrests Paul and sentences him to death. Not long after Shimeon (Peter) had been killed, Paul is decapitated at the same place, and the blood of the apostles mixes together. Bishop Linus takes Paul's body and buries it alongside Peter's in a house that becomes a place of prayer for the Christians. The narrator then gives details of the chronology of Paul's ministry from the time of his calling to the time of his death.

Later, two trees miraculously grow at the place where the blood of the apostles had been spilled. They perform many healings for those who believe, but for unbelievers they do nothing. Every year during the Easter Vigil, the trees would embrace each other at the moment of the passing of the peace in the liturgy—a symbol of the harmony of their preaching. Many, both Jew and gentile, are converted because of these miracles, until some mischievous Jews cut down the trees.

The text closes with an appeal for the scribe, the owner, and the hearers of the text to be brought to the glorious realm where the apostle resides.

Literary Background

Stylistic and manuscript evidence demonstrate that the author of the Petrine History of Shimeon Kepha the Chief of the Apostles. (ch. 4 in this volume) also produced this text. In fact, this Pauline account is the second in the cycle of the Acts of the Martyrs and Saints. Examples of literary dependence in the History of Shimeon Kepha the Chief of the Apostles allow us to date it no earlier than the sixth or seventh century, so a similar date should be assigned to this text. Its place of production and author are unknown.[1]

The author is clearly dependent upon the Acts of the Apostles for the early sections of the text, and the basic narrative of execution at the hands of Nero could have been taken from any number of sources. The narrator does connect with a particular detail from other accounts of Peter's death, namely his burial by Marcellus. In this story the elaborate tomb of Marcellus holds Peter's body for only a short time, because Linus the bishop then moves the body into a house along with the corpse of Paul. Only at a later date are the relics placed in a church. It is possible to read this as a justification for the joint apostolic cult site on the Appian Road south of Rome, although I have shown elsewhere that there were likely never any apostolic remains at that site.[2]

The unique material in this account is notable. For example, the author identifies the prefect of Rome as Tertullus. This was the name of an orator who was sent by the Jewish authorities to accuse Paul before the Roman procurator Felix in Caesarea Maritima (Acts 24:1–9). The memory of a legal charge being brought against Paul by a figure named Tertullus is here transferred to the Roman context. Also, while other traditions state that Paul and Peter died at different places and either on the same day or on the same date one or two years apart, here their deaths are separated seemingly by only a few days. Peter's death is recent enough that his blood still lies on the ground where Paul is decapitated, meaning that both apostles do

1. The claim of Clementine authorship at the end of the Petrine History of Shimeon (ch. 4 in this volume) is not repeated here.

2. David L. Eastman, *Paul the Martyr: The Cult of the Apostle in the Latin West*, WGRWSup 4 (Atlanta: Society of Biblical Literature, 2011), 94–114.

not die on June 29, their mutual feast day. Furthermore, this author adds a legend about two miraculous trees that grow on the spot of the apostolic deaths. The trees are emblematic of the author's larger literary project, which is to demonstrate the harmony of the apostles (*concordia apostolorum*). Peter and Paul were never at odds with each other; in fact, even the trees that rise to take their place greet and embrace each other. This witness to apostolic agreement allows them to continue preaching the gospel even from beyond the grave, and many come to faith in Christ as a result of the miracles they perform. In a sense the apostles are symbolically martyred a second time, when "the Jewish crucifiers" kill the trees. Finally, the author seeks to clarify the precise chronology of Paul's later life, beginning with his release from Rome and thus picking up the story where the Acts of the Apostles ends. He tells us precisely how long Paul preached after his first defense and claims that 2 Timothy was written at the time of his second imprisonment in Rome, which ended with his death.

Text

This edition of the text is based on a single manuscript from Kirkūk, Iraq, perhaps from the Monastery of Mār Thomas. In the eighteenth and nineteenth centuries, the East Syrian Christians of this region were labeled Nestorians, so the secondary literature sometimes refers to this as a "Nestorian" text, although there is nothing particularly Nestorian in its contents. Archbishop Khayyät of Diyarbekh made the manuscript available to Ignazio Guidi, who in turn permitted Paul Bedjan to publish an edition of the text. This translation is from the Bedjan edition and is the first available in English.

The History of the Holy Apostle My Lord Paul should not be confused with another Syriac history, the Martyrdom of Paul, the Elect Apostle of the Messiah, which was translated into French by François Nau in 1898.[3] Based on two manuscripts in the British Museum (Add. 12172 and Add. 14732), it is essentially a Syriac translation of the Greek Martyrdom of the Holy Apostle Paul in Rome and thus is not included in this volume.

3. François Nau, "La version syriaque inédite des martyres de S. Pierre, S. Paul et S. Luc d'après un manuscrit du dixième siècle," *ROC* 3 (1898): 39–57. The Syriac text of the Luke account is published later in that same volume, but Nau does not explain why he does not provide the Syriac texts for the accounts of Peter and Paul.

Select Bibliography

Baumstark, Anton. Pages 40–44 in *Die Petrus- und Paulusacten in der litterarischen Überlieferung der syrischen Kirche*. Leipzig: Harrassowitz, 1902.

Bedjan, Paul, ed. "History of the Holy Apostle my Lord Paul" (in Syriac). Pages 41–44 in *Acta martyrum et sanctorum*. Leipzig: Harrassowitz, 1890.

De Stefani, Luigi, trans. "Storia del Beato Apostolo S. Paolo." *GSAT* 14 (1901): 201–16.

Guidi, Ignazio. "Bemerkungen zum ersten Bande der syrischen Acta Martyrum et Sanctorum," *ZDMG* 46 (1892): 744–46.

Peeters, Paul. "Notes sur la légende des apôtres S. Pierre et S. Paul dans la littérature syrienne." *AnBoll* 21 (1902): 121–40.

ܬܫܥܝܬܐ ܕܫܠܝܚܐ ܩܕܝܫܐ ܡܪܝ ܦܘܠܘܣ

8. ܒܝܡܐ ܒܥܘܪܒܐ ܡܫܬܟܚܐ ܒܥܡܐ ܣܘܥܪܢܘܗܝ ܕܦܘܠܘܣ ܒܛܪܣܘܣ ܚܕܬܐܝܬ. ܘܟܠ ܗܘܐ ܚܕ ܡܬܕܡܪ ܒܥܒܕ ܒܠܚܘܕܘܗܝ ܐܝܟ ܡܢ ܕܠܚܢܫ ܥܠܡܐ ܚܕܝܢ ܐܢܘܢ.

9. ܦܘܠܘܣ ܕܝܢ ܡܢ ܒܬܪ ܕܢܦܩ ܡܫܡܫ ܒܪܘܚܐ ܩܕܡ ܢܐܘܢ ܘܐܡܪ: ܠܘܬ ܟܠܡܫܡܫܢܘܬܐ ܕܒܪܘܚܐ ܐܬܬܝ. ܘܚܘܐ ܘܡܚܐ ܫܒܚܐ ܒܐܬܘܬܐ ܘܒܐܬܕܪܬܐ ܕܐܡܪ. ܟܕ ܕܝܢ ܫܡܥܘ ܦܘܠܘܣ ܡܢ ܢܐܘܢ ܐܬܟܠܝ ܗܘܐ: ܐܢܫܐ ܕܐܬܬܢ ܡܫܟܢܐ، ܡܢܗ ܐܦ ܗܘܢ ܡܬܟܫܦܝܢ ܠܐܢܫܐ ܕܒܝܬܐ ܒܛܝܒܘܬܗ ܕܦܘܠܘܣ ܕܐܬܐ ܕܒܢܝ ܠܒܝܬܐ ܒܢܝ ܗܝܡܢܘܬܐ. ܘܟܕ ܐܫܬܡܥ ܦܘܠܘܣ ܟܠ ܗܠܝܢ ܕܡܫܡܗ ܡܢܘܬ ܘܟܠ ܒܢܝܗܘܢ. ܒܬܪ ܕܐܬܡܢܝ ܡܚܢܝܬܐ ܡܫܬܐܠܬܐ: ܘܐܦ ܒܗ ܒܢܝܗܘܢ ܠܟܠܗܘܢ ܘܠܐ ܡܫܚ ܡܢܗ ܠܡܫܬܘܬܐ ܘܡܫܝܚܐ: ܘܐܦ ܡܢ ܒܬܪܗ ܕܡܢܝܢ ܫܘܓܐܐ ܕܐܬܐ.

10. ܗܝܕܝܢ ܟܠ ܛܪܘܢܘܣ ܗܘܦܪܟܐ[1]: ܘܐܟܠ ܩܪܝܒܘܗܝ ܕܦܘܠܘܣ ܩܕܡ ܡܢܗ ܘܐܡܪ ܠܗ: ܕܒܢܝܢܘܗܝ ܦܘܠܘܣ ܠܟܠܗ ܕܝܘܢܐ ܒܪܘܫܠܡ. ܗܝܕܝܢ ܢܐܘܢ ܡܢܗ ܐܬܡܛܝ ܗܘܐ ܪܘܓܙܐ ܪܒܐ: ܘܡܢ ܗܘܐ ܘܐܫܪܘܗܝ ܠܦܘܠܘܣ. ܡܛܠ ܕܒܠܗܘܢ ܪܒ ܚܝܠܐ ܘܐܣܪܘ ܕܡܢܗ ܕܡܫܬܝܢ ܗܘܘ ܩܕܡܘܗܝ: ܡܫܡܫܘܗܝ ܗܘܘ ܘܗܘܘ ܘܫܠܡܘ ܘܫܠܝܚܘܗܝ ܡܬܕܪܬܐ ܕܛܠܐ ܠܟܠܡܫܝܚܐ ܕܡܪܝܐ.

1. From the Greek ὕπαρχος.

History of the Holy Apostle My Lord[1] Paul

8. Up to this point Luke accurately related the deeds of Paul in the Acts of the Apostles. For this reason we quickly passed over these things, as they are already known by the readers of scripture.

9. But after Paul made his defense before Nero and was set free, he again prepared for the ministry of preaching. He went and preached for ten years in Spain and the regions around there.[2] But after the blessed Peter had been crowned[3] by Nero, the brothers and sisters[4] whom Shimeon[5] had made disciples also began making disciples of others until the arrival of Paul in Rome for the second time. When Paul was told about the crowning of Shimeon, he hurried and came to Rome. After he had made disciples in many cities, he also brought into the household of Christ thousands in Rome who could not be counted, including a great multitude from the household of Caesar.[6]

10. Then Tertullus the prefect[7] accused Paul before Caesar. He said to him that Paul had made all of Rome into Christians. Then Nero Caesar was filled with great anger. He issued an order and arrested Paul, because all the commanders and noblemen of Caesar who had been in his presence had left him and changed their way of living, so that they could exercise the virtue[8] that is proper for disciples of the truth.

---

1. The term *marí* ("my lord") is frequently used in Syriac literature to refer to holy people.

2. On the traditions of Paul's visit to Spain, see Eastman, *Paul the Martyr*, 144–48.

3. That is, martyred. Crowning is one of dominant images attached to martyrdom.

4. Literally, "brothers," but earlier parts of the text specify that both men and women became disciples by Peter's preaching.

5. In this section the author refers to the apostle by both his Greek (Peter) and Semitic (Shimeon) names.

6. Phil 4:22.

7. Or *governor*. In Acts 24:1–9 an orator (ῥήτωρ) named Tertullus is hired by the Jewish religious authorities to accuse Paul before the Roman procurator Felix in Caesarea Maritima.

8. Both words in the expression "exercise the virtue" have connotations of asceti-

11. ܘܟܕ ܡܚܠ ܓܒܝܐ ܦܘܠܘܣ ܕܡܫܝܐ ܗܘܐ ܠܘܬ ܡܪܢ܆ ܡܠܟ ܠܘܬ ܛܝܡܬܐܘܣ ܠܟܡܝܪܘ
ܚܣܝܪܐ: ܕܗܘܐ ܥܡ ܕܐܚܐ ܕܐܬܡܠܝܘ ܡܠܦܢ: ܘܐܢܐ ܡܫܬܡܠܐ ܐܢܐ ܣܠܩ ܒܢܘܪܘܬܐ ܕܡܪܢܐ. ܟܕ ܗܟܝܠ ܐܬܢܟܣ
ܡܫܪ: ܥܠ ܦܘܠܘܣ ܡܢ ܥܠܡܐ ܡܓܕ̈ܦܢܘܬܐ ܕܗܘ̈ܝ ܥܠܘܗܝ ܡܢ ܪ̈ܫܝܥܐ: ܩܡ ܕܒܫܝܢܐ ܢܦܩܬ ܪܘܚܗ.
ܘܠܡܫܠܠ ܐܚܐ ܕܟܠܗ ܒܫܘܠܠܗ ܕܫܡܥܘܢ ܟܐܦܐ: ܕܒܪ[2] ܐܦ ܠܦܘܠܘܣ ܠܕܘܟܬܐ ܗܝ ܕܒܗ ܐܬܩܛܠ
ܫܡܥܘܢ: ܘܫܩܠܘܗܝ ܪܡܘ ܒܫܘܩܐ. ܘܣܠܩ ܕܡܗ ܥܡ ܕܡܗ ܕܛܘܒܢܐ ܫܡܥܘܢ ܟܐܦܐ.

12. ܘܗܘܐ ܫܓܘܫܝܐ ܣܓܝܐܐ ܒܥܠܡܐ: ܘܥܡܛܬܐ ܡܪܝܪܬܐ ܐܬܚܙܝܬ ܒܥܠܡܐ ܟܠܗ ܥܕܡܐ: ܥܠ ܕܐܬܛܠܡܘ
ܡܢ ܚܣܡܗܘܢ ܕܡܠܟ̈ܐ. ܘܩܡ ܠܣܘܣ ܡܕܒܪܢܐ: ܘܩܦܣ ܦܓܪܗ ܕܦܘܠܘܣ ܒܠܒܐ: ܘܩܒܪܗ ܒܐܪܥܐ
ܪܒܐ ܐܝܟܐ ܕܩܒܝܪ ܗܘܐ ܡܪܝ ܫܡܥܘܢ ܟܐܦܐ. ܠܗ ܒܩܒܪܗ ܕܡܪܝܡܘܬܗ: ܡܛܠ ܕܒܪ ܐܚܝ: ܐܬܚܙܝܘ
ܠܫܡܥܘܢ ܟܐܦܐ ܡܢ ܠܥܠ ܘܫܡܥܘܗܝ ܒܥܠܡܐ ܚܕ. ܘܚܒܐ ܕܐܚܐ ܐܬܐܚܕ ܥܡܗ ܐܦ ܦܓܪܗ ܕܛܘܒܢܐ
ܦܘܠܘܣ ܫܠܝܚܐ. ܘܗܘܐ ܒܥܠܡܐ ܗܘ ܕܫܡܫܝܢ ܗܘܘ ܒܗ ܒܟܠ ܙܒܢ ܠܡܓ̈ܪܬܐ. ܘܟܕ ܗܘܐ ܫܝܢܐ ܒܥܕܬܐ:
ܐܚܕܘ ܐܢܘܢ ܠܓܪ̈ܡܝܗܘܢ ܘܣܡܘ ܐܢܘܢ ܒܥܕܬܐ ܕܒܐܪܥܐ ܪܒܐ.

2. Bedjan suggests the reading ܕܒܪܘ (“they led”).

11. When Paul received a revelation that he was about to be taken away to our Lord, he wrote to Timothy, his approved disciple, "Look, the time has now come that I will be released, and I am being poured out[9] for the sake of the preaching of the truth." Thus, after Caesar had been agitated against Paul based on the pretext of the charges made against him by wicked people, he ordered that his head be cut off with a sword. A short time after the crowning of Shimeon Kepha, he also led Paul to that place where Shimeon had been killed. They cut off his head with a sword, and his blood mixed with the blood of the blessed Shimeon Kepha.[10]

12. There was a great commotion among the people, and bitter distress reigned in the whole church, because the people had been deprived of the presence of the apostles. Then Linus the bishop[11] issued an order and took the body of Paul by night and buried him with great honor in the same place that he had placed my lord Shimeon Kepha. This was not in the tomb of Marcellus,[12] because after a time they took Shimeon Kepha from there and placed him in a certain house. At that time the body of blessed Paul the apostle was also placed with him, and that house in which they were laid became a house of prayer for many. When there was peace in the church, they brought the two of them and placed them in a church with great honor.[13]

---

cal renunciation. Thus, these prominent Romans had left Nero's court in order to pursue lives of celibacy.

9. Phil 2:17; 2 Tim 4:6.

10. This contradicts the tradition that Peter died at the Vatican northwest of the city, while Paul died on the Ostian Road south of the city. However, the Christian poet Prudentius, writing at the turn of the fifth century, states that the apostolic blood had symbolically mixed in the marshes along the Tiber River, which "was made holy by two victories, for it witnessed both cross and sword when a rain of blood flowed over the same grass twice and soaked it" (*Perist.* 12.7–10).

11. The ordination of Linus by Peter is also recounted in the Liberian Catalog from 354 CE (*Chronica minora saec. IV. V. VI. VII.*, ed. T. Mommsen, MGH.AA 9 [Berlin: Weidmann, 1892], 73); Irenaeus (*Haer.* 3.3.3)—although Irenaeus states that Peter and Paul together ordained Linus; Eusebius (*Hist. eccl.* 5.6.1); Hist. Shim. 33; and Teach. Shim. 6. Cf. Pseudo-Abdias, *Pass. Pet.* 3.15; the apocryphal Epistle of Clement to James 2; and Tertullian, *Praescr.* 32, where Clement is identified as the one ordained by Peter as the second bishop of Rome.

12. Mart. Pet. 11; Pseudo-Linus, *Mart. Pet.* 16.

13. This description of a joint cult site including a large church is probably a reference to the catacombs (now St. Sebastian) on the Appian Road south of Rome. Evidence from graffiti places veneration of the apostles there at least as early as 258 CE,

13. ܡܠܟ ܗܟܝܠ ܢܪܘܢ ܕܢܬܕܪܫܘܢ ܦܘܠܘܣ ܠܗܠܝܢ ܘܫܡܥܘܢ ܟܐܦܐ. ܡܢ ܒܬܪ ܠܗ ܠܡܫܝܚܐ ܘܬܒܥܘܗ ܘܒܕܡܐ ܠܟܠܗ ܠܐܠܗܘܬܐ ܘܡܫܝܚܘܬܗ ܕܝܠܗ ܦܫܛ: ܟܦܪܝܢ ܒܗ ܘܚܕܐ ܟܠܗ̇ ܒܕܡܐ ܘܐܬܡܠܟܘ ܡܢ ܡܗܝܡܢܐ ܒܗܘܢ. ܘܐܬܦܢܝ ܟܐܦܐ ܐܡܪ ܠܢܪܘܢ ܒܗܠܝܢ ܐܒܘܗܝ ܕܦܘܠܘܣ: ܘܐܬܦܢܝ ܟܐܦܐ ܐܡܪ ܕܟܕ ܠܗܘܢ ܕܬܘܕܝܬܐ: ܟܕ ܗܠܝܢ ܒܥܝܢ ܟܐܦܐ ܐܡܪܝܢܢ. ܘܟܕ ܫܡܥ ܡܢ ܐܪܕܝܗ ܘܒܕܡܐ ܠܟܠܗܝܢ ܠܗܠܝܢ ܘܫܡܥܘܢ ܟܐܦܐ. ܐܬܡܠܟ[3] ܕܝܢ ܗܟܝܠ ܢܪܘܢ ܒܟܠܗ ܠܐܠܗܘܬܐ ܘܡܫܝܚܘܬܗ ܕܝܠܗ: ܘܗܘ ܗܘ ܒܬܪ ܠܗܠܝܢ ܘܟܠܗ ܘܫܡܗ ܕܦܪܘܩ. ܗܟܝܠ ܕܝܢ ܐܬܡܠܟ ܩܕܡ ܦܘܠܘܣ: ܘܦܘܠܘܣ ܒܠܘܕ ܒܗ ܒܟܠܗ ܒܡܫܝܚܘܬܐ ܒܪܢܫ ܠܐܡܪ ܒܟܦܪܝܢ ܠܗܘܐ ܒܗ.

14. ܘܟܕ ܫܡܥ ܒܪܘܚܐ ܗܠܝܢ ܕܢܫܡܥ ܒܟܠܗܘܢ ܕܗܘܐ ܘܩܝܡܐ: ܡܢ ܠܘܬ ܐܠܗܐ ܙܘܥܐ ܕܡܫܝܚܝܢ ܗܘܐ ܡܢ ܟܠܗܘܢ ܐܠܗܐ ܠܡܬܦܢܝܘ ܘܒܥܠܕܒܒܘܗܝ. ܘܐܬܦܢܝ ܗܘ ܣܦܪܐ ܘܗܝܠܐ ܙܘܥܐ ܒܗܘܢ ܡܫܬܡܫܝܢ ܗܘܘ: ܘܡܢ ܠܫܡܝܐ ܗܘ ܠܐܦܝܐ ܡܢ ܟܠ ܟܦܝܢ ܣܦܪܐ ܕܟܝܢ ܗܘܘ ܕܢܦܩܝܢ ܚܠܐ ܗܘ ܚܝܠܐ ܘܐܬܦܢܝܐ. ܒܘܪܟܬܐ ܟܠ ܐܝܟ ܐܝܟ ܕܒܬܘܪܬܐ ܕܐܬܪܘ ܫܡܗܘܢ ܢܫܒ ܗܘܐ: ܘܡܫܬܟܚ ܗܘܐ ܒܟܠ ܐܬܪܐ ܦܬܝܐ ܕܫܡܗܘܢ ܒܗ ܡܬܬܙܝܥ ܗܘܐ. ܘܡܠܟܘܬܐ ܕܟܠܐ ܒܢܦܫܬܐ ܕܒܝܫܐ ܢܦܩܪܐ ܕܪܥܝܐ ܗܘܝܢ ܗܘܘ. ܐܬܠܡܫ ܒܗܘܢ ܕܝܢ ܡܦܝܣ ܕܟܠܐ ܠܐܬܪܘܬܐ:

3. Read ܐܬܡܠܟܘ.

13. The time of the preaching of the blessed Paul, therefore, lasted for thirty-five years, from the nineteenth year of Tiberius until the thirteenth year of the reign of Nero Caesar.[14] There were twenty-one years until he was handed over by the Jews in Judea. Then he spent two further years in prison in Caesarea and two in Rome the first time he was there. Together with these were the ten other years,[15] so that altogether from his calling until his crowning there were thirty-five years. These victors were crowned in the thirteenth year of the reign of Nero, which is the thirty-sixth year of the passion of our Savior. Shimeon was crowned before Paul, and Paul was crowned after him in that same year on Thursday, the twenty-ninth day of the month of Tammuz.[16]

14. A little while later, in the places upon which the blood of the holy men flowed, two great trees sprang up that were different from all the other trees in regard to their leaves and their fruit. Many healings and great miracles were performed by them. When the word about this marvel spread, many people from everywhere were coming to see that new and amazing spectacle. Everyone was receiving from the trees a blessing, as if (from) the healing power of that place,[17] and they were healing all the severe maladies among those who approached them. There were ready healings for very many people for a long time.

It was said by them that a certain marvel occurred, which was difficult for the unbelievers to hear. Yet for those strong in faith, it was easy and simple to accept. For nothing is difficult for God, according to the word of the angel.[18] For it is said that on the night of the resurrection of our Savior at the time of the mysteries,[19] at the moment that the deacon instructed the people to offer the peace to each other, those trees used to bend toward each other and embrace each other for about one hour. By this they were demonstrating the harmony in their preaching, because not only in their

---

and Constantine built a basilica at the site during the first years when "there was peace in the church." See Eastman, *Paul the Martyr*, 71–114.

14. These dates would be approximately 33 to 67/68 CE.

15. In Spain (see above, §9).

16. Tammuz is the 10th month in the Syriac calendar and corresponds to July or to late June and early July. If the Thursday designation were taken seriously, then the calculation would yield a date of June 29, 67 CE. Note, however, that only Paul died on the traditional feast day of June 29, for Peter is said to have died some time earlier that year.

17. The Syriac here is obscure.

18. Gen 18:14.

19. That is, the Eucharist celebrated during the Easter Vigil.

ܘܠܫܡ̈ܥܝܢ ܘܡܫܝܚܘܬܐ ܠܫܡܫ ܗܘܐ ܒܡܫܡܫܗ: ܘܒܡܠ̈ܦܢܘܬܗ ܒܡܫܝܚܘܬܐ ܕܟܠܗ ܘܦܫܛ ܒܥܘܕܪܢܗ. ܠܐ ܓܝܪ
ܥܡܠ ܠܐܠܗܐ ܡܕܡ: ܐܝܟ ܡܫܠܡܢܘܬܗ ܘܡܠܐܟܐ. ܡܛܠ ܐܡܪܐ ܓܝܪ ܕܟܠܡܐ ܗܘ ܕܡܫܬܡܠܐ ܘܦܪܘܩ: ܟܕ ܒܝܬܐ ܘܐܪܙܐ:
ܕܪܒܐ ܘܡܢ ܡܫܡܫܢܐ ܕܟܠܗܘܢ ܡܠܟܐ ܠܥܒܝ̈ܕܐ: ܡܬܩܪܝܢ ܗܘܘ ܐܠܗܐ ܗܘܘ. ܘܐܝܟ ܗܢܐ ܚܕܐ ܠܥܒܝ̈ܕܐ ܒܥܡܡ
ܗܘܘ. ܘܒܗܘܢ ܟܠ ܐܦܘܠܘܢ ܘܟܪܙܘܬܐ ܡܟܪܙܝܢ ܗܘܘ: ܟܕ ܘܠܐ ܗܘܐ ܒܟܣܘ ܘܚܝܠܐ ܘܦܓܪܐ ܡܫܬܡܪܐ
ܗܘܐ: ܐܠܐ[4] ܐܦ ܗܘܐ ܒܥܘܠܗܘܢ ܐܝܩܘܢܐ[5] ܠܐ ܡܬܚܙܝܐ[6] ܘܡܥܒܘܕܗܘܢ ܘܒܠܥܘܡܐ ܡܩܝܡ. ܘܟܠ ܚܕܐ ܒܥܘܢܐ
ܒܝܬ ܦܠܚܘ ܡܬܝܒܠܐ ܠܟܠܗܘܢ ܢܦܫܐ[7] ܚܝܐ ܘܐܢܘܫܐ: ܘܡܢ ܐܬܪܘܬܐ ܡܫܬܡܠܝܐ ܡܢ ܓܫܡܝ ܗܘܘ. ܘܐܦ ܡܪ̈ܝܐ
ܘܡܘܕܝܐ ܘܡܩܝܡܐ ܫܘܬܐܐ ܡܬܬܠܒܫܝܢ ܗܘܘ ܒܟܠܟܐ ܗܘܐ. ܐܡܝܢܐ ܕܡܢ ܫܘܬܐܬܐ ܘܐܘܠܨܢܝܗܘܢ ܐܬܐܪܝܫ
ܫܡܝܐ ܒܡܘܕܝܐ ܕܟܘܦܐ: ܘܡܫܬܒܚܝܢ ܒܟܠܗ ܦܫܛܘ ܐܝܟ ܠܐܠܗܐ ܗܘܘ. ܘܡܛܠ ܕܠܐ ܫܪܐ ܗܘܐ ܒܟܝܢܐ
ܠܡܘܬܟܠܘ ܘܐܫܬܐܐ ܕܥܡܗܘܢ: ܐܦܠܐ ܗܘ ܐܠܗܐ ܗܘܘ.

15. ܗܠܝܢ ܗܟܢܐ ܕܐܬܡܠܟܘ ܕܡܢ ܦܘܠܘܣ ܡܫܝܚܐ ܗܘܐ ܐܬܚܙܝ. ܘܕܪܟܒܬܗ ܠܐܬܪ ܚܕܐ
ܘܒܝܬܗ ܕܟܠ ܐܬܪ. ܘܡܠܘܟܐ ܘܚܝܐ: ܟܕ ܩܪܝܐ ܘܡܩܘܒܠ ܢܡܘܣܐ ܕܥܡܗ ܢܒܥܘܢ. ܐܝܟ ܘܐܡܪܝܢ.

16. ܡܠܟܐ ܠܝܫܘܥ ܕܢܚܢ ܒܟܠܢܫܐ ܡܢ ܦܘܠܘܣ ܡܬܠܡܕܐ ܕܟܠ ܥܡܡܝܢ. ܘܠܐܠܗܐ ܫܘܒܚܐ.
ܐܝܟ ܘܐܡܪܝܢ.

4. From the Greek ἀλλά.
5. From the Greek εἰκών.
6. Read ܡܬܚܙܝܢܐ.
7. Bedjan suggests inserting ܗܘܐ here.

bodily lives, but even now in their deaths, they showed an infallible image of their agreement on divine matters.[20] Every year at that time the entire city went out there to see this marvel, and those from various places were also present. Many unbelievers, both Jews and gentiles, were being converted on account of this, so that jealousy was stirred up among the Jewish crucifiers by a crowd of their disciples, and at night they secretly cut down those trees. Because the world was not worthy of the gift of healing from them,[21] those trees did not spring up again.

15. This then is the history of my lord Paul the apostle, by whose prayers the church and its children[22] everywhere will be helped. May the scribe and the owner, together with the reader and the hearers,[23] be considered worthy to rejoice with him. Amen.

16. Thus concludes the history of the glorious one among the apostles, my lord Paul, the teacher of all the nations. Glory to God. Amen.

---

20. This appeal to the harmony of the apostles (*concordia apostolorum*) was a central element of Rome's claims to apostolic foundations and authority. See e.g., Charles Pietri, "Concordia Apostolorum et renovatio urbis (Culte des martyrs et propagande pontificale)," *MEFR* 73 (1961): 275–322; J. M. Huskinson, *Concordia Apostolorum: Christian Propaganda at Rome in the Fourth and Fifth Centuries*, BARIS 148 (Oxford: British Archaeological Reports, 1982).

21. Cf. Heb 11:38.

22. Literally, "sons."

23. The reference to a reader (or lector) and hearers strongly suggests that this text was meant to be read in a liturgical context. The request of a blessing for the scribe is not unknown (e.g., Hist. Shim. 37), yet here this request is extended to the owner of the actual manuscript, who may also have been the patron and paid for its production.

9. Martyrdom of Paul the Apostle and the Discovery of His Severed Head[1]

BHO 884, 898

Content

This Syriac text may be divided into three distinct sections. In part one the author provides a brief summary of Paul's biography, recounting his Jewish ancestry and eventual baptism by Ananias. After suffering many persecutions Paul comes to Rome and finds Peter there. They agree that Paul should focus his mission on the gentiles, while Peter will focus on the Jews. Nero sentences both of them to death, and as they are on the way to the executions, they lay hands on their disciples— Peter on Mark and Paul on Luke. After Paul and Peter are killed, their bodies are collected by the disciples and taken into the city. However, Paul's head is not found at that time. Later a shepherd finds and places it above his sheepfold. After dark a miraculous fire burns above the head, and the shepherd makes this known to the bishop, Xystus. Everyone believes that it is the head of Paul, but Xystus determines that they must verify this by seeing if the head will reattach to the body. It does so, and everyone glorifies God. The author specifies that thirty-five years passed between Paul's calling and his death: thirty-one spent as a traveling missionary, two in prison in Caesarea, and two in Rome. Every year the church continues to celebrate a feast in his honor.

Part two is identified as a historical account that should be placed at the beginning of the Pauline corpus. The author opens with an extended invocation of divine favor and mercy as he embarks upon the difficult task of recounting these important events. He promises to recount the events as accurately as possible. Then follows a biographical summary of Paul,

1. This title was given to the text by the modern editor.

describing his Jewish pedigree, his training as a Pharisee, his persecution of the followers of Christ, his participation in the killing of Stephen, and his fierce wrath toward the Christians.

At this point there is a one-page lacuna in the manuscript.

When the story picks up again, the author is giving details on Pauline chronology and the imprisonments in Caesarea Maritima and Rome. The narrator anticipates that some may reject his story, because Luke does not recount these things in the Acts of the Apostles. He counters that if Luke had recorded these things, then there would have been no need for further investigation. This gap prompted Eusebius to produce his history, which is presented as a positive outcome, and Christ's disciples are blessed for receiving by faith the traditions handed down to them by the fathers.

Part three is a brief reference to the martyrdom of Paul. Paul was decapitated in the time of Nero in the sixty-ninth year since the advent of Christ, and this account was translated from Greek into Syriac 436 years after Paul's death.

Literary Background

The literary context for the Martyrdom of Paul and the Discovery of His Severed Head is difficult to determine, for the three distinct sections were likely gathered by an editor from separate sources, as the manuscript and internal literary evidence suggest.[2] The common theme is Pauline chronology, but we should note that, for example, the explanation of the thirty-five years between Paul's Damascus Road experience and his death appears twice, as does the claim that Paul died in the thirty-sixth year after the death of Jesus. There is no progression of thought from one text to the next. Instead, it appears that an editor identified different texts about the chronology of Paul's life and copied them together in the same manuscript.

There is little that would allow us to assign them to a specific author or location, but several details could suggest Roman provenance (with the caveat that the different sections could originally come from different places). Part one places the apostolic division of the mission field in Rome instead of in Jerusalem (cf. Gal 2:7). This attempt to replace Jerusalem with Rome at a critical point in the history of the early church could

2. N.B. Although Rahmani puts the sections under a single title, there are two separate entries in the *BHO*.

reflect the Roman church's efforts to claim authority over other cities, particularly the churches of the East. The story of Paul's severed head is another piece of possible evidence for Rome. Bishop Xystus (Sixtus) is almost certainly Xystus II, who occupied the episcopal seat from 257–258 CE. Other literary evidence tells us that on June 29, 258, the Roman church celebrated some kind of festival in honor of Paul and Peter: "[Feast of] Peter in the Catacombs, of Paul on the Ostian Road, when Tuscus and Bassus were consuls." The nature of this festival is not specified in the sources, but such an event could prompt a foundation myth, and the discovery of Paul's head would explain the establishment of a Pauline cult on the Ostian Road.[3]

One final detail should be mentioned. At the end of part three, there is a notation that the text was translated from Greek into Syriac. We do not know if this is meant to apply to all sections of the text or only this final portion, but Greek was used by Roman Christians well into late antiquity. It was the official liturgical language until the middle of the fourth century and remained in parts of the liturgy as late as the eighth century. Thus, it is possible that a text (or texts) like this could have been produced in Rome in Greek. All the factors mentioned here, it must be emphasized, are highly speculative; so any suggestions of provenance must be offered tentatively.

The editor states at the end of part three that the text was translated from Greek into Syriac 436 years after Paul's death in 69 CE, or 499 CE. This corresponds to the claim that this translation was done in year 810 of Alexander the Great. Syriac manuscripts typically begin their dating from the Seleucid period and October 1, 311 BCE, so year 810 would be 499 CE. It is not certain that this date applies to all three parts of the text, but we may assign it to the Syriac translation of at least part of the text, with a date slightly earlier assumed for the Greek original.

The story of the rediscovery of Paul's head also appears in a slightly different, and likely later, version in Pseudo-Dionysius's *Epistle to Timothy* (ch. 12 of this volume).

3. Burying of the Martyrs (Dep. mart.). The text has survived because it was attached to the 354 Filocalian Calendar, a Roman civil calendar. See David L. Eastman, *Paul the Martyr: The Cult of the Apostle in the Latin West*, WGRWSup 4 (Atlanta: Society of Biblical Literature, 2011), 22–24; 95–97.

Text

The translation is the first in any modern language and is based on the edition by Rahmani from a single manuscript about which, unfortunately, he does not provide details concerning its provenance or location.

Select Bibliography

Peeters, Paul. "Notes sur la légende des apôtres S. Pierre et S. Paul dans la littérature syrienne." *AnBoll* 21 (1902): 121–40.

Rahmani, Ignatius Ephraem II, ed. "Pauli Apostoli martyrium et ipsius capitis truncati inventio." Pages 3–5 in *Studia Syriaca seu collectio documentorum hactenus ineditorum ex codicibus syriacis*. Monte Libano: Seminario Scharfensi, 1904.

[ܬܫܥܝܬܐ ܕܦܘܠܘܣ ܫܠܝܚܐ ܘܡܣܗܕܢܝܬܐ ܕܪܘܡܐ]

1. ܦܘܠܘܣ ܫܠܝܚܐ ܡܢ ܛܪܣܘܣ ܐܝܬܘܗܝ ܗܘܐ. ܡܢ ܡܕܝܢܬܐ ܕܩܝܠܝܩܝܐ. ܦܪܝܫܐ ܒܗܪܣܝܣ[1] ܕܝܠܗ. ܘܟܕ ܚܕܝ ܡܢ ܚܝܠܐ. ܐܬܪ̈ܘܬܐ ܣܓܝ̈ܐܬܐ ܘܡܕܝ̈ܢܬܐ ܘܩܘ̈ܪܝܬܐ ܐܠܦܝܢ. ܘܩܝܢܕܘܢܘܣ[2] ܘܠܐ ܒܡܕܡ ܫܠܐ ܘܫܡܫ ܚܠܦ ܫܡܗ ܕܡܫܝܚܐ. ܘܠܚܪܬܐ ܠܪܘܡܝ ܠܘܬ ܦܛܪܘܣ ܐܙܠ. ܘܟܕ ܦܘܠܚܢܐ ܕܐܚܘܗܝ ܥܒܕ ܗܘܐ. ܡܢܬܐ ܕܡܫܝ̈ܚܐ ܠܦܘܠܘܣ ܡܛܬ. ܠܦܛܪܘܣ ܕܝܢ ܚܒܠܐ ܕܡܘܬܐ. ܘܠܫܠܝ̈ܚܐ ܐܟܘܬܗ ܠܡܪܗ ܕܡܫܝܚܐ. ܦܝܣ ܠܘܬܗ ܕܒܟܝܢܘܬܐ ܡܪ̈ܝܬܐ ܢܟܘܬܗ ܠܐܪܡܝܗ. ܘܦܛܪܘܣ ܥܠܘܗܝ ܕܢܘܡܐ ܟܠܗ ܙܢܝܢ. ܘܗܘܐ ܡܚܝܡ ܚܢܢ ܙܡܢܐ ܕܝܢܗ. ܘܟܕ ܢܦܩ ܕܢܥܛܦܘܗܝ. ܐܝܟܢܐ ܫܡܥ ܐܢܐ ܕܒܥܘܬܐ ܠܡܠܟܘܬܗܘܢ ܦܛܪܘܣ ܠܡܪܘܗܝ ܘܦܘܠܘܣ ܠܠܘܩܐ. ܟܕ ܕܝܢ ܐܪܕܘܦ ܦܛܪܘܣ ܘܐܬܐܡܠܟ ܦܘܠܘܣ. ܘܫܠܝ̈ܚܐ ܥܡܗܘܢ ܡܢ ܐܡܟܢ ܕܐܬܐܬܡܟܪ ܥܡܗܘܢ. ܢܣܒ ܥܘܠܐ ܘܡܪܘܘܣ ܥܠܝܠܐ. ܘܐܟܠܗ ܦܓܪ̈ܝܗܘܢ ܠܡܕܝܢܬܐ. ܙܢܝܗ ܕܝܢ ܕܦܘܠܘܣ ܐܟܝ ܟܢܗ ܡܛܬܐ. ܘܠܐ ܐܫܬܟܚ. ܘܟܠܙ ܕܚܠܐ ܫܡܝܐ. ܟܕ ܙܕܩܐ ܟܒܪ ܒܫܘܟܠܐ. ܐܬܪ ܕܡܛܬܐ ܐܬܛܥܪܘ. ܐܥܒܪܗ ܠܙܢܝܗ. ܘܥܠܘܗܝ ܒܙܢܝܗ ܡܘܢܛܪܘ. ܘܐܬܠܐ ܫܡܥܘ ܠܟܠ ܡܢ ܛܒܐ ܕܒܢܘ. ܘܟܠܠܐ ܚܙܐ

1. From the Greek αἵρεσις.
2. From the Greek κίνδυνος.

[Martyrdom of Paul the Apostle and the Discovery of His Severed Head[1]]

1. The apostle Paul was from Tarsus, from the tribe of Benjamin, and he belonged to the Pharisee sect. After he was baptized by Ananias, he made disciples in many regions and great cities. He suffered and endured many dangers for the name of Christ, and finally he journeyed to Rome, where Peter was. They made a division of the inhabited earth—the portion of the gentiles going to Paul, and the nation of the Jews going to Peter[2]—and they converted many to the truth of Christ. Nero ordered that the two of them should die by harsh blows. Peter asked that he be crucified with his head downward, so that he may kiss the feet of his crucified master. When they were proceeding to be killed, they entrusted the laying on of hands of the priesthood to their disciples, Peter to Mark and Paul to Luke.[3] But after Peter was crucified and Paul was killed, along with many whom they had made disciples, Luke and Mark went out at night and carried their bodies into the city.[4] The head of Paul, however, was lost among those killed and was not found. A long time later, when a shepherd passed through the place where those killed were buried, he found Paul's head. He carried it with the head of his staff and went and put it above the sheepfold of his flock. After nightfall he beheld a fire break out above it, and he went and made this known to bishop Xystus[5] and the clergy. All of them understood

1. This title was given to the text by the modern editor.

2. Cf. Gal 2:7–9, where this division is agreed upon in Jerusalem. Paul's particular mission to the gentiles is also mentioned in Rom 1:5 and Acts 9:15.

3. These succession lines from Peter to Mark and from Paul to Luke follow the account in Irenaeus (*Adv. Haer*. 3.1.1); another version is cited in Eusebius (*Hist. eccl.* 5.8.3) and Tertullian (*Adv. Marc*. 4.5). In addition, Eusebius cites a passage from Clement of Alexandria that alleges the Peter-Mark connection (*Hist. eccl.* 6.14.6–7), and Eusebius himself affirms the Paul-Luke connection (*Hist. eccl.* 3.4.6–7).

4. Roman law and custom strictly forbade burials within the city walls, and this seems to have changed only in late antiquity with the burial of Christian holy people in intramural basilicas. See Eastman, *Paul the Martyr*, 24.

5. Xystus is an alternative spelling for Sixtus. Sixtus I is unlikely to be the bishop in question, for his tenure lasted approximately ten years during the reign of Hadrian. In

ܗܕܐ ܕܝܢ ܡܬܝܕܥܐ ܠܟܠ ܡܢܘ. ܘܟܠ ܐܝܟ ܠܡܫܡܫܢܘܬܗܘܢ ܐܫܬܡܫܘ ܘܠܡܠܟܘܬܗܘܢ. ܘܐܬܬܘܕܝܘ
ܠܗܘܢ. ܕܢܥܡܕܘ ܕܦܘܠܘܣ ܐܬܐ ܠܪܘܡܐ. ܐܡܪ ܠܗܘܢ ܒܡܫܡܫܢܘܬܗܘܢ. ܢܕܥ ܗܕܐ ܕܐܡܠܐ ܠܗ
ܠܟܠ. ܘܫܩܠܘܗ ܠܟܬܒܐ ܘܫܡܫܘܢܘܗܝ ܒܢܝܐ ܒܝܬܐ ܕܦܠܚܘ. ܘܐܦ ܗܕܐ ܘܡܬܚܙܝܢ ܠܥܕܬܗ. ܢܛܪܬܗܘܢ
ܕܦܘܠܘܣ ܐܠܗܘܢ. ܘܡܢ ܗܕܐ ܒܬܪܗ ܐܬܦܩ ܠܘܬܗ ܦܓܪܐ ܘܐܬܚܙܝ ܒܢܝܫܐ. ܐܝܟ ܗܘ ܕܠܐ ܐܬܦܫܩ
ܣܘܥܪܢܐ ܡܫܡܠܝܢ. ܘܐܡܪܝܢ ܕܡܢܘ ܐܝܬܘܗܝ ܘܡܟܢܫ ܠܟܢܘܫܬܐ ܗܘܐ ܕܝܢ ܡܢ ܩܕܡܘܗܝ ܠܥܘܠܡ ܫܘܒܚܐ.
ܐܠܗܐ ܘܡܫܡܫ ܥܡܗ. ܐܠܗܐ ܘܚܕܐ ܡܢ ܡܠܟܘܬܐ ܠܟܠ ܕܝܢ. ܘܐܬܐ ܒܫܡܗ ܐܦܝܣܩܦܐ ܕܐܬܦܩܕ. ܘܐܬܐ
ܒܪܘܡܐ. ܘܐܦܝܣ ܒܥܕܬܐ ܕܐܠܗܐ ܘܫܡܗ ܕܡܪܢ ܝܫܘܥ ܕܦܪܘܩܢ. ܗܘܐ ܡܢܗ ܒܟܠܗܝܢ ܕܘܟܝܬܐ ܕܡܠܟܘܬܐ.
ܒܪܘܡܐ ܒܝܘܡܐ ܕܝܢ ܘܟܠ ܚܝܠܐ ܒܥܕܢ ܘܐܦܠܐ ܒܠܚܘܕ ܒܥܘܠܡ ܕܢܣܒܘܢ ܡܫܡܫܢܝܢ.

2. ܫܪܒܐ ܕܡܬܐܡܪ ܥܠ ܦܛܪܘܣ ܘܦܘܠܘܣ ܫܠܝܚܐ

ܟܕ ܒܪܘܡܐ ܕܝܢ ܗܘܐ ܘܡܫܝܚܐ ܕܝܢ ܡܢ ܠܗܘܢ ܐܠܐ ܐܝܟ ܕܡܠܬܐ. ܒܥܘܕܪܢܐ ܘܡܫܡܫܢܘܬܐ
ܡܠܟܐ ܐܠܐ: ܘܡܥܠܝܐ ܠܟܠ ܘܥܒܕܐ ܕܐܠܗܐ ܕܐܬܚܙܝ ܩܕܡ ܐܠܐ. ܕܫܪܒܐ ܗܘܐ ܡܢ ܡܫܡܫܢܘܬܗ
ܕܦܛܪܘܣ ܐܝܟ. ܘܟܢܫܐ ܕܥܡܗ ܕܝܢ ܡܢ ܡܠܟܐ. ܟܠ ܕܝܢ ܡܢ ܠܐ ܡܫܡܫܢܘܬܐ ܒܗ ܕܒܥܠ

that it was the head of the corpse of Paul. Xystus said to them, "Let us observe a vigil and prayer all night, and let us bring out the corpse and put the head next to the feet. If the trunk turns around and is joined to its neck, then it will be acknowledged that it is [the head] of Paul." They proceeded in this way, and the entire body turned around and was joined to the head, as if a vertebra had never been severed. Those who saw it marveled and glorified God. From Paul's calling to the end of his life, there were thirty-five years: thirty-one when he was traveling around everywhere, two in prison in Caesarea,[6] and two in Rome. He became a martyr in the thirty-sixth year after the passion of our Savior. Behold, he was placed with great honor in the splendid churches of the empire in Rome, and every year on the twenty-ninth of Tammuz,[7] we celebrate the day of his festival.

2. The History That Should be Placed at the Beginning of the Book of Paul the Apostle

Because I am amazed, our honorable father,[8] at your love of learning and the persistence of your love, with reverence and obedience I am humbled. And to the narrow and straight[9] chasm of this narrative I direct myself, so that I may place this story before the book of Paul. I have taken this very great task upon myself out of fear of disobedience, because I know that in the Proverbs it is said, "A disobedient son will be given over to

---

the Liberian Catalog, Optatus assigns the dates 117–126 CE, while Eusebius gives the dates 119–128/129 (*Hist. eccl.* 4.4.1–4.5.5; *Chron.* Olympiad 224.3). Sixtus II (257–258 CE) is the more likely referent, for on June 29, 258, the Roman church celebrated the feast of "Peter in the Catacombs, of Paul on the Ostian Road." On the importance and limitations of this notation on the Roman calendar, see Eastman, *Paul the Martyr*, 95–97.

6. Caesarea Maritima.

7. Tammuz, the tenth month in the Syriac calendar, corresponds to the end of June and early July. Hence, the author is referring to the traditional June 29 date for the feast of Peter and Paul. However, it should be noted that in the Ethiopian Orthodox Church, the feast of Peter is observed on July 31 (Solomon C. Malan, *The Conflicts of the Apostles: An Apocryphal Book of the Early Eastern Church* [London: Nutt, 1871], 8 n. 2).

8. This invocation probably refers to a more senior ecclesiastical authority, not to God as Father, because the scribe asks for this father's prayers to help him get to God.

9. Matt 7:14.

ܠܗܘܢ ܕܢܦܩܬܐ ܡܬܐܡܪܐ. ܕܒܪܐ ܠܗܘܢ ܠܐ ܡܫܬܡܥܝܢ ܠܐܚܪܢܐ ܢܬܠܚܡܘܢ. ܗܘ ܕܝܢ ܕܫܬܡܥܘ ܠܒܪ ܡܢ ܗܢܐ ܗܘܘ. ܐܠܐ ܕܝܢ ܪܚܡܬܗ ܗܘܬ. ܘܟܕ ܒܕܡܘܬܐ ܠܟܠܐ ܡܕܡ ܘܡܕܡ ܦܩܐ ܢܦܫܢ ܢܬܩܪܒ ܠܘܬ ܐܠܗܐ. ܐܝܟ ܕܐܦ ܗܘܝܢ ܡܫܡܫܐ ܗܘ ܕܒܐ ܐܢܬܘܢ ܦܪܘܫ. ܟܕ ܡܕܒܪ ܒܪܘܚ ܠܐܦܣܛܘܠܘܣ ܫܡܥܘܢ ܡܫܢܝܬܐ ܐܢܫܐ ܕܐܦ ܐܬܐ ܟܕ ܡܢ ܪܘܡܐ ܕܐܬܪ ܕܡܫܬܢܝܢ ܐܠܗܘܗܝ: ܘܡܫܠܡܬ ܐܪܥܐ. ܠܐܚܐ ܕܡܕܝܢܬܐ ܠܠܡܐܢܐ[3] ܕܚܝܐ ܐܡܝܢ. ܟܕ ܡܥܒܪܐ ܐܢܐ ܗܘܝܬ ܒܥܕܢܐ. ܗܘܝܐ ܐܝܟ ܕܐܬܡܪ ܒܥܒܪܐ ܡܫܬܠܡܐܢܐ܀

3. ܦܘܠܘܣ ܗܟܝܠ ܒܒܪܐ ܡܢ ܐܠܗܘܗܝ ܗܘܐ ܓܢܣܗ.[4] ܡܢ ܫܪܒܬܐ ܕܒܢܝܡܝܢ ܦܪܝܫܐ ܕܝܢ ܒܐܘܪܚܗ ܕܢܡܘܣܐ. ܘܩܕܡ ܡܠܦܢܐ ܗܘܐ ܡܫܝܚܐ ܒܝܫܬܐܝܬ. ܒܥܡܡܐ ܕܗܘܐ ܠܐܘܪܚ. ܟܕ ܕܝܢ ܗܟܝܠ: ܠܦܪܘܫܘ ܘܐܠܗܘܗ ܚܝܐ ܕܡܫܝܚܐ ܒܗܕܐ ܗܘܐ ܪܕܦ ܗܘܐ ܕܝܢ ܘܟܠܗ ܠܥܕܬܐ ܕܐܠܗܐ. ܘܟܠ ܗܘܐ ܐܦ ܡܪܕ ܗܘܐ ܒܡܫܝܚܘ ܘܐܣܛܦܢܘܣ ܗܟܝܠ ܘܗܘܐ ܘܡܠܐ ܐܠܗܘܗܝ ܗܘܐ ܗܘܝܢ ܒܡܫܝܚܘ. ܟܕ ܡܕܡ ܠܗܘܢ ܒܥܠܡ ܐܢܫܐ ܕܠܗܘܢ ܐܠܝܢ ܕܪܕܦܝܢ ܗܘܘ ܠܗ. ܘܐܪܝܬܐ ܕܠܗܘܢ ܢܦܠ ܠܘܬ ܡܫܐ. ܘܡܕܝܢܬܐ ܒܗ ܡܬܩܪܝܐ ܡܬܡܛܝܐ ܗܘܬ. ܟܕ ܚܙܐ ܒܥܠܡܗ. ܕܠܒܢܝ ܡܠܬܐ. ܕܕܚܠܬ ܐܠܗܐ ܢܦܫܗ. ܘܡܣܬܬܐ ܐܠܗܘܗܝ ܘܪܘܪܒܬܐ ܗܘܝܢ ܕܡܢܗ ܠܡܫܠܡ ܚܒܝܫ ܗܘܘ ܗܘܘ. ܟܕ ܒܬܪܐ ܗܘܐ ܦܛܪܘܣ ܐܘ ܒܡܫܝܚܬܐ. ܗܘ ܕܒܗ ܠܐܦܣܛܠܘܣ ܡܫܒܪ ܗܘܐ ܕܡܢܐ ܕܚܝܠ ܐܠܗܐ ܘܡܠܐܟܐ ܪܘܪܒܬܐ. ܐܝܟ ܕܐܦ ܗܘ ܠܩܪܝܢܐ ܗܘܐ. ܘܟܘܠܐ ܐܬܐ ܡܫܬܠܡ ܒܟܠܗ

3. From the Greek λιμήν.
4. From the Greek γένος.

destruction,"[10] but the one who is obedient will be spared from this. But give me your prayers, so that like oars on both sides, they may give me wings and carry me to God. Just as that great Moses then stretched out his hands, when at that time he was helping Israel within the camp, so I also will be delivered from the spirits of the air that wage war on us[11] and will lead the ship of the word straight forward and will arrive with it in the port of peace.[12] I am now beginning with the affair and telling it truthfully just as it was.

3. The apostle Paul was from the Hebrew race, from the tribe of Benjamin, and from the Pharisee sect. He was first instructed in the law of Moses by the faithful teacher Gamaliel.[13] Moreover, he was dwelling in Tarsus, which is the main city of Cilicia,[14] and was persecuting and plundering the churches of God. In addition to this, he was also present at the killing of Stephen the apostle and martyr. He was at that time a partner in Stephen's killing, because he accepted the task of keeping the garments of all those who were stoning him, so that all their hands may be engaged in the killing.[15] He was also seen to be first among those causing a disturbance, because in every place that there were children of the word who feared God, he would diligently cast them down. Many and great were the things done by him against the church. The fury in him was beyond measure, because more and more he believed that he was demonstrating the fear of God and was setting many things right, as he also acknowledges in his epistle.[16] Luke also tells about it in his second book.[17] Not only did he hate and loathe the proclamation of the truth—as did a great portion of the Jews after him—but he was also displaying an exceedingly fierce anger greater than anyone else. For when he saw that the [Christian] proclamation was

---

10. The reference here is to Prov 13:1 in the Septuagint version, which does not agree with the MT, the Peshitta, or the Targum.

11. Exod 14:16–26.

12. Appeals for divine assistance in copying the Pauline epistles appear elsewhere in the Syriac manuscript tradition. See e.g., Amir Harrak, *Catalogue of Syriac and Garshuni Manuscripts: Manuscripts Owned by the Iraqi Department of Antiquities and Heritage*, CSCO 126 (Leuven: Peeters, 2011), 102–4.

13. Acts 22:3.

14. Literally, the "eye of Cilicia."

15. Acts 7:58.

16. Gal 1:13–14. Paul believed he was displaying devotion toward God at that time but later came to believe that he had been mistaken.

17. The Acts of the Apostles.

ܕܐܬܝܢ ܡܛܠܬܗ. ܕܠܗ ܒܠܚܘܕ ܐܝܟ ܣܘܓܐܐ ܕܝܘܬܪܢܐ ܐܫܬܡܠܝ: ܫܠܝܐ ܗܘܐ ܘܓܕܝܡ ܒܢܘܗܪܬܐ ܕܫܢܝܐ. ܐܠܐ ܐܦ ܙܘܓܐ ܒܥܝܠܐ ܡܚܘܐ ܗܘܐ ܠܗܢ ܡܢ ܦܠܘܗ ܒܡܠܐ. ܟܕ ܓܒܪ ܚܙܐ ܒܦܘܪܫܢܐ ܕܐܪܡܝܐ. ܘܠܡܫܠܠܐ ܕܫܢܝܐ ܕܦܘܫܩܐ: ܘܠܗܢ ܡܢ ܡܫܟܚܢܘܬܐ ܕܡܘܪܝܐ ܐܚܪܝܐ: ܚܕ ܡܛܠ ܗܕܐ. ܘܡܢ ܗܫܐ ܗܘܐ ܠܗ ܕܙܘܪܥܬܗ ܡܫܬܓܫܝܢ ܐܢܘܢ ܕܡܠܟܘܬܗܘܢ ܠܐ ܢܬܒܛܠ. ܡܫܓܫܬܐ ܓܝܪܬܐ ܘܐܣܟܝܡܬܐ ܠܡܫܩܠ ܒܢܝ ܒܝܬܐ ܒܟܢ ܗܘܐ ܐܝܟ ܕܐܘ ܡܢ ܡܠܟܘܬܐ ܕܫܢܝܐ ܢܦܩܬ ܐܢܘܢ: ܐܘ ܕܡܢ ܕܫܡܝܐ ...

[Here there is a one-page lacuna in the Syriac manuscript.]

4. ... ܒܒܝܬ ܐܣܝܪܐ ܕܡܐܣܝܪܝܢ܀ ܘܐܘܦ ܩܢܝܐ ܠܐܙܠܝܢ ܗܠܝܢ ܕܒܬܪ ܒܢܘܗܝ ܘܡܢܗܘܢ ܗܠܝܢ ܒܗܢ ܩܢܝܐ ܐܫܬܡܠܝ. ܐܝܟ ܕܢܫܡܥܘܢ ܩܢܝܐ ܦܠܚܝܢ ܡܢ ܦܪܣܐ ܕܠܗ ܘܣܒܪܐ ܠܡܫܡܠܝܘ ܠܐܠܗܝܢ ܘܡܫܡܘ܀ ܐܠܐ ܠܐ ܐܝܟ ܡܛܠ ܗܠܝܢ ܕܒܕܢ. ܘܡܛܠ ܒܗܠܝܢ ܕܐܣܬܪܝ ܒܠܚܘ ܦܠܓܐ ܕܦܪܩܣܝܣ[5] ܡܢ ܐܡܪ. ܕܒܗܘܐ ܗܠܝܢ ܠܐ ܫܡܥ. ܡܛܠ ܠܗ ܓܒܪ ܐܝܟ ܒܗܘܐ ܒܒܘܣܝܐ. ܐܘ ܢܟܝܢ ܠܐ ܡܫܡܠ ܐܝܟ ܒܪܢܫܐ ܕܒܠܘ ܦܪܩܣܝܣ. ܐܠܐ ܐܡܪ ܠܗ ܕܚܘܐ ܠܗ ܕܢܫܬܠܛ ܒܗܘܐ ܒܠ ܫܡܘܬܗ ܕܦܘܠܚܢܗ. ܕܒܗܘܐ ܗܘܐ ܡܫܝܐ ܐܝܟ. ܕܠܗ ܒܗܘܐ ܒܗܠܝܢ ܠܐܙܠܝܢ ܩܢܝܐ ܒܠܚܘܕ ܡܫܝܚ ܠܗ ܚܝܘܗܝ ܕܦܘܠܚܢܗ ܕܒܢܘܗܝ. ܘܐܫܬܠܝ ܠܗ ܒܠ ܫܡܘܬܗ. ܐܦܠܐ ܚܕ ܒܡܫܠܐ ܕܒܠ ܕܒܢܝܐ ܡܫܬܒܠܐ ܗܘܐ. ܐܠܐ ܡܛܠ ܕܒܠ ܫܡܘܬܗ ܗܘܐ ܠܐ ܐܫܬܠܝ. ܒܠܘ ܓܒܪ ܕܚܝܐ ܫܘܓܐܐ ܕܡܫܠܚܘܬܗ ܗܘܐ. ܐܬܬܫܝܡ ܡܫܝܚ ܠܐܦܣܩܘܗܝ ܗܘ ܘܐܫܠܡ ܠܗ ܒܠ ܕܒܢܝܐ ܘܠܡܫܝܚܐ ܒܪܚܝܐ ܛܒܐ ܐܘ ܢܟܝܢ ܡܫܠܡ. ܠܐܫܡܥܘܗܝ ܓܒܪ ܕܡܫܝܚܐ. ܟܕ ܒܫܡܝܐ ܘܒܡܫܝܚܘܬܐ ܐܝܟ ܕܚܝܠܐ ܕܡܢܗܘܢ ܘܐܢܫܝܐ ܒܡܫܡܫܝܢܘܬܐ ܘܐܟܘܬܐ ܕܡܫܚܠܦܢܘܬܐ ܡܫܡܫܝܢ ܢܘܪܐ ܗܘܝܢ ܕܡܫܠܡܘܬܐ ܕܡܫܝܐ܀ ܡܢܗ ܒܪܐ ܕܠܐ ܕܢܬܐܡܢ ܒܥܘܕܪ ܦܠܚܐ ܕܫܠܛܢܐ ܡܫܝܚܐ܀

5. From the Greek πράξεις.

shining forth, and that the word of truth was flourishing and prevailing greatly over the teaching of the Jews, he suffered because of this. And because he believed that it would be a great wrong if their doctrines were not suppressed, he took great pains and was diligent against the children of the church, so that either he might separate them from the teaching of truth or might be esteemed a worthy judge...

4. ... in the prison of Caesarea, and in addition the two years that he spent in Rome, and along with those ten latter years.[18] Thus, altogether there were thirty-five years from his calling until his perfection.[19] But let no one find fault with me about these things and reject these things that were done after the Book of the Acts[20] by saying that Luke did not mention these things. For one might rightly ask such a person this: "Our beloved, do you not accept that there were times after the Acts of the Apostles?" But he may say to me: "Show me that Luke tells about the martyrdom of Paul." And to this I respond: "If Luke had measured out for us in these two years alone the life of Paul in Rome and had told us about his martyrdom, then not even a single inquiry concerning the times would have been needed. But, because he did not write about Paul's martyrdom, which happened a long time after he wrote, the narrative was taken up from there by Eusebius, who wrote concerning the times and out of good will produced a history.[21] Oh, our beloved, accept this!" Indeed, Christ's disciples are heirs of the kingdom of heaven, because by persuasion and by faith they received the tradition of the fathers of doctrine as their building and the building of others.

Here ends the narrative that it is proper to place at the beginning of the book of Paul the apostle.

---

18. This is probably a reference to the tradition that Paul spent ten years traveling in Spain and the West after being released from Rome. See e.g., Hist. Paul 9 (ch. 8 in this volume).

19. A term used for martyrdom.

20. That is, the Acts of the Apostles.

21. This need to fill in the gap left by Luke is the author's primary justification for his own work and the work of others. In his *Chronicle*, Eusebius dates the deaths of Peter and Paul to 65 CE (*Chron*. Olympiad 211).

5. ܣܗܕܘܬܐ ܕܦܘܠܘܣ ܫܠܝܚܐ ܕܗܘܬ ܒܪܘܡܝ ܒܝܕ ܢܐܪܘܢ.

ܒܝ̈ܘܡܝ ܢܐܪܘܢ ܩܣܪ ܕܪ̈ܘܡܝܐ. ܐܣܝܪ ܒܪܘܡܝ ܦܘܠܘܣ ܫܠܝܚܐ. ܟܕ ܐܬܦܣܩ ܪܝܫܗ ܒܣܝܦܐ.
ܒܫܢܬܐ ܓܝܪ ܕܐܬܟܠܠ ܥܡܗ ܕܫܡܥܘܢ ܕܦܛܪܘܣ. ܐܓܘܢܐ[6] ܗܢܐ ܐܬܬܠܡ ܕܢܘܡܘܣ ܒܫܢܬܐ ܒܫܢܬ ܒܢܝܢܐ
ܐܝܟܢ ܒܫܢܝ ܘܐܬܩܛܠ ܒܗ. ܘܐܬܥܒܕ ܫܠܝܚܐ ܕܝܢܐ ܒܣܗܕܘܬܗ ܒܫܢܬܐ ܕܫܠܡ ܘܐܦܝܣ ܕܐܬܐܬܥܠܗ
ܕܦܪܘܡ ܡܢܘܬ ܡܫܝܚܐ. ܐܬܥܗܝ ܗܘܝܐ ܠܐ ܥܠܘܗܝ ܕܢܐ ܡܢ ܟܕ ܐܝܟܢ ܘܥܕܡܐ ܠܫܢܬܐ ܕܐܦܝܣܩܐ ܘܒܫܢܬ
ܕܠܒܫܢܪܘܣ ܡܫܝܚܐ. ܘܒܗ ܥܠܡܐ ܗܘܐ ܡܢ ܢܘܚܐ ܠܒܣܘܪܚܐ ܐܦܝܣ. ܒܫܢܬܐ ܩܕܝܫܬܐ. ܫܢܝܐ
ܐܘܫܢܝܬܐ ܘܐܟܠܡ ܘܫܠܡ܀ ܫܠܡܬ ܐܘܪܥܬ ܕܝܢܐ ܕܣܗܕܘܬܗ ܕܦܘܠܘܣ܀

6. From the Greek ἀγών, this term thus echoes the “good fight” language of 2 Tim 4:7: τὸν καλὸν ἀγῶνα ἠγώνισμαι.

5. The Martyrdom of Paul in Rome by the Hand of Nero

In the days of Nero, Caesar of the Romans, the apostle Paul became a martyr in Rome when his head was cut off by a sword. This was in the thirty-sixth year after the passion of our Savior.[22] The good fight[23] was fought in Rome on a Thursday in the month of Tammuz, on the twenty-ninth.[24] The holy martyr was perfected in martyrdom in the sixty-ninth year of the advent of our Savior Jesus Christ. Thus, altogether from the time when he became a martyr until the year 810 of Alexander the Macedonian, when this book was translated from Greek into Syriac for the first time, there were 436 years.[25] Accurately have I made known the time of the martyrdom of Paul.

---

22. The preceding text indicates that 35 years had elapsed, perhaps explaining why his death here is placed "in the 36th year."

23. Cf. 2 Tim 4:7.

24. See n. 7 above on the date.

25. The dating system in Syriac texts typically begins with the Seleucid period and October 1, 311 BCE. Thus, year 810 equals 499 CE. Correspondingly, the author dates Paul's martyrdom to 69 CE, and between his death and the translation of the text into Syriac there are 436 years, thus also yielding a date of 499 CE. On Syriac dating see Ludger Bernhard, *Die Chronologie der syrischen Handschriften*, VOHDSupp 14 (Wiesbaden: Steiner, 1971).

Part 3. Joint Martyrdom Accounts of Peter and Paul

10. Pseudo-Marcellus, *Passion of the Holy Apostles Peter and Paul*

CANT 193.1 / *BHL* 6657–6659

and

Acts of the Holy Apostles Peter and Paul

CANT 193.2 / *BHG* 1490–1491

Content

These two texts generally follow each other very closely, so they will be introduced together.

One of the places they diverge, however, is at the beginning of the text, where the Greek Acts of the Holy Apostles Peter and Paul (Greek Acts) includes twenty-one additional chapters relating the travels and adventures of Paul between Malta and Rome. Most notable among this additional material is a plot by some of the Jews in Rome to have Paul assassinated by the order of the emperor. Nero issues an edict to kill Paul on sight. The captain of one of Paul's ships happens to bear a strong resemblance to the apostle (primarily because he is bald) and is killed when he goes into Puteoli preaching the gospel. Nero and his conspirators are put at ease, yet meanwhile Paul has a disturbing dream about events in Rome and hastens his journey to the city. Word reaches Rome that Paul is still alive, and the Jewish leaders beg Simon the sorcerer to report the bad news to Nero.

Here the Latin *Passion of the Holy Apostles Peter and Paul* (Latin *Passion*) joins the story. Paul arrives in Rome and is approached by the Jewish leaders, who ask him to counter Peter's teachings against the law. Peter is made aware of Paul's presence in Rome and hurries to greet him, recount-

ing the threats to the faith caused by Simon the sorcerer. The apostles then collectively resolve a dispute between Jewish and gentile believers by emphasizing the universal nature of the gospel.

The apostolic preaching is so successful that some Jewish religious leaders and pagan priests set out to thwart Paul and Peter. Peter's preaching is causing aristocratic women—including the wife of Nero and the wife of the prefect Agrippa—to withdraw from sexual contact with their husbands, and Paul's preaching is causing members of the military and the imperial household to abandon their service. At this time Simon the sorcerer accuses the apostles of being frauds, but Peter counters him by performing miracles and casting out demons. Simon at last runs to Nero and warns that the Empire will fall unless these two threats are eliminated.

The Emperor summons the three of them into his presence, where the two sides argue about who is telling the truth about having divine power. Peter tells Nero to read the letter of Pontius Pilate to Claudius if he wants to know the truth about Christ and his apostles. The verbal sparring continues, and Peter defeats Simon in a contest of discerning each other's thoughts. Paul confirms that all of Peter's claims are true, and Simon finally claims that he will prove his power by ascending into heaven. He reminds Nero that he had already come back from the dead, although the narrator explains that Simon had only appeared to do so by deceiving a dimwitted executioner. The insults continue back and forth, as both sides plead their case before Nero. The Greek Acts lacks several sections of this banter but otherwise continues to parallel the Latin *Passion*.

In keeping with Simon's request, Nero constructs a tall tower in the city. All the people come to see whether Simon or Peter and Paul are telling the truth. Simon climbs the tower and begins to fly through the air, causing Nero initially to declare Simon the winner. But as Paul prays, Peter commands the demons to drop Simon. The sorcerer falls to his death. Nero arrests the apostles and instructs the prefect Agrippa to kill them. Paul is led away to his death—on the Ostian Road in the Latin *Passion*, but at an estate called Aquae Salvias in the Greek Acts. The Greek Acts here includes the story of a pious woman named Perpetua, who loans Paul a scarf to put over his eyes at the time of his execution. The apostle promises to return it to her after his death, which he does. Perpetua is blind in one eye, yet when she puts on Paul's bloody scarf, her eye is instantly healed.

The Latin *Passion* and the Greek Acts are parallel once again in their account of Peter being led away to crucifixion. A large crowd attempts to stop Nero from killing Peter, but the apostle calms the crowd, asks God to

care for the believers left behind, and goes quietly to his death. Suddenly holy men from Jerusalem appear and, together with a nobleman named Marcellus (who had previously been a follower of Simon the sorcerer), take Peter's body and bury it on the Vatican hill.

The Greek Acts then inserts a continuation of the Perpetua story. The soldiers who had met this woman on their way to kill Paul come upon her once again. They are amazed to hear the miracle of the scarf and immediately declare themselves servants of Christ, the master of Paul. They refuse to go back into the city to serve the Emperor. Perpetua brings the news to Nero and is arrested and thrown into prison. For their part, the newly converted soldiers are immediately executed. In prison Perpetua meets a Christian maiden named Potenziana and tells her all about the teachings of Paul. This Potenziana happens to be the sister of Nero's wife and convinces her sister and other aristocratic women to withdraw from their husbands. Nero tortures and executes Perpetua and has Potenziana burned alive.

Another account of the mysterious visitors from Jerusalem marks the rejoining of the two texts. They praise the Romans for being worthy of these two great martyr-patrons and predict the imminent demise of Nero. Soon after, as they had predicted, an uprising forces Nero to flee, and he dies a horrible death in the wilderness.

At another time some "Greeks" attempt to take the bodies of the apostles back to the East, but an earthquake stops them, and the Romans take their bodies to the catacombs on the Appian Road. From there the bodies are relocated—Peter to the Vatican and Paul to the Ostian Road. The Greek Acts closes by specifying the dates of the deaths of all the martyrs mentioned in the account, most importantly June 29 for the apostles.

Literary Background

There is no question that these two texts are connected. The overlap throughout most of the narrative reflects direct translation, so which text is the original? Both solutions have been proposed, but the literary evidence favors the Latin *Passion* as the original, for the Greek Acts gives indications of being a translation. Specifically, the Greek employs a number of terms that are direct transliterations from Latin, suggesting that the Greek version is a translation of the Latin, not the other way around. (This also suggests an audience that speaks Greek but would also be familiar with Latin. See more on this below in the discussion of provenance.) After the initial translation from Latin into Greek, the two texts had parallel but largely

separate histories of transmission. The Latin text was primarily preserved in Coptic, Arabic, and Old Irish. The Greek version was handed down in Armenian, Georgian, and Old Slavonic.[1]

The identity of the author of the Latin *Passion* and the Greek Acts is unknown. Tradition credits the text to Marcellus, the former disciple of Simon the sorcerer who comes to follow Peter, because there is a brief notation at the end of some of the Latin manuscripts: "I, Marcellus, have written what I saw." There is no historical evidence to link this text to anyone named Marcellus, and a first-century author can readily be eliminated from consideration. Nonetheless, the text is usually ascribed to Pseudo-Marcellus.

Both the Latin and Greek texts probably date from the fifth or sixth century. They incorporate elements from earlier martyrdom traditions, but they also alter those traditions to emphasize the harmony of the apostles (*concordia apostolorum*). In the opening scene in Rome, Peter and Paul are approached by a crowd of Jewish and gentile Christians. They are arguing among themselves about who is worthy of more honor. The Jewish believers claim pride of place based upon their lineage, while the gentiles retort that they at least accepted the gospel when it was preached to them and did not reject God's prophets. The tension between Jewish and gentile believers was a challenging issue for the early church, according to the letters of Paul and the Acts of the Apostles. Thus, in the Latin *Passion* and Greek Acts, Peter and Paul are tested on this point the first time they are together. They present a united front, thus illustrating that they are of one mind on this critical question and perhaps rehabilitating the scene of conflict in Antioch (Gal 2:11–21). Later, in the lengthy verbal exchange between the apostles and Simon the sorcerer, Paul and Peter explicitly reinforce each other's words. Nero first turns to Paul after Peter has spoken at length, and Paul confirms that everything is as Peter has said it. After Paul delivers a lengthy monologue, Nero turns to Peter, who confirms the truth of all the claims that Paul has just made. Peter's thoughts are Paul's, and Paul's teachings are Peter's. The final and perhaps most significant example of this harmonizing of the apostolic traditions concerns the accounts of their deaths. While the earlier renditions of the martyrdoms—including the

1. There exists one outlier to this general division. A codex of the sixteenth century contains a Greek translation of the Latin *Passion* as we have it, meaning that it does not include the additional material in the Greek Acts (i.e., the twenty-one opening chapters and the Perpetua story).

Martyrdom of Peter, Martyrdom of Paul, and the Pseudo-Linus versions of these—present Peter and Paul as dying at separate times, the Latin *Passion* and Greek Acts bring their executions together. Richard A. Lipsius has referred to this as the "catholicizing" of the tradition, demonstrating that Paul and Peter were fully united in life and in death and essentially correcting the other stories. For these reasons the Latin *Passion* and the Greek Acts are dated slightly later than the Pseudo-Linus texts, thus fifth or sixth century. Hennecke-Schneemelcher supports this date by suggesting that the text may come from the same chronological context as the Gelasian Decree (sixth century), which explicitly states that the apostles died "on one and the same day."

As I have shown elsewhere,[2] both texts are produced in Rome. The emphasis on apostolic harmony is emblematic of the Roman church's attempts to claim legitimacy and authority based on their dual apostolic foundation, although at the same time Peter is ultimately presented as superior to Paul. Peter is the one who speaks first to Nero, and he alone strikes down Simon from the sky. The accounts reflect firsthand knowledge of Roman geography and topography, and the closing story about the nefarious attempt by eastern Christians to remove the bodies of Peter and Paul from Rome reflects the Roman sentiment of privilege. The earthquake that prevents the translation of the relics is presented as miraculous, as if God or the apostles themselves had intervened to prevent the relocation (as some saints would reportedly do in later Medieval accounts). In fact, the Roman bishop Gregory I relates a version of the same story in a letter to the empress in Constantinople in 594. Gregory uses it to justify his decision not to send any apostolic relics to the East, for the earlier attempt to move the bodies had met with supernatural disapproval. On account of these details, Roman provenance for both seems certain.

Despite the many similarities between these two texts, the differences are also worthy of note. The editor of the Greek Acts adds material at the beginning of the text to relate more of Paul's journey to Rome. In this way the resulting text goes beyond a *passion* account into what we may call *acts* literature. Lipsius suggests that these initial chapters were added in the ninth century by an editor from southern Italy who wanted his region to figure prominently in the apostolic tradition. However, his arguments

2. David L. Eastman, *Paul the Martyr: The Cult of the Apostle in the Latin West*, WGRWSup 4 (Atlanta: Society of Biblical Literature, 2011), 62–69.

are weak and do not eliminate the possibility that these chapters were part of the Greek Acts in its original form. The Greek Acts also displays more concern with linking this story to the liturgical calendar. The specific dates of the deaths of Peter and Paul, the converted soldiers, Perpetua, and Potenziana are listed only at the end of the Greek Acts. The text therefore serves as a foundation story for multiple festivals in Rome. Not all differences between these texts are as innocuous as these, however. As I have shown elsewhere,[3] the Latin Passion places Paul's death on the Ostian Road, the dominant traditional site. In the Greek text, however, Paul dies on the estate at Aquae Salvias, several kilometers from the Ostian Road site. Gregory I supports this latter account in one of his letters, and so these two texts, although closely related, nevertheless also reveal rivalry in Rome concerning the Pauline cult sites.

Text

Both the Greek and Latin texts survive in numerous manuscripts from the Middle Ages. The translations are the first available in English based on the editions by Lipsius.[4]

Select Bibliography

Eastman, David L. *Paul the Martyr: The Cult of the Apostle in the Latin West*. WGRWSup 4. Atlanta: Society of Biblical Literature, 2011.

Erbetta, Mario, trans. "Gli Atti di Pietro e Paolo dello Ps. Marcello." Pages 178–92 in *Atti e leggende*. Vol. 2 of *Gli apocrifi del Nuovo Testamento*. 2nd ed. Turin: Marietti, 1978.

Hennecke, Edgar. "Acta Petri et Pauli (Ps.-Marcellus)." Pages 440–42 in vol. 2 of *New Testament Apocrypha*. Edited by Wilhelm Schneemelcher. English trans. edited by R. McL. Wilson. 5th ed. Louisville: Westminster John Knox, 1993.

---

3. Ibid.

4. The previous English translation of the Acts of Peter and Paul by Alexander Walker ("Acts of the Holy Apostles Peter and Paul," in *Apocryphal Gospels, Acts and Revelations*, ANCL 16 [Edinburgh: T&T Clark, 1870], 256–76) predates the publication of Lipsius's critical edition and is based on the seventeenth-century edition by Peter Lambeck.

Huskinson, J. M. *Concordia Apostolorum: Christian Propaganda at Rome in the Fourth and Fifth Centuries*. BARIS 148. Oxford: British Archaeological Reports, 1982.

Leloir, Louis, trans. "Actes de Pierre et Paul du Pseudo-Marcellus." Pages 1–34 in *Écrits apocryphes sur les apôtres: Traduction de l'édition arménienne de Venise*. CCSA 3. Turnhout: Brepols, 1986.

Lipsius, Richard A. Pages 2.1:284–366 in *Die apokryphen Apostelgeschichten und Apostellegenden*. Braunschweig: Schwetschke, 1887.

Lipsius, Richard A. and Max Bonnet, eds. "Acta Petri et Pauli catholica." Pages LVII–XC in vol. 1 of *Acta apostolorvm apocrypha post Constantinvm Tischendorf*. Leipzig: Mendelssohn, 1891. Repr., Hildesheim: Olms, 1972.

———, eds. *Passio sanctorum apostolorum Petri et Pauli*. Pages 119–77 in vol. 1 of *Acta apostolorvm apocrypha post Constantinvm Tischendorf*. Leipzig: Mendelssohn, 1891. Repr., Hildesheim: Olms, 1972.

———, eds. Πράξεις τῶν ἁγίων ἀποστόλων Πέτρου καὶ Παύλου. Pages 178–222 in vol. 1 of *Acta apostolorvm apocrypha post Constantinvm Tischendorf*. Leipzig: Mendelssohn, 1891. Repr., Hildesheim: Olms, 1972.

Migne, J.-P., trans. "Actes de saint Pierre et de saint Paul." Pages 715–31 in vol. 2 of *Dictionnaire des apocryphes*. Paris: Migne, 1858.

Moraldi, Luigi, trans. "Atti dei beati apostoli Pietro e Paolo dello Ps.-Marcello." Pages 1041–59 in vol. 2 of *Apocrifi del Nuovo Testamento*. Turin: Unione, 1971.

Vouaux, Léon. Pages 160–78 in *Les Actes de Pierre: Introduction, textes, traduction et commentaire* (Paris: Letouzey et Ané, 1922).

Walker, Alexander, trans. "Acts of the Holy Apostles Peter and Paul." Pages 256–76 in *Apocryphal Gospels, Acts and Revelations*. ANCL 16. Edinburgh: T&T Clark, 1870.

Passio sanctorum apostolorum Petri et Pauli

1. Cum uenisset Paulus Romam, conuenerunt ad eum omnes Iudaei dicentes: nostram fidem, in qua natus es, ipsam defende. non est enim iustum, ut cum sis Hebraeus ex Hebraeis ueniens, gentium te magistrum iudices, et incircumcisorum defensor factus tu cum sis circumcisus, fidem circumcisionis euacues. cum ergo Petrum uideris, suscipe contra eius doctrinam, quia omnem obseruationem nostrae legis euacuauit, exclusit sabbatismum et neomenias et legitimas ferias exinaniuit.

2. quibus Paulus respondit: me Iudaeum esse et uerum Iudaeum, hinc poteritis probare, cum et sabbatum obseruare et circumcisionem uere poteritis aduertere. nam sabbato die requieuit ab omnibus operibus Deus. nos habemus patres et patriarchas et legem. quid tale praedicat Petrus in regno gentium? sed et si forte aliquam uult introducere nouam doctrinam, sine conturbatione et sine inuidia et sine strepitu nuntiate ei, ut nos uideamus, et in uestro conspectu illum ego conuincam. quod si forte doctrina eius fuerit uero testimonio et Hebraeorum libris munita, decet nos omnes oboedire ei.

3. haec et his similia dicente Paulo perrexerunt Iudaei ad Petrum et dixerunt ei: Paulus ex Hebraeis uenit, rogat te ut uenias ad eum, quoniam hi qui eum adduxerunt dicunt non eum se posse dimittere, ut uideat quem uult, antequam eum Caesari insinuent.

Passion of the Holy Apostles Peter and Paul

1. When Paul had come to Rome, all the Jews came together to him, saying, "Protect our faith in which you were born. It is not right that you, who are a Hebrew of Hebrews, should consider yourself a teacher of the gentiles; or that you, who are circumcised, have become a defender of the uncircumcised and nullify faith in circumcision.[1] Therefore, when you see Peter, stand against his teaching, because he has nullified all observance of our law, has eliminated our Sabbath and new moons, and has decimated our lawful feasts."

2. Paul responded to them, "From now on you will be able to verify that I am a true Jew, when you will truly be able to observe the Sabbath and pay heed to circumcision. For on the Sabbath day God rested from all his works. We have the fathers and the patriarchs and the law. What sort of thing is Peter preaching in the kingdom of the gentiles? If by chance he wants to introduce any new teaching, then without any uproar or animosity or trouble tell him that we want to see him, and in your presence I will refute him.[2] But if by chance his teaching is supported by true testimony and the books of the Hebrews, then it is proper that we all obey him."

3. After Paul had said these and other similar things, the Jews hastened to Peter and said to him, "Paul came from the Hebrews and asks you to come to him, because those who brought him[3] are saying that they are not able to release him, so that he may see whomever he wishes, before they take him to Caesar."

1. Or "the faith of the circumcision." Cf. Gal 2:9–12.

2. Here Peter, not Paul, is seen as undermining traditional legal observance. On this reversal of roles, see David L. Eastman, "Confused Traditions? Peter and Paul in the Apocryphal Acts," in *Forbidden Texts on the Western Frontier: The Christian Apocrypha in North American Perspectives. Proceedings from the 2013 York University Christian Apocrypha Symposium* (Eugene, OR: Cascade, forthcoming).

3. That is, the Roman guards assigned to Paul.

audiens haec Petrus gaudio gauisus est magno et statim exsurgens perrexit ad eum. uidentes autem se prae gaudio fleuerunt et in amplexibus suis diutissime morati inuicem se lacrimis infuderunt.

4. cumque Paulus illi omnem textum suorum casuum indicasset et qualiter nauigii fatigationibus aduenisset et Petrus dixisset illi, quas a Simone mago pateretur insidias, abscessit Petrus ad uesperum, mane die altero reuersurus.

5. cumque aurora diei daret initium, ecce Petrus adueniens inuenit multitudinem Iudaeorum ante fores Pauli. erat autem inter Iudaeos Christianos et gentiles infinita conturbatio. Iudaei enim dicebant: nos genus sumus electum regale amicorum Dei, Abrahae, Isaac et Iacob et omnium prophetarum, cum quibus locutus est Deus, quibus ostendit mirabilia magna et secreta sua. uos autem ex gentibus, nihil in semine uestro magnum, nisi in idolis et sculptilibus inquinati et execrabiles extitistis.

6. haec et his similia dicentibus Iudaeis, gentes respondebant dicentes: nos mox ut audiuimus ueritatem, reliquimus errores nostros et secuti eam sumus. uos autem et paternas uirtutes scistis et prophetarum signa uidistis et legem accepistis et mare pedibus siccis transistis, et inimicos uestros demersos uidistis et columna nubis uobis per diem in caelo apparuit et ignis per noctem, et manna uobis de caelo data est, et de petra uobis aquae fluxerunt: et post omnia haec idolum uobis uituli fabricastis et adorastis sculptile. nos autem nulla signa uidentes credimus Deum hunc, quem uos non credentes dereliquistis.

7. haec et his similia contendentibus dixit apostolus Paulus, non debere eos has contentiones inter se suscipere, sed hoc magis adtendere, quia complesset Deus promissa sua, quae iurauit ad Abraham patrem nostrum,

Hearing these things Peter rejoiced greatly,[4] got up immediately, and went to him. Seeing each other, they wept for joy, and after embracing each other for a long time, they soaked each other with their tears.[5]

4. Then Paul recounted to Peter the entire story[6] of his misfortunes and how he arrived by the travails of sailing. Peter told him about the plots hatched by Simon the sorcerer that he was enduring. When it was evening, Peter departed to return at dawn on the next day.

5. When dawn brought the beginning of the day, behold, Peter came and found a multitude of Jews in front of the doors of Paul. There was a great disturbance between the Jewish and gentile Christians. The Jews[7] were saying, "We are the elect, royal race of the friends of God: Abraham, Isaac, Jacob, and all the prophets. When God spoke to them, he revealed to them great wonders and his secrets. However, you who are from the gentiles have nothing great in your lineage, but are polluted and accursed by your idols and statues."

6. After the Jews had said these and other similar things, the gentiles[8] responded, saying, "As soon as we heard the truth, we abandoned our errors and followed it. You, however, knew the powerful deeds of the fathers, and saw the signs of the prophets, and received the law, and crossed the sea with dry feet, and saw your enemies drowned. A pillar of smoke appeared for you in the sky by day, and a pillar of fire by night. Manna was given to you from heaven, and water flowed for you from a rock. But after all these things, you made for yourselves the image of a calf and worshiped a statue. We, however, saw no signs yet believe in this God, whom you unbelievers abandoned."

7. While they were arguing with these and other similar words, the apostle Paul said, "You should not take up these quarrels among yourselves. Rather, focus on the fact that God has fulfilled his promises, which he swore to Abraham our father, that in his seed all nations would have an

4. Literally, "rejoiced with great joy."

5. On the ubiquity of the image of an apostolic embrace in early Christian art, see Herbert L. Kessler, "The Meeting of Peter and Paul in Rome: An Emblematic Narrative of Spiritual Brotherhood," in *Studies on Art and Archeology in Honor of Ernst Kitzinger on His Seventy-Fifth Birthday*, ed. William Tronzo and Irving Lavin, DOP 41 (Washington: Dumbarton Oaks, 1987), 265–75.

6. The term refers to something that is woven, like a textile. The Greek translation of this text uses ὕφος ("web").

7. Here, Jewish believers in Christ.

8. Gentile believers in Christ.

quod in semine eius hereditarentur omnes gentes: non est enim personarum acceptio apud Deum. quicumque enim in lege peccassent, secundum legem iudicarentur; qui uero sine lege deliquissent, sine lege perirent. est enim in humanis sensibus tanta sanctitas, ut bona laudet naturaliter et puniat mala, quae inter se inuicem cogitationes aut accusantes puniat aut remuneret excusantes.

8. haec et his similia Paulo dicente factum est ut mitigati essent et Iudaei et gentes. sed principes Iudaeorum insistebant. Petrus uero his qui eum arguebant, quod synagogas eorum interdiceret, dixit: audite, fratres, Sanctum Spiritum promittentem patriarchae Dauid, quod de fructu uentris eius poneret super sedem suam. hunc ergo cui dixit Pater de caelis: filius meus es tu, ego hodie genui te, hunc crucifixerunt per inuidiam principes sacerdotum. ut impleret autem redemtionem necessariam saeculo, permisit se haec omnia sustinere, ut sicut ex costa Adae fabricata est Eua, sic ex latere Christi in cruce positi fabricaretur ecclesia, quae non haberet maculam neque rugam.

9. hunc Deus aditum aperuit omnibus filiis Abrahae et Isaac et Iacob, ut sint in fide ecclesiae et non in infidelitate synagogae. conuertimini ergo et intrate in gaudium Abrahae patris uestri, quia quod ei promisit Deus adimpleuit. unde et propheta canit: iurauit Dominus et non paenitebit

inheritance.[9] There is no favoritism with God. Whoever has sinned with the law is judged according to the law. And those who transgress without the law perish without the law.[10] In the human senses there is a very great sanctity that naturally praises good things and punishes evil things. It punishes those who are judging or accusing each other, or rewards those who forgive."[11]

8. After Paul had said these and other similar things, it came about that both the Jews and gentiles were pacified. But the leaders of the Jews were insistent. Peter said to those who were accusing him of renouncing their synagogues: "Hear, brothers,[12] the Holy Spirit promising to the patriarch David that he would place one from his own loins upon his throne. Therefore, the Father said this to him from heaven, 'You are my son. Today I have begotten you.'[13] But the leaders of the priests crucified him out of envy. In order that he might fulfill the necessary redemption for the world, he allowed himself to undergo all these things, so that just as Eve was formed from the rib of Adam,[14] so too from the side of Christ—who was placed on the cross—the church may be formed, which has neither stain nor wrinkle.[15]

9. "God opened this access to all the children of Abraham, Isaac, and Jacob, so that they might be in the faith of the church and not in the infidelity of the synagogue. Therefore, turn and enter into the joy of Abraham your father, because God has fulfilled what he promised to him. About this the prophet sings, 'The Lord has sworn and will not change his mind, you

---

9. Gen 18:18, 22:18.

10. Rom 2:11–12; Acts 10:34–35.

11. This section shows possible dependence on the writings of Pelagius: "I say that there is indeed in our souls (*animis*) a certain natural, I would say, sanctity. It presides in the stronghold of the soul and oversees the judgment of evil and good, so that it grants favor to true and right actions but condemns hurtful actions" (*Ep. Demet.* 4). The quarrel at hand, therefore, is an example of the "judging or accusing" that human nature should naturally punish. The editor of the parallel Greek Acts eliminates this possible Pelagian reference (Acts Pet. Paul 28).

12. In a first-century narrative setting, the leaders of the synagogues would generally be male, so I have preserved the gender-specific language of the original.

13. Ps 2:7, cited with reference to Christ in Acts 13:33; Heb 1:5, 5:5. Cf. Mark 1:11 and Luke 3:22, where a voice from heaven at Jesus's baptism says, "You are my son," but makes no reference to begetting.

14. Gen 2:21–22.

15. Eph 5:27.

eum, tu es sacerdos in aeternum secundum ordinem Melchisedech. sacerdos enim in cruce factus est, cum hostiam sui corporis et sanguinis pro omni saeculo sacrificium praebuisset.

10. haec et his similia dicentibus Petro et Paulo pars maxima populorum credidit, et perpauci fuerunt, qui non crediderunt, qui et ipsi simulata fide, non tamen aperte possent eorum neglegere monita uel praecepta. uidentes autem maiores synagogarum et gentium pontifices sibi per praedicationem eorum finem specialiter fieri, egerunt hoc ut sermo eorum in murmurationem populi ueniret.

unde factum est ut Simonem magum Neroni praeferrent et istos culparent. innumerabiles enim populi dum conuerterentur ad Dominum per praedicationem Petri, contigit etiam uxorem Neronis Liuiam et Agrippae praefecti coniugem nomine Agrippinam ita conuerti, ut a latere se suorum maritorum auferrent. per Pauli uero praedicationem multi deserentes militiam adhaerebant Deo, ita ut etiam ex cubiculo regis uenirent ad eum, et facti Christiani nollent ruerti ad militiam neque ad palatium.

11. hinc populis seditiosam murmurationem agentibus Simon excitatus est in zelum, et coepit de Petro multa mala dicere, dicens eum magum esse et seductorem. credebant autem illi hi qui mirabantur signa eius. faciebat enim serpentem aereum mouere se, et lapideas statuas et aereas ridere et mouere, se ipsum autem currere et subito in aëre uideri.

12. contra haec Petrus infirmos curabat uerbo, caecos uidere faciebat orando, daemonia iussu fugabat, interea et ipsos mortuos suscitabat. dicebat autem ad populum, ut ab eius seductione non solum fugerent, sed etiam detegerent eum, ne uiderentur diabolo consentire.

are a priest forever in the order of Melchizedek.'[16] He was indeed made a priest on the cross, when he provided the sacrifice of his own body and the offering of his own blood for the whole world."

10. After Peter and Paul had said these and other similar things, a great number of the people believed, but there were a few who did not believe.[17] Yet they, and those people who were like them in faith, were nevertheless certainly not able to ignore Peter and Paul's admonitions and teachings. However, when the leaders of the synagogues and the priests of the unbelievers saw that the preaching of Peter and Paul might bring about their end,[18] they arranged it that the teaching of Peter and Paul would be met with murmuring from the people.

Then it came about that they brought forth Simon, Nero's sorcerer, and accused Peter and Paul. At the time that innumerable people were being converted to the Lord through the preaching of Peter, it came to pass that the wife of Nero, Livia, and the wife of the prefect Agrippa, named Agrippina, were converted, so that they withdrew from the side of their husbands. Through the preaching of Paul many abandoned military service and clung to God, such that even from the bedchamber of the king they came to him.[19] And those who became Christians were unwilling to return either to military service or to the palace.

11. When the people began making a mutinous ruckus as a result, Simon's zeal was aroused, and he began to say many evil things about Peter—saying that he was a sorcerer and deceiver. Those who were amazed by Simon's signs believed him. He had, for instance, caused a bronze serpent to move and had made stone and bronze statues laugh and move, and he himself had run and suddenly seemed to be lifted into the air.

12. In response to these charges Peter was curing the sick by his word, making the blind see by his prayer, driving out demons by his command, and even raising the dead. He was speaking to the people, so that they would not only flee the seduction of Simon, but would also expose him, lest they seem to be conspiring with the devil.

---

16. Ps 110:4; applied to Christ in Heb 5:6, 10; 6:20; 7:17.

17. Cf. Matt 28:17.

18. Literally, "that their end particularly would come through their preaching."

19. Cf. Phil 1:12–13; 4:22. The Latin *cubiculum* can refer to a bedchamber but can also refer to the emperor's seat in the theater (Suetonius, *Nero* 12). The implication here is that even some of Nero's personal bodyguards were being converted and leaving the emperor's service. See e.g., Mart. Paul 1–2; Pseudo-Linus, *Mart. Paul* 1–5.

13. Sicque factum est ut omnes religiosi uiri execrantes Simonem magum, sceleratum eum adsererent; Simoni uero adhaerentes Petrum magum, quod ipsi erant cum Simone, falso testimonio adfirmarent. qui sermo usque ad Neronem Caesarem uenit; et Simonem magum ut ad se ingrederetur praecepit.

14. qui ingressus coepit stare ante illum et subito mutare effigies, ita ut fieret subito puer et posthaec senior, altera uero hora adolescentior. mutabatur sexu, aetate, et per multas figuras diaboli ministerio bachabatur. quod cum uideret Nero, uere hunc esse Dei filium aestimabat. Petrus uero apostolus dicebat hunc furem esse, mendacem, magum, turpem, sceleratum, apostaticum, et in omnibus quae sunt Dei praecepta aduersarium ueritatis, nihilque superesse nisi ut iussu Dei eius iniquitas manifestata omnibus panderetur.

15. tunc ingressus ad Neronem Simon dixit: audi me, bone imperator. ego sum filius Dei, qui de caelo descendi. usque modo Petrum qui se dicit apostolum solum patiebar; nunc ergo geminatum est malum. Paulus denique qui et ipse eadem docet et contra me sentit, simul dicitur cum eo praedicare. quos constat quia nisi de interitu eorum cogitaueris, regnum tuum stare non poterit.

16. tunc Nero sollicitudine cumulatus festinanter ad se eos iussit adduci. alia autem die cum introissent ad Neronem Simon magus et apostoli Christi Petrus et Paulus, Simon dixit: hi sunt discipuli illius Nazareni, quibus iam non est tam bene, ut sint de plebe Iudaeorum.

Nero dixit: quid est Nazareus?

Simon dixit: est ciuitas in Iudaea, quae semper aduersum uos fecit; haec Nazareth dicitur: ex ipsa fuit magister eorum.

17. Nero dixit: Deus omnem hominem monet et diligit; tu quare eos persequeris?

Simon dixit: istud hominum est genus, qui totam Iudaeam peruerterunt, ne mihi crederent.

Nero ad Petrum ait: quare tam perfidi estis uos uel genus uestrum?

tunc Petrus ad Simonem ait: omnibus inponere potuisti, mihi autem numquam; ipsos autem quos deceperas, per me Deus de suo errore reuo-

13. Thus it came about that all the pious people were cursing Simon the sorcerer and declaring that he was wicked. Those following Simon were asserting by false testimony that Peter was a sorcerer, because they were with Simon. This debate came even to the ears of the emperor Nero, and he ordered Simon the sorcerer to come to him.

14. After coming and standing before Nero, he suddenly began to change faces, such that he suddenly became a boy and after that an old man, but in another moment a younger man. He was changed in sex and age, and through many forms he was raging in the service of the devil. When Nero saw this, he supposed that this was truly the son of God. Peter the apostle was saying that this man was a thief, a liar, a sorcerer, foul, wicked, apostate, an adversary of the truth in all matters that are the commands of God, and that there was nothing left to do except, by the command of God, to make his iniquity openly manifest to all.

15. Then Simon went to Nero and said, "Hear me, good emperor. I am the son of God who descended from heaven. Until now I have put up with Peter, who says that he is the only apostle. Now this evil has been doubled, for there is also Paul, who teaches the same things and speaks against me, and at the same time is said to preach together with Peter. With regard to them, it is certain that unless you plot their destruction, your kingdom will not be able to stand."

16. Then Nero was overwhelmed with anxiety and immediately ordered them to be brought to him. On the next day, when Simon the sorcerer and the apostles of Christ, Peter and Paul, went in to Nero, Simon said, "Here are the disciples of that Nazarene, and it is not so good a thing for them that they are from the common folk of the Jews."

Nero said, "What is a Nazarene?"

Simon said, "There is a city in Judea[20] that always acts against you and is called Nazareth. Their teacher was from there."

17. Nero said, "God admonishes and esteems every person, so why do you persecute them?"

Simon said, "This is the race of people who have perverted all of Judea, so that they do not believe in me."

Nero said to Peter, "Why are you or your race so faithless?"

Then Peter said to Simon, "You were able to deceive everyone else, but never me, for through me God recalled from error those whom you had

20. Nazareth is in Galilee. This geographical error is another possible indication of the western provenance of the text.

cauit. et cum expertum tibi sit, quod me superare non possis, miror qua fronte in conspectu regis te iactes, ut putes per artem tuam magicam Christi discipulos superare.

18. Nero dixit: quis[1] est Christus?

Petrus dixit: hic est, quem hic Simon magus se esse adfirmat; hic autem est homo nequissimus et opera eius diabolica. si autem uis scire, bone imperator, quae gesta sunt in Iudaea de Christo, accipe litteras Pontii Pilati missas ad Claudium, et ita cognoscis omnia. Nero autem iussit eas accipi et in suo conspectu recitari. exemplar epistolae.

19. Pontius Pilatus Claudio suo salutem. nuper accidit quod ipse probaui, Iudaeos per inuidiam se suosque posteros crudeli condempnatione punisse. denique cum promissum haberent patres eorum quod illis Deus eorum mitteret de caelo sanctum suum, qui eorum rex merito diceretur, et hunc se promiserit per uirginem missurum ad terras,

20. is itaque me praeside in Iudaea Hebraeorum Deus cum uenisset, et uidessent eum caecos inluminasse, leprosos mundasse, paralyticos curasse, daemones ab hominibus fugasse, mortuos suscitasse, imperasse uentis, ambulasse siccis pedibus super undas maris et multa alia mirabilia fecisse: cum omnis populus Iudaeorum Dei filium hunc esse dicerent, inuidia contra eum ducti sunt principes sacerdotum et tenuerunt eum et mihi tradiderunt, et alia pro aliis mihi de eo mentientes dixerunt, istum magum esse et contra legem eorum agere.

21. ego autem credidi ita esse et flagellatum tradidi illum arbitrio eorum. illi autem crucifixerunt eum et sepulto custodes adhibuerent. ille autem militibus meis custodientibus die tertio resurrexit. in tantum autem exarsit nequitia Iudaeorum, ut darent pecuniam eis dicentes: dicite quia discipuli eius corpus ipsius rapuerunt. sed cum accepissent pecuniam,

1. A few manuscripts read *quid* ("What?").

deceived. Because you know by experience that you are not able to defeat me, I wonder in what guise you have brought yourself into the presence of the king, so that you believe you are able to overcome the disciples of Christ through your magical art."

18. Nero said, "Who is the Christ?"

Peter said, "He is the one who this Simon the sorcerer claims to be. But this man is completely worthless, and his deeds are diabolical. If you wish to know, good emperor, what were the deeds done by Christ in Judea, then get the letters of Pontius Pilate sent to Claudius, and you will know everything." Nero ordered them to be retrieved and read in his sight. This is a copy of the letter:[21]

19. "Pontius Pilate to Claudius, greetings. Recently it happened that I myself judged that through envy the Jews punished themselves and those coming after them with a cruel sentence. Their fathers had been promised that their God would send to them his own holy one from heaven, who would justly be called their king. And God promised that he would be sent to earth through a virgin.

20. "I was presiding in Judea of the Hebrews when God came down, and they saw him give sight to the blind, cleanse the lepers, cure the paralytics, drive demons from people, raise the dead, command the winds, walk upon the waves of the sea with dry feet, and perform many other wonders. When the whole populace of Jews was saying that he was the son of God, the leaders of the priests were driven by jealousy against him, seized him, and handed him over to me. And they told me many falsehoods about him and said that he was a sorcerer and had acted against their law.

21. "I believed that these things were so and handed him over to their judgment after he had been flogged. They crucified him and placed guards at his tomb.[22] However, while my soldiers were on guard, on the third day he rose again. The wickedness of the Jews was kindled to such a degree that they gave money to the guards, saying, 'Say that his disciples stole his

21. This letter is taken from Acts Pil. 13 (29). Quasten (1:116) suggests that it may be the letter that Tertullian claims was written from Pilate to Tiberius (*Apol.* 5, 21, 24). It must be distinguished from the equally spurious letters from Pilate to Tiberius produced in the Medieval period.

22. The pseudonymous author of this letter attempts to absolve Pilate of blame for anything but the flogging by making the historically impossible claim that the actual crucifixion was also carried out by the Jews.

quid factum fuerit tacere non potuerunt. nam et illum resurrexisse testati sunt se uidisse, et a Iudaeis pecuniam accepisse. haec ideo ingessi ne quis aliter mentiatur, et existimes credendum mendaciis Iudaeorum.

22. cumque perlecta fuisset epistola, Nero dixit: dic mihi, Petre, ita per illum omnia gesta sunt?

Petrus ait: ita, non te fallo; sic enim est, bone imperator. hic Simon plenus mendaciis et fallaciis circumdatus, ut putet se qui homo est, etiam hoc esse quod Deus est. in Christo enim est omnis summa uictoria per Deum et hominem, quem adsumpsit illa maiestas inconprehensibilis, quae per hominem hominibus dignata est subuenire. in isto autem Simone sunt duae substantiae, hominis et diaboli, qui per hominem conatur hominibus inpedire.

23. Simon dixit: miror te, bone imperator, hunc te alicuius momenti existimare, hominem inperitum, piscatorem, mendacissimum, et nec in uerbo nec in genere nec in aliqua praeditum potestate. sed ne diutius hunc patiar inimicum, modo praecipiam angelis meis, ut ueniant et uindicent me de isto.

Petrus dixit: non timeo angelos tuos, illi autem me poterunt timere in uirtute et confidentia Iesu Christi Domini mei, quem te esse mentiris.

24. Nero dixit: non times, Petre, Simonem qui diuinitatem suam rebus adfirmat?

Petrus dixit: diuinitas in eo est qui cordis rimatur arcana. dicat nunc mihi quid cogito uel quid facio. quam cogitationem meam, antequam hic mentiatur, prius tuis auribus insinuo, ut non audeat mentiri quae cogito.

Nero dixit: accede huc, et dic mihi quid cogitas.

Petrus dixit: iube mihi adferri panem ordeaceum et occulte dari.

body.'[23] But after they had taken the money, they were not able to be silent about what had happened, for they testified that he rose again and they saw him. But they took the money from the Jews. These things I have brought forth, lest someone should lie by telling a different story and you should judge that that story should be believed based on the lies of the Jews."

22. After the letter had been read, Nero said, "Tell me, Peter, were all these things done through him in this way?"

Peter said, "Yes, I am not lying. It was thus, good emperor. But this Simon is full of lies and encircled in deceit, so that he supposes that he, a man, is even what God is. In Christ is the full, ultimate victory through God and humanity[24]—which he assumed—and the incomprehensible majesty that deigned to come to humanity through a man. In that man Simon there are also two natures, that of humanity and that of the devil, who tries to ensnare humankind through a man."[25]

23. Simon said,[26] "I am amazed at you, good emperor, that you consider this man to be of any consequence, for he is an ignorant, lying fisherman and is gifted neither in word, nor in family descent, nor in any other authority. But I will no longer endure this enemy and will order my angels to come and avenge me on that man."

Peter said, "I do not fear your angels. They, however, will be able to fear me in the power and confidence of my Lord Jesus Christ, who you lie and say that you are."

24. Nero said, "Peter, do you not fear Simon, who confirms his divinity with deeds?"

Peter said, "Divinity is in the one who reveals the secrets of the heart.[27] Let him now say to me what I am thinking or what I am doing. But first I will whisper what I am thinking in your ears, before this man lies to you, so that he may not dare to lie about what I am thinking."

Nero said, "Come here, and tell me what you are thinking."

Peter said, "Order a barley loaf to be brought to me and given to me secretly." After what had been ordered was brought secretly and given to

---

23. Matt 28:11–15.

24. Literally, "through God and man."

25. The two natures of Christ (divine and human) are thus contrasted with the two natures of Simon (human and diabolical). Cf. Paul's "second Adam" argument in Rom 5:12–19 and 1 Cor 15:45–49.

26. Chapters 23–27 are likely the source for Pseudo-Abdias, *Pass. Pet.* 17–18.

27. Jer 17:10; Rev 2:23.

cumque hoc iussum fuisset occulte adferri et dari Petro, Petrus dixit: dicat nunc Simon, quid cogitatum, quid dictum, quidue sit factum.

25. Nero dixit: uis ergo ut credam quia haec Simon ignorat, qui et mortuum suscitauit et se ipsum decollatum post diem tertium repraesentauit, et quicquid dixit ut faceret, fecit?

Petrus dixit: sed coram me non fecit.

Nero dixit: sed me adstante haec omnia fecit; nam et angelos iussit ad se uenire, et uenerunt.

Petrus dixit: ergo si quod maximum est fecit, quare quod minus est non facit? dicat quid cogitauerim et quid fecerim

Nero dixit: quid dicis, Simon? ego me inter uos non conuenio.

Simon dixit: Petrus dicat, quid cogitem uel quid fecerim.

Petrus dixit: quid cogitet Simon, me scire docebo, dum fecerim quid cogitauerit.

26. Simon dixit: hoc scias, bone imperator, quia cogitationes hominum nemo nouit nisi unus Deus. ceterum Petrus mentitur.

Petrus dixit: tu ergo, qui filium Dei te esse dicis, dic quid cogitem; quid fecerim modo in occulto, si potes, exprime. Petrus enim benedixerat panem quem acceperat ordeaceum et fregerat et dextera atque sinistra in manica collegerat.

27. tunc Simon indignatus quod dicere non posset secretum apostoli, exclamauit dicens: procedant canes magni et deuorent eum in conspectu Caesaris. et subito apparuerunt canes mirae magnitudinis et impetum fecerunt in Petrum. Petrus uero extendens manus in orationem, ostendit canibus eum quem benedixerat panem; quem ut uiderunt canes subito nusquam conparuerunt.

Peter, he said, "Let Simon now say what was thought, what was said, and what was done."

25. Nero said, "Do you want me to believe that Simon does not know these things—he who raised the dead, and presented himself to me on the third day after he had been decapitated,[28] and did whatever he said he would do?"

Peter said, "But he did nothing in my presence."

Nero said, "But in my presence he did all these things, for he ordered angels to come to him, and they came."

Peter said, "If he has done the greatest thing, then why does he not do a lesser thing? Let him say what I thought and did."

Nero said, "What do you say, Simon? I myself cannot decide between you."

Simon said, "Let Peter say what I am thinking or what I did."

Peter said, "I will show that I know what Simon is thinking by doing what he was thinking."

26. Simon said, "Know this, good emperor, that no one knows the thoughts of people, except God alone.[29] But Peter is lying."

Peter said, "You, therefore, who say that you are the son of God, say what I am thinking and what I just did in secret. If you are able, say it." Peter had blessed the barley loaf that he had received, broken it, and gathered it under his sleeves in his right and left hands.

27. Then Simon was enraged that he was not able to tell the secret of the apostle, and he cried out, saying, "Let great dogs come and devour him in the sight of Caesar!" And suddenly dogs of amazing size appeared and made an attack on Peter.[30] Peter, however, extended his hands in prayer and showed the dogs the bread that he had blessed. As soon as the dogs saw it, they suddenly disappeared.

---

28. See §§31–32 below.

29. Cf. 1 Cor 2:11.

30. Cf. Pass. Apost. 7, where Paul is also included in this scene. Several medieval legends state that Simon was known to own a large, ferocious dog (e.g., Jacobus de Voragine [*Leg. aur.* 89], Nicephorus Callistus Xanthopulus [*Hist. eccl.* 11.27]), but it is unclear if there is a direct dependence on this text. For an explanation of Simon's association with dogs, see Alberto Ferreiro, "Simon Magus, Dogs, and Simon Peter," in *The Devil, Heresy, and Witchcraft in the Middle Ages: Essays in Honor of Jeffrey B. Russell*, ed. Alberto Ferreiro (Leiden: Brill, 1998), 45–89.

tunc Petrus dixit ad Neronem: ecce ostendi tibi scisse me quid cogitauerit Simon, non uerbis, sed factis; nam qui angelos promiserat contra me esse uenturos, canes exhibuit, ut se ostenderet non diuinos angelos sed caninos habere.

28. tunc Nero ad Simonem dixit: quid est, Simon? puto uicti sumus.

Simon dixit: hic et in Iudaea et in tota Palaestina et Caesarea ista mihi fecit, et saepe mecum certando ideo didicit, quia hoc eis erat contrarium: me ergo ut euaderet didicit hoc. nam cogitationes hominum nemo nouit nisi unus Deus.

et Petrus ad Simonem dixit: certe deum te esse mentiris. quare ergo non manifestas cogitationes singulorum?

29. tunc conuersus Nero ad Paulum sic ait: tu quare nihil dicis, Paule?

Paulus respondit: hoc scito, Caesar, quia si dimiseris istum magum tanta agere, magnum malum patriae tuae adcrescet, et regnum tuum ab statu suo deiciet.

Nero Simoni dixit: quid dicis tu, Simon?

Simon dixit: ego nisi me aperte demonstrauero deum esse, nemo mihi uenerationem debitam exhibebit.

Nero dixit: et quid modo moraris et non ostendis te deum esse, ut isti puniantur?

30. Simon dixit: iube mihi turrim altam fabricare ex lignis, et ascendam super eam, et uocabo angelos meos et praecipiam eis ut cunctis uidentibus in caelum perferant me ad patrem meum. hoc isti dum facere non potuerint, probabis eos homines esse inperitos.

Nero autem Petro dixit: audisti, Petre, quod Simon dixit? ex hoc apparebit quantam uirtutem habeat uel ipse uel Deus tuus.

Petrus dixit: optime imperator, si uelles, poteras intellegere quia daemonio plenus est.

Nero dixit: quid mihi uerborum ambages [circuitus] facitis? crastinus dies uos probabit.

Then Peter said to Nero, "Look, I have shown you that I know what Simon was thinking, not with words but with deeds, for he had promised that his angels would come against me, but he produced dogs. Thus, he has demonstrated that he has angels that are not divine, but canine."

28. Then Nero said to Simon, "Well, Simon? I think that we are beaten."

Simon said, "Here and in Judea and in all of Palestine and Caesarea he has done these things to me,[31] and by contending with me often, therefore, he has learned that this is hurtful to them. He thus learned this so that he might escape me, for no one knows the thoughts of people except God alone."[32]

And Peter said to Simon, "Certainly, you lie in saying that you are a god. Why, therefore, do you not reveal the thoughts of every person?"

29. Then Nero turned to Paul and said, "Why do you say nothing, Paul?"

Paul responded, "I know this, Caesar, that if you let that sorcerer go on doing such things, then great evil will increase upon your country, and your kingdom will be thrown down from its current position."

Nero said to Simon, "What do you say, Simon?"

Simon said, "Unless I openly show that I am a god, no one will offer the veneration that is due to me."

Nero said, "And why do you now delay and not show that you are a god, so that these men may be punished?"

30. Simon said, "Order a tall tower to be built for me out of wood. I will climb it and call upon my angels, and I will order them to carry me into heaven to my father with everyone watching. When those men are not able to do this, you will know that they are ignorant men."

Nero then said to Peter, "Peter, did you hear what Simon said? From this action it will be apparent how much power either he or your God has."

Peter said, "Greatest emperor, if you were willing, you would come to understand that he is full of a demon."

Nero said, "Why are you so evasive with your words to me? Tomorrow the day will test you."

---

31. Pseudo-Clement, *Hom.* 2.14–40; 3.1–4, 10, 29–58; 6.26–8.3; 16.1–18.23; 20.11–13.

32. The sense of this passage is somewhat obscure. Simon seems to be suggesting that Peter had learned the barley loaf defense based on previous showdowns with his dogs, but there is no indication of this in the Pseudo-Clementine *Homilies* or elsewhere.

31. Simon dixit: credis, bone imperator, quia magus sum, cum mortuus fuerim et resurrexerim?

egerat enim perfidus Simon praestigio suo, ut diceret Neroni: iube me decollari in obscuro et ibidem dimitti occisum, et si non tertia die resurrexero, scias me magum fuisse: si autem resurrexero, scias me esse filium Dei.

32. et cum hoc fieri iussisset Nero, in obscuro egit arte magica ut aries decollaretur; qui aries tamdiu Simon uisus est quamdiu decollaretur. decollatus autem in obscuro, cum scrutatus fuisset is, qui eum decollauerat, et caput eius protulisset ad lumen, inuenit caput berbicinum; sed nihil uoluit regi dicere, ne se ipsum detegeret qui iussus fuerat hoc in abditis perpetrare. hinc ergo dicebat Simon, se die tertia resurrexisse, quia caput et membra berbicis tulerat, sanguis uero ibidem congelauerat. et tertia die ostendit se Neroni et dixit: fac sanguinem meum qui effusus est extergi: quia ecce qui decollatus fueram, sicut promisi, die tertia resurrexi.

33. cum ergo dixisset Nero: crastinus dies uos probabit; conuersus ad Paulum ait: tu Paule, quare nihil loqueris? aut quis te docuit aut quem magistrum habuisti, aut qualiter in ciuitatibus docuisti, uel quales exstiterunt per tuam doctrinam? puto enim nullam te habere sapientiam, nec uirtutem aliquam posse perficere.

Paulus respondit: putas me contra hominem perfidum et desperatum magum maleficum, qui animam suam morti destinauit, cuius interitus et perditio cito adueniet, debere loqui? qui fingit se esse quod non est, et arte magica hominibus ad perditionem inludit?

34. huius tu uerba si uolueris audire uel fouere eum, perdes animam tuam et imperium tuum. hic enim homo pessimus est, et sicut Aegyptii magi Iamnes et Mambres qui Pharaonem et exercitum eius miserunt in

31. Simon said, "Do you believe, good emperor, that I am a sorcerer, although I was dead and resurrected?"

The treacherous Simon had put a plan in motion by his deceptiveness[33] and said to Nero, "Order me to be decapitated in the dark and my dead body to be left there. If I do not rise on the third day, then you will know that I am a sorcerer. If, however, I am resurrected, then you will know that I am the son of God."

32. And after Nero had ordered this to be done, in the dark Simon brought it about by his magical art that a ram was decapitated. This ram appeared to be Simon until it was decapitated. It was decapitated in the dark, but when it was examined, the one who had decapitated it and brought its head into the light discovered a ram's head. He decided to say nothing to the king, lest he get himself into trouble, because he had been ordered to do this in secret. Therefore, from then on Simon was saying that he had risen again on the third day, because he had taken the head and limbs of the ram, but the blood had congealed there. On the third day he showed himself to Nero and said, "Make my blood that was shed be wiped up, because look, I who was decapitated have risen again on the third day, as I promised."

33. After Nero had said, "Tomorrow the day will test you,"[34] he turned to Paul and said, "And you, Paul, why do you say nothing? Who taught you? Who was your master? How have you taught in the cities? What sorts of things have happened through your teaching? I think that you have no wisdom, nor are you able to demonstrate any power."

Paul responded, "Do you think that I should speak against a treacherous man and hopeless, wicked sorcerer, who has destined his soul to death, and whose destruction and ruin will come quickly? A man who forms himself into what he is not, and by his magical art fools people to their destruction?

34. "If you are willing to listen to his words or support him, then you will lose your soul and your kingdom. He is the worst kind of man, like the Egyptian sorcerers Jamnes and Mambres,[35] who led pharaoh and his

33. Cf. the account of Simon's faked resurrection in Pass. Apost. 2–3.

34. The repetition of Nero's quotation signals that chapters 31–32 were perhaps later insertions into the text.

35. These are the names traditionally ascribed to the sorcerers who opposed Moses in Exod 7–8. They are mentioned numerous times in ancient literature, including CD V, 18–19; Menaḥ. 85a; 2 Tim 3:8–9; Pliny the Elder, *Nat.* 30.1.11; Apuleius, *Apol.*

errorem, quousque demergerentur in mari: sic et hic per patris sui diaboli peritiam hominibus persuadet et multa mala facit per nicromantiam et cetera mala, si qua sunt apud homines, et sic multos incautos seducit ad temptationem imperii tui.

35. ego autem uerbum diaboli, quod per hunc hominem diffundi uideo, gemitibus cordis mei ago cum Spiritu Sancto, ut cito possit ostendi quid sit. nam quantum se exaltari putat ad caelos, tantum demergetur in infernis inferioribus, ubi est fletus et stridor dentium.

36. de doctrina autem magistri mei, de qua me interrogasti, non eam capiunt, nisi qui fidem mundi pectoris adhibuerint. nam quaecumque sunt pacis et caritatis, ea docui: per circuitum ab Hierusalem usque Illiricum repleui uerbum pacis.

37. docui, ut homines se inuicem diligant. docui ut inuicem se honore praeueniant. docui sublimes et diuites non se extollere et sperare in incerto diuitiarum, sed in Deo ponere spem suam. docui mediocres uictu et ues-

army into error until they were buried in the sea. He also persuades people through the skill of his father the devil[36] and does many evil things through necromancy, and other evil things besides. If somehow these things take place before the eyes of people, then he will thus lead astray many gullible people as a test of your empire.

35. "I, however, see the word of the devil, which is being poured out through this man. By the groanings of my heart I am acting with the Holy Spirit,[37] so that quickly [Simon] may be shown for what he is. For however much he thinks that he is lifted into the heavens, to that same degree he will be plunged into the depths of hell, where there is weeping and gnashing of teeth.[38]

36. "Concerning the teaching of my master, however, about which you asked me, no one can understand it except those who accept faith with a pure heart.[39] For whatever things concern peace and love, I have taught them. Throughout my journey from Jerusalem as far as Illyricum,[40] I have spread the word of peace.

37. "I have taught people to love one another. I have taught them to outdo one another in showing honor.[41] I have taught the lofty and the rich not to elevate themselves and hope in the uncertainty of riches, but to place their hope in God.[42] I have taught those with ordinary food and

---

90; and Numenius of Apamea (recorded in Eusebius, *Praep. ev.* 9.8.1). The Gelasian Decree lists an apocryphal work entitled the Repentance of Jannes and Jambres (an alternative spelling of Mambres), while Origen acknowledges that there is no record of them in scripture but claims that there exists "a secret book called the Book of Jamnes and Mambres" (*Comm. ser. Matt.* 28; 117 [quoted]). It is unclear how these references might relate to the text reconstructed in Albert Pietersma, ed. and trans., *The Apocryphon of Jannes and Jambres the Magicians: P. Chester Beatty XVI; (with new editions of Papyrus Vindobonensis Greek inv. 29456 + 29828 verso and British Library Cotton Tiberius B. v f. 87); with full facsimile of all three texts,* RGRW 119 (Leiden: Brill, 1994). On the various textual traditions related to these figures, see also Pietersma and R.T. Lutz, "Jannes and Jambres," in *OTP* 2:427–42. Palladius claims that their tomb in Egypt was guarded by demons (*Hist. laus.* 18.5–8).

36. Cf. John 8:44.

37. Rom 8:26.

38. Matt 8:12; 13:42, 50; 22:13; 24:51, 25:30; Luke 13:28.

39. 1 Tim 1:5; 2 Tim 2:22.

40. Rom 15:19.

41. Rom 12:10.

42. 1 Tim 6:17.

timento contentos esse. docui pauperes in sua egestate gaudere. docui patres docere filios suos disciplinam timoris Dei. docui filios obtemperare parentibus et monitis salutaribus. docui possidentes reddere tributum cum sollicitudine. docui negotiatores reddere uectigalia ministris reipublicae. docui uxores diligere uiros suos et timere eos quasi dominos. docui uiros fidem seruare coniugibus, sicut illi sibi seruare pudorem omnimodis uolunt. quod enim punit maritus in uxore adultera, hoc punit in marito adultero ipse Pater et conditor rerum Deus. docui dominos ut mitius cum seruis suis agant. docui seruos ut fideliter et quasi Deo ita seruiant dominis suis. docui ecclesias credentium unum et omnipotentem inuisibilem et inconprehensibilem colere Deum.

38. haec autem mihi doctrina non ab hominibus neque per hominem aliquem data est, sed per Iesum Christum et Patrem gloriae, qui mihi de caelo locutus est. et dum me mitteret ad praedicationem Dominus meus Iesus Christus, dixit mihi: uade et ego ero in te spiritus uitae omnibus credentibus in me; et omnia quaecumque dixeris aut feceris ego iustificabo.

39. Nero his auditis obstupuit et conuersus ad Petrum dixit: tu quid dicis?

et Petrus ait: omnia quaecumque locutus est Paulus uera sunt. nam multi anni sunt, per quos accepi litteras ab episcopis nostris, qui sunt in uniuerso orbe Romano, et paene omnium ciuitatum episcopi scripserunt mihi de factis et dictis eius. nam cum persecutor esset legis Christi, uox eum de caelo uocauit et docuit ueritatem, quia non erat per inuidiam

clothing to be content.[43] I have taught the poor to rejoice in their poverty.[44] I have taught fathers to teach their children the discipline of the fear of God.[45] I have taught children to obey their parents and the salvific admonitions.[46] I have taught those who have possessions to pay tribute out of duty. I have taught merchants to pay taxes to the servants of the republic.[47] I have taught wives to love their husbands and fear them as their masters.[48] I have taught husbands to be faithful to their wives, just as they wish to keep themselves blameless in every way.[49] That which a husband punishes in an adulterous wife, the father and maker of all things, God himself, punishes in an adulterous husband. I have taught masters to deal mildly with their servants.[50] I have taught servants to serve their masters faithfully and as if working for God.[51] I have taught assemblies[52] of believers to worship the one omnipotent, invisible,[53] incomprehensible God.

38. "This teaching was given to me not by a human source, nor through another person, but through Jesus Christ and the Father of glory, who spoke to me from heaven.[54] And when my Lord Jesus Christ sent me to preach, he said to me, 'Go, and I will be in you, the spirit of life for all those who believe in me. And I will forgive whatever things you have said or done.' "[55]

39. When he heard these things, Nero was stupefied and turned to Peter and said, "What do you say?"

And Peter said, "All the things that Paul said are true, because for many years I have received letters from our bishops, who are throughout the entire Roman world. Often the bishops of all the cities have written to me concerning his deeds and words. For when he was a persecutor of the law of Christ, a voice called to him from heaven and taught him the truth,

---

43. 1 Tim 6:8.
44. Cf. 2 Cor 6:10; Jas 1:9.
45. Cf. Eph 6:4.
46. Col 3:20; Eph 6:1.
47. Rom 13:5–7.
48. No such command is given even in the disputed Pauline epistles.
49. Col 3:18–19; Eph 5:22–28.
50. Phlm; Col 4:1; Eph 6:9.
51. Col 3:22–24; Eph 6:5–6.
52. Or "churches."
53. Col 1:15; 1 Tim 1:17.
54. Gal 1:1, 11–12.
55. The source of this quotation ascribed to Jesus is unknown. Cf. the command of Christ in Acts 22:21: "Go, for I will send you far away to the gentiles."

inimicus fidei nostrae sed per ignorantiam. fuerunt enim ante nos pseudochristi, sicut est Simon, fuerunt et pseudoapostoli, fuerunt et pseudoprophetae, qui contra sacros apices[2] uenientes euacuare studuerunt ueritatem. et contra hos necesse erat agere hunc uirum, qui ex infantia sua nihil aliud studii gesserat, nisi diuinae legis scrutari mysteria, in quibus hoc didicerat, ut defensor ueritatis et persecutor existeret falsitatis. quia ergo persecutio eius non ex aemulatione fiebat, sed ex defensione legis, ipsa ueritas eum de caelo adlocuta est dicens ei: ego sum ueritas quam defendis: cessa me persequi, quia ego ipsa sum pro qua uideris dimicare contra inimicos ueritatis. ergo cum cognouisset ita esse, deseruit quod defendebat et coepit defendere hanc quam persequebatur semitam Christi, qui est uia pure ambulantibus, ueritas nihil fallentibus et uita credentibus sempiterna.

40. Simon dixit: bone imperator, intellege conspirationem horum duorum aduersum me. ego enim sum ueritas et isti aduersum me sapiunt.

Petrus dixit: nulla ueritas in te est, sed ex solo mendacio omnia ista dicis et facis.

41. Nero dixit: Paule tu quid dicis?

Paulus dixit: quae a Petro audisti, hoc et a me dictum crede. unum enim sentimus, quia unum habemus Dominum Iesum Christum.

Simon dixit: putas me, bone imperator, cum his habere disputationem, qui aduersum me consensum fecerunt? et conuersus ad apostolos Dei dixit: audite, Petre et Paule; si hic uobis nihil possum facere, ueniemus ubi uos oportet me iudicare.

Paulus dixit: bone imperator, uide quales nobis minas ostendit.

Petrus dixit: cur non inrides hominem uanum et alieni capitis, qui ludificatus a daemoniis putat se manifestari non posse?

42. Simon dixit: ego uobis parco, quousque ostendam uirtutem meam.

Paulus dixit: quasi tu hinc exiturus sis sanus.

2. *Apex* refers to a small stroke of a letter. It is the same term used in the Vulgate of Matt 5:18.

because he was hostile to our faith not through jealousy but through ignorance.[56] Before us there were false christs, like Simon, and there were false apostles, and there were false prophets, who came against the sacred writings and were eager to nullify the truth. It was necessary to send this man against them—a man who from his youth had done nothing but search out the mysteries of the divine law, from which he learned so that he could be a defender of truth and a persecutor of falsehood. Therefore, because his persecution was done not out of rivalry but out of defense of the law, the truth itself spoke to him from heaven, saying to him, 'I am the truth that you are suppressing. Stop persecuting me, because I myself am the one for whom you seem to struggle against the enemies of truth.'[57] When he had realized that it was so, he abandoned what he was defending and began to defend that which he was persecuting—that is the path of Christ, which is the way for those walking in purity, the truth for those who are not deceivers, and the life eternal for those who believe."[58]

40. Simon said, "Good emperor, look at the conspiracy of these two against me. I indeed am the truth,[59] and they turn their thoughts against me."

Peter said, "There is no truth in you, but everything you say and do comes from only falsehood."

41. Nero said, "What do you say, Paul?"

Paul said, "Consider that the things you heard from Peter were also said by me. We feel the same way, because we have one Lord, Jesus Christ."

Simon said, "Do you think, good emperor, that I am going to dispute with these men, who have conspired against me?" And turning toward the apostles of God, he said, "Listen, Peter and Paul. If I am able to do nothing to you here, then we will go where it is right for me to judge you."

Paul said, "Good emperor, see what sorts of threats he hurls at us."

Peter said, "Why do you not laugh at this worthless and insane man, who is made sport of by demons and believes that he is not able to be exposed?"

42. Simon said, "I am putting up with you until I reveal my power."

Paul said, "[You speak] as if you will leave here unharmed."[60]

56. 1 Cor 15:8; Gal 1:15–16; Acts 9:3–9, 22:3–10, 26:9–18.

57. These words ascribed to Jesus are noticeably different from the accounts in Acts 9:3–9, 22:6–11, and 26:12–18.

58. John 14:6.

59. Cf. John 14:6, in direct response to Peter's words above.

60. The meaning of Paul's response is uncertain, although he is clearly predicting a bad end for Simon.

Petrus dixit: nisi uiderit Simon uirtutem Domini nostri Iesu Christi, non credit se Christum non esse.

Simon dixit: sacratissime imperator, noli istis credere, quia hi sunt qui circumciduntur et circumcidunt.

Paulus dixit: nos antequam ueritatem cognosceremus, carnis circumsionem tenuimus; at ubi ueritas apparuit, cordis circumcisione et circumcidimur et circumcidimus.

Petrus dixit: si mala est circumcisio, tu quare circumcisus es?

43. Nero dixit: ergo et Simon circumcisus est?

Petrus dixit: nec aliter poterat decipere animas, nisi se Iudaeum simularet et legem Dei docere ostenderet.

Nero dixit: tu, Simon, ut uideo, zelo duceris et ideo isto persequeris. est enim ut uideo, zelus magnus inter te et Christum eorum, et uereor ne ab eis conuincaris, et magnis malis consumptus esse uidearis.

Simon dixit: seduceris, imperator.

Nero dixit: quid est seduceris? hoc quod in te uideo hoc dico, euidenter te aduersarium esse Petri et Pauli et magistri eorum.

44. Simon dixit: Pauli Christus magister non fuit.

Paulus dixit: qui Petrum praesens docuit, ipse me per reuelationem instruxit. nam quod nos accusat circumcisos, dicat ipse, quare circumcisus sit.

Simon dixit: quare me hoc interrogatis?

Paulus dixit: est ratio ut te interrogemus.

Nero dixit: cur uereris respondere illis?

Simon dixit: ideo quia a Deo praecepta est circumcisio illo tempore quo ego eam suscepi.

45. Paulus dixit: audis, bone imperator, quid dixerit Simon? si ergo

Peter said, "Unless Simon sees the power of our Lord Jesus Christ, he will not believe that he is not the Christ."

Simon said, "Most holy emperor, do not believe those men, because they are circumcised and circumcise."[61]

Paul said, "Before we knew the truth, we held to the circumcision of the flesh. But where the truth has appeared, we are circumcised and circumcise with the circumcision of the heart."[62]

Peter said [to Simon], "If circumcision is evil, then why were you circumcised?"

43. Nero said, "Simon was circumcised?"

Peter said, "He would not otherwise have been able to deceive souls, unless he pretended to be a Jew and openly declared that he was teaching the law of God."

Nero said, "I see, Simon, that you are driven by jealousy and are therefore persecuting these men. I also see that there is great jealousy between you and their Christ. I fear that you will be conquered by them and seen to be overcome by great misfortunes."

Simon said, "You are mistaken, emperor."

Nero said, "What do you mean that I am mistaken? I say what I see in you, that you are obviously an enemy of Peter and Paul and their master."

44. Simon said, "Christ was not the master of Paul."

Paul said, "He who taught Peter in person instructed me through a revelation.[63] But because Simon attacks us for being circumcised, let him say why he was circumcised."

Simon said, "Why are you asking me this?"

Paul said, "It is right that we ask you."

Nero said, "Why are you afraid of answering them?"

Simon said, "I underwent circumcision, because at that time it was prescribed by God."

45. Paul said, "Do you hear, good emperor, what Simon said? If cir-

---

61. Simon is invoking a stereotype that Jews are untrustworthy because they mutilate their flesh. For example, circumcision was one of the practices specifically forbidden by Antiochus Epiphanes as part of his attempt to Hellenize the Jews in 165 BCE (1 Macc 1:48). Paul attacks his opponents in Philippi (the so-called "Judaizers") for promoting "the mutilation" (Phil 3:2), and the Roman historian Tacitus describes Jewish rites such as circumcision as "depraved and abominable" (*Hist.* 5.5).

62. Rom 2:28–29.

63. Gal 1:1, 11–12.

bona est circumcisio, quare tu circumcisos tradidisti, et coëgisti eos praecipitanter occidi?

Nero dixit: sed nec de uobis bene sentio.

Petrus et Paulus dixerunt: an tu de nobis sentias bene uel male, nom ad rem pertinet. nobis enim necesse est ut quod promisit magister noster fiat.

Nero dixit: quid si ego noluero?

Petrus dixit: non quod tu uolueris, sed quod nobis ille pollicitus est.

46. Simon dixit: bone imperator, hi homines circumuenerunt clementiam tuam et obligauerunt te.

Nero dixit: sed nec tu adhuc me de te confirmasti.

Simon dixit: quantis rebus bonis et signis a me tibi demonstratis miror quod adhuc dubitare uideris.

Nero dixit: ego neque dubito, neque cuiquam uestrum consentio. sed magis quod interrogo responde mihi.

47. Simon dixit: nihil tibi iam respondebo.

Nero dixit: ideo hoc dicis quia mentiris. et si ego tibi nihil possum facere, Deus qui potens est faciet.

Simon dixit: iam tibi responsurus non sum.

Nero dixit: sed nec ego te conputem aliquid esse. ut enim sentio fallax es in omnibus. sed quid plura? toti tres inconstabilitum animum uestrum ostendistis et me ita dubium in omnibus fecistis, ut non inueniam, cui credere possim.

48. Petrus dixit: ego unum esse Deum Patrem in Christo saluatore cum Sancto Spiritu creatorem omnium rerum praedico, qui fecit caelum et terram, mare et omnia quae in eis sunt, qui uerus rex est, et regni eius non erit finis.

Nero dixit: quis est rex Dominus?

Paulus dixit: saluator omnium gentium.

Simon dixit: ego sum quem dicitis; et sciatis, Petre et Paule, non uobis contingit quod cupitis ut martyrio uos digner.

cumcision is good, then why did you betray the circumcised and hastily gather them together to be killed?"

Nero said, "I am hearing nothing good from either of you two."

Peter and Paul said, "Whether you perceive good or evil from us is not relevant to the matter at hand. For us it is necessary that what our master promised should come about."

Nero said, "What if I am unwilling?"

Peter said, "It is not what you will that will happen, but what he has promised to us."

46. Simon said, "Good emperor, these men have taken advantage of your clemency and have ensnared you."

Nero said, "But up to now you have not proven to me anything about yourself."

Simon said, "After I have shown you so many great deeds and signs, I am amazed that you still seem to doubt."

Nero said, "I neither doubt nor agree with anything that any of you are saying. But answer me concerning what I am asking you."

47. Simon said, "I will not answer you now."

Nero said, "You say this because you are a liar. If I am not able to do anything to you, then the God who is able will do it."

Simon said, "I will no longer respond to you."

Nero said, "And I will consider you to be nothing. As I see it, you are deceitful in everything. But why should I say anything more? All three of you have demonstrated your unstable souls and have caused me to doubt everything such that I realize I am unable to believe anything."

48. Peter said, "I preach that there is one God, the Father, in Christ the Savior, together with the Holy Spirit, the creator of all things. He made heaven and earth, the sea and everything that is in them. He is the true king, and his kingdom will have no end."[64]

Nero said, "Who is this king and lord?"

Paul said, "The savior of all nations."

Simon said, "I am the one about whom you are speaking. But know, Peter and Paul, that although you want me to deem you worthy of martyrdom, it will not be granted to you."[65]

---

64. This creedal statement is taken from the Latin form of the Niceno-Constantinopolitan Creed and scriptural passages such as Ps 146:6; Luke 1:33.

65. While Peter had stated above that their martyrdom was promised by God (45), Simon here claims the divine authority to deny it to them.

Petrus et Paulus dixerunt: numquam tibi bene sit, Simon mage et amaritudinibus plene.

49. Simon dixit: audi, Caesar Nero, ut scias istos falsos esse et me de caelis missum: crastina die ad caelos uadam, ut hos qui mihi credunt beatos faciam; in istos autem qui me negare ausi sunt iram meam ostendam.

Petrus et Paulus dixerunt: nos olim uocauit Deus ad gloriam suam; tu autem a diabolo uocatus ad tormenta festinas.

50. Simon dixit: Caesar Nero, audi me. istos insanos a te separa, ut dum uenero ad patrem meum in caelis, possim tibi esse propitius.

Nero dixit: et unde hoc probamus quia in caelum uadis?

Simon dixit: iube turrim excelsam fieri ex lignis et trabibus magnis, ut ascendam in illam; et cum in illam ascendero, angeli mei ad me in aëra uenient: non enim in terra inter peccatores ad me uenire possunt.

Nero dixit: uolo uidere, si imples quod dicis.

51. tunc Nero praecepit in campo Martio turrim excelsam fieri et praecepit ut omnes populi et omnes dignitates ad istud spectaculum conuenirent. altera uero die in omni hoc conuentu iussit Nero Petrum et Paulum ad hoc spectaculum praesentari, quibus sic ait: nunc habet ueritas apparere.

Petrus et Paulus dixerunt: non enim nos eum detegimus, sed Dominus noster Iesus Christus, filius Dei, quem hic se ipsum esse mentitus est.

52. et conuersus Paulus ad Petrum dixit: meum est genibis positis Deum exorare, tuum est impetrare si quid uideris eum conari, quoniam tu prior electus es a Domino.

et positis genibus orabat Paulus. Petrus autem intuitus Simonem dixit: incipe, quod coepisti; adpropinquabit enim et tua detectio et nostra uocatio. uideo enim Christum meum uocantem me et Paulum.

53. Nero dixit: et quo ituri estis contra meam uoluntatem?

Petrus dixit: quo nos accersit Dominus noster.

Nero dixit: quis est dominus uester?

Petrus dixit: Dominus Iesus Christus, quem ego uideo nos uocantem.

Peter and Paul said, "May it never go well with you, Simon. You are a sorcerer and full of bitterness."

49. Simon said, "Listen, emperor Nero, so that you may know that those men are false and that I was sent from the heavens. Tomorrow I will depart into the heavens, so that I may make blessed those who believe in me. However, against those who dared to deny me I will show my anger."

Peter and Paul said, "God called us long ago for his glory, but you, who were called by the devil, are rushing to punishment."

50. Simon said, "Emperor Nero, listen to me. Separate these crazy men from yourself, so that when I go to my father in the heavens, I may be able to be gracious to you."

Nero said, "And how may we prove that you go into heaven?"

Simon said, "Order a very tall tower to be built out of wood and great timbers, so that I may ascend it. And after I climb upon it, my angels will come to me in the air.[66] They are not able to come to me on earth among sinners."

Nero said, "I want to see if you do what you say."

51. Then Nero ordered a very high tower to be built on the Field of Mars, and he ordered all the people and all the dignitaries to come together at this spectacle. On the next day Nero ordered Peter and Paul to be present at this spectacle before the whole assembly, and he said to them, "Now the truth will be evident."

Peter and Paul said, "We are not the ones exposing him, but it is our Lord Jesus Christ, the Son of God—who Simon has falsely asserted that he is."

52. Turning to Peter, Paul said, "It is up to me to entreat God on bended knees, and it is up to you to act, if you see him attempt anything, because you were chosen first by the Lord."[67]

Paul was praying on his knees, but Peter looked at Simon and said, "Go ahead with what you have started. Your exposure[68] indeed approaches, as does our calling. I in fact see my Christ calling me and Paul."

53. Nero said, "And where will you go against my will?"

Peter said, "Where our Lord summons us."

Nero said, "Who is your Lord?"

Peter said, "The Lord Jesus Christ, whom I see calling us."

---

66. According to Pseudo-Clement, *Hom.* 2.32, flight was another of Simon's powers.

67. The language of Petrine supremacy is placed in Paul's mouth.

68. That is, the moment at which you will be exposed as a fraud.

Nero dixit: ergo et uos in caelum ituri estis?

Petrus dixit: quo ipsi placuerit qui uocat nos.

Simon dixit: ut scias, imperator, istos fallaces esse, mox ut in caelum ascendero mittam ad te angelos meos et faciam te ad me uenire.

Nero dixit: fac ergo, quae dicis.

54. tunc ascendit Simon in turrim coram omnibus, et extensis manibus coronatus lauro coepit uolare. Nero ut uidit Petro sic ait: uerax homo est iste Simon, tu autem et Paulus seductores estis.

cui Petrus ait: sine mora scies nos ueraces esse Christi discipulos, hunc autem non esse Christum, sed magum et maleficum.

Nero dixit: adhuc perseueratis? ecce uidetis eum caelum penetrare.

55. tunc Petrus aspiciens Paulum dixit: Paule, erige caput et uide.

cumque eleuasset caput Paulus lacrimis plenus oculos, et uidisset Simonem uolantem, sic ait: Petre, quid cessas? perfice, quod coepisti. iam enim nos uocat Dominus noster Iesus Christus.

et Nero audiens eos subrisit et dixit: isti uident se uictos modo et delirant.

Petrus dixit: modo probabis nos non delirare.

Paulus ait Petro: fac iam, quod faciebas.

56. et aspiciens contra Simonem Petrus dixit: adiuro uos, angeli Satanae, qui eum in aëra fertis ad decipiendum hominum infidelium corda, per Deum creatorem omnium et per Iesum Christum quem tertia die a mortuis suscitauit, ut eum ex hac hora iam non feratis, sed dimittatis illum. et continuo dimissus cecidit in locum qui Sacra Uia dicitur, et in quattuor partes fractus quattuor silices adunauit, qui sunt ad testimonium uictoriae apostolicae usque in hodiernum diem.

Nero said, "And you are therefore going to go into heaven?"

Peter said, "We are going where it pleases the one who is calling us."

Simon said, "So that you may know, emperor, that these men are deceitful, as soon as I ascend into heaven, I will send my angels to you and will make you come to me."

Nero said, "Do what you are saying you will do."

54. Then Simon mounted the tower in the presence of all. With his arms extended and crowned with a laurel wreath, he began to fly. When Nero saw this he said to Peter, "This Simon is the true man, but you and Paul are deceivers."

Peter said to him, "Immediately you will know that we are the true disciples of Christ; this man, however, is not the Christ but a sorcerer and evildoer."

Nero said, "Do you persist even now? Look, you see that he is entering heaven."

55. Then Peter looked at Paul and said, "Paul, lift your head and see."

When Paul raised his head, his eyes full of tears, and saw Simon flying, he said, "Peter, why are you hesitating? Finish what you have started. Even now our Lord Jesus Christ calls us."

Hearing them, Nero scoffed and said, "These men see that they are now defeated and are going mad."

Peter said, "Now you will recognize that we are not mad."

Paul said to Peter, "Now do what you had started to do."

56. Looking toward Simon, Peter said, "You angels of Satan, who are carrying him in the air in order to deceive the hearts of unbelieving people, I command you through God, the creator of all things, and through Jesus Christ, whom he raised from the dead on the third day, not to carry him any longer but to let him go." And immediately he was dropped and fell onto the place called the Sacred Way.[69] He was broken into four parts and turned into four stones, which remain to the present day as a testimony to the apostolic victory.

---

69. The Sacred Way was the path of Roman triumphal processions, which began on the Capitoline Hill and passed through the Forum. The Apostolic Constitutions state that Simon was thrown to the earth as he was flying "in an unnatural way" (Apos. Con. 2.3.14), while Arnobius of Sicca claims that Simon tried to fly in a fiery chariot. Thrown down by the words of Peter, he broke his legs and soon after committed suicide (*Adv. nat.* 2.12).

57. tunc Nero teneri fecit Petrum et Paulum in uinculis; corpus autem Simonis iussit diligenter tribus diebus custodiri, putans eum resurgere tertia die.

cui Petrus dixit: hic iam non resurget, quoniam uere mortuus est et in aeterna poena dampnatus.

cui Nero dixit: quis tibi permisit tale scelus facere?

Petrus dixit: contentio eius, et si intellegas, multum est ei praestitum ut periret, ne tantas Deo ad multiplicationem supplicii sui inferret blasphemias.

Nero dixit: suspecto animo me esse fecistis, ideoque uos malo exemplo perdam.

Petrus dixit: non quae tu uis, sed quod promissum est nobis, necesse est consummari.

58. tunc Nero dixit ad praefectum suum Agrippam: homines inreligiosos necesse est male perdere, et ideo caris ferreis acceptis iubeo eos in Naumachia consumi et omnes huiuscemodi homines male consummari.

Agrippa praefectus dixit: sacratissime imperator, non congruenti exemplo iubes eos puniri.

Nero dixit: quare?

Agrippa dixit: quoniam Paulus innocens uidetur; Petrus autem homicidii reus est, insuper et inreligiosus.

57. Then Nero ordered Peter and Paul to be bound in chains. The body of Simon, however, he ordered to be kept carefully for three days, believing that he would rise again on the third day.

Peter said to him, "He will not now rise again, because he truly is dead and is damned to eternal punishment."

Nero said to him, "Who gave you permission to do such a wicked thing?"

Peter said, "On the contrary, if you want to understand, it is quite right for him to die, lest he commit such great blasphemies against God that he would multiply his own punishment."

Nero said, "You have made me mistrust you, and therefore I will destroy you with an evil punishment."

Peter said, "What has been promised to us, not what you wish, is what must be done."[70]

58. Then Nero said to his prefect Agrippa, "It is necessary to kill these impious men in a cruel way. Thus, after they have been tortured with iron claws,[71] I order that they be killed in the Naumachia[72] and that all people of this sort be put to death cruelly."

Agrippa the prefect said, "Most holy emperor, you order them to be punished with a penalty that does not fit their crimes."

Nero said, "Why?"

Agrippa said, "Because Paul seems to be innocent. Peter, however, is the one guilty of murder and is impious besides."

---

70. Cf. John 19:11.

71. Literally, "iron thistles" (*cardi*), torture devices designed to lacerate the skin as if one were carding wool.

72. The term *naumachia* refers to a mock sea battle or to the place where mock sea battles were staged. Nero was apparently the first emperor to put on such an event in an amphitheater (as opposed to in a dug basin) in 57 CE. He constructed this building on (or at least very near) the Field of Mars, opposite the Vatican hill (Suetonius, *Nero* 12.2–6; Cassius Dio, *Hist.* 61.9.5). Cassius Dio (*Hist.* 62.15.1) records that Nero staged a battle there in 64 CE, preceded by animal hunts and gladiatorial shows. Its exact location is unknown, but it is possible that the amphitheater and the place at which it was located could have taken on the name of the spectacles staged there. Archaeologists have identified a structure on the Vatican hill close to the Circus of Nero (where the obelisk stood) that may have been constructed for *naumachia* and was dedicated by Trajan in 109 CE. See Eva Margareta Steinby, ed., *Lexicon topographicum urbis Romae*, 5 vols. (Rome: Quasar, 1996), 3:338–39. This location is now the site of the Church of San Pellegrino in Vaticano (formerly San Pellegrino in Naumachia). If the topographical allusion in this text is taken to refer to the Trajanic structure, then this would be a clear anachronism.

Nero dixit: ergo quo exemplo peribunt?

Agrippa praefectus dixit: ut mihi uidetur, iustum est Paulo inreligioso caput amputari: Petrum autem eo quod insuper homicidium perpetrauerit, iube eum in cruce leuari.

Nero dixit: optime iudicasti.

59. et deducti sunt Petrus et Paulus a conspectu Neronis. Paulus decollatus est in uia Ostiensi.

60. Petrus autem dum uenisset ad crucem ait: quoniam Dominus meus Iesus Christus de caelo ad terram descendens recta cruce sublimatus est, me autem quem de terra ad caelum euocare dignatur, crux mea caput meum in terra debet ostendere, et pedes ad caelum dirigere: ergo quia non sum dignus ita esse in cruce sicut Dominus meus, girate crucem meam. at illi uerterunt crucem et pedes eius sursum fixerunt, manus uero deorsum.

61. conuenit autem innumerabilis multitudo maledicentes Caesarem Neronem, ita furore pleni ut uellent ipsum Caesarem incendere. Petrus autem prohibebat eos dicens: ante paucos dies rogatus a fratribus abscedebam, et occurrit mihi Dominus meus Iesus Christus, et adoraui eum et dixi: Domine, quo uadis? et dixit mihi: sequere me, quia uado Romam iterum crucifigi. et dum sequerer eum, redii Romam. et dixit mihi: noli timere, quia ego tecum sum, quousque introducam te in domum Patris mei.

Nero said, "By what punishment should they die, then?"

Agrippa the prefect said, "As it seems to me, it is fair to cut off the head of the impious Paul. As for Peter, however, because he also committed murder, order him to be hung on a cross."

Nero said, "You have pronounced an excellent judgment."

59. Peter and Paul were led away from the presence of Nero. Paul was decapitated on the Ostian Road.

60. However, when Peter came to the cross, he said, "Because my Lord Jesus Christ, who descended from heaven to the earth, was raised on an upright cross and has deigned to call me from the earth to heaven, my cross ought to place my head toward the earth and my feet directed toward heaven. Therefore, because I am not worthy to be on a cross in the way that my Lord was, turn my cross upside down." And they turned over the cross and attached his feet upward and his hands downward.[73]

61. A great multitude came together and hurled insults at the emperor Nero. They were so full of anger that they wanted to burn the emperor himself. Peter, however, stopped them, saying, "A few days ago I was leaving, because I had been begged to do so by the brothers and sisters. My Lord Jesus Christ ran up to me, and I worshiped him and said, 'Lord, where are you going?' He said to me, 'Follow me, because I am going to Rome to be crucified again.' While I was following him, I returned to Rome, and he said to me, 'Do not fear, for I am with you until the time that I lead you into the house of my Father.'

---

73. The description of his "hands downward" may suggest that the author believes Peter was fixed to the cross not in the traditional cruciform shape (*crux immissa*), but with hands and feet at full extension in opposite directions on a simple cross (*crux simplex*)—which could be no more than a wooden beam—or on a T-shaped cross (*crux commissa*). The form of ancient crucifixion has been the subject of several recent studies, e.g., John Granger Cook, "Envisioning Crucifixion: Light from Several Inscriptions and the Palatine Graffito," *NovT* 50 (2008): 262–85; idem, "Crucifixion as Spectacle in Roman Campania," *NovT* 54 (2012): 68–100; Gunnar Samuelsson, *Crucifixion in Antiquity: An Inquiry into the Background and Significance of the New Testament Terminology of Crucifixion*, WUNT 2/310 (Tübingen: Mohr Siebeck, 2011). On the development of Christian iconography of crucifixion scenes, see Felicity Harley-McGowan, "The Constanza Gem and the Development of Crucifixion Iconography in Late Antiquity," in *Gems of Heaven: Recent Research on Engraved Gemstones in Late Antiquity AD 200–600*, ed. Christopher Entwistle and Noel Adams, BMRP 177 (London: British Museum Press, 2011), 214–20.

62. et ideo, filioli, nolite inpedire iter meum. iam pedes mei uiam caelestem ambulant. nolite tristari, sed congaudete mecum, quia hodie laborum meorum fructum consequor. et cum haec dixisset, ait: gratias tibi ago, bone pastor, quia oues quas mihi credidisti compatiuntur mihi. peto ut participentur mecum de gratia tua. commendo tibi oues quas mihi credidisti, ut non sentiant se sine me esse, qui te habent per quem ego gregem hunc regere potui. et haec dicens emisit spiritum.

63. statim ibi apparuerunt uiri sancti, quos umquam nemo uiderat ante nec postea uidere potuerunt. isti dicebant se propter ipsum de Hierosolymis aduenisse, et ipsi una cum Marcello, inlustri uiro, qui crediderat et relinquens Simonem Petrum secutus fuerat, abstulerunt corpus eius occulte et posuerunt sub terebinthum iuxta Naumachiam in locum qui appellatur Uaticanus.

64. ipsi autem uiri qui se dicebant de Hierosolymis aduenisse, dixerunt ad omnem populum: gaudete et exultate, quia patronos magnos meruistis habere et amicos Domini Iesu Christi. sciatis autem hunc Neronem regem pessimum post necem apostolorum regnum tenere non posse.

65. accidit autem post haec ut odium exercitus sui et odium populi Romani incurreret; ita statuerunt ut publice cathomis tamdiu caederetur, quousque ut erat meritus expiraret. quod cum peruenisset ad eum con-

62. "Therefore, little children, do not impede my journey. Already my feet are walking on the heavenly road.[74] Do not be sad, but rejoice with me, because today I receive the fruit of my labors." After he had said these things, he said, "I thank you, good shepherd, because the sheep that you entrusted to me are suffering with me.[75] I pray that they may participate with me in your grace. I commit to your care the sheep that you entrusted to me, so that they may not notice that they are without me, because they have you, through whom I was able to direct this flock." After saying these things he gave up his spirit.[76]

63. Suddenly there appeared holy men, whom no one had ever seen before or was able to see afterward. They were saying that they had come from Jerusalem because of Peter.[77] They were together with Marcellus, a nobleman who had believed and had followed Peter after leaving Simon. They took away his body secretly and placed it under a turpentine tree next to the Naumachia in a place called the Vatican.

64. Those men who were saying that they had come from Jerusalem said to all the people, "Rejoice and be glad, because you have merited having the great patrons and friends of the Lord Jesus Christ.[78] Know, however, that this Nero, the most wicked king, is not able to keep his kingdom after the slaughter of the apostles."

65. It happened after these things that hatred from his own army and hatred from the Roman people rose up against [Nero]. Thus, they decided that he should be publicly beaten at a flogging post[79] for a long time, until he died in the way that he deserved. When news of this plan reached him,

---

74. Cf. Ignatius, *Rom.* 12.2, where Ignatius calls the Christians in Rome "the highway of those being killed for God."

75. Or "are showing sympathy for me." The fact that Peter then asks for these sheep also to partake in Christ's grace suggests to me that they are also sharing in Peter's suffering.

76. Cf. Matt 27:50; John 19:30.

77. Here Peter is singled out as the cause of their visit (*propter ipsum*), while the Greek Acts states that they had come "because of the holy and chief apostles," thereby highlighting Peter and Paul equally.

78. For a discussion of Paul and Peter as martyr-patrons of Rome and friends of Christ who could exert supernatural influence, see David L. Eastman, *Paul the Martyr: The Cult of the Apostle in the Latin West,* WGRWSup 4 (Atlanta: Society of Biblical Literature, 2011), 84–89.

79. On the origin of the obscure Latin word *cathomis*, see W. M. Lindsay, "'Glossae Collectae' in Vat. Lat. 1469. Catomvm. Navmachia," *ClQ* 15.1 (1921): 38–40.

silium, inruit in eum tremor et metus intolerabilis, et ita fugit ut ulterius non apparuerit. extiterunt autem qui dicerent, in siluis dum erraret fugiens frigore nimio et fame diriguisse et a lupis esse deuoratum.

66. sanctorum autem apostolorum dum a Graecis corpora tollerentur ad orientem ferenda, extitit terrae motus nimius. et occurrit populus Romanus et comprehenderunt eos in loco, qui dicitur Catacumba uia Appia miliario tertio; et ibi custodita sunt corpora anno uno et mensibus septem, quousque fabricarentur loca in quibus fuerunt posita corpora eorum. et illic reuocata sunt cum gloria hymnorum et posita sancti Petri in Uaticano Naumachiae et sancti Pauli in uia Ostiensi miliario secundo; ubi praestantur beneficia orationum in saecula saeculorum. amen.

trembling and unbearable fear fell upon him, and thus he fled and was never seen again. There were some who said that after fleeing he was wandering around in the forests, grew stiff from excessive cold and hunger, and was devoured by wolves.

66. However, when the bodies of the holy apostles were removed by some Greeks—bodies that they claimed had to be carried to the East—a huge earthquake occurred. The Roman people ran and seized these men at the place called the catacombs, on the Appian Road at the third milestone. There the bodies were kept for a year and seven months, until the places in which their bodies were placed could be built.[80] From there the bodies were retrieved with glorious singing and were deposited—that of holy Peter in the Vatican at the Naumachia, and that of holy Paul on the Ostian Road at the second milestone.[81] In those places the blessings of prayers are fully manifest forever and ever. Amen.

---

80. On the dual apostolic cult site on the Appian Road, which dates back at least to the third century based on archaeological evidence, see Eastman, *Paul the Martyr*, 71–114.

81. There are several accounts (including one by Gregory I) of a failed attempt to move the apostolic bodies to the East, see ibid., 110–14.

Πράξεις τῶν ἁγίων ἀποστόλων Πέτρου καὶ Παύλου

1. ἐγένετο μετὰ τὸ ἐξελθεῖν τὸν ἅγιον Παῦλον ἀπὸ Γαυδομελέτης τῆς νήσου ἐλθεῖν αὐτὸν ἐπὶ Ἰταλίαν. καὶ ἀκουστὸν ἐγένετο τοῖς Ἰουδαίοις τοῖς οὖσιν ἐν τῇ πρεσβυτέρᾳ τῶν πόλεων Ῥώμῃ ὅτι Παῦλος ᾐτήσατο πρὸς Καίσαρα ἐλθεῖν.

2. λύπῃ οὖν μεγάλῃ περιπεσόντες καὶ ἀθυμίᾳ πολλῇ εἶπαν πρὸς ἑαυτούς· οὐκ ἀρκεῖ ὅτι πάντας τοὺς ἀδελφοὺς καὶ τοὺς γονεῖς ἡμῶν ἔθλιψεν ἐν τῇ Ἰουδαίᾳ καὶ Σαμαρείᾳ καὶ ἐν πάσῃ τῇ Παλαιστίνῃ μόνος· καὶ οὐκ ἠρκέσθη ἐν τούτοις, ἀλλ' ἰδοὺ καὶ ἐνταῦθα ἔρχεται, δι' ἐπιθέσεως αἰτησάμενος Καίσαρα τοῦ ἀπολέσαι ἡμᾶς.

3. συνέδριον οὖν ποιήσαντες πάντες οἱ Ἰουδαῖοι κατὰ τοῦ Παύλου καὶ πολλὰ τρακταΐσαντες, ἔδοξεν αὐτοῖς προσελθεῖν Νέρωνι τῷ βασιλεῖ τῷ βασιλεύοντι ἐν ταῖς ἡμέραις ἐκείναις, ὥστε μὴ παραχωρῆσαι τὸν Παῦλον ἐλθεῖν ἐν τῇ Ῥώμῃ. ποιήσαντες οὖν εὐτρεπῆ οὐκ ὀλίγα δῶρα καὶ βαστάσαντες μεθ' ἑαυτῶν, μετὰ δεήσεως προσῆλθον αὐτῷ λέγοντες δεόμεθά σου, ἀγαθὲ βασιλεῦ, ἀποστεῖλαι κελεύσεις εἰς πάσας τὰς ἐπαρχίας τῆς ὑμετέρας εὐσεβείας περιεχούσας μὴ πλησιάσαι Παῦλον ἐν τούτοις τοῖς μέρεσιν· διότι οὗτος ὁ Παῦλος θλίψας πᾶν τὸ πατρῷον ἡμῶν ἔθνος ᾐτήσατο ἐλθεῖν ἐνταῦθα τοῦ καὶ ἡμᾶς ἀπολέσαι. καὶ ἀρκεῖ ἡμῖν, εὐσεβέστατε βασιλεῦ, τὴν θλίψιν ἣν ἔχομεν παρὰ Πέτρου.

4. ἀκούσας δὲ ταῦτα ὁ βασιλεὺς Νέρων ἀπεκρίθη αὐτοῖς· γίνεται κατὰ τὸ θέλημα ὑμῶν, καὶ γράφομεν πρὸς πάσας τὰς ἐπαρχίας ἡμῶν ἵνα παντελῶς μὴ ὁρμήσῃ ἐν τοῖς μέρεσιν Ἰταλίας. ὑπέβαλον δὲ καὶ Σίμωνι τῷ μάγῳ παρακαλέσαντες αὐτὸν ἵνα, ὡς εἴρηται, παντελῶς ἐν τοῖς μέρεσιν Ἰταλίας μὴ ἐπιβῇ.

Acts of the Holy Apostles Peter and Paul

1. It came about, after holy Paul set out from the island of Malta,[82] that he came to Italy. And it came to be heard by the Jews of that most venerable of cities, Rome, that Paul had asked to come to Caesar.[83]

2. Therefore, falling into great distress and losing heart, they said to themselves, "It does not suffice that he alone afflicted all our fellow Jews[84] in Judea and Samaria and all of Palestine. He was not satisfied by these things, but behold, he even comes here, having appealed to Caesar so that through an attack he may destroy us."

3. So after all the Jews had turned the Senate against Paul and had contrived many things, it seemed good to them to go to Nero, the emperor who was ruling in those days, so that he would not permit Paul to come to Rome. Therefore, after they had prepared many gifts and had deliberated among themselves, they went to him with their petition, saying, "We beg you, noble emperor, to send out orders to all the provinces under control of your piety that Paul should not come near to these regions. We ask this because this man Paul, who has afflicted the entire race of our people, has asked to come here so that he may also destroy us. And the distress that we have from Peter, most pious emperor, is already sufficient for us."

4. Having heard these things, the emperor Nero answered them, "It is done according to your will, and we are writing to all our provinces, so that he may certainly not drop anchor in the regions of Italy." And they informed even Simon the sorcerer, having summoned him so that, as has been said, Paul may not at all set foot in the regions of Italy.

---

82. Acts 27:39–28:10. The Greek form is Γαυδομελέτη, a name derived from the combined names of the adjacent islands Gozo (ancient Gaulos) and Malta (ancient Melita).

83. Acts 25:11–12

84. Literally, "brothers and fathers." It is highly unlikely, however, that first-century Jews would have considered those living in Samaria among this group.

5. τούτων δὲ οὕτως πραττόντων, τινὲς τῶν μετανοησάντων ἐξ ἐθνῶν καὶ βαπτισθέντων τῇ ἐπαγγελίᾳ τοῦ Πέτρου ἀπέστειλαν πρὸς τὸν Παῦλον πρέσβεις μετ' ἐπιστολῆς περιεχούσης οὕτως Παῦλε δοῦλε, γνήσιε τοῦ δεσπότου ἡμῶν Ἰησοῦ Χριστοῦ καὶ ἀδελφὲ Πέτρου τοῦ πρώτου τῶν ἀποστόλων, ἠκούσαμεν ἐκ τῶν διδασκάλων τῶν Ἰουδαίων τῶν ὄντων ἐν ταύτῃ τῇ μεγίστῃ τῶν πόλεων Ῥώμῃ ὅτι ᾐτήσαντο Καίσαρα τοῦ ἀποστεῖλαι ἐν πάσαις ταῖς ἐπαρχίαις αὐτοῦ, ἵνα ὅπου δᾶν εὑρεθῇς ἀποκτανθῇς. ἡμεῖς δὲ ἐπιστεύσαμεν καὶ πιστεύομεν ὅτι ὥσπερ οὐκ ἀποχωρίζει ὁ θεὸς τοὺς δύο φωστῆρας τοὺς μεγάλους οὓς ἐποίησεν, οὕτως οὐκ ἔχει μερίσαι ὑμᾶς ἀπ' ἀλλήλων, τοῦτ' ἔστιν οὔτε Πέτρον παρὰ Παύλου οὔτε Παῦλον παρὰ Πέτρον· ἀλλὰ κυρίως πιστεύομεν εἰς τὸν κύριον ἡμῶν Ἰησοῦν Χριστόν, εἰς ὃν ἐβαπτίσθημεν, ὅτι ἄξιοι γινόμεθα καὶ τῆς ὑμετέρας διδασκαλίας.

6. δεξάμενος δὲ ὁ Παῦλος τοὺς δύο ἄνδρας τοὺς ἀπεσταλμένους μετὰ τῆς ἐπιστολῆς, μηνὶ Μαΐῳ εἰκάδι, πρόθυμος ἐγένετο καὶ ηὐχαρίστησεν τῷ κυρίῳ καὶ δεσπότῃ ἡμῶν Ἰησοῦ Χριστῷ. ἀποπλεύσας δὲ ἀπὸ Γαυδομελέτης οὐκ ἔτι ἦλθεν διὰ Ἀφρικῆς ἐπὶ τὰ μέρη Ἰταλίας, ἀλλ' ἐπὶ Σικελίαν ἀνέδραμεν, ἕως οὗ ἦλθεν ἐν Συρακούσῃ τῇ πόλει μετὰ τῶν δύο ἀνδρῶν τῶν πεμφθέντων ἀπὸ Ῥώμης πρὸς αὐτόν.

7. κἀκεῖθεν ἀποπλεύσας παρεγένετο εἰς τὸ Ῥήγιον τῆς Καλαβρίας, καὶ ἀπὸ τοῦ Ῥηγίου ἐπέρασεν ἐν Μεσίνῃ, καὶ ὀρδινεύει[3] ἐκεῖ ἐπίσκοπον Βακχύλον ὀνόματι. ἐξελθόντος δὲ αὐτοῦ ἀπὸ Μεσίνης ἀπέπλευσεν ἕως Διδύμου, καὶ ἔμεινεν ἐκεῖ νύκτα μίαν· κἀκεῖθεν ἀποπλεύσας ἦλθεν εἰς Ποντιόλην τῇ δευτέρᾳ ἡμέρᾳ.

8. Διόσκορος δὲ ὁ ναύκληρος ὁ ἀπενέγκας αὐτὸν ἐν Συρακούσῃ, συμπαθῶν τῷ Παύλῳ, ὅτι τὸν υἱὸν αὐτοῦ ἐρρύσατο ἐκ θανάτου, ἐάσας τὸ ἴδιον πλοῖον ἐν Συρακούσῃ ἠκολούθησε μετ' αὐτοῦ ἕως Ποντιόλης. ἐκ δὲ τῶν μαθητῶν τοῦ Πέτρου εὑρεθέντες ἐκεῖ καὶ προσδεξάμενοι τὸν Παῦλον παρεκάλεσαν αὐτὸν μεῖναι πρὸς αὐτούς· καὶ ἔμεινεν ἑβδομάδα μίαν, κρυπτόμενος διὰ τὰς παραγγελίας τοῦ Καίσαρος.

9. πάντες δὲ οἱ τοπάρχαι ἐφύλαττον τοῦ πιάσαι καὶ ἀποκτεῖναι αὐτόν. Διόσκορος δὲ ὁ ναύκληρος, καὶ αὐτὸς ἀναφαλανδὸς ὑπάρχων, στιχάριον

3. From the Latin *ordino*. The number of loanwords in the text is an indication of the Greek text's dependence on a Latin original.

5. When these things had been done, some of the gentiles who had repented and been baptized through the proclamation of Peter[85] sent envoys to Paul with a letter saying, “Paul, servant and begotten of our master Jesus Christ, and brother of Peter the first of the apostles, we have heard from the teachers of the Jews who are in this greatest of cities, Rome, that they have asked Caesar to dispatch orders to all his provinces that you be killed wherever you may be found. But we believed and believe that just as God does not separate the two great lights that he made, so does he not plan to separate you from one another—that is, neither Peter from Paul, nor Paul from Peter. However, we rightly have faith in our Lord Jesus Christ, into whom we were baptized, because we are saints through your teaching.”[86]

6. But after receiving the two men sent with the letter on the 20th of May, Paul became eager and gave thanks to our Lord and master Jesus Christ. After sailing from Malta, he had not yet gone through Africa[87] into the regions of Italy. Instead, he landed on Sicily and went as far as the city of Syracuse with two of the men sent to him from Rome.

7. Having sailed off from there he came to Rhegium in Calabria,[88] and from Rhegium he passed into Messina. There he ordained a bishop named Bacchilus.[89] After leaving Messina he sailed as far as Didymus[90] and stayed there for one night. He sailed from there and came to Puteoli[91] on the second day.

8. But the ship captain Dioscorus, who had taken Paul to Syracuse, was favorable toward Paul, because he had delivered his son from death. He left his own boat in Syracuse and went with him as far as Puteoli. Some of the disciples of Peter who were there received Paul and begged him to stay with them. He stayed for one week, hidden because of the order of Caesar.

9. All the provincial governors were on alert to lay hold of and kill Paul. But Dioscorus the ship captain, who also was beginning to become bald,

---

85. The claim that Peter had preceded Paul to Rome and was the founder of the Roman church would support later papal claims to Petrine primacy. Cf. Acts Pet. 6, where Peter arrives to encourage a church that had already been founded by Paul.

86. This could be intended as a reference to Paul’s epistle to the Romans.

87. The sea journey to Rome would have passed very close to the northern coast of Africa near Carthage.

88. Acts 28:13.

89. Bacchilus (or Bachiritis) is traditionally considered the first bishop of Messina.

90. This is modern Isola Salina in the Tyrrhenian Sea. The name Didymus is likely derived from the twin volcanoes on the island.

91. Acts 28:13–14.

ναυκληρικὸν φορέσας καὶ παρρησιασάμενος τῇ πρώτῃ ἡμέρᾳ εἰς τὴν πόλιν Ποντιόλης ἐξῆλθεν. νομίσαντες οὖν ὅτι ὁ Παῦλός ἐστιν, ἐκράτησαν καὶ ἀπεκεφάλισαν αὐτόν, καὶ παρέπεμψαν τὴν κεφαλὴν αὐτοῦ πρὸς τὸν Καίσαρα.

10. προσκαλεσάμενος οὖν ὁ Καῖσαρ τοὺς πρώτους τῶν Ἰουδαίων ἀνήγγειλεν αὐτοῖς λέγων· χάρητε χαρὰν μεγάλην, ὅτι Παῦλος ὁ ἐχθρὸς ὑμῶν τέθνηκεν. καὶ ἐπέδειξεν αὐτοῖς καὶ τὴν κεφαλὴν αὐτοῦ. ποιήσαντες οὖν εὐφροσύνην μεγάλην τῇ ἡμέρᾳ ἐκείνῃ, ἥτις ἦν τεσσαρεσκαιδεκάτη τοῦ Ἰουνίου μηνός, ἕκαστος τῶν Ἰουδαίων ἐπληροφορήθη.

11. ὁ δὲ Παῦλος ἐν Ποντιόλῃ ὢν καὶ ἀκούσας ὅτι Διόσκορος ἀπεκεφαλίσθη, λυπηθεὶς λύπῃ μεγάλῃ, ἀτενίσας εἰς τὸ ὕψος τοῦ οὐρανοῦ εἶπεν· Κύριε παντοκράτωρ ἐπουράνιε, ὁ φανείς μοι ἐν παντὶ τόπῳ οὗ ἐπορεύθην διὰ τοῦ μονογενοῦς σου λόγου τοῦ κυρίου ἡμῶν Ἰησοῦ Χριστοῦ, ἐπιτίμησον τῇ πόλει ταύτῃ καὶ ἔκβαλε πάντας τοὺς πιστεύσαντας τῷ θεῷ καὶ ἀκολουθήσαντας τῷ λόγῳ αὐτοῦ.

12. εἶπεν οὖν αὐτοῖς· ἀκολουθεῖτέ μοι. καὶ ἐξελθὼν ἀπὸ Ποντιόλης μετὰ τῶν πιστευσάντων τῷ λόγῳ τοῦ θεοῦ, ἦλθον εἰς τόπον καλούμενον Βαΐας, καὶ ἀναβλέψαντες τοῖς ὀφθαλμοῖς αὐτῶν πάντες θεωροῦσι τὴν πόλιν ἐκείνην τὴν καλουμένην Ποντιόλην πεποντισμένην εἰς τὴν ὄχθαν τῆς θαλάσσης ὡσεὶ ὀργυίαν μίαν· καὶ ἐκεῖ ἔστιν ἕως τῆς σήμερον ἡμέρας εἰς μνημόσυνον ὑποκάτω τῆς θαλάσσης.

went out into the city of Puteoli on the first day, wearing his captain's tunic and speaking boldly. Therefore, believing that he was Paul,[92] they seized and decapitated him, and they sent his head to Caesar.

10. Then Caesar summoned the leaders of the Jews and reported to them, saying, "Rejoice greatly,[93] because your enemy Paul is dead." And he even showed them his head. Therefore, after they had held a great celebration on that day, which was the fourteenth day of the month of June, each of the Jews was fully satisfied.

11. But Paul, who was in Puteoli and heard that Dioscorus had been decapitated, was greatly distressed.[94] Looking intently to the height of heaven, he said, "Lord, all powerful heavenly one, you have given light to me in every place that I have gone through your only-begotten Word, our Lord Jesus Christ. Punish this city, but first bring out all those who have believed in God and followed his Word."

12. Then he said to them, "Follow me." And going out from Puteoli with those who had believed in the Word of God, they came to a place called Baiae.[95] Lifting up their eyes, they all beheld that city called Puteoli being plunged into the depths of the sea about one fathom. It is there beneath the sea,[96] even up to today, as a reminder.

---

92. The image of Paul as a bald man was well established in antiquity through the physical description in Acts Paul 3.3 and the iconographical tradition reflected on sarcophagi, gems, and gold glass. Paul's baldness was later parodied in the tenth-century *Philopatris* of Pseudo-Lucian (12): "I met a Galilean who was bald, had a pointed nose, and had ascended to the third heaven and learned unspeakable things" (2 Cor 12:2–4).

93. Literally, "Rejoice a great joy." This is one of several obvious Semiticisms in the text.

94. Literally, "distressed by a great distress."

95. Located at the northern edge of the Bay of Naples, this was a famous resort town in the later Roman Republic.

96. The reference here is somewhat obscure, but there are three possibilities: (1) The author may be referring to the remains of the Portus Julius, a harbor built by Marcus Agrippa in 37/36 BCE just west of Puteoli. Not long after its construction, it went out of use because of silting. Eventually, hydrothermal activity (bradyseism) caused the harbor area to sink into the sea. In his *Variae*, Cassiodorus includes a letter from Theodoric (*Var.* 1.25, ca. 507–511 CE) that may refer to repairs to the Portus Julius, which had been damaged (even possibly submerged) by the beginning of the sixth century. However, the manuscript evidence is quite complicated, leaving this reference uncertain. (2) The reference could be to other submerged remains near Puteoli on the Bay of Baiae. The area is famous for the destructive effect of its waves (Horace,

13. ἐξελθόντων δὲ αὐτῶν ἀπὸ Βαΐας, ἐγένοντο εἰς Γαΐτας, κἀκεῖ ἐδίδασκεν τὸν λόγον τοῦ θεοῦ· ἔμεινεν γὰρ ἐκεῖ τρεῖς ἡμέρας εἰς τὸν οἶκον Ἐράσμου, ὃν ἀπέστειλεν ὁ Πέτρος ἀπὸ Ῥώμης διδάξαι τὸ εὐαγγέλιον τοῦ θεοῦ. ἐξελθὼν δὲ ἀπὸ Γαΐτας ἦλθεν εἰς καστέλλιον[4] λεγόμενον Ταρακίνας, καὶ ἔμεινεν ἐκεῖ ἡμέρας ἑπτὰ εἰς τὸν οἶκον Καισαρίου τοῦ διακόνου, ὃν ἐχειροτόνησεν Πέτρος· κἀκεῖθεν ἀποπλεύσας διὰ τοῦ ποταμοῦ ἦλθεν εἰς τόπον καλούμενον Τρίβους Ταβέρνης.

14. οἱ δὲ σωθέντες ἐκ τῆς πόλεως Ποντιόλης τῆς ποντισθείσης ἀνήγγειλαν τῷ Καίσαρι εἰς Ῥώμην ὅτι Ποντιόλη ἐποντίσθη μετὰ παντὸς τοῦ ὄχλου αὐτῆς. καὶ ἐν λύπῃ μεγάλῃ γενάμενος ὁ βασιλεὺς διὰ τὴν πόλιν, προσκαλεσάμενος τοὺς πρώτους, τῶν Ἰουδαίων εἶπεν αὐτοῖς· ἴδε διὰ τὴν ὑπακοὴν ὑμῶν ἐποίησα ἀποκεφαλισθῆναι τὸν Παῦλον, καὶ διὰ τοῦτο ἐποντίσθη ἡ πόλις.

15. οἱ δὲ πρῶτοι τῶν Ἰουδαίων εἶπαν πρὸς τὸν Καίσαρα· εὐσεβέστατε βασιλεῦ, μὴ οὐκ εἴπαμέν σοι ὅτι πᾶσαν χώραν αὐτὸς ἐτάραξεν τῆς ἀνατολῆς καὶ τοὺς πατέρας ἡμῶν διέστρεψεν; προάγει οὖν, εὐσεβέστατε βασιλεῦ, ἵνα μία πόλις ἀπόληται καὶ μὴ τὸ βασίλειόν σου· τοῦτο γὰρ εἶχεν παθεῖν ἡ Ῥώμη. καὶ παρεμυθήθη ὁ βασιλεὺς ἀκούσας τοὺς λόγους αὐτῶν.

16. ὁ δὲ Παῦλος παρέμεινεν εἰς Τρίβους Ταβέρνης ἡμέρας τέσσαρας. καὶ ἐξελθὼν ἐκεῖθεν ἦλθεν εἰς Ἀππίου Φόρον καλούμενον Βικουσαράπη,[5] καὶ κοιμηθεὶς ἐκεῖ τὴν νύκτα ἐκείνην εἶδέν τινα καθήμενον εἰς καθέδραν χρυσῆν, καὶ

4. From the Latin *castellum*.

5. Βικουσαράπη = House or Domain (Latin *vicus*) of Sarapis, likely indicating that the area had a temple to the Egyptian god.

13. When they had set out from Baiae, they came to Gaeta. There Paul was teaching the word of God, for he stayed there for three days in the house of Erasmus,[97] whom Peter sent from Rome to teach the gospel of God. And going out from Gaeta, he came to the fortress called Terracina[98] and remained there for seven days at the house of Caesarius the deacon, on whom Peter had laid his hands. And having sailed off from there across the river he came to a place called the Three Taverns.[99]

14. But those who had been saved from the city of Puteoli, which had been plunged into the sea, reported to Caesar in Rome that Puteoli had been plunged into the sea with all its multitude. Because he was in great distress the emperor went through the city, summoning the leaders of the Jews, and he said to them, "Look, because of your obedience [to me] I had Paul beheaded, and because of that the city has been plunged into the sea."

15. But the leaders of the Jews said to Caesar, "Most pious emperor, did we not say to you that he stirred up the entire land of the East and disturbed our fathers? It is therefore preferable, most pious emperor, that one city be destroyed and not your kingdom, for Rome would have had to suffer this." And the emperor was relieved after he heard their words.

16. But Paul remained at the Three Taverns for four days. Setting out from there he came to the Forum of Appius,[100] called the House of Sarapis. While sleeping there that night, he saw someone sitting upon a golden

---

Carm. 2.18), and an early nineteenth-century traveler noted that the area "is lined with ruins, the remains of the villas and the baths of the Romans; some advance a considerable way out, and though now under the waves are easily distinguishable in fine weather" (John Chetwode Eustace, *A Classical Tour through Italy*, 6th ed. [London: Mawman, 1837], 4:410). (3) This reference to underwater ruins is a complete fabrication with no connection to any archaeological site.

97. This figure should be distinguished from Erastus, who was associated with Paul (Rom 16:23; 2 Tim 4:20, Acts 19:22).

98. Ancient Tarracina/Unxur. This is the first site mentioned on the Appian Road, although it would have been necessary to take the road for part of the trip from Baiae to Gaeta.

99. Acts 28:15. The Peutinger Map (ca. 300 CE) shows a sizable river flowing from the coast near Terracina through the mountains toward Ferentino. The Amaseno River, now little more than a stream, most closely follows the path of the ancient river that Paul allegedly would have crossed on the Appian Road by ferry.

100. Here the author is confused on the geography, for a trip from the south along the Appian Road would have reached the Forum of Appius first, then the Three Taverns (as in Acts 28). That the order is reversed here may indicate a lack of familiarity with the geography of the region.

παριστάμενον αὐτῷ πλῆθος μαύρων καὶ λεγόντων· ἐγὼ ἐποίησα σήμερον υἱὸν φονεῦσαι τὸν πατέρα αὐτοῦ.

ἄλλος δὲ ἔλεγεν ὅτι· κἀγὼ ἐποίησα πεσεῖν οἶκον καὶ φονεῦσαι γονεῖς μετὰ τέκνων. ἄλλοι μὲν ἄλλα ἐξηγοῦντο αὐτῷ πονηρὰ πολλά·

ἕτερος δὲ ἐλθὼν ἀνήγγειλεν αὐτῷ ὅτι· ἐγὼ ὠρδίνευσα ἵνα ὁ ἐπίσκοπος Ἰουβενάλιος, ὃν ἐχειροτόνησεν Πέτρος, μετὰ τῆς ἡγουμένης Ἰουλιανῆς κοιμηθῇ.

17. ἀκούσας δὲ ταῦτα πάντα κοιμώμενος εἰς αὐτὸν τὸν Ἀππίου Φόρον πλησίον Βικουσαράπης, εὐθέως καὶ παραχρῆμα ἀπέστειλεν ἐν Ῥώμῃ ἐκ τῶν ἀκολουθησάντων αὐτῷ ἀπὸ Ποντιόλης πρὸς τὸν ἐπίσκοπον Ἰουβενάλιον, λέγων τοῦτο αὐτὸ ὅπερ ἀπῄει ποιῆσαι.

18. καὶ δραμὼν τῇ ἑξῆς ἡμέρᾳ Ἰουβενάλιος ἔρριψεν ἑαυτὸν εἰς τὰ ἴχνη τοῦ Πέτρου κλαίων καὶ ὀδυρόμενος καὶ λέγων ὅτι· παραπεσεῖν ἀπῄειν. καὶ ἐξηγήσατο αὐτῷ τὸ κεφάλαιον καὶ εἶπεν· πιστεύω ὅτι αὐτός ἐστιν ὃν περιέμενες φωστῆρα.

ὁ δὲ Πέτρος πρὸς αὐτὸν ἔφη· πῶς ἐνδέχεται ἐκεῖνον εἶναι τελειωθέντος αὐτοῦ;

19. ὁ δὲ Ἰουβενάλιος ὁ ἐπίσκοπος ἔλαβεν τὸν ἀποσταλέντα παρὰ Παύλου πρὸς τὸν Πέτρον, καὶ αὐτὸς αὐτῷ ἀνήγγειλεν ὅτι ζῇ καὶ ἔρχεται, καὶ ὅτι ἐστὶν εἰς Ἀππίου Φόρον. καὶ ηὐχαρίστησεν καὶ ἐδόξασεν ὁ Πέτρος τὸν θεὸν καὶ πατέρα τοῦ κυρίου ἡμῶν Ἰησοῦ Χριστοῦ.

20. τότε προσκαλεσάμενος τοὺς πεπιστευκότας μαθητὰς αὐτοῦ ἀπέστειλεν αὐτοὺς πρὸς τὸν Παῦλον ἕως Τρίβους Ταβέρνης· ἔστιν δὲ τὸ διάστημα ἀπὸ Ῥώμης ἕως Τρίβους Ταβέρνης μίλια τριάκοντα ὀκτώ. καὶ ἰδὼν τούτους ὁ Παῦλος εὐχαριστήσας τῷ κυρίῳ ἡμῶν Ἰησοῦ Χριστῷ ἔλαβεν θάρσος. κινήσαντες δὲ ἐκεῖθεν ἐκοιμήθησαν εἰς πόλιν καλουμένην Ἀρικίαν.

throne, and a multitude of dark figures[101] was presented to him, and they were saying, "Today I have made a son kill his father."

And another said, "And I have made a house fall and kill the parents with the children." Still others related to him at length many evil deeds.

Yet another came and declared to him, "I arranged it so that the bishop Juvenal,[102] on whom Peter laid his hands, would sleep with the abbess Juliana."

17. After hearing all these things while sleeping at the Forum of Appius, close to the House of Sarapis, Paul immediately and without delay dispatched some of those who had followed him from Puteoli to bishop Juvenal in Rome, telling this very thing that had just happened.

18. And Juvenal hurried on the next day and threw himself at the feet of Peter, wailing and lamenting and saying what had just happened. And he related to him at length the most important point and said, "I believe that he is the light for whom you were waiting."

But Peter said to him, "How is it possible that that man is from the one who was perfected?"[103]

19. And Juvenal the bishop led to Peter the one who had been sent from Paul, and this man reported to Peter that Paul was alive and coming, and that he was at the Forum of Appius. And Peter gave thanks and praised the God and Father of our Lord Jesus Christ.[104]

20. Then, after gathering together his disciples who had come to believe, Peter sent them to Paul as far as the Three Taverns.[105] The distance from Rome to the Three Taverns is 38 miles. And when he saw them, Paul gave thanks to our Lord Jesus Christ and was encouraged. After moving from there, they spent the night at the city called Aricia.[106]

---

101. This is probably a euphemism for demons.

102. The name Juvenal is unknown among the bishops of Rome. This figure is not listed in the rank of Roman bishops given by Irenaeus (*Haer.* 3.3.3), Eusebius (*Hist. eccl.* 5.6), or any subsequent author.

103. Peter had heard that Paul had been killed, or "perfected," so he is naturally suspicious of a messenger coming now with news from Paul.

104. Cf. 2 Cor 1:3, Eph 1:3, Col 1:3.

105. Here the narrative rejoins a logical order of travel to Rome.

106. This city near Lake Nemi was the site of the Festival of Torches, a three-day annual celebration in honor of the goddess Diana (Ovid, *Fast.* 3.263–264, 267–270). According to Mart. Pet. 3 and Pass. Apost. 11, Simon the sorcerer is taken to Aricia after his fall from heaven and eventually dies there.

21. περίφημον δὲ ἐγένετο ἐν τῇ πόλει Ῥώμῃ ὅτι Παῦλος ὁ ἀδελφὸς Πέτρου ἔρχεται. οἱ δὲ πεπιστευκότες τῷ θεῷ ἔχαιρον χαρὰν μεγάλην. τάραχος δὲ μέγας ἐγένετο ἐν τοῖς Ἰουδαίοις, καὶ ἀπελθόντες πρὸς Σίμωνα τὸν μάγον παρεκάλουν αὐτὸν λέγοντες· ἀνάγαγε τῷ βασιλεῖ ὅτι οὐκ ἀπέθανεν ὁ Παῦλος, ἀλλὰ ζῇ καὶ ἦλθεν.

ὁ δὲ Σίμων πρὸς τοὺς Ἰουδαίους εἶπεν· τίς οὖν ἡ κεφαλὴ ἡ ἐλθοῦσα πρὸς τὸν Καίσαρα ἀπὸ Ποντιόλης; μὴ καὶ αὐτὴ οὐκ ἦν ἀναφαλανδός;

22. ἐλθόντος δὲ τοῦ Παύλου ἐν τῇ Ῥώμῃ, φόβος μέγας ἐπέπεσεν τοῖς Ἰουδαίοις. συνῆλθον οὖν πρὸς αὐτὸν καὶ παρεκάλουν αὐτὸν λέγοντες· τὴν πίστιν, ἐν ᾗ ἐγεννήθης, ταύτην διεκδίκησον· οὐ γὰρ δίκαιόν ἐστιν, ἵνα Ἑβραῖος ὢν καὶ ἐξ Ἑβριαίων ἑαυτὸν διδάσκαλον εἴπῃς ἐθνῶν καὶ ἐκδικητὴν τῶν ἀπεριτμήτων, καὶ αὐτὸς ὢν περιτετμημένος τὴν τῆς περιτομῆς καταργήσῃς πίστιν. ὅταν οὖν ἴδῃς Πέτρον, ἀνταγώνισαι κατὰ τῆς αὐτοῦ διδασκαλίας, ὅτι πᾶσαν <τὴν> τοῦ ἡμετέρου νόμου παραφυλακὴν κατήργησεν.

23. ἀποκριθεὶς δὲ ὁ Παῦλος εἶπεν αὐτοῖς· ἐὰν ᾖ ἡ διδασκαλία αὐτοῦ ἀληθής, τῇ τῶν Ἑβραίων βίβλων μαρτυρίᾳ ὠχυρωμένη, πρέπον ἐστὶν πάντας ἡμᾶς πειθαρχεῖν αὐτῷ.

24. ταῦτα καὶ τὰ τούτοις ὅμοια τοῦ Παύλου λέγοντος ἐγνώσθη τῷ Πέτρῳ ὅτι Παῦλος παραγέγονεν ἐν Ῥώμῃ, καὶ ἐχάρη χαρὰν μεγάλην, καὶ παραχρῆμα ἀναστὰς ἐπορεύθη πρὸς αὐτόν. ἰδόντες δὲ ἀλλήλους ἀπὸ τῆς χαρᾶς ἔκλαυσαν, καὶ ἐπὶ πολὺ περιλαβόντες ἑαυτοὺς τοῖς δάκρυσιν ἀλλήλους κατέβρεχον.

25. ὡς δὲ πάντων ὁ Παῦλος τῶν ἑαυτοῦ πράξεων τὸ ὕφος τῷ Πέτρῳ ἀπήγγειλεν, καὶ πῶς διὰ τῶν τοῦ πλοὸς κόπων παραγέγονεν, ὁμοίως καὶ Πέτρος εἶπεν αὐτῷ οἷα ἔπασχεν ὑπὸ Σίμωνος τοῦ μάγου, καὶ πάσας τὰς ἐνέδρας αὐτοῦ· καὶ ταῦτα εἰπὼν ἀνεχώρησεν πρὸς ἑσπέραν.

21. But it became known in the city of Rome that Paul, the brother of Peter, was coming. Those who had come to believe in God were rejoicing greatly.[107] But there was a great disturbance among the Jews, and they went to Simon the sorcerer and begged him, saying, "Report to[108] the emperor that Paul did not die, but is alive and has come."

But Simon said to the Jews, "Whose, then, is the head that came to Caesar from Puteoli? Was this not also the head of a bald man?"

22. When Paul came to Rome,[109] a great fear fell upon the Jews. Then they came to him and beseeched him, saying, "Defend this faith in which you were born, for it is not right that a Hebrew of Hebrews[110] should say that he himself is a teacher of gentiles and defender of the uncircumcised, or that you yourself, being circumcised, should undermine faith in circumcision.[111] Therefore, when you see Peter, confront his teaching, because he has undermined every observance of our law."[112]

23. But Paul answered and said to them, "If his teaching is true, confirmed by the witness of the Hebrew books, then it is fitting that all of us obey him."

24. After Paul had said these and other similar things, it became known to Peter that Paul was present in Rome. And he rejoiced greatly,[113] got up immediately, and went to him. Seeing each other, they wept for joy, and after embracing each other for a long time, they soaked each other with their tears.[114]

25. Paul reported to Peter the series of things he had done and how he had come through the trials of the sea voyage. Peter likewise told him the kinds of things he was suffering at the hands of Simon the sorcerer and all his treacheries. After saying these things, [Peter] withdrew when it was evening.

---

107. Literally, "rejoicing a great joy."

108. For this unusual use of ἀνάγω, see G. W. H. Lampe, *A Patristic Greek Lexicon* (Oxford: Oxford University Press, 1961), 100a.

109. From this point on the text closely parallels the Latin *Passion*.

110. Phil 3:5.

111. Or "the faith of the circumcision." Cf. Gal 2:9–12.

112. It is notable that the Jewish leaders see Peter, not Paul, as the greater immediate threat to the law. I have studied this dynamic further in Eastman, "Confused Traditions?"

113. Literally, "rejoiced a great joy."

114. On the ubiquity of the image of an apostolic embrace in early Christian art, see Kessler, "The Meeting of Peter and Paul in Rome," 265–75.

26. τῇ δὲ ἐπαύριον παραγενάμενος εὑρίσκει πλῆθος τῶν Ἰουδαίων πρὸ τῶν θυρῶν τοῦ Παύλου. ἦν δὲ μεταξὺ τῶν Ἰουδαίων χριστιανῶν τε καὶ ἐθνικῶν μεγάλη ταραχή. οἱ μὲν γὰρ Ἰουδαῖοι ἔλεγον· ἡμεῖς γένος ἐσμὲν ἐκλεκτόν, βασίλειον ἱεράτευμα, φυλῆς γε τοῦ Ἀβραὰμ καὶ Ἰσαὰκ καὶ Ἰακὼβ καὶ πάντων τῶν προφητῶν, μεθ᾽ ὧν ἐλάλησεν ὁ θεός, οἷς ἔδειξεν τὰ ἑαυτοῦ μυστήρια καὶ τὰ θαυμάσια αὐτοῦ τὰ μεγάλα. ὑμεῖς δὲ οἱ ἐξ ἐθνῶν, οὐδὲν μέγα ἐν τῷ σπέρματι ὑμῶν, εἰ μὴ ἐν εἰδώλοις καὶ γλυπτοῖς βέβηλοί τε καὶ βδελυκτοὶ γεγόνατε.

27. ταῦτα καὶ τὰ ὅμοια τούτοις λεγόντων τῶν Ἰουδαίων ἀπεκρίναντο οἱ ἐξ ἐθνῶν λέγοντες· ἡμεῖς ὡς ἠκούσαμεν τὴν ἀλήθειαν, εὐθέως ἠκολουθήσαμεν αὐτῇ, καταλιπόντες ἡμῶν τὴν πλάνην. ὑμεῖς δὲ καὶ τὰς πατρικὰς γνόντες δυνάμεις, καὶ τὰ προφητικὰ ὁρῶντες σημεῖα, καὶ νόμον δεξάμενοι, καὶ τὴν θάλασσαν ξηροῖς διαβεβηκότες τοῖς ποσίν, καὶ τοὺς ἐχθροὺς ὑμῶν βυθιζομένους ἰδόντες, καὶ στύλου πυρὸς ἐξ οὐρανοῦ ὑμῖν φαίνοντος τὴν νύκτα <καὶ νεφέλης ἡμέρας>, καὶ μάννα ὑμῖν ἐξ οὐρανοῦ δοθέντος καὶ ἐκ πέτρας στερεᾶς ὕδατος ὑμῖν ῥεύσαντος, μετὰ ταῦτα πάντα εἴδωλον ἑαυτοῖς μόσχου ἐτεκτήνατε καὶ προσεκυνήσασθε τῷ γλυπτῷ. ἡμεῖς δὲ οὐδὲν βλέποντες τῶν σημείων πιστεύομεν τοῦτον εἶναι σωτῆρα θεόν, ὃν ὑμεῖς ἐγκατελείπατε ἀπειθήσαντες.

28. ταῦτα καὶ τὰ τοιαῦτα αὐτῶν φιλονεικούντων εἶπεν ὁ ἀπόστολος Παῦλος μὴ χρῆναι αὐτοὺς τὰς τοιαύτας μεταξὺ ἀλλήλων ἔχειν ἀμφιβολάς, ἀλλὰ τοῦτο προσέχειν μᾶλλον, ὅτι πεπλήρωκεν ὁ θεὸς τὰς ἑαυτοῦ ἐπαγγελίας, ἃς ὤμοσεν Ἀβραὰμ τῷ πατρὶ ἡμῶν, ὅτι ἐν τῷ σπέρματι αὐτοῦ ἐνευλογηθήσονται πάντα τὰ ἔθνη· οὐ γὰρ ἔστι προσωποληψία παρὰ τῷ θεῷ.

29. ταῦτα τοῦ Παύλου λέγοντος κατεπραΰνθησαν οἵ τε Ἰουδαῖοι καὶ οἱ ἐξ ἐθνῶν. ἀλλ᾽ οἱ ἄρχοντες τῶν Ἰουδαίων ἐπετίθεντο τῷ Πέτρῳ. ὁ δὲ Πέτρος πρὸς τοὺς ἐλέγχοντας αὐτὸν ὅτι τὰς συναγωγὰς αὐτῶν ἀπηγόρευεν, εἶπεν· ἀκούσατε, ἀδελφοί, τοῦ ἁγίου πνεύματος περὶ τοῦ πατριάρχου Δαβὶδ ἐπαγγειλαμένου, ὅτι· ἐκ καρποῦ τῆς κοιλίας σου τεθήσεται ἐπὶ τοῦ θρόνου σου. τοῦτον οὖν, ᾧ ὁ πατὴρ εἶπεν· υἱός μου εἶ σύ, ἐγὼ σήμερον γεγέννηκά σε, ἐσταύρωσαν διὰ φθόνον οἱ ἀρχιερεῖς· ἵνα δὲ πληρώσῃ τὴν τοῦ κόσμου σωτηρίαν, συνεχώρησεν

26. On the next day Peter arrived and found a crowd of Jews in front of the doors of Paul. There was a great disturbance among the Jewish and gentile Christians, for the Jews were saying, "We are a chosen race, a royal priesthood,[115] of the tribe of Abraham, Isaac, Jacob, and all the prophets. God spoke with them and showed mysteries about himself and all his great wonders. But you are from the gentiles, and there is nothing great in your lineage, except that you have become defiled and abominable by your idols and graven images."

27. After the Jews had said these and other similar things, those from the gentiles answered, saying, "As soon as we heard the truth, we immediately followed it and abandoned our wandering. But you knew the powerful deeds of the fathers, had seen the prophetic signs, had received the law, had walked through the sea with dry feet, and had seen your enemies plunged into the sea. A pillar of fire from heaven appeared to you at night and a cloud by day; manna was given to you from heaven; and water flowed for you from a solid rock. And yet, after all these things you fashioned for yourselves an image of a calf and worshiped a statue. But we, who saw none of these signs, believe that this God is the savior, whom you abandoned in your disobedience."

28. As they were quarreling with these and other such words, the apostle Paul said, "You should not have such disputes among yourselves. Instead, turn your attention to the fact that God has fulfilled his promises, which he swore to our father Abraham, because in his seed all the gentiles have been blessed,[116] for there is no partiality with God."[117]

29. After Paul had said these things, both the Jews and the gentiles were assuaged, but the leaders of the Jews attacked Peter. To those accusing him of renouncing their synagogues Peter said, "Listen, brothers,[118] to what the Holy Spirit has proclaimed about the patriarch David, '[One] from the fruit of your loins will be placed upon your throne.'[119] But this one—to whom the Father said, 'You are my son; today I have begotten you'[120]—the chief priests crucified out of jealousy. In order that he might complete the salva-

115. 1 Pet 2:9.

116. Gen 18:18, 22:18.

117. Rom 2:11.

118. In a first-century narrative setting, the leaders of the synagogues would generally be male, so I have preserved the gender-specific language of the original.

119. Ps 132:11.

120. Ps 2:7; Acts 13:33; Heb 1:5, 5:5.

ταῦτα πάντα ἑαυτὸν παθεῖν. ὥσπερ οὖν ἐκ τῆς πλευρᾶς τοῦ Ἀδὰμ ἐκτίσθη ἡ Εὔα, οὕτως καὶ ἐκ τῆς πλευρᾶς τοῦ Χριστοῦ ἐκτίσθη ἡ ἐκκλησία, ἥτις σπῖλον οὐκ ἔχει οὐδὲ μῶμον.

30. τούτοις οὖν πᾶσιν ὁ θεὸς εἴσοδον ἤνοιξεν τοῖς υἱοῖς Ἀβραὰμ καὶ Ἰσαὰκ καὶ Ἰακώβ, τοῦ εἶναι αὐτοὺς ἐν τῇ πίστει τῆς ἐκκλησίας καὶ μὴ ἐν τῇ ἀπιστίᾳ διὰ τῆς συναγωγῆς. ἐπιστρέψατε οὖν καὶ εἰσέλθατε εἰς τὴν χαρὰν τοῦ πατρὸς ὑμῶν Ἀβραάμ, ὅτι ἃ ἐπηγγείλατο αὐτῷ ὁ θεὸς ἐπλήρωσεν· ὅθεν καὶ ὁ προφήτης λέγει· ὤμοσεν κύριος καὶ οὐ μεταμεληθήσεται· σὺ ἱερεὺς εἰς τὸν αἰῶνα κατὰ τὴν τάξιν Μελχισεδέκ. Ἱερεὺς γὰρ ἐν τῷ σταυρῷ γέγονεν, ἡνίκα τὴν ὁλοκάρπωσιν τοῦ ἰδίου σώματος καὶ αἵματος ὑπὲρ τοῦ κόσμου παντὸς θυσίαν προσήνεγκεν.

31. ταῦτα καὶ τὰ τούτοις ὅμοια λέγοντος τοῦ Πέτρου τὸ πλεῖστον τοῦ λαοῦ μέρος ἐπίστευσεν. συνέβη δὲ καὶ τὴν γυναῖκα Νέρωνος Λιβίαν καὶ τὴν Ἀγρίππα τοῦ ἐπάρχου σύζυγον οὕτως πιστεῦσαι, ὥστε καὶ περιελεῖν ἑαυτὰς ἀπὸ τῆς τῶν ἰδίων ἀνδρῶν πλευρᾶς. διὰ δὲ τῆς τοῦ Παύλου διδασκαλίας πολλοὶ καταφρονοῦντες τῆς στρατείας προσεκολλῶντο τῷ θεῷ, ὥστε καὶ ἀπὸ τοῦ κοιτῶνος τοῦ βασιλέως ἐλθεῖν τινας πρὸς αὐτόν· καὶ γενόμενοι Χριστιανοὶ οὐκ ἔτι ἠθέλησαν ὑποστρέψαι ἐν τῇ στρατείᾳ οὔτε ἐν τῷ παλατίῳ.

32. ὅθεν ὁ Σίμων ζήλῳ κινούμενος διεγείρεται, καὶ ἤρξατο περὶ Πέτρου πολλὰ λέγειν κακά, μάγον καὶ ἀπατεῶνα λέγων αὐτὸν εἶναι. ἐπίστευον δὲ αὐτῷ οἱ τὰ σημεῖα αὐτοῦ θαυμάζοντες· ἐποίει γὰρ ὄφιν χαλκοῦν κινεῖν ἑαυτόν, καὶ λιθίνους ἀνδριάντας γελάσαι καὶ κινῆσαι ἑαυτούς, αὐτὸν δὲ δραμεῖν καὶ αἰφνίδιον ἐν τῷ ἀέρι ἀρθῆναι.

33. κατέναντι δὲ τούτων ὁ Πέτρος ἀσθενοῦντας ἐθεράπευεν λόγῳ, τυφλοὺς ἀναβλέπειν ἐποίει προσευχόμενος, δαίμονας κελεύσματι ἐφυγάδευεν καὶ νεκροὺς ἤγειρεν. ἔλεγεν δὲ πρὸς τὸν λαόν, ἵνα μὴ μόνον ἀπὸ τῆς τοῦ Σίμωνος ἀπάτης φύγωσιν, ἀλλὰ καὶ δειγματίσουσιν αὐτόν, ὅπως μὴ φανῶσιν τῷ διαβόλῳ δουλεύοντες.

34. καὶ οὕτως γέγονεν ὥστε πάντας τοὺς εὐλαβεῖς ἄνδρας βδελύττεσθαι Σίμωνα τὸν μάγον καὶ ἀνόσιον αὐτὸν καταγγέλλειν. οἱ δὲ τῷ Σίμωνι κολληθέντες τὸν Πέτρον ἔλεγον εἶναι μάγον, ὅπερ αὐτοὶ σὺν τῷ Σίμωνι ὑπῆρχον· ὥστε τὸν

tion of the world, he allowed himself to suffer all these things. Thus, just as from the rib of Adam Eve was created, likewise from the rib of Christ the church was created, which has neither spot nor blemish.[121]

30. "Therefore, God opened an entrance to all these—the children of Abraham, Isaac, and Jacob—so that they might be in the faith of the church and not in faithlessness through the synagogue. Turn, therefore, and enter into the joy of our father Abraham, because God has fulfilled the things that were promised to him. For this reason the prophet says, 'The Lord has sworn and will not change his mind, "You are a priest forever according to the order of Melchizedek." '[122] For he became a priest on the cross, when he offered the whole burnt offering of his own body and blood as a sacrifice for the whole world."[123]

31. After Peter had said these and other similar things, the greater portion of the people believed. And it came to pass that Livia, the wife of Nero, and the wife of the prefect Agrippa[124] believed, so that they withdrew from the side of their own husbands. Through the teaching of Paul many despised military service and clung to God, such that some went to him even from the bedchamber of the emperor. Having become Christians, they did not wish to return to military service or to the palace.

32. Then Simon was stirred and aroused by zeal, and he began to say many evil things about Peter, namely that he was a sorcerer and a fraud. Those who were amazed by his signs believed him, for he was making a bronze serpent move by itself and stone statues laugh and move by themselves, and he made himself run and suddenly be raised into the air.

33. In response to these things Peter was healing the sick by his word, restoring sight to the blind by prayer, casting out demons by his command, and raising the dead. He was speaking to the people, so that they would not only flee from the deceit of Simon, but would also expose him, so that they might not seem to be serving the devil.

34. Thus it came about that all the pious people despised Simon the sorcerer and declared him profane. But those attached to Simon were saying that Peter was the sorcerer, because they were with Simon. Word of

---

121. Eph 5:27.

122. Ps 110:4; Heb 5:6, 10; 6:20; 7:17, 21.

123. 1 John 2:2.

124. She is identified as Agrippina in Pseudo-Marcellus, *Pass. Holy* 10, and is mentioned among a group of four of Agrippa's concubines in Mart. Pet. 4; Pseudo-Linus, *Mart. Pet.* 2; Hist. Shim. 29.

λόγον καὶ ἐπὶ Νέρωνος ἐλθεῖν τοῦ Καίσαρος, καὶ προστάξαι Σίμωνα τὸν μάγον πρὸς ἑαυτὸν εἰσαγαγεῖν.

35. ὁ δὲ εἰσελθὼν ἔστη ἔμπροσθεν αὐτοῦ καὶ ἤρξατο αἰφνιδίως μορφὰς ἐναλλάσσειν, ὥστε γενέσθαι αὐτὸν ἐξαίφνης παιδίον καὶ μετ᾽ ὀλίγον γέροντα, ἄλλοτε δὲ νεανίσκον, ἔχων ὑπουργὸν τὸν διάβολον. ὅπερ θεωρῶν ὁ Νέρων ἀληθῶς υἱὸν αὐτὸν εἶναι θεοῦ ὑπελάμβανεν. ὁ δὲ ἀπόστολος Πέτρος ἐδίδασκεν ψεύστην τε εἶναι καὶ μάγον, αἰσχρόν τε καὶ ἀνόσιον καὶ ἀποστάτην, καὶ ἐν πᾶσιν τῇ τοῦ θεοῦ ἀληθείᾳ ἐναντίον.

36. τότε εἰσελθὼν ὁ Σίμων πρὸς Νέρωνα εἶπεν αὐτῷ· ἄκουσον βασιλεῦ· εἰ μὴ τοὺς ἄνδρας τούτους ἐκδιώξεις ἐντεῦθεν, οὐ δυνήσεται στῆναι ἡ βασιλεία σου.

37. τότε ὁ Νέρων πλησθεὶς μερίμνης ἐκέλευσεν σπουδαίως αὐτοὺς πρὸς αὐτὸν ἀγαγεῖν. τῇ δὲ ἑξῆς ἡμέρᾳ εἰσελθόντων πρὸς Νέρωνα Πέτρου καὶ Παύλου, τῶν τοῦ Χριστοῦ ἀποστόλων ὁ Σίμων εἶπεν· οὗτοί εἰσιν οἱ μαθηταὶ τοῦ Ναζαρηνοῦ, οἷς οὐ πάνυ καλῶς ἔχει, ἵνα ὦσιν ἐκ τοῦ λαοῦ τῶν Ἰουδαίων.

Νέρων εἶπεν· τίς ἐστιν ὁ Ναζαρηνός;

Σίμων εἶπεν· ἔστιν πόλις ἐν τῇ Ἰουδαίᾳ, ἥτις ὑμῖν ἀεὶ ἐναντία γέγονεν, Ναζαρὲτ λεγομένη· ὁ οὖν διδάσκαλος τούτων ἐξ αὐτῆς γέγονεν.

38. τότε ὁ Πέτρος πρὸς τὸν Σίμωνα ἔφη· θαυμάζω ποίῳ χρώματι ἑαυτὸν ἐνώπιον τοῦ βασιλέως καταλαζονεύεις καὶ ὑπολαμβάνεις, ὅτι διὰ τῆς μαγικῆς σου τέχνης τοὺς τοῦ Χριστοῦ ὑπερνικήσεις μαθητάς.

39. Νέρων εἶπεν· τίς ἐστιν ὁ Χριστός;

Πέτρος εἶπεν· εἰ θέλεις γνῶναι, βασιλεῦ, τίς ἐστιν ὁ Χριστός, καὶ τὰ πραχθέντα ἐν τῇ Ἰουδαίᾳ περὶ τοῦ Χριστοῦ, λάβε τὰ γράμματα Ποντίου Πιλάτου τὰ πρὸς Κλαύδιον πεμφθέντα, καὶ οὕτως γινώσκεις πάντα. ὁ δὲ Νέρων ἐκέλευσεν αὐτὰ ἐνεχθῆναι καὶ ἐνώπιον αὐτῶν ἀναγνωσθῆναι. περιεῖχον δὲ οὕτως·

40. Πόντιος Πιλάτος Κλαυδίῳ χαίρειν. ἔναγχος συνέβη, ὅπερ αὐτὸς ἐγὼ ἐγύμνωσα· οἱ γὰρ Ἰουδαῖοι διὰ φθόνον ἑαυτούς τε καὶ τοὺς μετέπειτα ἰδίαις δειναῖς κρίσεσιν ἐτιμωρήσαντο. ἀμέλει ἐπαγγελίας ἔχοντες οἱ πατέρες αὐτῶν, ὅτι πέμψει αὐτοῖς ὁ θεὸς τὸν ἅγιον αὐτοῦ ἐξ οὐρανοῦ, ὅστις εἰκότως βασιλεὺς

this thus reached even up to the emperor Nero, and he ordered Simon the sorcerer to come before him.

35. Simon came and stood before him and at once began to change shapes, so that he suddenly became a child, and a little after this an old man. At another moment he was a young man, rendering service to the devil. When he beheld these things, Nero supposed that he truly was the son of God. But the apostle Peter was teaching that he was a liar and a sorcerer, shameful and profane and apostate, and in all things against the truth of God.

36. Then Simon came to Nero and said to him, "Listen, oh emperor. If you do not expel these men from here, then your kingdom will not be able to stand."

37. Then Nero was filled with anxiety and immediately ordered them to be brought to him. On the next day, after Peter and Paul, the apostles of Christ, had come in to Nero, Simon said, "These are the disciples of the Nazarene, and it is not at all good for them that they are from among the people of the Jews."

Nero said, "Who is the Nazarene?"

Simon said, "There is a city in Judea that has always been against you, and it is called Nazareth.[125] Their teacher comes from there."

38. Then Peter said to Simon, "I wonder in what form[126] you brag boldly about yourself before the emperor and suppose that through your magical art you will be victorious over the disciples of Christ."

39. Nero said, "Who is the Christ?"

Peter said, "If you wish to know, oh emperor, who is the Christ, and about the things done in Judea concerning the Christ, then take the letters sent by Pontius Pilate to Claudius, and thus you will know everything." Nero ordered them to be brought and read before them. They included the following:

40. "Pontius Pilate to Claudius, greetings. Lately there occurred something in which I myself was involved, for through jealousy the Jews have inflicted on themselves and those coming after them harsh punishments. Their fathers actually have promises that God will send to them the holy one from heaven itself. He would rightly be called their king, and God

125. Nazareth is not in Judea but in Galilee. This geographical error is another possible indication of the western provenance of the text.

126. Literally, "in what sort of skin."

αὐτῶν λεχθείη, τοῦτον ἐπηγγείλατο διὰ παρθένου ἐπὶ τὴν γῆν ἀποστεῖλαι. οὗτος τοίνυν ἐμοῦ ἡγεμονεύοντος ἦλθεν εἰς τὴν Ἰουδαίαν.

41. καὶ εἶδον αὐτὸν τυφλοὺς φωταγωγοῦντα, λεπροὺς καθαρίζοντα, παραλυτικοὺς θεραπεύοντα, δαίμονας ἀπὸ τῶν ἀνθρώπων φυγαδεύοντα, νεκροὺς ἐγείροντα, ἀνέμοις ἐπιτιμῶντα, ἐπὶ κυμάτων θαλάσσης πεζεύοντα καὶ πολλὰ ἕτερα ποιοῦντα θαυμάσια, καὶ πάντα τὸν τῶν Ἰουδαίων λαὸν υἱὸν αὐτὸν τοῦ θεοῦ λέγοντα. φθόνῳ οὖν οἱ ἀρχιερεῖς κατ᾽ αὐτοῦ κινούμενοι ἐκράτησαν καὶ ἐμοὶ αὐτὸν παρέδωκαν, καὶ ἄλλα ἀντ᾽ ἄλλων καταψευσάμενοι ἔλεγον μάγον αὐτὸν εἶναι καὶ ἐναντία τοῦ νόμου αὐτῶν πράττειν.

42. ἐγὼ δὲ πιστεύσας ταῦτα οὕτως ἔχειν μεμαστιγωμένον παρέδωκα αὐτὸν τῇ βουλῇ αὐτῶν· οἱ δὲ ἐσταύρωσαν αὐτὸν καὶ ταφέντος αὐτοῦ φύλακας κατέστησαν ἐπ᾽ αὐτόν. αὐτὸς δὲ τῶν στρατιωτῶν μου φυλαττόντων αὐτὸν τῇ τρίτῃ ἡμέρᾳ ἀνέστη. ἐπὶ τοσοῦτον δὲ ἐξεκαύθη ἡ τῶν Ἰουδαίων πονηρία, ὥστε δοῦναι ἀργύρια τοῖς στρατιώταις λέγοντες· εἴπατε ὅτι οἱ μαθηταὶ αὐτοῦ τὸ σῶμα αὐτοῦ ἔκλεψαν. ἀλλὰ αὐτοὶ λαβόντες τὰ ἀργύρια σιωπῆσαι τὸ γεγονὸς οὐκ ἠδυνήθησαν· κἀκεῖνοι γὰρ ἀναστάντα μεμαρτυρήκασιν ἑωρακέναι καὶ παρὰ Ἰουδαίων ἀργύρια εἰληφέναι. ταῦτα δὲ διὰ τοῦτο ἀνήγαγον τῷ κράτει σου, ἵνα μή τις ἄλλος ψεύσηται καὶ ὑπολάβῃς πιστεῦσαι ταῖς τῶν Ἰουδαίων ψευδολογίαις.

43. ἀναγνωσθείσης δὲ τῆς ἐπιστολῆς εἶπεν ὁ Νέρων· εἰπέ μοι, Πέτρε, οὕτως δι᾽ αὐτοῦ ἐπράχθη πάντα;

ὁ δὲ Πέτρος εἶπεν· οὕτως ἔστιν, βασιλεῦ. ὁ γὰρ Σίμων οὗτος πλήρης ψεύδους καὶ ἀπάτης ὑπάρχει, κἂν δοκῇ ἑαυτὸν τοῦτο εἶναι, ὅπερ οὐκ ἔστιν, θεός· ἐν δὲ τῷ κυρίῳ μου Ἰησοῦ Χριστῷ ἐστὶν πᾶσα ἡ ἄκρα νίκη, ὃς διὰ τὴν τῶν ἀνθρώπων σωτηρίαν ηὐδόκησεν διὰ τῆς θείας οἰκονομίας τοῖς ἀνθρώποις συναναστραφῆναι.

44. Σίμων εἶπεν· οὐκ ἀνέξομαί σου ἐπὶ πολύ, Πέτρε, ἀλλ᾽ ἄρτι προστάξω τοῖς ἀγγέλοις μου, ὅπως ἐλθόντες ἐκδικήσωσίν με ἀπὸ σοῦ.

Πέτρος εἶπεν· οὐ φοβοῦμαι τοὺς ἀγγέλους σου ἐκεῖνοι δὲ μᾶλλον ἐμὲ φοβηθήσονται ἐν τῇ δυνάμει τοῦ κυρίου μου Ἰησοῦ Χριστοῦ.

promised to send this one to earth through a virgin. When I was ruling, this one came to Judea.

41. "They saw him giving sight to the blind, cleansing lepers, healing paralytics, casting out demons from people, raising the dead, controlling the winds, walking upon the waves of the sea, and doing many other amazing things. And they saw all the people of the Jews saying that he was the son of God himself. Thus, the chief priests, incited by jealousy against him, seized him and handed him over to me. But they told one lie after another and were saying that he was a sorcerer and was acting against their law.

42. "I believed these things were so and had him flogged and handed over to their will. They crucified him[127] and, after he was buried, set a guard over him. However, while my soldiers were guarding him, on the third day he rose again. The wickedness of the Jews was kindled to such a degree that they gave money to the soldiers, saying, 'Say that his disciples stole his body.'[128] But those who had taken the money were not able to be silent about what had happened, for those men have testified that they saw him risen and that they have received money from the Jews. For this reason I have referred these things to your judgment, lest anyone else should lie and you should decide to believe the falsehoods of the Jews."

43. After the letter was read, Nero said, "Tell me, Peter, were all things done by him in this way?"

And Peter said, "It did happen in this way, oh emperor, for this Simon is full of falsehood and deceit, even if it may seem that he is what he is not, namely a god. There is complete and ultimate victory in my Lord Jesus Christ, who, for the sake of the salvation of humankind, was pleased through the divine economy[129] to live together with humankind."

44. Simon said, "I will bear with you no longer, Peter, but will now command my angels to come and avenge me on you."

Peter said, "I am not afraid of your angels. Instead, they will fear me in the power of my Lord Jesus Christ."

---

127. The pseudonymous author of this letter attempts to absolve Pilate of blame for anything but the flogging by making the historically impossible claim that the actual crucifixion was also carried out by the Jews.

128. Matt 28:11–15.

129. This concept, credited to Irenaeus of Lyons, includes all elements of God's interaction with the world, from creation through final redemption. See Eric Osborn, *Irenaeus of Lyons* (Cambridge: Cambridge University Press, 2001), 51–96.

45. Νέρων εἶπεν· οὐ φοβῇ τὸν Σίμωνα, Πέτρε, τὸν τὴν ἑαυτοῦ θεότητα πράγμασι βεβαιοῦντα;

Πέτρος εἶπεν· βασιλεῦ, ἐν ἐκείνῳ ἐστὶν ἡ θεότης, ὃς τὰ ἄδηλα ἐρευνᾷ τῆς καρδίας. νῦν οὖν εἰπάτω μοι τί διαλογίζομαι ἢ τί ποιῶ εἰς τὸν διαλογισμόν μου. πρὸ τοῦ ψεύσασθαι δὲ τοῦτον, τοῖς σοῖς ἐμφανίζω ὠσίν, ἵνα μὴ τολμήσῃ ψεύσασθαι τί διαλογίζομαι.

Νέρων εἶπεν· προσελθὼν ὧδε εἰπέ μοι, τί διαλογίζῃ.

Πέτρος εἶπεν· κέλευσον ἐνεχθῆναι ἄρτον κρίθινον καὶ λάθρα δοθῆναί μοι. καὶ εἶπεν πάλιν ὁ Πέτρος· εἰπάτω Σίμων νῦν τί τὸ διαλογισθέν, τί τὸ λεχθέν, τί τὸ γεγονός.

46. Missing

47. Σίμων εἶπεν· τοῦτο γίνωσκε, βασιλεῦ, ὅτι τοὺς διαλογισμοὺς τῶν ἀνθρώπων οὐδεὶς οἶδεν, εἰ μὴ εἷς ὁ θεός.

Πέτρος εἶπεν· σὺ οὖν ὁ λέγων ἑαυτὸν εἶναι υἱὸν θεοῦ, εἰπὲ τί ἐνθυμοῦμαι· τί ἄρτι πεποίηκα ἐν τῷ κρυπτῷ, σαφήνισον. ἦν δὲ ὁ Πέτρος εὐλογήσας ὃν εἰλήφει κρίθινον ἄρτον, καὶ κλάσας δεξιᾷ καὶ ἀριστερᾷ ἐν τοῖς χεριδίοις ἐσώρευσεν.

48. τότε ὁ Σίμων μὴ δυνηθεὶς εἰπεῖν τὸ τοῦ ἀποστόλου ἀπόρρητον, ἐβόησεν λέγων· ἐξελθέτωσαν κύνες μεγάλοι καὶ καταφαγέτωσαν αὐτὸν ἐνώπιον τοῦ Καίσαρος. καὶ ἐξαίφνης ἐφάνησαν κύνες μέγιστοι καὶ ὥρμησαν ἐπὶ τὸν Πέτρον. ὁ δὲ Πέτρος ἐκτείνας τὰς χεῖρας εἰς προσευχὴν ἔδειξεν τοῖς κυσὶν ὃν ηὐλόγησεν ἄρτον· ὃν ἰδόντες οἱ κύνες οὐκ ἔτι ἐφάνησαν ἀπὸ τῆς ὥρας ἐκείνης, ἀλλ' ἔφυγον.

τότε ὁ Πέτρος εἶπεν πρὸς Νέρωνα· ἰδού, βασιλεῦ, ἔδειξά σοι μάγον καὶ ἀπατεῶνα τὸν Σίμωνα εἶναι, οὐ ῥήμασιν ἀλλ' ἔργοις· ὁ γὰρ ἀγγέλους ὑποσχόμενος κατ' ἐμοῦ πέμπειν, κύνας παρήγαγεν, ἵνα δείξῃ ἑαυτὸν οὐ θεϊκοὺς ἔχειν ἀγγέλους ἀλλὰ κυνικοὺς δαίμονας.

49. τότε ὁ Νέρων πρὸς τὸν Σίμωνα εἶπεν· τί ἐστιν, Σίμων; νομίζω, ἡττήμεθα.

Σίμων εἶπεν· οὗτος καὶ ἐν τῇ Ἰουδαίᾳ καὶ ἐν ὅλῃ τῇ Παλαιστίνῃ καὶ Καισαρείᾳ τὰ αὐτά μοι ἐποίησεν.

45. Nero said, "Peter, do you not fear Simon, who has confirmed his divinity with deeds?"

Peter said, "Oh emperor, there is divinity in that man who searches out the unseen things of the heart. Therefore, let him now tell me what I am thinking or what I have under consideration. But before this man lies, I will say it into your ears, so that he may not dare to lie about what I am thinking."

Nero said, "Come here and tell me what you are thinking."

Peter said, "Order a barley loaf to be brought and given to me secretly." Then Peter said again, "Let Simon now say what was thought, what was said, and what was done."

46. *This section, which would correspond to Pseudo-Marcellus,* Pass. Holy *25, is absent from the Greek text.*

47. Simon said, "Know this, oh emperor, that no one knows the thoughts of people but God alone."[130]

And Peter said, "You, then, the one saying that you are the son of God, say what I am thinking. Reveal what I have just done in secret." But Peter had blessed the barley loaf that he had received, broken it into his right and left hand, and gathered it up in his sleeves.

48. Then Simon, being unable to say the apostle's secret, cried out, saying, "Let large dogs come forth and devour him in front of Caesar!" All of a sudden very large dogs appeared and attacked Peter. But Peter, after stretching out his hands for prayer, showed the dogs the bread that he had blessed. Seeing it, the dogs no longer appeared from that hour onward, but fled.

Then Peter said to Nero, "Look, oh emperor, I have shown you that Simon is a sorcerer and a cheat, not with words but with deeds. For he promised to send angels against me, but he produced dogs, thus showing that he has not divine angels but canine demons."[131]

49. Then Nero said to Simon, "Well, Simon? I think we have been beaten."

Simon said, "This man did things like this to me in Judea and in all of Palestine and Caesarea."[132]

---

130. Cf. 1 Cor 2:11.

131. Cf. Pass. Apost. 7, where Paul is also included in this scene. For further explanation of this story and the medieval associations of Simon with dogs, see the notes to Pseudo-Abdias *Pass. Pet.* 17–18 (ch. 3 in this volume).

132. Pseudo-Clement, *Hom.* 2.14–40; 3.1–4, 10, 29–58; 6.26–8.3; 16.1–18.23; 20.11–13.

50. τότε ὁ Νέρων πρὸς τὸν Παῦλον ἐπιστραφεὶς ἔφη· σὺ διὰ τί οὐδὲν λέγεις, Παῦλε;

ἀπεκρίθη ὁ Παῦλος καὶ εἶπεν· γίνωσκε τοῦτο, βασιλεῦ, ὅτι ἐὰν ἀπολύσῃς τὸν μάγον τοῦτον τοιαῦτα πράττειν, μέγιστον τῇ πατρίδι σου αὐξάνει, κακὸν καὶ τὴν βασιλείαν σου ἀπὸ τῆς ἰδίας στάσεως καταβιβάσει.

ὁ δὲ Νέρων τῷ Σίμωνι εἶπεν· τί λέγεις σύ, Σίμων, πρὸς ταῦτα;

ὁ δὲ Σίμων εἶπεν· ἐγὼ ἐὰν μὴ φανερώσω ἐμαυτὸν καὶ ὑποδείξω εἶναι θεόν, οὐδείς μοι τὸ ὀφειλόμενον ἀπονέμει σέβας.

Νέρων εἶπεν· καὶ νῦν τί χρονίζεις καὶ οὐκ ἀποδεικνύεις ἑαυτὸν θεόν, ὅπως ἂν οὗτοι τιμωρηθῶσιν;

51. Σίμων εἶπεν· κέλευσόν μοι πύργον οἰκοδομῆσαι ὑψηλὸν ἀπὸ ξύλων, καὶ ἀνελθὼν ἐπ' αὐτῷ καλέσω τοὺς ἀγγέλους μου καὶ προστάξω αὐτοῖς, ἵνα πάντων ὁρώντων ἀναγάγωσί με πρὸς τὸν πατέρα μου εἰς τὸν οὐρανόν. τοῦτο δὲ οὗτοι μὴ δυνάμενοι ποιῆσαι ἐλέγχονται ὅτι ἄνθρωποί εἰσιν ἀπαίδευτοι.

ὁ δὲ Νέρων τῷ Πέτρῳ εἶπεν· ἀκήκοας, Πέτρε, τὸ παρὰ Σίμωνος εἰρημένον; ἐκ τούτου φανήσεται, ὅσην δύναμιν ἔχει ἢ οὗτος ἢ ὁ θεὸς ὑμῶν.

Πέτρος εἶπεν· κράτιστε βασιλεῦ, εἰ θέλεις, δύνασαι νοῆσαι, ὅτι δαιμόνων πεπλήρωται.

Νέρων εἶπεν· τί μοι λόγων περιόδους ποιεῖτε; ἡ αὔριον ἡμέρα ὑμᾶς δοκιμάσει.

52. Σίμων εἶπεν· εἰ μὴ πιστεύεις, ἀγαθὲ βασιλεῦ, ὅτι μάγος οὐκ εἰμί, κέλευσον ἀποκεφαλισθῆναί με ἐν τόπῳ σκοτεινῷ, κἀκεῖ με ἐσφαγμένον κατάλειπε, καὶ ἐὰν τῇ τρίτῃ ἡμέρᾳ μὴ ἀναστῶ, γνῶθί με μάγον εἶναι· ἐὰν δὲ ἀναστῶ, γίνωσκε υἱόν με εἶναι τοῦ θεοῦ.

53. τοῦτο δὲ γενέσθαι κελεύσαντος τοῦ Καίσαρος ἐν τῇ σκοτίᾳ, τῇ μαγικῇ αὐτοῦ τέχνῃ ὁ Σίμων ἔπραξεν, ἵνα κριὸς ἀποκεφαλισθῇ· ἐπὶ τοσοῦτον δὲ ὁ κριὸς ὡς Σίμων ἐφάνη, ἕως οὗ ἀπεκεφαλίσθη ἐν τῇ σκοτίᾳ. ἐρευνήσας γὰρ ὁ ἀποκεφαλίσας αὐτὸν καὶ προαναγὼν εἰς τὸ φῶς τὴν κεφαλὴν εὗρεν αὐτὴν τὴν κεφαλὴν κριοῦ· ἀλλ' οὐδὲν τῷ βασιλεῖ εἰπεῖν ἐτόλμησεν, ἵνα μὴ μαστίξῃ αὐτόν, κελεύσαντι τοῦτο ἐν ἀποκρύφῳ πραχθῆναι. ἐντεῦθεν οὖν ἔλεγεν ἑαυτὸν ὁ Σίμων τῇ ἡμέρᾳ τῇ τρίτῃ ἐγερθῆναι, ὅτι τὴν κεφαλὴν τοῦ κριοῦ καὶ τὰ μέλη ἦρεν, τὸ δὲ αἷμα ἐκεῖσε προσεπέπηκτο, καὶ τῇ ἡμέρᾳ τῇ τρίτῃ ἔδειξεν ἑαυτὸν

50. Then turning to Paul, Nero said, "Why do you say nothing, Paul?"

Paul answered and said, "Know this, oh emperor, that if you permit this sorcerer to do such things, then very great evil will increase upon your country and will bring down your kingdom from its proper standing."

But Nero said to Simon, "Simon, what do you say to these things?"

Simon said, "Unless I show and demonstrate that I am a god, no one will render the reverence due to me."

Nero said, "And now why do you delay and not show that you are a god, so that these men may be punished?"

51. Simon said, "Order a tall tower to be built for me out of wood. After ascending it I will call my angels and give them orders, so that, when all are watching, they will carry me to my father in heaven. But these men, being unable to do this, will be put to shame, because they are ignorant men."

Nero said to Peter, "Did you hear, Peter, what was said by Simon? From this it will be revealed how much power either he or your God has."

Peter said, "Oh mightiest emperor, if you are willing, then you are able to perceive that he has been filled by demons."[133]

Nero said, "Why are you being so evasive with me? Tomorrow the day will test you."

52. Simon said, "If you do not believe, good emperor, that I am not a sorcerer, then order me to be decapitated in a dark place. Leave me there dead, and if I do not rise again on the third day, then know that I was a sorcerer. But if I rise again, then know that I am the son of God."[134]

53. After Caesar had ordered this to be done in the dark, Simon by his magical art made it so that a ram was decapitated. But the ram appeared very much like Simon until it was decapitated in the dark. After searching for the head, the one who had cut it off brought the head into the light and discovered that it was the head of a ram. But he did not dare to say anything to the emperor, who had ordered this to be done in secret, lest the emperor beat him. After that, then, Simon was saying that he had been raised on the third day, because he carried away the head and limbs of the ram, but the blood had congealed there. On the third day he showed himself to Nero and said to him, "Make my blood that was poured out be wiped up,

133. Both verbs are present tense, although we might expect the imperfect with ἄν to create the contrary-to-fact construction: "If you were willing, then you would be able to perceive." The parallel Latin passage contains such a construction (Pseudo-Marcellus, *Pass. Holy* 30).

134. Cf. the account of Simon's faked resurrection in Pass. Apost. 2–3.

τῷ Νέρωνι λέγων αὐτῷ· ποίησον ἐκμαγῆναι τὸ αἷμά μου τὸ ἐκχυθέν, ὅτι ἰδοὺ ἀποκεφαλισθεὶς καθὼς ὑπεσχόμην τῇ τρίτῃ ἡμέρᾳ ἀνέστην.

54. καθὼς δὲ εἶπεν ὁ Νέρων, ὅτι ἡ αὔριον ἡμέρα ὑμᾶς δοκιμάσει, στραφεὶς πρὸς τὸν Παῦλον λέγει· σὺ Παῦλε διὰ τί οὐδὲν φθέγγῃ;

55. ἀποκριθεὶς δὲ ὁ Παῦλος εἶπεν· τούτου τοὺς λόγους μὴ βουληθῇς ἀκούειν, βασιλεῦ. ἀπατεὼν γὰρ καὶ μάγος ἐστὶν καὶ εἰς ἀπώλειαν θέλει ἀγάγαι τὴν ψυχήν σου καὶ τὴν βασιλείαν σου. ὥσπερ γὰρ οἱ Αἰγύπτιοι μάγοι Ἰαννὴς καὶ Ἰαμβρὴς ἐπλάνησαν τὸν Φαραὼ καὶ τὸ στρατόπεδον αὐτοῦ, ἕως οὗ κατεποντίσθη ἐν τῇ θαλάσσῃ, οὕτως καὶ οὗτος διὰ τῆς τοῦ πατρὸς αὐτοῦ τοῦ διαβόλου παιδεύσεως πείθει τοὺς ἀνθρώπους πολλά κακὰ εἰς ἑαυτοὺς ποιεῖν, καὶ πολλοὺς τῶν ἀκεραίων ἐξαπατᾷ πρὸς πειρασμὸν τῆς βασιλείας σου.

56. ἐγὼ δὲ θαρρῶ τῇ δυνάμει τοῦ κυρίου μου Ἰησοῦ Χριστοῦ, ὅτι τάχιον φανερώσει αὐτὸν τὸ τίς ἐστιν, καὶ ὅσον δοκεῖ ἑαυτὸν ὑψῶσαι εἰς τὸν οὐρανόν, τοσοῦτον καταποντισθήσεται εἰς τὸν βυθὸν τοῦ ᾄδου, ὅπου ἐστὶν ὁ κλαυθμὸς καὶ ὁ βρυγμὸς τῶν ὀδόντων.

57. Νέρων εἶπεν· τίς ἐστιν ἡ τοῦ Χριστοῦ διδαχὴ τοῦ σοῦ διδασκάλου;

εἶπεν δὲ Παῦλος· περὶ τῆς τοῦ διδασκάλου μου διδαχῆς ἧς ἐπερώτησας, οὐ χωροῦσιν ταύτην εἰ μὴ οἱ καθαροὶ τῇ καρδίᾳ τὴν πίστιν προσιέμενοι. ὅσα γὰρ τῆς εἰρήνης ἐστὶν καὶ ἀγάπης, ταῦτα ἐδίδαξεν. κἀγὼ ἀπὸ Ἱερουσαλὴμ καὶ μέχρι τοῦ Ἰλλυρικοῦ πεπλήρωκα τὸν λόγον τῆς εἰρήνης, καθὼς παρ᾽ αὐτοῦ ἔμαθον.

because look, I who was decapitated have risen again on the third day, just as I promised."

54. After Nero said, "Tomorrow the day will test you,"[135] he turned to Paul and said, "And you, Paul, why do you say nothing?"

55. Paul answered and said, "Do not be willing to listen to the words of this man, oh emperor, for he is a deceiver and a sorcerer and wants to lead your soul and your kingdom to destruction. For just as the Egyptian sorcerers Jannes and Jambres misled Pharaoh and his army until it was plunged into the sea,[136] so also does this man—through the teaching of his father the devil[137]—persuade people to do many evil things to themselves. And he deceives many of the innocent as a test of your kingdom.

56. "But I am confident that by the power of my Lord Jesus Christ, he will quickly reveal [Simon] for what he is. And however much it seems that he is raised into heaven, to that same degree he will be plunged down into the depth of Hades, where there is weeping and gnashing of teeth."[138]

57. Nero said, "What is the teaching of Christ, your teacher?"

Paul said, "Concerning the teaching of my teacher about which you have asked, none comprehend it except the pure in heart who accept faith.[139] For whatever things relate to peace and love, I have taught them. From Jerusalem to Illyricum[140] I have set out fully the word of peace, just as I learned it from him.

---

135. The repetition of Nero's quotation signals that chapters 52–53 were perhaps later insertions into the text.

136. These are the names traditionally ascribed to the sorcerers who opposed Moses in Exod 7–8. They are mentioned numerous times in ancient literature, including CD V, 18–19; Menaḥ. 85a; 2 Tim 3:8–9; Pliny the Elder, *Nat.* 30.1.11; Apuleius, *Apol.* 90; and Numenius of Apamea (recorded in Eusebius, *Praep. ev.* 9.8.1). The Gelasian Decree lists an apocryphal work entitled the Repentance of Jannes and Jambres (an alternative spelling of Mambres), while Origen acknowledges that there is no record of them in scripture but claims that there exists "a secret book called the Book of Jamnes and Mambres" (*Comm. ser. Matt.* 28; 117 [quoted]). It is unclear how these references might relate to the text reconstructed in Pietersma, *The Apocryphon of Jannes and Jambres the Magicians*. On the various textual traditions related to these figures, see also Pietersma and Lutz, "Jannes and Jambres." Palladius claims that their tomb in Egypt was guarded by demons (*Hist. laus.* 18.5–8).

137. Cf. John 8:44.

138. Matt 8:12; 13:42, 50; 22:13; 24:51; 25:30; Luke 13:28.

139. 1 Tim 1:5; 2 Tim 2:22.

140. Rom 15:19.

58. ἐδίδαξα γὰρ, ἵνα τῇ τιμῇ ἀλλήλους προηγοῦνται· τοὺς ὑπερέχοντας καὶ πλουσίους μὴ ὑπεραίρεσθαι καὶ ἐλπίζειν ἐπὶ πλούτου ἀδηλότητι, ἀλλ᾽ ἐπὶ τῷ θεῷ τὴν ἐλπίδα αὐτῶν τίθεσθαι· τοὺς πτωχοὺς ἐν τῇ ἰδίᾳ χαίρειν πτωχείᾳ· τοὺς πατέρας διδάξαι τὰ τέκνα αὐτῶν παιδείαν τὴν ἐν φόβῳ θεοῦ· τὰ τέκνα πειθαρχεῖν τοῖς γονεῦσιν εἰς νουθησίαν σωτηριώδη. ἐδίδαξα τὰς ἐκκλησίας τῶν πιστευόντων πιστεύειν εἰς ἕνα θεόν, πατέρα παντοκράτορα, ἀόρατον καὶ ἀκατάληπτον, καὶ εἰς τὸν υἱὸν αὐτοῦ τὸν μονογενῆ τὸν κύριόν μου Ἰησοῦν Χριστόν.

59. αὕτη δέ μοι ἡ διδαχὴ οὐκ ἀπ᾽ ἀνθρώπων, οὐδὲ δι᾽ ἀνθρώπου, ἀλλὰ διὰ Ἰησοῦ Χριστοῦ ἐδόθη, τοῦ ἐκ τοῦ οὐρανοῦ μοι λαλήσαντος, ὃς καὶ ἀπέστειλέν με ἐπὶ τὸ κήρυγμα, εἰρηκώς μοι· πορεύου, ὅτι ἐγὼ ἔσομαι μετὰ σοῦ, καὶ πάντα ὅσα ἂν εἴπῃς ἢ ποιήσῃς ἐγὼ δικαιώσω.

60. ταῦτα ἀκούσας ὁ Νέρων ἐξέστη, καὶ στραφεὶς πρὸς τὸν Πέτρον εἶπεν· σύ τί λέγεις;

ὁ δὲ Πέτρος ἔφη· πάντα ὅσα ὁ Παῦλος ἐλάλησεν ἀληθῆ εἰσιν· καὶ γὰρ ἔκπαλαι πολλὰ ἐδεξάμην παρὰ τῶν ἡμετέρων ἐπισκόπων γράμματα, τῶν ὄντων εἰς πᾶσαν τὴν οἰκουμένην περὶ τῶν γενομένων καὶ λαλουμένων ὑπ᾽ αὐτοῦ. διώκτου γὰρ αὐτοῦ ὄντος τοῦ νόμου, φωνὴ αὐτὸν τοῦ Χριστοῦ ἐκ τοῦ οὐρανοῦ ἐκάλεσεν, καὶ ἐδίδαξεν τὴν ἀλήθειαν, ὅτι οὐκ ἦν ἐχθρὸς κατὰ φθόνον τῆς ἡμετέρας πίστεως ἀλλὰ κατὰ ἄγνοιαν. καὶ γὰρ ἐγένοντο πρὸ ἡμῶν ψευδόχριστοι ὡς καὶ ὁ Σίμων καὶ ψευδαπόστολοι καὶ ψευδοπροφῆται, οἵτινες κατὰ τῶν ἱερῶν χαραγμάτων ἐλθόντες ἐπετήδευσαν κενῶσαι τὴν ἀλήθειαν·

καὶ κατὰ τούτων οὖν ἀναγκαῖον ἦν τοῦτον προχειρίσασθαι τὸν ἄνδρα τὸν ἐκ παιδόθεν οὐδὲν ἕτερον παιδευθέντα, εἰ μὴ τοῦ θείου νόμου ἐρευνᾶν τὰ μυστήρια, ἐν οἷς τῆς ἀληθείας ἔκδικος καὶ τοῦ ψεύδους γένηται διώκτης. ἐπεὶ τοίνυν ὁ διωγμὸς αὐτοῦ οὐ διὰ φθόνον ἐγένετο, ἀλλὰ διὰ τὴν τοῦ νόμου ἐκδίκησιν, αὐτὴ ἡ ἀλήθεια ἐκ τοὺ οὐρανοῦ προσωμίλησεν αὐτῷ λέγουσα· ἐγώ εἰμι Ἰησοῦς, ὃν σὺ διώκεις· παῦσαι οὖν διώκων με, ὅτι ἐγώ εἰμι ἡ ἀλήθεια, ἧς ὑπεραγωνίζεσθαι φαίνῃ κατὰ τῶν ἐχθρῶν τῆς ἀληθείας. ὡς οὖν ἔγνω οὕτως εἶναι, καταλιπὼν

58. "For I have taught people to outdo one another in showing honor;[141] the lofty and the rich not to lift themselves up and hope in the uncertainty of wealth, but to place their hope in God;[142] the poor to rejoice in their poverty;[143] fathers to teach their children training in the fear of God;[144] children to be obedient to their parents as a salvific admonition.[145] I have taught the assemblies[146] of believers to believe in one God, the almighty Father, who is invisible[147] and incomprehensible, and in his only begotten Son, my Lord Jesus Christ.

59. "This teaching was given to me not by a human source, nor through a person, but through Jesus Christ, who spoke to me from heaven.[148] He sent me out to preach, having said to me, 'Go, because I will be with you, and I will forgive whatever things you have said or done.' "

60. After hearing these things Nero was amazed, and turning to Peter he said, "What do you say?"

And Peter said, "All the things Paul said are true, because for a long time I have received many letters from our bishops—who are in the entire world—about the things done and said by him. For when he was a persecutor of the law, the voice of Christ called him from heaven and taught him the truth, because he was an enemy of our faith not through jealousy but through ignorance. For before us there were false christs like Simon and false apostles and false prophets, who came against the sacred writings and set out to nullify the truth.

"It was necessary, therefore, to mobilize this man against them—a man who from his youth was trained in nothing but searching out the mysteries of the divine law, by which he became a champion of truth and a persecutor of falsehood. Therefore, because his persecution resulted not from jealousy but from defense of the law, the truth itself spoke to him from heaven, saying, 'I am Jesus, whom you are persecuting.[149] Stop persecuting me, because I am the truth for whom you appear to struggle against the enemies

141. Rom 12:10.
142. 1 Tim 6:17.
143. Cf. 2 Cor 6:10; Jas 1:9.
144. Cf. Eph 6:4.
145. Col 3:20; Eph 6:1.
146. Or "churches."
147. Col 1:15; 1 Tim 1:17.
148. Gal 1:1, 11–12.
149. Acts 9:5, 22:8, 26:15.

ὅπερ διεξεδίκα, ἤρξατο διεκδικῆσαι ταύτην τὴν τρίβον τοῦ Χριστοῦ ἣν ἐδίωκεν, ἥτις ἐστὶν ὁδὸς ἀληθείας τοῖς εἰλικρινῶς πορευομένοις ἐν αὐτῇ.

61. ταῦτα εἰρηκότος Πέτρου ὁ Σίμων εἶπεν πρὸς Νέρωνα· ἐννόησον, ἀγαθὲ βασιλεῦ, ὅτι συνέπνευσαν οὗτοι οἱ δύο κατ᾽ ἐμοῦ· ἐγὼ γάρ εἰμι ἡ ἀλήθεια, καὶ οὗτοι ἐναντία μου φρονοῦσιν.

Πέτρος εἶπεν· οὐδεμία ἐν σοὶ ἀλήθειά ἐστιν, ἀλλὰ πάντα ψευδῆ λέγεις.

62-66. Missing

67. Σίμων εἶπεν· ἀγαθὲ βασιλεῦ, οὗτοι οἱ ἄνθρωποι συνελογίσαντο τὴν εὐμένειάν σου καὶ συνέδησάν σε.

Νέρων εἶπεν· ἀλλ᾽ οὐδὲ σύ με περὶ σεαυτοῦ ἔτι ἐβεβαίωσας.

Σίμων εἶπεν· πόσων καλῶν πραγμάτων καὶ σημείων ὑπ᾽ ἐμοῦ σοι ὑποδειχθέντων θαυμάζω, ὅτι ἀμφισβητεῖς.

Νέρων εἶπεν· ἐγὼ οὐδενὶ ἐξ ὑμῶν συναινῶ· ἀλλ᾽ ὃ ἐρωτῶ σε, μᾶλλον ἀποκρίθητί μοι.

68. Σίμων εἶπεν· τὸ λοιπὸν οὐδέν σοι ἀποκρίνομαι.

Νέρων εἶπεν· ἐπειδὴ ψεύδῃ, διὰ τοῦτο ταῦτα λέγεις. τὸ λοιπὸν οὐδέν σε ἔτι λογίζομαι· ὡς γὰρ εὗρον, ψεύστης εἶ ἐν πᾶσιν. καὶ τί πολλὰ λέγω; οἱ τρεῖς ἐν πᾶσιν ἀμφισβητοῦντά με πεποιήκατε, ὥστε μὴ εὑρεῖν με τίνι πιστεῦσαι δυνηθῶ.

69. Πέτρος εἶπεν· ἕνα θεὸν καὶ πατέρα τοῦ κυρίου ἡμῶν Ἰησοῦ Χριστοῦ κηρύσσομεν, τὸν ποιήσαντα τὸν οὐρανὸν καὶ τὴν γῆν καὶ τὴν θάλασσαν καὶ πάντα τὰ ἐν αὐτοῖς, ὅς ἐστιν ἀληθινὸς βασιλεὺς καὶ τῆς βασιλείας αὐτοῦ οὐκ ἔσται τέλος.

Νέρων εἶπεν· τίς ἐστιν οὗτος ὁ βασιλεύς;

Παῦλος εἶπεν· Κύριος καὶ σωτὴρ πάντων τῶν ἐθνῶν.

Σίμων εἶπεν· ἐγώ εἰμι, ὃν λέγετε καὶ οἴδατε, Παῦλε καὶ Πέτρε, ἀλλ᾽ οὐ μὴ ἀποφήνωμαι καθ᾽ ὑμῶν· τοῦτο γὰρ ποθεῖτε, ἵνα τοῦ μαρτυρίου ὑμᾶς καταξιώσω.

of truth.'[150] As soon as [Paul] knew that it was so, he abandoned the things he was defending and began defending this way of Christ that he had persecuted—which is the path of truth for those going along it in purity."

61. After Peter had said these things, Simon said to Nero, "Understand, good emperor, that these two have conspired against me, for I am the truth,[151] and they turn their thoughts against me."

Peter said, "There is no truth in you, but you speak only lies."

62–66. *These sections, which would correspond to Pseudo-Marcellus,* Pass. Holy *41–45, are absent from the Greek text.*

67. Simon said, "Good emperor, these men have taken advantage of your good will and have entrapped you."

Nero said, "But you have not yet proven to me anything about yourself."

Simon said, "After you received so many good deeds and signs from me, I am amazed that you doubt."

Nero said, "I agree with nothing [that I have heard] from any of you, but rather answer me about what I am asking you."

68. Simon said, "I am not answering you any further."

Nero said, "Because you lie, you say these things. I no longer count you as anything, for as I have discovered, you are a liar in everything. And why do I say all these things? The three of you have made me a doubter about everything so that I find I am unable to believe anything."

69. Peter said, "We proclaim the one God and Father of our Lord Jesus Christ, who made heaven and earth and the sea and everything that is in them, who is the true king, and whose kingdom will have no end."[152]

Nero said, "Who is this king?"

Paul said, "The Lord and Savior of all nations."

Simon said, "I am he[153]—the one about whom you speak and whom you know, Paul and Peter. But I will not reveal myself against you, for you do this so that I may deem you worthy of martyrdom."[154]

---

150. This reference to Jesus as "the truth" is not found in Acts 9:3–9, 22:6–11, or 26:12–18.

151. Cf. John 14:6.

152. This creedal statement is taken from the Niceno-Constantinopolitan Creed and scriptural passages such as Ps 146:6, Luke 1:33.

153. Simon employs the expression ἐγώ εἰμι ("I am"), thus linking himself to God's self-identification in the Hebrew scriptures. Cf. Jesus's use of this phrase in e.g., John 8:58, 9:9.

154. Simon's words are somewhat confusing here, but he appears to be threatening to deny them the desired outcome of martyrdom.

Πέτρος καὶ Παῦλος εἶπον· μηδέποτέ σοι εἴη καλῶς, Σίμων μάγε καὶ πικρίας ἀνάμεστε.

70. Σίμων εἶπεν· ἄκουε, Καῖσαρ Νέρων, ἵνα γνῷς ψεύστας εἶναι τούτους, κἀμὲ ἐκ τῶν οὐρανῶν πεμφθέντα, τῇ αὔριον ἡμέρᾳ εἰς τοὺς οὐρανοὺς ἀνέρχομαι, ἵνα τοὺς πιστεύοντάς μοι μακαρίους ποιήσω· εἰς δὲ τούτους τοὺς τολμήσαντάς με ἀρνήσασθαι τὴν ὀργήν μου ἐνδείξομαι.

Πέτρος καὶ Παῦλος εἶπον· ἡμᾶς πάλαι ὁ θεὸς ἐκάλεσεν εἰς τὴν ἰδίαν δόξαν. σὺ δὲ ὑπὸ τοῦ διαβόλου κληθεὶς σπεύδεις πρὸς κόλασιν.

71. Σίμων εἶπεν· ἀγαθὲ βασιλεῦ, ἄκουσόν μου· τοῦς μαινομένους τούτους ἀποχώρισον ἀπὸ σοῦ, ἵνα ἐν τῷ πορεύεσθαί με εἰς τὸν οὐρανὸν πρὸς τὸν πατέρα μου δυνήσομαί σοι εἶναι

εὐΐλατος.

Νέρων εἶπεν· καὶ πῶς τοῦτο γνώσομαι, ὅτι εἰς τὸν οὐρανὸν ἀνέρχῃ;

Σίμων εἶπεν· κέλευσόν μοι πύργον γενέσθαι ὑψηλὸν ἀπὸ ξύλων καὶ δοκῶν μεγάλων, ἵνα ἐπ' αὐτὸν ἀνέλθων οἱ ἄγγελοί μου εἰς τὸν ἀέρα με εὕρωσιν· οὐ γὰρ δύνανται ἐπὶ τῆς γῆς μεταξὺ τῶν ἁμαρτωλῶν ἐλθεῖν πρός με.

72. τότε ὁ Νέρων προσέταξεν ἐν τῷ κάμπῳ Μαρτίῳ ὑψηλὸν γενέσθαι πύργον· καὶ πάντες οἱ λαοὶ καὶ πᾶσαι τῶν στρατιωτῶν αἱ ἀξίαι ἐπὶ τὸ θεωρῆσαι τοῦτον συνῆλθον. ἐν ταύτῃ οὖν τῇ συνδρομῇ ἐκέλευσεν ὁ Νέρων τὸν Πέτρον καὶ τὸν Παῦλον παραστῆναι, οἷς οὕτως εἶπεν· νῦν ἔχει ἡ ἀλήθεια φανερωθῆναι.

Πέτρος καὶ Παῦλος εἶπον· ἡμεῖς αὐτὸν οὐ παραδειγματίζομεν, ἀλλ' ὁ κύριος ἡμῶν Ἰησοῦς Χριστός, ὁ υἱὸς τοῦ θεοῦ τοῦ ζῶντος, ὃν ἑαυτὸν εἶναι ἀπετόλμησεν εἰπεῖν.

73. τότε ὁ Παῦλος πρὸς τὸν Πέτρον ἔφη· ἐμόν ἐστιν τῶν γονάτων τεθέντων τὸν θεὸν ἱκετεῦσαι· σὸν δέ ἐστι τὸ ἀνύσαι, εἴ τι ἂν ἴδῃς αὐτὸν ἐπιχειροῦντα· ὅτι σὺ πρῶτος ἐξελέχθης ὑπὸ τοῦ κυρίου.

καὶ θεὶς τὰ γόνατα ὁ Παῦλος προσηύχετο. ὁ δὲ Πέτρος πρὸς τὸν Σίμωνα εἶπεν· πλήρωσον ὃ ἐνήρξω· ἤγγισεν γὰρ ὁ σὸς παραδειγματισμὸς καὶ ἡ ἡμετέρα ἀνάκλησις· ὁρῶ γὰρ τὸν Χριστόν μου καλοῦντα ἐμέ τε καὶ τὸν Παῦλον.

74. Νέρων εἶπεν· καὶ ποῦ ἀπελεύσεσθε παρὰ τὴν ἐμὴν βούλησιν;

Πέτρος εἶπεν· ὅπου ἂν προσκαλέσηται ἡμᾶς ὁ κύριος ἡμῶν.

Νέρων εἶπεν· τίς ἐστιν ὁ κύριος ὑμῶν;

Πέτρος εἶπεν· Ἰησοῦς ὁ Χριστός, ὃν ἐγὼ ὁρῶ προσκαλούμενον ἡμᾶς.

Νέρων εἶπεν· οὐκοῦν καὶ ὑμεῖς εἰς τὸν οὐρανὸν μέλλετε ἀνελθεῖν;

Πέτρος εἶπεν· εἴ τι δόξει τῷ καλοῦντι ἡμᾶς.

Peter and Paul said, “May it never go well with you, Simon, you sorcerer who is full of bitterness.”

70. Simon said, “Listen, emperor Nero, so that you may know that these men are liars. But I was sent from the heavens, and tomorrow I will go up into the heavens, so that I may make blessed those who believe in me. But I will show my wrath to those who have dared to deny me.”

Peter and Paul said, “God called us long ago for his own glory. But you, who were called by the devil, are hurrying to punishment.”

71. Simon said, “Good emperor, listen to me. Separate these madmen from yourself, so that when I go to heaven to my father, it will be possible for me to be merciful to you.”

Nero said, “And how will I know that you are going away to heaven?”

Simon said, “Order a high tower to be built for me out of wood and great timbers, so that when I go up on it, my angels may snatch me up into the air, for they are not able to come to me on earth in the midst of sinners.”[155]

72. Then Nero ordered a high tower to be built on the Field of Mars, and all the people and all the lofty men among the military came together to see this. Then in the midst of this mob Nero ordered Peter and Paul to be present, and he said to them, “Now the truth will be revealed.”

Peter and Paul said, “We are not making a public example of him, but it is our Lord Jesus Christ, the Son of the living God, who he dared to say that he is.”

73. Then Paul said to Peter, “It is up to me to beseech God on bended knees, and it is up to you to put an end to it if you see him attempting anything, because you were chosen first by the Lord.”

Paul bent his knees and prayed, but Peter said to Simon, “Finish what you began, for your public shaming and our calling have arrived. For I see my Christ calling both me and Paul.”

74. Nero said, “Where will you go against my will?”

Peter said, “Wherever our Lord will call us.”

Nero said, “Who is your Lord?”

Peter said, “Jesus Christ, whom I see calling us.”

Nero said, “Are you also therefore about to go up into heaven?”

Peter said, “If it will seem good to the one calling us.”

---

155. According to Pseudo-Clement, *Hom.* 2.32, flight was another of Simon’s powers.

Σίμων εἶπεν· ἵνα γνῷς, βασιλεῦ, τούτους ἀπατεῶνας εἶναι, παραυτίκα οὖν ὡς ἀναβῶ εἰς τὸν οὐρανόν, πέμψω τοὺς ἀγγέλους μου πρός σε, καὶ ποιήσω σε ἐλθεῖν πρός με.

Νέρων εἶπεν· ποίησον ἐν τάχει· θέλω γὰρ ἰδεῖν εἰ πληροῖς ὃ λέγεις.

75. τότε ὁ Σίμων ἀνέβη ἐπὶ τὸν πύργον ἐνώπιον πάντων, καὶ ἐκτείνας τὰς χεῖρας ἐστεφανωμένος δάφναις ἤρξατο πέτασθαι. ὁ δὲ Νέρων ὡς εἶδεν αὐτὸν πετόμενον, ἔφη πρὸς τὸν Πέτρον· ἀληθινὸς ἄνθρωπός ἐστιν ὁ Σίμων, σὺ δὲ καὶ Παῦλος πλάνοι ἐστέ.

πρὸς ὃν ὁ Πέτρος ἔφη· παραχρῆμα γνώσῃ, βασιλεῦ, ἡμᾶς μὲν ἀληθινοὺς τοῦ Χριστοῦ εἶναι μαθητάς, τοῦτον δὲ μὴ εἶναι Χριστὸν ἀλλὰ μάγον καὶ κακοῦργον.

Νέρων εἶπεν· ἔτι ἐνίστασθε; ἰδοῦ θεωρεῖτε αὐτὸν ἀνερχόμενον εἰς τὸν οὐρανόν.

76. τότε ὁ Πέτρος ἀτενίσας τῷ Παύλῳ εἶπεν· Παῦλε, ἀνάνευσον καὶ ἴδε.

ἀνανεύσας δὲ ὁ Παῦλος πλήρης δακρύων καὶ θεασάμενος πετόμενον τὸν Σίμωνα εἶπεν· Πέτρε, τί παύῃ; τελείωσον ὃ ἐνήρξω· ἤδη γὰρ προσκαλεῖται ἡμᾶς ὁ κύριος ἡμῶν Ἰησοῦς Χριστός.

καὶ ὁ Νέρων ἀκούσας αὐτῶν ὑπεμειδίασεν καὶ εἶπεν· οὗτοι βλέπουσιν ἑαυτοὺς ἡττημένους ἄρτι καὶ ληροῦσιν.

Πέτρος εἶπεν· ἄρτι γνώσῃ μὴ εἶναι ἡμᾶς λήρους.

ἔφη δὲ ὁ Παῦλος τῷ Πέτρῳ· ποίησον τὸ λοιπὸν ὃ ποιεῖς.

77. τότε ὁ Πέτρος ἀτενίσας κατὰ τοῦ Σίμωνος εἶπεν· ὁρκίζω ὑμᾶς, οἱ ἄγγελοι τοῦ σατανᾶ οἱ φέροντες αὐτὸν εἰς τὸν ἀέρα πρὸς τὸ ἀπατᾶν τὰς τῶν ἀπίστων ἀνθρώπων καρδίας, τὸν θεὸν τὸν κτίστην τῶν ἁπάντων καὶ κύριον Ἰησοῦν τὸν Χριστόν, ὃν τῇ τρίτῃ ἡμέρᾳ ἤγειρεν ἐκ τῶν νεκρῶν, ἵνα ἀπὸ ταύτης τῆς ὥρας μηκέτι αὐτὸν βαστάξητε, ἀλλ' ἐξεάσατε αὐτόν. καὶ παραχρῆμα ἀπολυθεὶς ἔπεσεν εἰς τόπον λεγόμενον Σάκρα Βία, ὅ ἐστιν ἱερὰ ὁδός· καὶ

Simon said, "So that you may know, oh emperor, that these men are frauds, as soon as I ascend into heaven, I will send my angels to you, and I will make you come to me."

Nero said, "Do it quickly, for I wish to see if you might accomplish what you say."

75. Then Simon went up onto the tower in front of everyone, and crowned with laurels he stretched out his hands and began to fly. When Nero saw him flying, he said to Peter, "The true man is Simon, but you and Paul are deceivers."

Peter said to him, "Immediately you will know, oh emperor, that we are the true disciples of Christ, but that this man is not Christ but a sorcerer and evildoer."

Nero said, "Do you still resist? Look, you see that he is going up into heaven."

76. Then Peter looked intently at Paul and said, "Paul, lift your head and see."

After Paul lifted his head, full of tears, and saw Simon flying, he said, "Peter, why do you do nothing? Finish what you have started, for already our Lord Jesus Christ is calling to us."

Having heard these things, Nero smirked and said, "These men see that they are defeated and now are going mad."

Peter said, "Now you will know that we are not mad."

Paul said to Peter, "Do what is left for you to do."

77. Then Peter cast an intense gaze at Simon and said, "You angels of Satan that are carrying him into the air in order to deceive the hearts of faithless people, through God the creator of all things and the Lord Jesus Christ, whom he raised from the dead on the third day, I command that from this time you no longer carry him but let him go." Immediately he was let go and fell to the place called the *Sacra Via*, which is the sacred way.[156]

---

156. The author transliterates and then translates the Latin expression *Sacra Via*, suggesting that the audience is not expected to be familiar with Latin. The Sacred Way was the path of Roman triumphal processions, which began on the Capitoline Hill and passed through the Forum. Regarding Simon's fall, the Apostolic Constitutions state that Simon was thrown to the earth as he was flying "in an unnatural way" (Apos. Con. 2.3.14), while Arnobius of Sicca claims that Simon tried to fly in a fiery chariot. Thrown down by the words of Peter, he broke his legs and soon after committed suicide (*Adv. nat.* 2.12).

τέσσαρα μέρη γενόμενος τέσσαρας σίλικας[6] συνήνωσεν, οἵ εἰσιν εἰς μαρτύριον τῆς τῶν ἀποστόλων νίκης ἕως τῆς σήμερον ἡμέρας.

78. τότε ὁ Νέρων θυμοῦ πλησθεὶς κρατήσας τὸν Πέτρον καὶ τὸν Παῦλον ἐποίησεν ἐν δεσμοῖς γενέσθαι· τὸ δὲ σῶμα τοῦ Σίμωνος ἐκέλευσεν ἐπιμελῶς ἐν τρισὶν ἡμέραις φυλαχθῆναι, νομίζων ἐγερθῆναι αὐτὸν τῇ τρίτῃ ἡμέρᾳ.

πρὸς ὃν ὁ Πέτρος εἶπεν· οὗτος οὐκέτι ἐγείρεται, ἐπειδὴ ἀληθῶς τέθνηκεν, εἰς τὴν αἰώνιον κατακριθεὶς κόλασιν.

ὁ δὲ Νέρων εἶπεν αὐτῷ· τίς σοι ἐπέτρεψεν τοιοῦτον πρᾶγμα ποιῆσαι δεινόν·

Πέτρος εἶπεν· ἡ ἔρις αὐτοῦ καὶ ἡ πονηρὰ ἔννοια καὶ αἱ βλασφημίαι αὐτοῦ παρέσχον αὐτῷ τὸ ἀπολέσθαι.

Νέρων εἶπεν· ὕποπτόν μοι λογισμὸν πεποιήκατε, διὰ τοῦτο κακῶς ἀπολέσω ὑμᾶς.

Πέτρος εἶπεν· οὐχὶ ὃ θέλεις σὺ γίνεται, ἀλλ᾽ ὃ ἐπηγγείλατο ἡμῖν ὁ Χριστός, χρεία ἐστὶν πληρωθῆναι.

79. τότε ὁ Νέρων εἶπεν πρὸς Ἀγρίππαν τὸν ἔπαρχον· ἀνθρώπους ἀθρησκεύτους κακῶς ἀπολέσθαι χρή· ὀγκινάραις[7] οὖν σιδηραῖς τυφθέντας κελεύω αὐτοὺς ἐν τῷ ναυμαχίῳ τόπῳ ἀναλωθῆναι, καὶ πάντας τοὺς τοιούτους κακῶς συντελεσθῆναι.

Ἀγρίππας ὁ ἔπαρχος εἶπεν· ἀγαθὲ βασιλεῦ, οὐχ ἁρμόζει οὕτως αὐτοὺς τιμωρηθῆναι ὡς ἀθρησκεύτους ὄντας.

Νέρων εἶπεν· διὰ τί;

Ἀγρίππας εἶπεν· ἐπειδὴ ὁ Παῦλος ἀθῷος φαίνεται· ὁ δὲ Πέτρος φόνου ἔνοχός ἐστιν, ἔτι δὲ καὶ ἀθρήσκευτος.

6. From the Latin *silices*.

7. This variant is preferable to the reading κινάραις favored by Lipsius.

He was broken into four parts and turned into four stones, which are there as a witness of the victory of the apostles up to today.

78. Then Nero was filled with rage, seized Peter and Paul, and threw them into chains. But he ordered the body of Simon to be guarded carefully for three days, thinking that he would be raised again on the third day.

Peter said to him, "This man will never again be raised, because he has truly died and has been condemned to eternal punishment."

But Nero said to him, "Who commanded you to do such a wicked thing?"

Peter said, "His quarreling and wicked mind and his blasphemies have sentenced him to be destroyed."

Nero said, "You have made me suspicious of you, and therefore I will destroy you in a cruel way."

Peter said, "What you wish will not come about, but what Christ has promised to us must be fulfilled."

79. Then Nero said to Agrippa the prefect, "It is necessary that these impious men be destroyed in a cruel way. After they have been beaten with iron claws, I order them to be killed in the placed called Naumachia,[157] and all the people of this sort[158] to be put to death cruelly."

Agrippa the prefect said, "Good emperor, it is not proper that they have vengeance taken upon them as if they were impious."

Nero said, "Why?"

Agrippa said, "Because Paul seems not guilty, but Peter is guilty of murder and is impious."

---

157. The term *naumachia* refers to a mock sea battle or to the place where mock sea battles were staged. Nero was apparently the first emperor to put on such an event in an amphitheater (as opposed to in a dug basin) in 57 CE. He constructed this building on (or at least very near) the Field of Mars, opposite the Vatican hill (Suetonius, *Nero* 12.2–6; Cassius Dio, *Hist.* 61.9.5). Cassius Dio (*Hist.* 62.15.1) records that Nero staged a battle there in 64 CE, preceded by animal hunts and gladiatorial shows. Its exact location is unknown, but it is possible that the amphitheater and the place at which it was located could have taken on the name of the spectacles staged there. Archaeologists have identified a structure on the Vatican hill close to the Circus of Nero (where the obelisk stood) that may have been constructed for *naumachia* and was dedicated by Trajan in 109 CE. See Steinby, *Lexicon topographicum urbis Romae*, 3:338–39. This location is now the site of the Church of San Pellegrino in Vaticano (formerly San Pellegrino in Naumachia). If the topographical allusion in this text is taken to refer to the Trajanic structure, then this would be a clear anachronism.

158. That is, the Christians.

Νέρων εἶπεν· ποίῳ οὖν μόρῳ ἀπολοῦνται;

Ἀγρίππας ὁ ἔπαρχος εἶπεν· ὡς ἐμοὶ καταφαίνεται, δίκαιόν ἐστιν, Παῦλον ὡς ἀθρήσκευτον ὄντα τὴν κεφαλὴν ἀποτμηθῆναι. τὸν δὲ Πέτρον διὰ τὸ καὶ φόνον ἀνύσαι, ἐπὶ σταυροῦ ἀρθῆναι.

Νέρων εἶπεν· κράτιστα ἔκρινας.

80. καὶ ἀπήχθησαν ὅ τε Πέτρος καὶ ὁ Παῦλος ἀπὸ προσώπου Νέρωνος λαβόντες τὴν ἀπόφασιν. ἀπαγομένου δὲ τοῦ Παύλου ὥστε αὐτὸν ἀποκεφαλισθῆναι ἀπὸ τῆς πόλεως ἄχρι μιλίων τριῶν, ἦν σιδηροδέσμιος· οἱ δὲ φυλάσσοντες αὐτὸν στρατιῶται τρεῖς ἦσαν ὄντες γένους μεγάλου. ἐξελθόντων δὲ αὐτῶν τὴν πόρταν ὡσεὶ τόξου βολῆς τὸ μῆκος, ὑπήντησεν αὐτοῖς γυνὴ θεοσεβής, καὶ θεωρήσασα τὸν Παῦλον σιδηροδέσμιον συρόμενον ἐσπλαγχνίσθη αὐτῷ καὶ ἔκλαυσεν σφοδρῶς· τὸ δὲ ὄνομα τῆς γυναικὸς Περπετούα ἐλέγετο· ἦν δὲ μονόφθαλμος. καὶ ἰδὼν αὐτὴν ὁ Παῦλος κλαίουσαν, λέγει αὐτῇ· δός μοι τὸ ὠράριόν σου, καὶ ὡς ὑποστρέφω, δίδωμί σοι αὐτό. ἡ δὲ λαβοῦσα τὸ ὠράριον προθύμως ἔδωκεν.

οἱ δὲ στρατιῶται προσεγέλασαν καὶ εἶπαν τῇ γυναικί· διατί θέλεις ἀπολέσαι τὸ φακιόλιόν[8] σου, γύναι; οὐκ οἶδας, ὅτι ἀποκεφαλισθῆναι ὑπάγει;

ἡ δὲ Περπετούα πρὸς αὐτοὺς εἶπεν· ὁρκίζω ὑμᾶς κατὰ τῆς σωτηρίας Καίσαρος, εἰς αὐτὸ τὸ φακιόλιον δήσατε αὐτοῦ τοὺς ὀφθαλμούς, ὅταν ἀποτέμνητε αὐτοῦ τὴν κεφαλήν. ὃ καὶ γέγονεν. ἀπεκεφάλισαν δὲ αὐτὸν εἰς μάσσαν καλουμένην Ἄκουαι Σαλβίας, πλησίον τοῦ δένδρου τοῦ στροβίλου. ὡς δὲ ἠβουλήθη ὁ θεός, πρὶν ὑποστρέψαι τοὺς στρατιώτας, ἀπεδόθη τῇ γυναικὶ τὸ φακιόλιον, ἔχον σταγόνας αἵματος· καὶ ὡς ἐφόρεσεν αὐτό, εὐθέως καὶ παραχρῆμα ἀνεῴχθη αὐτῆς ὁ ὀφθαλμός.

81. οἱ δὲ ἀπαγαγόντες στρατιῶται τὸν ἅγιον Πέτρον, ὡς ἦλθον αὐτὸν σταυρῶσαι, εἶπεν πρὸς αὐτούς ὁ μακάριος· ἐπειδὴ ὁ κύριός μου Ἰησοῦς Χριστὸς

8. From the Latin *faciale*.

Nero said, "By what sort of death should they be killed then?"

Agrippa the prefect said, "It seems to me that it is just for Paul to have his head cut off as an impious man, but that Peter, on account of the murder that he committed, should be fixed on a cross."

Nero said, "You have judged most excellently."

80. Peter and Paul were led away from the presence of Nero after they received their sentence. They led Paul three miles outside the city in order to decapitate him, and he was bound in irons.[159] The three soldiers guarding him were of a large race.[160] After they left the gate and had traveled about the distance of a bow shot, a pious woman came to meet them. When she saw Paul being dragged along and bound in chains, she felt great pity for him and wept bitterly. The name of the woman was Perpetua, and she had only one eye. Seeing her crying, Paul said to her, "Give me your scarf, and as I am returning I will give it back to you." She took the scarf and gave it to him willingly.

The soldiers approached the woman and said to her, "Why do you want to lose your scarf, woman? Do you not know that he is going to be beheaded?"

Perpetua said to them, "I adjure you, by the well-being of Caesar, to place this scarf on his eyes when you cut off his head." And it happened in that way. They decapitated him at the estate called Aquae Salvias, near the pine tree. But just as God wished, before the soldiers returned, the scarf, which was covered with blood, was given back to the woman. As soon as she put it on, immediately and at that moment her eye was opened.

81. But as for the soldiers who had led away holy Peter, as soon as they came to crucify him, the blessed one said to them, "Because my Lord

159. This account of Paul's martyrdom varies significantly from the brief reference in Pseudo-Marcellus, *Pass. Holy* 59. See Eastman, *Paul the Martyr*, 62–69. Perpetua is identified in other versions of this legend as Plautilla (Pseudo-Linus, *Mart. Paul* 14–17) or Lemobia (Pseudo-Dionysius, *Ep. Tim.* 8).

160. The stories of the soldiers accompanying and evangelized by Paul do not agree with each other. In Mart. Paul 2–5, Nero is deserted by three bodyguards named Justus, Orion, and Hephaestus; Paul evangelizes two Romans (the prefect Longinus and a centurion named Cescus); and Nero send two soldiers to ensure that Paul has been killed (Parthenius and Pheres). In Pseudo-Linus, *Mart. Paul* 14–15, there are two soldiers involved in the parallel Plautilla story (Parthenius and Feritas), while three other Roman officials (two prefects and a centurion: Longinus, Megistus, and Acestus) seek salvation from Paul. Likewise, in Pseudo-Abdias, *Pass. Paul* 8, Nero despatches two soldiers to oversee the execution (Ferega and Parthenius). The number of soldiers thus varies, but only in this text is there a reference to their deaths as Christian martyrs.

ἐκ τοῦ οὐρανοῦ ἐπὶ τῆς γῆς κατέβη, ὀρθῷ τῷ σταυρῷ ὑψώθη· ἐμὲ δὲ ὃν ἀπὸ τῆς γῆς εἰς οὐρανὸν καλέσαι καταξιοῖ, ὁ σταυρός μου τὴν κεφαλήν μου κατὰ γῆν ὀφείλει δεῖξαι καὶ πρὸς τὸν οὐρανὸν κατευθῦναι τοὺς πόδας μου. ἐπεὶ οὖν οὐκ εἰμὶ ἄξιος οὕτως ἐν τῷ σταυρῷ εἶναι ὡς καὶ ὁ κύριός μου, ἀντιστρέψατε τὸν σταυρόν μου. κἀκεῖνοι εὐθέως ἀντέστρεψαν τὸν σταυρὸν καὶ τοὺς πόδας αὐτοῦ ἄνω προσήλωσαν.

82. συνῆλθεν δὲ ἀναρίθμητον πλῆθος λοιδοροῦντες τὸν Καίσαρα θυμοῦ πεπληρωμένοι, ὥστε αὐτὸν βουλεύεσθαι κατακαῦσαι. ὁ δὲ Πέτρος διεκώλυεν αὐτοὺς λέγων· πρὸ ὀλίγων ἡμερῶν παρακληθεὶς ὑπὸ τῶν ἀδελφῶν ἀνεχώρουν, καὶ ἐθεώρησα τὸν κύριόν μου Ἰησοῦν Χριστόν· καὶ προσκυνήσας αὐτῷ εἶπον· Κύριε, ποῦ πορεύῃ; καὶ εἶπέν μοι· ἀκολούθει μοι, ὅτι ἐν Ῥώμῃ ἀπέρχομαι πάλιν σταυρωθῆναι. καὶ ἐν τῷ ἀκολουθεῖν με αὐτῷ ὑπέστρεψα πάλιν εἰς Ῥώμην. καὶ εἶπέν μοι· μὴ φοβοῦ, ὅτι μετὰ σοῦ εἰμι, ἕως οὗ εἰσαγάγω σε εἰς τὸν οἶκον τοῦ πατρός μου.

83. διὰ τοῦτο, τεκνία μου, μὴ ἐμποδίσητε τὴν ὁδόν μου· ἤδη γὰρ οἱ πόδες μου τὴν οὐράνιον ὁδεύουσιν ὁδόν. μὴ οὖν λυπεῖσθε, ἀλλὰ συγχάρητέ μοι μᾶλλον, ὅτι σήμερον τῶν πόνων μου τὸν καρπὸν ἐπιτυγχάνω. καὶ τοῦτο εἰπὼν προσηύξατο οὕτως· εὐχαριστῶ σοι, ἀγαθὲ ποιμήν, ὅτι κατηξίωσάς με τῆς ὥρας ταύτης· ἀλλὰ δέομαί σου, τὰ πρόβατα ἃ ἐπίστευσάς μοι μὴ αἰσθανθῶσι χωρισμόν μου, σὲ ἔχοντα δι' οὗ ἐγὼ τὴν ποίμνην ταύτην ἠδυνήθην ποιμᾶναι. καὶ τοῦτο εἰπὼν παρέδωκεν τὸ πνεῦμα.

84. παραυτίκα δὲ ἐφάνησαν ἅγιοι ἄνδρες, οὓς οὐδέποτέ τις πρότερον ἑωράκει οὐδὲ μετὰ ταῦτα θεάσασθαι ἠδυνήθη· οὗτοι ἔλεγον ἑαυτοὺς ἀπὸ Ἱεροσολύμων παραγενέσθαι, ἅμα Μαρκέλλῳ ἀνδρὶ ἰλλουστρίῳ,[9] ὅστις ἦν τῷ Χριστῷ πεπιστευκώς, καὶ καταλιπὼν τὸν Σίμωνα τῷ Πέτρῳ ἠκολούθει. ἦραν δὲ τὸ σῶμα τοῦ ἁγίου Πέτρου λάθρα πιστοὶ καὶ ἔθηκαν αὐτὸ ὑπὸ τὴν τερέβινθον πλησίον τοῦ ναυμαχίου εἰς τόπον καλούμενον Βατικάνον.

οἱ δὲ τρεῖς στρατιῶται οἱ τὴν κεφαλὴν ἀποτεμόντες τοῦ ἁγίου Παύλου, ὡς μετὰ τρεῖς ὥρας τὴν αὐτὴν ἡμέραν ἦλθον μετὰ τῆς βούλλας,[10] ἀπάγοντες αὐτὴν τῷ Νέρωνι, καὶ ὑπαντήσαντες τῇ Περπετούᾳ λέγουσιν αὐτῇ· τί ἐστιν γύναι; ἰδοὺ πείσματι ἀπώλεσας τὸ φακιόλιόν σου.

---

9. From the Latin *illustrius*.

10. From the Latin *bulla*.

Jesus Christ came down from heaven to the earth and was raised up on an upright cross, as for me—whom he deigned to call from the earth to heaven—my cross must place my head down to the ground and my feet directed toward heaven. Because I am not worthy to be on a cross in the way my Lord was, turn my cross upside down." They immediately inverted the cross and nailed his feet upward.

82. A countless mob gathered, reviling Caesar and filled with rage, such that they wanted to burn him alive. But Peter prevented them, saying, "A few days ago I was departing, because I had been exhorted to do so by the brothers and sisters,[161] and I saw my Lord Jesus Christ. I worshiped him and said, 'Lord, where are you going?' And he said to me, 'Follow me, because I am going to Rome to be crucified again.' In following him I turned back again to Rome. And he said to me, 'Do not fear, because I am with you until I lead you into the house of my Father.'

83. "Therefore, my little children, do not hinder my way, for my feet are already traveling on the heavenly road.[162] Thus, do not grieve, but rather rejoice with me, because today I receive the fruit of my labors." After saying this he prayed in this way, "I thank you, good shepherd, because you have deemed me worthy of this hour. But I beg you that the sheep that you entrusted to me would not notice my departure, because they have you through whom I was able to shepherd this flock." Saying this, he gave up his spirit.[163]

84. Immediately holy men appeared, whom no one had ever seen before nor was able to see after these things. These men said that they came from Jerusalem along with Marcellus, a nobleman who, after he had believed in Christ, left Simon and followed Peter. The faithful secretly took the body of holy Peter and placed it under a turpentine tree next to the Naumachia at a place called the Vatican.

But as for the three soldiers who had cut off the head of holy Paul, three hours later on that same day they were going with the decree[164] and taking it back to Nero. They met Perpetua and said to her, "Well, woman? Look, because of your confidence you have lost your scarf."

---

161. Literally, "the brothers," but textual evidence points to this being a mixed group.

162. Cf. Ignatius, *Rom.* 12.2, where Ignatius calls the Christians in Rome "the highway of those being killed for God."

163. Matt 27:50; John 19:30.

164. This is a reference to Paul's death warrant issued by Nero.

ἡ δὲ πρὸς αὐτοὺς ἔφη· καὶ τὸ φακιόλιον ἔλαβον, καὶ ὁ ὀφθαλμός μου ἀνέβλεψεν· καὶ ζῇ κύριος ὁ θεὸς τοῦ Παύλου, ὅτι κἀγὼ παρεκάλεσα αὐτόν, ἵνα ἀξιωθῶ δούλη γενέσθαι τοῦ κυρίου αὐτοῦ.

τότε οἱ στρατιῶται οἱ τὴν βούλλαν ἔχοντες, γνωρίσαντες τὸ φακιόλιον καὶ ἰδόντες ὅτι ἀνεῴχθη αὐτῆς ὁ ὀφθαλμός, ἔκραξαν φωνῇ μεγάλῃ ὡς ἐξ ἑνὸς στόματος καὶ εἶπον· καὶ ἡμεῖς δοῦλοί ἐσμεν τοῦ δεσπότου τοῦ Παύλου.

ἀπελθοῦσα οὖν ἡ Περπετούα ἀπήγγειλεν εἰς τὸ παλάτιον τοῦ βασιλέως Νέρωνος, ὅτι οἱ στρατιῶται οἱ ἀποκεφαλίσαντες τὸν Παῦλον λέγουσιν ὅτι οὐκ ἐμβαίνομεν ἔτι εἰς τὴν πόλιν· ἡμεῖς γὰρ πιστεύομεν τῷ Χριστῷ, ὃν Παῦλος ἐκήρυξεν, καὶ Χριστιανοί ἐσμεν. τότε ὁ Νέρων θυμοῦ πλησθεὶς ἐκέλευσεν τὴν Περπετούαν τὴν τοὺς στρατιώτας μηνύσασαν φυλακισθῆναι σιδηροδέσμιον· τοὺς δὲ στρατιώτας τὸν μὲν ἕνα ἀποκεφαλισθῆναι ἐκέλευσεν, τὸν δὲ ἄλλον διχοτομηθῆναι, καὶ τὸν ἕτερον λιθοβοληθῆναι ἔξω τῆς πόρτης ὡς ἀπὸ μιλίου ἑνὸς τῆς πόλεως. ἡ δὲ Περπετούα ἦν ἐν τῇ φυλακῇ.

ἐν αὐτῇ δὲ τῇ φυλακῇ ἦν τηρουμένη Ποτεντζιάνα, κόρη εὐλαβής, διότι ἦν εἰρηκυῖα· καταλιμπάνω τοὺς γονεῖς μου καὶ πᾶσαν τὴν ὑπόστασιν τοῦ πατρός μου, καὶ θέλω Χριστιανὴ γενέσθαι. συγκολληθεῖσα οὖν αὕτη τῇ Περπετούᾳ ἐξηγήσατο αὐτῇ πάντα τὰ περὶ τοῦ Παύλου, καὶ πλεῖον ἠγωνίσατο περὶ τῆς εἰς Χριστὸν πίστεως. ἡ δὲ γυνὴ τοῦ Νέρωνος ἀδελφὴ ὑπῆρχεν τῆς Ποτεντζιάνας, καὶ λάθρα ἐδήλου αὐτῇ περὶ τοῦ Χριστοῦ, ὅτι αἰωνίαν χαρὰν βλέπουσιν οἱ πιστεύοντες εἰς αὐτόν, καὶ ὅτι ὅλα τὰ ὧδε πρόσκαιρά εἰσιν, τὰ δὲ ἐκεῖ αἰώνια· ὥστε καὶ αὐτὴν φυγεῖν ἐκ τοῦ παλατίου καί τινας τῶν συγκλητίδων μετ' αὐτῆς. τότε ὁ Νέρων πολλαῖς βασάνοις τιμωρήσας τὴν Περπετούαν, τέλος

But she said to them, "I have received my scarf, and my eye has recovered its sight. The Lord, the God of Paul, lives, because I also called upon him, so that I might be deemed worthy to become a servant of his Lord."

Then the soldiers who had the decree, after they recognized the scarf and saw that her eye had been opened, cried out with a loud voice as if from one mouth and said, "We also are the servants of the master of Paul!"

Perpetua therefore departed and announced in the palace of the emperor Nero that the soldiers who had decapitated Paul say, "We will no longer enter the city, for we believe in Christ, whom Paul preached, and we are Christians." Then Nero was filled with rage and ordered Perpetua, who had informed him about the soldiers, to be thrown into prison bound in chains. And as for the soldiers, he ordered one to be beheaded, another to be sawn in two, and the other to be stoned outside the gate about one mile from the city. But Perpetua was in prison.

In this same prison was being held Potenziana,[165] a pious maiden, because she had said, "I am leaving my parents and all the support of my father, and I wish to become a Christian." Therefore, she attached herself to Perpetua and learned from her everything about Paul, and she contended[166] even more for the faith in Christ. But the wife of Nero was the sister of Potenziana, and Potenziana secretly explained to her about Christ, namely that those who believe in him see everlasting joy, and that everything here is temporary, but there it is eternal. As a result even she fled from the palace—and some of the women of senatorial rank with her. Then Nero

165. The name Potenziana (Potentiana) is considered to be another form of Pudentiana. Roman pilgrim itineraries as early as the seventh century report that a saint and martyr by this name was buried in the Cemetery of Priscilla alongside Praxedes (Salzburg Itinerary; Libri de locis sanctorum martyrum). Later tradition made them the daughters of Pudens (mentioned in 2 Tim 4:21) and both martyrs (*AASS* Mai. 4 [1685], 296–301). Scholars agree that these spurious acts—and perhaps the figure of Pudentiana herself—were created due to a misunderstanding of the name of a basilica built in the fourth century in honor of Pudens (*ecclesia Pudentiana* = Santa Pudenziana; see Richard Krautheimer, *Corpus basilicarum christianarum Romae*, MACr 2,3 [Vatican City: Pontificio Istituto di Archeologia Cristiana, 1967], 3:277–302). Pudentiana was taken as a proper name instead of an adjective, and a legend was created to explain the naming of a church in her honor. Her acts are not attested until the eighth century, according to Rodolfo Amedeo Lanciani, *Pagan and Christian Rome* (Boston: Houghton and Mifflin, 1899), 112. However, we might speculate that our text represents an earlier attempt to insert Potenziana into the martyrological record.

166. Cf. the use of the same verb to describe Paul's struggles in 2 Tim 4:6–8.

δήσας λίθον μέγαν εἰς τὸν τράχηλον αὐτῆς ἐκέλευσεν ῥιφῆναι εἰς κρημνόν. κεῖται δὲ τὸ λείψανον αὐτῆς εἰς πόρταν Νωμεντάναν. ἡ δὲ Ποτεντζιάνα καὶ αὐτὴ ὑπομείνασα κριτήρια πολλά, τέλος δὲ ποιήσαντες ἐσχάραν, ἔκαυσαν εἰς μίαν ἡμέραν.

85. οἱ δὲ ἅγιοι ἄνδρες οἱ εἰπόντες ἐξ Ἱεροσολύμων παραγενέσθαι, οὓς οὐδεὶς πρώην ἑωράκει, εἶπον πρὸς πάντα τὸν λαόν· χαίρετε καὶ ἀγαλλιᾶσθε, ὅτι μεγάλους πάτρωνας ἠξιώθητε ἔχειν τοὺς ἁγίους ἀποστόλους καὶ φίλους τοῦ κυρίου Ἰησοῦ Χριστοῦ. γινώσκετε δὲ τοῦτον τὸν Νέρωνα τὸν πονηρότατον βασιλέα μετὰ τὴν σφαγὴν τῶν ἁγίων ἀποστόλων μηκέτι αὐτὸν δύνασθαι τὴν βασιλείαν κατασχεῖν.

86. συνέβη δὲ μετὰ ταῦτα μισηθῆναι τὸν Νέρωνα ἀπὸ παντὸς τοῦ στρατοῦ αὐτοῦ καὶ τοῦ λαοῦ τῶν Ῥωμαίων, ὥστε κρῖναι εἰς ἑαυτοὺς δημοσίᾳ τοῦτον τύψαι, ἕως οὗ, ὡς ἦν ἄξιος, τυπτόμενος ἐκπνεύσῃ. ὡς οὖν ἤκουσεν ὁ Νέρων ταῦτα, ἐπέπεσεν αὐτῷ φόβος καὶ τρόμος ἀνυπόστατος, καὶ οὕτως ἔφυγεν, ὥστε μὴ ὁραθῆναι αὐτὸν ἔτι. ἔλεγον δέ τινες, ὅτι ὡς ἐπλανᾶτο ἐν ταῖς ὕλαις φεύγων, ἀπὸ τοῦ ψύχους καὶ τοῦ λιμοῦ ἀτέψυξεν, καὶ ὑπὸ λύκων καπεβρώθη.

87. τὰ δὲ τῶν ἁγίων ἀποστόλων σώματα συνέβη ὑπὸ τῶν ἀνατολικῶν ἐπαρθῆναι τοῦ κομίσαι αὐτὰ ἐν τῇ ἀνατολῇ. ἐγένετο δὲ σεισμὸς μέγας ἐν τῇ πόλει· καὶ δραμόντες οἱ λαοὶ τῶν Ῥωμαίων κατέλαβον αὐτοὺς ἐν τόπῳ λεγομένῳ Κατακούμβας ὁδῷ τῆς Ἀππίας τῆς πόλεως τρίτου μιλίου· κἀκεῖ ἐφυλάχθησαν τὰ σώματα τῶν ἁγίων, ἐνιαυτὸν ἕνα καὶ μῆνας ἓξ μέχρι τοῦ κτισθῆναι αὐτοῖς τόπους, ἐν οἷς ἀποτεθῶσιν. καὶ τὸ μὲν τοῦ ἁγίου Πέτρου σῶμα εἰς τὸν Βατικάνον τόπον πλησίον τοῦ ναυμαχίου μετὰ δόξης καὶ ὕμνων ἀνεκλήθη, τὸ δὲ τοῦ ἁγίου Παύλου εἰς τὴν Ὀστησίαν ὁδὸν ἀπὸ μιλίων δύο τῆς πόλεως· ἐν οἷς τόποις διὰ τῶν προσευχῶν αὐτῶν εὐεργεσίαι πολλαὶ παρέχονται τοῖς πιστοῖς ἐν τῷ ὀνόματι τοῦ κυρίου ἡμῶν Ἰησοῦ Χριστοῦ.

88. ἐτελειώθη δὲ ὁ δρόμος τῶν ἁγίων ἀποστόλων τε καὶ μαρτύρων τοῦ Χριστοῦ Πέτρου καὶ Παύλου μηνὶ Ἰουνίῳ κθ· τῶν δὲ τριῶν στρατιωτῶν μηνὶ

took vengeance upon Perpetua with many tortures. At last he bound a large stone to her neck and ordered her to be thrown over a cliff, and her remains lie at the Nomentan gate.[167] But Potenziana herself endured many trials, and at last they made a furnace and burned her there one day.

85. Then holy men came saying that they were from Jerusalem, and no one had ever seen them before. They said to all the people, "Rejoice and be glad, because you have merited to have as your great patrons the holy apostles and friends of the Lord Jesus Christ.[168] Know that this Nero, the most wicked emperor, is no longer able to keep his kingdom after the slaughter of the holy apostles."

86. It came about after these things that Nero was so hated by his entire army and by the Roman people that they decided among themselves to beat him publicly until, as he deserved, he died from being beaten. When Nero heard these things, fear and uncontrollable trembling fell upon him, and thus he fled, so that he might never be seen again. Some said that as he was wandering and fleeing into the forest, he died from cold and hunger and was eaten by wolves.

87. It then happened that people from the East dug up the bodies of the holy apostles in order to carry them away to the East. But there was a great earthquake in the city, and the people of Rome ran out and seized them in a placed called the catacombs on the Appian Road, three miles from the city. There the bodies of the saints were kept for a year and six months, until the places were built for them in which they are placed.[169] The body of holy Peter was brought back with praise and singing to the Vatican near the Naumachia, and the body of holy Paul to the Ostian Road at the second milestone from the city. In these places through their prayers, many good deeds are done for the faithful in the name of our Lord Jesus Christ.[170]

88. The race of the holy apostles and martyrs of Christ, Peter and Paul, was completed on June 29. That of the three soldiers was completed on July

---

167. This gate is located on the northeast side of Rome near the camp of the Praetorians. I can find no evidence that a church or shrine for Perpetua was ever built there.

168. For a discussion of Paul and Peter as martyr-patrons of Rome and friends of Christ who could exert supernatural influence, see Eastman, *Paul the Martyr*, 84–89.

169. On the mention of a version of this story in a letter of Gregory I, see ibid., 110–14.

170. Graffiti from the catacombs (St. Sebastian) in Rome demonstrate that pilgrims had been seeking the apostles' prayers on their behalf since at least the third century (ibid., 72–73, 84–89).

Ἰουλίῳ δευτέρᾳ· τῆς δὲ ἁγίας Περπετούας καὶ Ποτεντζιάνας τῷ αὐτῷ Ἰουλίῳ μηνὶ ὀγδόῃ· χάριτι καὶ φιλανθρωπίᾳ τοῦ κυρίου ἡμῶν Ἰησοῦ Χριστοῦ, μεθ' οὗ τῷ πατρὶ ἅμα τῷ ἁγίῳ πνεύματι δόξα, κράτος καὶ τιμὴ νῦν καὶ ἀεὶ καὶ εἰς τοὺς αἰῶνας τῶν αἰώνων. ἀμήν.

2,[171] and on July 8 for holy Perpetua and Potenziana.[172] In the grace and love of our Lord Jesus Christ, to whom, together with the Father and the Holy Spirit, be glory, power, and honor now and always and forever and ever. Amen.

---

171. See n. 160 above on the various identifications of the soldiers in the Paul story. The Roman liturgical calendar known as the Burying of the Martyrs (*Depositio martyrum*) dates from 336 CE and shows no evidence of a festival for three soldiers. However, an eighth-century manuscript of the so-called Martyrology of Jerome, which may have its roots in the sixth century, lists a feast in Rome for "Orion with the others" (*Orion cum aliis*) on July 1 (the *kalends* of July). In Mart. Paul 2, one of the soldiers who abandons Nero because of Paul's preaching is named Orion, so perhaps this text reflects this festival. The evidence is tenuous, however. See J. B. de Rossi and Louis Duchesne, eds., *Acta sanctorum novembris* (Brussels: Société des Bollandistes, 1894), 2.1:85 (Cod. Bern.).

172. There is no record of July 8 as the feast day for Perpetua and Potenziana in the Burying of the Martyrs or the Martyrology of Jerome. The traditional feast day for Potenziana was May 19 until the 1969 revision of the Roman calendar, when her name was removed because her acts were considered spurious.

11. Passion of the Apostles Peter and Paul

CANT 194 / *BHL* 6667

Content

Peter and Paul enter Rome, seemingly together, and are received by the many Christians already in that city. They renew their acquaintance with a relative of Pontius Pilate, whom they had known in Judea. Meanwhile, a skilled sorcerer named Simon comes to Nero's attention. Nero initially orders his arrest but ends up inviting him into his household. He asks Simon where he comes from, and the sorcerer claims that he comes from the East, was rejected and crucified by the Jews, and rose on the third day. He offers to prove to Nero that he can rise from the dead, and the emperor finally agrees to this test. Simon deceives his would-be executioner in a dark chamber and reappears "resurrected" when Nero is in the presence of the Roman Senate. Nero invites Simon into his inner bedchamber, where Simon reveals to him the full power of his witchcraft.

Later Nero takes Simon with him to a meeting of the Senate, introducing him as a man sent by God, and Simon invites the Senators to have him conjure any of their dead relatives. The unnamed relative of Pontius Pilate stands up and denounces Simon, who reacts by making more explicit his claim to divine authority by identifying himself as the Christ. Pilate's relative tells Nero to invite Peter and Paul to settle the question, because surely they will be able to recognize the Christ. Nero leaves the Senate chamber only to discover that Simon had also been outside speaking to the people while he was inside with the Senate. Amazed by this feat, the emperor erects a statue in his honor.

On the next day Peter and Paul are brought to Nero. They deny that Simon is the Christ, and Simon denies that they are truly Peter and Paul. A series of contests of supernatural power then occurs. Peter shows his ability to discern the inner thoughts of Simon and defeat the sorcerer's phantom attack dogs. Then, Simon fails to raise from the dead a young relative of

Caesar, but Peter succeeds. Finally, Simon states that he will fly into heaven as the ultimate proof of his power. Paul and Peter, aware that their deaths are imminent, pray to God as Simon begins his spectacle. Peter rebukes the demons carrying Simon, who falls to the earth and later dies.

Nero determines to kill the apostles, so the Christians beg Peter to leave the city. He finally agrees, leaving the believers in the care of Paul. But as he leaves the city, he is met by a vision of Jesus, who says he is going to be crucified again. Peter understands that this is a prediction of his own passion and returns to the city. Meanwhile, the emperor has been waiting for Simon to rise again, but the rotting corpse shows no signs of life. Nero is enraged anew and orders the execution of the apostles. The prefect, here named Clement, sentences Paul to decapitation and Peter to crucifixion. Peter and Paul are killed (with the specific date given) and then received into heaven, while Simon is taken to hell.

Literary Background

This text is constructed from various sources. The story of Simon's faked resurrection is an expansion, or at least a further explanation, of an event referred to in Pseudo-Marcellus, *Pass. Holy* 25 / Acts Pet. Paul 46, where Simon deceives an executioner and the emperor himself. The text also follows Pseudo-Marcellus's *Passion of the Holy Apostles Peter and Paul* and the Greek Acts of the Holy Apostles Peter and Paul in its recounting of a verbal debate between Simon and the apostles in the presence of Nero, a contest of supernatural power involving ravenous dogs conjured by Simon and dispelled by Peter, and the ultimate showdown when Simon attempts to fly. Chapters 8–12 also show dependence on Pseudo-Hegesippus. The dates of the sources from which the author borrows makes a date in the latter sixth century or early seventh century most likely. This is supported by the specific date given for the apostolic martyrdoms—June 29, 57 CE—which is otherwise first attested in a chronicle from 533 CE.

The author is unknown, as is the place of provenance. Rome is often assumed, but the differences from Pseudo-Marcellus's *Passion* and the Greek Acts of Peter and Paul may suggest another location in the Latin West.

Although the Passion of the Apostles Peter and Paul follows Pseudo-Marcellus's *Passion* and the Greek Acts of Peter and Paul in its emphasis on the unified apostolic mission in Rome, it nevertheless contains some dramatic details that distinguish it. Simon's ability to disappear, reappear, and bilocate is not otherwise attested, even in the accounts of his sorcery

in the Pseudo-Clementine literature. The presence of a relative of Pontius Pilate in Rome becomes an important factor in driving the plot but is also not mentioned in any other account. Indeed, it is an odd claim that the apostles would be friendly with a family member of the one who had sentenced Jesus to death. Perhaps this is explained by the fact that Christ plays a more central role in this story, because of Simon's explicit claims to be the Christ. In addition, while the story of the dogs conjured by Simon appears in Pseudo-Marcellus's *Passion* and the Greek Acts of Peter and Paul, the editor of this text preserves the incident in a corrupted form. Several lines are missing that explain the placement and movement of the bread between Peter and Simon, so the story as it appears here does not readily make sense. The final chapter of this text relates the gruesome reality that Simon will not rise again, despite Nero's hopes, and the name of the prefect who ultimately sentences Paul and Peter to death is Clement, not Agrippa as we find in other sources. This alteration of the name is particularly notable, given that other versions of Peter's death identify Clement as the bishop who succeeds him (Pseudo-Abdias, *Pass. Pet.* 15) or even the author of his martyrdom account (Hist. Shim. 37). The identification of someone named Clement as the one responsible for the apostles' deaths might constitute further evidence of this editor's lack of familiarity with the Roman traditions.

Text

The critical edition by Lipsius is based on two manuscripts: British Museum Add. 11880 (ninth century) and Florence Bibl. aedil. eccl. 132 (eleventh century). This first English translation is from the Lipsius edition.

Select Bibliography

Erbetta, Mario, trans. “Passione latina di Pietro e Paolo.” Pages 193–98 in *Atti e leggende*. Vol. 2 of *Gli apocrifi del Nuovo Testamento*. 2nd ed. Turin: Marietti, 1978.

Lipsius, Richard A. Pages 2.1:366–80 in *Die apokryphen Apostelgeschichten und Apostellegenden*. Braunschweig: Schwetschke, 1887.

Lipsius, Richard A., and Max Bonnet, eds. “Passio apostolorum Petri et Pauli.” Pages XC–XCIV and 223–34 in vol. 1 of *Acta apostolorvm apocrypha post Constantinvm Tischendorf*. Leipzig: Mendelssohn, 1891. Repr., Hildesheim: Olms, 1972.

Passio apostolorum Petri et Pauli

1. In diebus illis cum introissent Romam beatus Petrus et Paulus discipuli Domini nostri Iesu Christi, secundum uoluntatem Dei a diuersis fidelibus qui Christo crediderant excepti sunt. frequentabant autem domum cuiusdam Pontii Pilati parentis propter notitiam quando Pilatus praesidatum gesserat in Iudaea. post paucos uero dies Nerone imperatore procedente quidam Simon nomine ei adductus est. hic magus erat non mediocriter doctus, sed perfectus in omni artis ipsius iniquitate. cum autem hoc Nero imperator cognouisset, artius eum iubet a militibus custodiri: quique per fantasiam artis suae nusquam conparuit. audiuit itaque Nero imperator, quia Simon, quem antea custodiri iusserat, nusquam conparuisset: et mirari satis coepit.

post aliquot autem dies Nerone imperatore procedente ut sacrificia diis suis offerret, et ecce subito Simon magus imperatori Neroni apparuit dicens: quid est, domine imperator, quia me quaeris? ecce ego sum Simon, quem ante hos dies a militibus iussisti custodiri. ne me fugacem aestimes

Passion of the Apostles Peter and Paul

1. In those days after the blessed Peter and Paul, the disciples of our Lord Jesus Christ, had entered Rome, by the will of God they were received by the many faithful who had believed in Christ.[1] They frequently visited the home of a certain relative of Pontius Pilate, because they had been acquainted when Pilate was governor[2] in Judea. After a few days, when Nero had risen to become emperor, a certain man named Simon became attached to him.[3] This Simon was a very skilled sorcerer, accomplished in every despicable aspect of his art. When the emperor Nero had become aware of this, he strictly ordered that Simon be held in custody by soldiers.[4] But Simon, through the deception of his art, could not be found anywhere. So the emperor Nero heard that Simon, whom he had ordered to be held in custody by soldiers, could not be found anywhere, and he was considerably amazed.

However, after a few days, when Nero had risen to become emperor, and as he was offering sacrifices to his own gods, behold, suddenly Simon the sorcerer appeared to the emperor Nero saying, "Why, lord emperor, are you looking for me? Behold, I am Simon, whom a few days ago you ordered to be held in custody by soldiers. Do not think that I am going to

---

1. Unlike other accounts in this volume, this text states that Peter and Paul entered Rome at the same time, not one before the other.

2. Pilate was technically the prefect (*praefectus*) of Judea, but the text here follows the designation of governor (*praesidatus*) as in the Latin Vulgate. In the biblical account Pilate's wife is the only relative mentioned (Matt 27:19).

3. Nero became emperor in late 54 CE, so the author places the arrival of Peter and Paul in Rome prior to that date.

4. Suspicion, and even legal suppression, of those labeled "magicians" was a feature of the Roman world: "There was the danger of being prosecuted for magic-working under the law; then there were the police actions that the authorities might take at any given time to eliminate magic-workers from their midst, either executing them or expelling them" (Matthew W. Dickie, *Magic and Magicians in the Greco-Roman World* [London: Routledge, 2001], 142).

et inuentum perdere uelis, ultro me tibi obtuli.

dicit ei Nero imperator: nihil sit, quod timeas; libere ambula et in palatio meo assiduus esto.

2. Simon ergo exhilaratus a Nerone iam non recessit. quem interrogauit Nero dicens: obsecro te, dic mihi quod genus hominis es, uel unde fueris ortus?

Simon dicit: ortus sum ex Fenice, de oriente missus a maiestate, ut quae dicebam Iudaeis, crederent mihi. illi uero non solum credere noluerunt, sed et me cruci adfixerunt, et post diem tertiam a morte suscitatus sum. nam ut scias manifesta me loqui, iube ut ueniat unus de speculatoribus[1] et ante conspectum tuum caput meum auferat; et scies quid facere possim. Nero autem talibus uerbis nullo modo credebat. illo tamen cogente et nimium suadente speculator uenit.

cui Nero imperator ait: uade et abscide caput eius, et uideamus, si uere a maiestate missus est.

tunc Simon Neroni dixit: loco tenebroso hoc fieri iube et mundissimo, ne quis sanguinem meum calcet et uobis mali aliquid contrariique proueniat. introiuit autem locum tenebrosum speculator, in quo lampada ardens missa est, ut caput Simonis gladio amputaret.

uocauit ergo Nero cubicularium suum dicens: caput illud in sportam mittite et desuper contexite, et anulo meo signabo et in cubiculum pono. et ita factum est. die quoque alio Nero ad cubicularium suum dicit: date locum, uideamus caput hominis, ne forte nobis prae timore mentitus sit, et uoluit ingenio mori, quia probare non poterat, quod ipse esset opinatissimus ille Christus. cubicularius autem attulit sportam, et aperuit Nero

1. This term is transliterated into Greek in Mark 6:27 (σπεκουλάτορα).

flee, and do not wish to lose what you have found. Besides, I have offered myself to you."

The emperor Nero said[5] to him, "You have nothing to fear. Move about freely and remain always in my palace."

2. Simon was very pleased and did not depart anymore from Nero. Nero questioned him, saying, "I beg you to tell me what race you are or where you were born."

Simon said, "I was born in Phoenicia[6] but was sent from the East by the divine majesty, so that the Jews would believe the things that I was saying to them. Not only did those people refuse to believe me, but they even nailed me to a cross, and after the third day I was raised from the dead. So that you may know that I am telling the plain truth, order one of your executioners to come and cut off my head in your sight, and you will know what I am able to do." Nero, however, by no means believed such words. Nevertheless, after Simon had compelled and urged him excessively, the executioner came.

The emperor Nero said to him, "Go and cut off his head, and let us see if he was truly sent by the divine majesty."

Then Simon said to Nero, "Order this to be done in a dark and very clean place, lest someone tread on my blood and something evil or unfortunate happen to you."[7] The executioner entered a dark place in which a burning torch was set up, so that he could cut off Simon's head with a sword.

Nero then called to his chamber-servant, saying, "Put (pl.) that head into a basket and put a cover on it. I will seal it with my ring and place it in my bedchamber." And thus it was done. On the next day Nero said to his chamber-servant, "Tell me the place, and let us see the man's head, lest he perhaps deceived us before out of fear and naturally wished to die, because he was not able to prove that he himself was that very famous Christ."[8] The

5. This author frequently employs the historical present.

6. Justin Martyr (*1 Apol.* 26) and Hippolytus (*Haer.* 6.7.1) claim that Simon was from a village called Gitta in Samaria. [N.B.: The references for Hippolytus follow the numbering system in the most recent edition by M. Markovich (*Hippolytus: Refutatio omnium haeresium*, PTS 25 [Berlin: de Gruyter, 1986]). In earlier editions of the *Haeresium*, the sections were divided differently, so section 6.7 here corresponds to section 6.2 in older editions and translations.]

7. The "you" is plural here, perhaps warning of possible consequences for the empire as a whole.

8. Nero seems to know the general story of Jesus, thus explaining Simon's earlier claims to crucifixion and resurrection after three days. The notion that Simon

imperator et agnouit sigillum suum. et inuenit caput arietis, quod per fantasiam nusquam conparuit. et Nero mirari coepit et praecepit uenire senatum et omnibus retulit gestum rei et multi eorum mirabantur.

3. die igitur tertio, cum intraret Nero curiam senatus, et ecce Simon apparuit in medio eorum, et adorans imperatorem clara uoce dixit: ego sum quem ante diem tertium iussisti decollari; et ecce suscitatus sum. Nero autem amplius mirari coepit et omnes qui cum eo erant; et iussit ei pro hoc facto statuam poni. tunc Simon ait: nunc multa uobis ostendam, ut intellegatis quia a maiestate missus sum.

Nero imperator dixit: licet nihil facias, iam credam tibi quia quodcumque uis possis facere. et post multa quae dicta sunt, Nero in palatium suum discessit; iussit autem et Simonem secum ingredi. et cum simul intus essent, introierunt in cubiculum interius: et nescio quas iniquas et magicas sanctiones faciens Neroni, plurimas ei ostendit artis suae uirtutes.

4. die autem alio Nero Simonis manum tenens ad curiam senatus simul processerunt. cumque sederet Nero senatui sic ait: patres conscripti, magnum hominem Deus patriae nostrae misit. hic est, quem offenderunt Iudaei et morti tradiderunt.

chamber-servant brought the basket, and the emperor Nero opened it and recognized his seal. And he found the head of a ram,[9] because through deception Simon could not be found anywhere. Nero was amazed and ordered the Senate to come. He reported the affair to all, and many of them were amazed.

3. On the third day, when Nero entered the chamber of the Senate, behold, Simon appeared in the midst of them. Addressing the emperor he said in a loud voice, "I am the one whom you ordered to be decapitated three days ago. Behold, I have been raised."[10] Nero and all those who were with him were all the more amazed, and he ordered that a statue for Simon be set up in honor of this deed.[11] Then Simon said, "Now I will show you many things, so that you may understand that I was sent by the divine majesty."

The emperor Nero said, "Even if you do nothing, I already believe that you are able to do whatever you want to do." After many things were said, Nero departed to his palace and ordered Simon to go with him. When they were together inside, they went into the inner bedchamber. Performing for Nero I know not what diabolical and magical spells, Simon revealed to him the many powers of his art.

4. On another day Nero took Simon's hand, and they proceeded to the Senate chamber together. When Nero sat down, he spoke thus to the Senate, "Senators, God sent a great man to our country. Here he is, a man whom the Jews beat and handed over for death."

---

would commit suicide, because he knew he was about to be discovered as a fraud, also appears in Hippolytus, *Haer.* 6.20.3. [N.B.: All references to section 6.20 in Hippolytus correspond to section 6.15 in older editions and translations.]

9. According to the Pseudo-Clementine *Homilies* (2.32, 34), Simon could allegedly turn himself into animals.

10. Hippolytus recounts that Simon attempted to prove that he was Christ by having his followers bury him alive, claiming that he would rise again on the third day. "He remained there to this day … for he was not the Christ" (*Haer.* 6.20.3–4).

11. Justin Martyr records that a statue for Simon stood between two bridges on the Tiber (*1 Apol.* 26). He probably misinterpreted the inscription on the statue, but it is not impossible that followers of Simon used this statue as a focus of worship. See Richard A. Lipsius, *Die apokryphen Apostelgeschichten und Apostellegenden* (Braunschweig: Schwetschke, 1887), 2.1:33–35; Otto Zwierlein, *Petrus in Rom: Die literarischen Zeugnisse*, 2nd ed. (Berlin: de Gruyter, 2010), 129–34. This would assume, of course, that Simon ever actually had disciples in Rome.

cumque omnes mirarentur, Simon dixit: si quis uestrum parentem proprium aut aliquem de amicis suis quem antea amisit uidere desiderat, dicat mihi et statim ei apparebit.

adstans autem erat et unus ex parentibus Pontii Pilati, qui eo tempore permanebat quando Pilatus praesidatum gesserat in Iudaea; et nunc cognoscens ipsum non esse Christum, sic ait: optime imperator, ego quidem rem gestam in Iudaea bene noui; hunc autem hominem ignoro, licet aliqua quae dicit sunt uerisimilia. sed iube interrogem eum publice quod scio et cognoscam utrum uere ipse sit Christus an non.

imperator Nero ait: interroga eum, si quid tibi uidetur.

parens uero Pontii Pilati dicit ei: quid uocaris?

ille autem ait: ego sum Christus, quem caesum flagellis Iudaei tradiderunt crucifigi.

ille uero plenius cognoscens quia ipse Christus non esset sed Simon magus, ait: mentiris; sed tu es Simon magus: modo enim te integre cognoui. tu enim prius et legem sequebaris Christianam; sed quia uictus es a Petro illo, qui uere discipulus Christi fuit, a Iudaea discessisti. omnibus mentiri potes praeter mihi, quia omnia quae ibi gesta sunt optime noui. unde conuersus ad imperatorem sic ait: oro, domine imperator, quia hic sunt in ciuitate uestra Petrus et Paulus discipuli Christi illius, iube uenire eos ut se inuicem cognoscant.

Simon uero turbatus coepit imperatori dicere: iube ueniant, et si uere Petrus et Paulus sunt, cognoscunt me.

Nero imperator ait: requirite eos, et in crastinum facite eos ad nos uenire.

5. Exeunte uero imperatore eadem hora uidit turbam magnam collectam ante palatium et interrogauit quid hoc esset. dictumque est ei: quia ille qui uobis intus loquebatur, ipse etiam hic ad populum loquitur, et uerba

And while everyone was marveling, Simon said, "If any one of you desires to see his relative or any one of his friends whom he has lost previously, let him say it to me, and immediately that person will appear to him."[12]

Then one of the relatives of Pontius Pilate stood up—one who remained from that time when Pilate was governor in Judea. He recognized right away that Simon was not the Christ and said, "Greatest emperor, I was indeed well acquainted with the affair in Judea. However, I do not know this man, although some things he says seem to be true. But give the order for me to question him publicly on what I know, and I will recognize whether he truly is the Christ or not."

The emperor Nero said, "Question him, if it seems good to you."

The relative of Pontius Pilate said to him, "What is your name?"

And Simon said, "I am the Christ, whom, after I was beaten with whips, the Jews handed over to be crucified."

That man, knowing full well that he was not the Christ but Simon the sorcerer, said, "You are lying, but you are Simon the sorcerer. I know you quite well, in fact. You previously used to follow the Christian way of life, but because you were defeated by that man Peter, who was truly a disciple of Christ, you departed from Judea.[13] You are able to lie to everyone except me, because I know very well all the things that happened there." Then turning to the emperor he said, "I ask you, lord emperor—because here in your city are Peter and Paul, the disciples of that Christ—order them to come, so that they may recognize each other."

Being unsettled, Simon began to say to the emperor, "Order them to come, and if they are truly Peter and Paul, then they will recognize me."

The emperor Nero said, "Look for them, and see to it that they come to us tomorrow."

5. After the emperor left, he saw in that same hour a large crowd gathered in front of the palace, and he asked what was going on. Someone said to him, "That man who was speaking to you inside is speaking here to the people and is saying to the people the same words that he was saying

12. In Pseudo-Clement, *Hom.* 2.32, a former disciple of Simon states that his abilities included conjuring images at banquets.

13. Acts 8:4–24, although Peter and John rebuked, rather than "defeated," Simon in that encounter. The reference to Simon's defeat and departure from Judea seems to come from the Acts of Peter, where Peter twice claims to have driven Simon from Judea because of his treatment of a woman named Eubula (Acts Pet. 17; 23).

quae in conspectu uestro dicebat ipsa etiam populo dicit. imperator Nero et omnis senatus mirati sunt, quomodo in una eademque hora et in palatio in conspectu imperatoris fuisset, et foris ad populum loqueretur. unde hoc diuinitati redigens iussit ei aliam erigi statuam habentem facies duas, unam intendentem ad senatum et aliam ad populum.

6. sequenti uero die introiuit Simon ad Neronem in cubiculum, quia carissimus factus ei fuerat, et ait: Hic sunt illi duo quos parens Pontii Pilati magnos esse proposuit. sed audi, imperator, diutius uiuere non debent, quia isti totam Iudaeam subuerterunt. nam Petrus et Paulus alii sunt.

Nero autem iussit colligi senatum et Petrum et Paulum introduci. quibus ait: quid uocamini?

responderunt: Petrus et Paulus discipuli Domini Iesu Christi.

tunc ostendit eis Simonem dicens: nostis hominem hunc?

et dixerunt: nouimus magum peruersum ualde.

subridens uero Nero dixit: quid uocatur?

dixerunt: Simon. iste et ad nos uenit et baptizatus uoluit uirtutem diuinam pretio conparare. unde maledictus et condemnatus a nobis discessit in suam perditionem. nam Christus non est quem[2] esse se dicit: etsi alios per iniquitates suas inducit, nos tamen nullo modo fallere potest.

Nero imperator dicit: quis est Christus, cuius uos discipulos esse dixistis?

Petrus et Paulus dixerunt: si uis scire, lege omnes uirtutes et doctrinas eius, et uera praeclara mirabilia, et inuenies Christum. nam iste fallax est et iniquus.

7. Nero imperator ait: et iste multa mirabilia fecit me praesente et quicquid uolui statim demonstrauit mihi.

---

2. Read *quemadmodum*.

in your presence." The emperor Nero and the whole Senate were amazed at how in that same hour he had been in the palace in the sight of the emperor and outside speaking to the people. Ascribing this to divinity, Nero ordered that another statue be erected for him having two faces, one directed toward the Senate and the other toward the people.[14]

6. On the following day Simon went into Nero in his bedchamber, because he had become very dear to him, and he said, "They are here, those two men whom the relative of Pontius Pilate declared to be great. But listen, emperor. They should not live any longer, because they turned all of Judea upside down. These men are not Peter and Paul."[15]

Nero then ordered that the Senate be gathered and that Peter and Paul be brought in. He said to them, "What are your names?"

They responded, "Peter and Paul, disciples of the Lord Jesus Christ."

Then he showed Simon to them, saying, "Do you know this man?"

And they said, "We know this wicked sorcerer very well."

Smiling, Nero said, "What is his name?"

They said, "Simon. He came to us, and after he was baptized, he wanted to purchase divine power for a price. Rebuked and condemned, he departed from us into his own destruction,[16] for he is not the Christ as he says he is. He seduces others through his evil deeds, but he is in no way able to deceive us."

The emperor Nero said, "Who is the Christ, whose disciples you have said you are?"

Peter and Paul said, "If you wish to know, read about all his virtues and his teachings, which are both true and clearly wondrous, and you will find Christ. But that man with you is deceitful and perverted."

7. The emperor Nero said, "That man did many miracles in my presence, and he immediately demonstrated for me whatever I wanted."

---

14. Simon's disciple in the Pseudo-Clementine *Homilies* says that "he becomes two-faced" (Pseudo-Clement, *Hom.* 2.32). In regards to Simon's alleged divinity, Hippolytus records that followers of Simon worshiped "an image of Simon fashioned into the image of Jupiter" (*Haer.* 6.20.1), and Robert P. Casey argues that "the cultus of Simon was regularly performed before statues of Zeus" ("Simon Magus," *BegC* 5:154).

15. Literally, "Peter and Paul are other men."

16. In Acts 8 Simon is confronted by Peter and John, not Peter and Paul. Paul had his own confrontation with a *μάγος* named Bar-Jesus in Acts 13:6–12. However, according to the Acts of Peter, Simon attempted to buy power from Peter and Paul in Jerusalem after seeing the miracles they performed (Acts Pet. 23).

Petrus et Paulus dicunt: si quid fecit, per fantasiam ad praesens et in aenigmate fecit; nam uerissimum aliquid nec fecit nec aliquando facturus est.

Simon dixit: dicat Petrus quid nunc facere cogito.

Petrus uero silentio panem petiit et sub manica tenens dixit Simoni: fac quod cogitas, ut cognoscant omnes quia fantasticum est omne quod facis. Simon autem continuo eleuata manu digitos excussit, et apparuerunt subito quasi canes ingentes et impetum magnum in Petrum et Paulum fecerunt, ita ut omnes exterriti fugerent. Petrus quoque proiecto in terra pane, canes statim fantastici nusquam conparuerunt.

et ait Simoni: si uera sunt quae fecisti, quare panis remansit in manu tua, et qui comederent nusquam conparuerunt?

Nero etiam imperator Simoni mago sic ait: puto, uicti sumus.

Simon dixit: audi, imperator bone, ut isti sciant quae ego eis aliquando ostendi.

conuersus itaque ad Paulum Nero dicit ei: Paule, quid dicis?

cui ait: hunc nisi citius perdideris, malum grande adcrescet patriae tuae.

8. contigit autem eo tempore, ut adulescens quidam nobilis etiam propinquus Caesaris moreretur, quem multi in ciuitate dolebant. admonebant autem plerique experimentum quarentes utrum posset Petrus adulescentem mortuum suscitare, quia iam celeberrimus a diuersis in his operibus habebatur; sed apud gentiles difficile credebatur. alii autem Simonem adduci dicebant, ut eum si posset a morte suscitaret. utrique ergo ubi

Peter and Paul said, "If he did something, he did it up until now through deception and in an illusion, for neither did he do anything that was really true, nor is he going to do anything."

Simon said, "Let Peter say what I now have in mind to do."

Without a word Peter asked for bread, and holding it under his sleeve he said to Simon, "Do what you have in mind to do, so that all may know that everything you do is an illusion." Simon immediately raised his hand and thrust forth his fingers, and suddenly there appeared what seemed to be enormous dogs. They viciously attacked Peter and Paul, and everyone fled out of fear. Peter threw the bread on the ground, and at once the imaginary dogs were nowhere to be found.

And he said to Simon, "If the things you did are true, then why did the bread remain in your hand, while those who would eat have disappeared?"[17]

The emperor Nero then said to Simon the sorcerer, "I think we are beaten."

Simon said, "Listen, good emperor, so that your people may know the things that I showed them at another time."[18]

Then turning to Paul, Nero said to him, "Paul, what do you have to say?"

Paul said to him, "Unless you destroy this man quickly, great evil will increase upon your country."

8. At that time it happened that a certain young man died.[19] He was noble and related to Caesar, and many in the city were mourning him.[20] And many were recalling their own experience and asking whether Peter would be able to raise the dead youth, because he was already considered

---

17. The narrative resembles other accounts in which Simon and Peter have a showdown that involves the discernment of each other's unspoken intentions, bread, and dogs (Pseudo-Abdias, *Pass. Pet.* 17–18; Pseudo-Marcellus, *Pass. Holy* 27; Acts Pet. Paul 48). However, the author of this text presents a corrupt version of the story, for it makes no sense that the bread is suddenly in Simon's hand. Notably, the author also inserts Paul into the account, in order to emphasize the mutuality of the apostles. For further explanation of this story and the medieval associations of Simon with dogs, see the notes to Pseudo-Abdias, *Pass. Pet.* 17–18 (ch. 3 in the present volume).

18. Simon seems to be invoking Peter and Paul as witnesses of his former deeds of power. Indeed, despite the vitriol reserved for Simon by early Christian writers such as Justin, Irenaeus, and Hippolytus, none of them questions his power as a sorcerer.

19. Chapters 8–12 appear to be dependent on Pseudo-Hegesippus, *Exc. Hier.* 3.2.

20. The death and resurrection of a youth attached to Nero is also a theme in e.g., Acts Pet. 25–26 and Mart. Paul. 1–2.

fuerat corpus directi sunt. conuenientibus etiam multis senatoribus qui fuerant cum Nerone, quarentes cognoscere utrum aliquis ex ipsis posset iuuenem de morte suscitare, respondens Petrus dixit: qui se potentiorem offert, accedat prius et uirtute qua dicit posse mortuum resuscitet.

tunc Simon conditionem proposuit, si ipse mortuum resuscitaret, continuo Petrus occideretur; si uero Petrus praeualuisset, in Simonem sententia uerteretur. et quieuit Petrus conditioni propositae. accessitque Simon ad lectulum defuncti, incantare atque inmurmurare dira carmina coepit. et post horam multam caput mouere uisus est qui mortuus fuerat. et mox clamor ingens omnium qui aderant surrexit, quod iam uiueret adulescens. ira ergo et indignatio ab omnibus surrexit in Petrum, quod ausus esset praeferre se tantae potentiae.

9. tunc sanctus Petrus apostolus petiit silentium dicens: si uiuit defunctus loquatur, et si resuscitatus est surgat, ambulet, fabuletur. fantasma, non ueritas est quod uidetur caput mouisse. deinde uero dicit: separetur a lectulo Simon et uideamus si iterum se mortuus mouere possit. quo facto remansit corpus exanime sicuti fuerat. adstitit itaque Petrus longius a lectulo et intra se orationem cum lacrimis faciens magna uoce dicit: adulescens, surge, sanet te Dominus Iesus Christus. et statim surrexit adulescens et locutus est et ambulauit et cibum sumpsit: et dedit eum matri suae. qui cum rogaretur ut ab eo non discederet, ait: nolite solliciti esse: non delinquetur ab eo qui illum fecit resurgere.

very famous in different places for these kinds of deeds.[21] But among the unbelievers[22] there was significant doubt about him. Others were saying that Simon should be brought, so that, if possible, he might raise him from the dead. Therefore, both were brought to where the body was. After a large number of Senators who were with Nero had come together, they wanted to know whether either of those men would be able to raise the young boy from the dead. Peter responded, saying, "The one who presents himself as more powerful, let him come forth—the one who previously said that by his power he is able to raise the dead."

Then Simon proposed a condition: If he were to raise the dead, then Peter would be killed immediately. But if Peter were to prevail, then the sentence would be turned against Simon. Peter agreed to the proposed condition. Then Simon approached the bed of the deceased, and he began to offer incantations and murmur abominable chants. After a long time the head that had been dead seemed to move, and immediately a great cry arose among those who were present, because the youth was now alive. Anger and indignation, therefore, rose up from everyone against Peter, because he had dared to claim superiority to such power.

9. Then holy Peter the apostle asked for silence, saying, "If he is living, let the dead man speak. And if he has been revived, let him get up, walk, and talk. It is an illusion, not the truth, that the head seems to have moved." Then he said, "Let Simon be taken away from the bed, and let us see if the dead man is able to move again." After this was done, the body remained lifeless just as it had been. So Peter stood at a distance from the bed and within himself offered a prayer with tears. Then he said with a loud voice, "Young man, get up! May the Lord Jesus Christ heal you!" And immediately the young man arose, spoke, walked around, and ate food. And Peter gave him to his mother.[23] When she asked Peter not to leave him, he said, "Have no fear. The one who raised him up will never abandon him."

---

21. E.g., Acts 9:36–42.

22. Literally, "the gentiles," but the term is used by Christian authors to describe anyone outside their faith.

23. Cf. Luke 7:15.

motus est autem omnis populus aduersus Simonem, ut lapidaretur. et dixit Petrus: sinite: non est ei parum quod cognoscit suas artes nihil ualere. uiuat magis et Christi regnum crescere uideat et per inuidiam cottidie torqueatur.

10. ille autem fugiens Neroni dixit se in urbe iam habitare non posse, quoniam a Galilaeis offensus fuisset. pollicetur ergo uolatum, quod in caelum portaretur et petiit imperatorem ut turris lignea fabricaretur ei et in monte Capitolino ei construeretur. constituto ergo die conuenit omnis populus a minimo usque ad maximum uidere quod Simon implere promiserat. iussit autem Nero non discedere Petrum et Paulum, sed adduci ad spectaculum istud. dixitque eis Nero: ecce quod parat facere Simon multum est. sed ut credam quod aliis atribus omnia faciet, uolo uidere uirtutem uestram, ut probem quod non de caelo uenit.

Petrus et Paulus dixerunt: nos homines sumus et potestatem nullam habemus, nisi Deus noster qui eum in conspectu uestro confundere potest.

conuersus Petrus ad Paulum ait: genibus fixis oremus Dominum nostrum. et ita orare coeperunt.

et Paulus Petro dicit: fac quod coepisti: adpropinquat enim de mundo transitus noster.

audiens hoc Nero dicit: et quo ituri estis ab ante meam potestatem?

Paulus dicit: ignoramus Domini uoluntatem, quo nos duci iubet; hoc tamen scimus quia cito sumus ituri.

Simon dicit: optime imperator, ut eos scias esse fallaces, nunc tibi probabo.

All the people, however, moved toward Simon to stone him,[24] and Peter said, "Leave him alone. It is sufficient[25] for him to know that his arts are powerless. Let him live longer and see the kingdom of Christ arise, and let him be tormented every day out of envy."

10. However, that man fled to Nero and said that he was no longer able to live in the city, because he had been insulted by the Galileans.[26] Therefore, he promised that he would fly—that he would be carried into the sky—and he asked the emperor to build a wooden tower for him and then construct it for him on the Capitoline Hill.[27] Therefore, on the appointed day all the people from the least to the greatest gathered to see what Simon had promised to accomplish. Nero ordered that Peter and Paul should not leave, but should be brought to this spectacle. Nero said to them, "Behold, what Simon is preparing to do is a great thing. But so that I may believe that he can do anything by his other arts, I wish to see your power, so that I may verify that it does not come from heaven."

Peter and Paul said, "We are men and have no power, except that our God is able to thwart him in your sight."

Peter turned to Paul and said, "Let us pray to our Lord on our knees."[28] And so they began to pray.

Then Paul said to Peter, "Do what you started to do. Our departure from the world draws near."

Hearing this Nero said, "And where will you go that is outside my authority?"

Paul said, "We do not know the will of the Lord or where he commands us to be led. However, we know that we will go soon."

Simon said, "Oh great emperor, so that you may know that they are deceitful, I will now prove it to you."

---

24. Hippolytus at one point compares Simon to a Libyan sorcerer named Apsethus, who was burned alive by a mob when they realized that he had duped them by his phony magic tricks (*Haer.* 6.7.2–6.8.4).

25. Literally, "It is not not enough."

26. Only Peter was from Galilee, while Paul was from Cilicia. The term is being used here for Christians in general.

27. Flight was another of Simon's alleged powers (Pseudo-Clement, *Hom.* 2.32).

28. The basilica of Santa Francesca Romana (Santa Maria Nova) in Rome sits in the ancient Forum just below the Capitoline Hill, Simon's launching site. The church displays a stone that is said to have the imprints made by the knees of Peter and Paul when they knelt to pray. See David L. Eastman, *Paul the Martyr: The Cult of the Apostle in the Latin West*, WGRWSup 4 (Atlanta: Society of Biblical Literature, 2011), 108.

imperator Nero dicit: comple, quod facturus es, et faciam de illis quodcumque uolueris.

11. Simon autem ascendens turrem extensis manibus coepit in altum uolare, omnisque populus ut uidit clamare nimium coepit. Nero autem Petro et Paulo dicit: uidetis, quia uere a maiestate missus est quem magum esse dixistis; uos potius estis hominum seductores.

Petrus ait: scimus quia post paululum cum Christo erimus.

Nero autem ait: adhuc perseueratis in uanitate hac? ego enim uideo eum paene iam caelum introire, et conamini eum adhuc falsum dicere?

Paulus autem Petro dicit: erige oculos et mentem ad Deum et ora. cumque eleuasset Petrus caput lacrimis plenus et Neronem uidisset mirari uolantem Simonem in aëre, dixit ei Paulus: quid dicis, Petre famule Christi? hodie nos iste impius perdet, si Simon iste adhuc in sua praeualuerit potestate.

haec Nero cum audisset sic ait inridens eos: isti iam delirant.

Petrus uero cum magna constantia dicit ei: modo scies, imperator quia non deliramus.

Paulus Petro dicit: fac quod faciebas: ora Deum omnipotentem ut suam potentiam ostendat et inimici confundat astutiam.

Petrus autem iterum faciem eleuans in caelum extensis manibus ait: increpo uos, daemonia qui eum fertis, per Deum Patrem omnipotentem et per Iesum Christum filium eius, ut sine mora eum dimittatis. omnes enim dicent quia ipse est saluator huius mundi. cumque hoc diceret, uenit Simon ex alto in terram, et crepuit medius; nec tamen continuo exanimatus est, sed fracto debilitatoque corpore, ut poenam suam et ruinam cognosceret, ad locum qui uocatur Aricia sublatus, post paululum cum diabolo eius anima discessit in Gehennam.

The emperor Nero said, "Finish what you are going to do, and I will do with them whatever you wish."

11. Simon climbed the tower and, with hands outstretched, began to fly into the sky. All the people, as they saw this, began to raise a tremendous shout. Nero said to Peter and Paul, "You see that the one whom you said was a sorcerer was in fact sent by the divine majesty, but you deceive people."

Peter said, "We know that after a little while we will be with Christ."

Then Nero said, "Even now do you persist in this foolishness? Just now I saw him go into the sky, and you are still trying to say that he is a fraud?"

Paul said to Peter, "Lift your eyes and mind and pray to God." And when Peter, his eyes filled with tears,[29] lifted his head and saw that Nero was amazed at Simon flying in the sky, Paul said to him, "What do you say, Peter, servant of Christ? Today that impious man will kill us, if that Simon now prevails over us in his own power."

When Nero heard these things, he laughed at them and said, "Now they are going mad."

With great resolve Peter said to him, "You will know without any doubt, emperor, that we are not mad."

Paul said to Peter, "Go back to doing what you were doing. Ask the omnipotent God to show his power and thwart the craftiness of the enemy."

Peter then lifted his face again to the sky, stretched out his hands, and said, "I rebuke you, you demons who are carrying him, through God the almighty Father and Jesus Christ his Son. Let go of him right now, and all will say that Christ is the Savior of this world." When he said this, Simon fell from the heights to the earth and crashed in the midst of them. However, he was not killed immediately but lay there with his body broken and debilitated, so that he might be aware of his punishment and ruin.[30] He was carried to the place which is called Aricia,[31] and after a little while his soul descended with the devil into hell.

---

29. Cf. Pseudo-Marcellus, *Pass. Holy* 55, and Acts Pet. Paul 76, where Paul is the one with tears in his eyes.

30. The Apostolic Constitutions state that Simon was thrown to the earth as he was flying "in an unnatural way" (Apos. Con. 2.3.14), while Arnobius of Sicca claims that Simon tried to fly in a fiery chariot. Thrown down by the words of Peter, he broke his legs and soon after committed suicide (*Adv. nat.* 2.12).

31. Cf. Mart. Pet. 3. Aricia was home to a temple of Diana near Lake Nemi, "Diana's Mirror," where the goddess was honored with a three-day festival each August (Ovid, *Fast.* 3.263–264, 267–270).

12. quo audito Nero deceptum se et destitutum dolens tanti casu amici, quem subito sibi sublatum plangebat, uirum sibi utilem et necessarium rei publicae, indignatus quaerere coepit causas, quibus Petrum occideret.

et quia iam tempus aderat quo sancti apostoli ad suum Dominum uocarentur, denique dato praecepto ut comprehenderentur, rogabatur Petrus a diuersis Christianis ut alio se loco conferret. quibus ille resistebat dicens, nequaquam se facturum ut tamquam metu mortis territus effugeret; bonum esse pro Christo pati, qui pro omnibus se obtulit; semper docebat, illam non esse mortem pro Christo, sed inmortalitatem et uitam aeternam potius praedicabat. haec et alia Petrus loquebatur eis qui eum fugere suadebant. sed plebs ne se inter procellas fluctuantes gentilium destitueret hoc ei suadebant. uictus itaque Petrus omnium fletibus cessit promisitque egredi urbem.

proxima ergo nocte celebrata oratione uale omnibus faciens, relicta omni plebe cum Paulo, solus coepit proficisci. ut autem uentum est ad portam urbis, uidet sibi Christum occurrere; et adorans eum cum ingenti gaudio dicit: Domine, quo uadis?

dicit ei Iesus: uenio iterum crucifigi.

intellexit ergo Petrus pro sua hoc dictum passione, quod in eo Christus passurus uideretur, qui in omnibus martyribus suis pati cognoscitur: et conuersus ad urbem in loco quo fuerat redit, captusque est a persecutoribus sequenti die cum conseruo suo Paulo.

13. custodierat autem Nero corpus Simonis putans eum sicuti ante fuerat resuscitari. at ubi cognouit eum iam in fetore et putredine uersum, partes corporis eius obrui praecepit. accensus autem iracundia magna aduersus Petrum et Paulum sic ait Clementi praefecto urbis: Pater Clemens, isti homines increduliores sunt nimis, et possunt omnino nostram disper-

12. When he heard this, Nero began to mourn the fact that he had been cheated and deprived by the fall of such a great friend. He was wailing for the one who suddenly was taken from him, a man useful to himself and necessary for the republic, and in anger he began to look for reasons that he might strike down Peter.

Because the time had now arrived when the holy apostles were being called to their Master, the order was then given that the apostles should be arrested. Peter was begged by many Christians to go somewhere else. He resisted these people, saying that he would by no means flee on account of being terrified by the fear of death. He also said that it is good to suffer for Christ, who offered himself for all. He was always teaching that that which is done for Christ is not death, but he preached instead that it is immortality and eternal life. Peter said these and other things to those who were persuading him to flee. But the people, being tossed about amid the uproar of their fellow countrymen, did not desist and persuaded Peter to do this. And so, after being convinced, Peter left while all were weeping and promised to go out of the city.

Therefore, on the next night, after he offered a prayer, he said farewell to all. Having left all the people with Paul, he began to set out alone. However, as he came to the gate of the city, he saw Christ coming to meet him. He worshiped him with great joy and said, "Lord, where are you going?"

Jesus said to him, "I am going to be crucified again."

Peter understood that this was said about his own passion, because in him Christ—who is understood to suffer in all his martyrs—would be seen to suffer. Peter therefore turned back, returning to the city in the place where he had been, and he was seized by the persecutors on the following day, along with his fellow servant Paul.

13. Nero had been caring for the body of Simon, counting on the fact that he would be resurrected just as he had before. But, when he recognized from the terrible smell and rottenness that Simon was decomposing,[32] he began to bury the parts of his body. Aroused by great anger against Peter and Paul, he spoke thus to Clement,[33] the prefect of the city, "Father Clement, those men are far too impious, and they are able to destroy our religion

32. Literally, "being altered."

33. The prefect is identified as Agrippa in the other accounts in this volume.

dere religionem, si eos adhuc uiuere passi fuerimus. sed accipiant utrique cardos ferreos et inuicem se lacerare cogantur.

Clemens praefectus ait: optime imperator, quoniam Paulus non tantum incredulior apparet, aliter ipse pereat.

Nero imperator dicit: quomodo uis pereant.

tunc Clemens praefectus urbis dedit sententiam dicens: Paulus contumax contra Romanum imperium capitali sententia puniatur, Petrus autem qui carminibus suis homicidium perpetrauit crucifigatur. postulauit autem Petrus ut inuersis uestigiis crucifigeretur, eo quod indignum se iudicaret eo modo crucifigi quo Dominus et magister eius Iesus Christus filius Dei crucifixus est. passi sunt autem tertio kalendarum Iuliarum, Nerone bis et Pisone consulibus.

ipsi uero in caelum recepti sunt, Simon autem deductus est in infernum. nam qui in Christo credunt, uiuent cum eo semper in gloria sempiterna per omnia saecula saeculorum. amen.

completely if we allow them to live any longer. But let them take iron claws[34] and be forced to beat each other in turn."

Clement the prefect said, "Greatest emperor, because Paul seems to be not so impious, let him die some other way."

The emperor Nero said, "Let them die as you wish."

Then Clement the prefect of the city gave the sentence, saying, "Paul, the insolent one against Roman power, let him be punished by the sentence of decapitation. But Peter, who committed murder by his incantations, let him be crucified." Peter, however, asked that he be crucified upside down, because he considered himself unworthy to be crucified in the way that his Lord and Master Jesus Christ, the Son of God, had been crucified. They suffered on the third kalends of July, when Nero for the second time and Piso were consuls.[35]

And Peter and Paul were received into heaven, but Simon was led away into hell, for those who believe in Christ will live with him forever in eternal glory, forever and ever. Amen.

---

34. These instruments of torture, described as "thistles" (*cardi*), were designed to lacerate the skin as if one were carding wool.

35. June 29, 57 CE.

12. Pseudo-Dionysius, *Epistle to Timothy on the Death of the Apostles Peter and Paul*

CANT 197 / *BHL* 6671

Content

The author ("Dionysius") opens the text, which is presented as a letter, with praise for Timothy because he had endured many hardships alongside Paul. He then turns to an encomium of Paul himself as a great teacher, a destroyer of sin and demons, an enemy of the Jews, and a builder of the church. However, Paul will no longer be able to send letters, and the author laments the loss of such a great spiritual father. The disciples of Paul are left destitute by the death of their teacher, who was able to open and explain the Scriptures to them. Now they should weep like the prophets in the Hebrew Scriptures.

Dionysius claims to have been an eyewitness to the martyrdoms of Paul and Peter and bemoans that the two pillars of the church died on the same day and left the Christians as orphans. Dionysius encourages Timothy to hold a festival in honor of the suffering of the apostles and describes the scene as they were led away to their martyrdoms. The two were ultimately separated, and the author followed Paul to the end. The author shifts back into mourning and claims to have seen Paul and Peter ascending into heaven together after their deaths. Here he inserts the story of a pious woman named Lemobia. She had given Paul a veil with which he could collect his own blood, and he miraculously returned it to her before ascending into heaven. The topic shifts again suddenly as the author recounts the discovery of a mysterious head. It was believed to be the head of the apostle and soon was reunited with Paul's body.

Literary Background

This letter is ostensibly from Dionysius the Areopagite, an Athenian converted by Paul in Acts 17, to Timothy, one of Paul's closest disciples. However, it belongs not to the first century but to the late antique period, when traditions about the apostles' deaths were expanding. The text is certainly pseudepigraphical and anonymous, and this Pseudo-Dionysius should not be confused with the Christian theologian and Neoplatonic philosopher of the fifth or sixth century.

The provenance of the letter is a challenging issue. Textual evidence suggests that the epistle was written in Greek, but no copy of the Greek original survives. (Reports in the secondary literature of Greek manuscripts in Florence and Vienna are inaccurate.) Versions of the letter survive in a number of ancient languages, including Latin, Syriac, Armenian, Georgian, Arabic, and Ethiopic. Among these there are noticeable differences between the western (Latin) and eastern (Syriac, Armenian, Georgian, Arabic, and Ethiopic) versions. The eastern versions, for example, include substantial additional theological commentary, and the distinctions are significant enough to suggest separate transmission histories for the Latin and eastern texts. Dionysius claims to be writing from Rome, where he had been an eyewitness to Paul's martyrdom, but there are indications against this. He makes statements that suggest a lack of familiarity with the layout of the city; his version of the discovery of Paul's head in the Latin version gives the name of the bishop as Fabellius, a name that does not appear on the list of Roman bishops; and he identifies Fabellius as the *patriarch* of Rome, a term that is first employed by Justinian I in Constantinople in the sixth century to refer to the heads of the five primary episcopal sees: Rome, Constantinople, Alexandria, Antioch, and Jerusalem.[1] Ultimately, the provenance cannot be established, but Constantinople is a possibility. It would explain the production of the text in Greek, the proliferation of the letter in a variety of eastern languages, the inaccuracies in Roman topography, and the use of the term *patriarch* for the bishop.

The employment of the term *patriarch* suggests a date no earlier than the middle of the sixth century and the reign of Justinian, while the earliest textual witness to this epistle is a Syriac manuscript dated to the seventh

1. Adrian Fortescue, *The Orthodox Eastern Church* (Piscataway, NJ: Gorgias Press, 2001), 21–25. The Council in Trullo officially recognized and ranked these five sees in 692, but Justinian is the first to refer to their bishops as *patriarchs*.

century. Taken together, these parameters point to a fairly specific period of time—the second half of the sixth or the first half of the seventh century.[2]

Among the collection in this volume, Pseudo-Dionysius's *Epistle to Timothy* stands out in being written as a letter, instead of being a *passion* or *acts* account. Dionysius employs elements of the Greek and Roman literary genre *consolation*, seeking to assuage Timothy's grief. At the same time, however, he promotes this same grief, seeking to motivate Paul's disciple to establish a feast in honor of his teacher.

Several key themes emerge in this epistle. The first is intimacy—the intimacy between Paul and Timothy, the intimacy between Paul and Dionysius (who at one point suggests that these events might seem "easy" to Timothy, because he did not have to witness them), and the intimacy between Paul and Peter. Indeed, the author makes much of the tearful scene as the apostles are separated from each other to go to their deaths—a scene that later prompted the founding of a church in honor of this emotional parting (see n. 31 in the translation section of this chapter). In this way the Dionysian author reflects the emphasis on the harmony of the apostles (*concordia apostolorum*) that is evident in Pseudo-Marcellus's *Passion of the Holy Apostles Peter and Paul* and the Greek Acts of the Holy Apostles Peter and Paul, two texts that likely come from a similar chronological context. A second theme is the miraculous nature of these events. The story of Lemobia and her veil is clearly dependent on the account of Plautilla in Pseudo-Marcellus's *Passion* and Perpetua in the Greek Acts of Peter and Paul. Not only does Paul borrow a scarf and return it posthumously to its owner, but in this case the return is accompanied by a heavenly vision of the apostles entering the city together dressed in radiant clothing and bearing the triumphant crowns of martyrs. A third theme is the density of scriptural allusions in the text. As we might expect, the author repeatedly cites letters from the Pauline corpus, particularly the Pastoral Epistles and the foreshadowing of Paul's death in 2 Timothy. But the author also frequently refers to figures and passages from the Hebrew Bible. Jacob, David,

2. Richard A. Lipsius (*Die apokryphen Apostelgeschichten und Apostellegenden* [Braunschweig: Schwetschke, 1887], 227–31) originally assigned the text to Gaul in the ninth century, but the discovery of the seventh-century manuscript caused him to reconsider. He finally proposed that the original letter may be earlier than he had thought, but the Latin version alone could not be dated earlier than the ninth century. There is, however, no evidence to support this proposed gap of several centuries between the western and eastern editions of the text.

Jeremiah, Amos, and Joel are among those evoked to express the author's angst at the death of Paul and Peter, and now Timothy must take up the mantle from Paul, just as Elisha did from Elijah.

One comment on the current form of the text is in order. The story of Paul's head was probably not part of the original letter. It is absent from a number of the eastern manuscripts, and even when it does appear in those texts it does so at different points in the story. The Latin editor has added it to the end of the text with an awkward statement that Peter's head remained attached to his body, no doubt meant to transition the reader to the story of a head (Paul's) that did not remain attached. This is a clear seam in the text and points to a later insertion. In addition, as the Martyrdom of Paul the Apostle and the Discovery of His Severed Head (ch. 9) in this volume attests, the story of Paul's rediscovered head had its own, separate history of transmission. It was probably added to this epistle as further evidence of the supernatural signs that resulted from the martyrdoms of the two greatest pillars of the church.

Text

The text survives in numerous manuscripts in the languages discussed above. This translation is the first of the Latin text produced by Albin Brunet and Henri Quentin.[3] Their edition is an update of the work of Bonino Mombrizio, with substantial dependence on the edition by Paulin Martin. The manuscripts contain numerous orthographical variations, most of which have been standardized here for the sake of the reader.

Select Bibliography

Eastman, David L. "The Epistle of Pseudo-Dionysius the Areopagite to Timothy Concerning the Deaths of the Apostles Peter and Paul: A New Translation and Introduction." In *New Testament Apocrypha: More Noncanonical Scriptures*. Edited by Tony Burke and Brent E. Landau. Grand Rapids: Eerdmans, forthcoming.

Leloir, Louis. *Écrits apocryphes sur les apôtres : Traduction de l'édition arménienne de Venise.* CCSA 3. Turnhout: Brepols, 1986, 173–88.

---

3. The volume refers to the editors as "Two monks of Solesmes." I am grateful to Père Louis Soltner of the Benedictine Abbeye Saint-Pierre in Solesmes for providing me the internal records that identify these previously anonymous scholars.

Lipsius, Richard A. Pages 42–44 in *Die apokryphen Apostelgeschichten und Apostellegenden*. Braunschweig: Schwetschke, 1890.

Malan, Solomon C., trans. "The Epistle of S. Dionysius the Areopagite to S. Timothy." Pages 230–43 in *The Conflicts of the Apostles: An Apocryphal Book of the Early Eastern Church*. London: Nutt, 1871. This translation is from the Ethiopic version.

Martin, Paulin. "Dionysii Areopagitae." Pages 241–54, 261–76 in *Analecta sacra spicilegio solesmensi* 4: *Patres antenicaeni*. Edited by Joannes B. Pitra. Paris: Roger and Chernoviz, 1883.

Mombrizio, Bonino. "Epistola beati Dionisii ariopagite de morte apostolorum Petri et Pauli ad Timotheum." Pages 354–57, 709–10 in volume 2 of *Sanctuarium seu Vitae sanctorum*. New edition by Albin Brunet and Henri Quentin. Paris: Fontemoing, 1909.

Watson, W. Scott. "An Arabic Version of the Epistle of Dionysius the Areopagite to Timothy." *AJSL* 16.4 (1900): 225–41.

Epistola beati Dionisii Ariopagite
de morte apostolorum Petri et Pauli ad Thimotheum

1. Saluto te dominum discipulum et filium spiritualem ueri patris et boni amatoris qui consumasti uoluntatem magistri tui et substinuisti cum eo tribulationes et omnes passiones et perpessus es omnes agones et flagella. recepisti etiam cum eo famem et sitim et suscepisti omnia obprobria et contemptus et cruciatus et irrogationes et uenumdatus cum eo fuisti in laboribus omni tempore et afflictionibus cum dolore et amaritudine in perturbationibus et temptationibus et diligentia portasti inuictum ministerium in abstinentiis uigiliis et orationibus et gratiis in fortitudine et agone in peregrinationibus cum eo contemptus et flagellatus odio habitus et abiectus ab inimicis et amicis. nunquam ab obedientiam piger fuisti nec ad obsequium spiritualis magistri tui exacerbatus et tractus per uicos flagellatus et dilaceratus confractus et conuiciatus in omni loco cum eo. naufragium passus in mari cum eo conturbatus in nauibus uulneratus in ciuitatibus in angustia et contumeliis conuiciis et obprobriis in carceribus die et nocte cum eo in uinculis et uectibus in manicis ferreis in tribulationibus comitatus eum. et non solum haec sed grauiora et innumerabilia tormenta et agones passus es cum eo qui fuit pater patrum.

2. doctor doctorum et pastor pastorum qui crucifixus fuit mundo et Domini nostri Iesu Christi in corpore suo stigmata portauit. abyssum sapientiae fistulam altissonam praedicatorem ueritatis infatigabilem Paulum dico nobilissimum apostolum qui ecclesias illuminauit confirmauit Christianos et confregit portas peccati rhumphea[1] bis acuta. fugauit gentiles deiecit templa idolorum et diruit aras et confregit idola abominabilia et destruxit altaria eorum deiecit et humiliauit habitacula daemonum et

1. From the Greek ῥομφαία.

Epistle of Blessed Dionysius the Areopagite to Timothy on the Death of the Apostles Peter and Paul

1. I greet you, honored disciple and spiritual son of our true father and good friend, you who fulfilled the will of your master, underwent with him trials and all kinds of sufferings,[1] and bore steadfastly contests and floggings. You also accepted with him hunger and thirst, and you received all kinds of abuse and contempt and tortures and oppression. You also were sold with him, laboring at all times and in afflictions with pain and bitterness. Amid perturbations and trials and with diligence you carried out your ministry, unconquered in self-denying vigils and prayers and acts of grace in strength and in struggle. On voyages with him you were scorned and flogged, held in contempt and cast out by enemies and friends. Never were you reluctant to be obedient or to yield to your spiritual master, afflicted and dragged through the streets, flogged and torn apart, broken to pieces and reviled in every place with him. You endured shipwreck on the sea, tossed about with him in ships. You were wounded in cities, in distress and in abuses, insults, and reproaches, in prisons day and night with him, in chains and in iron bars and shackles. In these trials you were his companion. You suffered not only these, but harsher and innumerable torments and struggles with him.

2. He was the father of fathers, the teacher of teachers, and the shepherd of shepherds. He was crucified to the world, and he bore the marks in his own body of our Lord Jesus Christ.[2] I am speaking of Paul, the deep well of wisdom, the greatest pitch-pipe and tireless preacher of truth, the noblest apostle who brought light to the churches, who strengthened the Christians, and who destroyed the gates of sin, like a sword twice-sharpened. He put to flight the unbelievers and threw down the temples of idols. He demolished altars. He broke into pieces the abominable idols and destroyed their altars. He threw down and humiliated the dwelling places of

1. The list that follows is reminiscent of 2 Cor 6:4–5; 11:23–27.

2. Gal 6:14, 17.

cessare fecit solemnitates et obsequia eorum. hic uere terrestris angelus et homo caelestis imago et similitudo diuinitatis credentium gloria. amicus poenitentium generis sui aduocatus dilectus et desideratus a gentibus dispersionis hostis fuit Iudaeorum odio habitus a Phariseis. dissipator synagogae eorum aedificator ecclasiae sanctorum et instans in sollicitudine spirituali. scutum[2] fidei minister Christi praeco euangelii eius os diuinum et lingua spiritualis. scrutator diuinorum eloquiorum inquisitor perditorum pater pupillorum et studiosus iudex uiduarum confortator debilium fortitudo confractorum. nauis ornata uelis oppugnans fluctibus furibundis nauclerus industrius in sapientia spirituali disponens bene omnia affectuose desiderans inuariabilem unitatem inimicus haereticorum et mente corruptorum pater diligens et pastor optimus magister optimus et dulcis et spiritualis doctor. hic sanctus artifex gloriosus architectus et studiosus pugil sanctus et dignissimus et deiformis spiritus omnes nos dereliquit nos inquam inopes et indignos in hoc mundo contemptibili et maligno et ingressus est ad Christum Deum suum et Dominum et amicum.

3. heu frater mi dilecte animae meae ubi est spiritualis pater tuus bone discipulae magistri amator? unde ulterius salutabit te? de mari aut de arida de Galatia aut de Hipsania? ab Asia aut a Corintho? ecce enim orphanus

2. From the Greek σκῦτος.

demons and caused their festivals and their worship to cease.[3] He was truly an earthly angel and a heavenly man, the image and likeness of divinity,[4] the glory of believers. He was a friend of the penitent, an advocate for his own race,[5] esteemed and longed for by the peoples of the diaspora. He was an enemy of the Jews, held in contempt by the Pharisees, the destroyer of their synagogue.[6] He was a builder of the assembly of the saints and present to those in spiritual anxiety. He was a shield of faith,[7] a servant of Christ,[8] a herald of his gospel, a divine mouth, and a spiritual tongue. He was an examiner of divine utterances, a seeker of the lost,[9] a father of orphans, a zealous defender of widows,[10] a comforter of the lame, the strength of the broken.[11] He was an ornate ship with sails, attacking on the raging waves. He was a shipmaster diligent in spiritual wisdom, arranging all things well out of affection and longing for unwavering unity. He was an enemy of heretics and those corrupt in mind, a diligent father and most excellent shepherd, a very great master and a pleasant and spiritual teacher. He was a holy craftsman, a glorious architect, and an eager boxer.[12] He was holy and most worthy, and his divinely formed spirit has abandoned us all. I say that we are poor and unworthy in this contemptible and wicked world, but he went forth to Christ his God and Lord and friend.

3. Oh, my brother, dear to my soul, where is your spiritual father, oh good disciple and lover of his master? From what far off place will he greet you? From the sea or from the desert? From Galatia or from Spain? From Asia or from Corinth? Behold, you have indeed been made an orphan

---

3. Acts 19:24–41.

4. Cf. Acts Paul Thec. 3.3, where Paul is described as follows: "A man small of stature, with a bald head and crooked legs, in a good state of body, with eyebrows meeting and nose somewhat hooked, full of friendliness. *Sometimes he appeared like a man, but other times he had the face of an angel*" (emphasis added).

5. Rom 9:3.

6. The author distinguishes between Paul's advocacy for "his own race" and his antagonism toward "the Jews" and "the Pharisees." It is not clear how these elements hold together, given that Paul trumpeted his credentials as both a Jew and a Pharisee, e.g., Rom 11:1; Phil 3:5. See also Acts 23:6, 26:5.

7. Eph 6:16.

8. Rom 15:16; 1 Cor 4:1; 2 Cor 11:23.

9. Luke 19:10.

10. Ps 68:6.

11. Ps 145:14; 146:8.

12. 1 Cor 9:26.

factus es et remansisti solus. cessauit et consumatus est cursus tuus quem faciebas cum spirituali patre tuo uel quo ad eum festinus accedebas. et iam nequaquam scribet tibi manu sua sanctissima dicens: fili carissime. sed nec ad te mittet ulterius uocando: festina uenire ad me expecto enim te in tali et tali ciuitate. o carissime frater Thimothee perfecisti quod mihi scripsisti et dixisti: si audisti ubi est magister meus notifica mihi ut uadam ad eum. hodie completum est quod Dominus discipulis suis dixit: quoniam desiderabitis unam horam magistri et minime uidebitis.

uae mihi frater Thimothee. quod hoc accidit nobis [dies] tristitiae et tenebrarum et damni quia orphanati sumus? quis dabit oculis nostris aquas et pupillis nostris fontes lachrimarum ut ploremus die et nocte lumen ecclesiarum quia extinctum est? complica frater libros prophetarum et signa super eos quia neminem habemus interpretem parabolarum et paradigmatum et eloquiorum ipsorum et dicamus et nos cum Amos propheta: pasco ego in locis desertis et in pascuis ubi non sunt pascua. ubi sunt lamentationes Hieremiae prophptae dicentis: cor meum conturbatum est ab afflictione et gemitu et non est mihi consolatio et requies? uae mihi frater mi Thimothee iam non uenient ad te epistolae eius in quibus scriptum sit: Paulus modicus seruus Iesu Christi et iam non scribet de te ibi ulterius ciuitatibus dicens: suscipite filium meum dilectum Thimotheum. uae mihi frater. uae mihi. quis non induet fletum et gemitum aut quis non uestietur lugubribus et mente attonitus non obstupescet? o frater carissime spiritalis sacerdos minister Christi et ecclesiae induere ciliciis[3] et lamento

3. From the Greek κιλίκιον for "hair shirt." See, e.g., Ps 35:13.

and have remained alone. He has departed, and your course is complete,[13] which you were making with your spiritual father, or because of which you were proceeding quickly to him. And now by no means will he write to you with his most holy hand, saying "Most beloved son."[14] And he will not send to you from far away, calling, "Make haste to come to me.[15] I am waiting for you in such and such a city." Oh, dearest brother Timothy, you have finished your course, because you wrote and said to me: "If you have heard, where is my master? Tell me, so that I may hurry to him." Today is fulfilled what the Lord said to his disciples, "Although you will desire your master for one hour, you will not see him."[16]

Woe to me, brother Timothy, because this day of sadness and shadows and loss has befallen us, for we have been orphaned. Who will give water to our eyes and fountains of tears to us orphans, so that we may weep day and night[17] for the light of the churches, because it has been extinguished? Brother, fold up the books of the prophets and place a seal upon them, because we have no interpreter of their parables and examples and pronouncements. We should therefore say, like Amos the prophet, "I am feeding in deserted places and in pastures where there is no food."[18] Where are the lamentations of Jeremiah the prophet, who said, "My heart is overwhelmed by suffering and groans. There is no consolation or rest for me."[19] Alas, my brother Timothy. Now his epistles will not come to you, in which it is written, "Paul, the humble servant of Jesus Christ."[20] And no longer will he write about you to the citizens, saying, "Receive my beloved son, Timothy."[21] Alas, my brother! Woe is me! Who will not put on wailing and groaning? Or who will not be clothed with garments of lamentation or astounded and confounded in their minds? Oh, dearest brother and spiritual priest, servant of Christ and the church, be clothed with sackcloth and

13. 2 Tim 4:7.
14. Cf. 2 Tim 1:2.
15. Cf. 2 Tim 4:9.
16. This may be a reference to John 7:34.
17. Cf. Jer 9:1.
18. This quotation does not correspond to any passage in Amos.
19. Lam 1:20–21.
20. Rom 1:1; Phil 1:1; Titus 1:1.
21. Cf. 1 Cor 4:17, 16:10–11; Phil 2:19; 1 Thess 3:2.

quia uox in rhama audita est ploratus et ululatus.[4] et non tantum ploratus et ululatus sed mortis et orphanitatis.

hae duae plagae terribiles et amarae in die una nobis uenerunt et completum est in nobis dictum Iacob patriarchae: dum Ioseph adhuc perditus esset et Symeon non rediret. ecce et enim Petrus fundamentum ecclesiarum et gloria sanctorum apostolorum recessit a nobis orphanos dereliquit. Paulus quoque gentium familiaris consolator parentum defecit nobis et ulterius non inuenitur. et completum est in uos uerbum Dauid dicentis: posuerunt morticina seruorum tuorum escas uolatilibus caeli et carnes sanctorum tuorum bestiis terrae. ubi est cursus Pauli et labor sanctorum pedum eius euaserunt enim uincula et carceres et ligno constricta et uecte. sed nec manus eius industriae tradentur amodo alligari uinculis ferreis. ubi est os loquens et lingua consulens et spiritus beneplacens Deo suo?

4. o frater mi Thimothee sollemnisemus pro eo qui non eget orationis patrocinio. quis non ploret et ululet? nam qui meruerunt gloriam et honorem apud Deum tanquam malefactores traduntur in mortem. o frater mi Thimothee si uidisses agones consumationis eorum defecisses quidem prae tristitia et dolore. quoniam autem non interfuisti facile tibi ui detur opus agonis ipsorum. quis non fleret hora illa quando praeceptum sententiae egressum in eos est ut Petrus silicet crucifigeretur et Paulus decollaretur? uidisses utique tunc turbas Iudaeorum et gentilium multitudines percutientes eos illudentes eis et spuentes in facies eorum ipsi uero quieti et tranquilli extiterunt sicut agni innocentes et mansueti. aduenientе autem terribili tempore consumationis eorum cum separarentur ab inuicem

4. MS *hululatus*.

weeping,[22] because in Ramah is heard a voice of wailing and shrieking—and not only of wailing and shrieking but of death and orphanage.[23]

These two terrible and bitter blows have come to us in one day.[24] Now is fulfilled in us what was said by Jacob the patriarch: "Joseph has already been lost, and Simeon has not returned."[25] Behold, indeed Peter, the foundation of the churches and the glory of the holy apostles, has departed from us and left us orphans. Paul also, the familiar comforter of the nations, has deprived us of a parent and is no more. In you has been fulfilled the word of David, who said, "They put out the carcasses of your servants as food for the birds of the sky and the flesh of your saints for the beasts of the earth."[26] Where are Paul's course and the labor of his holy feet? They have escaped chains, prisons, and the shackles of the stocks with their heavy bar. His diligent hands will no longer be given over to binding by iron chains. Where is his mouth speaking? And where is his tongue giving counsel? And where is his spirit that is so pleasing to his God?

4. Oh, my brother Timothy, let us hold a feast for him who does not need to defend his speech. Who would not mourn and wail, for [Peter and Paul] have earned glory and honor before God, because they were handed over to death like evildoers?[27] Oh, my brother Timothy, if you had seen the trials of their end, you certainly would have died from sadness and anguish. However, because you were not present, the struggle of their contest seems easy to you. Who would not weep in that hour, when the order of the sentence was carried out against them, so that Peter of course was crucified, and Paul was decapitated? You certainly would have seen then the uproar among the Jews and the crowds of unbelievers striking them, mocking them, and spitting in their faces. But they stood forth calm and tranquil, just like innocent and mild lambs.[28] When the terrible moment of their end had come, however, and they were separated from each other,

22. Joel 1:13.
23. Cf. Jer 31:15; Matt 2:18.
24. The author here reflects the tradition that Peter and Paul died on the same day.
25. Gen 42:36.
26. Ps 79:2.
27. 1 Pet 2:12.
28. Cf. Isa 53:7; Matt 10:16.

ligauerunt columnas mundi non utique absque fratrum gemitu et ploratu. tunc inquit Paulus Petro: pax tecum fundamentum ecclesiarum et pastor ouium et agnorum Christi.

Petrus autem ad Paulum inquit: uade inquit in pace praedicator bonorum mediator et dux salutis iustorum.

5. cum autem elongassent eos ab inuicem secutus sum magistrum meum Paulum non enim in eodem uico occiderunt eos. in hora autem illa tristitiae plena frater mi dilecte dicente carnifice Paulo collum parare tunc beatus apostolus suspexit in caelum muniens frontem et pectus suum signo crucis et dixit: Domine mi Iesu Christe in manus tuas commendo spiritum meum. et tunc absque tristitia et compulsione extendit collum et suscepit coronam.

6. uae mihi quoniam in illa hora intuitus sum corpus sanctum sanguine innocenti cruentum.

7. heu mihi pater mi spiritualis et magister et doctor. non quidem reus tali morte extitisti. nunc ergo quo ibo te quaerere gloria Christianorum et laus? quis conticescere fecit uocem tuam fistula altissona plectrum psalterii decachordi?[5] ubi te quaeram instructor meus? ubi te quaeram ac inueniam? o dux uere quid dicam discipulis tuis? dicam ne te captum aut uinculatum? aut quis eorum utilis erit tibi et mittam eum ad te? sed de caetero nemine nostrum indiges aut aliorum. nam introisti ad Deum tuum et Dominum quem desiderasti et toto affectu concupisti uae mihi quoniam manus illas

5. This phrase employs three Greek loan words: πλῆκτρον, ψαλτήριον, and δεκάχορδον.

then the soldiers bound the pillars of the world, and the brothers[29] left each other with groaning and weeping.

Then Paul said to Peter, "Peace to you, founder of the churches and shepherd of the sheep and lambs of Christ."[30]

Peter then said to Paul, "Go in peace, preacher of good tidings, mediator and chief of the salvation of the just."[31]

5. When they separated them from each other, I followed my master Paul, because they did not kill them in the same part of the city. In that hour there was great sadness, my beloved brother, when the executioner told Paul to prepare his neck. Then the blessed apostle looked up into heaven and strengthened his forehead and chest with the sign of the cross. He said, "My Lord Jesus Christ, into your hands I commit my spirit."[32] Then without sadness or compulsion he extended his neck and received his crown.

6. Woe is me, because in that hour I gazed upon the holy body stained with innocent blood![33]

7. Oh, my spiritual father and master and teacher, you were indeed not worthy of such a death. Now where will I go to look for you, oh glory and praise of the Christians? Who silenced your voice, oh greatest pipe and plectrum of the ten-stringed lyre? Where may I seek you, oh my teacher? Where may I seek and find you? Oh true leader, what should I say to your disciples? Should I not say that you were arrested and enchained? Or who among them will be useful to you, and should I send him to you? But from now on you have no need of us or of any others. You have gone to your God and Lord, whom you have sought and desired with all your heart.

---

29. The image of Peter and Paul as brothers appears in several of these martyrdom texts, reinforcing their unity in life and death.

30. John 21:15–17.

31. Roman tradition fixed the site of this final farewell on the Ostian Road, just south of the Gate of St. Paul. This prompted the founding of a small church, known as the Chapel of the Farewell, the Chapel of the Parting, or the Chapel of Saints Peter and Paul. A plaque on the church bore an inscription featuring the parting greetings from this text. Mussolini tore down the church, but the plaque can still be seen in the church of Santissima Trinita dei Pellegrini in the Piazza dei Pellegrini in Rome. See Mariano Armellini, *Le chiese di Roma dal secolo IV al XIX*, 2nd ed. (Rome: R.O.R.E., 1942), 2:1148–49.

32. Ps 31:5; Luke 23:46.

33. The Syriac version of this letter inserts here the story of the discovery of Paul's head during the time of Xystus (Sixtus). An alternative version of this same story appears below in §9.

innocentes cathenis duplicibus in Hierusalem ligatas in Roma dissoluerunt. Dauid propheta plangebat Absalon filium suum et dicebat: uae mihi pro te fili mi. uae mihi ego autem uae mihi pro te magister. uere uae mihi. amodo cessauit et deficit conuersus discipulorum tuorum Romam uenientium et quaerentium uos. iam nemo dicturus est: eamus et uideamus doctores et interrogemus eos qualiter regere nos oporteat ecclesias nobis commissas et interpretabuntur nobis praecepta Domini nostri Iesu Christi et eloquia prophetarum Hierusalem. et Roma praua amicitia aequales factae sunt in malo. Hierusalem crucifixit Dominum Iesum Christum: Roma uero apostolos eius interemit. Hierusalem autem seruit ei quem crucifixit. Roma autem sollemnisando glorificat quos interemit.

8. attende miraculum uide prodigium frater mi dilecte die uictimationis illorum nam praesto fui in tempore separationis illorum. post mortem autem illorum uidi eos inuicem manu ad manum intrantes portas urbis et indutos ueste luminis et coronis claritatis et lucis ornatos. non autem ego solus uidi sed Lemobia pedisequa serte regis quae discipula erat Pauli. et cum duceretur ad mortem martyrii Paulus et egrederetur ex urbe occurrit ei pedissequa illa flens cum lamento tunc dixit ei Paulus: noli flere sed da mihi uelum quo operitur caput tuum et statim tibi restituam. percutiente autem carnifice et amputante Pauli caput tunc beatissimus in ipso ictu explicuit uelum et collegit sanguinem proprium in uelo ligauitque uelum et obuoluit et tradidit illi feminae.

et conuerso carnifici militi dixit sancta Lemobia: ubi dimisisti magistrum meum Paulum?

respondit miles: cum socio enim iacet ibi extra urbem in ualle pugilum et uello tuo uelata est facies eius.

Woe is me, because they bound in double chains those innocent hands, and in Rome they freed them. David the prophet was bewailing his son Absalom, saying, "Woe is me on account of you, my son. Woe is me!"[34] But I say, woe is me on account of you, master. Truly, woe is me! From now on your disciples will no longer come and look for you in Rome. Now no one will say, "Let us go and see the teachers,[35] and let us ask them how we should oversee the churches that were commissioned to us. They will interpret for us the teachings of our Lord Jesus Christ and the oracles of the prophets." Jerusalem and Rome are made equals in evil in a hideous friendship: Jerusalem crucified the Lord Jesus Christ, and Rome slew his apostles. Jerusalem serves the one it crucified. Rome celebrates with a feast the ones it slew.[36]

8. Oh, beloved brother, listen to a miracle and behold a sign that occurred on the day of their sacrifice, for I was present at the time of their departure. After their deaths I saw them one after the other entering the gates of the city hand in hand, and I saw them dressed in garments of light and adorned with bright and radiant crowns. I was not the only one who saw this, but Lemobia, a handmaid in the service of the emperor and a disciple of Paul, also saw it.[37] When Paul was being led to a martyr's death and was leaving the city, he met this handmaid, who was weeping with sorrow. Then Paul said to her, "Do not weep, but give me the veil that is covering your head, and I will give it back to you immediately." After the executioner had struck and cut off the head of Paul, the most blessed man spread out the veil on the wound and collected his own blood with the veil. He then tied the veil, wrapped it, and gave it back to that woman.

When the executioner was returning, the holy Lemobia said to the soldier, "Where did you send my master Paul?"

The soldier responded, "He lies together with his friend there outside the city in the valley of the fighters,[38] and his face is covered with your veil."

34. 2 Sam 19:4.

35. The attention here shifts back to Paul and Peter together.

36. This is a reference to the June 29 joint feast of Peter and Paul.

37. Cf. Pseudo-Linus, *Mart. Paul* 14–17, where she is called Plautilla, and Acts Pet. Paul 80–84, where she is named Perpetua.

38. We cannot identify this location precisely, but a clue may come from the Syriac, Arabic, Armenian, and Ethiopic translations of this account. These versions employ terms that sound similar to each other but have no meaning in those languages: *Armeno* in Syriac, *Armanum* in Arabic, *Arerminon* in Armenian, and *Armaten or Armatul* in Ethiopic. It is possible that these forms are all taken from the Latin

ipsa autem respondens ait: ecce nunc intrauerunt Petrus et Paulus induti ueste praeclara et coronas fulgentes luce radiantes habebant in capitibus suis. et protulit uelum sanguine cruentatum et monstrauit eis. propter quod opus quamplures crediderunt in Domino et facti sunt Christiani.

9. et nunc frater mi Thimothee quos dilexisti et toto corde desiderabas Saul dico regem et Ionatam filium eius in uita sua non sunt separati nec in morte. et ego etiam non sum separatus a domino magistro meo nisi cum nos separauerunt homines iniqui et pessimi. et separatio haec huius horae non erit semper. anima eius cognoscit dilectos etiam si ne hoc quod ei loquantur qui tunc elongati sunt. in die autem resurrectionis iactura magna erit separari ab eis. sed uere uae his filiis frater mi qui priuati sunt patre spirituali quibus priuatus est grex. et nobis etiam frater uae qui priuati sumus magistris nostris spiritualibus qui collegerunt intellectum et scientiam ueteris ac nouae legis et colligauerunt in suis epistolis ex quibus unus dicebat: si in ecclesia non fuerit qui interpraetetur qui legit lector sileat.

However, she responded and said, "Behold, Peter and Paul have already entered, dressed in radiant garments, and they had on their heads shining crowns radiating light." And she took out the veil stained with blood and showed it to them. On account of this deed, very many believed in the Lord and became Christians.

9. And now, my brother Timothy, the ones whom you loved and longed for with all your heart are not separated in death, just as they were not separated in life—like king Saul and his son Jonathan.[39] I also was not separated from my lord and master, except when evil and wicked men separated us. The separation of this hour will not be forever. His spirit knows his beloved,[40] even if those who were separated at that time do not speak. On the day of the resurrection, however, it will be a great loss to be separated from them.[41] But truly, my brother, woe to these children[42] that were deprived of a spiritual father. This flock has been deprived. Woe even unto us, brother, who have been deprived of our spiritual masters, those who gathered the understanding and knowledge of the old and new law and bound them up in their epistles. One of them said, "If there is not in the assembly one who may interpret, then let the reader be silent."[43]

Armamentaria, a term used for the gladiatorial training facility (also known as the *Ludus Magnus*) located in a valley next to the Roman Coliseum. If this identification is correct, then the author of the epistle has made two mistakes. Domitian constructed the *Armamentaria* at the end of the first century CE in the valley between the Esquiline and Caelian hills, so it would not have existed at the time of Paul's death. Second, the *Armamentaria* was built in a location that had been within the city walls since the construction of the Servian Wall in the fourth century BCE. Thus, Paul in fact would not have been lying "outside the city." The chronological and spatial problems likely indicate a lack of familiarity with the layout of Rome. Even in an otherwise spurious text such as this, we might still expect an author familiar with Roman topography to get certain details right. See also Eva Margareta Steinby, ed., *Lexicon topographicum urbis Romae* (Rome: Quasar, 1996), 1.126; 3.196–97.

39. 2 Sam 1:23.

40. Cf. 2 Tim 2:19.

41. The argument seems to be that Peter and Paul will never be separated from each other or from their Lord. Therefore, if any are separated from the apostles on the day of resurrection, then they will necessarily be separated also from the Lord, which will be for them a great loss. It is possible, however, that the text is corrupt here, and another meaning is intended.

42. Literally, "sons," but the author is referring to Christians in general.

43. Cf. 1 Cor 14:27–28.

et nunc frater dilecte et amice spiritus mei Thimothee festina rogare Dominum oratione et ieiunio uigiliis et laboribus ut donet tibi Dei gratiam magistri tui sicut donauit Heliseo discipulo Heliae quando perdurauit cum eo et non recessit ab eo quandiu subleuauit eum in alto ab eo Deus. substinebat enim malitias impiorum et eos qui ex inuidia loquebantur ei dicentes: ecce discipulus pseudo prophetae et transgressoris legis. haec audiuit et in nullo diffusus est a magistro suo. et propter hoc adeptus est quod petebat geminum spiritum. et quamuis multos haberet Paulus discipulos in nullo tamen requieuit spiritus eius sicut in te qui substinuisti cum eo temptationes et tribulationes quas perpessus es cum laetifico affectu. uere tu solus dignus es carismata talia adipisci. notum sit tibi insuper quoniam gloriosum Petrum deposuerunt de ligno et caput eius corpori adhaerebat.

cum autem Paulum decollauerunt caput eius separauerunt a corpore proiicientes in uallem separatim a corpore et prae multitudine occisorum qui interfecti fuerunt in illa die disparuit et non fuit inuentum inter interfectos caput sancti Pauli in illa ualle. Christiani autem omnes sciebant quod caput sancti Pauli non erat inuentum. post multum autem temporis mandauit rex mundari fossam. et cum mundaretur proiectum est caput sancti Pauli cum aliis purgamentis. quidam autem pastor iuxta locum iter faciens leuauit illud in uirga sua et fixit iuxta caulas ouium suarum. uidit autem in eadem nocte super caput illud lucem et gloriam ineffabilem et hoc per tres noctes continuas uidit. et tunc ingressus urbem significauit domino suo quod uiderat. egressus autem dominus eius uidit ut pastor uiderat et cum festinatione nuntiauit Fabellio patriarchae[6] romano et omnibus presbyteris et principibus populi et egressi multi uiderunt et dixerunt inuicem: uere hoc est caput Pauli.

6. From the Greek πατριάρχης.

And now, my beloved brother and spiritual friend Timothy, make haste to seek the Lord with prayer and fasting, with vigils and great effort, so that he may give to you the grace of God that your master had, just as he gave the grace of Elijah to his disciple Elisha, when Elisha stayed with Elijah and did not depart until God took Elijah from him into heaven. Elisha also endured the attacks of the impious and those who out of envy said to him, "Behold the disciple of a false prophet and transgressor of the law." He heard these things but did not separate from his master. For this reason he obtained it, because he was seeking the same spirit.[44] In the same way Paul had many disciples, yet on none of them did his spirit rest as much as it did on you. You endured with him trials and tribulations, which you endured with a joyful heart. You alone are truly worthy to receive such charismatic gifts. May it be credited to you from above, since they hung glorious Peter on a cross, and his head remained with his body.

When they decapitated Paul, however, they separated his head from his body and threw it into a valley separate from the body. It disappeared among the multitude of the dead who had been killed on that day, and the head of holy Paul was not found among the killed in that valley. However, all the Christians knew that the head of holy Paul had not been found. After a long time, the emperor ordered a trench to be dug. When it was dug, the head of holy Paul was thrown in with the other remains. However, a certain shepherd making a journey near the place picked up the head on his staff and attached it next to the sheepfolds of his own sheep. On that same night he saw above that head a light and unspeakable glory, and he saw this three nights in a row. Then he entered the city and told his master what he had seen. His master went out and saw the same thing the shepherd had seen. Quickly he announced it to the Roman patriarch Fabellius[45] and to all the presbyters and leaders of the people. Many went out to see it, and they said the same thing: "Truly this is the head of Paul."

---

44. 2 Kgs 2:1–15. The source of the quotation about Elisha is unknown. There is no parallel in 2 Kgs, nor is there any reference to Elijah's being called a "false prophet and transgressor of law." The author of this text is most likely taking charges levied against Paul and retroactively applying them to Elijah, in order to strengthen the comparison between Elisha and Timothy.

45. This name is not among any list of Roman bishops. Sabellius was a third-century theologian in Rome, but he was condemned as a heretic and unlikely to be confused with a bishop.

egressus autem patriarcha cum turbarum multitudine portauerunt illud super mensam auream et attentabant ponere cum corpore Pauli sed patriarcha prohibuit dicens: nos scimus quod multi fideles occisi sunt in hac urbe et dispersa sunt in tempore illo membra eorum a gentibus et non sunt iuncta unde non audeo alterius caput corpori sancti Pauli adiungere sed exponamus corpus sancti Pauli et ponamus caput ad pedes corporis orantes et petentes misericordiam Dei ut si caput hoc abscissum est ab hoc corpore conuertatur corpus et iungatur capiti. et firmata est sententia haec ad arbitrium patriarchae et hoc ideo quod nihil dubietatis aut haesitationis occurrere poterat et fecerunt ut dixerat patriarcha et dum oraret uersum est corpus et adhesit capiti et coniunctum est in iunctura colli in locum suum et omnes qui uiderunt admirati sunt. dantes gloriam Deo et sciuerunt quod corpus erat Pauli immaculati qui fuit seruus et apostolus Domini nostri Iesu Christi quem decet gloria laus et cultus cum Patre et Spiritu Sancto nunc et semper et in saecula saeculorum.

The patriarch went out with a great multitude. They carried the head on a golden table and wanted to place it with the body of Paul, but the patriarch prohibited it, saying, "We know that many faithful people were killed in this city, and in that time their members were scattered by the unbelievers and not joined together. Thus, I do not dare to join the head to the body of holy Paul. Let us set out the body of holy Paul and place the head at the feet of the body. Then let us pray and seek the mercy of God, so that if this head was torn off this body, then the body will turn and be joined to the head." This idea, according to the judgment of the patriarch, was accepted, and there was no doubt or hesitation that the body would be able to go to meet the head. And they did as the patriarch had said. While he was praying, the body turned and joined to the head. It was connected to the joint of the neck in its proper place, and all who saw it were amazed and gave glory to God. They knew that it was the body of the immaculate Paul, who was a servant and apostle of our Lord Jesus Christ. To him be glory, praise, and adoration, with the Father and the Holy Spirit, now and always and forever and ever.

13. Teaching of Shimeon Kepha in the City of Rome

CANT 199 / *BHO* 936

Content

The text had opened with a summary of some stories from the Gospels and an account of the arrival of Peter, here called Shimeon Kepha, in Rome (chs. 1–5). In the midst of a sermon, where this translation begins, Shimeon turns his attention to Simon the sorcerer. He admonishes the crowd not to be fooled by Simon's deceptions; rather, they should bring him to a public competition, where the true worker of miracles will be identified by his ability to perform a sign. Some people go to Simon and invite him to this confrontation, confident that he can do anything he wants and will overcome Shimeon.

The body of a dead man happens to be passing, and the crowd decides that raising him will be the basis of the competition. Simon is granted the first opportunity but fails to raise the man, despite his many incantations. Shimeon approaches and immediately raises him in the name of Jesus Christ. The crowd declares that Peter's Christ is true and calls for Simon to be stoned. The sorcerer manages to escape the mob, and the entire city embraces Shimeon. The apostle is invited to live in the house of the young man he had raised from the dead. Through his preaching and continued deeds of power, many Jews and gentiles become disciples in Rome. He strengthens the church in Rome and throughout Italy and presides for twenty-five years.

Later Nero arrests Shimeon and puts him in prison. The apostle knows his death is imminent, so he ordains Ansus (probably Linus) to take his place as bishop and continue his teaching. When the emperor orders Shimeon to be crucified and Paul decapitated, the whole church rises up in protest at the loss of the apostles. The bishop takes the bodies away at

night and buries them, and this location becomes a place of meeting for the Christians.

Nero loses the kingdom as if by divine judgment, and the persecution quiets down for a time. The author closes with the comment that many years later there was a famine in Rome but offers no explanation of the significance of this event.

Literary Background

The majority of this text, as the title suggests, is dedicated to a lengthy sermon delivered by Peter in Rome after he arrives from Antioch. It is a summary of basic Christian doctrine and theology, including a brief account of the death of Jesus. At the point that our translation joins the narrative, Peter is turning his attention to Simon the sorcerer, and the conflict with Simon will ultimately lead to his martyrdom. This portion of the text may depend loosely on the lost Syriac translation of the Acts of Peter and the Syriac translation of the Pseudo-Clementine literature. In turn, this text was likely a source for the History of Shimeon Kepha the Chief of the Apostles (ch. 4 in this volume).[1]

The most promising indicators of date occur in Peter's sermon in sections prior to those translated here. Peter employs strong Trinitarian language and identifies Christ as the creator, not a creature, which signals a date after the dogmatic councils of the fourth century. Moreover, Peter's declaration that Christ "mixed his divinity with our humanity" suggests a Miaphysite author reacting to the christological controversies of the late fifth and early sixth centuries. A manuscript in the National Library of Russia in St. Petersburg has been dated to the sixth century. If this date is accurate, then it would establish the *terminus ante quem* for the text.

The author is unknown. The provenance is likely Syria or another region in the East, because Syriac was the original language of production, and the author espouses a Miaphysite Christology, which was typical of certain regions in the East after the Council of Chalcedon in 451 CE.

The martyrdom section translated here focuses on Shimeon's (Peter's) conflict with Simon the sorcerer, his triumphant preaching in the city of Rome, his establishment of the apostolic succession by ordaining his suc-

---

1. See the introduction to the History of Shimeon for a discussion of this dependence.

cessor, his execution by Nero, and the establishment of a joint cult site for the relics of Peter and Paul.

The Teaching of Shimeon Kepha in the City of Rome should not be confused with another text of a similar title, the Preaching of Peter (Kerygma Petrou), a product of the second half of the second century CE. In order to distinguish our text, the phrase "in the City of Rome" is typically included in its title.

Text

The text is witnessed by six manuscripts. The standard critical edition is by William Cureton and is the basis for the translation.

Select Bibliography

Baumstark, Anton. Pages 40–44 in *Die Petrus- und Paulusacten in der litterarischen Überlieferung der syrischen Kirche*. Leipzig: Harrassowitz, 1902.

Cureton, William, trans. "Doctrine of Simon Cephas in the City of Rome." Pages 35–41 and 173–77 in idem, *Ancient Syriac Documents: Relative to the Earliest Establishment of Christianity in Edessa and the Neighbouring Countries*. London: Williams & Norgate, 1864.

Haase, Felix. Page 205 in *Apostel und Evangelisten in den orientalischen Überlieferungen*. NTAbh 9.1–3. Münster: Aschendorff, 1922.

Hennecke, Edgar. "Doctrina Petri (syriaca)." Page 437 in vol. 2 of *New Testament Apocrypha*. Edited by Edgar Henncke and Wilhelm Schneemelcher. English trans. edited by R. McL. Wilson. 5th ed. Louisville: Westminster John Knox, 1993.

Lipsius, Richard A. Pages 2.1:206–7 in *Die apokryphen Apostelgeschichten und Apostellegenden*. Braunschweig: Schwetschke, 1887.

Peeters, Paul. "Notes sur la légende des apôtres S. Pierre et S. Paul dans la littérature syrienne." *AnBoll* 21 (1902): 121–40.

Pratten, Benjamin P., trans. "The Teaching of Simon Cephas in the City of Rome." *ANF* 8:673–75.

ܡܣܗܕܘܬܗ ܕܫܡܥܘܢ ܟܐܦܐ

6. ܠܐ ܢܛܥܝܢܟܘܢ ܫܡܥܘܢ ܚܪܫܐ ܒܕܓܠܘ̈ܬܐ ܕܡܚܘܐ ܠܟܘܢ ܕܠܐ ܒܟܕܐ ܐܝܟ ܕܠܐܢܫܐ ܘܠܐ ܗܘܝܐ. ܘܠܐ ܚܕܟܘܢ
ܕܢܦܪܫܘܢ ܡܕܡ ܕܚܙܝܢ ܘܫܡܥܝܢ. ܚܕܪܘ ܗܘ ܡܟܝܠ ܐܬܘ ܘܚܙܘ ܐܚ̈ܐ ܕܟܢܫܐ ܡܠܟܗ ܡܕܝܢܬܟܘܢ. ܘܓܠܘ ܠܟܘܢ
ܐܬܐ ܡܕܡ ܕܢܚܒ ܡܕܡܥܟܘܢ. ܗܘܘ ܐܢܫܐ ܕܚܙܝܢ ܐܢܬܘܢ ܕܥܕܟ ܟܢܘ ܟܠܗܘܢ ܐܬܐ ܕܡܠܟܘܢ ܗܘ ܕܐܬܡܗܝܢ ܒܗ.
7. ܘܒܚܕ ܒܫܒܬܐ. ܚܕܪ ܐܬܟܢܫܘ ܗܘܘ ܠܫܡܥܘܢ ܚܪܫܐ. ܘܐܡܪܘ ܗܘܘ ܠܗ ܐܢܫܐ ܟ̈ܢܫܐ ܕܟܢܫܘ.
ܐܝܟ ܓܒܪܐ ܕܐܫܬܟܚ ܒܟܠ. ܘܐܝܬ ܒܗ ܚܝܠܐ ܕܠܟܠܡܕܡ ܐܚܝܕ. ܟܕ ܐܬܐ ܡܕܡ ܩܕܡ ܟܘܠ. ܘܚܙܐ ܗܘܐ
ܫܡܥܘܢ ܓܠܓܠܬܐ ܕܡܥܒܪ ܠܫܡܝܐ.
8. ܘܟܕ ܗܟܢܐ ܐܡܪܝܢ ܗܘܘ ܠܗ ܐܫܬܡܠܠ ܠܒܪ ܗܘܐ ܫܥܬܐ ܚܕ ܒܪܗ ܕܚܕ ܡܢ ܪ̈ܫܐ ܘܕܝ̈ܢܐ ܘܫ̈ܠܝܛܢܐ
ܕܒܗܘܢ. ܘܐܡܪܘ ܗܘܘ ܠܗ ܥܠܘܗܝ ܟܕ ܚܫܝܫ ܗܘܐ. ܘܐܢܫܐ ܡܢܗܘܢ ܕܢܚܐ ܠܗ ܒܗܝ ܫܥܬܐ. ܗܘ ܗܘ ܫܪܪ
ܘܩܘܝܡ ܘܡܫܬܡܠܠ. ܘܟܬܪܘ ܐܪܟܢ ܡܢ ܒܟܠܡܕܡ ܕܐܡܪ ܠܝ. ܘܐܡܪܘ ܗܘܘ ܠܗ ܠܫܡܥܘܢ ܚܪܫܐ
ܡܛܠ ܕܐܝܬ ܗܘ ܩܕܡ ܐܝܬ ܠܫܡܥܘܢ ܓܠܓܠܬܐ ܗܘܪܒܐ. ܘܟܕ ܗܘ ܚܕܝܢ ܡܕܡܘܗܝ. ܐܝܬ ܗܘܐ ܚܝܠܐ ܕܒܗ
ܟܕ ܡܕܡܠܬ. ܫܡܥܘܢ ܕܝܢ ܢܛܠܝܬ ܡܪܟ ܗܘܐ ܐܪ̈ܙܘܗܝ ܕܡܫܬܐ ܘܫܡܫܘܗܝ ܗܘܘ ܠܟܪ̈ܗܐ ܡܕܡܘܗܝ. ܘܢܣܒ
ܗܘܐ ܠܟܡܫܐ ܘܠܟܡܫܠܐ. ܘܫܡܫܐ ܡܬܟܒܐ ܗܘܐ. ܟܕ ܐܡܪ ܗܘܐ ܩ̈ܠܐ ܡܫܬܐܠܐ. ܡܫܘܡ ܕܝܢ ܒܫܒܬܐ ܐܡܪ ܗܘܐ.
ܘܡܫܘܡ ܒܫܡܫܐ ܘܠܐ ܡܕܠܐ. ܘܐܓܪ ܗܘܐ ܓܘܪܐ ܡܫܓܠܐ ܘܡܕܡ ܠܐ ܗܘܐ ܗܘܐ ܘܠܐ ܐܫܬܟܪ. ܘܫܥܬܐ ܗܘ ܒܟܪ̈ܗܘ
ܪ̈ܡܐ ܗܘܐ.
9. ܘܒܬܪ ܒܫܒܬܐ ܩܪܐ ܗܘܐ ܫܡܥܘܢ ܟܐܦܐ ܠܐܚܘ̈ܬܐ ܠܘܬܗ ܕܫܥܬܐ ܗܘ. ܘܩܐܡ ܗܘܐ ܩܕܡ ܟܠܗ
ܟܢܫܐ ܕܩܐܡ ܗܘܐ ܠܐܡܝ. ܒܫܡܗ ܕܝܫܘܥ ܡܫܝܚܐ ܗܘ ܕܪܟܒ ܗܘܘ ܩܕܝܫ̈ܐ ܠܐܘܪܫܠܡ ܘܐܚܝ ܡܫܡܫܢܝ

6. "Do not let Simon the sorcerer deceive you with the apparent deeds that he shows you but are not real, as though you were people without understanding who do not know how to discern what they see and hear. Therefore, send and summon him to where your entire city is gathered. Choose for yourselves some sign for us to perform in your presence. Whichever one you see performing that sign, it will be up to you to believe in him."

7. In that hour they sent and summoned Simon the sorcerer, and the men who followed his teaching said to him, "Because you are a man who we believe has the power to do anything, perform some sign in front of us all, and this Shimeon the Galilean, who preaches Christ, will see it."

8. As they were saying this to him, a dead man happened to be passing by, the son of one of the leaders who was well known and famous among them. All those who were gathered said to him, "Whichever one of you restores this dead man to life, he is true and to be believed and accepted, and we will all follow him in everything that he says to us."

And they said to Simon the sorcerer, "Because you were here before Shimeon the Galilean, and we knew you before him, you show the power that is in you first." But Simon reluctantly drew near to the dead man, and they set down the bier in front of him. He looked to the right and the left and gazed up into heaven. He then spoke many words—some of them he said aloud, and some of them secretly and not aloud. He waited for a long time, but nothing happened and nothing was done, and the dead man kept lying on his bier.[1]

9. At that moment Shimeon Kepha confidently drew near to that dead man and cried out in front of the entire crowd that was standing there, "In the name of Jesus Christ, whom the Jews crucified in Jerusalem and in

1. In other accounts of a similar story, Simon initially seems to make the dead man move, and the crowd thinks he has brought him back to life. See e.g., Pseudo-Abdias, *Pass. Pet.* 16.

ܣܡ ܠܗ. ܩܘܡ ܡܢ ܬܡܢ. ܘܚܙܘ ܕܡܠܠܗ ܕܩܕܡܘܗܝ ܚܙܐ ܗܘܐ ܡܫܡܫܬܐ ܗܘ ܩܘܡ ܗܘܐ ܡܢ ܒܝܬܐ. ܘܚܕܐ ܡܠܗ ܒܥܠ ܘܐܬܕܡܪ. ܘܐܡܪܘ ܗܘܘ ܠܗ ܠܫܡܥܘܢ. ܕܗܪܟ ܗܘ ܡܫܝܚܐ ܕܡܒܪܢ ܐܢܬ ܠܗ ܘܩܘܡ ܫܠܝܚܐ ܘܐܡܪܘ. ܬܠܡܝܕܝ ܫܡܥܘܢ ܣܢܐ ܘܡܬܚܝܠܐ ܕܟܠ. ܫܡܥܘܢ ܕܝܢ ܒܥܠܕܒܒܐ ܘܪܘܓܙܐ ܗܘܐ ܠܗ ܟܠܗ ܘܢܝܚܐ ܠܡܫܡܥܬܐ ܗܘ ܕܢܝܚܐ. ܦܠܛ ܗܘܐ ܡܢܗܘܢ ܡܢ ܗܘܠܐ ܠܡܕܝܢܬܐ ܘܡܢ ܕܪܬܐ ܠܕܪܬܐ ܘܠܐ ܫܒܩ ܗܘܐ ܠܬܠܡܝܕܘܗܝ ܒܗܘ ܡܘܡܠ.

10. ܡܕܝܢܬܐ ܕܝܢ ܟܠܗ ܐܣܝܪܐ ܗܘܬ ܠܫܡܥܘܢ ܒܟܠ ܘܡܬܒܠܒܠܝܢ ܗܘܘ ܣܓܝܐܐ ܘܡܬܚܠܚܠܝܢ. ܟܕ ܡܢ ܐܬܪܐ ܘܠܐܬܪܬܐ ܠܐ ܫܠܐ ܗܘܐ ܕܢܬܒ ܒܡܕܝܢܬܐ ܕܡܫܝܚܐ. ܘܡܬܬܟܝܢ ܗܘܘ ܒܗ ܫܠܝܚܐ. ܘܡܦܪܢܣ ܕܝܢ ܐܚܘܗܝ ܕܗܘ ܕܢܝܚܐ ܗܘܐ ܐܘܟܠܗ ܗܘܐ ܒܥܕܗ ܠܫܡܥܘܢ، ܒܟܠ ܠܒܠܗ ܘܡܚܠܗ ܗܘܐ ܐܟܢ ܕܪܘܚ. ܟܕ ܡܬܡܢܝܢ ܗܘܐ ܗܘ ܘܒܢܝ ܒܠܗ ܡܠܗܘܢ، ܒܫܡܫܐ ܕܒܪܗ ܗܘ ܕܐܠܗܐ ܚܝܐ. ܘܐܬܬܠܡܕܘ ܗܘܘ ܠܗܢ ܫܠܝܚܐ ܡܢ ܡܗܘܝܐ ܘܡܢܐܠ. ܘܟܕ ܫܡܥܬ ܗܘܬ ܚܝܘܬܐ ܒܡܠܟܘܬܗ ܒܠ ܗܘܐ ܠܗܢ ܒܢܬܐ ܒܪܗܘܡܐ ܘܒܩܕܝܫܬܐ ܘܚܝܘܬܗ ܘܡܗܝܡܢܘܬܐ ܠܟܠܗܘܢ ܕܒܢܝ ܐܠܗܐ ܘܫܡܫ ܗܘܐ ܠܗܢ ܕܪܕܝܐ ܕܡܕܒܪܢܘܬܐ ܕܦܩܘܕܐ ܒܫܪܝܪ ܘܫܡܫ ܫܢܝܢ.

11. ܘܡܢ ܒܬܪ ܗܠܝܢ ܫܢܝܐ ܠܒܥܘܬܐ ܗܘܐ ܢܘܪܝ ܩܣܪ. ܘܫܒܩܗ ܗܘܐ ܒܝܕ ܐܚܪܢܐ. ܘܫܪܐ ܗܘܐ ܕܢܦܩ ܗܘܐ ܠܗ. ܘܩܪܐ ܗܘܐ ܠܐܢܫܘܗ ܡܩܡܩܡܐ ܘܥܒܕܗ ܗܘܐ ܐܦܣܩܘܦܐ[1] ܣܠܩܘܗܝ ܒܪܗܘܡܐ. ܘܗܘܝ ܗܠܝܢ ܐܡܪ ܗܘܐ

1. From the Greek ἐπίσκοπος.

whom we believe, rise up from there!" At the word of Shimeon the dead man came back to life and got up from the bier.

All the people saw and were amazed, and they said to Shimeon, "The Christ whom you preach is true."

And many cried out and said, "Let Simon, the sorcerer and deceiver of us all, be stoned!" But because everyone was running to see the dead man who was now alive, Simon escaped them by going street-to-street and courtyard-to-courtyard, and he did not fall into their hands on that day.

10. But the entire city took Shimeon Kepha and received him gladly and affectionately. When he did not cease doing signs and wonders in the name of Christ, many believed in him. Cuprinus, the father of the one who was alive again, brought Shimeon Kepha with him into his house and received him as it was proper. Then he and all the children of his house believed in Christ, that he is the Son of the living God. Many Jews and gentiles there became disciples.[2] There was great rejoicing in his teaching, and he built up the church there in Rome, in the cities around it, and in all the villages of the people of Italy. And he served there as the overseer of the Mass for twenty-five years.[3]

11. After these years Nero Caesar seized him and put him in prison. Shimeon knew that Nero would crucify him, and he called Ansus[4] the deacon and made him bishop of Rome in his place.[5] Shimeon said these and other things that were his own [teachings].[6] He also ordered that

2. Cf. Peter's role in the salvation of the household of Cornelius and other gentiles in Acts 10:1–11:18.

3. This is a way of identifying him as the bishop.

4. From other accounts we know that this figure should be Linus. The initial *lamadh* can signify the direct object, but here it is part of the name. The copyist seems confused by the distinction and is inconsistent in his rendering of the name. See William Cureton, *Ancient Syriac Documents: Relative to the Earliest Establishment of Christianity in Edessa and the Neighbouring Countries* (London: Williams & Norgate, 1864), 176.

5. This passage has close parallels to Hist. Shim. 33. The ordination of Linus by Peter is also recounted in the Liberian Catalog from 354 CE (*Chronica minora saec. IV. V. VI.VII.*, ed. T. Mommsen, MGH.AA 9 [Berlin: Weidmann, 1892], 73); Irenaeus (*Haer.* 3.3.3)—although Irenaeus states that Peter and Paul together ordained Linus; and Eusebius (*Hist. eccl.* 5.6.1). Cf. Pseudo-Abdias, *Pass. Pet.* 15; the apocryphal Epistle of Clement to James 2; and Tertullian, *Praescr.* 32, where Clement is identified as the one ordained by Peter as the second bishop of Rome.

6. The Syriac is obscure here.

ܗܘ ܫܡܥܘܢ ܘܡܛܪܐ ܠܘܬ ܐܦ ܐܢܬܝܬܐ ܕܐܝܟ ܪ̈ܘܫ ܠܗ ܦܩܕܗ ܗܘܐ ܠܐܝܫܘܥ ܕܗܘܐ ܡܠܟ ܩܕܡ ܥܡܐ ܟܕ ܐܡܪ
ܗܘܐ ܠܗ ܕܟܠ ܕܢܬܠ ܚܝܠܐ ܘܥܠܬܝܬܐ. ܠܐ ܗܘܐ ܡܬܚܙܐ ܩܕܡ ܥܡܐ ܡܢܩ ܐܚܪܢܐ ܕܠܐ ܪܕܩ.

12. ܟܕ ܕܝܢ ܦܛܪ ܗܘܐ ܫܡܥܘܢ ܕܦܪܚ ܗܘܐ ܫܡܥܘܢ ܠܥܠ ܪܗܛ ܐܝܟ ܕܗܘ ܦܪܚ ܗܘܐ ܡܢ ܫܡܝܐ ܘܕܢܚܬܘܢܝܗܝ
ܗܘܐ ܪܗܛ ܕܦܪܚܘܗܝ. ܗܘܐ ܗܘܐ ܦܪܘܣܐ ܫܡܝܐ ܠܥܡܐ ܘܥܡܐ ܡܪܢܝܬܐ ܒܥܠܡܐ ܟܝܬܐ. ܐܝܟ ܕܐܬܦܠܓܘ
ܗܘܘ ܡܢ ܚܝܠܐ ܕܫܡܝܐ. ܘܩܡ ܗܘܐ ܐܝܫܘܥ ܡܕܒܪܢܐ ܘܩܫܫ ܗܘܐ ܦܛܪܘܣ ܒܥܠܡܐ. ܘܩܒܪ ܗܘܐ ܐܢܘܢ ܒܐܝܩܪܐ
ܪܒܐ ܘܗܘܐ ܗܘܐ ܠܐܡܝܢ ܒܫܡܗ ܪܘܚܐ ܠܟܢܫܐ.

13. ܘܒܗ ܒܝܘܡܐ ܗܘ ܐܝܟ ܕܡܢ ܕܢܐ ܕܒܝܬܐ ܡܠܟ ܗܘܐ ܢܪܘܢ ܡܠܟܘܬܗ ܘܒܪܗ. ܘܗܘܘ ܡܠܟܐ ܡܠܟܐ ܡܢ
ܪܘܡܝܐ ܕܐܝܟܢ ܗܘܐ ܠܟܢܫܗܘܢ ܢܪܘܢ ܫܡܥ. ܘܡܢ ܟܠܗ ܫܢܝܐ ܫܠܝܚܐ ܕܡܠܟܘܬܗܘܢ ܪܒܐ ܕܩܕܝܫܐ ܕܝܫܘܥ ܗܘܘ
ܡܢ ܠܥܠܡܐ ܟܕ ܪܘܚܐ ܗܘܐ ܐܝܟܐ ܕܒܥܘܬܗܘܢ ܒܫܠܡܐ ܪܘܚܐ ܘܒܫܠܡܐ ܐܠܗܐ. ܫܠܡ ܕܝܢ ܘܗܘܘ ܗܘܐ ܒܫܢܐ
ܪܒܐ ܒܪܘܚܐ ܡܫܝܚܐ.

14. ܫܠܡܬ ܡܠܟܘܬܗ ܕܫܡܥܘܢ ܟܐܦܐ.

Ansus should teach before the people, saying to him, "Alongside the New Testament and the Old, let nothing else that is not right be read in front of the people."[7]

12. But when Caesar ordered that Shimeon be crucified head downward, as he himself had requested from Caesar, and that the head of Paul be cut off, there was a great commotion among the people and bitter distress in the whole church, because they were deprived of the presence of the apostles. Ansus the bishop arose and took their bodies by night and buried them with great honor, and that place became a meeting house for many.[8]

13. In that time, as if by a judgment of justice, Nero left his kingdom and fled. There was a brief respite from the persecution that Nero Caesar had stirred up against them. Many years after the great crowning of the apostles, who had left the world, while the handing down of their priesthood was continuing in all of Rome and all of Italy,[9] it happened that there was a great famine in the city of Rome.[10]

14. Here ends the teaching of Shimeon Kepha.

---

7. Shimeon is forbidding the reading of unapproved, extrabiblical texts. The language here is clearly anachronistic, for there was no "New Testament" in Peter's time.

8. This may be a reference to the joint apostolic cult site on the Appian Road. See David L. Eastman, *Paul the Martyr: The Cult of the Apostle in the Latin West*, WGRW-Sup 4 (Atlanta: Society of Biblical Literature, 2011), 71–114.

9. This likely refers to the passing on of episcopal authority through the laying on of hands.

10. Famines were a common occurrence in antiquity. See e.g. Peter Garnsey, *Famine and Food Supply in the Graeco-Roman World* (Cambridge: Cambridge University Press, 1988); Bruce Winter, "Acts and Food Shortages," *BIFCS* 2:59–78; Kenneth S. Gapp, "The Universal Famine under Claudius," *HTR* 28.4 (1935), 258–65.

14. Doctrine of the Apostles

BHO 81–82

Content

In the sections prior to what is translated here, the author asserts that after the events of Pentecost, the apostles put in place certain regulations concerning worship, the church calendar, the roles and qualifications of church leaders, and various other issues. Then follows a gazetteer of apostolic missions. Different regions from Britain to India are described as having received "the apostles' hand of priesthood" from certain apostles, probably a reference to the ordination of bishops through the laying on of hands.

The final section of the text refers to the apostolic deaths. The author specifies that Luke reported the deeds of the apostles in Acts and handed these things down through Aquila and Prisca (Priscilla), two of the traditional missionary partners of the apostle Paul. They remained with Luke until his death, just as several of Paul's disciples had done with him all the way to Rome. The text then makes a sudden turn to Peter (Shimeon Kepha) and states that Nero killed him with the sword in Rome.

Literary Background

The Doctrine of the Apostles survives in three known manuscripts in the British Library, with the earliest dating from the fifth or sixth century: Add. 14644 (fifth/sixth cent.), Add. 14531 (seventh/eighth cent.), and Add. 17193 (874 CE). William Cureton had planned to publish an introduction to accompany his edition and translation of the text, but his death left this work undone. Benjamin P. Pratten, extrapolating from notes left by Cureton, includes this text in his *Syriac Documents Attributed to the*

First Three Centuries,[1] but there is no reason for suggesting a date so much earlier than the manuscript evidence supports.[2] With regard to author and provenance, Ms. Add. 14644 credits it to the apostle Addeus, who is said to have been active in the regions of Edessa and Mesopotamia. This Syriac text likely was produced in the Christian East, but the ascription to a first-century apostle is specious.

This text is an example of a church order document, of which we have several from early Christianity with similar names, e.g., the Didache (Teaching of the Twelve Apostles) from the late first or early second century and the third-century Teaching of the Apostles (Didascalia apostolorum). The latter is also preserved in Syriac but was translated from a lost Greek original. In order to distinguish it from our text, we have adopted the title The Doctrine of the Apostles.[3]

The Doctrine of the Apostles notably also includes the gazetteer. This section of the text depends on earlier such lists recounting the missionary fields of the apostles. In Eusebius of Caesarea's *Ecclesiastical History*, he cites Origen as providing a brief list in his *Commentary on Genesis*.[4] In other cases these lists are associated with the "seventy (or seventy-two) apostles" mentioned in Luke 10:1. On the Seventy Apostles of Christ is a text falsely ascribed to Hippolytus of Rome that seeks to recount the missionary activities of this broader group of apostles, rather than just the core twelve. Another work entitled the Acts of the Seventy Apostles was once credited to Dorotheus of Tyre but has been shown to be a work of pseudepigraphy. These examples attest to the interest among early Christians to establish what happened to the apostles and how the gospel came to various regions of the world. The Doctrine of the Apostles fits squarely within this tradition.

Of primary interest in all such lists are the two greatest apostles, Paul and Peter, and their stories are the focus of the final lines of the text. However, here we find an interesting variation in the text. The author brings Paul

1. Benjamin P. Pratton, *Syriac Documents Attributed to the First Three Centuries* (Edinburgh: T&T Clark, 1871). N.B.: Pratten incorrectly lists Add. 17193 as Add. 14173.

2. The text was later cited by John of Damascus (eighth century) and Bar Hebraeus (twelfth/thirteenth century).

3. Other titles in manuscripts include "The Canons of the Rites and Laws that the Apostles Established" and "The Canons of the Apostles."

4. Eusebius of Caesarea, *Hist. eccl.* 3.1, citing a section from Origen (*Comm. Gen.* 3) that is not extant. This is text 16 in chapter 15 of this volume.

to Rome to face Emperor Nero and does not finish the story, but instead states that Nero killed Peter (Shimeon Kepha) with the sword. This is obviously a divergence from the dominant tradition that is attested throughout this volume. Paul is the one killed by the sword, and Peter dies by crucifixion. I have described this elsewhere as "Apostolic Confusion,"[5] in which the traditions about Peter and Paul are mixed and/or inverted. It is not surprising that the death of Peter would be emphasized in relation to Rome, because earlier in the text the author claims, "The city of Rome and all of Italy, Spain, Britain, and Gaul, along with the rest of the countries around them, received the apostles' ordination to the priesthood from Shimeon Kepha, who went there from Antioch. He was the ruler and leader in the church that he built there and in the regions around it" (Doct. Apost. 35). Shimeon Kepha, not Paul, was the primary founder of the Roman church, yet it is still surprising to find Peter being killed in the Pauline fashion.

In the history of transmission, one scribe sought to correct this. In British Library Add. 17193, the scribe adds the phrase "crucifying him on a cross." Thus, the final line in that manuscript reads: "And Nero Caesar killed him [i.e., Paul] with a sword and Shimeon Kepha, crucifying him on a cross in the city of Rome." This correction also requires the insertion of an implied *Waw* ("and"), which is not in the text, yet the end result is to bring this account into line with the dominant apostolic traditions. In his English translation of this text, William Cureton introduces his own editorial change. He correctly omits the reference to the crucifixion in his critical edition and translation, but he also inserts the absent *Waw* ("and"), thus yielding: "And Nero the Emperor slew him [Paul] with the sword, and Simon Cephas, in the city of Rome."[6] Inserting the comma after "sword" creates the impression that the reference to death by the sword should apply only to what comes before—the reference to Paul. The mention of Shimeon Kepha is somehow a new topic, and Peter's method of death simply goes unstated, rather than stated in a nontraditional way. Cureton's

5. David L. Eastman, "Confused Traditions? Peter and Paul in the Apocryphal Acts," in *Forbidden Texts on the Western Frontier: Christian Apocrypha in North American Perspectives*, edited by Tony Burke and Brent E. Landau, Eugene, OR: Cascade, forthcoming.

6. William Cureton, trans., "The Doctrine of the Apostles," in idem, *Ancient Syriac Documents: Relative to the Earliest Establishment of Christianity in Edessa and the Neighbouring Countries* (London: Williams & Norgate, 1864), 35.

translation therefore agrees with tradition but does not accurately reflect the Syriac text.

Overall, then, this text displays both dependence on earlier sources and unique characteristics.

Text

The manuscripts cited above are the basis for the edition by William Cureton on which the translation is based.

Select Bibliography

Cureton, William, trans. "The Doctrine of the Apostles." Pages 24–35 and 166–73 in idem, *Ancient Syriac Documents: Relative to the Earliest Establishment of Christianity in Edessa and the Neighbouring Countries*. London: Williams & Norgate, 1864.

Lagarde, A. P. de, ed. Pages 32–44 in *Reliquiae iuris ecclesiastici antiquissimae syriace*. Vienna: Teubner, 1856.

Peeters, Paul. "Notes sur la légende des apôtres S. Pierre et S. Paul dans la littérature syrienne." *AnBoll* 21 (1902): 121–40.

Pratten, Benjamin P., trans. "The Teaching of the Apostles." Pages 35–49 in *Syriac Documents Attributed to the First Three Centuries*. Edinburgh: T&T Clark, 1871.

ܡܟܬܒܢܘܬܐ ܕܡܫܝܚܐ

40. ܒܬܪ ܕܝܢ ܐܘܢܓܠܣܛܐ[1] ܗܘܐ ܠܗ ܒܡܟܬܒܢܘܬܐ ܗܕܐ ܘܟܠܗ ܗܘܐ ܢܓܝܪܐ ܕܣܘܥܪܢܘܗܝ ܕܡܫܝܚܐ
ܘܛܟܣܐ[2] ܘܢܡܘܣܐ[3] ܕܐܠܗܘܬܐ ܕܒܡܘܠܕܗ. ܘܐܝܟܢܐ ܕܐܦ ܠܐ ܗܘܐ ܚܕ ܚܕ ܡܢܗܘܢ ܒܡܟܬܒܢܘܬܗ ܡܡܠܠ
ܕܒܬܪ ܗܠܝܢ ܘܕܡܫܝܚܐ ܡܢ ܗܠܝܢ ܟܠܗ ܗܘܐ ܘܟܢ ܟܕ ܦܪܨܘܦܘܗ ܘܐܟܬܒܘܗ ܠܟܢܘܫܝܗܘܢ. ܘܟܠܗܘܢ
ܗܘܘ ܠܗ ܒܝܕܐ ܒܬܪܐ ܕܫܘܪܝܗ ܐܝܟ ܕܟܕ ܗܘܐ ܒܟܠܟܠܗ ܢܦܩܘܢ ܘܐܪܥܐ ܕܡܢ ܒܛܘܦܣܐ.

1. From the Greek εὐαγγελιστής.
2. From the Greek τάξις.
3. From the Greek νόμος.

40. But Luke the evangelist took care to write down the heroic deeds of the Acts of the Apostles, the rules and laws of the ministry of their priesthood, and where each one of them went. Thus, with care Luke wrote these things and more than these, and he placed them in the hand of Priscus and Aquilus,[1] his disciples. They accompanied him until the day of his death, just as Timothy and Erastus of Lystra[2] and Menaeus,[3] the first disciple of the apostles,[4] had accompanied Paul until he went up to the city of Rome,

1. Aquila and Prisca (Priscilla in Acts) were a husband and wife team that partnered with Paul at several points (Acts 18:2–3, 18–19, 24–26; Rom 16:3–5; 1 Cor 16:19; 2 Tim 4:19). The traditional connection between Paul and Luke probably accounts for the claim that they were Luke's disciples. The Syriac author has modeled the masculine name Aquilus on the Greek form Ἀκύλας, rather than on the Latin *Aquila*. Notably, the name Priscus involves changing the feminine name Πρίσκα/Πρίσκιλλα (Prisca/Priscilla in the Vulgate) to a more typically masculine form (Priscus in Latin). It would appear, therefore, that the Syriac author thinks, or wants us to believe, that both of these important early figures were male. Cf. the sixth-century Palestinian Aramaic text of 1 Cor 16:19 in the Codex Climaci Rescriptus, which gives the names as Aq(u)ilus and Prisca (ܐܩܝܠܘܣ ܘ ܦܪܝܣܩܐ). See Christa Müller-Kessler and Michael Sokoloff, eds., *A Corpus of Christian Palestinian Aramaic* (Groningen: Styx, 1998), IIB:87.

2. Timothy and Erastus are mentioned together in Acts 19:22. According to Acts 16:1, Timothy was from Lystra. A certain Erastus is sent to Macedonia with Timothy (Acts 19:22), but Erastus's place of origin is never specified. This is almost certainly not meant to be the Corinthian city official in Rom 16:23. A third mention of an Erastus (2 Tim 4:20) could be either of these figures, or neither.

3. Cureton (*Ancient Syriac Documents*, 173) suggests the name should be Manaen, who is mentioned in Acts 13:1 as a member of the community in Antioch. A figure named Menaeus is not known in the New Testament, which would make his designation as the "first disciple" peculiar.

4. The scribe has perhaps mistakenly placed the *seyame* (plural indicator) over "apostle" instead of "disciple." If the *seyame* were moved over "disciple," then these three figures would be collectively and more logically identified as "the first disciples of the apostle."

ܘܩܒܠܘܗ̇ ܠܦܓܪܐ ܩܕܝܫܐ ܕܫܠܝܚܐ ܒܝܕܐ ܕܗܠܟ ܒܪܗܘܡܐ ܡܕܝܢܬܐ. ܕܐܝܬ ܗܘܐ ܒܗܘܢ ܠܪܗܛܘ
ܪܗܛܪܐ.[4] ܘܫܡܗ ܗܘܐ ܢܪܘܢ ܗܢܐ ܒܫܢܬܐ ܠܗ ܠܡܫܬܗ ܒܬܪ ܒܪܗܘܡܐ ܡܕܝܢܬܐ܀

4. From the Greek ῥήτωρ.

because he stood up against Tertullus the orator.[5] And Nero Caesar killed Shimeon Kepha with a sword in the city of Rome.[6]

5. The term orater (ῥήτωρ) is the same term used to describe the Tertullus hired by the Jewish religious authorities to accuse Paul before Felix in Caesarea Maritima (Acts 24:1–9). Cf. Hist. Paul 10, where Tertullus is described as a prefect (also with a Greek loan word, ὕπαρχος).

6. On the author's confusion (or at least conflation) of the apostolic deaths, see Eastman, "Confused Traditions?"

Part 4. Patristic Literature

15. Early Christian and Patristic References to the Deaths of Peter and Paul

The martyrdom accounts of the apostles are not the only references to these events in early Christian literature. As early as the end of the first century CE, other authors refer to these events, even if only obliquely at first. In the patristic period such references become more common and explicit as the legacy of apostolic martyrdom is evoked in various contexts and for various reasons.[1] This chapter presents a broad selection of the most significant examples, without making any claims to being exhaustive.

1. See, e.g., George E. Demacopoulous, *The Invention of Peter: Apostolic Discourse and Papal Authority in Late Antiquity*, Divinations: Rereading Late Ancient Religion (Philadelphia: University of Pennsylvania Press, 2013); Marcus Bockmuehl, *Simon Peter in Scripture and Memory: The New Testament Apostle in the Early Church* (Grand Rapids: Baker Academic, 2012); David L. Eastman, *Paul the Martyr: The Cult of the Apostle in the Latin West*, WGRWSup 4 (Atlanta: Society of Biblical Literature, 2011).

1. 1 Clement 5.1–7[1]

ἀλλ' ἵνα τῶν ἀρχαίων ὑποδειγμάτων παυσώμεθα, ἔλθωμεν ἐπὶ τοὺς ἔγγιστα γενομένους ἀθλητάς· λάβωμεν τῆς γενεᾶς ἡμῶν τὰ γενναῖα ὑποδείγματα. διὰ ζῆλον καὶ φθόνον οἱ μέγιστοι καὶ δικαιότατοι στῦλοι ἐδιώχθησαν καὶ ἕως θανάτου ἤλθησαν. λάβωμεν πρὸ ὀφθαλμῶν ἡμῶν τοὺς ἀγαθοὺς ἀποστόλους· Πέτρον, ὃς διὰ ζῆλον ἄδικον οὐχ ἕνα οὐδὲ δύο, ἀλλὰ πλείονας ὑπήνεγκεν πόνους καὶ οὕτω μαρτυρήσας ἐπορεύθη εἰς τὸν ὀφειλόμενον τόπον τῆς δόξης. διὰ ζῆλον καὶ ἔριν Παῦλος ὑπομονῆς βραβεῖον ἔδειξεν· ἑπτάκις δεσμὰ φορέσας, φυγαδευθείς, λιθασθείς, κῆρυξ γενόμενος ἔν τε τῇ ἀνατολῇ καὶ ἐν τῇ δύσει τὸ γενναῖον τῆς πίστεως αὐτοῦ κλέος ἔλαβεν· δικαιοσύνην διδάξας ὅλον τὸν κόσμον καὶ ἐπὶ τὸ τέρμα τῆς δύσεως ἐλθὼν καὶ μαρτυρήσας ἐπὶ τῶν ἡγουμένων, οὕτως ἀπηλλάγη τοῦ κόσμου καὶ εἰς τὸν ἅγιον τόπον ἐπορεύθη, ὑπομονῆς γενόμενος μέγιστος ὑπογραμμός.

2. Martyrium et Ascensio Isaiae 4:2–4[2]

[στερεώμα]τος αὐτοῦ ἐ[ν εἴδει] ἀνθρώπου βασιλέως ἀνόμου μητραλῴου ὅστι[ς] αὐτὸς ὁ βασιλεὺς οὗτος τὴν φυτ[ε]ίαν ἣν φυτεύσουσιν οἱ δώδεκα ἀπόστολοι

1. Annie Jaubert, ed., *Clément de Rome: Épître aux Corinthiens*, SC 167 (Paris: Cerf, 1971), 106–8.

2. Paolo Bettiolo, *Ascensio Isaiae: textus*, CCSA 7 (Turnhout: Brepols, 1995), 145.

1. 1 Clement 5.1–7 (80–130 CE)

But so that we may cease with the ancient examples, let us come to the athletes who are nearest to us, and let us take up the examples from our time. On account of jealousy and envy the greatest and most righteous pillars were persecuted and fought to the death. Let us place before our eyes the noble apostles. Because of unjust jealousy Peter endured hardships, and not once or twice but many times. Thus, after bearing witness he went to the place of glory that was due him. On account of jealousy and conflict Paul pointed the way to the prize for perseverance. After he had been bound in chains seven times, driven into exile, stoned, and had preached in both the east and the west, he received the noble glory for his faith, having taught righteousness to the whole world and having gone even to the limit of the west. When he had borne witness[1] before the rulers, he was thus set free from the world and taken up to the holy place, having become the greatest example of perseverance.

2. Martyrdom and Ascension of Isaiah 4:2–4 (100–130 CE)

[2]*After this has taken place, Beliar, the great ruler and king of this world, will descend—the one who has ruled it since it came into being. He will descend from his firmament* in the form of a man, who is a lawless king and a murderer of his mother. He himself, this king, will persecute the plant that the

1. By this time the verb μαρτυρέω does not appear to have taken on the technical meaning of *dying as a martyr*, as argued by, e.g., Boudewijn Dehandschutter, "Some Notes in 1 Clement 5, 4–7," in *Fructus centesimus: Mélanges offerts à Gerard J. M. Bartelink à l'occasion de son soixante-cinquième anniversaire*, ed. Antoon Bastiaensen et al., IP 19 (Steenbrugis: Abbatia S. Petri, 1989), 83–89; Thomas A. Robinson, *Ignatius of Antioch and the Parting of the Ways: Early Jewish-Christian Relations* (Grand Rapids: Baker Academic, 2009), 156–57. Cf. Robert F. Stoops, "If I Suffer … Epistolary Authority in Ignatius of Antioch," *HTR* 80 (1987): 165–67, who argues that the verb does mean *to die as a martyr* in 1 Clement, Acts, and Revelation.

2. These opening lines in italics are based on the Ethiopic translation. I include them in the translation to provide some context for the fragmentary Greek text.

τοῦ ἀγαπητοῦ διώξε[ι], καὶ [τ]ῶν δώδεκα [εἷς] ταῖς χερσὶν αὐτοῦ π[αραδ]οθήσεται. οὗτος [ὁ ἄρ]χων ἐν τῇ εἰδέᾳ τοῦ βασιλέως ἐκείνου ἐλεύσεται, [κ]αὶ αἱ δυνάμεις πᾶσαι [ἐλ]εύσ[ον]ται τ[ο]ύτ[ου τ]οῦ κό[σμου] …

3. Ignatius of Antioch, *Epistula ad Ephesios* 12.1–2[3]

[1] οἶδα τίς εἰμι καὶ τίσιν γράφω. ἐγὼ κατάκριτος, ὑμεῖς ἠλεημένοι· ἐγὼ ὑπὸ κίνδυνον, ὑμεῖς ἐστηριγμένοι. [2] πάροδός ἐστε τῶν εἰς θεὸν ἀναιρουμένων, Παύλου συμμύσται, τοῦ ἡγιασμένου, τοῦ μεμαρτυρημένου, ἀξιομακαρίστου, οὗ γένοιτό μοι ὑπὸ τὰ ἴχνη εὑρεθῆναι, ὅταν θεοῦ ἐπιτύχω, ὃς ἐν πάσῃ ἐπιστολῇ μνημονεύει ὑμῶν ἐν Χριστῷ Ἰησοῦ.

4. Apocalypsis Petri 14:4–6[4]

καὶ πορεύου εἰς πόλιν ἄρχουσαν δύσεως, καὶ πίε τὸ ποτήριον ὃ ἐπηγγειλάμην σοι ἐν χειρεὶ[5] τοῦ υ(ἱο)ῦ τοῦ ἐν Ἅιδου, εἵνα[6] ἀρχὴν λάβῃ αὐτοῦ ἡ ἀφάνια· καὶ σὺ δεκτὸς τῆς ἐπαγ᾽γελεί[ας.

3. Michael W. Holmes, *The Apostolic Fathers: Greek Texts and English Translations*, 3rd ed. (Grand Rapids: Baker, 2007), 192.

4. Peter van Minnen, "The Greek Apocalypse of Peter," in *The Apocalypse of Peter*, ed. Jan N. Bremmer and István Czachesz, SECA 7 (Leuven: Peeters, 2003), 38–39. This reading of the so-called Rainer Fragment (P.Vindob.G 39756) is confirmed in Thomas J. Kraus and Tobias Nicklas, eds., *Das Petrusevangelium und die Petrusapokalypse: die griechischen Fragmente mit deutscher und englischer Übersetzung*, GCS NS 11 (Berlin: de Gruyter, 2004), 127. Kraus and Nicklas cite van Minnen's reconstruction several times in support of their edition.

5. Read χειρί.

6. Read ἵνα.

twelve apostles of the beloved one will plant, and one of the twelve[3] will be given over into his hands. This leader will come in the likeness of that king, and all the powers of this world will be present …[4]

3. Ignatius of Antioch, *Epistle to the Ephesians* 12.1–2 (110–125 CE)

[1] I know who I am and to whom I am writing. I am condemned, while you have received mercy. I am in danger, while you are secure. [2] You are the highway of those being killed for God.[5] You are fellow initiates of the mysteries with Paul, the one who was sanctified, who was well attested,[6] who is worthy of blessing. May I be found in his footsteps when I attain to God—that is, in the footsteps of the one who remembers you in Christ Jesus in every letter.[7]

4. Apocalypse of Peter 14:4–6 (100–140 CE)

Go to the city that rules over the West, and drink the cup that I promised you,[8] which is in the hands of the son of the one who is in Hades, so that his destruction may begin. And you … acceptable … of the promise.[9]

---

3. This is understood as a reference to Peter's death at the hands of Nero.

4. On early Christian interpretation of this eschatological figure, see L. J. Lietaert Peerbolte, *The Antecedents of Antichrist: A Traditio-Historical Study of the Earliest Christian Views on Eschatological Opponents*, JSJSup 49 (Leiden: Brill, 1996), 194–205; Antonio Acerbi, *L'Ascensione di Isaia: Cristologia e profetismo in Siria nei primi decenni del II secolo* (Milan: Università Cattolica del Sacro Cuore, 1989), 83–98.

5. See possible references to this passage in Pseudo-Marcellus, *Pass. Holy* 62 (ch. 10a is this volume); Acts Pet. Paul 83 (ch. 10b in this volume).

6. The verb could also be rendered "martyred," but it is not clear that μαρτυρέω had the technical sense of dying for one's faith by the time of Ignatius. See note 1 above on the translation of 1 Clement.

7. Phil 1:3–4.

8. Cf. Mark 10:37–39, where Jesus tells James and John that they will drink the cup he is drinking.

9. By comparing the fragmentary Greek with two Ethiopic manuscripts, Dennis D. Buchholz constructed the following corrected text: "Go out, therefore, and go to the city which is (in) the West and drink the wine about which I have told you, from the hand of my son who is without sin, that his work of destruction may begin. But you (sg.) (are) chosen by the promise which I have promised you. And send out, therefore, into all the world my story in peace. For the Fountain of My Word has rejoiced at the promise of life, and suddenly the world has been snatched away." It is not clear to me

5. Polycarp, *Epistula ad Philippenses* 9.1–2[7]

παρακαλῶ οὖν πάντας ὑμᾶς πειθαρχεῖν τῷ λόγῳ τῆς δικαιοσύνης καὶ ὑπομένειν πᾶσαν ὑπομονήν, ἣν καὶ εἴδατε κατ' ὀφθαλμοὺς οὐ μόνον ἐν τοῖς μακαρίοις Ἰγνατίῳ καὶ Ζωσίμῳ καὶ Ῥούφῳ ἀλλὰ καὶ ἐν ἄλλοις τοῖς ἐξ ὑμῶν καὶ ἐν αὐτῷ Παύλῳ καὶ τοῖς λοιποῖς ἀποστόλοις. πεπεισμένους ὅτι οὗτοι πάντες οὐκ εἰς κενὸν ἔδραμον ἀλλ' ἐν πίστει καὶ δικαιοσύνῃ, καὶ ὅτι εἰς τὸν ὀφειλόμενον αὐτοῖς τόπον εἰσὶ παρὰ τῷ κυρίῳ ᾧ καὶ συνέπαθον. οὐ γὰρ τὸν νῦν ἠγάπησαν αἰῶνα, ἀλλὰ τὸν ὑπὲρ ἡμῶν ἀποθανόντα καὶ δι' ἡμᾶς ὑπὸ τοῦ θεοῦ ἀναστάντα.

6. Irenaeus of Lyons, *Aduersus haereses* 3.1.1[8]

ὁ μὲν δὴ Ματθαῖος ἐν τοῖς Ἑβραίοις τῇ ἰδίᾳ αὐτῶν διαλέκτῳ καὶ γραφὴν ἐξήνεγκεν εὐαγγελίου, τοῦ Πέτρου καὶ τοῦ Παύλου ἐν Ῥώμῃ εὐαγγελιζομένων καὶ θεμελιούντων τὴν ἐκκλησίαν· μετὰ δὲ τὴν τούτων ἔξοδον, Μάρκος, ὁ μαθητὴς καὶ ἑρμηνευτὴς Πέτρου, καὶ αὐτὸς τὰ ὑπὸ Πέτρου κηρυσσόμενα ἐγγράφως ἡμῖν παραδέδωκεν· καὶ Λουκᾶς δέ, ὁ ἀκόλουθος Παύλου, τὸ ὑπ' ἐκείνου κηρυσσόμενον εὐαγγέλιον ἐν βίβλῳ κατέθετο.

7. Paul Hartog, *Polycarp's Epistle to the Philippians and the Martyrdom of Polycarp: Introduction, Text, and Commentary*, OAF (Oxford: Oxford University Press, 2013), 88.

8. Adelin Rousseau and Louis Doutreleau, eds., *Irénée de Lyon: Contre les hérésies Livre III*, vol. 2, SC 211 (Paris, Cerf, 1974), 22–24. The Greek of this text survives only in various fragments, this one preserved in Eusebius of Caesarea, *Hist. eccl.* 5.8.2–3. The text survives complete in an early Latin translation: *Ita Matthaeus in Hebraeis ipsorum lingua scripturam edidit Euangelii, cum Petrus et Paulus Romae euangelizarent et fundarent Ecclesiam. Post uero horum excessum, Marcus discipulus et interpres Petri et ipse quae a Petro adnuntiata errant per scripta nobis tradidit. Et Lucas autem spectator Pauli quod ab illo praedicabatur Euangelium in libro condidit.*

5. Polycarp, *Epistle to the Philadelphians* 9.1–2 (110–135 CE)

I encourage you all, then, to obey the teaching about righteousness and to discipline yourselves with all the discipline that you saw with your own eyes—not only in the blessed men Ignatius, Zosimus, and Rufus, but also in others from among your number, and in Paul himself, and in the other apostles. Be assured that all of these did not run in vain, but in faith and righteousness, and that they are in the place that is due them in the presence of the Lord, with whom they suffered. For they did not love the present age but the one who died for us and was raised again by God for our sake.[10]

6. Irenaeus of Lyons, *Against the Heresies* 3.1.1 (ca. 174–189)[11]

Matthew produced a written account of the gospel among the Hebrews in their own dialect, while Peter and Paul were preaching in Rome and laying the foundations of the church. After their departure[12] Mark, the disciple and interpreter of Peter, handed down to us in writing the things that were preached by Peter; and Luke, the follower of Paul, wrote down in a book the gospel preached by that man.

---

that Buchholz's reconstruction is clarifying at every point. For example, how could Nero be called "my son who is without sin"? See *Your Eyes Will Be Opened: A Study of the Greek (Ethiopic) Apocalypse of Peter*, SBLDS 97 (Atlanta: Scholars Press, 1988), 230, 232.

10. Polycarp alludes to Phil 2:16 and 2 Tim 4:6–8 in the context of a discussion about Paul's martrydom. For further discussion of this passage, see David L. Eastman, "Paul as Martyr in the Apostolic Fathers," in Todd D. Still and David E. Wilhite, eds., *The Apostolic Fathers and Paul*, PPSD 2 (London: T&T Clark, forthcoming).

11. In *Haer.* 3.3.3 Irenaeus identifies Eleutherus (ca. 174–189) as the Roman bishop at the time he was producing the text.

12. That is, their deaths.

7. Canon Muratori 34–39[9]

Acta aute(m) omniu(m) apostolorum sub uno libro scribta sunt. Lucas obtime Theofile conprindit quia sub praesentia eius singula[10] gerebantur sicuti et semote passione(m) Petri euidenter declarat sed et profectione(m) Pauli ab urbe ad Spania(m) proficiscentis.

8. Tertullian, *Apologeticum* 5.3[11]

Consulite commentarios uestros, illic reperietis primum Neronem in hanc sectam cum maxime Romae orientem Caesariano gladio ferocisse. tali dedicatore damnationis nostrae etiam gloriamur: qui enim scit illum, intellegere potest non nisi grande aliquod bonum a Nerone damnatum.

9. Tertullian, *De praesciptione haereticorum* 36.1–3[12]

[1] Age iam, qui uoles curiositatem melius exercere in negotio salutis tuae, percurre ecclesias apostolicas apud quas ipsae adhuc cathedrae apostolorum suis locis praesident, apud quas ipsae authenticae litterae eorum recitantur sonantes uocem et repraesentantes faciem uniuscuiusque. [2] proxima est tibi Achaia, habes Corinthum. si non longe es a Macedonia, habes

---

9. Henry M. Gwatkin, ed., *Selections from Early Writers Illustrative of Church History to the Time of Constantine*, updated ed. (London: Macmillan, 1911), 84. Variations in Latin orthography are evident here: *scribta* for *scripta*; *obtime* for *optime*; *conprindit* for *comprendit*.

10. MS *sincula*.

11. Eligius Dekkers and Attilio Carpin, eds., *Tertulliano Difesa del Cristianesimo: Apologeticum*, CCSL 1 (Rome: San Clemente; Bologna: Studio Domenicano, 2008), 138–40.

12. F. Refoulé, ed., *Tertullien Traité de la prescription contre les hérétiques*, SC 46 (Paris: Cerf, 1957), 137–38.

7. Muratorian Canon 34–39 (170–400 CE)[13]

However, the acts of all the apostles are written in one book. Luke recounts for the most excellent Theophilus individual events that took place in his presence, as is evident by the omission of the passion of Peter and the departure of Paul, who went from the city [Rome] to Spain.[14]

8. Tertullian, *Apology* 5.3 (197 CE)

Consult your annals. There you will find that Nero was the first to rage with the imperial sword against this way of life, when it was rising to great prominence in Rome. We even rejoice in our condemnation by such an author, for whoever knows him is able to understand that nothing was condemned by Nero except that which is very good.[15]

9. Tertullian, *Prescription against Heretics* 36.1–3 (203 CE)

[1] Come now, you who wish to exercise your curiosity more in the matter of your salvation. Pass through the apostolic churches in which the very seats of the apostles still preside in their places, in which are read aloud their own authentic letters, which take up the voice and represent the presence of each one.[16] [2] Achaia is very near to you, so you have Corinth.

---

13. The date of this document is disputed. The traditional date of ca. 170 has been defended by e.g., Bruce M. Metzger, *The Canon of The New Testament: Its Origin, Development, and Significance* (Oxford: Clarendon, 1987), 191–201. A third-century date has been proposed by Jonathan J. Armstrong, "Victorinus of Pettau as the Author of the Canon Muratori," *VC* 62 (2008): 1–34. A fourth-century date has been espoused by e.g., Albert C. Sundberg, Jr., "Canon Muratori: A Fourth Century List," *HTR* 66 (1973): 1–41; and later by Geoffrey Mark Hahneman, *The Muratorian Fragment and the Development of the Canon*, OTM (Oxford: Clarendon, 1992). This fourth-century dating was exposed to a systematic critique by J. Verheyden, "The Canon Muratori: A Matter of Dispute," in *The Biblical Canons*, ed. Jean-Marie Auwers and H. J. de Jonge, BETL 163 (Leuven: Leuven University Press, 2003), 487–556.

14. The author assumes that Luke was present for Paul's two-year incarceration in Rome but not for any of the significant subsequent events there.

15. This passage does not name Peter and Paul among those who fell victim to Nero's raging, but the subsequent passages from Tertullian will make this connection clear.

16. The reading of the letters makes it as if the apostles themselves are present and speaking.

Philippos; si potes in Asiam tendere, habes Ephesum; si autem Italiae adiaces, habes Romam unde nobis quoque auctoritas praesto est. [3] ista quam felix ecclesia cui totam doctrinam apostoli cum sanguine suo profuderunt, ubi Petrus passioni dominicae adaequatur, ubi Paulus Iohannis exitu coronatur, ubi apostolus Iohannes posteaquam in oleum igneum demersus nihil passus est, in insulam relegatur.

10. Tertullian, *Aduersus Marcionem* 4.5.1[13]

Uideamus quod lac Paulo Corinthii hauserint, ad quam regulam Galatae sint recorrecti, quid legant Philippenses Thessalonicenses Ephesii, quid etiam Romani de proximo sonent, quibus euangelium et Petrus et Paulus sanguine quoque suo signatum reliquerent.

11. Tertullian, *Scorpiace* 15.1–3[14]

[1] Quae tamen passos apostolos scimus, manifesta doctrina est. hanc intellego solam Acta decurrens, nihil quaero. [2] carceres illic et uincula et flagella et saxa et gladii et impetus Iudaeorum et coetus nationum et tribunorum elogia et regum auditoria et proconsulum tribunalia et Caesaris nomen interpretem non habent. quod Petrus caeditur, quod Stephanus opprimitur, quod Iacobus immolatur, quod Paulus distrahitur, ipsorum

13. Claudio Moreschini and René Braun, eds., *Tertullien Contre Marcion Tome IV*, SC 456 (Paris: Cerf, 2001), 82.

14. August Reifferscheid and George Wissowa, eds., *Quinti Septimi Florentis Tertulliani Opera*, vol. 1, CSEL 20 (Vienna: Tempsky, 1890), 178.

Because you are not far from Macedonia, you have Philippi. If you are able to go into Asia, you have Ephesus. Because you are close to Italy, you have Rome, from which the authority extends also over us. [3] How blessed is that church on which the apostles poured out their whole teaching with their own blood—where Peter equaled the passion of the Lord,[17] where Paul was crowned with a death like John,[18] and where the apostle John was later plunged into boiling oil but suffered nothing, and so was exiled to an island.[19]

10. Tertullian, *Against Marcion* 4.5.1 (ca. 207–208 CE)

Let us look at what milk the Corinthians drank from Paul, by what standard the Galatians were corrected, what the Philippians, Thessalonians, and Ephesians are reading, even what the nearby Romans are saying—those to whom Peter and Paul left the gospel sealed with their own blood.

11. Tertullian, *Antidote for the Scorpion's Sting* 15.1–3 (ca. 211–212 CE)

[1] We know that the apostles endured sufferings; the teaching is clear. I learn this just by scanning through the acts.[20] I do not need to search for it. [2] There are the prisons, the chains, the beatings, the large stones, the swords, the attacks by the Jews, the mobs of unbelievers,[21] the indictments by tribunes, the hearings in front of kings, the judgment seats of proconsuls, and the name of Caesar—these do not need an interpretation. That Peter is beaten, that Stephen is crushed, that James is sacrificed, that

17. Peter was also crucified.

18. This is John the Baptist, who was beheaded according to Mark 6:14–29; Matt 14:1–12; Luke 9:7–8; Josephus, *Ant.* 18.5.2.

19. Tradition identifies John the apostle with John the author of Revelation, who had his visions while on the island of Patmos (Rev 1:1–4, 9). However, based on the writings of Papias available to him, Eusebius suggests that John the apostle should be distinguished from John the presbyter, the true author of Revelation (*Hist. eccl.* 3.39.5–6). The Acts of John places the apostle in Ephesus, not Rome, and Tertullian is the earliest known source for the story that John survived boiling oil in Rome.

20. This could be a reference specifically to the Acts of the Apostles, but Tertullian then refers to traditions not recorded in that text—i.e., the deaths of James and Paul—so I take this as a reference to apostolic acts more broadly.

21. Literally, "gentiles." The use of this term to describe unbelievers is common among early Christian authors.

sanguine scripta sunt. [3] et si fidem commentarii uoluerit haereticus, instrumenta imperii loquentur, ut lapides Hierusalem. uitas Caesarum legimus: orientem fidem Romae primus Nero cruentauit. tunc Petrus ab altero cingitur, cum cruci adstringitur. tunc Paulus ciuitatis Romanae consequitur natiuitatem, cum illic martyrii renascitur generositate.

12. Apocryphon Iacobi 5.9–20[15]

Ⲏ ⲛⲧⲉⲧⲛⲥⲁⲩⲛⲉ ⲉⲛ ϫⲉ ⲙⲡⲁⲧⲟⲩⲣ ϩⲩⲃⲣⲓⲍⲉ ⲙⲙⲱⲧⲛ ⲁⲩⲱ ⲙⲡⲁⲧⲟⲩⲣ ⲕⲁⲧⲏⲅⲟⲣⲓ ⲙⲙⲱⲧⲛ ϩⲛⲛ ⲟⲩϫⲓ ⲛϭⲁⲛⲥ ⲟⲩⲇⲉ ⲙⲡⲁⲧⲟⲩⲱⲧⲡ ⲧⲏⲛⲉ ⲁϩⲟⲩⲛ ⲁⲩϣⲧⲉⲕⲟ ⲟⲩⲧⲉ ⲉⲙⲡⲁⲧⲟⲩϭⲁⲉⲓⲉ ⲧⲏⲩⲧⲛ ϩⲛ ⲟⲩⲙⲛⲧⲁⲛⲟⲙⲟⲥ ⲟⲩⲧⲉ ⲙⲡⲁⲧⲟⲩⲣ ⲥⲧⲁⲩⲣⲟ[ⲩ][16] ⲙⲙⲱⲧⲛ ϩⲛⲛ ⲟⲩⲙⲛⲧ<ⲁ>ⲗⲟⲅⲟⲥ ⲟⲩⲧⲉ ⲙⲡⲁⲧⲟⲩⲧⲱⲙⲥ ⲧⲏⲛⲉ ϩⲛⲛ ⲟⲩϣⲟⲩ[17] ⲛⲧⲁϩⲉ ϩⲱⲱⲧ ⲁⲃⲁⲗ ϩⲓⲧⲟⲟⲧϥ ⲙⲡⲡⲟⲛⲏⲣⲟⲥ.

13. Peter of Alexandria, Περὶ *μετανοίας* / *Epistola canonica* 9[18]

οὕτως ὁ πρόκριτος τῶν ἀποστόλων Πέτρος πολλάκις συλληφθεὶς καὶ ἀποκλεισθεὶς καὶ ἀτιμασθεὶς ὕστερον ἐν Ῥώμῃ ἐσταυρώθη. ὁμοίως καὶ ὁ περιβόητος Παῦλος πλεονάκις παραδοθεὶς καὶ ἕως θανάτου κινδυνεύσας, πολλά τε ἀθλήσας καὶ καυχησάμενος ἐν πολλοῖς διωγμοῖς καὶ θλίψεσιν ἐν τῇ αὐτῇ πόλει καὶ αὐτὸς μαχαίρᾳ τὴν κεφαλὴν ἀπεκείρατο.

14. Lactantius, *De mortibus persecutorum* 2.5–8[19]

[5] Cumque iam Nero imperaret, Petrus Romam aduenit et editis quibusdam miraculis, quae uirtute ipsius Dei data sibi ab eo potestate faciebat, conuertit multos ad iustitiam Deoque templum fidele ac stabile conlocauit. [6] qua re ad Neronem delata cum animaduerteret non modo Romae,

---

15. Harold W. Attridge, ed., *Nag Hammadi Codex I (The Jung Codex): Introductions, Texts, Translations, Indices*, NHS 22–23 (Leiden: Brill, 1985), 1:34–36.

16. In the manuscript the Chi-Rho symbol is inserted in the verb "crucified" in place of the letters ⲧⲁⲩⲣ.

17. Read ⲟⲩϣⲱⲥ. Here Attridge follows the emendation of Schenke in reading ⲟⲩϣⲱⲥ (shamefully) instead of ⲟⲩϣⲟⲩ (in sand). See Attridge, *Nag Hammadi Codex I*, 2:15.

18. *Reliquary of ancient ecclesiastical laws / reliquiae iuris ecclesiastici antiquissimae*, ed. Paul de Lagarde (Leipzig: Teubner, 1856), 68.

19. Alfons Städele, ed., *Laktanz de mortibus persecutorum: Die Todesarten der Verfolger*, FontC 43 (Turnhout: Brepols, 2003), 94–96.

Paul is dragged away—these things are written with their own blood. [3] If a heretic wants to place faith in a record, then the archives of the empire will speak, as will the stones of Jerusalem. We read the lives of the Caesars. Nero was the first who stained with blood the rising faith in Rome. At that time Peter was bound around the body by another when he was bound to the cross. At that time Paul obtained the birth of Roman citizenship, when he was born again there by the nobility of martyrdom.[22]

12. Apocryphon of James 5.9–20 (late 2nd or 3rd cent. CE)

[Jesus speaking to Peter] Or do you not know that you will be mistreated, and unjustly accused, and imprisoned, and condemned unlawfully, and crucified for no reason, and buried, as I myself was by the evil one?

13. Peter of Alexandria, *On Repentance / Canonical Epistle* 9 (306 CE)

Thus the chief of the apostles, Peter, who had often been arrested and thrown into prison and treated poorly, was finally crucified in Rome. Likewise also the famous Paul—who had frequently been handed over and in danger to the point of death, and who had endured many trials and had boasted in his many persecutions and afflictions[23]—had his head cut off with a sword in that same city.

14. Lactantius, *On the Deaths of the Persecutors* 2.5–8 (313–316 CE)

[5] While Nero was ruling, Peter came to Rome. After he had performed certain miracles, which he was doing by the strength of God himself that had been given to him by God, he converted many to righteousness and established for God a faithful and steadfast temple. [6] This matter was reported to Nero. When he observed that not only in Rome, but every-

22. This passage played an important role for the idealization of Paul's martyrdom as part of the construction of North African Christian identity. See David L. Eastman, *Paul the Martyr: The Cult of the Apostle in the Latin West*, WGRWSup 4 (Atlanta: Society of Biblical Literature, 2011), 160–63.

23. Rom 5:3–5; 2 Cor 11:16–31.

sed ubique cotidie magnam multitudinem deficere a cultu idolorum et ad religionem nouam damnata uetusta transire, ut erat execrabilis ac nocens tyrannus, prosiliuit ad excidendum caeleste templum delendamque iustitiam et primus omnium persecutus Dei seruos Petrum cruci adfixit, Paulum interfecit. [7] nec tamen habuit inpune. respexit enim Deus uexationem populi sui. deiectus itaque fastigio imperii ac deuolutus a summo tyrannus impotens nusquam repente comparuit, ut ne sepulturae quidem locus in terra tam malae bestiae appareret. [8] unde illum quidam deliri credunt esse translatum ac uiuum reseruatum Sibylla dicente: matricidam profugum a finibus [terrae] esse uenturum, ut, qui[20] primus persecutus est, idem etiam nouissimus persequatur et Antichristi praecedat aduentum.

15. Eusebius of Caesarea, Papias, and Dionysius of Corinth in *Historia ecclesiastica* 2.25.5–8[21]

ταύτῃ γοῦν οὗτος, θεομάχος ἐν τοῖς μάλιστα πρῶτος ἀνακηρυχθείς, ἐπὶ τὰς κατὰ τῶν ἀποστόλων ἐπήρθη σφαγάς. Παῦλος δὴ οὖν ἐπ᾿ αὐτῆς Ῥώμης τὴν κεφαλὴν ἀποτμηθῆναι καὶ Πέτρος ὡσαύτως ἀνασκολοπισθῆναι κατ᾿ αὐτὸν ἱστοροῦνται, καὶ πιστοῦταί γε τὴν ἱστορίαν ἡ Πέτρου καὶ Παύλου εἰς δεῦρο κρατήσασα ἐπὶ τῶν αὐτόθι κοιμητηρίων πρόσρησις, οὐδὲν δὲ ἧττον καὶ ἐκκλησιαστικὸς ἀνήρ, Γάϊος ὄνομα, κατὰ Ζεφυρῖνον Ῥωμαίων γεγονὼς ἐπίσκοπον· ὃς δὴ Πρόκλῳ τῆς κατὰ Φρύγας προϊσταμένῳ γνώμης ἐγγράφως διαλεχθείς. αὐτὰ δὴ ταῦτα περὶ τῶν τόπων, ἔνθα τῶν εἰρημένων ἀποστόλων τὰ ἱερὰ σκηνώματα κατατέθειται, φησίν·

20. Or *qui[a]*.

21. Eduard Schwartz, ed., *Eusebius Werke 2.1*, GCS 9.1 (Leipzig: Hinrichs, 1903), 176–78.

where, a great multitude was daily turning away from the worship of idols and, condemning their old ways, going over to a new religion, he—being an abominable and wicked tyrant—sprang forth to tear down the heavenly temple and abolish righteousness. He was the first of all to persecute the servants of God. He nailed Peter to a cross and killed Paul. [7] However, he did not get away without punishment. God took note of the distress of his people. Thrown down from the pinnacle of imperial power and deprived of the highest position, the powerless tyrant suddenly disappeared, so that not even the burial place of so wicked a beast could be found on earth. [8] As a result some deluded people believe that he was taken away and kept alive—as the Sibyl says, "The mother-killer and fugitive will come from the ends of the earth"[24]—so that he who was the first persecutor[25] might also be the last and may precede the coming of the antichrist.

15. Eusebius of Caesarea, Papias, and Dionysius of Corinth in *Ecclesiastical History* 2.25.5–8 (ca. 325 CE)[26]

After [Nero] had made clear that he was indeed the foremost enemy of God among them, he was stirred up for the slaughter of the apostles. It is therefore recorded that Paul was beheaded in Rome itself and that Peter was likewise crucified under him. This story is confirmed in that Peter and Paul are addressed in the cemeteries there up to today.[27] Likewise an ecclesiastical man named Gaius, who was born under Zephyrinus, bishop of the Romans, was disputing in writing with Proclus, a leader of the Kataphrygian sect.[28] He said these things about the places where the holy bodies[29] of the aforementioned apostles lie:

---

24. Sib. Or. 8.70-71.

25. The reading without the proposed *[a]* in *qui[a]* is preferable. The addition of *[a]* would yield: "so that because he was the first persecutor, he might also be the last."

26. Eusebius quotes both Papias and Dionysius. The date given is for the final form of the *Hist. eccl.*, which was produced over the course of several decades. The writings of Papias are dated to ca. 130–140 CE, and those of Dionysius to ca. 170 CE.

27. Graffiti in the catacombs (St. Sebastian) on the Appian Road south of Rome demonstrate that pilgrims had been appealing to the apostles as martyr-patrons since at least the third century. See Eastman, *Paul the Martyr*, 72–73, 84–89.

28. This is a term used for the Montanists.

29. Or "dwellings."

> ἐγὼ δὲ τὰ τρόπαια τῶν ἀποστόλων ἔχω δεῖξαι. ἐὰν γὰρ θελήσῃς ἀπελθεῖν ἐπὶ τὸν Βασικανὸν[22] ἢ ἐπὶ τὴν ὁδὸν τὴν Ὠστίαν, εὑρήσεις τὰ τρόπαια τῶν ταύτην ἱδρυσαμένων τὴν ἐκκλησίαν.

ὡς δὲ κατὰ τὸν αὐτὸν ἄμφω καιρὸν ἐμαρτύρησαν, Κορινθίων ἐπίσκοπος Διονύσιος ἐγγράφως Ῥωμαίοις ὁμιλῶν, ὧδε παρίστησιν·

> ταῦτα καὶ ὑμεῖς διὰ τῆς τοσαύτης νουθεσίας τὴν ἀπὸ Πέτρου καὶ Παύλου φυτείαν γενηθεῖσαν Ῥωμαίων τε καὶ Κορινθίων συνεκεράσατε. καὶ γὰρ ἄμφω καὶ εἰς τὴν ἡμετέραν Κόρινθον φυτεύσαντες ἡμᾶς ὁμοίως ἐδίδαξαν, ὁμοίως δὲ καὶ εἰς τὴν Ἰταλίαν ὁμόσε διδάξαντες ἐμαρτύρησαν κατὰ τὸν αὐτὸν καιρόν.

καὶ ταῦτα δέ, ὡς ἂν ἔτι μᾶλλον πιστωθείη τὰ τῆς ἱστορίας.

16. Eusebius of Caesarea, *Historia ecclesiastica* 3.1[23]

Πέτρος δ᾽ ἐν Πόντῳ καὶ Γαλατίᾳ καὶ Βιθυνίᾳ Καππαδοκία τε καὶ Ἀσίᾳ κεκηρυχέναι τοῖς [ἐκ] διασπορᾶς Ἰουδαίοις ἔοικεν· ὃς καὶ ἐπὶ τέλει ἐν Ῥώμῃ γενόμενος, ἀνεσκολοπίσθη κατὰ κεφαλῆς, οὕτως αὐτὸς ἀξιώσας παθεῖν. τί δεῖ περὶ Παύλου λέγειν, ἀπὸ Ἱερουσαλὴμ μέχρι τοῦ Ἰλλυρικοῦ πεπληρωκότος τὸ εὐαγγέλιον τοῦ Χριστοῦ καὶ ὕστερον ἐν τῇ Ῥώμῃ ἐπὶ Νέρωνος μεμαρτυρηκότος; ταῦτα Ὠριγένει κατὰ λέξιν ἐν τρίτῳ τόμῳ τῶν εἰς τὴν Γένεσιν ἐξηγητικῶν εἴρηται.

22. The reading Βατικανόν is attested in only a few of the manuscripts.
23. Schwartz, *Eusebius Werke*, 188.

> I can show the trophies[30] of the apostles. For if you are willing go to the Vatican or the Ostian Road, you will find the trophies of those who have laid the foundations of this church.

Dionysius, bishop of the Corinthians, attests that they both died as martyrs at the same time. In writing to the Romans, he states:

> Therefore, you also through such an admonition have mingled the seed that sprouted among the Romans and Corinthians through Peter and Paul. For both of them planted here in Corinth and likewise taught us;[31] and in the same way after teaching together in Italy, they suffered martyrdom at the same time.[32]

[I have quoted] these things, so that the facts[33] of this account might be believed even more.

16. Eusebius of Caesarea citing Origen in *Ecclesiastical History* 3.1 (ca. 325 CE)

Peter seems to have preached in Pontus, Galatia, Bithynia, Cappadocia, and Asia to the Jews of the Diaspora. After he finally came to Rome, he was crucified with his head downward, as he thought it proper for him to suffer.[34] Why is it necessary to speak about Paul, who had fully explained the gospel of Christ from Jerusalem to Illyricum and was at last martyred in Rome under Nero? Origen speaks about these things in writing in the third book of his commentaries on Genesis.[35]

---

30. These are the tombs of the apostles (Eastman, *Paul the Martyr*, 21–24).

31. Cf. 1 Cor 3:5–9.

32. The claim that Paul and Peter died at the same time is supported by Jerome, *Vir. ill.* 5; *Tract. Ps.* 96.10; and Maximus of Turin, *Serm.* 1.2; 2.1; 9.1. A similar passage credited to Damasus of Rome is spurious, as shown by Cuthbert H. Turner, ed., *Ecclesiae occidentalis monumenta iuris antiquissima* (Oxford: Clarendon: 1899–1939), 1.2:157. Cf. early Christian authors who claim that they died on the same date but a year apart: Ambrose of Milan, *Virginit.* 19.124; Augustine, *Serm.* 295.7; 381.1; Prudentius, *Perist.* 12.5, 21–22; Gregory of Tours, *Glor. mart.* 28; and Arator, *Act. apost.* 2.1247–49.

33. Literally, "the things of this account."

34. Matthew C. Baldwin (*Whose Acts of Peter? Text and Historical Context of the Actus Vercellenses*, WUNT 2/196 [Tübingen: Mohr Siebeck, 2005], 71–73) claims that this is the earliest reference to Peter's inverted crucifixion.

35. This section of Origen's commentary does not survive.

17. John Chrysostom, *Aduersus oppugnatores uitae monasticae* 1.3[24]

τὸν Νέρωνα πάντως ἀκούετε (καὶ γὰρ ἐπίσημος ὁ ἀνὴρ ἀπὸ τῆς ἀσελγείας ἐγένετο, πρῶτος καὶ μόνος εὑρὼν ἐν ἀρχῇ τοιαύτῃ καινούς τινας ἀκολασίας καὶ ἀσχημοσύνης τρόπους)· οὗτος ὁ Νέρων τὸν μακάριον Παῦλον (καὶ γὰρ ἔτυχε κατὰ τοὺς αὐτοὺς ἐκείνῳ γενόμενος χρόνους) τοιαῦτα ἐγκαλῶν, οἷάπερ ὑμεῖς τοῖς ἁγίοις τούτοις ἀνδράσι (παλλακίδα γὰρ αὐτοῦ σφόδρα ἐπέραστον πείσας τὸν περὶ τῆς πίστεως δέξασθαι λόγον, ἔπειθεν ὁμοῦ καὶ τῆς ἀκαθάρτου συνουσίας ἀπαλλαγῆναι ἐκείνης)· τοιαῦτα γοῦν ἐγκαλῶν ἐκεῖνος, καὶ λυμεῶνα καὶ πλάνον καὶ τὰ αὐτὰ, ἅπερ ὑμεῖς φθέγγεσθε, τὸν Παῦλον ἀποκαλῶν, τὸ μὲν πρῶτον ἔδησεν, ὡς δὲ οὐκ ἔπειθε τῆς πρὸς τὴν κόρην ἀποσχέσθαι συμβουλῆς, τέλος ἀπέκτεινε. τί οὖν ἀπὸ τούτου γέγονε βλάβος τῷ παθόντι κακῶς; τί δὲ ὄφελος τῷ δράσαντι κακῶς; τί μὲν οὐκ ὄφελος τῷ τότε ἀναιρεθέντι Παύλῳ; τί δὲ οὐ βλάβος τῷ ἀνελόντι Νέρωνι; οὐχ ὁ μὲν ὥσπερ ἄγγελος πανταχοῦ τῆς οἰκουμένης ᾄδεται (τὰ γὰρ παρόντα τέως ἐρῶ)· ὁ δὲ, ὥσπερ ὄντως λυμεὼν καὶ δαίμων ἄγριος πρὸς πάντας διαβέβληται;

18. John Chrysostom, *De laudibus sancti Pauli apostoli* 4.15[25]

εἴπω σοι καὶ ἑτέρωθεν δύναμιν κηρύγματος θαυμαστὴν καὶ παράδοξαν, καὶ δείξω σοι καὶ διὰ τῶν πολεμούντων αἰρόμενον αὐτὸν καὶ αὐξανόμενον; τῷ Παύλῳ τούτῳ ποτέ τινες πολεμοῦντες, ἐκήρυττον τουτὶ τὸ δόγμα ἐν Ῥώμῃ. βουλόμενοι γὰρ τὸν Νέρωνα παροξῦναι πολεμοῦντα τῷ Παύλῳ, ἀναδέχονται καὶ αὐτοὶ κηρύττειν, ἵνα μᾶλλον πλατυνθέντος τοῦ λόγου, καὶ πλειόνων γινομένων μαθητῶν, θερμότερος ὁ θυμὸς τοῦ τυράννου γένηται, καὶ ἀγριωθῇ τὸ θηρίον. καὶ τοῦτο αὐτὸς ὁ Παῦλος Φιλιππησίοις ἐπιστέλλων ἔλεγε· γινώσκειν ὑμᾶς βούλομαι, ἀδελφοὶ, ὅτι τὰ κατ᾽ ἐμὲ μᾶλλον εἰς προκοπὴν τοῦ εὐαγγελίου ἐλήλυθεν· ὥστε τοὺς πλείονας τῶν ἀδελφῶν πεποιθότας τοῖς δεσμοῖς μου, περισσοτέρως τολμᾷν ἀφόβως τὸν λόγον λαλεῖν. τινὲς μὲν καὶ διὰ φθόνον καὶ

24. PG 47:323–24.
25. PG 50:493.

17. John Chrysostom, *Against the Opponents of the Monastic Life* 1.3 (ca. 376 CE)

You have heard a lot about Nero, for he was a man who was famous for his wicked lifestyle. He was the first and only one who found in such a position of leadership some new forms of intemperance and opportunities for disgraceful conduct. This Nero accused the blessed Paul—for it happened that they both lived at the same time—with the very sorts of charges that you bring against these holy men.[36] For Paul had persuaded Nero's very beloved mistress to accept the teaching of the faith and likewise to withdraw from impure sexual intercourse. Accusing Paul of such things, that man called him a corrupter and deceiver, the very things that you say. First he put [Paul] in chains, but because this did not persuade him to agree to stay away from the young woman, he finally killed him. What harm came from this to the one suffering unjustly? And what was the benefit to the one acting wickedly? What benefit did not come to Paul, who was killed at that time? And what harm did not come to Nero, who killed him? Is not the one praised everywhere on the earth as a herald.[37] For I am speaking of the things of this life. And is not the other remembered by everyone with contempt as a destroyer and a savage demon?

18. John Chrysostom, *On the Praises of Saint Paul* 4.15 (ca. 390 CE)

Should I tell you in another way about the marvelous and incredible power of preaching, and should I show you that [Paul] was lifted up and strengthened even through those waging war against him? At that time some of those fighting against this man Paul were preaching their doctrine in Rome. For wishing to spur on Nero—who was waging war against Paul—they took up preaching, so that after the word had been spread more and many had become disciples, the wrath of the tyrant would burn hotter, and the beast would be made more savage. "I want you to know, brothers, that the things that have happened to me have turned out even more for the advancement of the gospel, so that the majority of the brothers, who have been encouraged by my chains, dare to speak the word more fearlessly.

36. These are the monks of Chrysostom's time who are being criticized for their promotion of chastity. They are being persecuted like Paul, while their critics are acting like Nero.

37. Or *angel*.

ἔριν, τινὲς δὲ καὶ δι' εὐδοκίαν τὸν Χριστὸν κηρύσσουσιν· οἱ μὲν ἐξ ἐριθείας, οὐχ ἁγνῶς, οἰόμενοι θλῖψιν ἐπιφέρειν τοῖς δεσμοῖς μου· οἱ δὲ ἐξ ἀγάπης, εἰδότες ὅτι εἰς ἀπολογίαν τοῦ εὐαγγελίου κεῖμαι. τί γάρ; πλὴν παντὶ τρόπῳ, εἴτε προφάσει, εἴτε ἀληθείᾳ, Χριστὸς καταγγέλλεται. εἶδες πῶς πολλοὶ ἐξ ἐριθείας ἐκήρυττον; ἀλλ' ὅμως καὶ διὰ τῶν ἐναντίων ἐκράτει.

19. John Chrysostom, *Homiliae in epistulam ii ad Timotheum* 10.1–2[26]

A. *On 2 Tim 4:9–13*

[1] καὶ κύριος ἀποδημίας οὐκέτι ἦν· δεσμωτήριον ᾤκει, καὶ συνεκέκλειστο ὑπὸ Νέρωνος, καὶ ὅσον οὔπω ἔμελλε τελευτᾷν. ἵνα οὖν μὴ τοῦτο γένηται πρὸ τοῦ τὸν μαθητὴν ἰδεῖν, διὰ τοῦτο αὐτὸν καλεῖ, θεάσασθαι ποθῶν πρὸ τῆς τελευτῆς, καὶ ἴσως πολλὰ παραθέσθαι· διό φησι· σπούδασον πρὸ χειμῶνος ἐλθεῖν πρός με.

B. *On 2 Tim 4:16*

[2] ποίαν δὲ πρώτην ἀπολογίαν λέγει; παρέστη ἤδη τῷ Νέρωνι, καὶ διέφυγεν· ἐπειδὴ δὲ τὸν οἰνοχόον αὐτοῦ κατήχησε, τότε αὐτὸν ἀπέτεμεν.

C. *On 2 Tim 4:17–18*

[2] καὶ ἐρρύσατό με ἐκ στόματος λέοντος· καὶ ῥύσεταί με ὁ Κύριος ἀπὸ παντὸς ἔργου πονηροῦ. ὅρα πῶς παρὰ μικρὸν ἦλθεν ἀποθανεῖν. εἰς αὐτὸν τοῦ λέοντος ἐνέπεσε τὸν φάρυγγα. λέοντα γὰρ τὸν Νέρωνά φησι διὰ τὸ θηριῶδες καὶ ἰσχυρὸν τῆς βασιλείας αὐτοῦ καὶ ἀκατάπληκτον. καὶ ἐρρύσατό με, φησὶν, ὁ Κύριος, καὶ

26. PG 62:655–57.

Some preach Christ out of envy and strife, while others preach out of good will. Some do it out of contention and not from pure motives, thinking that they will add on to my chains. Others preach out of love, knowing that I am heading for a defense of the gospel. What then? Only that in every way, either out of falsehood or truth, Christ is being preached."[38] Do you see how many were preaching out of contention? But nevertheless, he was triumphing through his opponents.[39]

19. John Chrysostom, *Homilies on 2 Timothy* 10.1–2 (ca. 393 CE)

A. *On 2 Tim 4:9–13*

[1] He was no longer in control of his movements. He lived as a prisoner and was locked away by Nero, and he was not yet at the point of death. Thus, so that this [i.e., his death] might not happen before he saw his disciple [Timothy], he therefore called him, longing to see him before death and probably to commit to him many things. For this reason he says, "Hurry to come to me before winter."

B. *On 2 Tim 4:16*

[2] What kind of "first defense" is [Paul] talking about? He had already stood before Nero and escaped. But after he taught his cupbearer,[40] Nero beheaded him.

C. *On 2 Tim 4:17–18*

[2] "And he delivered me out the mouth of the lion," and, "The Lord will protect me from every evil deed." See how close he came to dying. He had fallen into the very throat of the lion. He says that Nero is a lion because of his ferocity and the violence and brashness of his kingdom. "And he delivered me," he says, and, "The Lord will deliver." If [the Lord] will

38. Phil 1:15–18.

39. On the possible role of intra-Christian conflict in the death of Paul, see David L. Eastman, "Jealousy, Internal Strife, and the Deaths of Peter and Paul: A Reassessment of *1 Clement*," *ZAC* 18 (2014): 34–53.

40. The cupbearer is identified as Patroclus in Mart. Paul 1–2; Pseudo-Linus, *Mart. Paul* 2–5.

ῥύσεται. εἰ ῥύσεται πάλιν, πῶς ἔλεγεν ὅτι Ἤδη σπένδομαι; ἀλλὰ πρόσεχε τῇ φωνῇ· ἐρρύσατό με, φησὶν, ἐκ στόματος λέοντος. καὶ πάλιν ῥύσεται, οὐκέτι ἐκ στόματος, ἀλλά τί; ἀπὸ παντὸς ἔργου πονηροῦ. τότε μὲν γάρ με τῶν κινδύνων ἐξήρπασεν· ἐπειδὴ δὲ τὸ ἱκανὸν τῷ εὐαγγελίῳ γέγονε, ῥύσεταί με πάλιν ἀπὸ παντὸς ἁμαρτήματος. τουτέστιν, οὐκ ἀφήσει καταγνωσθέντα ἀπελθεῖν. καὶ γὰρ καὶ τοῦτο, τὸ δυνηθῆναι μέχρις αἵματος ἀντικαταστῆναι πρὸς τὴν ἁμαρτίαν καὶ μὴ ἐνδοῦναι, ἑτέρου λέοντός ἐστι ῥύσασθαι, τοῦ διαβόλου.

20. John Chrysostom, *Homiliae in Acta apostolorum* 46[27]

λέγεται Νέρωνος καὶ οἰνοχόον καὶ παλλακίδα ἀσπάσαι· πόσα οἴεσθε κατ' αὐτοῦ εἰρηκέναι αὐτοὺς διὰ τοῦτο; ἀλλ' οὐ δικαίως. εἰ μὲν γὰρ ἐπὶ ἀσελγείᾳ ἠσπάσατο, ἢ ἐπὶ πονηροῖς πράγμασιν, εἰκότως· εἰ δὲ ἐπὶ βίῳ ὀρθῷ, τίνος ἕνεκεν;

21. Jerome, *Tractatus in Psalmos* 96:10[28]

Hic oritur questio: si Dominus custodit animas sanctorum suorum, et de manu peccatori[bu]s liberat, quomodo in persecutione martyres opprimuntur? quomodo Petrum et Paulum Nero impius una die data sententia morte damnauit, si custodit Dominus animas sanctorum suorum? diligenter attendite quid dicat. custodit Dominus animas sanctorum suorum: animas dixit, non corpora. nolite timere eos, ait, qui occidunt corpora, animas autem non possunt occidere; sed eum timete, qui corpus et animam potest occidere in Gehennam. quomodo ergo custodit Dominus animas sanctorum suorum? in martyrio. pretiosa in conspectu Domini mors sanctorum eius. in martyrio ideo sanguis effunditur, ut anima de temptationibus liberetur: ut relinquat breuem uitam, et migret ad aeternam: ut relin-

27. PG 60:325.

28. Germain Morin, ed., *S. Hieronymi presbyteri opera, Pars II: Opera homiletica*, CCSL 78 (Turnhout: Brepols, 1958), 445–46.

deliver again, then why does [Paul] say, "I am already being poured out as a drink offering"? Pay attention to what he says: "He delivered me out of the mouth of the lion." And again, "He will deliver"—not out of the mouth, but what?—"from every evil deed. For at that time [the Lord] snatched me away from dangers, but because enough has been done for the gospel, he will again rescue me from all sin. In other words, he will not permit me to depart condemned."[41] For being able to resist sin to the point of shedding blood[42] and not giving in, this is being delivered from another lion, the devil.

20. John Chrysostom, *Homilies on Acts* 46 (ca. 400 CE)

It is said that [Paul] welcomed both the cupbearer and the concubine of Nero. What sorts of things do you suppose they said against him because of this? But they did not do so rightly. For if he welcomed them for licentiousness or wicked deeds, then rightly [did they speak against him]. But if for proper living, then for what reason [did they speak against him]?

21. Jerome, *Tractate on the Psalms* 96:10 (ca. 389–391 CE)

Here the question is raised: If the Lord preserves the souls of his saints and frees them from the hand of sinners, then how were the martyrs overcome by persecution? How did the impious Nero condemn Peter and Paul with a death sentence given on one day, if the Lord preserves the souls of his saints? Pay careful attention to what he says: "The Lord preserves the souls of his saints." He says souls, not bodies. "Do not fear those," he says, "who kill your bodies but cannot kill your souls. But fear the one who is able to cast body and soul into Gehenna."[43] How then does the Lord preserve the souls of his saints? In martyrdom: "Precious in the sight of the Lord is the death of his saints."[44] In martyrdom, therefore, the blood is poured forth, so that the soul may be freed from temptations, leave behind this brief life, and depart to the eternal one; and so that it may leave behind persecution

41. These final lines are unknown in the Pauline corpus. Chrysostom seems to be taking up the voice of Paul, but it is unclear where where Chrysostom as Paul ends and Chrysostom speaking in his own voice resumes.

42. Heb 12:4.

43. Matt 10:28.

44. Ps 116:15.

quat persecutionem, et uadat ad coronantem Dominum nostrum Iesum Christum. cui est honor et gloria in saecula saeculorum. amen.

22. Jerome, *De uiris illustribus* 1, 5[29]

[1] Simon Petrus, filius Iohannis, prouinciae Galileae uico Bethsaida, frater Andreae apostoli et princeps apostolorum, post episcopatum Antiochensis ecclesiae et praedicationem dispersionis eorum qui de circumcisione crediderant, in Ponto, Galatia, Cappadocia, Asia et Bithynia, secundo Claudii anno, ad expugnandum Simonem magum, Roman pergit ibique uiginti quinque annis cathedram sacerdotalem tenuit usque ad ultimum annum Neronis. id est, quartum decimum. a quo et adfixus cruci, martyrio coronatus est, capite ad terram uerso et in sublime pedibus eleuatis, adserens se indignum qui sic crucifigeretur ut Dominus suus … sepultus Romae in Uaticano, iuxta uiam triumphalem, totius orbis ueneratione celebratur.

[5] et quia in actis apostolorum plenissime de eius conuersatione scriptum est, hoc tantum dicam, quod, post passionem Domini uicesimo quinto anno, id est secundo Neronis eo tempore quo Festus procurator Iudaeae successit Felici, Romam uinctus mittitur et, biennium in libera manens custodia, aduersum Iudaeos de aduentu Christi cotidie disputauit. sciendum autem in prima satisfactione, necdum Neronis imperio roborato

29. Ernest Cushing Richardson, ed., *Hieronymus Liber de viris inlustribus, Gennadius Liber de viris inlustribus*, TUGAL 24 (Leipzig: Hinrichs, 1896), 6–10.

and hurry forth to our Lord Jesus Christ, who offers a crown. To him be honor and glory forever and ever. Amen.

22. Jerome, *On Illustrious Men* 1, 5 (392–393 CE)

[1] Simon Peter, the son of John, was from the village of Bethsaida in the province of Galilee, the brother of the apostle Andrew and chief of the apostles. After being bishop of the church in Antioch and preaching to the diaspora of those who had believed in circumcision in Pontus, Galatia, Cappadocia, Asia, and Bithynia, he went to Rome in the second year of [the reign of] Claudius to defeat Simon the sorcerer. There he held the priestly chair for twenty-five years, until the final year of Nero's reign, which was year fourteen.[45] He was nailed to a cross by Nero and crowned with martyrdom, with his head turned toward the earth and his feet lifted skyward, for he claimed that he was unworthy of being crucified in the same way as his Lord … He was buried at Rome on the Vatican hill, next to the Triumphal Way, and is venerated with honor throughout the whole world.

[5] Because his manner of life was written about extensively in the Acts of the Apostles, I will say only this: In the twenty-fifth year after the passion of the Lord—that is, the second year of [the reign of] Nero, at the time that Festus, the procurator of Judea, succeeded Felix[46]—[Paul] was sent in chains to Rome. For two years he remained in free custody[47] and argued daily with the Jews about the coming of Christ. It must be known, however, that at Paul's first defense, the power of Nero had not yet been strengthened, nor had his wickedness burst forth to such a degree as the

45. 67/68 CE Nero died on June 9, 68 CE, so if he had any hand in Peter's death, it had to occur in 67 according to this account.

46. 55/56 CE. This would place the death of Jesus in 32/33 CE and would assign the beginning of the term of Porcius Festus to 55/56 CE. Both of these dates are disputed. On the dates of Jesus's death, see e.g., Karl Paul Donfried, "Chronology of the Life of Jesus," *ABD* 1:1015–16; Raymond E. Brown, *An Introduction to the New Testament* (New York: Doubleday, 1997), 429. On the date of Festus as procurator, see David L. Eastman, "Paul: An Outline of His Life," in Mark Harding and Alanna Nobbs, eds., *All Things to All Cultures: Paul among Jews, Greeks and Romans* (Grand Rapids: Eerdmans, 2013), 49–50.

47. Cf. Acts 28:16, where Paul is under "military custody," meaning that he is allowed to live in a private dwelling but is guarded by a soldier. On the different categories of imprisonment, see Richard J. Cassidy, *Paul in Chains: Roman Imprisonment and the Letters of St. Paul* (New York: Crossroad, 2001), 37–43.

nec in tanta erumpente scelera quanta de eo narrant historiae, Paulum a Nerone dimissum, ut euangelium Christi in Occidentis quoque partibus praedicaretur, sicut ipse scribit in secunda ad Timotheum, eo tempore quo et passus est, et de uinculis dictat epistulam: in prima mea satisfactione nemo mihi adfuit, sed omnes me dereliquerunt; non eis inputetur. Dominus autem mihi adfuit et confortatuit me, ut per me praedicatio conpleretur et audirent omnes gentes, et liberatus sum de ore leonis, manifestissime leonem propter crudelitatem Neronem significans. et in sequentibus, liberauit me ab ore leonis, et statim, liberauit me Dominus ab omni opere malo et saluabit in regnum suum caeleste, quod scilicet praesens sibi sentiret inminere martyrium. nam in eadem epistula praemiserat: ego enim iam inmolor et tempus resolutionis meae instat. et hic ergo, quarto decimo Neronis anno eodem die quo Petrus, Romae pro Christo capite truncatur, sepultusque est in uia Ostiensi anno post passionem Domini tricesimo septimo.

23. Asterius of Amasea, *Homiliae* 8.16, 33 (*In sanctos principes apostolos Petrum et Paulum*)[30]

16. χρόνου δὲ προϊόντος τὴν βασιλεύουσαν τῶν ἀνθρώπων πόλιν καταλαβὼν ἐκεῖθεν ἐπὶ τὴν βασιλείαν ἀνέδραμεν. ἀναρριπισθεὶς γὰρ ὁ Νέρων εἰς ὀργὴν ὥς ποτε κατὰ τὴν Παλαιστίνην Ἡρώδης ἡνίκα βασιλέα τὸν Χριστὸν οἱ μάγοι διήγγελλον, ὑπερβαίνει μὲν τοὺς ἄλλους τῶν κολάσεων τρόπους, ψηφίζεται δὲ τὸν τρισμακάριον ξύλῳ προσηλωθῆναι σταυροῦ, ἵνα μὴ μόνον πεζεύων θάλασσαν Πέτρος τὸν Δεσπότην μιμῆται, ἀλλὰ καὶ ἐπὶ τοῦ ξύλου κρεμάμενος. ὅμως ὡς εὐλαβὴς καὶ σοφὸς κἀν τῷ καιρῷ τῆς ἀγωνίας εἰδὼς τίς διαφορὰ Κυρίου πρὸς δοῦλον μίαν ᾔτησε παρὰ τῶν ἐχθρῶν χάριν μήτοι γε ἐν ὁμοίῳ τῷ σχήματι τῷ ξύλῳ προσαγαγεῖν, ἀλλὰ τὴν κεφαλὴν τῷ προσγείῳ μέρει τοῦ σταυροῦ προσηλώσαντας. οὐ γὰρ ἄξιον οὐδὲ ἐν πάθει τῶν ἴσων τὸν δοῦλον τῷ Δεσπότῃ τυχεῖν. εἶπεν καὶ ἔτυχεν ὧν ἐβούλετο καὶ διὰ τοῦ σταυροῦ πρὸς

30. Cornelis Datema, ed., *Asterius of Amasea: Homilies I–XIV* (Leiden: Brill, 1970), 96–97, 106.

histories tell about him. Paul was released by Nero, so that he might preach the gospel of Christ also in the western regions, just as he himself writes in his second letter to Timothy at the time that he suffered, which he dictated while in chains: "At my first defense no one was with me; everyone abandoned me, but let it not be held against them. The Lord, however, was with me and comforted me, so that through me the teaching may be completed and all the gentiles might hear. And the Lord freed me from the mouth of the lion." Obviously he uses "lion" because of the cruelty of Nero. In what follows he says, "He freed me from the mouth of the lion," and just after this, "The Lord freed me from every wicked deed and will save me into his celestial kingdom," because he certainly sensed that his martyrdom was imminent. For in the same epistle he declared, "I am already being offered as a sacrifice, and the time of my release is at hand." Therefore, in the fourteenth year of Nero and on the same day as Peter, Paul was decapitated in Rome for Christ. He was buried on the Ostian Road in the thirty-seventh year after the passion of the Lord.[48]

23. Asterius of Amasea, *Homily* 8.16, 33 (*On the Holy Princes of the Apostles Peter and Paul*) (380–415 CE)

16. When the time came [Peter] came to the city that ruled over all people, and from there he returned to the kingdom. For Nero was rekindled in his anger—just as Herod had been at one time in Palestine, when the magi proclaimed Christ the king.[49] He passed over the other methods of torture and decided to nail the triple-blessed one to the wood of a cross, so that Peter might imitate his Lord not only in walking on the sea, but also in hanging on a tree. Nevertheless, as a pious and wise man, even in a time of suffering, he knew the difference between a master and his servant, and he asked one favor from his enemies: that they place him on the cross not in the same position [as the Lord], but with his head toward the bottom of the cross, for it is not proper even in suffering that the servant should be equal to his master.[50] He spoke and it happened as he requested. Adorned

48. 67/68 CE.

49. Matt 2:1–12. According to Matthew, Herod responded by killing all the male children in and around Bethlehem who were two years old and younger (2:16–18).

50. Cf. Matt 10:24; John 13:16, 15:20.

τὸν σταυρωθέντα καὶ ἀναστάντα ἀπῆλθεν, αὐτὸς μὲν τὸν τοῦ μαρτυρίου ἀναδησάμενος στέφανον, ἡμῖν δὲ τούτων τῶν ἑορτῶν καταλιπὼν τὰς αἰτίας.

33. ἐπειδὴ γὰρ πᾶσαν ἐκπεριελθὼν τὴν οἰκουμένην καὶ θεὶς ἐπὶ τῆς λυχνίας τὸν λόγον μέγαν ἀνῆψε τῆς εὐαγγελικῆς γνώσεως τὸν πυρσόν, ἀφίκετο μὲν καὶ πρὸς Ῥωμαίους, ὡς βασιλεύουσαν πόλιν, ἵνα τοὺς κρατοῦντας τῶν πάντων ἀνθρώπων μυσταγωγήσας καὶ πείσας καὶ κτησάμενος μαθητὰς ἐκ τοῦ περιόντος τοῖς ἄλλοις ἀνθρώποις προσομιλοίη. εὑρὼν δὲ καὶ τὸν Πέτρον ἐκεῖ, τῆς αὐτῆς ἐργάτην σπουδῆς, καὶ ἱεράν τινα καὶ ἔνθεον ξυνωρίδα ζευξάμενος ἐν συναγωγαῖς τοὺς ὑπὸ νόμον ἐπαίδευεν, ἐν ἀγοραῖς τοὺς ἐθνικοὺς προσεκτᾶτο· καὶ ποικίλος ἦν τῶν ἀγαθῶν διδάσκαλος θεοῦ γνῶσιν ἐμφανίζων τὴν καθαρὰν καὶ ἀκίβδηλον, ἠθικῆς ἀρετῆς κανόνας θεσμοθετῶν ἀκριβεῖς, ἀπελαύνων πόρρω τῶν ἀνθρώπων χορείας καὶ μέθην καὶ πᾶσαν τὴν ἀκόλαστον ἡδυπάθειαν, ᾗ μάλιστα καὶ τὸ πλῆθος ἅπαν καὶ ὁ τότε βασιλεύων ἐνείχετο. καθήψατο τοίνυν σφοδρῶς τοῦ Νερῶνος ἡ τῆς ἀρίστης καὶ σώφρονος πολιτείας εἰσαγωγή· καὶ πλέον ἀλγήσας τῆς ἡδονῆς καταλυομένης ἢ εἰ τῆς βασιλείας αὐτῆς ἐξεβάλλετο. καὶ γαρ ἦν, εἴπερ τις ἄλλος, σοφιστὴς ἡδονῶν, τρυφῶν καὶ καταυλούμενος, βλὰξ καὶ θηλυδρίας, πορνῶν ἐπιστάτης, οὐ βασιλεὺς ἀνδρῶν. πῶς γὰρ ἂν ἑτέρων ἐκράτησεν ὁ ἄρχειν ἑαυτοῦ μὴ μαθών; μίαν ἔθετο φροντίδα, ὅπως ἂν

with the crown of martyrdom, through the cross he went away to the one who was crucified and rose again, but he left behind for us the occasions for these feasts.

33. When [Paul] had gone around the entire world and had placed the great word upon the lampstand,[51] he lit the torch of the knowledge of the gospel. Then he arrived at Rome, the ruling city, so that after initiating and persuading the rulers of all the people and making disciples in that region, he might go on to speak with other people.[52] There he found Peter, a worker with the same zeal. After joining with him in a certain holy and godly community, he was teaching those under the law in the synagogues and winning over the gentiles in the marketplaces. He was a skilled teacher of good things, making clear the pure and untainted knowledge of God. He set down the precise standards of moral virtue, driving out among the people from that time forward dancing, drunkenness, and every unbridled lust, in which the whole multitude and the one ruling at that time were entangled. The introduction of the most excellent and temperate[53] way of life was a direct assault on Nero. Nero suffered much from the loss of pleasure, as if he had been thrown out of his kingdom. For he was, if anything, a master of pleasures, delicate and a flute player,[54] sluggish and effeminate, a commander of harlots, not a king of men.[55] For how could the one who did not know how to control himself rule over others? He made it his one

51. The image of a lampstand appears in Rev 1:20 with reference to the seven churches of Asia Minor, of which Ephesus is one. This could be an oblique reference to the fact that Paul brought the gospel to the Ephesians.

52. Asterius may have in mind Rom 15:23–24, where Paul tells the Romans that he plans to visit them but then move to preach in Spain.

53. Or "chaste," thus highlighting the curbing of Nero's sensual lusts.

54. Nero was famous for his love of singing and playing the lyre, even in public and at the Olympic Games of 67 CE. According to the Roman historians Suetonius, *Nero* 42; Tacitus, *Ann.* 14.15; and Cassius Dio, *Hist.* 61.21, some found such performances disgraceful. The famous image of Nero fiddling while Rome burned is derived from the accounts by Suetonius (*Nero* 38) and Cassius Dio (*Hist.* 62.18), who claim that Nero sang "The Capture of Troy" as Rome was burning during the great fire of 64. Tacitus dismisses this story as a rumor (*Ann.* 15.39).

55. Charges of sexual deviance and effeminacy against Nero originated with Roman authors such as Suetonius (*Otho* 12; *Nero* 29). See e.g., Megan Rowland, "Effeminacy as Imperial Vice in Suetonius' Nero and Caligula," *Classicum* 36.2 (2010): 23–30; Jason von Ehrenkrook, "Effeminacy in the Shadow of Empire: The Politics of Transgressive Gender in Josephus's *Bellum Judaicum*," *JQR* 101 (2011): 145–63.

ἐκκόψειε ἐκ τῆς πόλεως τὸν τῆς εὐσεβείας καὶ σωφροσύνης διδάσκαλον. καὶ ζηλώσας τὸν Ἡρώδην τῆς γνώμης ἀπάγει τοὺς ἀποστόλους εἰς δεσμωτήριον, ὡς τὸν Ἰωάννην ἐκεῖνος, ἔχων δὲ καθ' ὁμοιότητα ἄλλην Ἡρωδιάδα τὴν ἀκόλαστον καὶ φιλήδονον γνώμην ζητοῦσαν Πέτρου καὶ Παύλου τὴν κεφαλὴν ἀμφοτέρους ἀνέδησε τῷ στεφάνῳ τοῦ μαρτυρίου· τὸν μὲν τῷ ξύλῳ προσηλώσας, τοῦ δὲ Παύλου τὴν κεφαλὴν ἐκτεμών, ἡμῖν δὲ καὶ τῷ κόσμῳ καταλιπὼν τὸ τῶν ἁγίων πάθος πανήγυριν καὶ τοσαύτης ἑορτῆς ἀφορμήν.

24. Sulpicius Severus, *Chronicon* 2.28–29[31]

[28] Apostolorum actus Lucas edidit usque in tempus, quo Paulus Romam deductus est Nerone imperante: qui non dicam regum, sed omnium hominum et uel inmanium bestiarum sordidissimus dignus extitit, qui persecutionem primus inciperet: nescio an et postremus explerit, siquidem opinione multorum receptum sit, ipsum ante antichristum uenturum. huius uitia ut plenius exponerem res admonebat, nisi non esset huius operis tam uasta ingredi: id tantum annotasse contentus sum, hunc per omnia foedissima et crudelissima eo processisse, ut matrem interficeret, post etiam Pythagorae cuidam in modum sollemnium coniugiorum denuberet;

31. Charles Halm, ed., *Sulpicii Severi libri qui supersunt*, CSEL 1 (Vienna: Gerold, 1866), 82–84.

concern to remove from the city the teacher of piety and temperance.[56] Emulating Herod in his thinking, he sent the apostles to prison, just as Herod had done to John, for he had another who in appearance was like Herodias—unbridled and fond of pleasure in her thinking—and was seeking the heads of Peter and Paul.[57] He adorned both of them with the crown of martyrdom. One he nailed to a cross, while he cut off the head of Paul. But for us and the world he left behind the suffering of the saints as a holiday and an occasion for such a great feast.[58]

24. Sulpicius Severus, *Chronicle* 2.28–29 (404 CE)

[28] Luke related the acts of the apostles up to the time that Paul was brought to Rome, when Nero was ruling. I will not say that he stands out just as the worst of rulers, but as the worst of all people and even of wild beasts. He was the first to initiate a persecution. I do not know whether he will be the last, if indeed, as it has been passed down by the opinion of many, he will return before the antichrist.[59] That question would require that I expound extensively on his vices, but it is not the purpose of this work to take up so vast a topic. I have limited myself to note this—that he went so far in all his extremely repulsive and cruel actions that he killed his mother[60] and even married a certain Pythagoras in the manner of the

56. Or "chastity."

57. In Mark 6:17–28 (parallels in Matt 14:3–11; Luke 3:19–20) Herodias conspires to have John the Baptist beheaded by Herod, for John had condemned the unlawful marriage between Herod and Herodias. Herodias's daughter dances at a feast, and in response Herod promises her up to half his kingdom. Prompted by her mother, the girl asks for John's head on a platter. It is unclear who the Neronian equivalent to Herodias is meant to be. Nero was married three times (Claudia Octavia 54–62, Poppaea Sabina 62–65, and Statilia Messalina 65–68) but was known to have other lovers, as well.

58. The two references to the liturgical calendar suggest that this homily was written for the festival day of Peter and Paul (June 29).

59. The linking of Nero with an antichrist figure also appears in Mart. Ascen. Isa. 4:2–4 (text 2 in this chapter); Sib. Or. 5.28–34, 361–85; Commodian, *Instr.* 41; Lactantius, *Mort.* 2.8 (text 14 in this chapter); Augustine, *Civ.* 20.19.3. Central to this connection is the theory that 666, the "number of the beast" in Rev 13:18, is a direct reference to Nero through the use of gematria (assigning a numerical value to words or names). Most scholars accept the theory that 666 is an oblique reference to Nero, but it must be noted that Nero is called the beast, not the antichrist. In fact, there is no antichrist figure in Revelation.

60. Suetonius, *Nero* 34; Tacitus, *Ann.* 14.3–8. Both authors record that it took Nero

inditumque imperatori flammeum; dos et genialis torus et faces nuptiales, cuncta denique, quae uel in feminis non sine uerecundia conspiciuntur, spectata. reliqua uero eius incertum pigeat an pudeat magis disserere. hic primus Christianum nomen tollere agressus est: quippe semper inimica uirtutibus uitia sunt et optimi quique ab improbis quasi exprobrantes aspiciuntur. namque eo tempore diuina apud urbem religio inualuerat, Petro ibi episcopatum gerente et Paulo, posteaquam ab iniusto praesidis iudicio Caesarem appellauerat, Romam deducto: ad quem tum audiendum plures conueniebant, qui ueritate intellecta uirtutibusque apostolorum, quas tum crebro ediderant, permoti ad cultum Dei se conferebant. etenim tum illustris illa aduersus Simonem Petri ac Pauli congressio fuit. qui cum magicis artibus, ut se deum probaret, duobus suffultus daemoniis euolasset, orationibus apostolorum fugatis daemonibus, delapsus in terram populo inspectante disruptus est.

[29] interea abundante iam Christianorum multitudine accidit ut Roma incendio conflagraret, Nerone apud Antium constituto. sed opinio omnium inuidiam incendii in principem retorquebat, credebaturque imperator gloriam innouandae urbis quaesisse. neque ulla re Nero efficiebat, quin ab eo iussum incendium putaretur. igitur uertit inuidiam in Christianos, actaeque in innoxios crudelissimae quaestiones: quin et nouae mortes excogitatae, ut ferarum tergis contecti laniatu canum interirent, multi crucibus affixi aut flamma usti, plerique in id reseruati, ut cum defecisset dies, in usum nocturni luminis urerentur. hoc initio in Christianos

solemn conjugal rites. The bridal veil was placed upon the emperor. The dowry and the bridal bed, the wedding torches, and all the things that even among women are not looked upon without a sense of modesty—these were all displayed.[61] As for his other actions, I cannot say if they would provoke more disgust or shame.

He was the first to attempt to eliminate the Christian name. Of course, vices are always at odds with virtues, and the best men are looked at by the wicked as if they are reproaching them. For at that time the divine religion had grown strong in the city. Peter was filling the role of bishop there, and Paul had been brought to Rome after he appealed to Caesar because of the unjust sentence of the governor.[62] Many then gathered to hear him and turned to the worship of God, because they were moved by the truth they came to understand and the powerful deeds of the apostles, which they then performed frequently. Indeed, at that time the famous showdown of Peter and Paul with Simon took place. In order to prove that he was a god, Simon by his magical arts flew into the air, carried by two demons. After the demons fled due to the prayers of the apostles, he fell to the earth with all the people watching and was broken into pieces.

[29] Meanwhile, as the multitude of Christians was then growing very large, it came about that Rome was consumed by a fire while Nero was staying at Antium.[63] The opinion of all turned back upon the leader the blame for the fire, and the emperor was believed to have been seeking the glory of a rebuilt city. Nero could not by any means prevent the belief that the fire had been ordered by him. Thus, he turned the blame against the Christians, and the cruelest tortures were inflicted upon the innocent. Even new forms of death were imagined, and as a result [the Christians] were covered with the skins of wild animals and died by being torn apart by dogs. Many were crucified or burned with fire, and very many were set aside for the purpose of nightly illumination after day had ended.[64] In this

---

several attempts to kill his mother, Agrippina.

61. Tacitus, *Ann.* 15.37, is equally critical of Nero's lack of decorum in the marriage to Pythagoras. According to Suetonius (*Nero* 28–29) and Cassius Dio (*Hist.* 62.28, 63.13), while Nero was still married to Pythagoras, who played the role of his husband, he also forced a boy named Sporus to be castrated and marry him as his "wife."

62. Acts 25:9–12.

63. Tacitus, *Ann.* 15.39.

64. Suspicions about Nero's role in the fire and his subsequent cruelty to Christians are recorded by Pliny the Elder, *Nat.* 17.1; Suetonius, *Nero* 16, 38; Tacitus, *Ann.* 15.44; Cassius Dio, *Hist.* 62.16–18.

saeuiri coeptum. post etiam datis legibus religio uetabatur, palamque edictis propositis Christianum esse non licebat. tum Paulus ac Petrus capitis damnati: quorum uni ceruix gladio desecta, Petrus in crucem sublatus est. dum haec Romae geruntur, Iudaei, praesidis sui Festi Flori iniurias non ferentes, rebellare coeperunt. aduersus eos Uespasianus proconsulari imperio a Nerone missus multis grauibusque proeliis deuictos coegit intra muros Hierosolymae confugere. interim Nero iam etiam sibi pro conscientia scelerum inuisus, humanis rebus eximitur, incertum an ipse sibi mortem consciuerit: certe corpus illius non repertum. unde creditur, etiam si se gladio ipse transfixerit, curato uulnere eius seruatus, secundum illud, quod de eo scriptum est: et plaga mortis eius curata est, sub saeculi fine mittendus, ut mysterium iniquitatis exerceat.

25. Macarius of Magnesia, Ἀποκριτικὸς ἢ Μονογενὴς πρὸς Ἕλληνας 4.4.1–3, 4.14.1–2, 7[32]

A. [4.4.1] ἴδωμεν δ' ἐκεῖνο τὸ ῥηθὲν τῷ Παύλῳ· εἶπε δὲ δι' ὁράματος ὁ Κύριος ἐν νυκτὶ τῷ Παύλῳ· μὴ φοβοῦ, ἀλλὰ λάλει, ὅτι μετὰ σοῦ εἰμι καὶ οὐδεὶς ἐπιθήσεταί σοι τοῦ κακῶσαί σε. καὶ ὅσον οὐδέπω ἐν Ῥώμῃ κρατηθεὶς τῆς κεφαλῆς ἀποτέμνεται οὗτος ὁ κομψός, ὁ λέγων ὅτι ἀγγέλους κρινοῦμεν,

32. Richard Goulet, ed., *Macarios de Magnésie: Le monogénès*, TT 7 (Paris: Vrin, 2003), 2:246, 274–78.

way ferocity against Christians had its beginning. Afterward, even their religion was forbidden by laws that were put in place; and based on edicts that were put forth publicly, it was not permitted to be a Christian. At that time Paul and Peter were condemned to death. One of them had his head cut off, while Peter was raised up on a cross.

While these things were happening in Rome, the Jews began to rebel, because they would not endure the harms inflicted on them by their governor Festus Florus.[65] Vespasian was sent against them by Nero with the authority of a proconsul, and in numerous and great battles he forced the conquered to seek refuge within the walls of Jerusalem. Meanwhile, Nero, who now even looked upon himself with disgust because of an awareness of his wicked deeds, withdrew from human affairs, and it was uncertain if he had caused his own death. His body was never found. As a result it was believed that, even if he had stabbed himself with a sword, he was saved from his wound, which had healed. This belief came about because of what had been written about him: "And his mortal wound was healed,"[66] and at the end of the age he must be sent out to practice the mystery of wickedness.[67]

25. Macarius of Magnesia, *Answer Book or The Only Begotten to the Pagans* 4.4.1–3, 4.14.1–2, 7 (late fourth or early fifth century)

In this text Macarius responds to a series of criticisms of Christianity. In 4.4 he highlights the charge that the deaths of Paul and Peter were not in line with the promises that God had made to them. His response comes in 4.14.

A. [4.4.1] Let us consider what was said to Paul, "The Lord spoke to Paul at night through a vision, 'Do not fear, but speak, because I am with you, and no one will attack you to do you harm.' "[68] He had hardly arrived in Rome when this excellent fellow was arrested and had his head cut off—

65. This must be Gessius Florus, who was the Roman procurator of Judea from 64 to 66 CE. According to Josephus, Florus was openly antagonistic toward the Jews (*J.W.* 2.14.5–9) and ultimately provoked the Jewish Revolt (*Antiq*. 20.11.1).

66. Rev 13:3.

67. Many authors record the idea that Nero had not died but was going to return to seek revenge on the Roman Empire, e.g., Suetonius, *Nero* 57; Tacitus, *Hist*. 2.8; Cassius Dio, *Hist*. 66.19; Sib. Or. 5.137–54, 214–27, 361–85; Dio Chrysostom, *Pulchr*. (Or. 21) 10. This may be the fear reflected in Rev 13:3. Several men later claimed to be the risen Nero, but each was discovered to be a fraud.

68. Acts 18:9–10.

[2] οὐ μὴν ἀλλὰ καὶ Πέτρος λαβὼν ἐξουσίαν βόσκειν τὰ ἀρνία, τῷ σταυρῷ προσηλωθεὶς ἀνασκολοπίζεται· καὶ ἄλλοι δὲ μυρίοι τούτοις ὁμόδοξοι οἱ μὲν ἐκαύθησαν, οἱ δ᾽ ἄλλοι τιμωρίαν ἢ λώβην δεξάμενοι διεφθάρησαν. [3] τοῦτο δ᾽ οὐκ ἄξιον θεοῦ γνώμης, ἀλλ᾽ οὐδ᾽ ἀνδρὸς εὐσεβοῦς, εἰς αὐτοῦ χάριν καὶ πίστιν πλῆθος ἀνδρῶν ἀπανθρώπως κολάζεσθαι, τῆς προσδοκωμένης ἀναστάσεως καὶ ἐλεύσεως οὔσης ἀδήλου.

B. [4.14.1] λοιπὸν τὴν ὑπόθεσιν Πέτρου καὶ Παύλου καὶ τῶν ὁμογνωμόνων αὐτοῖς ἐπισκεπτέον, πῶς εἰπὼν Πέτρῳ· Βόσκε τὰ ἀρνία μου, καὶ Παύλῳ· λάλει, μὴ σιώπα, ὅτι μετὰ σοῦ εἰμι καὶ οὐδεὶς κακώσει σε, ἀμφοτέρους διάφορον τιμωρίαν δέξασθαι συνεχώρησεν. [2] ὃν μὲν γὰρ σταυρούμενον, ὃν δ᾽ ἀποτεμνόμενον ὁρῶν ἐκαρτέρησε καὶ μάλα πρεπόντως· οὐ πρὸ τῶν ἀγώνων οὐδὲ τῶν τῆς διδασκαλίας παιδευμάτων καὶ πράξεων, ἀλλὰ μετὰ τοὺς ἱδρῶτας, οὓς ὑπέμειναν εὐσεβῶς, διδάσκοντες γῆν, θάλασσαν πολλῆς ταραχῆς ἐκπραΰνοντες, νήσους ἐν βυθῷ πλάνης κεκλιμένας ἐγείροντες, τὰ ὑπ᾽ οὐρανὸν φωτὸς ἀκηράτου γεμίζοντες, ψυχὰς ἐσπιλωμένας ἐν πονηρίᾳ καθαίροντες, φρόνημα τετρωμένον καὶ μικροῦ δεῖν ἐσβεσμένον νουθεσίαις ἐξάπτοντες, τῆς παρακοῆς τὰ βέλη συντρίβοντες καὶ τῶν ἁμαρτημάτων τὰ ξίφη συγκόπτοντες, τῶν καταπονουμένων γενναίως προϊστάμενοι καὶ τῶν ἀδικουμένων ὑπέρμαχοι δυνατώτατοι, τῶν ἀπολωλότων ζητητῆρες ἄριστοι, καὶ τῶν καταπιπτόντων ἔρεισμα καὶ βοήθημα, πολλὰ θαυμασίων ἔργων τῷ κόσμῳ μηνύσαντες σταυρῷ καὶ τμήσει τὸν βίον ἐζημιώσαντο ... [7] ἵνα γοῦν μετὰ πολλὰ τῶν καλῶν ἀγωνισμάτων ὑστάτῳ καμάτῳ στεφαν[ῖται] ἀπέλθωσι, συνεχωρήθησαν εἰσελθεῖν εἰς τὸ μέγα τῶν πόνων καὶ ἐπίσημον θέατρον, καὶ ὁ μὲν τομὴν κεφαλῆς, ὁ δὲ σταυρὸν ὑπελθεῖν, δι᾽ ὧν ἡ τοῦ δράκοντος σπεῖρα συνεκόπη· ὁ μὲν γὰρ τῆς κεφαλῆς τμηθεὶς αἵματι καὶ γάλακτι τὸν ὄφιν εἰς λιχνείαν ὥσπερ ἐδελέασεν, ὁ δὲ τῷ σταυρῷ τοῦτον εὐτόνως συνέκοψε.

the very one who had said, "We will judge angels."[69] [2] But in fact also Peter, who had received the authority to feed the sheep,[70] was nailed and fixed to a cross. Some of the countless others who agreed with them were burned alive, while others were killed by being subject to torture or mutilation.[71] [3] It is not worthy of the purpose of God, nor even of a pious man, that a multitude of people should be savagely chastised because of his grace and their faith in him, while the expected resurrection and appearance remain unseen.

B. [4.14.1] Furthermore, we must consider the question about Peter and Paul and those who agreed with them. After saying to Peter, "Feed my sheep,"[72] and to Paul, "Speak, and do not be silent, because I am with you and no one will do you any harm,"[73] how did [the Lord] permit each of them to undergo a different form of suffering? For he endured seeing one of them crucified and the other decapitated. And yet, very appropriately [this took place] not before their struggles or their teaching about doctrine or their acts, but after the hardships that they faithfully endured. They instructed the earth; they calmed the sea, which was very tumultuous; they raised up islands that were lying in the depth of error; they filled everything under heaven with a pure light; they purified souls that were defiled by fornication; they kindled by their admonitions the spirit that had been wounded and nearly snuffed out; they demolished the weapons of disobedience and broke the swords of sinfulness; they nobly protected those who had been crushed and were the most powerful defenders of the oppressed; they were the most excellent seekers of those who were lost; they were a support and help to those who had fallen. After revealing to the world many of their miraculous deeds, they lost their lives by crucifixion and beheading ... [7] In order, then, that after the many deeds of their excellent contests, they might depart crowned by their final labor, they were allowed to go into the great and glorious theater of sufferings. One went to decapitation, the other to crucifixion. Through these deaths the coil of the serpent was cut to pieces, for it was as if the one who was decapitated enticed the serpent to a feast with his blood and the milk, and the other one vigorously cut him to pieces with the cross.[74]

69. 1 Cor 6:3.

70. John 21:15–17.

71. Cf. Heb 11:35–38.

72. John 21:17, which is followed by a prediction of Peter's death.

73. Acts 18:9–10.

74. The Greek here is somewhat obscure, but the idea seems to be that Paul lured

26. Augustine of Hippo, *Sermones*

A. 293A augm. (*De oboedientia*) 16[33]

Pretiosa in conspectu Domini mors iustorum eius. inde pretiosa mors Petri, inde pretiosa mors Pauli, inde pretiosa mors Uincentii, inde pretiosa mors Cypriani. unde pretiosa? ex caritate pura et conscientia bona et fide non ficta. uidit autem hoc anguis ille, uidit hoc antiquus serpens ille honorari martyres, templa deseri: astuta illa et uenenosa contra nos uigilantia sua, quia non potuit Christianis deos falsos, fecit martyres falsos. sed o uos, catholica germina, comparate nobiscum paululum istos martyres falsos martyribus ueris, et pia fide distinguite quod conatur diabolus fallacia uenenosa confundere.

B. 295.1, 7[34]

[1] Istum nobis diem beatissimorum apostolorum Petri et Pauli passio consecrauit. non de obscuris aliquibus martyribus loquimur. in omnem terram exiit sonus eorum, et in fines orbis terrae uerba eorum. isti martyres uiderunt quod praedicauerunt, secuti aequitatem, confitendo ueritatem, moriendo pro ueritate.

---

33. François Dolbeau, "Nouveaux sermons de saint Augustin pour la conversion des païens et des donatistes," *REAug* 38 (1992): 74–75.

34. PL 38:1348–52.

26. Augustine, *Sermons*

A. 293A augm. (*On Obedience* 16) (404 or 405 CE)

Precious in the sight of the Lord is the death of his just ones.[75] Therefore the death of Peter is precious; therefore the death of Paul is precious; therefore the death of Vincent[76] is precious; therefore the death of Cyprian is precious. On what account are they precious? Because of a pure affection and a good conscience and a faith that is not false. That snake, however, sees this. That ancient serpent sees that the martyrs are honored and the temples are deserted. He carefully concocted cunning and poisonous plots against us, and because he was not able to wield influence over Christians by false gods, he created false martyrs. But oh you, catholic sprouts, compare with us a little those false martyrs with the true martyrs, and by pious faith discern that the devil is trying to cause confusion by a poisonous fraud.[77]

Sermons 295–299C and 381 were all preached in different years on the feast of Peter and Paul (June 29). They include allusions to the apostolic deaths, but here I focus on passages with specific references to the martyrdoms.

B. 295.1, 7 (405–410 CE)

[1] This day has been consecrated for us by the martyrdoms of the most blessed apostles Peter and Paul. We are not talking about some obscure martyrs. Their sound has gone out into all the earth, and their words to the ends of the wide world.[78] These martyrs had seen what they proclaimed. They pursued justice by confessing the truth and by dying for the truth.

---

the serpent into the open, and then Peter delivered the deathblow. This imagery links the two deaths symbolically but also implicitly suggests a chronological relationship, with Paul's death first, followed by Peter. This runs counter to what we find in other sources, which suggest Peter died first. On the milk flowing from Paul's body, see Mart. Paul 5 (ch. 5 in this volume).

75. Ps 116:15.

76. Vincent was a deacon of Saragossa in Spain who died during the persecution under Diocletian.

77. Augustine is writing against the "false" Donatist martyrs in general, but he may have in mind the Circumcellion sect in particular. Members of this group reportedly jumped off cliffs in order to make themselves martyrs.

78. Ps 19:4; Rom 10:18.

[7] ecce ostendit illi Dominus quae illum oporteret pati pro nomine eius. post exercuit illum in labore. ipse in uinculis, ipse in plagis, ipse in carceribus, ipse in naufragiis. ipse illi procurauit passionem: ipse perduxit ad istum diem. unus dies passionis duobus apostolis. sed et illi duo unum erant: quanquam diuersis diebus paterentur, unum erant. praecessit Petrus, secutus est Paulus.

C. 297.5[35]

Attende apostolum Paulum, quoniam et ipsius hodie dies festus est. concordem uitam ambo duxerunt, socium sanguinem ambo fuderunt, coelestem coronam ambo sumpserunt, diem hodiernum ambo consecrauerunt.

D. 298.1[36]

Per angustias passionum, per uiam spinis plenam, per tribulationes persecutionem, ut transeant postea fideles, apostolos duces habuerunt. beatus Petrus primus apostolorum, beatus Paulus nouissimus apostolorum, qui rite coluerunt eum qui dixit: ego sum primus, et ego sum nouissimus, ad unum diem passionis sibi occurrerunt primus et nouissimus.

E. 299.8[37]

Sed quid est illud, fratres, quem non moueat? alter, inquit, te cinget, et feret quo tu non uis. non ergo uolens Petrus ad tantam gratiam passionis aduenit?

35. PL 38:1361.

36. D. C. Lambot, ed., *Sancti Aurelii Augustini Sermones selecti duodeviginti*, SPM 1 (Utrecht: Spectrum, 1950), 95.

37. PL 38:1373.

[7] Behold, the Lord showed [Paul] the things that he would have to suffer for the sake of his name. After that he trained Paul with hard labor—with chains, with beatings, with imprisonment, and with shipwrecks.[79] He secured for Paul his suffering and brought him to this very day. There is one day for the suffering of the two apostles, but those two are also one. Although they suffered on different days, they are one. Peter went first, and Paul followed.

C. 297.5 (405–410 CE)

Turn your attention to the apostle Paul, because today is also his feast day. They both [Peter and Paul] led a harmonious life; they both shed their blood together; they both received a heavenly crown; they both consecrated this present day.

D. 298.1 (428 CE)

In order that later the faithful could pass through the distresses of their sufferings, through the road full of thorns, and through the trials of persecutions, they had the apostles as their leaders. The blessed Peter was the first of the apostles, while the blessed Paul was the last of the apostles.[80] They rightly worshiped the one who had said, "I am the first and the last,"[81] and the first and the last [of the apostles] ran to meet each other on the one day of their passion.[82]

E. 299.8 (418 CE)

But what is this, brothers and sisters? And who would not be impacted by it? "Another," [Jesus] said, "will bind you and lead you where you do not

79. 2 Cor 11:23–27.

80. Cf. 1 Cor 15:9, where Paul calls himself the "least" (Vulgate: *minimus*) of the apostles.

81. Rev 1:17.

82. The image of Peter and Paul running to embrace each other in Rome was a common iconographical trope. See Herbert L. Kessler, "The Meeting of Peter and Paul in Rome: An Emblematic Narrative of Spiritual Brotherhood," in *Studies on Art and Archeology in Honor of Ernst Kitzinger on His Seventy-Fifth Birthday*, ed. William Tronzo and Irving Lavin, *DOP* 41 (Washington: Dumbarton Oaks, 1987), 265–75.

ecce Paulus, ego enim iam immolor, et tempus resolutionis meae instat; uidetur in his uerbis exsultande quasi festinare ad passionem: huic autem, alter te cinget, et feret quo tu non uis. uolens Paulus et nolens Petrus? imo si intelligamus, uolens Paulus et uolens Petrus, et nolens Paulus et nolens Petrus.

F. 299A.1[38]

Unus dies duorum martyrum et duorum apostolorum: quantum ecclesiae traditione percepimus, non uno die passi sunt, et uno die passi sunt. hodie prior passus est Petrus, hodie posterior passus est Paulus: aequauit meritum passionem, caritas occurrit ad diem; hoc egit in eis, qui erat in eis, qui in eis patiebatur, qui cum eis patiebatur, qui adiuuabat certantes, qui coronabat uincentes.

G. 299C.1[39]

Beati apostoli Petrus et Paulus diuersis temporibus sunt uocati, et uno die coronati. Petrum Dominus uocauit ante omnes, Paulum post omnes. apostolorum Petrus primus, Paulus nouissimus: adduxit eos ad unum diem primus et nouissimius. pulcherrima integritas perseuerat, quando cum primis extrema concordant.

H. 381[40]

Petri et Pauli apostolorum dies, in quo triumphalem coronam, deuicto diabolo, meruerunt, quantum fides Romana testator, hodiernus est. quibus solemnis festiuitas exhibetur, solemnis etiam sermo reddatur. laudes audiant

38. D. G. Morin, ed., *Sancti Augustini Sermones post Maurinos reperti*, MATS 1 (Rome: Poliglotta Vaticana, 1930), 308.

39. Morin, *Sancti Augustini Sermones post Maurinos*, 521–22.

40. PL 39:1683.

want to go."[83] Therefore, did Peter not go willingly to so great a grace as his suffering? Look at Paul: "I am now being offered as a sacrifice, and the time of my departure has come."[84] In these words he seems to be rejoicing, as if he is rushing to his suffering. For this other one, however, "Another will bind you and lead you where you do not want to go." Was Paul willing and Peter unwilling? If we were to understand it completely, Paul was willing, and Peter was willing. And Paul was unwilling, and Peter was unwilling.

F. 299A.1 (year uncertain)

There is one day for two martyrs and two apostles. We have received this much from the tradition of the church: that they did not suffer on one day, and they did suffer on one day. Today Peter suffered first, and today Paul suffered later.[85] Their merit made their suffering equal, and their love made itself evident on this day. He brought this about in them—the one who was in them, who was suffering in them, who was suffering with them, who was helping them as they did battle, and who crowned them when they were victorious.

G. 299C.1 (year uncertain)

The blessed apostles Peter and Paul were called at different times but crowned on one day. The Lord called Peter before all the others and Paul after all the others. Peter was the first of the apostles, Paul the last. He who is the first and the last[86] led them to the same day. A most beautiful integrity is maintained when the last things agree with the first.

H. 381 (year uncertain)

As the Roman faith attests, today is the day of the apostles Peter and Paul, on which they earned a victor's crown, because the devil was defeated. For them a formal feast is held, and so let a formal sermon also be given. Let them hear praises from us, and let their prayers pour forth for us. The

83. John 21:18.

84. 2 Tim 4:6.

85. The implication is that they suffered on the same date but not in the same year. Cf. 298.1 above, where Augustine speaks of "the one day of their passion."

86. Rev 1:17.

a nobis, preces fundant pro nobis. sicut traditione patrum cognitum memoria retinetur, non uno die passi sunt per coeli spatia decurrente. natalitio ergo Petri passus est Paulus, non quo ex utero matris in numerum fusus est hominum, sed quo ex uinculo carnis in lucem natus est angelorum; ac per hoc ita singuli dies dati sunt duobus, ut nunc unus celebretur ambobus.

27. Orosius, *Aduersus paganos* 7.7[41]

Auxit hanc molem facinorum eius temeritas impietatis in Deum. nam primus Romae Christianos suppliciis et mortibus affecit ac per omnes prouincias pari persecutione excruciari imperauit ipsumque nomem exstirpare conatus beatissimos Christi apostolos Petrum cruce, Paulum gladio occidit. mox aceruatim miseram ciuitatem obortae undique oppressere clades. nam subsequente autumno tanta urbi pestilentia incubuit, ut triginta milia funerum in rationem Libitinae uenirent. Britannica deinde clades e uestigio accidit, qua duo praecipua oppida magna ciuium sociorumque clade et caede direpta sunt. praeterea in Oriente magnis Armeniae prouinciis amissis Romanae legiones sub iugum Parthicum missae, aegreque Syria retenta est. in Asia tres urbes, hoc est Laudicia Hierapolis Colossae, terrae motu conciderunt. at uero Nero postquam Galbam in Hispania imperatorem creatum ab exercitu cognouit, totus animo ac spe

41. Charles Zangemeister, ed., *Pauli Orosii historiarum adversum paganos Libri VII*, CSEL 5 (Vienna: Gerold, 1882), 454–55.

memory, based on the tradition of the learned fathers, maintains that they did not suffer on one day between sunrise and sunset. Paul suffered on the birthday of Peter—not on the day that he was added to the number of men from his mother's womb, but on the day that he was born from the bondage of the flesh into the light of the angels. For this reason, while each had a separate day [of martyrdom], now both are celebrated on one day.

27. Orosius, *Against the Pagans* 7.7 (416–418 CE)

The rashness of [Nero's] impiety toward God added to his mass of crimes. For he was the first to inflict torments and death on the Christians in Rome and ordered that they be tortured with a similar persecution throughout all the provinces. He attempted to eradicate the name itself and killed the most blessed apostles of Christ—Peter on a cross, and Paul with a sword. Soon disasters sprang up from every side to weigh upon that most unfortunate city. In that following autumn, so great a plague oppressed the city that 30,000 funerals were recorded in the counting of Libitina.[87] Then Britain immediately suffered disasters, for two of the main towns were plundered, and a great number of citizens and their allies were injured and killed.[88] Furthermore, in the east the great provinces of Armenia were lost. Roman legions were placed under Parthian control, and Syria was barely retained.[89] In Asia earthquakes destroyed three cities—Laodicea, Hierapolis, and Colossae.[90] But after Nero learned that Galba had been declared emperor by the army in Spain,[91] he completely lost all spirit and hope. Because he

---

87. Libitina was the Roman goddess of funerals and burial. Horace (*Sat.* 2.16.19) uses her name as a metonymy for death, and this is probably the intended usage here.

88. Tacitus, *Ann.* 14.31–37 and *Agr.* 16.1–2; Cassius Dio, *Hist.* 62.1–12. Boudicca, wife of the client king Prasutagus, led the Iceni and Trinovantes in a revolt against the Roman governor in 60 CE. They sacked the cities of London and Verulamium and the colony at Colchester before being defeated by the Roman forces.

89. Tacitus, *Ann.* 15.1–17; Cassius Dio, *Hist.* 62.19–26.

90. This report by Orosius is often cited relevant to the dating of Colossians, but the report by Tacitus (*Ann.* 14.27) only states that Laodicea was destroyed by an earthquake in 60/61 CE. Tacitus says nothing about Colossae. See Eduard Lohse, *Colossians and Philemon*, trans. William R. Poehlmann and Robert J. Karris, Hermeneia (Philadelphia: Fortress, 1971), 8–9.

91. In fact, Galba insisted that he be declared a legate of the Senate, not Nero's replacement, in 68 CE. Following Nero's death he did march to Rome, but his imperial pretentions were short-lived, for he was assassinated on January 15, 69 CE. Tacitus

concidit. cumque incredibilia perturbandae, immo subruendae reipublicae mala moliretur, hostis a senatu pronuntiatus et ignominiosissime fugiens, ad quartum ab urbe lapidem sese ipse interfecit, atque in eo omnis Caesarum familia consumpta est.

28. Leo I, *Sermo* 82.6–7 (*In natali apostolorum Petri et Pauli*)[42]

[6] Ad quam beatus coapostolus tuus, uas electionis, et specialis magister gentium Paulus occurrens, eo tibi consociatus est tempore, quo iam omnis innocentia, omnis pudor, omnisque libertas sub Neronis laborabat imperio. cuius furor per omnium uitiorum inflammatus excessum, in hunc eum usque torrentem suae praecipitauit insaniae, ut primus nomini Christiano atrocitatem generalis persecutionis inferret, quasi per sanctorum neces gratia Dei posset exstingui: quibus hoc ipsum erat maximum lucrum, ut contemptus uitae huius occiduae, perceptio fieret felicitatis aeternae. pretiosa est ergo in conspectu Domini mors sanctorum eius. nec ullo crudelitatis genere destrui potest sacramento crucis Christi fundata religio. non minuitur persecutionibus Ecclesia, sed augetur; et semper Dominicus ager segete ditiori uestitur, dum grana, quae singula cadunt, multiplicata nascuntur. unde duo ista praeclara diuini seminis germina in quantam sobolem pullularint, beatorum millia martyrum protestantur; quae apostolicorum aemula triumphorum, urbem nostram purpuratis et longe lateque rutilantibus populis ambierunt, et quasi ex multarum honore gemmarum conserto uno diademate coronarunt.

42. PL 54:425–27.

had attempted to perpetrate incredible deeds of wickedness to throw into disorder and even destroy the republic, the Senate declared him an enemy of the state.[92] Fleeing in the most shameful fashion, he killed himself at the fourth milestone from the city, and in him the whole family of the Caesars came to an end.[93]

28. Leo I, *Sermon* 82.6–7 (*On the Birthday of the Apostles Peter and Paul)* (441 CE)

[6] Your [Peter's] blessed fellow apostle Paul, the vessel of election[94] and particular teacher of the gentiles, came there. He was united with you at that time, when all innocence, all modesty, and all freedom was being suppressed under the rule of Nero. Nero's fury, inflamed by the excess of every kind of vice, cast him headlong into the heat of his insanity, so that he was the first to introduce the savagery of a general persecution of the Christian name, as if the grace of God could be extinguished by murdering the saints. For them, in fact, this very thing was the greatest gain—that contempt for this perishable life might result in receiving eternal happiness. "Precious," therefore, "in the sight of the Lord is the death of his saints."[95] By no type of cruelty can religion based on the mystery of the cross of Christ be destroyed. The church is not diminished by persecutions, but increased. The Lord's field is adorned with a richer crop, while the grains—which fall one at a time—spring up multiplied.[96] Thus, these two glorious grains of divine seed have yielded so great a progeny that thousands of blessed martyrs have borne witness. Their triumphs are equal to those of the apostles, and they have encircled our city both far and wide with people clad in purple and red, as if they form a crown of one united diadem out of the beauty of many gems.[97]

(*Hist.* 1), Suetonius (*Galba*), and Plutarch (*Galba*) tell similar versions of the story. They may have all been dependent on the same source, possibly Pliny the Elder's *A fine Aufidi Bassi*, although this is disputed. Cf. Cassius Dio, *Hist.* 63–64.

92. The disasters throughout the empire are seen as divine retribution for Nero's many crimes (which also included murder and matricide), but the assassinations of Peter and Paul finally provoke God's vengeance.

93. Nero was the last emperor in the Julio-Claudian dynasty.

94. Acts 9:15.

95. Ps 116:15.

96. Cf. John 12:24.

97. The sacred sites of Christian martyrs surrounded the city of Rome, forming

[7] de quo praesidio, dilectissimi, diuinitus nobis ad exemplum patientiae et confirmationem fidei praeparate, uniuersaliter quidem in omnium sanctorum commemoratione laetandum est, sed in horum excellentia patrum merito est exsultantius gloriandum, quos gratia Dei in tantum apicem inter omnia Ecclesiae membra prouexit, ut eos in corpore, cui caput est Christus, quasi geminum constituerit lumen oculorum. de quorum meritis atque uirtutibus, quae omnem loquendi superant facultatem, nihil diuersum, nihil debemus sentire discretum: quia illi[43] et electio pares, et labor similes, et finis fecit aequales. sicut autem et nos experti sumus, et nostri probauere maiores, credimus atque confidimus, inter omnes labores istius uitae, ad obtinendam misericordiam Dei, semper nos specialium patronorum orationibus adiuuandos: ut quantum propriis peccatis deprimimur, tantum apostolicis meritis erigamur. per Dominum nostrum Iesum Christum, cui est cum Patre et sancto Spiritu eadem potestas, una Diuinitas in saecula saeculorum. amen.

29. John Malalas, *Chronographia* 10.34–37[44]

[34] ὁ δὲ ἀπόστολος Πέτρος δι' εὐχῆς αὐτοῦ ἐφόνευσε τὸν Σίμωνα τὸν μάγον θελήσαντα ἀναληφθῆναι. εἶπε γὰρ ὁ Σίμων τῷ Πέτρῳ, ὅτι· εἶπες ὅτι Χριστὸς ὁ θεός σου ἀνελήφθη. ἰδοὺ κἀγὼ ἀναλαμβάνομαι. καὶ εἶδεν αὐτὸν ὁ Πέτρος

43. MS *illos*.

44. Hans Thurn, ed., *Ioannis Malalae Chronographia*, CFHB.SB 35 (Berlin: de Gruyter, 2000), 192–94.

[7] Most beloved ones, on behalf of this cohort[98] that was divinely prepared for us as an example of endurance and the confirmation of our faith, we must rejoice everywhere in commemoration of all the saints. But it is right that we must boast even more joyfully in the excellence of these fathers, whom the grace of God has carried to so great a height among all the members of the church that he has established them in the body—whose head is Christ[99]—as the twin light of the eyes. Concerning their merits and virtues, which surpass all ability to speak about them, there is no difference, and we should not think there is any distinction, because they were equal in their calling, alike in their labor, and faced equal deaths. However, just as we have experienced and our ancestors have demonstrated, we believe and are confident that amid all the toils of this life, we must always be helped by the prayers of these special patrons, in order to attain the mercy of God.[100] Thus, however much we are pressed down by our sins, by that much we are raised up by the apostolic merits, through our Lord Jesus Christ, to whom, together with the Father and Holy Spirit, be the same authority, one God forever and ever. Amen.

29. John Malalas, *Chronography* 10.34–37 (ca. 565–575 CE)

This chronicle incorporates legends from a variety of sources. After explaining that Peter and Simon the sorcerer had been performing rival miracles in Rome, the author links the death of Simon with the executions of Peter and Paul.

[34] Through prayer the apostle Peter killed Simon the sorcerer, who had wanted to be taken up. For Simon had said to Peter, "You say that Christ your God ascended. Look, I also am being taken up." Peter saw that

---

a kind of crown for the city. Suzanne Lewis ("Function and Symbolic Form in the Basilica Apostolorum at Milan," *JSAH* 28.2 [1969]: 92) has suggested that Ambrose attempted to imitate this sacred "crown" around Rome by establishing martyr shrines around the outskirts of Milan. See also Eastman, *Paul the Martyr*, 122–23. During the Carolingian Renaissance, similar imagery was used to describe the ring of martyr shrines around Verona, which created a city "surrounded (*circumuallata*) by the holiest guardians" (Versus de Verona 56).

98. The Latin term can apply specifically to a cohort or band of soldiers.

99. Eph 1:22.

100. Pilgrims in Rome, for example, left graffiti appealing to the martyr-patrons Paul and Peter for their prayers as early as the third century (Eastman, *Paul the Martyr*, 72–73, 84–89).

κουφιζόμενον διὰ τῆς μαγείας εἰς τὸν ἀέρα ἐν μέσῳ τῆς πόλεως. Ῥώμης· καὶ ηὔξατο ὁ Πέτρος καὶ κατηνέχθη Σίμων ὁ μάγος ἐκ τοῦ ἀέρος εἰς τὴν γῆν ἐπὶ τὴν πλατεῖαν καὶ ἐψόφησεν. καὶ τὸ λείψανον αὐτοῦ κεῖται ἐκεῖ ἕως ἄρτι ὅπου ἔπεσεν, καὶ ἔχει πέριξ κάγκελλον λίθινον· καὶ ἀκούει ὁ τόπος ἐκεῖνος ἔκτοτε τὸ Σιμώνιον.

[35] ἀκούσας δὲ Νέρων ὁ βασιλεύς, ὅτι ἐφονεύθη ὑπὸ τοῦ Πέτρου ὁ Σίμων, ἠγανάκτησεν· καὶ ἐκέλευσεν αὐτὸν συσχεθέντα ἀποθανεῖν. καὶ ᾗ μόνον ἐκρατήθη ὁ ἅγιος Πέτρος, ἐπέδωκε τὸ ἔνδυμα τῆς ἐπισκοπῆς Ῥώμης Λίνῳ ὀνόματι, μαθητῇ αὐτοῦ· ἠκολούθει γὰρ αὐτῷ, ὅτε ἐκρατήθη. ὁ δὲ αὐτος ἅγιος Πέτρος γέρων ὑπῆρχε τῇ ἡλικίᾳ διμοιριαῖος, ἀναφάλας, κονδόθριξ, ὁλοπόλιος τὴν κάραν καὶ τὸ γένειον, λευκός, ὑπόχλωρος, οἰνοπαὴς τοὺς ὀφθαλμούς, εὐπώγων, μακρόρινος, σύνοφρυς, ἀνακαθήμενος, φρόνιμος, ὀξύχολος, εὐμετάβλητος, δειλός, φθεγγόμενος ὑπὸ πνεύματος ἁγίου καὶ θαυματουργῶν. καὶ ἐγένετο μετὰ τὸν ἅγιον Πέτρον τὸν ἐπίσκοπον ἤτοι πατριάρχην Ῥώμης ὀνόματι Λίνος, καθὼς ὁ σοφὸς Εὐσέβιος ὁ Παμφίλου ἐχρονογράφησεν. ὁ δὲ ἅγιος Πέτρος ὁ ἀπόστολος ἐμαρτύρησεν σταυρωθεὶς κατακέφαλα, τοῦ αὐτοῦ ἀποστόλου ὁρκώσαντος τοῦτο τὸν ἔπαρχον, ὅτι· μὴ ὡς ὁ κύριός μου σταυρωθῶ. καὶ ἐτελειώθη ὁ ἅγιος Πέτρος ἐπὶ τῆς ὑπατείας Ἀπρωνιανοῦ καὶ Καπίτωνος.

[36] ὁμοίως δὲ καὶ κατὰ τοῦ Πιλάτου ἠγανάκτησεν ὁ αὐτὸς βασιλεὺς Νέρων, καὶ ἐκέλευσεν αὐτὸν ἀποκεφαλισθῆναι, λέγων· διὰ τί ἐξέδωκε τὸν δεσπότην Χριστὸν τοῖς Ἰουδαίοις, ἄνδρα ἄμεμπτον καὶ δυνάμεις ποιοῦντα; εἰ γὰρ ὁ αὐτοῦ μαθητὴς τοιαῦτα θαυμάσια ἐποίει, ὁποῖος ὑπῆρχεν ἐκεῖνος δυνατός.

[37] ἐπὶ δὲ τῆς αὐτοῦ βασιλείας κατέφθασεν εὐθέως ἐν τῇ Ῥώμῃ καὶ ὁ ἅγιος Παῦλος πεμφθεὶς ἀπὸ τῆς Ἰουδαίας χώρας παραστάσιμος· καὶ ἐμαρτύρησε καὶ αὐτὸς ἀποτμηθεὶς τὴν κεφαλὴν τῇ πρὸ γ' καλανδῶν ἰουλίων ἐπὶ τῆς ὑπατείας Νέρωνος καὶ Λεντούλου. καὶ ἐκέλευσεν ὁ βασιλεὺς Νέρων τὰ σώματα τῶν ἁγίων ἀποστόλων ταφῇ μὴ παραδοθῆναι, ἀλλ' ἄταφα μεῖναι. ὑπῆρχεν δὲ ὁ Παῦλος ἔτι περιὼν τῇ ἡλικίᾳ κονδοειδής, φαλακρός, μιξοπόλιος τὴν κάραν καὶ τὸ γένειον, εὔρινος, ὑπόγλαυκος, σύνοφρυς, λευκόχρους, ἀνθηροπρόσωπος,

he was being raised up into the air through magic in the middle of the city of Rome. Peter prayed, and Simon the sorcerer was brought down out of the air to the earth. And he died in the street. His remains lie there where he fell up to today and have a stone railing around them. From then on that place has been called the Simonium.[101]

[35] When the emperor Nero heard that Simon had been slain by Peter, he was angry and ordered him to be arrested and killed. As soon as holy Peter was arrested, he handed over the vestment of the Roman episcopacy to one named Linus, his disciple, for Linus was following Peter when he was arrested. This same Peter was an old man, of average height, with a bald forehead, short hair, completely gray on his head and his beard, light (skinned), pale, with wine-colored eyes, a substantial beard, a sizable nose, and eyebrows that met. He had good posture and was prudent, quick to anger, changeable, and fearful.[102] He spoke through the Holy Spirit and performed wonders. And after the holy bishop Peter, a man named Linus became patriarch of Rome, just as the wise Eusebius Pamphilius chronicled.[103] But holy Peter the apostle died as a martyr, being crucified with his head downward, because the apostle had bound the prefect by an oath, "Do not let me be crucified as my Lord was." The holy Peter was killed during the consulate of Apronianus and Capito.[104]

[36] Likewise the emperor Nero was angry with Pilate and ordered him to be decapitated, saying, "Why did he hand over the Lord Christ to the Jews, a man who was innocent and performed powerful deeds? For if his disciple did such wonders, how powerful that man was."

[37] During Nero's reign, right afterward, holy Paul came to Rome, having been sent from Judea to stand trial. He died as a martyr by being decapitated three days before the calends of July, during the consulship of Nero and Lentulus.[105] The emperor Nero ordered the bodies of the holy apostles not to be handed over for burial, but to remain unburied. But when Paul was still alive, he was short in stature, bald, partially gray on his head and his beard, with a good nose, grayish eyes, eyebrows that met, light complexion, a florid face, a substantial beard, and a cheerful countenance.

101. I can find no other record of a place by this name.

102. Note the similarities to the description of Paul below (§37), which is based on Acts Paul 3.3.

103. Eusebius, *Hist. eccl.* 3.2, 3.13, 3.21.

104. 59 CE.

105. June 29, 60 CE.

εὐπώγων, ὑπογελῶντα ἔχων τὸν χαρακτῆρα, φρόνιμος, ἠθικός, εὐόμιλος, γλυκύς, ὑπὸ πνεύματος ἁγίου ἐνθουσιαζόμενος καὶ ἰώμενος.

30. Gregory of Tours, *De gloria martyrum* 1.27–28[45]

[27] Petrus apostolus ob humilitatem docendam caput desuper tondi[46] instituit; qui ab apostolis ceteris episcopus ordinatur, Romae cathedram locauit. cuius oratione uel Pauli Simonis magi calliditas uel detecta est uel obruta. extant hodieque apud urbem Romanam duae in lapide fossulae, super quem beati apostoli, deflexu poplite, orationem contra ipsum Simonem magum ad Dominum effuderunt. In quibus cum de pluuiis limphae collectae fuerint, a morbidis expetuntur, haustaeque mox sanitatem tribuunt. sanctus uero Petrus apostolus, ut praefati sumus, post Neroniana ac Simoniaca bella ad crucem uenisset, impleto iam felicis trophei certamine, resupinis ad caelum uestigiis se expetiit crucifigi, indignum se uociferans ut Dominum exaltari. sicque dirigens spiritum uiuacem in astris, sepultus est in templo quod uocitabatur antiquitus Batecanum … Hoc enim sepulchrum sub altare collocatum, ualde rarum habetur …

[28] Paulus uero apostolus post reuolutum anni circulum ipsa die, qua Petrus apostolus passus, apud urbem Romam gladio percussus occubuit. ex cuius sacro corpore lac defluxit et aqua. nec mirum, si lac eius manauit

45. Bruno Krusch, ed., *Gregorii episcopi Turonensis miracula et opera minora*, *MGH.SRM* 1.2 (Hannover: Hahn, 1969), 53–55.

46. Some MSS say *tundi* (beaten), but *tondi* is clearly the preferable reading.

He was prudent, moral, sociable, and pleasant. He was inspired by the Holy Spirit and performed healings.

30. Gregory of Tours, *On the Glory of the Martyrs* 1.27–28 (586–588 CE)

[27] In order to teach humility, the apostle Peter had his head shaved from above.[106] He was ordained bishop by the other apostles and established his seat in Rome. By the eloquence of Peter and Paul the craftiness of Simon the sorcerer was revealed and overpowered. Today in the city of Rome there are two depressions in the stone on which the blessed apostles, on bended knee, poured forth their request to the Lord against that sorcerer Simon. When rainwater has been collected in them, the sick come seeking it. After they drink it, it soon restores them to health.[107] The holy apostle Peter, as we said before, went to the cross after his wars with Nero and Simon [the sorcerer]. After he had completed his contest for the blessed trophy, he asked to be crucified with his feet upward toward heaven, crying out that he was unworthy to be raised up as his Lord was. And so, sending his living spirit into the stars, he was buried in the church that in more ancient times was called the Vatican … This sepulcher is located under the altar and is accessed very rarely.

[28] One year later, on the same day that the apostle Peter had suffered, the apostle Paul died in the city of Rome by being struck with a sword. Milk and water flowed from his holy body. It is not surprising if milk flowed

106. Gregory's note that Peter had his head shaved "from above" (*desuper*) may relate to a controversy in late antiquity over the form of the tonsure. The "Roman tonsure" involved shaving the hair into the shape of a crown and was traditionally believed to hearken back to Peter, although there is no evidence for this. Gregory elsewhere claimed, for example, that his uncle, Nicetius, was destined from birth to become a bishop, because his hair naturally grew in the shape of a *corona* (*Vitae patrum* 17.1). This form was juxtaposed with the "Insular (or Celtic) tonsure." The exact form of it remains unclear, but it involved cutting the hair from ear to ear. Ecclesiastical writers, and even the Fourth Council of Toledo in 633 CE, condemned this latter style, and some claimed that it could be traced back to Simon the sorcerer. On the tonsure debate, see Edward James, "Bede and the Tonsure," *Peritia* 3 (1984): 85–98; Daniel McCarthy, "On the Shape of the Insular Tonsure," *Celtica* 24 (2003): 140–67.

107. The basilica of Santa Francesca Romana (Santa Maria Nova) in Rome displays a stone that is said to have the imprints made by the knees of the apostles when they knelt to pray. This church sits in the ancient Forum just below the Capitoline Hill, Simon's supposed launching site. See Eastman, *Paul the Martyr*, 108.

ex corpore, qui gentes incredulas et parturiuit et peperit ac lacte spiritali nutritas ad cibum solidum scripturarum sanctarum opaca reserando perduxit.

from his body, for he had labored and given birth to the unbelieving gentiles. He had fed them with spiritual milk and led them to the solid food of the holy Scriptures by disclosing the things that were obscure.[108]

108. 1 Cor 3:2. Cf. Heb 5:12; 1 Pet 2:2.

Bibliography

Acerbi, Antonio. *L'Ascensione di Isaia: Cristologia e profetismo in Siria nei primi decenni del II secolo*. Milan: Università Cattolica del Sacro Cuore, 1989.

Alibert, Dominique. "Vision du monde et imaginaire dans quelques textes de la collection dite du Pseudo-Abdias." *Apocrypha* 11 (2000): 207–26.

Armellini, Mariano. *Le chiese di Roma dal secolo IV al XIX*. 2nd ed. Rome: R.O.R.E., 1942.

Armstrong, Jonathan J. "Victorinus of Pettau as the Author of the Canon Muratori." *VC* 62 (2008): 1–34.

Attridge, Harold W., ed. *Nag Hammadi Codex I (The Jung Codex): Introductions, Texts, Translations, Indices*. NHS 22–23. Leiden: Brill, 1985.

Baldwin, Matthew C. *Whose Acts of Peter? Text and Historical Context of the Actus Vercellenses*. WUNT 2/196. Tübingen: Mohr Siebeck, 2005.

Barnes, Timothy David. *Tertullian: A Historical and Literary Study*. 2nd ed. Oxford: Clarendon, 1985.

Bauckham, Richard. "The Martyrdom of Peter in Early Christian Literature." *ANRW* 26.1:539–95. Part 2, *Principat*, 26.1. Edited by H. Temporini and Wolfgang Haase. Berlin: de Gruyter, 1992.

Bauman, Guy Caesar. "The Miracle of Plautilla's Veil in Princeton's Beheading of Saint Paul." *Record of the Art Museum, Princeton University* 36.1 (1977): 2–11.

Baumstark, Anton. *Die Petrus- und Paulusacten in der litterarischen Überlieferung der syrischen Kirche*. Leipzig: Harrassowitz, 1902.

Beard, Mary, John North, and Simon Price. *Religions of Rome: Volume 1: A History*. Cambridge: Cambridge University Press, 1998.

Bedjan, Paul, ed. *Acta martyrum et sanctorum*. Leipzig: Harrassowitz, 1891.

Bernhard, Ludger. *Die Chronologie der syrischen Handschriften*. VOHD-Supp 14. Wiesbaden: Steiner, 1971.

Bettiolo, Paolo. *Ascensio Isaiae: Textus*. CCSA 7. Turnhout: Brepols, 1995.

Bickerman, E.J. *Chronology of the Ancient World.* 2nd ed. Ithaca, NY: Cornell University Press, 1980.

Bockmuehl, Marcus. *The Remembered Peter in Ancient Reception and Modern Debate.* WUNT 1/262. Tübingen: Mohr Siebeck, 2010.

———. *Simon Peter in Scripture and Memory: The New Testament Apostle in the Early Church.* Grand Rapids: Baker Academic, 2012.

Bovon, François. "The Synoptic Gospels and the Noncanonical Acts of the Apostles." *HTR* 81.1 (1988): 19–36.

Bovon, François, and Pierre Geoltrain, eds. *Écrits apocryphes chrétiens.* Vol. 1. Pléiade 442. Paris: Gallimard, 1997.

Bremmer, Jan N., ed. *The Apocryphal Acts of Paul and Thecla.* Kampen: Kok Pharos, 1996.

———. *The Apocryphal Acts of Peter: Magic, Miracles, and Gnosticism.* SECA 3. Leuven: Peeters, 1998.

Brown, Raymond E. *An Introduction to the New Testament.* ABRL. New York: Doubleday, 1997.

Buchholz, Dennis D. *Your Eyes Will Be Opened: A Study of the Greek (Ethiopic) Apocalypse of Peter.* SBLDS 97. Atlanta: Scholars Press, 1988.

Burke, Tony, and Brent E. Landau, eds. *Forbidden Texts on the Western Frontier: Christian Apocrypha in North American Perspectives.* Eugene, OR: Cascade, forthcoming.

Casey, Robert P. "Simon Magus." *BegC* 5:151–64.

Cassidy, Richard J. *Paul in Chains: Roman Imprisonment and the Letters of St. Paul.* New York: Crossroad, 2001.

Cook, John Granger. "Crucifixion as Spectacle in Roman Campania." *NovT* 54 (2012): 68–100.

———. "Envisioning Crucifixion: Light from Several Inscriptions and the Palatine Graffito." *NovT* 50 (2008): 262–85.

Côté, Dominique. *Le thème de l'opposition entre Pierre et Simon dans les Pseudo-Clémentines.* Études Augustiniennes, Série Antiquités 167. Paris: Institut d'Études Augustiniennes, 2001.

Cureton, William. *Ancient Syriac Documents: Relative to the Earliest Establishment of Christianity in Edessa and the Neighbouring Countries.* London: Williams & Norgate, 1864.

Datema, Cornelis, ed. *Asterius of Amasea, Homilies I–XIV.* Leiden: Brill, 1970.

De Stefani, Luigi, trans. "Storia del Beato Apostolo S. Paolo." *GSAT* 14 (1901): 201–16.

Dehandschutter, Boudewijn. "Some Notes in 1 Clement 5, 4–7." Pages 83–89 in *Fructus centesimus: Mélanges offerts à Gerard J. M. Bartelink à l'occasion de son soixante-cinquième anniversaire*. Edited by Antoon Bastiaensen, G. J. M. Bartelink, A. Hilhorst, and C. H. Kneepkens. IP 19. Steenbrugis: Abbatia S. Petri, 1989.

Dekkers, Eligius, and Attilio Carpin, eds. *Tertulliano Difesa del Cristianesimo: Apologeticum*. CCSL 1. Rome: San Clemente; Bologna: Studio Domenicano, 2008.

Demacopoulos, George E. *The Invention of Peter: Apostolic Discourse and Papal Authority in Late Antiquity*. Divinations: Rereading Late Ancient Religion. Philadelphia: University of Pennsylvania Press, 2013.

Dickie, Matthew W. *Magic and Magicians in the Greco-Roman World*. London: Routledge, 2001.

Dolbeau, François. "Nouveaux sermons de saint Augustin pour la conversion des païens et des donatistes," *REAug* 38 (1992): 50–79.

Donfried, Karl Paul. "Chronology of the Life of Jesus." *ABD* 1:1015–16.

Duchesne, Louis. "Les Anciens Recueils dans légendes apostoliques." Pages 67–79 in *Compte rendu du troisième congrès scientifique international des catholiques*. Brussels: Société belge de librairie, 1895.

Eastman, David L. "Confused Traditions? Peter and Paul in the Apocryphal Acts." In *Forbidden Texts on the Western Frontier: Christian Apocrypha in North American Perspectives*. Edited by Tony Burke and Brent E. Landau. Eugene, OR: Cascade, forthcoming.

———. "The Epistle of Pseudo-Dionysius the Areopagite to Timothy Concerning the Deaths of the Apostles Peter and Paul: A New Translation and Introduction." In *New Testament Apocrypha: More Noncanonical Scriptures*. Edited by Tony Burke and Brent E. Landau. Grand Rapids: Eerdmans, forthcoming.

———. "Jealousy, Internal Strife, and the Deaths of Peter and Paul: A Reassessment of *1 Clement*." *ZAC* 18 (2014): 34–53.

———. "The Matriarch as Model: Sarah, the Cult of the Saints, and Social Control in a Syriac Homily of Pseudo-Ephrem." *JECS* 21 (2013): 241–59.

———. "Paul: An Outline of His Life." Pages 34–56 in *All Things to All Cultures: Paul among Jews, Greeks and Romans*. Edited by Mark Harding and Alanna Nobbs. Grand Rapids: Eerdmans, 2013.

———. "Paul as Martyr in the Apostolic Fathers," in Todd D. Still and David E. Wilhite, eds., *The Apostolic Fathers and Paul*. PPSD 2. London: T&T Clark, forthcoming.

———. *Paul the Martyr: The Cult of the Apostle in the Latin West*. WGRW-Sup 4. Atlanta: Society of Biblical Literature, 2011.

Ehrenkrook, Jason von. “Effeminacy in the Shadow of Empire: The Politics of Transgressive Gender in Josephus’s *Bellum Judaicum*.” *JQR* 101 (2011): 145–63.

Elliott, J. K. *The Apocryphal New Testament*. Oxford: Clarendon, 1993.

Erbetta, Mario. *Atti e leggende*. Vol. 2 of *Gli apocrifi del Nuovo Testamento*. 2nd ed. Turin: Marietti, 1978.

Eustace, John Chetwode. *A Classical Tour through Italy*. 6th ed. London: Mawam, 1837.

Ferreiro, Alberto. “Simon Magus, Dogs, and Simon Peter.” Pages 147–200 in *Simon Magus in Patristic, Medieval, and Early Modern Traditions*. Edited by Alberto Ferreiro. Studies in the History of Christian Traditions 125. Leiden: Brill, 2005.

Flamion, J. “Les Actes de Pierre.” *RHE* 11 (1910): 19–28.

Fortescue, Adrian. *The Orthodox Eastern Church*. Piscataway, NJ: Gorgias, 2001.

Fossum, Jarl E. *The Name of God and the Angel of the Lord*. WUNT 1/36. Tübingen: Mohr, 1985.

French, Valerie. “Midwives and Maternity Care in the Roman World.” *Helios* 13.2 (1986): 69–84.

Gapp, Kenneth S. “The Universal Famine under Claudius.” *HTR* 28 (1935): 258–65.

Garnsey, Peter. *Famine and Food Supply in the Graeco-Roman World*. Cambridge: Cambridge University Press, 1988.

Geoltrain, Pierre, and Jean-Daniel Kaestli, eds. *Écrits apocryphes chrétiens*. Vol. 2. Pléiade 516. Paris: Gallimard, 2005.

Giles, John Allen, ed. *The Uncanonical Gospels and Other Writings, Referring to the First Ages of Christianity, in the Original Languages: Collected together from the Editions of Fabricius, Thilo, and Others*. London: Nutt, 1852.

Goulet, Richard, ed., *Macarios de Magnésie: Le monogénès*. TT 7. Paris: Vrin, 2003.

Guidi, Ignazio. “Bemerkungen zum ersten Bande der syrischen Acta Martyrum et Sanctorum.” *ZDMG* 46 (1892): 744–58.

Gwatkin, Henry W., ed. *Selections from Early Writers Illustrative of Church History to the Time of Constantine*. Updated ed. London: Macmillan, 1911.

Haase, Felix. *Apostel und Evangelisten in den orientalischen Überlieferungen*. NTAbh 9.1–3. Münster: Aschendorff, 1922.

Hahneman, Geoffrey Mark. *The Muratorian Fragment and the Development of the Canon*. OTM. Oxford: Clarendon, 1992.

Harley-McGowan, Felicity. "The Constanza Gem and the Development of Crucifixion Iconography in Late Antiquity." Pages 214–20 in *Gems of Heaven: Recent Research on Engraved Gemstones in Late Antiquity AD 200–600*. Edited by Christopher Entwistle and Noel Adams. BMRP 177. London: British Museum Press, 2011.

Halm, Charles, ed., *Sulpicii Severi libri qui supersunt*. CSEL 1. Vienna: Gerold, 1866.

Harnack, Adolf von. *Militia Christi: Die christliche Religion und der Soldatenstand in den ersten drei Jahrhunderten*. Tübingen: Mohr, 1905.

Harrak, Amir. *Catalogue of Syriac and Garshuni Manuscripts: Manuscripts Owned by the Iraqi Department of Antiquities and Heritage*. CSCO 126. Leuven: Peeters, 2011.

Hartog, Paul. *Polycarp's Epistle to the Philippians and the Martyrdom of Polycarp: Introduction, Text, and Commentary*. OAF. Oxford: Oxford University Press, 2013.

Harvey, Susan Ashbrook. *Scenting Salvation: Ancient Christianity and the Olfactory Imagination*. Berkeley: University of California Press, 2006.

Hennecke, Edgar, and Wilhelm Schneemelcher, eds. *New Testament Apocrypha*. English trans. edited by R. McL. Wilson. 5th ed. Vol. 2. Louisville: Westminster John Knox, 1993.

Holmes, Michael W. *The Apostolic Fathers: Greek Texts and English Translations*. 3rd ed. Grand Rapids: Baker, 2007.

Huskinson, J. M. *Concordia Apostolorum: Christian Propaganda at Rome in the Fourth and Fifth Centuries*. BARIS 148. Oxford: British Archaeological Reports, 1982.

James, Edward. "Bede and the Tonsure." *Peritia* 3 (1984): 85–98.

Jaubert, Annie, ed. *Clément de Rome: Épître aux Corinthiens*. SC 167. Paris: Cerf, 1971.

Jensen, Robin Margaret. *Understanding Early Christian Art*. New York: Routledge, 2000.

Jones, F. Stanley, trans. "History of Simon Cephas, the Chief of the Apostles." In *New Testament Apocrypha: More Noncanonical Scriptures*. Edited by Tony Burke and Brent E. Landau. Grand Rapids: Eerdmans, forthcoming.

Kelley, Nicole. *Knowledge and Religious Authority in the Pseudo-Clementines: Situating the 'Recognitions' in Fourth Century Syria*. WUNT 2/213. Tübingen: Mohr Siebeck, 2006.

Kessler, Herbert L. "The Meeting of Peter and Paul in Rome: An Emblematic Narrative of Spiritual Brotherhood." Pages 265–75 in *Studies on Art and Archeology in Honor of Ernst Kitzinger on His Seventy-Fifth Birthday*. Edited by William Tronzo and Irving Lavin. DOP 41. Washington: Dumbarton Oaks, 1987.

Konstan, David. *Friendship in the Classical World*. Cambridge: Cambridge University Press, 1997.

———. "Patrons and Friends." *CP* 90 (1995): 328–42.

Kraus, Thomas J., and Tobias Nicklas, eds. *Das Petrusevangelium und die Petrusapokalypse: die griechischen Fragmente mit deutscher und englischer Übersetzung*. GCS NS 11. Berlin: de Gruyter, 2004.

Krautheimer, Richard. *Corpus basilicarum christianarum Romae*. MACr 2,3. Vatican City: Pontificio Istituto di Archeologia Cristiana, 1967.

Krusch, Bruno, ed., *Gregorii episcopi Turonensis miracula et opera minora*. MGH.SRM 1.2. Hannover: Hahn, 1969.

Lagarde, A. P. de, ed. *Reliquiae iuris ecclesiastici antiquissimae syriace*. Vienna: Teubner, 1856.

Lambot, D. C., ed. *Sancti Aurelii Augustini Sermones selecti duodeviginti*. SPM 1. Utrecht: Spectrum, 1950.

Lampe, G. W. H. *A Patristic Greek Lexicon*. Oxford: Oxford University Press, 1961.

Lanciana, Rodolfo Amedeo. *Pagan and Christian Rome*. Boston: Houghton and Mifflin, 1899.

Leloir, Louis. *Écrits apocryphes sur les apôtres: Traduction de l'édition arménienne de Venise*. CCSA 3. Turnhout: Brepols, 1986.

Lewis, Suzanne. "Function and Symbolic Form in the Basilica Apostolorum at Milan." *JSAH* 28.2 (1969): 83–98.

Lindsay, W. M."'Glossae Collectae' in Vat. Lat. 1469. Catomvm. Navmachia," ClQ 15 (1921): 38–40.

Lipsius, Richard A. *Die apokryphen Apostelgeschichten und Apostellegenden*. Braunschweig: Schwetschke, 1883–1890.

Lipsius, Richard A., and Max Bonnet, eds. *Acta apostolorvm apocrypha post Constantinvm Tischendorf*. Vol. 1. Leipzig: Mendelssohn, 1891. Repr., Hildesheim: Olms, 1972.

Lohse, Eduard. *Colossians and Philemon*. Translated by William R. Poehlmann and Robert J. Karris. Hermeneia. Philadelphia: Fortress, 1971.

MacDonald, Dennis R. "Apocryphal and Canonical Narratives about Paul." Pages 55–70 in *Paul and the Legacies of Paul*. Edited by William S. Babcock. Dallas: Southern Methodist University Press, 1990.

———. *The Legend and the Apostle: The Battle for Paul in Story and Canon*. Philadelphia: Westminster John Knox, 1983.

Malan, Solomon C. *The Conflicts of the Apostles: An Apocryphal Book of the Early Eastern Church*. London: Nutt, 1871.

Martin, Paulin. "Dionysii Areopagitae." Pages 241–54, 261–76 in *Analecta sacra spicilegio solesmensi* 4: *Patres antenicaeni*. Edited by Joannes B. Pitra. Paris: Roger and Chernoviz, 1883.

McCarthy, Daniel. "On the Shape of the Insular Tonsure." *Celtica* 24 (2003): 140–67.

Meeks, Wayne, and John T. Fitzgerald, eds. *The Writings of St. Paul*. 2nd ed. New York: Norton, 2007.

Metzger, Bruce M. *The Canon Of The New Testament: Its Origin, Development, and Significance*. Oxford: Clarendon Press, 1987.

———. *A Textual Commentary on the Greek New Testament*. 2nd ed. New York: United Bible Societies, 1994.

Migne, J.-P. *Dictionnaire des apocryphes*. Vol. 2. Paris: Migne, 1858.

Minnen, Peter van. "The Greek Apocalypse of Peter." Pages 15–39 in *The Apocalypse of Peter*. Edited by Jan N. Bremmer and István Czachesz. SECA 7. Leuven: Peeters, 2003.

Mombrizio, Bonino. "Epistola beati Dionisii ariopagite de morte apostolorum Petri et Pauli ad Timotheum." Pages 354–57, 709–10 in vol. 2 of *Sanctuarium seu Vitae sanctorum*. New edition by Albin Brunet and Henri Quentin. Paris: Fontemoing, 1909.

Mommsen, T., ed. *Chronica minora saec. IV. V. VI. VII*. MGH.AA 9. Berlin: Weidmann, 1892.

Moraldi, Luigi. *Apocrifi del Nuovo Testamento*. Vol. 2. Turin: Unione, 1971.

Moreschini, Claudio, and René Braun, eds. *Tertullien Contre Marcion Tome IV*. SC 456. Paris: Cerf, 2001.

Morin, Germain, ed. *S. Hieronymi presbyteri opera, Pars II: Opera homiletica*. CCSL 78. Turnhout: Brepols, 1958.

———. *Sancti Augustini Sermones post Maurinos reperti*. MATS 1. Rome: Poliglotta Vaticana, 1930.

Müller-Kessler, Christa, and Michael Sokoloff, eds. *A Corpus of Christian Palestinian Aramaic*. Vol. IIB. Groningen: Styx, 1998.

Nau, François. "La version syriaque inédite des martyres de S. Pierre, S. Paul et S. Luc d'après un manuscrit du dixième siècle." *ROC* 3 (1898): 39–57.

Nordheim, Eckhard von. "Das Zitat des Paulus in 1 Kor 2,9 und seine Beziehung zum koptischen Testament Jakobs." *ZNW* 65 (1974): 112–20.

Osborn, Eric. *Irenaeus of Lyons*. Cambridge: Cambridge University Press, 2001.

Peebles, Rose Jeffries. *The Legend of Longinus in Ecclesiastical Tradition and in English Literature, and Its Connection with the Grail*. Baltimore: Furst, 1911.

Peerbolte, L. J. Lietaert. *The Antecedents of Antichrist: A Traditio-Historical Study of the Earliest Christian Views on Eschatological Opponents*. JSJSup 49. Leiden: Brill, 1996.

Peeters, Paul. "Notes sur la légende des apôtres S. Pierre et S. Paul dans la littérature syrienne." *AnBoll* 21 (1902): 121–40.

Pervo, Richard I. *Acts: A Commentary*. Hermeneia. Minneapolis: Augsburg Fortress, 2009.

———. *The Making of Paul: Constructions of the Apostle in Early Christianity*. Minneapolis: Augsburg Fortress, 2010.

Pharr, Clyde. "The Interdiction of Magic in Roman Law." *TAPA* 63 (1932): 269–95.

Pietersma, Albert. *The Apocryphon of Jannes and Jambres the Magicians: P. Chester Beatty XVI ; (with new editions of Papyrus Vindobonensis Greek inv. 29456 + 29828 verso and British Library Cotton Tiberius B. v f. 87); with full facsimile of all three texts*. RGRW 119. Leiden: Brill, 1994.

Pietersma, Albert, and R. T. Lutz. "Jannes and Jambres." Pages 227–42 in vol. 2 of *Old Testament Pseudepigrapha*. Edited by James H. Charlesworth. 2 vols. New York: Doubleday, 1983.

Pietri, Charles. "Concordia Apostolorum et renovatio urbis (Culte des martyrs et propagande pontificale)." *MEFR* 73 (1961): 275–322.

Poupon, Gérard. "Les 'Actes de Pierre' et leur remaniement." *ANRW* 25.6:2363–83. Part 2, *Principat*, 25.6. Edited by Wolfgang Haase. Berlin: de Gruyter, 1988.

———. "La passion de saint Pierre apôtre: Introduction, texte et traduction." Master's thesis, Université de Genève, 1975.

Pratten, Benjamin P. *Syriac Documents Attributed to the First Three Centuries*. Edinburgh: T&T Clark, 1871.

———, trans. "The Teaching of Simon Cephas in the City of Rome." *ANF* 8:673–75.

Rahmani, Ignatius Ephraem II, ed. "Pauli Apostoli martyrium et ipsius capitis truncati inventio." Pages 3–5 in *Studia Syriaca seu collectio documentorum hactenus ineditorum ex codicibus syriacis*. Monte Libano: Seminario Scharfensi, 1904.

Refoulé, F., ed. *Tertullien Traité de la prescription contre les hérétiques*. SC 46. Paris: Cerf, 1957.

Reifferscheid, August, and George Wissowa, eds., *Quinti Septimi Florentis Tertulliani Opera*. Vol. 1. CSEL 20. Vienna: Tempsky, 1890.

Reinhartz, Adele. "The Vanishing Jews of Antiquity." *Marginalia*. http://marginalia.lareviewofbooks.org/vanishing-jews-antiquity-adele-reinhartz/.

Richardson, Ernest C. *Hieronymus Liber de viris inlustribus*. TUGAL 14. Leipzig: Hinrichs, 1896.

Robinson, Thomas A. *Ignatius of Antioch and the Parting of the Ways: Early Jewish-Christian Relations*. Grand Rapids: Baker Academic, 2009.

Rossi, Giovanni B. *La Roma sotterranea cristiana*. Rome: Litografia Pontificia, 1864–1877.

Rossi, J. B. de, and Louis Duchesne, eds. *Acta sanctorum novembris*. Vol. 2.1. Brussels: Société des Bollandistes, 1894.

Rousseau, Adelin, and Louis Doutreleau, eds. *Irénée de Lyon: Contre les hérésies Livre III*. Vol. 2. SC 211. Paris, Cerf, 1974.

Rowland, Megan. "Effeminacy as Imperial Vice in Suetonius' Nero and Caligula." *Classicum* 36.2 (2010): 23–30.

Saller, Richard P. *Personal Patronage under the Early Empire*. Cambridge: Cambridge University Press, 1982.

Salonius, A. H. "Martyrium beati Petri apostoli a Lino episcopo conscriptum." Pages 22–58 in *Societas scientiarum fennica—Commentationes humanarum litterarum* 1.6. Helsinki: Helsingfors, 1926.

Samuel, Alan E. *Greek and Roman Chronology: Calendars and Years in Classical Antiquity*. Handbuch der Altertumswissenschaft 1.7. Munich: Beck, 1972.

Samuelsson, Gunnar. *Crucifixion in Antiquity: An Inquiry into the Background and Significance of the New Testament Terminology of Crucifixion*. WUNT 2/310. Tübingen: Mohr Siebeck, 2011.

Schwartz, Daniel R. "'Judaean' or 'Jew'? How Should We Translate Ioudaios in Josephus?" Pages 3–27 in *Jewish Identity in the Greco-Roman World/Jüdische Identität in Der Griechisch-Römischen Welt*. Edited by Jörg Frey, Daniel R. Schwartz, and Stephanie Gripentrog. Leiden: Brill, 2007.

Schwartz, Eduard, ed. *Eusebius Werke* 2.1. GCS 9.1. Leipzig: Hinrichs, 1903.

Schwartz, Seth. "How Many Judaisms Were There? A Critique of Neusner and Smith on Definition and Mason and Boyarin on Categorization." *JAJ* 2 (2011): 208–38.

Snelders, Bas. "The *Traditio legis* on Early Christian Sarcophagi." *AnTard* 13 (2005): 321–33.

Snyder, Glenn. *Acts of Paul: The Formation of a Biblical Canon.* WUNT 2/352. Tübingen: Mohr Siebeck, 2013.

Städele, Alfons, ed. *Laktanz de mortibus persecutorum: Die Todesarten der Verfolger*. FontC 43. Turnhout: Brepols, 2003.

Steinby, Eva Margareta, ed. *Lexicon topographicum urbis Romae.* 5 Volumes. Rome: Quasar, 1996.

Stoops, Robert F. "If I Suffer . . . Epistolary Authority in Ignatius of Antioch." *HTR* 80 (1987): 161–78.

Sundberg, Albert C., Jr. "Canon Muratori: A Fourth Century List." *HTR* 66 (1973): 1–41.

Tajra, Harry W. *The Martyrdom of St. Paul: Historical and Judicial Context, Traditions, and Legends*. WUNT 2/67. Tübingen: Mohr Siebeck, 1994.

———. *The Trial of St. Paul: A Judicial Exegesis of the Second Half of the Acts of the Apostles.* WUNT 2/35. Tübingen: Mohr, 1989.

Thomas, Christine M. *The Acts of Peter, Gospel Literature, and the Ancient Novel: Rewriting the Past.* New York: Oxford University Press, 2003.

Thurn, Hans, ed. *Ioannis Malalae Chronographia.* CFHB.SB 35. Berlin: de Gruyter, 2000.

Todman, Donald. "Childbirth in Ancient Rome: From Traditional Folklore to Obstetrics." *ANZJOG* 47.2 (2007): 82–85.

Turner, Cuthbert H., ed. *Ecclesiae occidentalis monumenta iuris antiquissima.* 9 vols. Oxford: Clarendon, 1899–1939.

Van Dam, Raymond. *Remembering Constantine at the Milvian Bridge.* Cambridge: Cambridge University Press, 2011.

Verheyden, J. "The Canon Muratori: A Matter of Dispute." Pages 487–556 in *The Biblical Canons.* Edited by Jean-Marie Auwers and H. J. de Jonge. BETL 163. Leuven: Leuven University Press, 2003.

Verrando, G. N. "Osservazioni sulla collocazione cronologica degli apocrifi Atti di Pietro dello Pseudo-Lino." *VetChr* 20 (1983): 391–426.

Vouaux, Léon. *Les Actes de Paul et ses lettres apocryphes: Introduction, textes, traduction et commentaire.* Paris: Letouzey et Ané, 1913.

———. *Les Actes de Pierre: Introduction, textes, traduction et commentaire.* Paris: Letouzey et Ané, 1922.

Walker, Alexander, trans. "Acts of the Holy Apostles Peter and Paul." Pages 256–76 in *Apocryphal Gospels, Acts and Revelations*. ANCL 16. Edinburgh: T&T Clark, 1870.

Watson, W. Scott. "An Arabic Version of the Epistle of Dionysius the Areopagite to Timothy." *AJSL* 16 (1900): 225–41.

Winter, Bruce W. "Acts and Food Shortages." *BIFCS* 2:59–78.

Zangemeister, Charles, ed. *Pauli Orosii historiarum adversum paganos Libri VII*. CSEL 5. Vienna: Gerold, 1882.

Zwierlein, Otto. *Petrus in Rom: Die literarischen Zeugnisse*. 2nd ed. UALG 96. Berlin: de Gruyter, 2010.

Scripture Index

General Index

CPSIA information can be obtained
at www.ICGtesting.com
Printed in the USA
FFOW04n2210240715
15479FF